KU-483-742

Colour, Confusion and Concessions

THE HISTORY OF THE CHINESE IN SOUTH AFRICA

Colour, Confusion and Concessions

The History of the Chinese in South Africa

Melanie Yap and Dianne Leong Man

Hong Kong University Press
香港大學出版社

Hong Kong University Press
139 Pokfulam Road, Hong Kong

ISBN 962 209 423 6 (Hardback)
ISBN 962 209 424 4 (Paperback)

Printed in Hong Kong by Color Print Co.

Contents

Sources of Illustrations

Most of the illustrations in this book have been donated by individuals to form part of the South African Chinese History Project's collection. Page numbers and sources for the other photographs are as follows:

Abbreviations:	*TLWE*	*Transvaal Leader Weekly Edition*
	TWI	*Transvaal Weekly Illustrated*

Page	Source
2, 4	courtesy of Dr Oscar Norwich
11	Cape Archives Depot, No M164 and No. E3417
23	Natal Archives Depot, No. C993
38	*TLWE*, 3 August 1907
46/7	McGregor Museum, Kimberley
91	*TLWE*, 10 December 1906
92	Liberation Museum, Beijing, courtesy of Jonathan B. Thompson
94	Natal Archives Depot, No. C51
107	*TLWE*, 19 May 1906
110	*TLWE*, 20 May 1905
113	Local History Museum, Durban. No. Q/81/8/9 and Q/81/6/5
114	Simmer & Jack Mine
115	Johannesburg Public Library
116	University of the Witwatersrand Library
117/8	Johannesburg Public Library
120	Simmer & Jack Mine
121	*The Star Weekly Edition*, 16 February 1907
123	*TLWE*, 1 December 1906
130	*TLWE*, 19 May 1906
132	Krugersdorp Municipality
133	*TLWE*, 6 July 1907
148	*TWI*, 28 November 1908
154	*TWI*, 22 August 1908
161	*TWI*, 15 February 1908
165	*TWI*, 8 February 1908
175	*TLWE*, 20 May 1905
311	Baileys African Photo Archives
358	(centre photograph) University of the Witwatersrand Library
364	*Daily Dispatch*, 9 April 1970

Acknowledgments

This book belongs to the Chinese people of South Africa and all who contributed to its creation. The Chinese Association of South Africa (CASA) and the Transvaal Chinese Association have remained steadfast in their hope that this work would eventually be completed, and we appreciate their trust. Thanks must go too to the Eastern Province Chinese Association and the other member associations of CASA who assisted us — Kimberley Chinese Association, Pretoria Chinese Association, Western Province Chinese Association and East London Chinese Association.

There are several individuals who deserve special mention. Lynette Man played a significant role in the project's research, specializing in the legal aspects of the community's history and assisting in the analysis of legislation. Stanley May sacrificed much time in translating essential documents from Chinese into English and providing us with the necessary background for their interpretation. Paul Vink, Rodney Man and Eric Yenson have been our mainstays, unstinting with their expertise and advice and unfailingly generous with their assistance. Professor Peter Li of the University of Saskatchewan, Canada, read the manuscript and offered invaluable criticism and advice. Professsor Charles van Onselen of the University of the Witwatersrand, Johannesburg, read an early draft of the first chapters and provided us with much appreciated guidance on historical perspectives.

We are most grateful to Hong Kong University Press for their patience, professionalism and precision. Our research was made possible by many institutions, organizations and individuals, and to each of these, we wish to express our heartfelt gratitude. A full list of those to whom we are indebted appears from p. 437 to 442.

Acknowledgements

This book belongs to the Chinese people of South Africa and all who contributed to its creation. The Chinese Association of South Africa (CASA) and the Transvaal Chinese Association have remained steadfast in their hope that this work would eventually be completed, and we appreciate their trust. Thanks must go too to the Eastern Province Chinese Association and the other member associations of CASA who assisted us — Kimberley Chinese Association, Pretoria Chinese Association, Western Province Chinese Association and East London Chinese Association.

There are several individuals who deserve special mention. Lynette Man played a significant role in the project's research, specialising in the legal aspects of the community's history and assisting in the analysis of legislation. Stanley May sacrificed much time in translating essential documents from Chinese into English and providing us with the necessary background for their interpretation. Paul Vink, Rodney Man and Eric Yenson have been our mainstays, unstinting with their expertise and advice and unfailingly generous with their assistance. Professor Peter Li of the University of Saskatchewan, Canada, read the manuscript and offered invaluable criticism and advice. Professor Charles van Onselen of the University of the Witwatersrand, Johannesburg, read an early draft of the first chapters and provided us with much appreciated guidance on historical perspectives.

We are most grateful to Hong Kong University Press for their patience, professionalism and precision. Our research was made possible by many institutions, organisations and individuals, and to each of these, we wish to express our heartfelt gratitude. A full list of those to whom we are indebted appears from pp. 437 to 442.

Introduction

South Africa's Chinese constitute one of the smallest and most identifiable minority groups in arguably the most race-conscious country in the world. In this divided society, they have lived in limbo, neither dark enough to be Black nor light enough to be White. Their story is one of adaptation, of trying to fit into a society which had no place for them and of striving to find some niche in today's post-apartheid South Africa. The present community numbers around 20 000 people, or 0.04% of South Africa's population, and is made up of those who can trace their forefathers' arrival in the country back for three to five generations, as well as new immigrants from Taiwan, Hong Kong and mainland China.

For more than 300 years Chinese have been part of the fascinating mix of people who make up the inhabitants of the southern tip of Africa. Too minuscule in number to warrant any serious historical attention, they were unknown and largely forgotten in the wider South African context. The intention behind this work is to fill a gap in available histories by producing the first comprehensive record of the Chinese in South Africa from the earliest times to the present. A key objective is to correct the widely held misconception that the present-day Chinese are descendants of the labourers contracted to work on the Reef gold mines at the turn of the century.

This is not a history of South Africa, but a somewhat introspective account of the Chinese people of South Africa. Many themes raised in this book are well-documented in other works, for example, indentured mine labour, passive resistance, apartheid and the application of discriminatory laws such as Group Areas. The difference here is that attention is directed largely at the Chinese and those historical developments which shaped the community. We have put the Chinese on centre stage and this has of necessity shifted the focus away from other major players in South Africa's history. While this approach may open us to charges of having 'the tail wag the dog', we believe it is important to record minority group experiences which would otherwise be lost. Attempts have nonetheless been made to place this story within a broader South African, Chinese and international context.

Mention should be made of the way in which this work has been written. Each chapter begins with a brief outline which provides a framework for its contents. The main text serves as the detailed record of the community's history, documenting all major developments from the 1660s to the 1990s. The short story 'insets' are asides which would interrupt the flow of the main text, but nonetheless offer interesting insights into or more information on the people and subjects discussed. Of equal importance is the inclusion of photographs to bring the history of the community to life. The level of detail on regional developments may seem superfluous or even repetitious to some readers, but is necessary to serve as a record of the activities of communities in each area.

As for terminology, most Chinese regard the word 'Chinaman' as a slur. Its use in this work is unavoidable because of the extent of its occurrence in early documents. It and other derogatory racial terms have been used only in context in direct quotations. Without becoming embroiled in the political connotations of race terminology, we have chosen to use the term 'non-White' as a more practical and accurate description for people of colour than 'Black' which was once used as a generic term for all people who were not White. 'Black' refers to the indigenous African people, 'Coloured' to those of mixed racial descent and 'Indian' to those originating from the Indian sub-continent. Chinese names are rendered in the forms most familiar locally. We have used the Wade-Giles system of romanization with its Hanyu Pinyin equivalent in parentheses.

This work is developed thematically and follows a largely chronological sequence. Time periods overlap in several chapters to allow for a thorough discussion of each theme. Beginning with references to earliest Chinese contact with Africa, this account outlines the arrival of Chinese in the Cape from 1660 and events in China which precipitated the migration of thousands to foreign shores in the 19th century. It reflects the settlement of independent traders in most centres of South Africa prior to the mass importation of over 60 000 Chinese labourers to work the gold mines of the Witwatersrand in 1904. Chinese participation in Mahatma Gandhi's passive resistance campaign as well as the social and political development of the community in the early part of the 20th century are discussed. Attention is paid to the Chinese position in relation to the Japanese, the response to the Sino-Japanese War from 1937 and the emphasis on education to secure the future of the community. The impact of apartheid on the Chinese is examined with particular reference to Group Areas, Immigration and Separate Amenities laws. The work concludes with the dismantling of apartheid, the country's historic all-race elections in 1994 and the challenges confronting Chinese in the new South Africa.

The map of South Africa has since been redrawn to incorporate the former Black 'homelands' and to create nine provinces. We however refer only to the original four provinces or colonies which existed in the time period covered in this work – namely,

Cape, Natal, Orange Free State and Transvaal. South Africa's nine new provinces are Western Cape, Eastern Cape, Northern Cape, KwaZulu Natal, Free State, Gauteng, Mpumalanga, Northern Province and North West Province.

Documenting this history has been a community project, funded and supported by organizations countrywide as well as individuals who also provided information and photographs. The work was launched as the South African Chinese History Project by the Transvaal Chinese Association and from 1988 was conducted under the auspices of the community's national representative body, the Chinese Association of South Africa.

Not being historians, we embarked on this project somewhat naively, without any realization of the extent and scope of such an undertaking. Ignorant of the fact that Chinese settlement in South Africa could be traced back to the 17th century, we were also unaware of the problems of trying to find information on a virtually invisible minority. We learned as we worked, conducting more than 200 personal interviews, visiting most centres where Chinese lived to gain insights into local conditions and scouring cemeteries for evidence of early settlement. Much time was spent in state archives, libraries and museums to trace records on Chinese and to read newspapers dating from the 1860s. Two slide presentations were produced to publicize the project, to raise funds and to elicit further information from the community and historical groups.

Research proved more difficult than initially anticipated. The Chinese 'disappeared' in official records such as censuses and statistics where their small numbers led to their being incorporated into larger groups such as 'Asiatic' or 'Coloured'. Information searches were complicated by the ambitious time scale covered, variant spellings for Chinese, including Chinees, Chinezen, Sjinees and Sjinezen and the need to understand Dutch, Afrikaans, English, French and Chinese. Much assistance had to be sought particularly for the translation of Chinese language documents. South Africa's distance from Britain, Taiwan and China limited access to potentially useful archival resources. It is regrettable that most Chinese regional associations as well as the Chinese Consulate-General which was based in Johannesburg for 90 years, apparently kept few records of their activities. Notable exceptions were the Eastern Province Chinese Association and the Uitenhage Chinese Association which generously offered the history project free access to their files.

Writing the community's story has been like putting together a complicated jigsaw puzzle. Many pieces of information were collected and only after each had been verified and analyzed could we see what kind of picture was emerging. A few pieces may be missing or incomplete and lack of knowledge may have led us to err in some assessments. For this, we ask your indulgence. We have also had to deal with issues which aroused controversy within the community. Varying and sometimes conflicting accounts were given to us in interviews, but we have tried to reflect all sides in dealing with subjects such as the Chinese group area in Port Elizabeth or the role and contribution of particular individuals in the community. Some community members expressed vehement opposition to our making any mention of gambling activities such as fah-fee. We have tried to walk the middle road, including all the information we considered necessary to produce a fair and balanced account.

Many community members said this project started too late, and should have included elders who had died over the past 20 or 30 years. While the perspectives of these, the first generation of settlers, would have been invaluable, we also realized that research could probably only have been conducted earlier with grave handicaps. Throughout the 1960s and the 1970s, the community was pervaded by a sense of fear and the need to maintain a low-profile. Within a repressive political system, they were wary of the possibility of a backlash and any who asked questions were regarded with suspicion. Only by the late 1980s were circumstances right for this project. Being part of the closely-knit Chinese community enabled us to gain access to a wide cross-section of people, most of whom spoke frankly of their experiences and gave freely of their time.

In the 1990s we were fortunate to be invited to participate in three international conferences on Overseas Chinese. Contact with Chinese scholars made us realize that the experiences of the Chinese in South Africa should not be seen in isolation but had a place in the wider context of contemporary Chinese studies. Awareness of issues such as migratory patterns and ethnic identity prompted us to examine more closely their relevance locally. The South African Chinese pattern of migration could in many respects be regarded as a microcosm of Chinese migration worldwide and we hope this work will provide material of use to those interested in comparative Chinese studies.

We regret that this book has taken so many years to complete and that many of the people we interviewed have not lived to see in print the anecdotes they recounted. But the passage of time has also proved to be a boon ... history was being made while the project was in progress. Political changes in South Africa make it logical for this work to conclude in 1994 with the democratic, all-race elections which marked the end of an era for the Chinese and all South Africa. Bringing the book up to date has however left little leeway for the safety of hindsight which historians recommend, and it is for this reason that the final chapter is not an analysis but simply a record of current developments.

Nearing the end of nine years' work makes us realize how inadequate the words 'thank you' are to express our debt to the countless people who have shown their support in so many ways. There were those who shared their stories with us, the generous donors who made the research possible and all those who sought out old documents and photographs. There were those who gave unstintingly of their time to translate interviews and documents and families around the country who were warmly hospitable. Colleagues and acquaintances offered valuable snippets of advice and information, volunteers gamely accompanied us on many a foray through the veld in search of neglected graves while libraries, archives and museums countrywide gave us access to their records. Finally, of course, there are those very special people, our families and friends, without whose support, encouragement and belief in us, this work could not have been completed. Thank you.

Melanie Yap
Dianne Leong Man
Johannesburg, South Africa
October 1996

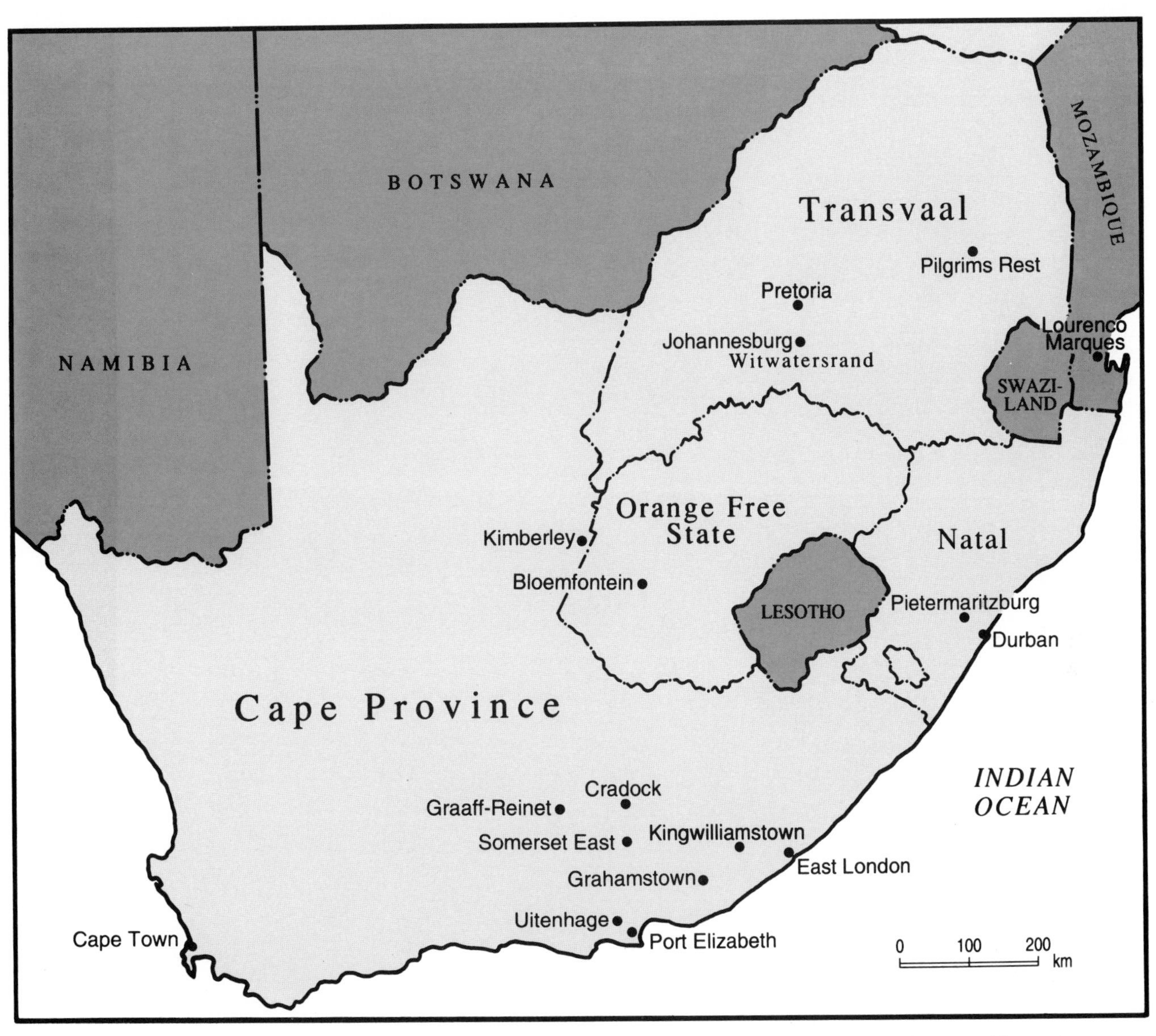

This map reflects the boundaries of the four provinces (formerly colonies and independent republics) of South Africa which are discussed in this work. Cities and towns shown are those referred to in the text.

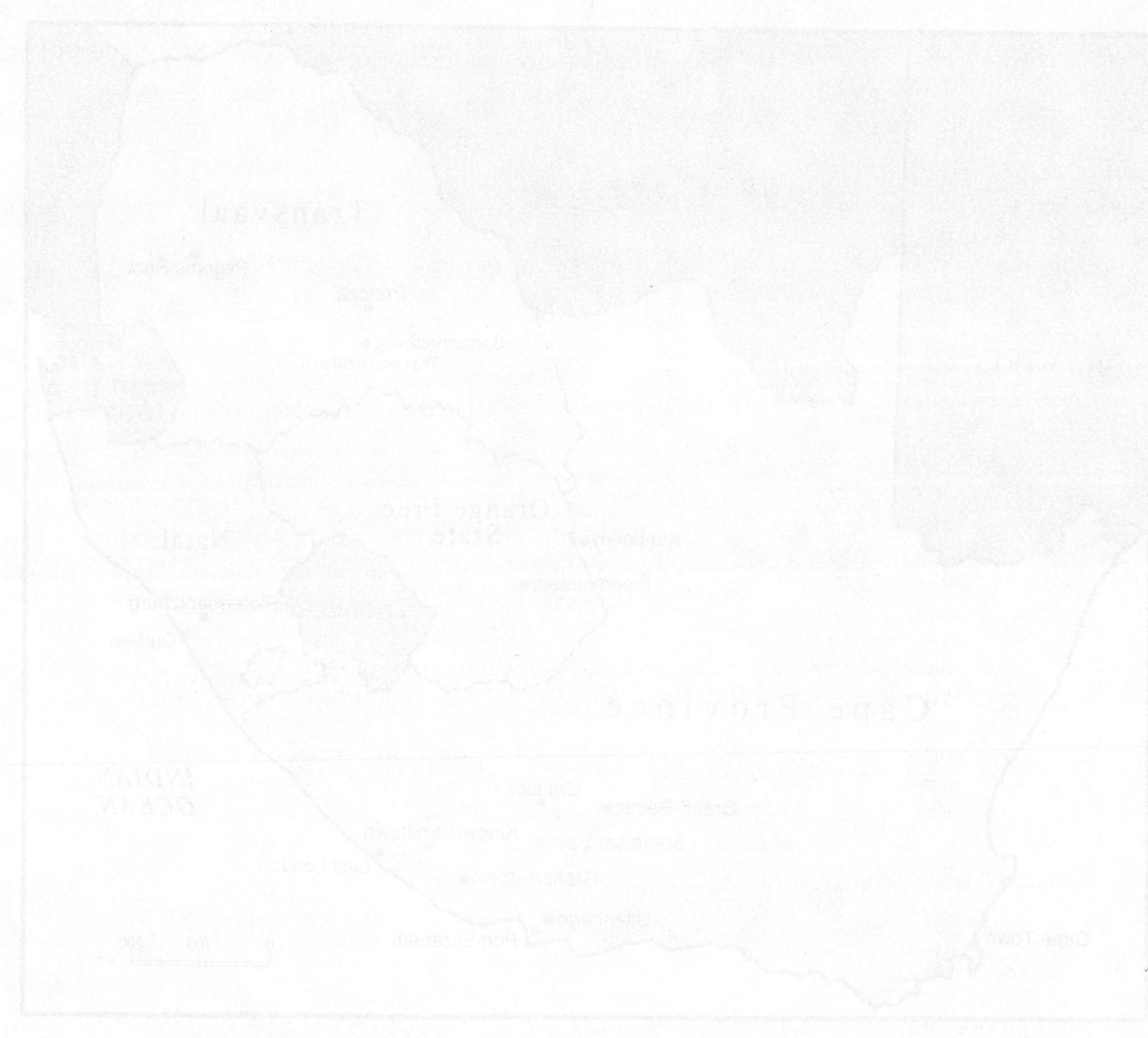

1

Convicts and Coolies 1660 – 1880

What kind of contact existed between China and Africa? Why did Chinese first come to South Africa? Beginning with earliest references to Chinese contacts with Africa, this chapter outlines the arrival of Chinese in the Cape as exiles and convicts during the 17th century and then as indentured labourers during the 19th century. Their presence was noticed from the outset, making them a ready target for racist rhetoric in those territories which were to become the British colonies of the Cape and Natal. Always the smallest of minorities, the Chinese were an adjunct to the multi-hued society being forged on the southern tip of Africa.

EARLY CONTACT

Chinese links with the continent of Africa can be traced back for nearly 2000 years. During the Han dynasty (208 BC to 220 AD) Chinese travellers recounted tales of ancient Egypt, opening the Silk Road to carry Chinese silk to the west and take home glass and coloured glazes from north Africa.[1] This cultural and commercial interchange appears to have continued in the centuries which followed, with tales of strange gifts such as a live rhinoceros, magicians, jugglers and large birds' eggs being sent to the Chinese court from remote corners of Africa.[2]

During the T'ang dynasty (618 to 907), Chinese records reflected knowledge of Berbera (also called Bobali) on the Somali coast, and Malindi in Kenya. They described a country producing ivory, rhinoceros horn and ambergris, whose people drank the blood of cattle mixed with milk and who hunted with poisoned arrows.[3] The earliest record of a Chinese setting foot on African soil dates back to around the year 750 AD. Captured in battle with the Arabs near Samarkand, Du Huan, an officer, disappeared for 12 years. On his return to China, he wrote of his experiences among Black people in a country called Molin, probably the border of today's Eritrea.[4]

Arab vessels plied a busy trade route to China's southern ports and slaves from Zanzibar and Madagascar were sent to China. It was only during the Ming dynasty (1368 – 1644) that Chinese ships actually sailed to Africa.[5] Early maps offer concrete evidence that the Arabs and Chinese knew more about the southern part of Africa than most historians have recognized. In 1320, more than 150 years before the Portuguese explorer Bartholomew Dias told Europe that South Africa existed, Chinese cartographer Chu Ssu-pen (Zhu Siben) compiled a map revealing the triangular shape of the southern African sub-continent. Ch'uan Chin's map, 82 years later, fills in more detail, showing inland waters and possibly the Orange River flowing westward. Between 1405 and 1433,

Ming dynasty cartographer Ch'uan Chin produced this map of the world in 1402, showing the continent of Africa on the extreme left.

the most famous explorer of the Ming Dynasty, Cheng Ho (Zheng He), undertook seven expeditions in the Indian Ocean, the nautical chart of his voyages reflecting the extent of Chinese knowledge of this region.[6]

Noted Sinologist, J.L. Duyvendak asserted it was a *giraffe* which first prompted the Chinese to sail to Africa in 1417, on an expedition to Malindi on Kenya's coast. He said in the Somali language, a giraffe was called a 'girin' which to the Chinese would sound much like 'ki-lin' — a mythical animal which could be equated to the unicorn. Legend had it that the appearance of the 'ki-lin' was evidence of Heaven's favour and augured well for an emperor's rule. So when ambassadors from Malindi visited the Chinese court in 1415 taking with them a gift of a giraffe, they were warmly welcomed and honoured by a Chinese escort, which accompanied them all the way home to the east African coast.

The appearance of a giraffe in China was immortalized in poetry and painting, and lavishly described in such verses of praise:

> Truly was produced a K'i-lin whose shape was high 15 feet,
>
> With the body of a deer and the tail of an ox, and a fleshy boneless horn,
>
> With luminous spots like a red cloud or a purple mist,
>
> Its hoofs do not tread on (living) beings and in its wanderings it carefully selects its ground,
>
> It walks in stately fashion and in its every motion it observes a rhythm,
>
> Gentle is this animal that in all antiquity has been seen but once ...[7]

Small wonder that Africa was an area of much interest to early Chinese explorers!

Limiting the focus of this work to southern Africa however, fragments of information point to Chinese contact with the sub-continent over the past 1000 years. Chinese porcelain dating from the Sung dynasty (960 – 1279) has been found in Zimbabwe,[8] and inhabitants of Ndarangwa in Zimbabwe's Honde Gorge have, for generations, used the Chinese character for the surname 'Tien' [田] as a decorative motif on walls and clay pots.[9]

Even in South Africa, porcelain dating from the Sung dynasty is said to have been found at an excavation at Mapungubwe, in the northern Transvaal.[10] While finds of pottery do not necessarily point to direct human contact, evidence suggests the Chinese, or some Mongolian people, visited South Africa before Black tribes moved south in the 16th century. Bushman paintings once assumed to be foreigners wearing peaked Chinese and peg-topped Mongolian hats have been found at Magdala, near Barkly East in the north eastern Cape province, and along the Kei and White Kei Rivers near East London. In the 1920s, Brother Otto, a Trappist monk at the Marianhill monastery in Natal, made painstaking sketches of Bushmen paintings in rock shelters, at least two of which were possibly inspired by some oriental people. Renowned anthropologist Raymond Dart said these finds were highly significant in demonstrating 'an extremely ancient cultural impact upon the aboriginal Bushman'.[11]

He also speculated that the peaked straw hats, characteristic of Lesotho headgear, originated from contact with the Orient when the Basotho people lived further north,

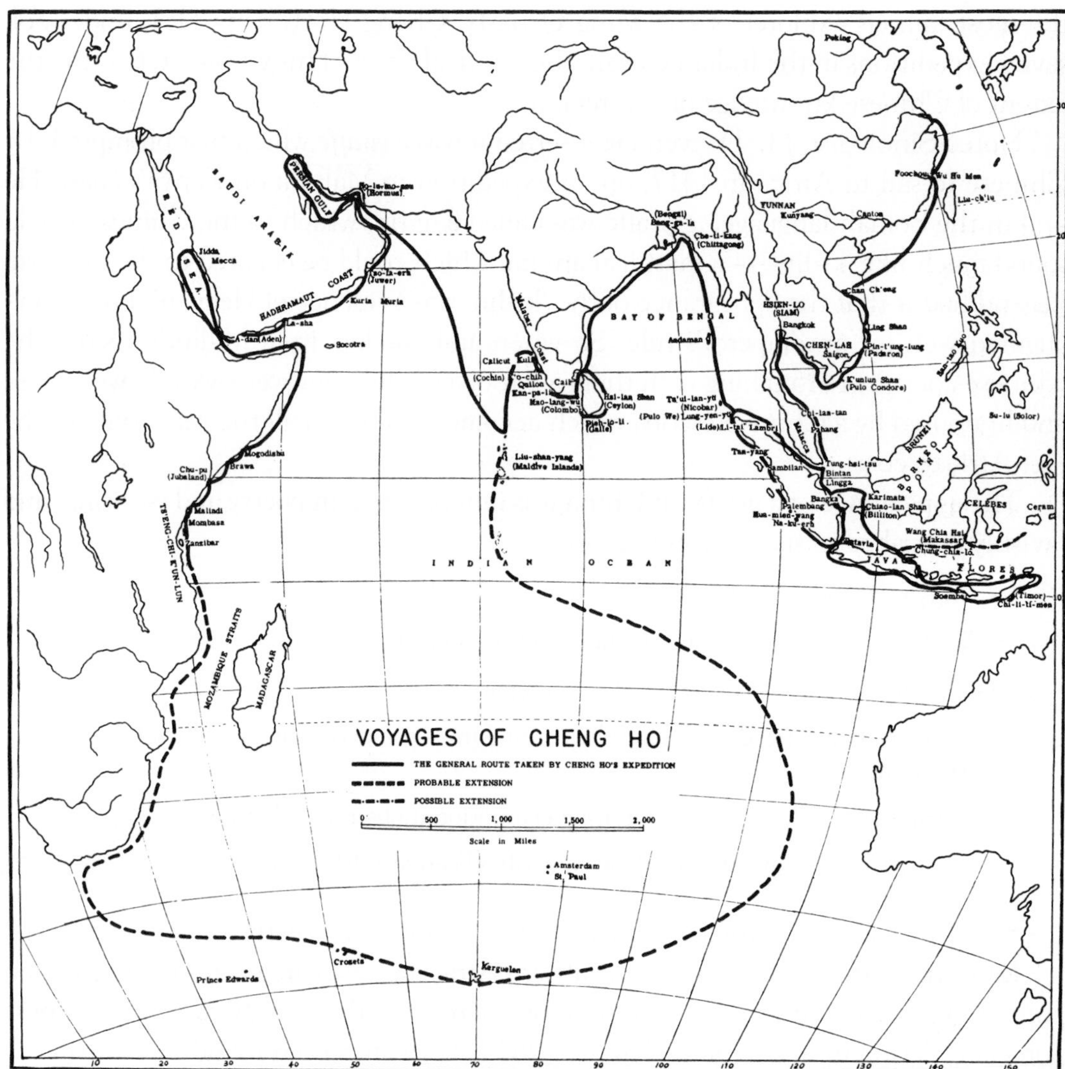

This nautical chart of the route traversed by Ming dynasty explorer, Admiral Cheng Ho, reflects the possible extent of Chinese knowledge of the Indian Ocean area.

or were adopted from the 'Bust-Hottentot' communities of the eastern Cape. Of these nomadic tribes, he wrote:

> So Chinese did these Kei River people appear to early Dutch settlers that they called them Snese Hottentoten: Chinese Hottentots.[12]

Chroniclers of the early Cape described inhabitants in the vicinity of the Great and Little Fish Rivers, near East London, as 'a tribe of Hottentots of somewhat lighter colour, yellower than the others, called on that account Chinese Hottentots',[13] and a people 'with curling hair, ... called Little Chinese.'[14]

Perhaps it was simply these names which gave rise to flights of fancy on the origins of the Khoikhoi (also called Hottentots) and speculation that they were descendants of Chinese sailors who visited the African coast. While it is highly improbable that any such Chinese temporarily settled in Africa before European colonization, the theories, nevertheless, make for interesting if somewhat 'popular' reading.[15] In brief, the story goes that before the year 1300 navigators from south China, called Manzi, were frequent visitors to the east and west coasts of South Africa. Remaining ashore for five to six months for the south-west winds to aid the voyages of their junks, they mixed closely with the local people ... a possible explanation for the Mongolian characteristics of the Hottentots.[16] Surmising that Port Nolloth was 'the home of the true yellow Hottentots, the Snese, or Chinese Hottentots of the old Cape Dutch', one writer points to the tonal similarity between the Hottentot and Chinese languages, adding that 'any number of Chinese ships must have been wrecked on the Namaqualand coast from 945 to at least 1295'.[17]

In this vein, the Bahurutsi tribe of Bechuanas (Tswanas) has been linked to similar origins. Said to trace their history back to the middle of the 13th century when the Chinese abandoned their trips to the southern African coast, they too wore peak-topped, oriental hats. 'These Chinese-Bantus were referred to as the abandoned people, Awatwa, a name later given to the Bushmen.'[18]

CHINESE CONVICTS ARRIVE IN THE CAPE : 1660 – 1795

European expansion towards the East necessitated navigation around southern Africa and from the end of the 15th century, Portuguese ships bypassed the Cape. Although English, French and Dutch East India companies all considered establishing a base in Table Bay for their ships, only the Dutch did so in 1652. Not intended to be a colony or settlement, the Cape of Good Hope was founded as a refreshment station with a hospital, granary and garden to supply fresh provisions for Dutch ships traversing the busy sea route between the Netherlands and Asia.[19] It served as an outstation for the vast trading empire controlled by the Dutch East India Company (VOC)[20] from Batavia (Djakarta) in Java, Indonesia.

The Cape, populated by Khoikhoi herdsmen and San (Bushman) hunters, held the promise of rich agricultural potential in fertile soil, fresh water and a temperate climate. Difficulties however in developing intensive cultivation prompted the first Cape commander, Jan van Riebeeck, to suggest that agriculture be handed over to freeburghers (free citizens) who would perhaps labour more diligently on their own land than as Company employees. Settlement of freeburghers was encouraged by grants of land and these former VOC employees formed the nucleus of the permanent White population which would increase slowly in the following years.[21]

Sufficient labour to develop the Cape's resources was cause for much concern from the outset of the establishment of the refreshment station. The indigenous Khoikhoi people were reluctant to become labourers and Van Riebeeck persistently pleaded for the services of slaves. On several occasions he also asked the Company to send him a few Chinese to introduce agricultural and fishing skills.[22] The Chinese in Java, however, did not regard the Cape as a worthwhile risk and the India Council informed Van Riebeeck: 'We have not been able to persuade any Chinese to leave their country for such a distant land and with such uncertain prospects.'[23] Just a few years later, in 1656, the Council said it was trying to find some 'industrious Chinese' to promote agriculture but again confessed defeat ... 'We would have liked to send you some Chinese volunteers for agricultural purposes but all were unwilling and could not be persuaded to go.'[24]

Slavery played an important part in the Dutch East India Company's activities in the Indies and its introduction in the Cape set the pattern for relations between racial groups which would be marked by the dominance of Whites over Blacks. The following description of the legal status of slaves as defined in Roman law sums up the position of those consigned to the Cape:

> ... slaves have not any of those rights and privileges which distinguish the state of the free in civil society; they cannot marry, they do not possess the right of disposing of their children, even if they be minors, they cannot possess any money or goods in property ... they cannot make a will, and they are therefore considered in the civil law as not existing.[25]

From 1658 the Company imported slaves and used the Cape as a penal settlement for its unwanted criminals, political exiles and other undesirables from the East Indies.[26]

So, ironically, the first Chinese to arrive in the Cape were not the farmers with knowledge of rice and sugar planting, the fishermen, carpenters, masons and craftsmen that both Van Riebeeck and his successors sought. Instead, they were a few among the thousands of convicts, banished from Batavia, either for debts owed the Company or for offences and crimes largely unspecified in the Cape records.[27]

The exiles were Indian, Singhalese, Javanese, Chinese and other Indonesians. And since most Chinese in Batavia at the time were from Fukien (Fujian), it is likely the Chinese who came to the Cape were Fukienese. The first Chinese convict to arrive appears to have been a man named 'Wancho', sent on the *Arnhem* in 1660.[28] Four years later, Ytcho Wancho was caught attacking a slave woman in the Cape with a knife. After unsuccessfully trying to hang himself, he was sentenced to a flogging and then banished to serve out his term on Robben Island which lies seven kilometres off Cape Town's coast.[29]

Although never numbering more than 50 to 100 at any one time, some Chinese left traces of their existence in legal documents, wills and petitions. In an extensively researched work on the Chinese at the Cape during the Dutch occupation from 1652 to 1795, historian James Armstrong sketched a vivid picture of the lives of these exiles. As convicts they were, in everything but name, Company slaves. The numbers who died were high ... and red tape, strung out from distant Batavia, added to their hardships. In one case, a convict sentenced to serve 10 years at the Cape was found 22 years later still there![30] The Chinese convicts were employed as basketmakers, fishermen and masons.

In Batavia, the Dutch feared economic competition from Chinese settlers and imposed restrictions on their trade and movement. This led in 1740 to a massive uprising which saw the massacre of thousands of Chinese and the deportation of many back to China, or to Ceylon (Sri Lanka) and the Cape.[31] When the Chinese convicts in the Cape had completed their terms or when they were pardoned, they either returned to Batavia or chose to remain in the Cape as 'free' Blacks, the status accorded to former slaves who had won their liberation. 'Free Blacks', during the Company period, was a term which included Chinese and generally referred to all free people wholly or partially of African or Asian descent. It did not however seem to be applied to the indigenous Khoisan people.[32] As a description it was a misnomer since the majority of free Blacks were from Asia — India, Ceylon, Indonesia and China.[33]

In 1722 the Chinese with other free Blacks were formed into a type of citizens' defence force in the Table Valley — their task being to deal with emergencies such as fire or ships being stranded in Table Bay.[34] In very rare instances did free Blacks own fixed property, although the more affluent among them did own slaves. From 1752, freed men were given all the privileges and rights of burghers (citizens) but they were certainly never regarded as the equals of Whites. In the 1790s, free Blacks had to carry passes if they wished to leave town, a requirement not made of free-born citizens.[35]

Some Prosperous 'Free' Chinese

A difficulty in researching individual Chinese in the Cape's early days is the variety of spellings given to a single name, for example the names Onka, Onko, Onkonko, Oquanko, Loquanko and Hoquanko all refer to the same person. While most of the individuals' names do not appear to be 'Chinese', it is likely they were simply transcribed to match a sound more familiar to the Dutch, and some Chinese probably adopted Dutch names.

One of these was perhaps the first free Chinese in the Cape, Abraham de Vyf, also known as 'Tuko de Chinees'. He was accepted into the Reformed Church and baptized in 1702, 'an unprecedented event at the Cape'. The Church Council also noted that another two Chinese were receiving religious instruction. Abraham de Vyf accumulated some property and intended to return to Batavia, but died in 1713, leaving his widow, Maria Jacobs Eenre and three children, Daniel, Christina and Beatrix de Vyf.

A rather prosperous Chinese was Horloko, a goldsmith and interpreter. His will in 1724 named three sons and a daughter, living in Quintangh province in China — probably the southern province of Kwangtung (Guangdong). Another successful individual was Oquanko who lived in the Cape for at least 10 years and who, in 1726, owned one female and five male slaves. He was a baker, and it seems likely that a 1727 edict forbidding the sale of baked goods in the streets of Cape Town, was specifically directed against him. That year the licensed bakers complained of unfair competition from Chinese bakers sending their 'boys' into the streets.[36]

Some of the Chinese exiles deported from Batavia were exempted from serving hard labour during their terms of banishment, and instead, paid a 'special tax'.[37] Virtually all Chinese within the ranks of the free Blacks were former convicts. Their numbers were few ... there were only two in 1725, rising to 16 in 1750 and then declining to three in 1774.[38] Nevertheless the Dutch settlers saw them as 'unwelcome competitors' in activities such as baking, petty trading, shopkeeping and ships' provisioning, and also accused them of receiving stolen goods, thus encouraging theft.[39]

One major chronicler of the Cape at the time, Otto Friedrich Mentzel, claimed they did not deal with thieves among the slaves, but received goods from sailors smuggling items from the ships. Of the Chinese traders he said:

> ... it is dangerous to generalize and condemn them all as rogues. Some of them will show more consideration to those who owe them money than Europeans do. I have met people to whom Asiatic dealers had given various commodities such as tea, chinaware and Eastern fabrics on long credit, even until their return from Holland. On the whole these Chinese live a humble, quiet and orderly life at the Cape.[40]

From the 1740s, it appears the handful of free Chinese (probably no more than 12 men) ran restaurants, sold vegetables, and were active as traders, chandlers and craftsmen. Describing their activities, Mentzel wrote:

> Some of these Chinese are expert fishermen as well as good cooks. Fried or pickled fish with boiled rice is well-favoured by soldiers, sailors and slaves. When the fierce North-Westers blow, crayfish, crabs, seaspiders and 'granelen' are cast ashore. They are jealously collected by these Orientals, cooked and sold ... These Asiatics likewise keep small eating houses where tea and coffee is always to be had; they specialise in the making of kerri-kerri. One need not be squeamish in patronising their cookshops since they keep the places scrupulously clean and do not touch the food with their fingers. When they themselves feed they cut the meat, fish, etc., into small slices and put the food in their mouths with chopsticks of white wood or ivory. They manipulate these sticks with such skill that no crumb escapes their attention.[41]

Another of Mentzel's observations covered Chinese handiwork:

> The Chinese are the only candlemakers at the Cape, for though the homemade farm candle is serviceable, it cannot be compared in appearance with the handiwork of the Chinamen. Though made of mutton fat they are as white and well-shaped as wax candles.[42]

Other chroniclers too referred fleetingly to the few Chinese they encountered in the Cape. One remarked on seeing a tame tyger-wolf (spotted hyena) which had been reared from birth by a Chinese,[43] and another described his landing at the Cape in 1772, in these words:

> We were hardly come to an anchor, before a crowd of black slaves and Chinese came in their small boats to sell and barter, for clothes and other goods, fresh meat, vegetables, and fruit, all of which our crew were eager to procure.[44]

Among the Chinese in the Cape, several are known to have signed official documents in Chinese characters. Although this was not proof that they were literate in Chinese, sufficient numbers must have been able to read for the Company to post important edicts in Chinese as well as in Malay, Javanese and Dutch.[45] Several Dutch statutes relating specifically to Chinese forbade them to wear 'European clothing' and imposed a high customs duty on the export of Chinese corpses. Furthermore, the estate of a Chinese who died without leaving a will was divided equally between a widow and sons, with daughters only being entitled to half of their mother's share.[46]

Petitions lodged in the Cape Archives offer some insights into the concerns and the hardships encountered by the convict and 'free' Chinese. In 1733 two men asked to be relieved of hard labour, stating that they had been in the Cape for 20 years and were growing too old to work. It appears the authorities only then discovered that although the men had been banished to the Cape for life, no mention had been made of their being condemned to hard labour![47] Ten years later 38 Chinese appealed for permission to return to Batavia, several having served their punishment in chains and others wishing to be pardoned.[48] In a rather plaintive series of petitions from 1724, a Chinese named Pang Sisay appealed repeatedly for pardon. Aged 65 years, he said he had been sentenced to hard labour but was continually sick and unable to work. The records only reflected that he had been banished for 'some offence', but the man's pleas appear to have gone unheeded.[49] Many Chinese requested permission to manumit their slaves or to be allowed to return to Batavia.

In contrast to the trickle of Chinese into the colony, there is at least one instance of a Chinese being banished from the Cape to Batavia shortly after the British took control of the Cape in 1806. He was Simon Arnold, 37, who was tried for theft and exiled to Batavia in 1807.[50] As single men, the handful of free Chinese practised polygamy and obtained wives by purchasing female slaves.[51] Of all owners applying to free their slaves, four percent were Chinese. Many of these stated they wished to marry their freed slaves.[52] That several Chinese had children by slave women is clear from various petitions in which they applied for the manumission of their children. In 1737 Limkoksaaij asked for the freedom of his 18-year-old daughter, Cornelia, whose mother was Sophia of Angie, a Company slave, and in 1765 Liminionko requested the manumission of his slave Dina, and the two children he had procreated by her.[53]

Few as the Chinese were in the Cape's early days, they warranted a separate burial ground, near the gallows.[54] Quite where this was is difficult to say since varying descriptions have been given on its position. It has been said to lie north west of Cape Town, perhaps on the site now occupied by Gallows Hill Road,[55] but another observer has placed it south of the city.[56] The only description of a Chinese burial was recorded by Thunberg in the late 1700s:

> In their burying ground at a short distance from the city, small ratans are stuck up, fastened together with cotton thread, so as to form an arch or a vaulted roof over the tomb.[57]

The numbers of free Chinese declined through the latter part of the 18th century. Since only two Chinese women are known to have come to the Cape (neither of whom had children), any offspring of the 17th and 18th century Chinese would have become part of the Cape's emerging Coloured population.[58] The term 'Coloured' is generally used in South Africa to denote persons of mixed racial descent.

BRITISH SEEK CHINESE LABOUR

From the time of the Dutch occupation, the boundaries of White settlement in the Cape had been steadily pushed eastwards and northwards. Hunting and trading expeditions regularly set out in search of ivory and cattle, 'trekboers' (nomadic farmers) sought out grazing lands in outlying country areas and pioneers dispersed into the hinterland. White settlers first encountered Blacks along the eastern Cape frontier. Xhosa moving westward across the Fish River in search of hunting and grazing land for their cattle crossed paths with colonists moving eastward over the Gamtoos River, and there the struggle for land gave rise to bitter conflicts.

Control of the Cape changed hands three times between 1795 and 1806, passing from the declining Dutch East India Company to the British, then back to the Batavian Republic in the Netherlands and the colony was eventually formally placed under British rule. Immigrants had arrived from France, Germany and other parts of central Europe to swell the White population to 26 568 in 1806.[59] British rule introduced new influences challenging the cultural uniformity of a society which was largely Dutch-speaking and under the sway of the Calvinist Dutch Reformed Church. English replaced Dutch as the official language, religious toleration was extended, many trade restrictions were removed and measures abolishing slavery were introduced.[60]

The persistent shortage of cheap labour in the colony continued to motivate periodic calls for the importation of Chinese workers. And it was not long before artisans were smuggled out of China to work as contract labourers for the Cape colonial government. As early as 1804, a Cape official, John Barrow, had proposed the settlement of 10 000 Chinese farmers in the Cape, Stellenbosch and Drakenstein districts. He suggested the grant of free land to enable the industrious Chinese not only to supply local markets but to produce sufficient surplus for export. This importation 'would prove a more valuable gold mine to the colony, than those which are supposed to exist'.[61]

Nothing came of the suggestion, although in later years the view was expressed that Chinese would be most useful as 'artificers, mechanics, and domestic servants' in Cape Town and smaller towns.[62] In 1810, a Chinese cabinet maker named Iyou appealed to the Governor of the Cape for permission to remain in the colony until his health improved. A traveller aboard the *Fort William* bound for India, he expressed the wish to settle in the Cape.[63]

Nearly 50 Chinese artisans arrived in the Cape in the following years. In 1814, Capt. T.T. Harington, brought 23 Chinese craftsmen to erect his new home and establish the gardens at Seaforth, in Simonstown, Cape. They included 3 carpenters, 3 masons, 2 stonecutters and 15 farmers.[64] Faced with this example, the Governor of the Cape, Lord Charles Somerset, may have been influenced in his decision to request 25 Chinese artificers to serve the Cape's Colonial Government. In April 1815, Harington transported these artisans from Canton to Cape Town aboard the *Scaleby Castle*.

Referring to the Chinese government's prohibition on the emigration of any Chinese, Harington offered no guarantee that the labourers were able or qualified. They had been brought aboard secretly, just before the ship's departure and their capabilities were taken on 'general assurance only'.

> The 25 consisted of a Foreman and 12 ordinary masons, a Foreman and 10 ordinary carpenters and one 'carpenter and painter'.

Their three-year contract stated they would serve His Majesty's Government at the Cape of Good Hope 'in our several capacities, faithfully, honestly and industriously, at

Table Bay in the 17th century offered early sailors a spectacular view of its major landmark, Table Mountain.

The Chinese Junk, Keying, as seen in 1848. It was believed to be the first junk to round the Cape of Good Hope, arriving at Gravesend in England 477 days after departing from Canton.

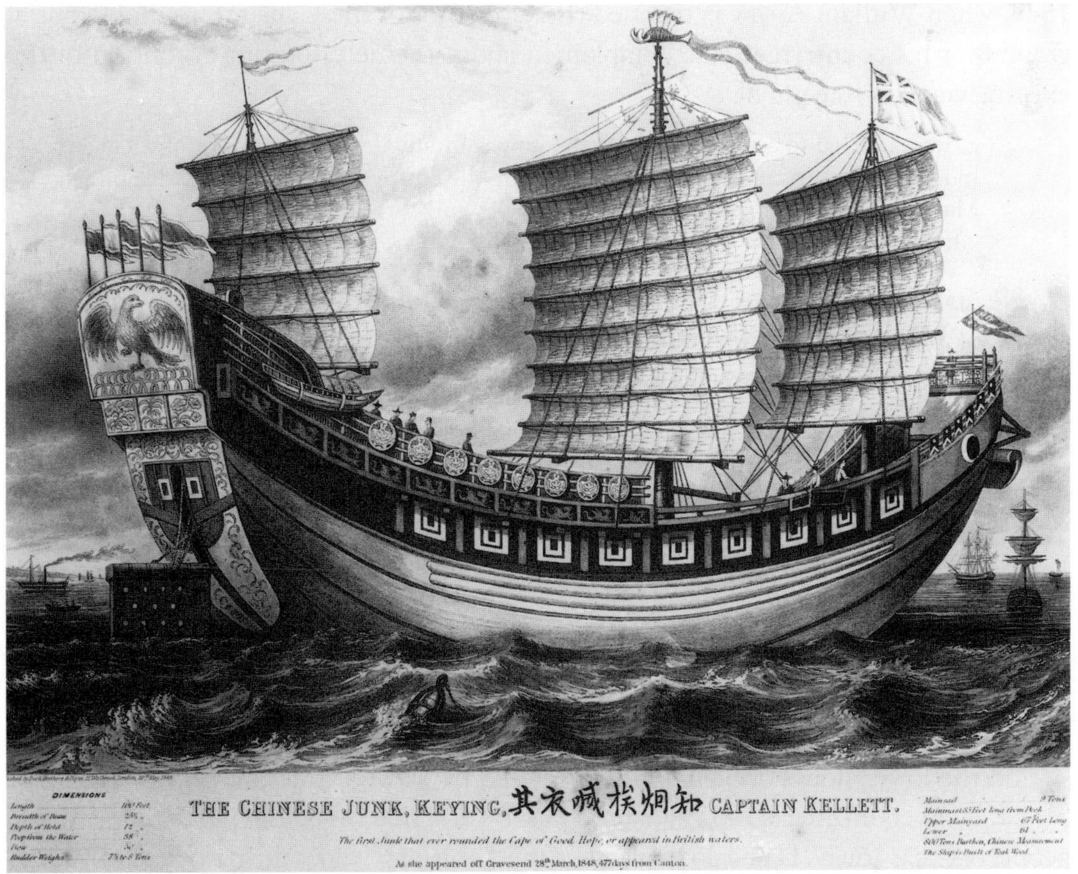

the wages of Eight Spanish Dollars per month with wholesome food and suitable lodging; and we also acknowledge to have received from Captain Thomas Talbot Harington three months advance of wages previous to our leaving China.'[65]

It appears four of these men were sent to work on the Drostdy at George, but returned to Cape Town after a few months, dissatisfied with their working conditions. One was subsequently employed at Knysna, and 10 others were still working in 1822. Some of these workmen built the belfry and wooden campanile of the English chapel in the Naval Yard at Simonstown.[66]

A number of Chinese indentured labourers from St Helena were also sent to the Cape after Britain took control of the small Atlantic Ocean island in 1834. The Cape Archives contain various petitions relating to the plight of these labourers. Many appealed to be sent home to China, or to be returned to St Helena. Some stated they were too old to continue working while others asked for an increase in their maintenance allowance. It is difficult to judge how many Chinese from St Helena were in the Cape but an amount of £252/16/6 was spent on their maintenance between 1 January 1847 and 30 June 1848.

EARLY CHINESE CEMETERY IN THE CAPE

Reference has already been made to a cemetery set aside for those Chinese who were sent to the Cape from Batavia. This was most probably the site referred to, on 26 March 1829, when William Assaw petitioned the Governor of the Cape for a suitable burial ground for his countrymen. He complained about the deteriorating condition of the existing cemetery saying he

> ... was shocked to see the entire of the graves totally defaced and most of them hidden from view, a heap of rubbish covering the entire of the grave ground. The Malaye's (sic) grave ground, at the height of Wall Street, is close to that of the Chinese ...

He questioned whether the ground had been purchased by the Malay community, and if so, asked the governor to allow another portion of land for Chinese interment. An official note attached to this petition states that the site concerned

> appears to have been appropriated many years ago by the Chinese as a place of Interment but neglected of late years in consequence of the comparative small numbers of that nation who continue to reside in this Colony — on which account also the said piece of ground has been encroached upon by the Malayes to enlarge their adjoining burial ground.[67]

Within a matter of months, Assaw's request was granted and a piece of land was ceded 'in full and free property to the Chinese of this Town, for the sole and express purpose of a Burial place, the undermentioned piece of ground, situated on the side of the Lions Rump, Cape Town'. The government surveyor's map of the cemetery shows a site on the lower slopes of Signal Hill, bordered by Dawes Street, just off Longmarket Street. It covers an area of 6817 square feet and is described as belonging to the 'Chinese people of Cape Town'. Dated 26 November 1830, the map values the property at £1000.[68]

The Chinese of St Helena

The tiny island of St Helena, 3000 km north west of Cape Town, in the south Atlantic Ocean, is perhaps best known as the place of exile of self-proclaimed French Emperor, Napoleon Bonaparte. Discovered by Portuguese sailor, Juan de Nova Castella, in 1502, it was used as a refreshment station by Portuguese ships traversing the sea route between Europe and Asia. St Helena was first colonized by the British, then the Dutch, and in 1673 ceded to the United English East India Company.

In May 1810, the Company imported fifty Chinese labourers from Canton (Guangzhou) to work in St Helena. They soon proved their value to the island and another 150 were requisitioned.

> "They were divided into two tribes according to their place of origin and were accompanied by priests and interpreters. Rules for the employment and control of the Chinese were laid down, and as late as 1828 these are to be found in the island bye-laws, showing that the scheme continued to be useful to the Colony.
>
> It seems that the number of Chinese stabilized at about 400 for some time. China Lane and masonry bearing Chinese characters remain today to remind St Helenians of the industrious and skilled workmen who contributed so much during some of the most eventful years of the island's history."[69]

One of the labourers returned home 'with a tidy sum of money' to import silk worms from China. But although a silk-worm farm was started in 1828, it failed to become a profitable industry.[70] Most of the labourers were employed in farming, and some worked as mechanics. Their contracts were for three years, later extended to five years, and although some chose to return to China, they were soon replaced by Chinese sailors off passing ships.[71]

Writing on the role of these labourers, the island governor, Major General Alexander Beatson, said,

> "In respect of the Chinese, they are a good deal employed in agriculture; that is, in fencing the lands, in paring and burning, in driving carts, in planting and gathering potatoes, and many other offices; and some are already become expert ploughmen ...
>
> The Company pay the labourers a shilling a day, and finds them in rations; and by this mode, their military services may be at command, and very useful in aiding the corps of artillery, in dragging of cannon, and carriage of ammunition; in short, in employments similar to those of the artillery Lascars in India. As they are all placed under the direction of European overseers, it cannot be doubted that much more labour is obtained from them than if they were left to themselves."[72]

In 1818 it appears fights broke out between the two Chinese groups on the island — those from Canton and others from Macao. Two Chinese were shot in the incident.[73]

When St Helena became a Crown Colony in 1834, the British government faced the problem of repatriating the Chinese. Many were sent to Cape Town where they were given an allowance by the government.

Of the Chinese who remained on St Helena, the former Commissioner of Crown Property, John Charles Mellis, wrote in 1875: '... it is regretted that such industrious men have quite disappeared. A year or two ago the last remaining Chinaman died at a good old age ... the only records of their time exist in the Chinese cemetery, at a spot called New Ground, and an extremely picturesque little Jos house at Black Square; but both of these are fast falling into decay.'[74]

Chinese buried there probably included Atim, a middle aged man who died in the old Somerset Hospital on 5 May 1836[75] and the poor soul, known only as 'a Chinaman' called Attick or Artick. A sparse death notice in the Cape records reveals that he died in a pauper asylum at the age of 64 on 3 November 1846, leaving no children and no belongings.[76]

Ten years after being granted the land, community leaders erected walls around the cemetery and advised the Chinese of Cape Town to apply to be buried there. They published the following notice in the *Cape of Good Hope Gazette* on 1 May 1840:

Notice to the Chinese

William Assier, Assam, and Achin, headmen of the Chinese people resident in this Colony, having, by permission of His Excellency the Governor, had appropriated to them a plot of ground as a Burial place for the people of that nation, and having built, by subscription amongst themselves, enclosure walls, &c. around the same, hereby give notice, that all natives of China, and their wives lawfully married, or children by said marriages, may claim for themselves or deceased relatives the right of burial therein free, upon application to either of the headmen above named.[77]

For as long as the present-day Chinese community can remember, at the twice-yearly festivals of tomb-sweeping and honouring the dead in April and August, visits have been paid to this graveyard. Because no tombstones remain, flowers are left at the gateway.[78] Chinese were not only buried in the cemetery at Signal Hill. There is a record of one Chinese who was interred in the Anglican graveyard of St George's, on a site fronting Somerset Road. He was J.J. Arshut, of Barrack Street, who died in 1853. His tombstone, carrying an inscription in both English and Chinese characters, survives at Cape Town's Maitland cemetery.[79]

CHINESE LABOUR: OPPOSED AT THE OUTSET

Between 1849 and 1882, the British-controlled colonies of the Cape and Natal experimented on a small scale with the importation of Chinese labour. Groups of Chinese were indentured both by independent farmers and agents as well as by government departments. The often bitter public opposition to the arrival of Chinese shaped legislative measures, in later years, to restrict and eventually prohibit Asiatic immigration into South Africa.

On 12 January 1849, the *Norfolk*, en route from China, docked in Port Elizabeth's Algoa Bay with a cargo of tea and a few Chinese artisans 'who will enter the service of Mr J.O. Smith, in their several callings of cooks, gardeners, carpenters etc.'

Recording the arrival of the Chinese, the local newspaper added:

> We understand that Mr Smith likewise expects a batch of men from Orkney in Scotland. When these have arrived, their union with the Chinamen will afford a

The First Chinese Community Leader

Probably the first Chinese 'community' leader in the Cape was a man known as William Assaw, Assue or Assier. These names crop up in various records between 1829 and 1840; the first name William is consistent in all the references; and the similarity in the surnames is too coincidental to ignore. Perhaps the various spellings arose as different individuals wrote down the name according to its sound.

Nevertheless, this man emerges as an articulate individual who spoke up on behalf of the Chinese in the Cape, appealing first for a Chinese cemetery and later requesting assistance for Chinese labourers from St Helena. William Assaw may well have been illiterate in English, for one of his petitions was signed with a cross, yet he certainly knew whom to engage to prepare his petitions to officials.

Addressing the Cape Governor in a letter dated 26 March 1829, William Assaw, said he was 'a native of China' who intended shortly to leave the colony. He however expressed his concern about obtaining some land for burying his countrymen, 'as it will be of infinite pleasure to Petitioner in case his request is granted before his departure'.[80] Evidently Cape officials regarded him as a spokesman for the community since the cover sheet of the title deed to the Chinese burial ground refers to 'William Assaw as representing the Chinese Population of Cape Town'.[81]

Despite stating that he intended leaving, it is possible he simply visited China then returned to the Cape. By April 1838, one William Assue appeared to be caring for a number of Chinese labourers who had been transferred from St Helena to the Cape. On behalf of 10 of these 'aged and worn out' strangers, he petitioned the Cape governor for their sixpence a day allowance to be increased to a shilling. A police report attached to this petition, of 17 April 1838, states:

> "Among these Pensioners there are some not too old to do something for themselves. I have no doubt they do contrive to earn a little, and which, the Chinese being so remarkable in their patriotic feelings, they share with those who from extreme age are really incapacitated from working. It strikes me that to allow these people a Shilling a day as applied for, independent of free lodgings which the Government also provides, would be setting a premium on idleness, and that meat being so dear the Pensioners might very well eat fish thrice a week so long as the present scarcity may continue and the allowance would then be found ample for their support."[82]

Undeterred by this refusal, Assue submitted another petition just two weeks later in which he cited 'the great rise in the articles ...[the former labourers]... consume, even fish and rice', and his conviction that food would not 'soon be cheaper'. His persistence paid off and he was granted 9d a day for the labourers' maintenance.[83]

His name surfaces yet again two years later, this time as 'William Assier'. A notice published in the *Cape of Good Hope Gazette* on 1 May 1840 cites him as one of the 'headmen' of the Chinese resident in the colony. In this notice, he and others said they had collectively raised funds to enclose the Chinese burial ground and would consider applications from all Chinese for burial there. Bearing in mind that it was a William Assaw who first asked for a Chinese cemetery, it is highly likely he is the same person.

> kind of literal representation of the 'ends of the earth being brought together'. And no human agency has contributed more towards this consummation than the enterprizing commercial spirit.[84]

Over the next 30 years the large-scale importation of Chinese labour for public works and local farming was a recurring theme of discussion in the colony. A shipload of Chinese, bound for Cuba, passed by the Cape in 1853 prompting officials to discuss the subject. The authorities however dismissed the issue as not 'expedient now to embark in an endeavour to introduce this class of Emigrants into the Colony of the Cape of Good Hope.'[85]

Despite the worldwide clamour for cheap labour, some Chinese did not willingly leave their homes for foreign lands. When a Spanish ship, the *Rosa del Turia*, carrying Chinese coolies from Macao to Havannah stopped at Algoa Bay for provisions in 1872, a Cape newspaper reported there were 317 'coolies' on board — 48 had died from sickness on the voyage and 22 had jumped overboard and drowned.[86]

Again addressing the subject of the cheap labour shortage on Cape farms, the newspaper argued that 'Chinamen are manifestly unsuited to the requirements of our pastoral and agricultural employers'.[87] In 1874, the Cape Parliament toyed with the idea of introducing no more than 400 Chinese labourers to assist the Public Works department in building railways. The high cost per head, treaty arrangements and safeguards required by the Imperial Chinese government, however, kept the issue in the realm of discussion only.

In a succinct summary of prevailing attitudes relating to the question of labour supply, John X. Merriman, Commissioner of the Ministerial Department of Crown Lands and Public Works, wrote in a memorandum:

> ... in the Cape the Government is called on to 'Survey mankind from China to Peru,' in the hope of creating and maintaining a class of cheap labourers, who will thankfully accept the position of helots, and not be troubled with the inconvenient ambition of bettering their condition.[88]

In the following years, the 'shall we, shan't we' approach to importing Chinese labour continued. Influential editorial writers argued that the Cape government should look more closely at aiding immigration from Europe since they would find it difficult to control the importation of Asiatics. In February 1876, the following observation appeared in a Cape Town newspaper:

> Chinamen are industrious, saving, sober, peaceful people; and they succeed in making a livelihood, and even in acquiring what is to them wealth, where an Englishman would starve. But on the other hand, they rarely or never take root in the country where they settle; they leave their women behind them, and they invariably endeavour to carry out their own laws and social system — by secret means, if necessary — in the place where they have temporarily taken up their abode.[89]

For local farmers, the long-term implications were academic. They faced an immediate, and pressing labour shortage, which some hoped could be alleviated by Chinese. Replying to a petition from an Albany farmer, in October 1882, to import Chinese labourers, with the same concessions granted to White immigrants, the Colonial Secretary wrote:

> I feel bound to say that the Government would regard the introduction of Chinese in any number as a step fatal to the future of this colony, destroying as it would any hope of creating an European population other than capitalists and landowners and with these views, it would be idle for me to hold out any hopes of assistance in the introduction of what I believe might prove a serious danger to the community.[90]

Yet private enterprise had already embarked on introducing this 'danger' into the Cape. On 10 November 1881, a group of Chinese labourers from Foochow (Fuzhou) aboard the British barque, *Ambassador*, arrived in Port Elizabeth.[91] The group consisted of 20 men, two of whom had died on the passage from China.[92] Rumours had run rife that the new arrivals would number 250, and scathing remarks condemning Chinese were widely circulated.

Unbridled racism marked a lengthy article which appeared in *The Friend of the Free State*, a newspaper published in Bloemfontein in the Orange Free State, and written by columnist 'Devoir'.

> Two hundred and fifty John Chinamen have been safely landed in the Colony, with a cargo of jingalls, Chinese fireworks, and other furious abominations; chopsticks, fat dogs, edible birds nests, and an assortment of buttons and peacock's feathers for those who may be raised to the distinction of mandarin by the present Secretary for Native Affairs ...
>
> The lower class of Chinese are filthy, dirty, terrible thieves, and I know many instances of their treachery. They are nearly all opium smokers, and great gamblers. A Chinaman will gamble away his wife, his wife's relations, and then try his hand on his own relatives ...
>
> Hanging has no effect on a Chinaman ... Decapitation is the only punishment they fear. ... When all the dogs in Cape Town are polished off, a supply will be sent from China. There is a dark tale that the Chinese are very fond of babies; this, however, I am not going to assert ... [93]

That the 250 'Chinamen' used as the basis for this racist diatribe numbered only 18 did not deter Kimberley's *Diamond Fields Advertiser* from reprinting the column, in full, under the heading, 'That Heathen Chinee Again'.[94] The Cape Argus, however, dismissed 'Devoir' as being motivated by feelings of resentment, concluding with a tongue-in-cheek invitation:

> We also make no assertions as to babies; but if John will come and make a series of square meals of every cur in Cape Town he will earn our eternal gratitude.[95]

The *Graaff Reinet Advertiser* described the Chinese as 'human rubbish' and 'moral plagues', making dark predictions on the future of the colony if Chinese were allowed to gain a foothold.[96] In Natal, an appeal was made for the adoption of a protective immigration policy to 'shut our gates against the Chinese coolie'.[97]

Injecting a measure of balance to these views, the *Cape Argus* questioned whether 'the landing of any inoffensive man on these shores should be prevented on account of his race'.

> We are not concerned to paint in any glowing colours the Chinese character; although we have on many occasions spoken of the miserable hypocrisy of objecting to the Chinaman as a colonist on the self-contradictory grounds that he gambles

> away his gains, and that he saves all he can; or that he only wishes to return to his own land, and that he will take possession of the land to which he comes. ... the Chinaman is certainly not the immigrant we would wish to see here if we could otherwise supply the place which he would fill; but if he comes, it will be because there is a practical need for his services. Petty plodding industries and small gains, such as attract the Chinese, will never bring the European settler to South Africa ... In any Chinese Immigration which may find its way to our shores, not less than in the European Immigration which we hope will go on, we shall learn in the long run that things will find their own level, despite all our fluster.[98]

The newspaper added that even opponents of Chinese immigration 'would not drive off, because of objections to his race or colour, a Chinaman who had paid his own passage here, and who was willing to do work which the white man was glad to pay for, but which the black man would not do. Whatever vices the Chinaman may be guilty of, laziness is not one of them.'

In the face of the furore, another group of Chinese disembarked from the *Notting Hill*, in December 1881 and were transported from Port Elizabeth to Cradock. And 10 Chinese were recorded as passengers for Port Elizabeth when the *Berwickshire* docked in the same month.[99]

CHINESE LABOURERS IN CRADOCK

In the course of 1882 more Chinese labourers arrived in the Eastern Cape, their sojourn remarkable mainly for the attention it attracted. The saga of the ill-fated passengers aboard the S.S. *Bylgia* aptly illustrated some of the hazards and hardships which accompanied such a venture. Fewer than 80% of the 152 labourers who set sail from Hong Kong for Algoa Bay survived the sea voyage of more than three months, and virtually all aboard ship were ill when the vessel was forced to dock in quarantine at Port Natal.

According to official medical reports, 1 died by accident and 26 of trichinosis, caused by the poor quality of provisions and water on board ship. Of the 126 who landed, half were suffering from diarrhoea, pain in their joints, fever and colic and a further seven later died in a typhoid state. Most of the survivors made a rapid recovery once they were treated to 'fresh air, fresh vegetables and meat, large in quantity and good in quality'. The Inspector for Emigrants in Hong Kong said he had had every reason to believe the men should reach their destination alive since they were nearly all skilled artisans and superior in physique to the majority of Chinese who left the port.[100]

By September 1882 the labourers were ready to take up their contracts, one of which was extending the railway line between the Eastern Cape towns of Cradock and Colesberg. Seventy men were sent aboard the S.S. *Dunkeld* to Port Elizabeth where their arrival was greeted with 'some excitement' by local residents. Speculating that some of the Chinese had been suffering from scurvy, a local newspaper noted: 'Those we saw looked fine healthy men, most of them young men. They were sent off to Cradock by rail, and, we believe, will be employed in the construction of the Cradock Extension line.'[101] Another Eastern Cape newspaper however pointed out that whatever disease had plagued the labourers, '... it is something very, very bad', and speculated on the moral evils and opium dens which the Chinese would introduce.[102]

For the labourers themselves, the controversy surrounding their importation was only beginning. Shortly after their arrival in Cradock, they refused to work, claiming that they were not being paid the wages stipulated in their contracts. Their employer, G.R. Davies, airing his grievances in the press, wrote that they had been influenced by 'three Chinese residing at Cradock, formerly gaol birds'. After stopping their food supplies and thrashing one of the ringleaders, work on the railway resumed.[103]

Describing the incident as 'A Bad Spec', the *Graaff Reinet Herald* commented:

> ... It was understood that the men with the pigtails were to be employed on the Cradock-Colesberg railway line, but as we are informed, a hitch has occurred which bids fair to assume considerable proportions ... Some of the pigtails proved to be equal to the occasion, and denied that they had ever signed or entered into any agreement at all ...[Davies], knowing that he is being cheated and that the agreement, if forthcoming, would be found all fair and square, would like to see his rebellious charges compelled to go to work ... Possibly when the copy of that agreement ... arrives from Hongkong, it will be found that Johnny Chinaman will still find some legal excuse for evading its provisions.[104]

An East London resident, however, saw the incident differently. Arguing against agents such as Davies and 'flooding the Colony with cheap labour', he wrote:

> ... This agent for the benighted Chinee carts his precious, and let us hope his unprofitable cargo to Cradock, hurries them before the Resident Magistrate to sign an agreement — some of their countrymen, however, are there before them and probably keenly remembering the suffering caused by the tender mercies of a previous coolie agent, tenders them, as in duty bound, some good practical and wholesome advice, for this they are branded as 'gaol birds.' Can it be possible that strangers in this colony can legally be coerced into signing agreements, can be sentenced to starvation, and to be beaten by others than magistrates and judges — life and property in that case are no longer safe. Our friend, G.R. Davies, however, is not easily abashed by small difficulties; he proceeds as per confession to put on the thumbscrews, in the shape of starvation. Even this does not subdue them all, for one at least receives a 'reprimand' with a stick — it is not stated to what part of the body applied, but probably the soles of the feet — thus compelling him to go on his knees before the chief man ...
>
> The cry hitherto has been that the Chinese are required in this country to compete with the native. How false that is can now plainly be seen by the arrival of these 70 Chinese artizans, evidently to cheapen the cost of European labour.[105]

A month after the initial group of 70 Chinese were despatched to work in Cradock, the remaining 43 of their countrymen arrived in Port Elizabeth. With no place to go and none assuming responsibility for their presence, they were the object of much curiosity as they waited to hear their fate outside the magistrate's court in the city.

> A benevolent Malay by name Ismail, a basket maker, gave them food and secured a night's lodging for them ... On the stoep of the Court House they presented a pitiable sight.[106]

Despite their plight, the new arrivals soon displayed a natural curiosity about their surroundings. The following account described their antics.

> Yesterday the band of Celestials were to be observed taking 'stock' of the town, the

> famous Donkin-street occupying a deal of their attention, while some took a lively interest in the working of a smithy in Main-street, and to his credit be it remarked, an unusually foolish looking Chinaman passed the greater part of the day in the congenial companionship of the 'cabbies', who appeared to highly relish his society and his pantomimic enquiries into the mysteries of their profession. Should the weather get a little cooler, it is highly probable that the Hill will be visited by our illustrious strangers — at present they shy at anything approaching exertion, and enjoy themselves in such shade as the streets afford.[107]

How long these workers enjoyed their enforced idleness is not known, but more than likely the agent who recruited them soon claimed his charges and put their services to use in the Eastern Cape. In addition to working on the railway line, Chinese labourers also built the 3000 to 4000 yards of stone wall enclosing the Cradock race course. Their work was described as 'neatly and well done.'[108]

CHINESE CONTRACT LABOUR IN NATAL

In south-eastern Africa, adjoining the Cape, the Colony of Natal was also under British rule and populated largely by Zulus as well as White settlers, many of whom had emigrated from England and Scotland in the 1850s. Although Blacks performed manual work for most Whites, coastal planters establishing sugar and cotton industries were unable to attract sufficient labourers.[109] They urged the importation of either Indian or Chinese labourers ... and in 1858, 'the manager of the Umzinto Sugar Company brought from Java a few Chinese and Malay labourers used to the cultivation of sugar-cane.'[110]

But it was the mass importation of Indian labourers from 1860 which added a forceful new element to Natal's population structure. More than 6000 indentured labourers, over two-thirds male, were imported from Madras, and a few from Calcutta. For the time being, the sugar cane plantations had the labour they needed,

> but neither the planters nor the Colony in general seem to have faced the sociological implications of the new venture nor indeed to have shown the most elementary human compassion and understanding towards the immigrants who were mainly regarded as 'hands' and no more.[111]

Indian immigration stopped temporarily in 1866, but by the 1870s, the colonists once again sought supplies of labour. Chinese were suggested as potential candidates, although enquiries on their suitability proved discouraging. Commenting on the subject, the Colonial Secretary of Hong Kong, in a letter to the Colonial Secretary of Natal, stated:

> ... it seems right that you should be made to understand, in the first instance, that a Chinaman does not, in the proper sense of the word, *emigrate*, but simply goes to a foreign country with a view of making money and of returning to his home.[112]

He added that a Chinese would want more money than the 10 to 15 shillings a month apparently offered to farm labourers, 'and he would expect to earn it without too much laborious physical work, and without denying himself reasonable indulgence in what he considers the luxuries of life.' Furthermore, he said, should the Chinese find the Colony suitable, their friends and their friends' friends would follow in the same way as the Californian emigration commenced.

The Immigration Agent for Natal, H. Firth, pointed out that Indians would 'be content to work for nearly four times less the amount of wages'.[113] He said he could recruit Chinese labourers at £11 monthly, foremen at £25, blacksmiths, carpenters and brickmakers at £20, masons and wellsinkers at £16 and bricklayers at £15. Since these were 'relatively excessive' wages, he said he expected the Colony would prefer to recruit 400 Indian labourers.

Elderly community members have long maintained that Chinese helped build the Durban harbour, and these claims have since been substantiated by archival documents and newspaper clippings.[114] From 1875, the Natal colonial government imported Chinese artisans and labourers on a small scale for the colony's roadmaking, harbour and other public works projects. On 16 August 1875, 75 Chinese and 34 French Creoles arrived from Mauritius to work for the Colonial Engineer's Department.[115] It is interesting to note the way in which their arrival was recorded in the 'Shipping' column of the local newspaper:

> The *Rio* arrived yesterday from Mauritius with 3 passengers, 75 Chinese, & 34 French coolies, and a general cargo.[116]

The contingent included 'a great many craftsmen such as carpenters, masons etc. ... and after being taken to the civil engineer in whose department they are intended to serve, [they] were marched to the coolie barracks where preparations were made to receive them'.[117] By January 1876 there were 53 Chinese males resident in Pietermaritzburg, the capital of Natal, about 80 km inland from Durban.[118] Chinese carpenters and masons were also sent to the outlying area of Estcourt and to work on the Tugela Bridge at Colenso.

Later that year, in August 1876, one of the labourers, Simcaw or Akou, aged 47, died intestate in the Durban Hospital. Scanty records state he was from 'Fookhoug', China, and his worldly possessions amounted to a mere £1-7-5, of which £1-5-0 was used for a coffin.[119]

CONTROVERSY RAGES OVER CHINESE HARBOUR WORKERS

No sooner had Chinese workers arrived to work at the harbour in late 1875 when 33 mechanics and workmen at the Durban Harbour petitioned the Colonial Secretary expressing their fears that these Chinese would 'throw some of us out of work'.[120] Vocal opposition to their importation was expressed at a crowded public meeting in Durban's Council Chambers as the 'artizans, mechanics and labourers of Durban' argued that the future of British workmen in the colony was at stake.

Among the many 'reasons' cited for the wish to keep the Chinese out were — they were barbarous and uncivilized, they were adepts in thieving, they were immoral, and they lived on rice and fowls borrowed or stolen from their neighbours.[121] Several speakers stated the settlement of Whites would be adversely affected and the meeting unanimously

The Case of Ah Hing

Official records throw little light on the everyday lives and concerns of the Chinese who arrived in Natal to work as contract labourers, either on the sugar cane fields or on public works projects. One exception is an early petition, dated 28 June 1878, involving the case of 72-year-old Ah Hing.

One might well ask how a man of such an age could be working as a labourer, since the first large batch of Chinese workers only arrived in Natal three years earlier, in August 1875. Perhaps he was one of the group of Chinese imported nearly two decades previously to work on the Umzinto Sugar Company's cane fields, in 1858. In a petition to the Natal Governor, thirteen Chinese who described themselves as traders and labourers in the colony, pleaded for the release from jail of aged Ah Hing, who had been convicted of 'maliciously wounding cattle'.

They stated he had worked on a sugar and coffee plantation in Victoria County but 'that his mind had given way long before said offence was charged against him, and that he is now from old age and infirmity in a semi state of mental derangement and physically in very feeble health'. Adding that he could not live very long 'and it is amongst the Chinese considered the very greatest of calamities to die out of their own country', the petitioners asked for permission to send him back to China at their own expense.

Asked to comment on this appeal, the superintendent of the Durban jail said Ah Hing was in fact nearly 80 years old and had been unfit for hard labour since his admission. He added that he had 'given no trouble' in prison.

The judge in the case said although the evidence was 'altogether circumstantial', both he and the jury had had no doubt as to the prisoner's guilt. No evidence had been given on Ah Hing's state of mind, nor had he smoked or chewed opium. He concluded: 'Prisoner attempted to cut his throat immediately after suspicion was cast upon him.' Replying to the petitioners, the Governor turned down their request for remission of Ah Hing's sentence and said he saw no grounds for interfering with the court's sentence.[122]

adopted a petition calling on the government to stop further importation of Chinese labourers.

In defence of the Chinese, another speaker, a Mr Escombe, pointed out any increase in immigration would benefit all in the colony, distributing taxation more equitably and promoting the construction of public works. Describing the Chinese as an enterprising people, he said 'the injustice done to them would remain a stigma upon the land to which we belonged'. While he did not favour their passage being paid for them, he stated that:

> There was very much in the character of these people to favour their introduction, and it was only right to give them fair play - and wrong to prejudge them before they had been tried (shouts of 'We know them well enough; we don't want to try them').[123]

As a result of this stormy meeting, one D.P. Carnegie published an impassioned 15-page tract to spell out his opposition to the Chinese and to answer those who had

The Wharf in Durban, 1879. Chinese artisans were among the labourers employed on Durban's harbour works from 1875.

defended them. He warned that Western civilization was endangered by this 'influx of heathenism' and it was absurd to contend that Chinese were the oldest nation in the world, renowned for strides in civilization, science and education. He dismissed as 'sheer nonsense' the view that the British mechanic could hold his own against the Chinese.[124]

A local newspaper, the *Natal Mercury*, expressed its support for halting further Chinese importation. In a lengthy editorial it argued that those who had defended the 'irrepressible "Chinee" ' represented employers whose interests were opposed to those of the workers.[125]

The Chinese themselves did not, however, face this barrage of abuse silently. To ensure that his views gained some exposure, one Chinese merchant paid for special advertisements to be printed in the *Natal Mercury* just a few days later. The advertisements, in the form of a letter replying to accusations against the Chinese, stated the recently imported Chinese labourers had been 'wholly and emphatically deceived'. Instead of receiving the wages they expected, they had 'to work for little or nothing to enable them to pay back their passage money'. The merchant said the labourers would gladly return to Mauritius, 'the sooner the better, instead of allowing the people of Natal to harmonise and harbour such arbitrary feelings, and run down a nation without justifiable cause or reason.'[126]

Less than a month after this outcry, 28 European mechanics at Durban's Harbour Works were discharged from service, while the Chinese remained. Reporting the incident, the *Natal Mercury* said:

> Not a little consternation was caused yesterday at the Point, when it was observed that the 'blue ensign' had been affixed reversed on a pole, as a signal — so it was taken to be — of distress...
>
> The Chinese are retained, and the mechanics being thus suddenly thrown out of employ think they have just cause for complaint.[127]

Notwithstanding all the protest, another group of five Chinese arrived from Mauritius aboard the schooner *Alice* in October 1875,[128] and work progressed at the harbour. The only incident involving Chinese in the following months was an accident on the Breakwater at the Point when a Chinese worker was hit by a truck.[129] In the next year, 1876, the newspaper remarked favourably on the increase in Natal's population, adding that a good many settlers had originated from Mauritius.

> More than a hundred Chinamen have come from thence, and although their advent caused a species of small panic amongst the artisans here, the demand for workmen is such that the fact does not appear to have disturbed the conditions of the labour market.[130]

It is not known whether these Chinese artisans and labourers remained in Natal or returned to Mauritius. At least 10 were still employed by the colonial government in 1886, but by 1887, only two were reported to be living in the barracks of the Point, the quarters adjoining Durban's harbour.[131]

Over the following years discussion on the importation of Chinese labourers went as far as a proposal to appoint Chinese consular representatives in the Cape Colony. In 1891 Cape authorities asked the British government whether such a proposal would 'convey tacit approval of introduction of Chinese as settlers'. The reply was reassuringly direct:

> Her Majesty's Government are of opinion that the appointment of a Chinese Consul for the Cape Colony, if made, would not commit the Colonial Government directly or indirectly to adopt any policy with regard to Chinese immigration which would not have been adopted if there were no Chinese Consul.

It was pointed out that the Chinese government was not likely to appoint consuls in places where there were not a considerable number of Chinese subjects.[132]

More independent immigrants — among whom were the forefathers of the South African-born Chinese — arrived in the country from the 1870s onwards. They left southern China, as did thousands of their compatriots, to seek new opportunities in foreign lands. The reasons for their exodus lay in China and the impact of western penetration into the 'Middle Kingdom'.

2

From China to South Africa

Why did so many thousands leave China in the 19th century? From which parts of China did the early Chinese settlers in South Africa originate? This chapter outlines social and economic conditions in the declining Ch'ing dynasty which, combined with foreign domination, drove Chinese to seek opportunities abroad. From the 1870s, leaving their homes in southern Kwangtung (Guangdong), adventurous men travelled first to Mauritius and then to South Africa in search of the fabled "Gold Mountain".

Chinese perceived their country as the centre of the world, using the words 'Middle Kingdom' (中國 — Jung Gwo) to denote China. The beginning of Chinese history is obscure, some writers dating the first dynasty of Huang Ti (the Yellow Emperor) as early as 2697 B.C.[1] While dates before 841 B.C. are probably legendary,[2] they nevertheless point to the antiquity of Chinese society and culture.

Over the millennia, different dynasties formed an empire in which intellectual pursuits such as philosophy, art and literature made China one of the world's great civilizations. During the reign of the last Manchu rulers known as the Ch'ing (Qing) dynasty, the country was in the 18th century, 'the most populous and possibly the most prosperous realm on the planet'.[3] Yet this proud self-sufficiency was shattered by the combined forces of internal decay and foreign incursion which changed the face of China in the 19th century.

While the Western world had taken advantage of the industrial revolution and the European powers were expanding their empires, China in the mid-19th century again faced the decline of a dynasty which had turned corrupt and oppressive. Prosperity had led to a massive growth in population, without the necessary increase in agricultural activity to feed China's 412-million people.[4] As dykes and canals to maintain the country's irrigation farming system deteriorated, greedy officials sought new ways to tax the already overburdened peasants and to embezzle imperial revenue.

To worsen the rapidly deteriorating economic situation, Nature threw in the devastation of famine, drought, floods, typhoons, epidemics and locust plagues. Between 1830 and 1839, 136 districts in China were beset by some natural disaster.[5] Hunger was rife, bandits roamed the land and peasant revolts reflected the rapid breakdown of the social order. In the 20 years between 1850 and 1870, China experienced 'what was probably the greatest wave of peasant wars in history'. Often instigated by secret societies opposed to the Ch'ing rulers, these peasant uprisings involved millions and for a few years made the country virtually ungovernable.[6]

> Such was the Chinese system of government, where so much depended on the monarch, that both the dynasty and the Empire, with mediocrity or worse at the helm, stumbled into defeat and almost into disintegration.[7]

PRESSURE FROM THE WEST

The determined drive by Western powers to increase trade and other contacts with China aggravated the country's internal upheaval and marked the end of her independence. In relations with the outside world, China had steadfastly maintained a 'closed door' policy, strictly controlling trade and unwilling to establish diplomatic ties.

From 1757, commerce in China was conducted under the 'Canton System', which restricted all foreign merchants to one port — that of Canton (Guangzhou) — and regulated their terms of trade.[8] Only officially authorized Chinese firms, the Cohong, were permitted to import and export goods, giving them a monopoly and creating 'a highly influential trading aristocracy'.[9]

Canton, in its prime position at the mouth of the Pearl River, became the trading hub of the empire. The production of tea, silk, cotton and porcelain increased, artisans and traders flocked to the port city where work was plentiful and an intricate river transport network developed for produce from all parts of the country to reach Canton. As the West's purchases from China escalated, so did Britain's need to balance its trade and to reduce the massive payments of silver it was making for its tea imports. Tea had virtually become a necessity of English life, with imports amounting to £15 million in 1785.[10]

The Chinese, however, were not interested in British products. As Emperor Chi'en Long wrote to King George III, in 1790:

> ... Our Celestial Empire possesses all things in prolific abundance and lacks no product within its own borders. There was therefore no need to import the manufactures of outside barbarians in exchange for our own produce ...[11]

For the West, opium was the answer. The drug, used by the Chinese only for medicinal purposes from the 13th century, was banned by imperial edict in 1729. Yet British and American merchants, bent on profits, took to large scale opium-smuggling. Aided by corrupt officials, opium smuggled from India became widely available to all

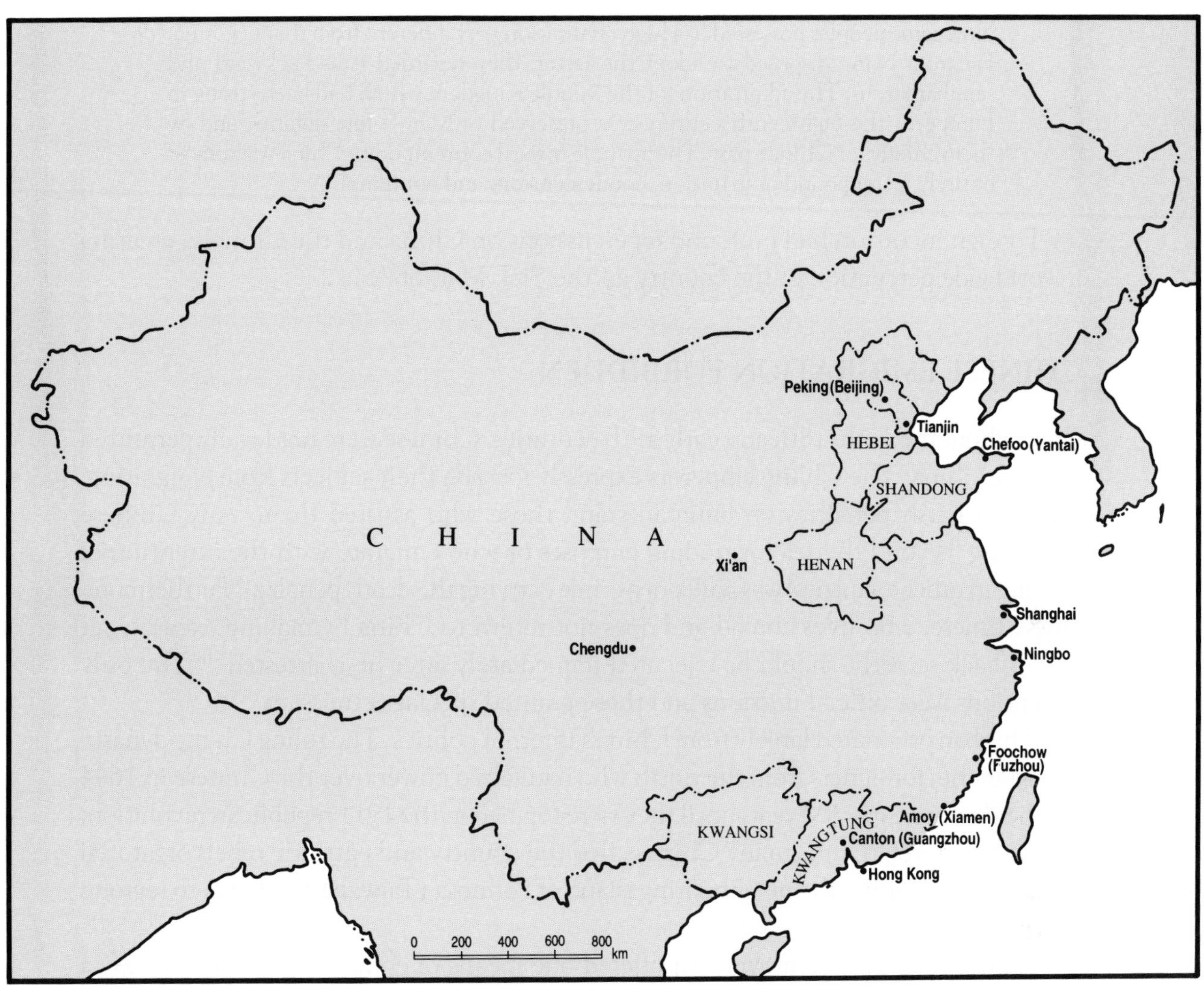

Early immigrants to South Africa originated from the southern Chinese province of Kwangtung (Guangdong). The map also shows the northern provinces from which Chinese labourers were recruited for mines in the Transvaal from 1904.

classes of Chinese. By the 1830s, Chinese purchase of opium outstripped the value of their exports, silver poured out of the country and the number of opium-addicts was estimated to run into millions.[12]

In a vain bid to halt the illicit traffic, Commissioner Lin Tse-hsu (Lin Ze-xu), ordered the destruction of all stores of opium held by foreign merchants in Canton. Tensions grew and in 1839 the first Opium War started. By the time hostilities ended with the 1842 Treaty of Nanking, China was required to pay heavily for the war, to cede Hong Kong to the British and to open five ports to foreign trade.

Not only did this mark the end of the 'Canton System', it also set the pattern for future relations with foreign powers. China again suffered defeat in the second Opium War, from 1856 to 1860, and over the next 20 years, China was forced into a series of unequal treaties which opened the country to Western economic and social penetration.[13]

> Now came peoples possessed of a high civilization very different from that of China. Far from being disposed to adopt the latter, they regarded it as backward and semibarbarous. The admiration for the Middle Kingdom which had been strong in Europe in the eighteenth century was preserved only by a few savants, and by them chiefly for China's past. The attitude toward contemporary China was almost entirely a compound of irritation, condescension, and contempt.[14]

Foreign incursion had profound repercussions on China and the Chinese, creating a worldwide perception of the country as 'the Sick Man of Asia'.

CHINESE EMIGRATION FORBIDDEN

Throughout the 17th, 18th and early 19th centuries, Chinese were not legally permitted to leave China. The Ch'ing emperors expressly forbade their subjects from emigrating, imposing harsh penalties on emigrants and those who assisted them. Any Chinese travelling 'beyond the sea for trading purposes or who emigrate with the intention of settling in other countries' was guilty of a crime carrying the death penalty.[15] Furthermore, 'any Chinese, who lives abroad and does not return to China by making excuses, yet comes back secretly, should be executed immediately after he is arrested'.[16] The only exceptions were official missions and those granted special permission.

This ban originated largely from China's internal politics. The ruling Ch'ing dynasty was Manchu, foreigners from the north who had seized power over the Chinese in 1644 and held it for nearly 300 years until they were toppled in the 1911 republican revolution. Under this 'foreign' rule, many Chinese fled the country and patriotic rebels organized uprisings, often using the neighbouring island of Formosa (Taiwan) and Japan to regroup their forces.

Restricting Chinese movement offered one means of containing opposition. As a sign of submission to the Manchus, Chinese were also required to shave the front of their heads and wear their hair in queues or pigtails ... the strange style which was so often caricatured in the West in the late 19th century. Despite the laws forbidding emigration, headmen often arranged passages for Chinese wishing to leave the country secretly aboard foreign trading vessels and illegal emigration continued throughout the 18th and early 19th centuries.

CHINESE COOLIE TRAFFIC TAKES HOLD

Different explanations have been given for the origin of the word 'coolie', widely used to describe Indian and Chinese labourers sent to work under contract in foreign lands. It has been incorrectly suggested that it stems from the Chinese words, 'k'u-li' meaning bitter strength or labour, but the word most probably derives from the Tamil word 'kuli', meaning 'hire', and is an Indian term adopted by foreigners to describe menial labourers in China as well as India.[17] The Chinese coolie traffic developed in the wake of the western world's burgeoning industrialization, the abolition of slavery and increasing demand for labour in South America, the West Indies, America and Australia in the mid-19th century. Despite the Chinese ban on emigration, unscrupulous middlemen,

The Manchu Dynasty: The Ch'ings

The people of China consist of 56 different ethnic groups, more than 90% of whom are the Han, or Chinese. The remaining ethnic minorities, scattered throughout the country and in the border regions developed different languages, cultures and social and political institutions. Among these were the Mongolians and the Manchus, the only non-Chinese rulers to conquer the whole of China in its approximately 3 600 years of recorded history.[18]

Originating from Manchuria on the north eastern border of China, the Manchu people belonged to a tribe called Chin. Taking advantage of the decline of the Chinese Ming dynasty, Manchu leaders overran the Chinese capital of Peking (Beijing) and established their control there in 1644. Their new empire was named Ch'ing meaning Purity.[19]

In the first 40 years of the Ch'ing dynasty's rule, the Manchus faced determined resistance to their conquest ... one of their most colourful opponents being the pirate, Cheng Ch'eng-kung, also known as Koxinga. Because of his and other Ming loyalists' activities along the Chinese coast, assisted by the local people, the Manchus ordered the evacuation of the coastal population, from Shantung to Kwangtung. Cheng Ch'eng-kung died in 1662 and only in 1683 were Chinese once more allowed to live on the coast of Fukien.

Although they adopted much of Chinese civilization, the Manchus tried to keep themselves aloof from their subjects. One of the most noticeable elements of their rule was the decree that all male Chinese should shave part of their heads and wear a queue or 'pigtail', which was a Manchu form of headdress, as a symbol of loyalty to the dynasty.[20]

compradors and coolie brokers took advantage of the highly profitable business of trading in human cargo.

Conditions in China contributed to the trade — poverty, debt and desperation drove many to seeking out any opportunity for work. By kidnapping, fraud and deceit, thousands were lured onto ships to be dumped in plantations, mines and wherever cheap labour was needed in foreign lands. Many were never to return home.

> The laborers were under contract, but at the end of their term of service they were continued in their servitude for alleged debt, crimes and other fictitious charges. They were treated as slaves, were lashed, beaten and tortured. Their condition was so wretched that they often sought relief in death.[21]

This merciless traffic, described as 'the buying and selling of pigs'[22] or the 'piglet trade' after the pigtails worn by the Chinese,[23] reached its heyday in the 1850s. It was during this time that China was forced to bow to western demands in the aftermath of the Opium Wars, and the weakened dynasty allowed western powers increasing rights on Chinese soil. People in the southern provinces of China reacted angrily to the many abuses, but the Chinese government was largely indifferent and made no serious attempts to end it.[24]

After numerous requests by American and British representatives, details were eventually worked out for 'controlled voluntary emigration'[25] culminating in the

Emigration Convention of 1866 which established a comprehensive system for Chinese to work and settle outside of China.[26] The Convention was signed by the British and French Ministers at Peking with Prince Kung as representative of the Emperor of China. Aware of the dangers of forced emigration, the Chinese government added that those who kidnapped Chinese to send them abroad would be put to death.

Marking the beginning of the Chinese government's official relaxation of its prohibition on all emigration, Prince Kung stated in the Convention:

> The Chinese Government throws no obstacle in the way of free emigration, that is to say, to the departure of Chinese subjects embarking of their own free will and at their own expense for foreign countries, but that all attempts to bring Chinese under an engagement to emigrate, otherwise than as the present regulations provide, are formally forbidden, and will be prosecuted with the extreme rigour of the law.[27]

The British and French, however, objected to the Chinese requirement that contracted labourers be given their return passage after five years' service, arguing this would make the scheme too costly. The Chinese government refused to alter the Convention, which was therefore not ratified and of no binding effect.[28] In the years which followed the Chinese nevertheless used the Convention as the fixed rule for the engagement of Chinese labour.[29]

Only in 1893 did the Chinese government finally annul its 182-year-old ban on emigration and abolish the law of 1712 which prohibited people from emigrating and returning. From 1899 Chinese diplomats abroad, were, for the first time, instructed to help and protect Chinese emigrants.[30]

IMPETUS TO LEAVE SOUTH CHINA

The southern province of Kwangtung (Guangdong) was hard hit not only by the political and economic forces at play in China, but also the destructive power of natural disasters. Lives disrupted by civil upheaval in the wake of the Opium Wars were further burdened by drought and famine. When Canton (Guangzhou) lost its unique trading monopoly, many faced unemployment as commerce shifted to the other four newly opened treaty ports of Shanghai, Ningbo, Amoy (Xiamen) and Foochow (Fuzhou). Exports of tea through Canton slumped by two-thirds in tonnage from 76 million pounds in 1845 to 24 million pounds in 1858.[31]

> Hundreds of thousands of boatmen and porters in central and southern China were thrown out of work, and it was from among this army of unemployed that several of the leaders of the Taiping rebellion emerged.[32]

The Taiping Rebellion constituted the most serious popular threat to the ruling dynasty, combining elements of Western Christianity with traditional Chinese religious beliefs. Led by Hung Hsiu-ch'uan, a Hakka peasant who had studied under a Protestant missionary in Canton, the movement aimed to overthrow the Manchus. Hung founded his own 'dynasty' called the 'Heavenly Kingdom of Great Peace' in 1851. His followers cut off their queues and established a rebel capital at Nanking which they held for 11 years.[33] The rebellion lasted for 14 years from 1850 to 1864, and more than 20 million died before it was suppressed.[34]

While the Taiping Rebellion was just one of the many revolts which plagued China in the mid-19th century, its significance lies in the immediate impetus it gave to emigration from south China, and in later years, to its impact on the overthrow of the Ch'ing dynasty and the formation of a republic.

> When the radical reform movement gained control in the twentieth century, it owed much to the efforts of Chinese who had gone overseas. Some of the zeal of the emigrants is traceable to T'ai P'ings who, escaping after the collapse of their cause, kept alive abroad the desire for change. Sun Yat-sen, the archrevolutionist of the first quarter of the twentieth century, seems in his youth to have had close contact with groups of T'ai P'ing origin.[35]

By the mid-19th century, the population of Kwangtung had swelled substantially; political instability combined with economic uncertainty and widespread poverty made it necessary for many to seek new horizons. Whether as refugees or enterprising young men in search of better opportunities, the people of south China saw emigration as a solution. Among the first Chinese exposed to foreign trade and influence, they were prepared to set forth into the unknown and to venture beyond the confines of China.

THE NEW WORLD BECKONS

South East Asia was a natural choice for many emigrants from China. Not too far away, the newly ceded British colony of Hong Kong offered a springboard to the opportunities of a wider world. Thousands of Chinese made their way to British Malaya and Singapore, where it was no secret that the British favoured the immigration of the Chinese described as 'a hardworking and money-loving people'.[36] This migration to the 'Nanyang', the countries adjoining the southern seas of China, saw Chinese settling in Thailand, Malaysia and Indonesia, both as independent merchants or artisans and as contract labourers.

From 1848 Chinese emigration to the 'new world' gained momentum. Word of fabulous finds of gold were a lure to all. Spurred further by internal upheaval and famine, 'The tide of Chinese emigration ... became a flood and beyond the power of the government to control.'[37] Many men left in search of that fabled gold, heading for San Francisco, the place they called 'Gold Mountain', (Gam Saan in Cantonese) or to British Columbia in Canada, Melbourne in Australia, Otago in New Zealand or even, from the 1870s, to the southern end of the African continent.

Unlike many emigrants who set out with their wives and children to build new lives in foreign lands, the Chinese ventured forth as lone men ... cherishing hopes of accumulating wealth and returning home to China some day. It was estimated that in some villages at least one member of every family had gone overseas. While abroad, the men would send money home on a regular basis. Such remittances were important not only for the family, but for the village economy in general. In later years it was the overseas Chinese who helped to finance factories, schools and even ancestral homes in their villages.[38]

In the 19th century Chinese women seldom, if ever, accompanied their menfolk abroad. Chinese custom dictated that the first duty of married women was to their parents-in-law and women remained in China to care for their husbands' families.[39] These wives had to fend for themselves and raise children, but many were independent enough to earn their own living through occupations such as rice-growing, silk production or fish farming.[40]

In their new country of adoption Chinese men would either lead a bachelor existence, or take advantage of Chinese law which permitted a man to have as many concubines as he could financially support by cohabiting with a local woman.[41] Only years later, when they were financially established, did some of them return to China to fetch wives or children.

ORIGINS OF THE SOUTH AFRICAN CHINESE

Most South African-born Chinese are descendants of independent immigrants who arrived in the country from the 1870s onwards. They originated from two areas, about 400 km apart, in the Kwangtung (Guangdong) province of south China and could be

Cantonese-speaking Chinese originated from villages in the vicinity of Canton (Guangzhou) while the Hakkas emigrated largely from areas surrounding Moiyean (Meixian).

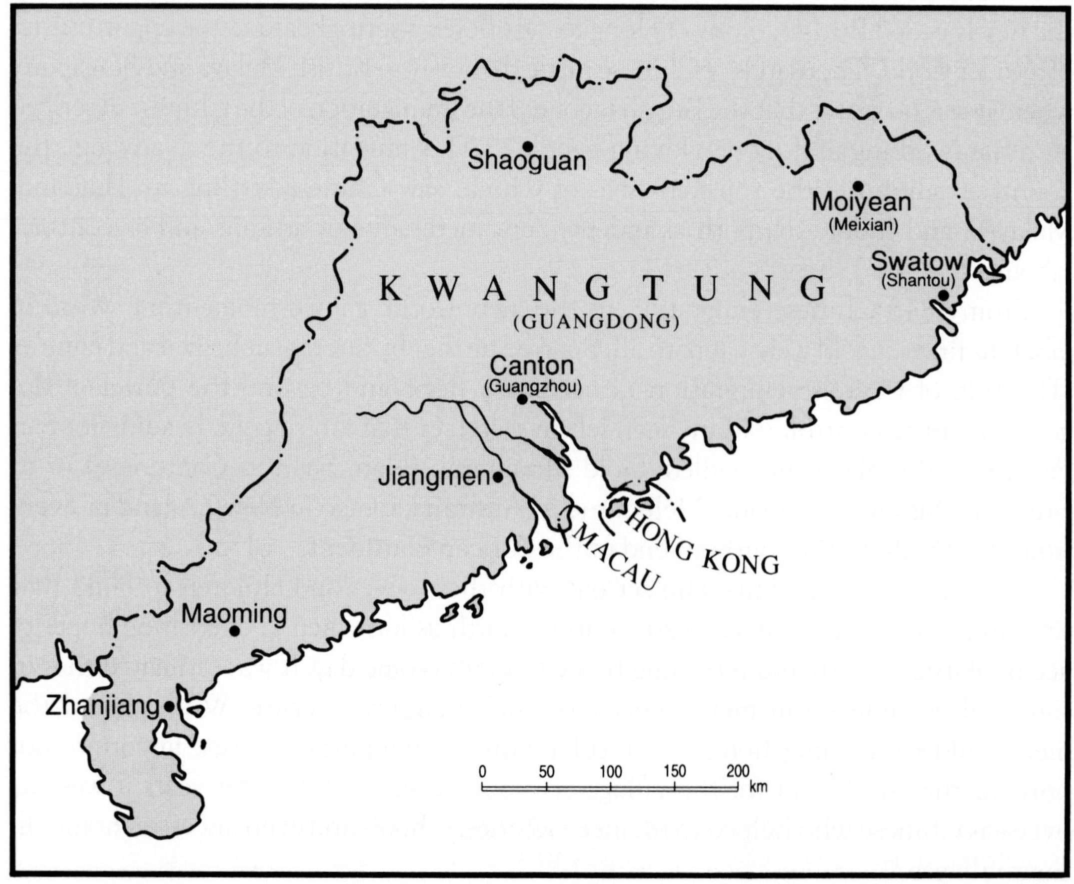

The Cantonese

The name 'Cantonese', as used in this work, describes the dialect spoken by people originating from the south western districts of Kwangtung (Guangdong) province in south China. Five percent of all Chinese speak a dialect of Cantonese, which differs from one district to another, and is quite distinct from northern dialects.[42]

The Cantonese-speaking people of Kwangtung are generally considered to be descendants of northern refugees and soldiers who made their way down south between 1500 and 2000 years ago. Through intermarriage with the local Yueh people who lived south of the Yangtze river, they became known as the Punti (Bendi) or 'local' people and eventually settled in the most fertile areas of the rich Pearl River Delta.

There they established the provincial capital of Canton (Guangzhou) which, from the 7th to the 19th centuries, was effectively the trading capital of China. Its position at the mouth of the Pearl River made it the centre of an intricate inland river transport system and the busy coastal sea route.

Merchants, artisans, farmers, peasants were drawn to the bustling and prosperous port city. Although densely populated, the delta plains provided rich crops of rice, mulberry bushes, vegetables and sweet potatoes. From the mid-19th century however economic, political and natural disasters befell Kwangtung in particular, and China in general.

Emigration gained momentum and the Cantonese dispersed, virtually to all corners of the earth. Today Cantonese predominate among Chinese settlements in South Vietnam, Hong Kong, North America, Canada, Australia and New Zealand.[43]

The majority of South African Cantonese originate from the Sam Yup area — or Three Counties, of Namhoi (Nanhai), Suntak (Shunde) and Punyi (Panyu). A few families too emigrated from Toishan and Chungsan.

ethnically distinguished as Cantonese and Moiyeanese (or Hakka). They spoke different dialects, practised different customs and their relations both in their home province and abroad were marked by traditional animosity ... despite the fact that outsiders saw them all simply as 'Chinese'.

The Cantonese came mainly from villages south of the city of Canton (Guangzhou), in the counties of Namhoi (Nanhai), Suntak (Shunde) and Punyi (Panyu). These villages are virtually all within a 20 km radius of one another, and the Cantonese were often referred to as 'Namsoon', [南順] from the first syllables of Namhoi [南海] and Suntak [順德]. They originated predominantly from a cluster of villages surrounding the market town of Lok Chung [樂從]. These villages include Peng Po [平步], Siu Po [小布], Lo Chau [鷺洲], Sui Tung [水籐], Sha Kiu [沙教], Kiu Tak [教德], Kot Ngon [葛岸], Ma Kiu [馬教], Leung Kiu [良教], Leung Kiu Sha [良教沙] and Sha Liu [沙寮].

The Hakka who settled in South Africa were mainly the 'Moiyeanese' who emigrated from the Moiyean (Mei Hsien/Meixian) [梅縣] region in north east Kwangtung. Many came from the districts of Nam Kou [南口], Song Kou [松口], Shi Yung [西陽], Lo Tian

The Moiyeanese 'Hakka'

The Hakka are the refugees of China. Their name means 'guest people' or 'stranger people' and in their gradual dispersal throughout that vast land, they have remained a group apart — retaining their own customs, language and habits. Their origins have been the subject of controversy with their detractors claiming they were not true Chinese of the Han race and they were 'rootless vagabonds'.[44]

It is, however, widely accepted that their ancestors came from the Yellow River delta in north China, settling in the central Chinese province of Honan which, during the Han dynasty (208 BC to 220 AD), was the seat of Chinese culture and civilization.

Threatened by invasions of the Tartars and Mongols from the north as well as the civil chaos accompanying the rise and fall of dynasties, their history since the fourth century is an account of at least five major migrations. From 317 AD to 879 AD, they left Honan, following the Yangtze River to Chekiang and Kiangsi. From 880 AD, many moved further south, to Fukien (Fujian), and from 1127 a mass migration took the Hakka to the hilly regions of north and east Kwangtung (Guangdong).

Yet another migratory wave was spurred by the Manchu conquest of China in 1644 and the Hakka spread further afield — to the central and coastal regions of Kwangtung, to Kwangsi, Kweichow, Szechwan and the islands of Taiwan and Hainan. The devastating Taiping Rebellion of 1850 to 1864, led by a Hakka and strongly supported by his people, forced many Hakka to flee China as refugees, heading for South East Asia and the 'new world'.

Among the characteristics which distinguished them from other Chinese was their refusal to bind the feet of their women despite this countrywide practice in the days of the dynasties. In general, Hakka women have been said to be more self-reliant than non-Hakkas, enjoying close to equal status with men and shouldering heavy farm work from ploughing to harvesting.

The distinctiveness of the Hakkas has made them the subject of much study and criticism. At times, depending on the pronunciation and stress, the word 'Hakka' itself has carried derogatory overtones. Writers have questioned why the Hakka have no name for themselves except one meaning foreigners, but other scholars have described them as a 'distinct and virile strain of the Chinese race' whose instincts for survival forged them into adventurous, patriotic, independent people. Supporting claims for the northern Chinese origins of the Hakkas, writers have cited the similarity between their language and those spoken in the north. Four percent of all Chinese speak Hakka.

Scattered throughout China but particularly in Kwangsi, Kiangsi and Fukien, the Hakka concentration also remained strong in the mountainous region of north-east Kwangtung called the Kaiyin (Jiaying) district with Moiyean (Meixian) at its centre. Unlike the fertile delta plains, much of the hilly land was barren and the Hakkas eked out a living growing rice and potatoes.[45]

The majority of the Hakka who emigrated to South Africa originate from the Moiyean area, hence the description they generally use for themselves as 'Moiyeanese'.

[羅田] and Mei Nam [梅南]. Emigration from this area was so extensive that Moiyean was often referred to as the 'home of the overseas Chinese'. It was estimated in the late 1980s that 1 530 000 Chinese living overseas originated from the prefecture of Moiyean.[46] While the generic term 'Hakka' applies to the 'guest people' spread throughout China, 'Moiyeanese' refers specifically to the Hakka from the Moiyean region.

To understand some of the former antagonism between the Cantonese and Moiyeanese, it is necessary to review briefly their contact in China. As relative latecomers from the north to the southern province of Kwangtung, it was perhaps inevitable that they clashed with local Cantonese over access to land and water.[47] In 1854 local feuds erupted into widespread violence between the two groups which lasted for 14 years. Thousands were left homeless, villages were destroyed and, by 1868, the Hakka retreated to the north eastern areas of Kwangtung.[48]

Denounced by the Cantonese as 'guest bandits',[49] the Hakka preserved their own ethnic habits and distanced themselves from the Cantonese. Differences between the two groups were evident in their dialects, customs, dress and traditional dishes. Generally, Chinese from the north tended 'to be taller by an average of two or more inches, heavier, less dark of complexion, with less broad noses, more conservative, and less high-strung' than Chinese in the south.[50]

Many early emigrants took with them the 'ethnic' dislikes of their homeland, and, until as late as the 1970s, marriages between Cantonese and Moiyeanese in South Africa were rare and often actively discouraged. In China, however, both groups were caught up in the political and economic chaos of the late 19th century. For many, emigration offered some hope for survival. For the Cantonese, the ports of Macao and Hong Kong were close at hand, and for the Moiyeanese, the port of Swatow (Shantou) [汕頭] was within reach to take them to greener pastures.

Ethnic differences between the two groups have, in the 1990s, largely been forgotten, but they played an important role in the formation and functioning of early Chinese organizations in South Africa. Clan members, bearing a common surname, formed the nucleus of community organizations. They offered material and moral support for newcomers, training them to adapt to foreign ways and enabling them to settle and survive in a new land, without forgetting their obligations to those left in China.

As with new immigrants everywhere, the gradual growth of the Chinese community was effected through the process of 'chain migration', in which an established immigrant would assist a relative or member of the extended clan, that is, anyone with the same surname, to join him. Kinship ties extended beyond immediate family to a clan which included five or more generations tracing their lineage back to a common ancestor. Most Chinese migrants were related by ties of a common dialect or place of origin and tended to congregate in the same areas.[51]

Bonds of clan and kinship were probably the major factors leading to the concentration of the Cantonese and Moiyeanese in different parts of South Africa. For many years Moiyeanese tended to predominate in the coastal towns, particularly Port Elizabeth, East London, Cape Town and Durban, while the Cantonese were more numerous in the Pretoria/Witwatersrand/Vereeniging area, which includes the metropolis of Johannesburg.

Chinese Sojourner Mentality

An important characteristic which contributed to the way in which Chinese were received in the lands to which they travelled was their so-called 'sojourner mentality'. It has been said this attitude of regarding their stay abroad as merely a sojourn prevented the Chinese from making long-term commitments to the new countries in which they found themselves, but it was not a uniquely Chinese trait for pioneering migrants.[52]

Undeniably most Chinese — both contract labourers and 'free' settlers — retained many of the cultural values and traditions of their homeland. As one writer described it:

> 'The Chinese emigrant was unique because he saw his departure as only a temporary solution to pressuring poverty and deprivation at home. Whether he found himself in the tin mines and plantations of Malaya, or panning for gold in the rivers of California, his first thoughts were for his family and kinsmen in the village where he grew up, and to which he hoped eventually to return...
>
> The Chinese sojourner lived in a nether world — suspended between a social system that is physically inaccessible and the present society which he is either unable or unwilling to fully participate in...
>
> However while he was overseas, even for a limited time, the sojourner and his fellow countrymen banded together to replicate miniaturized Chinese worlds. These were the famed Chinatowns, common throughout the world wherever a sizeable Chinese population congregated...[The Chinese] seem to have a penchant for grouping together and transplanting certain features of the culture, institutions and social organizations of their homeland...'[53]

Varying forms of discrimination in the new countries to which the Chinese emigrated however served to ensure that they remained aliens. They were stereotyped and blamed for a host of social evils. Not accepted in general society, it was natural to retain a firm hold on their own institutions which linked them to a Chinese world that they knew and understood.

TO SOUTH AFRICA VIA MAURITIUS

The island of Mauritius in the Indian Ocean became a key port of call along the busy shipping trade route around the Cape between Asia and Europe in the mid-19th century. It was here that many Chinese stopped over, for a few months or even years, before making their way to South Africa. From Hong Kong, Macao, Canton or Swatow, Chinese venturing overseas could board one of the many ships operating on the lucrative Chinese/ Indian trade routes to the other major continents.[54]

Many secured their passage on ships carrying Indian contract labourers from Calcutta to Mauritius. The introduction of regular trips there by the British India Steam

Navigation Company further facilitated Chinese emigration from South East Asian ports. Other shipping companies such as the Union Castle Line, the Clan Line, the Ellerman and Harrison Line and the P & O Line which plied routes around the coast of Africa all called in at the Mauritian island harbour of Port Louis.[55]

Mauritius had already been populated by Chinese from the end of the 18th century, but from 1845 increasing numbers of merchants made their way to the small island where they became an integral part of its developing economy. In a comprehensive analysis of the spread of the Chinese in areas around the Western Indian Ocean, historian Huguette Ly-Tio-Fane Pineo maintains Mauritius played a pivotal role in 'distributing' Chinese emigrants to Reunion, the Seychelles, Madagascar and South Africa from 1880 to about 1940. Despite a steady influx of Chinese immigrants into Mauritius in the 1880s, the community's numbers dwindled, reflecting their even higher rate of emigration.

Barred from owning land in Mauritius, established Chinese traders diverted accumulated capital into new businesses in neighbouring Indian Ocean countries. These businesses were then managed by new immigrants, who were relatives of the Chinese owners and had served a short 'apprenticeship' in Mauritius. Explaining the clan network which organized the 'importation' and 'exportation' of Chinese to and from Mauritius, Ly-Tio-Fane Pineo writes:

> Leaders of the organisation had devised a method of procedure for the selection of emigrants in China, and had organised their transport to Mauritius. After their reception in the island, they were given a training designed to familiarize them with the Western mode of life. Newcomers usually began their training by performing such simple jobs as cooking or going to the market: next after having mastered the rudiments of language they were made to serve the shop clients under the supervision of the shop manager. These simple tasks gave them the opportunity to acquire the first elements of Western culture.[56]

After spending some time in Mauritius, these immigrants were then despatched further afield bearing letters of introduction to assist them in settling into new communities in neighbouring countries. Most of the new immigrants to Mauritius were Moiyeanese who, from 1895, arrived in increasing numbers to jeopardize the existing dominance of the Cantonese. Ethnic feuds developed, weakening the established system of controlled immigration. To counter this, Cantonese who had left Mauritius for Madagascar then effectively prevented any Hakkas from settling in Madagascar. Ly-Tio-Fane Pineo states this underlines the extent to which ethnic clan groups assisted the settlement of new immigrants.[57]

It was via Mauritius that many Chinese made their way to the shores of southern Africa. News of the discovery of diamonds in 1867, and then the fabulous wealth of the gold reef in 1886 was an irresistible attraction for both the adventurous and the determined. Between 1888 and 1898, nearly 1800 Chinese sailed from Port Louis, Mauritius — the vast majority of them bound for Algoa Bay (Port Elizabeth), less than 200 for Durban and a mere handful for East London, and the Mocambican port of Delagoa Bay.[58] As the nearest port to the gold fields of the Witwatersrand and Johannesburg, the town of Lourenco Marques at Delagoa Bay was a convenient disembarkation point for travellers.

Chinese in Mocambique

Many of the early Chinese in Mocambique were artisans, originating from the Sze Yup counties of Kwangtung province. The first immigrants arrived in the last quarter of the 19th century, settling mainly around the ports of Lourenco Marques and Beira. One of the pioneers was Ja Assam, a carpenter and builder, who donated a plot of land for the Lourenco Marques Chinese to establish the 'Chinese Pagoda' in 1903. It was a community association which later started a Chinese school in the city.

In 1893, there were 52 Chinese in Lourenco Marques, increasing to 287 in 1903. Beira, in 1900, had a Chinese population of 84. Apart from the independent artisans, many Chinese worked for the sugar and mining companies of Manica-e-Sofala. Chinese also played a role in the construction of the railway line between Beira and Umtali (Zimbabwe) from 1892 to 1898 and the railway line between Lourenco Marques and Komatipoort (South Africa) between 1886 and 1894.[59]

Consul-General Lew Yuk Lin, and his daughter, May, visited some of the merchants in Lourenco Marques, Mocambique, in 1907.

For some Chinese, their settlement in South Africa may have been purely accidental. Elderly community members often tell how some early Chinese haphazardly boarded ships in search of Gam Saan or Gold Mountain [金山], the name given to San Francisco when gold was first found there in 1848. To confuse matters, both Melbourne in Australia and Johannesburg in South Africa were called New Gold Mountain [新金山]. Not too sure where this fabled place was, they set sail aboard any ship bound for 'Gold Mountain'. So, the story goes, many arrived in Johannesburg only to discover it wasn't San Francisco![60]

Whatever their expectations, the Chinese had reached the southern tip of Africa, equipped with little more than the determination to make something of their lives. From the 1870s, they settled in the Cape, Natal, and later the Transvaal, only to discover that being Chinese limited their opportunities and made them outsiders in a land where race drew the dividing line.

Emigrants made their way to South Africa via the tiny island of Mauritius, a stop-over on the shipping trade routes to India and China.

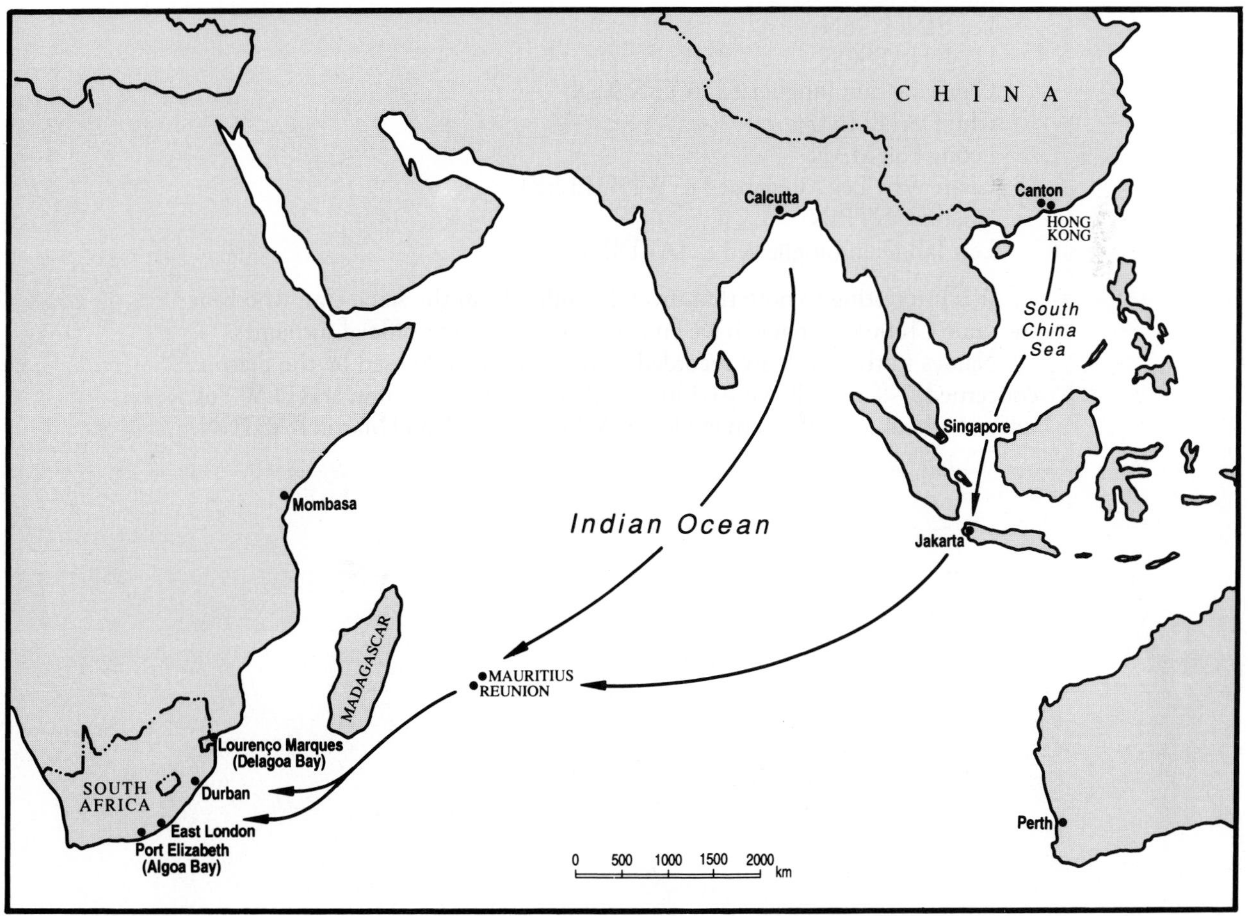

Anomalies in South African Chinese Surnames

Some confusion has accompanied the use of Chinese surnames in South Africa. Since Chinese traditionally give their surnames first, followed by their given names, immigration authorities and other officials often recorded the forenames as surnames and vice versa. Later generations have found themselves obliged to continue using, for example, a grandfather's given names as the family surname.

For this reason some families have 'surnames' which are not traditional Chinese surnames and because names were spelled phonetically, some have been anglicized to sound more western than Chinese. In the eastern Cape many Chinese have double-barrelled surnames made up of the two characters of a forefather's given names.

In the following examples, the actual Chinese surname of the forbear appears first, followed by the given name which has since become the family's official 'surname' in capital letters.

Wong Hop Sin (anglicized to HOPTION)
Wong LUNKING
Wong KOLLING
Foo KIM SING
Hsieh DATE CHONG
Lim WING KING
Lee SING GEN
Lee CHAPSON
Chu Ying Sun (anglicized to YENSON)
Chu DATELING
Leong Fok MAN
Chan Why Lee (anglicized to WHITELEY)
Chan FONTBIN
Lew Jah Dien (anglicised to JARDINE)

It is interesting to note that several families from the same clan who bear the same Chinese surname have ended up with different official surnames.

Names in this work are recorded in the written style used by the persons concerned — some following Chinese style e.g. LEUNG Quinn and LEW Yuk Lin and others in the Western mode e.g. William ASSUE and Martin EASTON.

3

Under British Rule

How were Chinese received in the British colonies of Natal and the Cape? How did they adapt to a new environment, protect their interests as an identifiable minority and create a community? In this analysis, Chinese settlement from the 1870s is described regionally, discriminatory legislation is outlined and the effects of the Chinese Exclusion Act in the Cape in 1904 are discussed.

South Africa in the 1860s was not a single, united country but an assortment of African territories, British colonies (the Cape of Good Hope and Natal) and independent Boer republics (the Orange Free State and Transvaal). It was an economically undeveloped and sparsely populated land, its inhabitants involved mainly in subsistence farming. Inland transport was primitive, with the ox-wagon providing the chief means of carrying wool, hides and skins from the interior to the coastal ports.

Of the four White-occupied territories, each of which exercised its own form of government, the Cape Colony was the most economically advanced. In 1865 it had a population of some 500 000 people, mainly Blacks and Coloureds with some 181 600 Whites. Cape Town was the centre for manufacturing and commerce and the only town with a population of more than 10 000 people. Natal's population was half that of the Cape, with a total of 278 806, made up of Blacks, Indians and fewer than 18 000 White inhabitants. From the late 1860s however the discovery of diamonds in the northern Cape and then gold in the Transvaal had far-reaching consequences for the economic structure of the whole country.[1] From all parts of the world, speculators arrived in their thousands transforming rural backwaters into industrialized centres in just a few decades.

The gradual settlement of 'free' Chinese coincided with the often hostile reception given to the groups of Chinese contract labourers imported to work both in Natal and the eastern Cape during the 1870s and 1880s. Their advent did not go unnoticed, and in some instances mere rumour of their arrival was enough to spark publicity out of all proportion to their numbers or any 'threat' they could pose to the settled community. Although the views of Blacks at the time are not known, Whites expressed prevailing prejudices against alien races quite clearly in their local newspapers. In both Natal and the Cape, the governments remained intent on shaping colonies in which the interests of White settlers were paramount.

Because the Chinese encountered differing conditions under British rule from that imposed in the independent Boer republics, this chapter will focus only on Natal and the Cape. Distinct 'communities' developed in various parts of these colonies, and this outline follows a regional approach to give a comprehensive account of circumstances in each town where Chinese settled. While it is possible that some indentured labourers remained in Natal and the Cape after the expiry of their contracts, the majority of early Chinese settlers were independent men who sought new opportunities in a land of promise. It was only much later, well after the turn of the century, that the first Chinese women joined their husbands in southern Africa.

NATAL

The port of Durban in the 1870s was already a busy, bustling and picturesque collection of wattle and daub houses, corrugated iron buildings and brick shops and warehouses.[2] Although farming in Natal was hampered by poor transport and the hazards of its subtropical climate, coastal planters succeeded in establishing a commercially viable sugar industry and wool became the chief commercial product in the interior. More than half of the White population, mainly artisans and shopkeepers, lived in Pietermaritzburg and Durban.[3] Home of South Africa's first railway line, Durban gradually developed the necessary transportation network to make it a key South African port.

The first Chinese settler in Durban may well have been a trader known as 'Gumption' who arrived in 1866.[4] He was soon followed by other independent merchants who had established grocery businesses by 1875. At that time more than 70 Chinese artisans and labourers, contracted to work for the colonial government, were the focus of controversy for outspoken opponents of Chinese immigration. In a strong letter to the *Natal Mercury*, a Chinese merchant defended the habits and customs of his race, saying thousands of Chinese had emigrated to all parts of the world and had 'never met with such ... indignation and ignominy'.[5]

Objecting to remarks in the paper's editorial on Chinese being aggressive and acquisitive, he said a Chinese 'has always a desire to make an honest livelihood by his industry and energy ... confines himself to very strict habits and customs, ... has always moved and associated with all classes, white or coloured, rich or poor ... is harmless and friendly with all, without distinction of colour or position.'

The letter, dated 13 September 1875 and signed 'A Chineese (sic) Merchant', concluded with a brief outline on how non-indentured Chinese first arrived in Natal.

> ... six of my countrymen — merchants, had arrived in Natal from Mauritius a few months previous to this for the purpose of establishing business and traffic in the land, who have extensive firms both in Mauritius and India, and have been residing there for the last 30 years and upwards, and have always moved and associated in all circles and classes of men, and have always been highly esteemed and respected as merchants and regret very much to learn that my countrymen are so indignantly and embitterly looked down upon by the working class of Europeans of Natal.[6]

After the initial outcry against any large-scale importation of Chinese labourers abated, individual Chinese made their way into the colony, establishing small businesses and laundries, mainly in the vicinity of the port city of Durban, and Natal's capital, Pietermaritzburg, about 80 km inland.

Rumours that some 250 Chinese labourers would be arriving in the Cape in 1881 prompted the *Natal Mercury* to state firmly that Chinese were not wanted in Natal.

> Excepting in the most infinitismal numbers they must act as a drawback to the prosperity of any European colony. The Chinaman is insidiously working his way into Natal, and our police court reports are already beginning to tell of a dozen of the pigtail wearers being fined for gambling on a Sunday morning. We have little fear, however, that these alien people will be allowed to crowd upon us in any numbers which might be detrimental to the welfare of the Europeans of nearly all classes.[7]

Nonetheless the paper itself was soon scolded for the attention it paid to the novelty of a Chinese presence in Natal. Writing for *The Friend* newspaper in the Orange Free State, a columnist remarked:

> The *Natal Mercury* might fairly be dubbed a mo(u)rning paper. The number of lengthy death notices that appear in its columns are positively enough to send a man melancholy mad. The *Natal Mercury* actually devoted some of its *valuable space* to record the death of a Chinaman. Whether he was the only Chinaman Natal had, or whether the editor wished people to understand that Chinamen (like donkeys) *do die sometimes*, I could not make out.[8]

A charge often levelled against Chinese in the nineteenth century was that they were not 'settlers' who would contribute to the future of a country. It was said they sought only to make money before returning home to their families. While this was probably true of many men, of all races, who ventured out into an unknown world alone, quite a few Chinese demonstrated their wish to make South Africa their home. By 1884, lawyers were enquiring into the possibility of Chinese becoming citizens of their land of adoption.[9] And two years later, 19 Chinese petitioned the Governor of Natal to allow them to become naturalized British subjects. Stating that they had resided in Natal for several years, they described themselves as 'quiet, sober and industrious men'. Since only those of European birth or descent were entitled to naturalization, they appealed for a change to be made in the law.[10] Signatories to this petition included James Sansuy, L. Changson, R.Y. Chapson, Youngson, H.J. Ahlee, H. Hopson, P. Tetlong, Chongson, Vounfook and others. Descendants of some of these settlers were still resident in Durban and other parts of South Africa in the 1990s.

Not only would naturalization have made it easier for Chinese to obtain trading licences, it would also have paved the way for them to bring their families out to join them. The Governor considered their request seriously enough to draw up an amendment to the naturalization law, but fears about such a measure being generally accepted led to it being shelved.[11]

Anti-Asiatic Measures Introduced

Natal was granted Responsible Government by Britain in 1893. At that time, the population of the colony was estimated to be 470 000 Blacks, 45 000 Whites and 46 000 Indians.[12] The Chinese were a negligible minority, totalling only 77 males (38 in Pietermaritzburg, 33 in Durban and 4 in Umlazi) in 1891.[13] White merchants had over the years expressed alarm at the growth of the Indian population, and particularly what they labelled 'unfair competition' by Indian traders who had entered the colony in the wake of Indian indentured labourers.

Steps were soon taken against the Asiatics generally and since this term included Chinese, they too were affected by measures restricting Asiatic immigration and trading rights. The Colonial Patriotic Union collected signatures from more than 5000 Natal residents who argued that 'the low moral tone and insanitary habits of Asiatics are a constant source of danger to the progress and health of the European population'.[14]

Legislation was duly enacted which required new immigrants to pass an education test in a European language. In addition to the Immigration Restriction Act 1 of 1897, the Dealers Licensing Act 18 of 1897 allowed local authorities wide discretionary powers to decide whether or not to grant any Asiatic trading licences. When the Dundee Local Board issued a trade licence to Hoi Lee in November 1897, protests by ratepayers promptly led to the licence being revoked. The reason for the cancellation was simply his nationality as a Chinese.[15]

Statistics provided by the Immigration Restriction Department in the following years show the effectiveness of the new measure in stemming the trickle of Chinese into Natal. In the first six months of 1897, 15 Chinese were refused entry.[16] Between 1900 and 1904 a total of 752 Chinese were turned away and only 54 admitted, either because they passed the education test, or could prove they had previously resided in the colony.[17] Many appeals to bring relatives into Natal were refused. When Alfred Edward Chongson, a grocer who traded under the name Cheong Long & Co. in Grey Street from the 1880s, applied for permission to bring his brother-in-law and later his 12-year-old son into the colony, both requests were denied. Immigration authorities expressed their suspicions that some Chinese with permission to bring in wives and children were in fact bringing in other people's relatives.[18]

Those Chinese already residing in Natal had to obtain domicile certificates to re-enter the colony. This led to a few cases where Chinese, stranded outside Natal, wrote desperate letters appealing to business contacts and acquaintances to vouch for them. Kongheng, also called Hinglong, went on a short business trip to neighbouring Delagoa Bay but soon discovered he was barred from returning to his shop in Pietermaritzburg. Only when one of his suppliers stated they had recently done business with him and his employee confirmed he was the legal owner of a shop in Berg Street, was he sent a certificate enabling him to return.[19] The shipping company, King & Sons, refused to sell a ticket to Longfoon to travel from Canton, China, until a circuit court judge wrote to the immigration authorities vouching for Longfoon's respectability and previous residence of about 15 years in Natal.[20]

The imminent introduction of Chinese labour on a large scale into the Transvaal led Natal authorities to tighten immigration regulations further and to introduce the Transit Immigrants Act no. 7 of 1904. This allowed for all Chinese contracted as labourers in the territories adjoining Natal to be confined to compounds during their stay in Natal and prohibited anyone in the colony from harbouring or employing such Chinese.

The law, however, also had a direct impact on the 'free' Chinese settlers in Natal. They were required to furnish their fingerprints for a special domicile certificate proving their status as residents in Natal and to carry the certificate with them at all times. Within days of these regulations being published, on 19 September 1904, 97 Durban Chinese residents signed a petition objecting to giving fingerprints. They said: 'throughout the East the fingerprint system exists for the identification of criminals ... [and] your Petitioners feel that some other means might be found for the identification of Chinese residents without putting upon them the slur ... of compelling identification by means of [such] a system...'

They said as 'industrious, loyal and law-abiding citizens' they were aggrieved by the regulations and appealed 'for the issue of passes under circumstances less objectionable to your Petitioners'. The Colonial Secretary replied the fingerprinting requirement was for the protection of the Chinese themselves and the government was not prepared to modify the conditions under which the certificates were granted.[21]

At this time Chinese in Natal numbered a mere 165 people — 161 men and 4 women.[22] The majority lived in Durban, but 66 were working in Pietermaritzburg. Although subjected to immigration and trade restrictions, they were permitted to purchase fixed property, a 'right' which gave them advantages over their compatriots in the Transvaal who were totally excluded from landownership. From 1896, Asiatics in Natal were prohibited from participating in parliamentary elections, but it is not known whether any Chinese were ever included on the municipal voters' rolls. No formal Chinese organization seems to have existed in Natal prior to 1904, but new settlers probably worked towards this objective and in later years formed the Natal Chinese Association.

CAPE COLONY

No specific legislation barred the entry of Chinese into the Cape until 1904, and after the Chinese government withdrew restrictions on emigration in 1866, independent Chinese gradually made their way into the colony. News of the discovery of diamonds in the northern Cape in 1867 attracted fortune hunters from all parts and by the late 1870s an impressive railway system linked the port cities of the Cape Colony with the mecca of Kimberley.[23]

The official census, taken on 5 April 1891, recorded the presence of 215 Chinese men in the Cape Colony. There were 185 in Kimberley, 19 in Port Elizabeth, 5 in the districts around Cape Town[24] and the remaining 6 were probably in outlying areas. Following existing transportation routes into the interior, Chinese in later years scattered more widely, but fair numbers remained concentrated in Kimberley, the Eastern Cape and the environs of Cape Town.

By the turn of the century Chinese were among the thousands of refugees from the Transvaal who fled to the Cape. The outbreak of the Anglo-Boer War in 1899 and hostilities which lasted three years turned vast areas of the Transvaal, northern Cape, Orange Free State and Natal into battle zones. After the war, many returned to the Transvaal, but quite a few Chinese chose to remain in the Cape. The introduction of the Chinese Exclusion Act in 1904 initiated stringent restrictions on immigration, but the Chinese in the Cape generally enjoyed more rights than the Chinese in the Transvaal. As a testimony to the Cape's liberal tradition, they were permitted to own fixed property and subject to educational, property and income qualifications, could be registered as parliamentary voters in terms of the Franchise and Ballot Act of 1892.

The caption to the original copy of this picture reads: 'A Chinaman's Shop'. It was one of many Chinese shops in early Kimberley.

The Malay Camp, on the outskirts of the city of Kimberley, consisted of a motley assortment of tin shanties which housed people of all races.

KIMBERLEY — DIAMOND CITY

Wild, frenzied and chaotic, Kimberley in the 1870s typified a bustling mining camp in its heyday. Tales of fortunes made and lost overnight on the diamond diggings were legend. Prospectors and adventurers flocked in their thousands to the tent town first called De Beers New Rush, then Colesberg Kopje and eventually Kimberley.

One of the first Chinese there was teenager Foo Nim, who arrived in the late 1860s. He is said to have taken a month to walk 850 km from Durban to Kimberley, living off what he could find on the way and the hospitality of passers-by.[25] Foo Nim stayed on in Kimberley to become a prosperous merchant and community leader.

No available evidence points to any Chinese having worked as a diamond digger, although many survived as shopkeepers and laundrymen, living in the Malay Camp on the outskirts of the town. Started by Malay transport drivers, the Malay Camp was a motley collection of 'squalid, tightly packed', makeshift hovels and shacks[26] which served as home for the Coloureds, Indians and Chinese. For most, life was a hand-to-mouth existence, described by one observer in these words:

> Has the average European any idea of the way in which the Celestial shopkeepers manage to meet the requirements of their customers? I really do not think so, nor can he obtain one without visiting their places of business. Take a walk round the outskirts, especially in the neighbourhood of the Malay Camp, and just see what these almond-eyed strangers are doing. Of the buildings it may be said that they are made of the zinc lining from packing cases. The stock-in-trade consists of vegetables, groceries, sweets, and a few articles of Kafir truck. At the door stands one of the proprietors, ready to dart in any direction to waylay a possible customer, and he can buy anything in stock in the most minute quantities. A pennyworth of sugar or coffee, half a candle, a fraction of a pumpkin or cabbage: such divisions scarcely call for comment. When, however, it comes to retailing a spoonful of condensed milk, it almost seems there should be some restriction, for it opens the way to adulteration, at which John Chinaman is an adept. That so-called milk is sold in this way is a fact, and so are tinned jams and similar articles, and I can only say that if such things are permitted, there should be the very closest scrutiny of these places of business. Much of the food sold from them must be unwholesome, from the fact of decaying vegetables being huddled together in a close, oven-like room with the open cans, and the owners sleeping in the shop. To go near one of the places sends a shudder through one, and to eat anything out of them must be highly injurious.[27]

Quite how any customer departed with his purchase of a 'spoonful of condensed milk' or jam is left to the reader's imagination!

From their early association with Kimberley's Malay Camp, the Chinese incorporated the name into their vocabulary (Malaikam in Cantonese and Malaikim in Hakka) and used it to describe the areas where Chinese congregated both in Port Elizabeth and in Johannesburg.

Kimberley's earliest known Chinese grave is that of a man identified as 'Canton Chinaman' who was buried in the Pioneer Park cemetery in 1882. By 1890 the Chinese population in the town numbered some 180 and, like every group in those rough and tumble days, they saw their share of murder and mayhem.

Old timers talked for years of the scandal when four Chinese were charged with the murder of Ah Sam during an argument over *fan tan*, a game involving betting on numbers of counters or beans. It all happened on 11 April 1890 when a few men gathered at a house in the Malay Camp to gamble. One man grabbed Ah Sam by the throat, pushed him against a wall and started beating him. Others joined in and suddenly Ah Sam cried out he had been stabbed. His assailants fled ... and one, Lo Chin, even managed to flee the Cape Colony.

But, obviously, a Chinese man on the run couldn't escape detection for long. After two weeks as a fugitive, he was arrested in the tiny Transvaal town of Christiana, about 170 km away from Kimberley. Extradition papers had to be drawn up for the Transvaal (South African Republic) authorities to transfer him to the Cape.[28]

Chinese Traders Defend Rights

Discussion on the importation of Chinese to supplement the labour needs of Kimberley's diamond mines in 1881 once again focused attention on the group which newspapers had dubbed 'Heathen Chinee'.[29] Writing under the nom-de-plume, 'One who knows

The oldest remaining Chinese gravestone in Kimberley's Pioneers Cemetery is inscribed 'Canton Chinaman'. It marks the resting place of John Misiyoude who died in 1882 or 1887, aged 37 years.

John Chinaman', a Kimberley resident listed reasons for his dislike of the Chinese as a race. He said they would soon desert the work for which they were introduced to compete with White men.

> ... their well known dishonesty, which is of a most cunning nature, would become a most serious matter ... and if we suffer so severally from the thieving of the comparatively simple native, how should we fare in the hands of these keen and subtle robbers? ... they go a long way to ruin the trade of any place they settle in, as in a financial sense they absorb all they possibly can and give out nothing. As far as I know of their customs the only advantage we should derive from them ... would be that we should probably have a better supply of vegetables, as they seem to possess the power of making them grow on almost a barren rock.[30]

One of the earliest Chinese settlers in Kimberley, Foo Nim, became a successful trader with several shops and died in 1901.

Although no Chinese labourers were imported for the mines, in 1890 the Kimberley settlers were already the target of abuse by the town's White traders who cast slurs on their race and cried 'unfair competition'. A Storekeepers Protection Association was formed in a bid to halt the 'Chinese invasion', to restrict all Chinese trade to areas called 'locations' and to prevent the further development of Chinese businesses in the Cape.[31] Words were bandied back and forth as the Chinese were accused of a host of social and moral evils.

Three representatives of the Chinese shopkeepers eloquently defended their people against the barrage of 'charges' levelled and outlined their case in a lengthy letter to the local *Diamond Fields Advertiser* newspaper on 4 April 1890. The men, Foo Nim, T.

Machow and H.J. Ah Lee, stated that Chinese wished to work and trade legitimately and denied that they cut prices to undersell White shopkeepers. They pointed out that many of them were naturalized British subjects, they paid tax and municipal rates on their properties and contrary to accusations that they ate and drank little or nothing, they enjoyed a good meal as much as any man.

> True we do not run into debt at our butchers, but for this fault we would crave forgiveness. As to drinking nothing, while we are certainly abstemious, any canteen keeper can tell you that we are not total abstainers ... 'We gamble.' Well, amongst ourselves we like to risk a little now and then, but so soon as you have suppressed the Totalisator, abolished the Share Market, and rendered card playing at your clubs punishable by expulsion, we undertake to emulate your admirable example.
>
> 'We smoke opium.' Without enquiring whether the practice in strict moderation is injurious or no, we would ask: From whom do we procure the opium? If it be wicked for us to smoke it, it must be a thousand times more sinful for you to sell it to us. But you who make the laws practically encourage its sale.
>
> 'We are immoral.' You here ask us to prove a negative. Your charge is 'vague and embarrassing' as your lawyers call it, and we refuse to plead, or we would allude to China as a country where the marriage tie is held in more inviolate sanctity than certain European nations that we know of.'

They concluded by stating that they had answered each accusation directed at them and trusted that British fairplay would not permit injustice to be done to the Chinese. Despite such reasoned and placatory arguments, opposition to Chinese immigration persisted. Over the next two years, outspoken editorial writers and correspondents reflected ever more antagonism, making misleading, exaggerated and distorted references to Chinese settlement. More than in any other area, the Kimberley Chinese in the 1890s were the target of strident racism in the local press. Although their numbers were insignificant in relation to the total population, letter writers referred constantly to the 'Chinese deluge' or 'Yellow invasion' and urged action to 'prevent the Colony from being swamped by a vast horde of uncanny Mongols'.[32]

Much of this opposition had its roots not only in the prevailing British colonial desire to shape South Africa into a White man's country but also in Kimberley's rather unique economic circumstances. White traders, already under siege by the De Beers Diamond Company's monopoly, reacted vociferously when threatened by new competitors. The saga of 'Perkin Aja Mahen' who was also styled the 'Chinese Prophet' (see inset story) is a striking example of the attitudes of the times and of the ease with which the press was able to inflame public sentiment against the Chinese.

Probably 'inspired' by a suggestion in government circles that a Chinese consular office be established in the Cape, Kimberley's *Diamond Fields Advertiser* printed a lengthy series of correspondence in which a fictitious Chinese consul taunted the public and drew forth a barrage of White abuse. The Chinese tried to defend themselves, denying the existence of any consular representative, but they had become a ready target for vendors of public opinion.

The Strange Case of 'The Chinese Prophet'

In the six weeks between the end of September and mid-November 1891, the *Diamond Fields Advertiser* published a series of inflammatory letters, supposedly written by a Chinese, named 'Perkin Aja Mahen'. This sparked off a wave of correspondence, much of it racist and insulting, which called for a boycott of Chinese traders and the extermination of the 'Asiatic plague'.

Describing 'Perkin' as the 'African Chinese Prophet', various letter writers condemned his 'pig-tailed impudence' and suggested he be hanged by his hair. Whether 'Perkin' was the creation of a satirical editorial writer or a gifted trouble-maker bent on stirring up anti-Chinese feeling is open to speculation. His name bears no resemblance to that of a Chinese, although 'Perkin' is suggestive of the Chinese capital 'Peking'.

On 25 September 1891 'Perkin' fired his first salvo. His letter, carrying the address 'Selby Street', Kimberley announced the appointment of a Chinese Consul for Kimberley.

'We have been treated at all times by the European merchants as 'wild dogs', and we have to suffer all their remarks. But now we have our representative, who is well aware of all the commercial treaties between England and China, where will the 'Funny Ferries' of West End fame put his nose now when we have our Consulate here.... We have already subscribed £1000 towards building a church for the Chinese congregation ... We have made Kimberley our adopted home, and as long as there are diamonds in De Beers Mine, we will never leave this place. Therefore it will only be idle for those Africander agitators to try to get us out of this place. We don't drink champagne at one guinea a bottle. That is the reason we are so prosperous in every branch of trade. We are already 700 strong in this place ... and before long we hope to import our own goods, and open shops in Dutoitspan Road ...'[33]

The impact was immediate. Under the nom-de-plume of a 'Knight of Labour', an angry resident described this as a menacing letter which should arouse the people of Kimberley against the Chinese, and others retaliated in the same vein.

'Perkin' went on to claim he had been a schoolmaster and also attached to the Chinese Embassy in London. But his letters degenerated rapidly into rambling replies to critics in which the grammar and spelling made his remarks nonsensical. Offering an explanation, the *Diamond Fields Advertiser* editor commented at the end of one such letter: 'The literary beauties of the above would have been spoiled by the application of an unsympathetic sub-editorial pen.'

Just eight days after 'Perkin's' first letter was published, the newspaper printed a seven-verse satire on the man they called 'The Chinnese (sic) Consul'. Describing him as peculiar, the verses made fun of his language and logic, claimed the Chinese hadn't donated much to charity and said it was a cheek for them to maintain that Whites also gambled.[34]

After the flurry of correspondence generated by Perkin's letters, the following letter appeared on 24 October 1891, headlined:

The Chinese Population of Kimberley
Poor Perkin Killed Off!

Sir,

We, the undersigned Chinamen, resident in Kimberley, will be obliged, if you will allow us through the medium of your paper to inform the public of these Fields that the silly letters, which have recently appeared in your columns over the signature —'Perkin Aja Mahen' — do not emanate from, and have not been written by any person of our nationality, and that the only object of these letters has been to stir up ill-feeling towards us.

There is no Chinese Consul in Kimberley, and the Chinese inhabitants of Kimberley see no necessity for obtaining one, being confident of just and fair treatment and protection under the laws of this country.

The statement that there are 700 Chinese resident on these Fields is a gross exaggeration; our number do not exceed 150. Finally, we have not the slightest intention of importing our goods direct from Europe or Asia, being perfectly satisfied to make our purchases from the local wholesale houses.

It was signed by Messrs H.J. Ahlee, J. Machan and others. No editorial comment or explanation followed this letter, but a regular correspondent expressed the wish that it be totally ignored by the Kimberley municipality and the community.[35] 'Perkin', however, made a final appearance in the newspaper's letters page. Saying he had been on holiday in Natal, he was pleased that nothing had happened to the Chinese community and expressed his support for the Indian community's 'agitation to the north'. He thanked the newspaper editor for 'past favours' and thereafter remained silent.[36]

That the newspaper did not 'prove' Perkin's existence or apologize in any way for the letters published perhaps indicates its active role in an unsavoury campaign to discredit the Chinese community of Kimberley and South Africa.

Forging a Community

Confronted by antagonism from the populace at large, it was inevitable that the Chinese should group together to protect their interests. They met socially to gamble and to exchange local news in their home tongues, and soon established an informal community organization.

By 1890, the Chinese residents of Kimberley jointly despatched a letter welcoming the new Governor of the Cape, Henry Loch. The governor replied warmly and diplomatically:

> It affords me much satisfaction to learn from your address your appreciation of the constitutional rights and privileges which as subjects of the British Empire you now enjoy, and it gives me pleasure to receive the assurances of your steadfast loyalty to Her Most Gracious Majesty the Queen.
>
> ... I can assure you that ... I shall always be pleased to watch over the interests of the Chinese who may be residents therein, whether naturalized British subjects or not.[37]

Although this assurance was more polite than real, it encouraged the conviction that the Chinese could approach the highest authorities in the land directly to intervene on their behalf.

Just a few years later, in 1895, the Kimberley Chinese collected money to build the 'Kaiyin Fee Gon' [嘉應會館] in the town. Five counties around Moiyean make up the Kaiyin (Jiaying) district in north-east Kwangtung, and the club's name therefore indicates a predominance of Moiyeanese over Cantonese in Kimberley's early days. Elderly community members said the club was built by Chinese labourers, who also added extensions to it in 1900. It was built in the traditional Chinese style consisting of a series of rooms around an open courtyard.[38] Situated at Number 1, China Street in the Malay Camp, the club gave the community a venue to gather over weekends — to gamble, to exchange news and to bid in the 'fee' or 'hui' money-lending scheme. Often described as a Chinese banking system, the 'fee' was used by Chinese worldwide as a means of raising capital and investing excess funds. For early settlers in South Africa, it played a vital role in developing a community network and assisting with the immigration of relatives and has remained a popular funding method.

Unlike other areas where intense rivalry marked relations between the Moiyeanese and Cantonese, all Kimberley Chinese shared the club's facilities, and no serious differences appeared to surface. By 1904, the Chinese population in Kimberley numbered 210 men and 4 women, and the town of Mafeking, not far away, counted 31 Chinese men among its residents.[39] It is interesting to note that until the 1990s Kimberley was the only South African city which housed a traditional Chinese temple, or Guan Ti. When it was first established no community member can recall, but a few altars to various gods were maintained at the 'Kaiyin Fee Gon', probably from the turn of the century, and can still be seen at the headquarters of the Kimberley Chinese Association clubhouse in York Street.

EASTERN CAPE SETTLEMENT

The Eastern Cape was for many years the second largest area of Chinese settlement in South Africa, after the Transvaal. Often referred to as 'settler country' since becoming home to more than 4000 British immigrants in 1820, this was frontier territory with hills and valleys covered in thick bush and vast tracts of farmland. Towards the end of the 19th century, both Port Elizabeth and East London were ports of call along the sea route from Mauritius, offering natural entry points into the country for the Chinese. Port Elizabeth was the largest town in the area and a flourishing commercial centre, trading in ivory, ostrich feathers, wool, mohair and hides while East London had the distinction of being the country's only river port.[40]

Landing at Port Elizabeth in the early days was quite an experience since passengers had to be transferred from ships to smaller boats in swaying wicker baskets. For new arrivals, confronted by rocky beaches and buildings balanced on the sides and top of a very steep hill, their first sight of the town was often disappointing.[41] But the panoramic views from the hills offered some compensation and the bustling activity of Port Elizabeth's streets and markets meant opportunities for enterprising settlers.

When the first Chinese settled in the Eastern Cape is not known, but old gravestones indicate the presence of some Chinese as early as 1878. In cemeteries throughout the country the graves of the first Chinese to be buried in the area were generally called the local 'Dai Buk Gung' (大伯公). The designation means 'Great Grand Uncle' and those graves were honoured by the local communities, either as caretakers of the burial ground, or simply as the first Chinese to be buried there.

The oldest Chinese grave still in existence in the Eastern Cape is in Uitenhage, which lies 34 km north west of Port Elizabeth. Dated the 4th year of the reign of the Emperor Kwong Si, which was 1878, the stone marks the final resting place of Fok Yuen Yin, a native of Ma Kau village, in the Suntak district of Kwangtung. While he may not have been the first Chinese in the area, his grave points to the early presence of Chinese who, by 1901, numbered 89 in Uitenhage. These men ran 44 small businesses until an outbreak of the plague led to the closure of eight Chinese shops in the town.[42]

In Somerset East, about 185 km north of Port Elizabeth, one of the first Chinese settlers in the town lies in a lonely grave overgrown with grass and weeds. His tombstone carries no date, but he is believed to have died sometime in the 1880s. Some say he was the first Chinese in Somerset East who was so lonely that he committed suicide in a deserted kloof outside the town. Another story, more probable, is that he worked for some Chinese in the town but was accused of theft. Unable to live with this 'loss of face', he committed suicide. His ghost is said to haunt the area, appearing as a fiery ball on dark nights.[43]

Originally erected in the mid-1880s, the tombstone of Port Elizabeth's 'Dai Buk Gung' (大伯公) — the earliest Chinese grave in the city — was set in the base of this structure and a 'new' stone placed above it in 1906.

The man reputed to have been the first Chinese in East London adopted the unlikely English name of 'Ching Chong'. The story goes that he stepped off a boat and walked up a street on the city's West Bank. Some local children followed him, chanting the common insult 'Ching Chong, Ching Chong'. Liking the sing-song sound, and unaware of its connotations, he named himself 'Ching Chong'. The story is corroborated by a tombstone in the West Bank cemetery where Ching Chong buried his son, 'Kong Chow' in 1902.

The grave of an early Chinese settler in Somerset East, believed to have died in the 1880s, is marked by a simple stone tablet.

In Port Elizabeth, three memorials in the North End cemetery mark the graves of the first Chinese to die in that city. They are called 'Dai Buk Gung' (first great grand uncle), 'Yee Buk Gung' (second) and 'Saam Buk Gung' (third). The original headstones, dating from the mid-1880s, have been preserved in the bases of cement structures, and 'new' tombstones dated 1906 installed above them. Elderly community members claimed the graves were those of sailors off passing ships, but it is possible they were contract labourers brought to Port Elizabeth in November 1881. Recording the arrival of these Chinese, a local newspaper remarked:

> A large number of Chinamen have recently arrived here, and are proving themselves to be most useful individuals in the capacity of household servants.[44]

For new arrivals, the undoubted attractions inland were the business opportunities created by Kimberley's diamond fields and the Transvaal's gold mines. Within the eastern Cape, Chinese settled in Port Elizabeth and the neighbouring town of Uitenhage while a handful followed the rail routes to places such as Somerset East, Graaff Reinet and Cradock and a few headed for Kingwilliamstown, Grahamstown and Queenstown.

By 1884 several Chinese from Mauritius had established small businesses in Port Elizabeth. Between 1888 and 1891, at least 116 Chinese left the Mauritian capital of Port Louis for Algoa Bay. The majority of these must have made their way further into the interior since official records show only 19 Chinese resident in Port Elizabeth in 1891.[45] In the two years between 1896 and 1898, more than 1200 Chinese embarked in Mauritius for Port Elizabeth.[46] This influx however came to a temporary standstill when the Anglo-Boer War erupted in the Transvaal in 1899.[47] Instead of arriving by sea, numbers of Chinese fleeing hostilities in the north made their way overland to the Eastern Cape, some to remain permanently.

Public records throw little light on the activities and everyday concerns of the Chinese in the Eastern Cape before 1904. Perhaps the very lack of documentation is a reflection of the extent to which they tried to stay out of the limelight, going about their businesses and their lives as inconspicuously as possible. A few newspaper clippings focus mainly on brushes with the law and prevailing prejudices towards Asiatics.

Of the Eastern Cape newspapers, the *Graaff-Reinet Advertiser* was particularly vocal in its opposition to Chinese immigration, stating that the presence of 'these almond eyed sons of Confucius' was 'a stumbling block to all European enterprise and progress'.[48] When the town's citizens appealed for a poll tax to be imposed on Asiatics in May 1897, it was claimed that the influx of Asiatics had increased to an alarming extent and was a danger to health and prosperity.[49] There were two Chinese in Graaff Reinet in 1897, increasing to 15 by early 1898.[50] This situation prompted the newspaper to adopt the argument used worldwide by opponents of Asiatic immigration, namely that the arrival of Chinese would spread disease. In its leader the newspaper stated:

> In almost every respect, these undesirable visitors to our shores are a prolific source of annoyance and danger — socially, commercially and morally.[51]

Because the *Graaff Reinet Advertiser* made no bones about its attitude towards Chinese, it paid closer attention to them than other recorders of events of the day. This has at least left us an interesting insight into the reception the new arrivals encountered in Port Elizabeth and how they were generally perceived.

Arriving in a new Land

The following newspaper report offers an insight into the first experiences of many Chinese when they arrived in South Africa in the late 1890s. Printed in an Eastern Cape newspaper, the *Graaff Reinet Advertiser* on 12 September 1898, it is entitled 'Another Asiatic Invasion':

Port Elizabeth has lately experienced what was little short of an invasion of the yellow race. Carrying among her complement of passengers the *Doune Castle* had on board 128 Chinese and 24 Indians, who had booked from Mauritius for that port. The yellow boys and their swarthy companions were set ashore early in the morning, and their arrival kept the Customs House officials busy for two or three hours. The scene outside the Customs House at the North Jetty was a busy and animated one. Each emigrant had taken the precaution of providing himself with quite an imposing amount of baggage, as curious in its composition as it was large in bulk. Each emigrant stood anxiously guarding his belongings, and as the majority did not understand English, it was indeed amusing to see their puzzled looks of bewilderment as they were peremptorily told to open up and unpack. Nothing escaped the penetrating eyes of the officials, and their scrutiny of each man's goods and chattels was of the most searching description. But John Chinaman is not a man of deep emotions, and as he saw perhaps some of his most cherished treasures so rudely knocked about, he merely nodded his muddled head, gaped a little wider, and blinked. Then when the officer had chalked his chattels as passable, John's moment of triumph arrived, and with feverish haste, and an unbusiness-like regard for order, he stuffed his goods back again, and waddled away with them to be taken in charge by the grinning coolie. One or two were asked what was their object in coming over here. All answered alike. It was to 'makee monee'. But whether they will succeed in 'makee monee' or not, one thing is certain, and that is that the municipal and sanitary authorities will have an extra amount of work on their hands, for it is this unchecked, or at least unguarded, emigration of irresponsible foreigners that lead to the spread of pestilence and disease. For instance, it is only necessary to mention the present local small-pox outbreak which was brought there by the unguarded visitation of Indians.

HOW NEW SETTLERS SURVIVED

Chinese immigration to South Africa was not part of any organized importation scheme. Virtually all the new settlers were individuals, men who either arrived on their own, or in the company of a relative or friend, and then set about earning a living. Most of them started small grocery businesses, laundries and market gardens. In a strange land, with little or no understanding of English, they resorted to the age-old means of overcoming communication barriers — sign language.

Elderly community members often tell how one of the essential tools in any new business was a broomstick or walking stick. In makeshift shops, where packing cases served as counters, customers used the stick to point to the goods they wanted — and by displaying the number of coins required, the shopkeeper was able to state his selling price. One item which was never sold was the last packet or tin of goods in any range of products ... the shopkeeper needed to use it as a sample for re-ordering.[52]

Old residents of Port Elizabeth also recall the existence of Chinese market gardens in the Baakens River Valley in 1895, fondly reminiscing that there 'fresh vegetables were to be had at any time'.[53] Describing the picturesque corners of Port Elizabeth early this century, author Lawrence Green wrote of the Chinese market gardeners:

> Chinese growers took their vegetables from door to door in pannier baskets. Even in those days some people enjoyed the authentic Chinese dishes; meat and fish cooked with sesame or peanut oil and mild spices; mushrooms and bamboo shoots, shrimps and almonds and soya sauce; cakes flavoured with powdered ginger.[54]

Finding that they were able to survive by dint of hard work and perseverance, the Chinese passed on word to male relatives and kinsmen to join them. Only much later when they were more firmly established would they either have sent for their wives and children or gone home to China or Mauritius to marry and then return. Chinese women only arrived in South Africa after the turn of the century and their role will be more fully examined in later chapters.

Although Port Elizabeth did not experience anything like the anti-Chinese virulence in Kimberley, underlying opposition to Chinese settlement remained a feature of the times. At a Port Elizabeth Town Council meeting in January 1899, a councillor called for volunteers to go out to meet ships carrying Asiatics, and to shoot any who attempted to land. Asiatics 'are expected by steamer daily. The feeling is very strong that the Government ought to do something.'[55]

PORT ELIZABETH'S 'MALAIKIM'

From the turn of the century, the Chinese congregated near the eastern edge of Port Elizabeth around Evatt Street where it intersects with Russell and Hartman roads. They called this area, 'Malaikim', most probably adopting the name from Kimberley where Chinese lived mainly in the Malay Camp. Port Elizabeth had already become a busy trading centre and fair numbers of Chinese moved to Port Elizabeth after initially working in Kimberley.[56]

In 1901, at least three Chinese businesses were operating in Evatt Street: Ah Yan's grocery store, the Hoplee China Laundry and Jonson and Co, grocers and general dealers.[57] In the following years, more Chinese moved into the area, as residents and traders, transforming 'Malaikim' into a mini-Chinatown where food of every description was available and where Chinese met in small clubs, gambling and opium 'dens' or visited the resident herbalist for medical advice.

In the early years of the 20th century Chinese already dominated Port Elizabeth's laundry business. Of the city's eleven laundrymen, eight were Chinese. They were: For

On of Thomas Street, South End; Hop Lee of Evatt Street; Man Lee of Walmer Road, South End; Quang Chong of Westbourne Road; Quong Lee of Evatt Street; Sam Lee of Mackay Street, Richmond Hill; Sing Lee of Evatt Street and Soon Lee of Robson Street, the Hill.[58]

At least one clan organization had already been formally established by 1902. Called the 'Nam Hoi and Sun Tak Club of Canton Chinese at Port Elizabeth and Uitenhage', it most probably operated as a mutual benefit society which offered financial support to new settlers. Organizations like these were established by emigrant Chinese worldwide to run the 'fee' or 'hui' (會) money-lending scheme and to provide capital for members to establish a new business, or to pay their passage to visit their families in China. Clearly wishing to build up goodwill on a wider basis than only among Chinese, the Nam Hoi and Sun Tak club collected £37-2-0 from its members which was sent to King Edward VII of Great Britain in honour of his coronation on 9 August 1902.[59] They were notified that their donation had been sent to King Edward's Hospital Fund for London.

By 1903, officials recorded a total of 179 Chinese grocers in Port Elizabeth,[60] and White traders soon expressed their antagonism towards such competition. Welcoming moves by the local council to establish a separate township for Asiatics, they claimed Chinese shopkeepers were selling short weights and asked for the appointment of an inspector of weights and measures. They formed a Grocers' Association to protect their interests and levelled other accusations against the Chinese:

> It was also pointed out that in nearly every case where the [White] merchants had been robbed, the Chinese were the receivers of the stolen goods. That they broke all sanitary laws by sleeping in the same room as that in which they sell their goods; that they were debasing the trade generally.[61]

Like any group, the Chinese had rogues in their ranks, but did not deserve to be labelled thieves or crooks as a whole. Most simply tried to eke out what living they could, scrimping and saving in the hopes of either returning home to China or bringing their families out to join them. By 1904, Chinese in the Eastern Cape and outlying districts numbered 806, including only 9 women. It was most probable that none of these women was Chinese by birth, but were enumerated as such if they had married Chinese men.

At least 12 Chinese were registered as voters in the Port Elizabeth electoral division in 1905. Mainly general dealers and shop assistants, they included several well-known community members such as Ho Carson, Li Green, Warson James, William James, Wong William Singson and Chain Guide Wing. Listed as qualified to vote for members of the Legislative Council and the House of Assembly, most of these were also named in the electoral rolls for 1907 and 1913.[62]

Of all Chinese who settled in the coastal towns, the Moiyeanese were predominant. Varying reasons have been offered for this — perhaps the Cantonese were more enterprising and adventurous, whereas the Moiyeanese settled where they landed, unwilling to venture further inland. It seems most likely that clan members trailed their kinsmen, and after the first Cantonese had paved the way to the small inland towns and up north to the Transvaal, their relatives followed.

Eastern Cape Chinese Population – 1904

District	*Males*	*Females*	*Total*
Port Elizabeth	498	1	499
East London	93	6	99
Uitenhage	88	2	90
Somerset East	22	–	22
Kingwilliamstown	18	–	18
Albany	17	–	17
Cradock	17	–	17
Queenstown	16	–	16
Bedford	6	–	6
Graaff Reinet	5	–	5
Middelburg	4	–	4
Steynsburg	3	–	3
Wodehouse	3	–	3
Aliwal North	1	–	1
Britstown	1	–	1
Colesberg	1	–	1
Hanover	1	–	1
Humansdorp	1	–	1
Tarka	1	–	1
Lusikisiki	1	–	1
TOTAL	797	9	806

Census of the Colony of the Cape of Good Hope, 17 April 1904.[63]

CAPE TOWN

Small numbers of Chinese first arrived in Cape Town from 1660, and the formal establishment of a 'new' Chinese cemetery there in 1840 points to the continued settlement of a sprinkling of individuals, if not a community as such. Whether they came as lone adventurers off passing ships or made their way overland to Cape Town from Kimberley or Port Elizabeth, numbers of Chinese were living and working in the city by the end of the 19th century. In June 1899, the Cape Colonial government turned down a request by two Chinese grocers in Cape Town to be naturalized. Both stated they had resided in the colony for more than six years.[64]

By 1900 however the Chinese in Cape Town warranted enough attention for a deputation to request restrictions to be placed on Chinese immigration.[65] It is likely shopkeepers who had fled the Witwatersrand and Kimberley with the outbreak of the Anglo-Boer War were in the vanguard of such anti-Chinese moves. When plague broke out in Cape Town in 1901, Chinese laundries were believed to be particularly dangerous in encouraging its spread — although only one case actually occurred on Chinese premises. Writing about Chinese laundries, a local newspaper correspondent said:

> The enterprising Celestial finds them a very paying investment. I have noted at least a couple of dozen in different parts of the city during my slum tours, more than one would expect considering the population and the quantity of washing given out direct to the coloured women. The majority of these so-called laundries will be found amongst the most undesirable surroundings ... He hangs out his sign with 'Ah Sing', or 'San Lui', or 'Yo Sam', or some such picturesque patronymic, with 'New Laundry' in large letters underneath. Every place that opens is called 'New Laundry'. It looks attractive. The old places are still designated 'New Laundry'. It is rather confusing to the stranger, who, however, tumbles in time, to this gentleman of Oriental Wiliness.[66]

The 1904 census recorded the presence of 328 Chinese men and one woman in Cape Town and its suburbs.[67]

CAPE PROHIBITS CHINESE IMMIGRATION

Following the example set by Natal's legislators, the Cape introduced a law against Asiatic immigration without specifically naming it as such. The Immigration Restriction Act of 1902 effectively barred Asiatics by its demand that prospective immigrants be able to read and write a European language. But the threat of the 'yellow peril' loomed ever larger in the public mind as it became clear that mine owners and the British administration in the Transvaal were intent on importing Chinese labourers in large numbers to work the Witwatersrand gold mines. A wide variety of organizations and newspapers reflected increased opposition to Chinese settlement in South Africa.

> John Chinaman is in every way unfitted to be a fellow citizen in this country, and yet as such he is steadily and quietly taking up his abode in the seaport towns, working out the European trader and introducing habits and customs which it is to our interest to keep out of the country.[68]

This time the persistent appeals to keep Chinese out of the Cape were heeded. Fearing that some of the indentured Chinese labourers might make their way into the Cape, the colony introduced the first legislation in South Africa specifically against the Chinese.

When the Chinese Exclusion Bill passed its second reading, virtually all parliamentary members expressed support for strong measures to 'curtail the evil' of a Chinese influx and to 'Exclude all Chinese from South Africa'. Only one member, a Mr Oats, criticized the restrictions the law would place on Chinese already in the colony and said the measure was 'retrogressive, barbaric and savage'.[69]

The Chinese Exclusion Act of 1904 prohibited Chinese from entering and residing in the Cape Colony and instituted a comprehensive system for the registration and control of the 1380 Chinese already present within its borders. Special 'Certificates of Exemption' had to be carried by all Chinese in the Cape and renewed every year. Penalties included fines, imprisonment and deportation. It was this certificate which the Chinese scornfully referred to as a 'dog licence'.[70]

Far-reaching in its implications for the rights of Chinese in the colony, the Chinese Exclusion Act contained the following provisions:

- No 'Chinaman' except those born British subjects or naturalized in the Cape could enter or reside in the colony, and each of these needed to obtain a Governor's Certificate of Exemption.
- All Chinese in the colony when the Act was promulgated were to be registered and issued with a Minister's Certificate of Exemption.
- Every male 'Chinaman' reaching the age of 18 had to apply for a certificate.
- Certificates of Exemption were to be produced on demand from any official and renewed every year before 15 January.
- Movement from one part of the Cape to another, even for a visit, had to be reported to the local magistrate.
- No liquor, mining, general dealer's, importer's, hawker's or other licence whatever to carry on a trade were to be issued nor any property hired out to Chinese not possessing a Certificate of Exemption.
- The resident magistrate was required to register all Chinese present in his district every year.
- No Certificates of Naturalization were to be issued to Chinese under any circumstances after the promulgation of the Chinese Exclusion Act.
- Chinese convicted twice of assault, gambling, keeping a brothel or any crime before a high court would be deported to China after serving their sentences.
- Only Chinese holding the Governor's Certificate of Exemption could be registered as voters.
- Officials were empowered to search any premises for Chinese illegally in the colony and a magistrate was entitled to call on all Chinese in his district to appear before him simultaneously to produce their Certificates of Exemption.
- Ships' captains and owners of vehicles entering the Cape were obliged to report the presence of any Chinese. Should any Chinese not be eligible to be in the colony, the ships' captains and vehicle owners were to return them back to their place of origin.
- Police and railway officials were empowered to prevent the entry of any Chinese without valid certificates into the Cape and officials who accepted railway tickets without examining Certificates of Exemption would be dismissed.
- Contravention of the law carried a fine of up to £100 or one year's imprisonment as well as deportation from the Cape.

For identification purposes Chinese requesting Certificates of Exemption had to submit all their fingerprints, be physically examined for distinguishing marks and sign their application forms in English and Chinese. The law contained a total of 36 sections and those who had to bear their brunt colloquially dubbed the measures 'the 36 unjust laws'.[71]

The Chinese Exclusion Act was promulgated on 22 September 1904, and a few days later plans were set in motion to erect a temporary detention station for Chinese immigrants on Robben Island, a few kilometres off Cape Town's coast. This oval-shaped

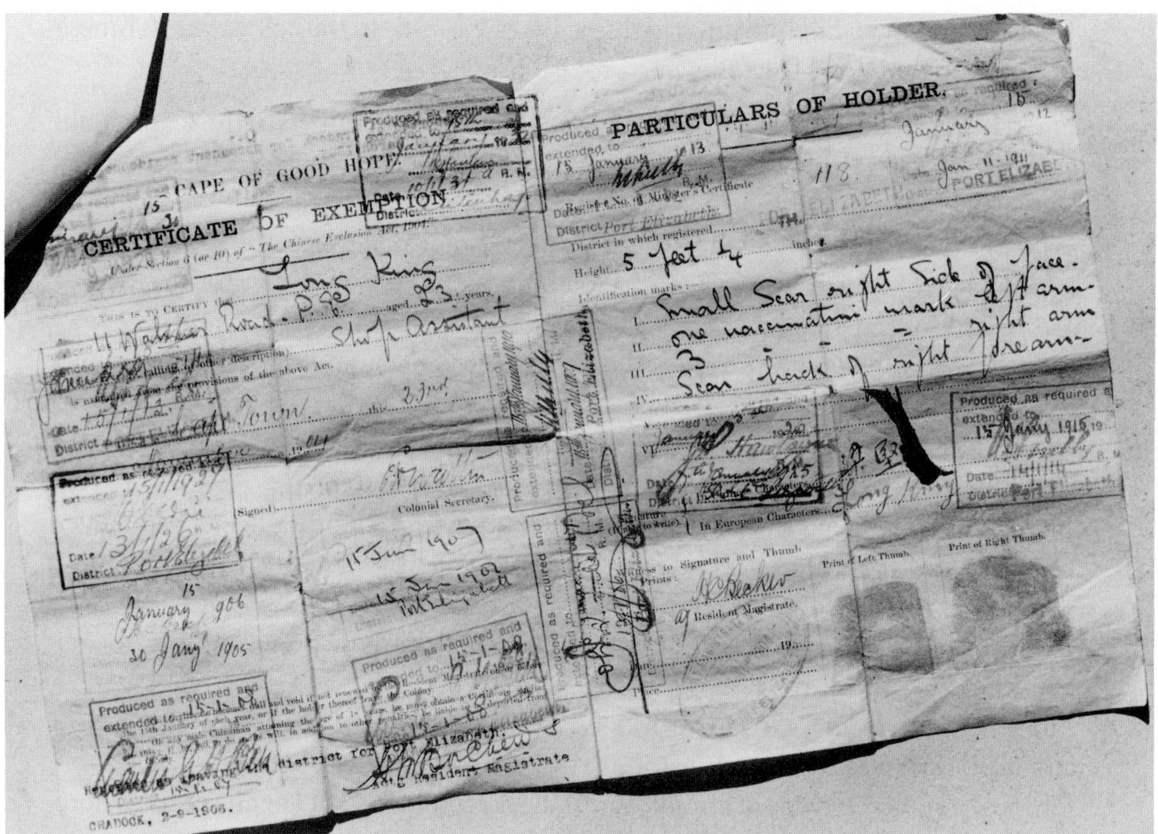
CAPE OF GOOD HOPE.
CERTIFICATE OF EXEMPTION.
PARTICULARS OF HOLDER.
Long King
Shop Assistant
Height 5 feet 4 inches
Identification marks:
I. Small Scar on right side of face.
II. One vaccination mark left arm
III. Scar back of right forearm
Colonial Secretary.
Produced as required and extended to
In European Characters
Print of Left Thumb.
Print of Right Thumb.
Resident Magistrate.
CRADOCK, 2-9-1906.

The infamous 'dog licence' — the piece of paper which Cape Chinese had to carry with them at all times and produce on demand. This much-worn Certificate of Exemption, issued in terms of the Chinese Exclusion Act of 1904, belonged to Long King of Uitenhage.

piece of land, covering an area of only 5.2 square kilometres, took its name from the Dutch word 'robbe' — a reference to the island's population of seals. Characterized by a rocky coastline, Robben Island was, from the earliest days of the Cape settlement, a penal colony and in later years became the 'home of lepers, lunatics, lawbreakers, the chronic sick and paupers'.[72]

The idea of establishing a detention station for the Chinese on Robben Island was probably based on New York's Ellis Island where new arrivals to America were held for questioning and the completion of immigration formalities. To investigate the eligibility of Chinese immigrants to enter the Cape, officials requested the erection of two buildings, accommodating 20 to 24 men and women separately. Initial estimates for wood and iron buildings were about £1000, excluding transportation of building materials to the island, and doubts were expressed on the acceptability of this amount. The Commissioner of Robben Island suggested using tents instead of buildings, but it seems the idea of a detention station was eventually dropped.[73]

For the Chinese as a whole, the 1904 Exclusion Act necessitated the formation and strengthening of community organizations and forced the Chinese to look to themselves to maintain and protect the tenuous position they held in the Cape.

OPPOSITION TO EXCLUSION ACT

Scattered in small concentrations throughout the colony, the Chinese naturally congregated on an informal, social basis. Clan organizations were operating in Kimberley as well as in Port Elizabeth by the early years of this century.

It is likely all the regional Chinese associations in the Cape, which exist to this day, were formed specifically to protest against the Chinese Exclusion Act. These were the East London, Port Elizabeth, Kimberley and Cape Town Chinese associations. This assumption is partially borne out by interviews with elderly community members as well as the fact that references to these organizations only appear in official documents after the promulgation of the law.[74]

To implement the Chinese Exclusion Act, officials needed to register all Chinese males in the Cape and obtain identification details. East London's 100 Chinese promptly communicated their outrage to the British Secretary of State for the Colonies and the Chinese Minister in London. They objected particularly to officials requiring them to strip for the purpose of finding identification marks on their bodies.

Asked to report on this complaint, the Medical Officer of Health for the Cape, Dr C. E. J. Gregory, pointed out the difficulties in identifying Chinese. To Western eyes, most Chinese appeared the same; they generally had few obvious identification marks, and even with complete stripping it had been 'found impossible to observe reliable and distinctive marks'. Dr Gregory added the Chinese in East London were the first to object strongly to the implementation of the law, 'a circumstance which was the more noticeable inasmuch as in many other Districts of the Colony no opposition was made'. Their appeal to the Chinese Minister however brought the welcome news, in a telegram to the East London Chinese Association, that they would not be required to strip.[75]

Both the East London and Port Elizabeth Chinese raised £1000 to pay for a delegate to travel to London to petition the Chinese Minister.[76] In Cape Town and elsewhere, the Chinese also raised strong objections to the taking of thumbprints, claiming that in China such prints were only taken from criminals condemned to execution. The same issue was to be raised in the Transvaal a few years later and dramatic steps taken to resist its enforcement.

The implementation of the law brought in its wake a host of administrative queries and highlighted anomalies such as the fact that no provision was made for Chinese to leave the colony and return. Only those with Governor's Certificates — proving they were British subjects or naturalized — could re-enter the Cape. Two years later an amendment to the law enabled resident Chinese to obtain permits to visit China. Since trading licences could only be granted to those Chinese who obtained Certificates of Exemption, postmasters who issued these had to consult with local magistrates on each individual case.[77]

Chinese soon found themselves running foul of the law, and facing deportation, for simply moving home from one Cape Town suburb to another. By the end of 1905, 12 Chinese were under sentence of deportation, but it was decided to suspend the ruling in these cases since many Chinese were not fully aware of the requirement that they had to notify the authorities of any and every change of address. Officials even advised

Issue of Licences to Chinamen.

ACT 37 OF 1904

(Promulgated 22nd September. 1904.)

The attention of Postmasters who issue Licences is specially directed to Section 17 of the above Act, which reads as follows :—

"No Liquor. Mining. General Dealer's. Importer's. Hawker's or other Licence whatever to carry on a trade shall be issued to any Chinaman who is not the registered owner of a Certificate of Exemption under this Act. nor shall any such Chinaman have any direct or indirect interest in any such Licence in this Colony. and no Chinaman not being the registered owner of a Certificate aforesaid shall be permitted to enter into a contract of labour either as a labourer in mining. agriculture, or any other pursuit, as a domestic servant or as a laundry man. or to be an assistant to a person holding any of the Licences mentioned in this section of the Act."

Postmasters are requested to exercise great care in issuing Licences to Chinamen. Should a Chinaman apply for a Licence and not be in possession of the necessary Certificate. he should be referred to the Magistrate of the District who grants such Certificates.

When a Licence is issued to a Chinaman the number, date and place of issue, of the Certificate of Exemption should be endorsed on the back of the Licence form and Counterfoil and should also be shown on the P. 259 (detailed statement only.)

R. HENDERSON,
Accountant.

G. P. O.. Cape Town.

6th October, 1904.

400-10-4

The above notice instructed postmasters in the Cape Colony on the terms under which they should issue licences to Chinese.

the Cape Town Chinese Association to apply to the Supreme Court to challenge magistrates' decisions to deport Chinese for not reporting their change of address.

The president of the Cape Town Chinese Association, the Reverend Baker, told officials many Chinese were ignorant of English and did not fully understand the regulations. He offered to have a detailed Chinese translation circulated in the community.[78]

FORMATION OF CAPE COLONY CHINESE ASSOCIATION

It is most probable that the Chinese Exclusion Act of 1904 was the catalyst for the formation of a new, broadly based organization to represent the 1380 Chinese in the colony. A photograph, taken in Cape Town in 1906, records the presence of at least 19 representatives of Chinese groups who constituted the 'Cape Colony Chinese Association'. Ornately embellished, the photograph features a banner stating the

The first broadly based Chinese community organization was the Cape Colony Chinese Association, representatives of which were photographed in 1906. The aims of the organization are outlined in the Chinese inscriptions on the pillars, written by Consul-General Lew Yuk Lin.

association's name (written by the Consul General for China, Lew Yuk Lin), the dragon flag of the Manchu Ch'ing dynasty and probably the association's own flag. Inscriptions on the pillars declare the organization's commitment to fight for the rights of the Chinese.

Loosely translated, the inscriptions state:

> We who now live in South Africa temporarily face unjust laws. We are being driven out, because the Ch'ing government is weak ... We miss our homeland, China. We hope our people will waken, strengthen and conquer the world ... Nothing is impossible. Everything depends on enthusiasm ... We each have our duty, to remember the best traditions of our ancestors and to see to our future.

The Cape Colony Chinese Association represented Chinese associations in Cape Town, Port Elizabeth, Kimberley and East London. Over the next few years it appealed directly and through the office of the Imperial Chinese Consulate-General for a relaxation in the Chinese Exclusion Act.

In 1908, the association's spokesman, Hing Woo, gave evidence before the government's Select Committee on Asiatic Grievances and asked for Chinese to be treated in the same way as other aliens. He pointed out they were adversely affected in terms of immigration, naturalization and freedom to participate in both municipal and parliamentary elections in the Cape. Since the introduction of the Exclusion Act, unlike other Asiatics, Chinese were prohibited entry and excluded from naturalization rights. He requested they be treated as all other ratepayers to qualify for a municipal franchise, and that naturalized subjects be given the same parliamentary franchise rights as other British born subjects.[79]

Chinese also objected to deportation for petty crimes and requested the authorities to recognize the various Chinese Associations since such organizations were able to exercise a measure of control over the community. Hing Woo, president of the Cape Town Chinese Association, said that if the associations were recognized, 'The Government would have better control over them [the Chinese] and the good ones would not suffer because of the bad ones.'[80]

He told the committee that fair numbers of Chinese men were married and there were about 12 to 14 wives in Cape Town. None of these women was, however, Chinese and his own wife was 'colonial'. The Select Committee made no recommendations on the specific complaints of the Chinese in relation to the Chinese Exclusion Act and only advised the government to recognize the various Chinese Associations throughout the Colony in dealing with matters affecting Chinese residents.[81]

Action was also taken on the diplomatic front. Since the importation of Chinese labourers to the Reef gold mines in 1904, an Imperial Chinese Consulate-General was established in Johannesburg, and through this office, Cape Chinese also directed petitions for the repeal of the law. The acting Consul-General, Liu Ngai, addressed several letters to the Cape Prime Minister, John X. Merriman, stating that the Chinese Exclusion Act constituted class legislation which placed 'an undeserved stigma on the subjects of a nation in amity with Great Britain'.

Acknowledging the letters and confirming that deputations from the Chinese were being met on the subject, the Prime Minister replied:

> The whole subject is fraught with great difficulty. I will ask you to consider that what you call the hardships and disabilities are the result of what may be called the conflict of civilizations ... It would be far indeed from the intention of any person in this country who has the smallest knowledge of affairs to reflect upon the Chinese. Their matchless industry, their intelligence and their proverbial integrity command the admiration of all who have studied their economic history.
>
> But it is also undoubtedly true that the introduction of Chinese civilization into South Africa (admirable as it is) would from our point of view be no more desirable than an European settlement in China would probably be to the authorities of that country. It is for these reasons that certain disabilities have been imposed, in the administration of which I take leave to assure you that every effort will be made to avoid unnecessary hardship to individuals already domiciled in the country.[82]

Acting Consul-General Liu submitted the Exclusion law was too drastic, and requested the government to consider amendments allowing for the entry of educated Chinese. A year later, he again raised the question, pointing out that the numbers of both the Chinese labourers on the Reef and independent Chinese in the Cape had declined. He said legislative amendments would not increase the Chinese population 'but would be the means of removing the regrettable impression that Chinese subjects of any class are undesirable under any circumstances'.[83]

Interestingly enough, this letter was circulated among Cabinet Ministers and drew forth the following revealing comments:

> 'I must say that this letter makes one feel rather ashamed.'
>
> 'That is so!'
>
> 'Yes, but the Rand Magnates are to blame for it. Surely the Union Parliament will deal with this question during their first session.'
>
> 'Self preservation is the first Law of Nature'
>
> 'Can we do more than say 'Wait for Union'?'[84]

In the official reply to Acting Consul-General Liu, the Prime Minister said pending changes in the form of government, he was not at liberty to make any radical change in the present position of Chinese. He, however, gave the assurance that each case would be considered on its merits.[85]

Although various Chinese organizations and the Consulate-General submitted numerous petitions for the repeal of the law, the Chinese Exclusion Act of 1904 was enforced for 29 years and effectively halted Chinese immigration into the Cape.

4

Under Boer Rule

Why were people of colour subjected to many more restrictions in the independent Boer republics than in the British colonies? How did Chinese cope with anti-Asiatic laws from 1885? Which community organizations were formed to meet social and political needs? This chapter outlines the prohibition on Chinese settlement in the Orange Free State, the numerous restrictions which existed in the South African Republic (Transvaal), the effects of the Anglo-Boer War and Chinese opposition to the importation of Chinese mine labourers in 1904.

Far north of the Cape, beyond the Orange and the Vaal rivers, lay the sprawling, landlocked territories known as Trans-Orangia and Transvaal. It was there that Dutch-speaking pioneers established independent republics to preserve their own way of life and to escape British rule. But the discovery of untold mineral wealth deep in the interior of the country and the influx of immigration it triggered was to destroy any hope these frontiersmen had of being left alone.

For the Chinese, and all people of colour, life in these territories was subject to many more restrictions than they had encountered either in the Cape or Natal. From the outset the pioneers who forged these independent republics sought to create a totally different society, 'a new Eden where there was to be no question of equality between White and Black.'[1]

In the early 19th century, the frontiers of White settlement had gradually extended north of the Cape as nomadic farmers (*trekboers*) crossed the Orange River in search of grazing land for their cattle. The Great Trek, from 1836 to 1854, however marked the organized migration of thousands of people away from British rule in search of new terrain where they could be free and independent. These Dutch-speaking pioneers were called Voortrekkers and later became known as Boers or Afrikaners.

It was estimated that some 14 000 had left the Cape by 1845. With all their worldly possessions packed onto ox-wagons, fully armed and driving their herds of livestock, entire families ventured into the interior. They were accompanied by their Coloured servants — cattle herders, workers and domestics — who numbered as many as the Voortrekkers themselves.[2] Historians have listed many and varied reasons for this exodus including resentment towards the granting of equal civil rights to the Coloured people in the Cape, the emancipation of slaves, the anglicization of public institutions such as schools and courts and the trekkers' need for land.[3]

Despite numerous hostile encounters with Black tribes, land disputes and disunity within their own ranks, the Voortrekkers established a short-lived Boer republic in Natal, as well as separate states in the areas north of the Orange and Vaal Rivers. All these territories were either annexed or put under British sovereignty at some stage between 1840 and 1885, but the Orange Free State and the South African Republic (Transvaal) did win recognition from Britain of their independence. The constitutions of both these independent republics reflected their concern for group survival and entrenched a racial basis for the suffrage.

African chiefdoms struggled to retain their own states in the face of White expansion but the new republics managed to incorporate fair numbers of Blacks as labourers. In the Transvaal, Afrikaners in three areas around Potchefstroom, Soutpansberg and Lydenburg united to form the South African Republic (known as the Zuid Afrikaansche Republiek or ZAR) in 1861. A significant and much quoted article of the ZAR's constitution was its clear statement of its attitude towards people of colour: 'The people are not prepared to allow any equality of the non-white with the white inhabitants, either in Church or State'.[4]

Until the discovery of the mineral wealth which transformed the economy of southern Africa, the White population of the Afrikaner republics remained small and thinly spread, numbering no more than 45 000 in 1870 — when the Cape Colony had nearly 200 000 White inhabitants.[5] Rumours, rumblings and then actual gold strikes in the eastern Transvaal in the 1870s attracted foreigners in ever-increasing numbers into the territory. In 1877 Britain temporarily annexed the ZAR, but eventually granted the Boers limited self-rule in a republic, subject in some respects to British intervention.

From 1886 however an 80 km ridge in the southern Transvaal, known as the Witwatersrand (ridge of white waters) drew world attention. It was here that prospectors uncovered the main gold reef which would become the 'richest treasure chest ever opened by man'.[6] For the Boers who had established strong, self-sufficient farming communities, the gold finds meant the end of their rural tranquillity 'and they were catapulted into the maelstrom of the international power struggle of that time'.[7] They retained control of the ZAR until the end of the 19th century and the eruption of the devastating Anglo-Boer War. This tumultuous conflict between a world power and some 50 000 Boers lasted for more than two years — from 1899 until 1902 — culminating in the demise of the Afrikaner republics and the re-establishment of British rule throughout South Africa.

This chapter will outline the conditions Chinese encountered in the Boer republics, their exclusion from the Orange Free State and the numerous legal restrictions imposed on them in the ZAR. The formation of Chinese social organizations is examined and the outline is developed up to 1905, shortly after Britain and the mine owners of the Transvaal embarked on the mass importation of Chinese labourers to work the Witwatersrand goldfields.

OFS EXCLUDES CHINESE

No Chinese settled anywhere in the Orange Free State until late in the 20th century. From 1854, this independent republic forbade Asiatics from owning property. It was a territory in which Dutch was the sole official language, citizenship was extended to Whites resident there for six months and the franchise was open only to male citizens registered for military service.[8] It appears after English-speaking traders objected to the admission of Asiatics in the 1880s, the Volksraad (the People's Council and law-making body) passed a measure which prohibited any Asiatic from living in the Orange Free State.[9] This 1891 law, which remained on the statute books for nearly 100 years, stated:

> No Arab, 'Chinaman', Coolie, or other Asiatic Coloured person (excluding the inhabitants of the Cape Colony known under the name of Malays) may settle in this State for the purpose of carrying on a commercial business or farming or otherwise remain there for longer than two months without first having obtained special permission from the State President. A period of twelve months ending 11th September, 1891, allowed to each such person as is already in the State to quit, after that to be deported without compensation.[10]

This law prohibited Asiatics from living in the Orange Free State, while any who wished to travel through it to other parts of the country were only permitted to be within its borders for 72 hours.[11] Only in 1986 was the legislation amended to allow Chinese officially to reside in the province.

IN SEARCH OF GOLD

Some Chinese ventured into the ZAR as early as 1876. In a deep valley on the eastern escarpment of the Transvaal, the boom town of Pilgrim's Rest had become the legendary El Dorado for diggers, drawn to its rich hoard of alluvial gold. It boasted a community of colourful characters from the Californian and Australian gold fields, a newspaper, stores, bars and a church hosting services in a tent.[12]

By July 1876, seven Chinese were among the many prospectors who converged on Pilgrim's Rest. Their appearance caused some concern to the local Gold Commissioner who promptly consulted his superiors in Pretoria about the action to be taken.

> It appears that these people have come with the view to investigate the inducements held out by this Country as a field for immigration from China and should the report sent home by these strangers be favourable it is not improbable that a rather extensive immigration may set in as has been the case in Australia and California.

> I have been informed that it is the intention of the Chinese now arrived to apply for licences to follow the occupation of gold diggers, but I am in doubt as to whether they would be considered 'white' within the meaning of the Gold Law.

The reply he received from the the State Secretary was short and to the point:

> Until further instructions, do not allow them under any circumstances to take out licences for any purpose. They can't be considered 'White Men'.[13]

New gold strikes continued to attract diggers to the eastern Transvaal, particularly in the De Kaap vicinity of Barberton. Chinese too joined the swelling ranks of hopefuls. In September 1886 three Chinese, described as 'sons of the Celestial Empire' travelled through Pretoria en route for Barberton. Remarking on their presence, one newspaper said:

> Whether they entertain the idea of digging or of carrying on trade at the Fields has not transpired. The law prohibits their holding or working claims on the Goldfields, but Ah Chin and Li Chung will doubtless find means to obtain a living notwithstanding legal disabilities and local prejudices.[14]

Chinese Tobacco Farmer

The small eastern Transvaal town of Barberton, lying in the De Kaap Valley, was the site of the first rich gold finds in the South African Republic. Prospectors flocked to the area before the Witwatersrand's even wealthier cache was unearthed in 1886. By the turn of the century, one enterprising Chinese farmer had established himself as a tobacco grower — and this newspaper report printed in the *Graaff Reinet Advertiser* on 27 March 1903 throws some light on how he made his living.

An Industrious Chinaman

On the banks of the Queen's River in De Kaap Valley, a little over five miles from Barberton Camp, is a 'John Chinaman', with the good old English name of Wilson. He is a fine specimen of his race, industrious, plodding, sober, saving, but remarkably shrewd. Being an old hand on various American tobacco plantations, he has located himself as a tenant farmer in this valley, having an eye and something more to the main chance, he is making good use of his travels and past experiences, the latter gained in more distant and prosperous countries.

On his lands can be seen from nine to ten acres of tobacco plants as roughly and carelessly grown as nature permits, minus any attempt at class cultivation. In his sphere of usefulness as a tenant farmer looking after his own concerns he has found that it is more profitable for him to grow leaf tobacco for the native snuff trade and leave the fastidious pipe smoker to his less experienced but more ambitious neighbours.

Mr Wilson, of De Kaap Valley, does not care one jot for texture, flavour or combustion, he is now busy reaping his crop of tobacco, which is certainly not less than three quarters of a ton to the acre. He has disposed of the whole crop, when dry, to a Barberton Kaffir store dealer, for a price which would turn any Cuban or Virginian grower green with envy. If the Johannesburg capitalists had allowed Mr Chamberlain to go to Barberton, he could have been shown something to tax, without the aid of champagne glasses.

The arrival of more Chinese a few months later however prompted another newspaper to take a stand against this influx and to warn of the possible consequences:

> Of course (says the *Natal Advertiser*) it will be with the diggers of De Kaap to say whether or not they are to allow the Chinese to come in to undersell them in labour and goods and to reap the benefit of the hard work of the White man. A number of Chinese have arrived here from Mauritius and Australia, and they also are on their way to the De Kaap Gold-fields. We understand that they have with them a good deal of money, and that they expect to be able to invest it well at the Fields.[15]

Ironically enough, most Chinese who came to the southern part of Africa in the 1870s and 1880s were lured by the prospect of digging for gold, yet it was this very opportunity which was denied them. Although the gold laws of the time did not specifically prohibit Chinese from prospecting, it seems authorities administered these to ensure only Whites were permitted diggers' licences. Only much later did the Gold Law No. 15 of 1898 prevent any Coloured person from obtaining a licence to dig for precious metals.

In this respect the history of the Chinese in South Africa differs markedly from that of their settlement in other parts of the world. On both the Californian goldfields in America and the Victoria diggings in Australia in the 1850s, Chinese were part and parcel of the frenetic gold rushes. Taxes and other restrictions were introduced in later years, but Chinese miners toting picks and shovels were a relatively common sight around mining camps.[16]

It was, however, another gold strike which was to have far-reaching repercussions for the future of the Transvaal and South Africa. Early in 1886, the discovery of the edge of the Witwatersrand's main gold-bearing reef, with its promise of untold riches, triggered off the world's greatest gold rush. Within a few months, tranquil farmlands were transformed into a hubbub of activity. Thousands of fortune seekers descended with their makeshift tents and shanties, laying the foundations of the mining camp which would become the metropolis of Johannesburg.

Speculators, financiers, entrepreneurs and artisans arrived hot on the heels of the diggers. In wood and iron buildings around a central market square, traders opened up shops and the new settlement grew by leaps and bounds. Diggings stretched out for more than 60 km along the Main Reef and within two years the town of Johannesburg boasted 77 bars, 43 hotels and 12 billiard saloons.[17]

A few Chinese were undoubtedly among the many who flocked to the new city of gold. Establishing small businesses, they survived as shopkeepers, laundrymen, market gardeners and farmers. By 1890, just four years after the founding of Johannesburg, at least 121 Chinese were known to be resident in the town.[18] From this centre they spread to surrounding districts, several making their homes in Pretoria, Germiston, Springs, Heidelberg, Roodepoort, Krugersdorp, Potchefstroom and outlying rural areas of the Transvaal.

RESTRICTIVE LEGISLATION IN FORCE

Inequality between Whites and people of colour was entrenched in the Transvaal from the early days of the Boer republic. From 1855 no person of colour could become a citizen of the Transvaal republic, and only citizens were permitted to own land.[19] Even before the Witwatersrand gold finds attracted people of all races, the ZAR had already enacted Law 3 of 1885 to restrict Asiatic rights in the Transvaal. Prompted by fears of what was regarded as an invasion of Indian traders, the law was based on the general principle that 'no equality between the white and coloured races shall be tolerated.'[20]

The Chinese were equally affected by anti-Asiatic legislation, for Law 3 of 1885 stipulated that any of the native races of Asia, including the 'Coolies', Arabs, Malays and Mohammedan subjects of the Turkish Dominion were prohibited from acquiring citizenship rights in the ZAR. They were also precluded from owning any fixed property, were required to register with a district magistrate within eight days of arrival and pay a fee of £25. As British subjects, Indians claimed the protection of the London Convention which had accorded them the liberty to enter, travel, reside and trade freely in the Transvaal. Indian merchants of a superior class, at the time usually called 'Arabs', objected to being relegated to the same category as 'Coolies', Chinese etc.[21] After protracted correspondence between the ZAR and British governments, the law was amended in 1887 to allow Asiatics the right to buy fixed property in streets or locations set aside for them, and the registration fee was lowered to £3. Law 3 of 1885 was however not strictly enforced, perhaps because of the difficulties in fixing locations and the possibility of opposition from Britain.[22]

In response to repeated appeals by the White business sector for more stringent measures to limit Asiatic immigration and trade, the ZAR government did pass various resolutions affecting Asiatics in the closing years of the 19th century. These included:

Volksraad Resolutions

5 July 1888	–	To institute an enquiry into and prohibit the residence of Asiatics on business premises not in locations.
5 August 1892	–	To take stringent measures to prevent Coolies, Chinese or Asiatics from trading in towns.
	–	To move all Coolie shops opened after 1889. [Repealed in 1898]
8 September 1893	–	To apply Law 3 of 1885 strictly to confine Asiatics to trade and live in locations.
	–	To have every 'Chinaman' apply for a special pass on payment of £25, renewable annually.
	–	To arrest and fine or imprison any Chinese who did not produce the pass on demand to an official, and to banish any repeat offenders from the ZAR.
20 March 1894	–	To allow only licence holders or their heirs to reside on stands in Braamfontein. (This measure prevented Asiatics from using White nominees to lease premises for them.)
November 1898	–	To move all Asiatics to locations before 1 January 1899.
26 June 1899	–	State President's proclamation setting aside certain streets, areas and locations for occupation and trade by Coolies, Asiatics etc. in terms of Law 3 of 1885.

Early Chinese Graves in Johannesburg

Johannesburg's first cemetery was laid out in January 1887 in an area which is today virtually part of the city centre. It occupied 12 stands bounded by De Villiers, Bree, Harrison and Diagonal streets. Because the area was not enclosed in any way,

> wagons and cattle were frequently driven over the graves and it was soon inadequate owing to the high death rate in Johannesburg at that time. Later in the year those buried there were exhumed and reinterred in the new cemetery on the farm Braamfontein.[23]

It is not known whether any Chinese were buried in the first cemetery, but a separate section was set aside for them in the Braamfontein cemetery. Burial records for the Chinese in the first 10 years of this cemetery's existence have unfortunately been lost, although an ornate headstone still marks what is believed to be the grave of the first Chinese to be buried in the city. The stone carries no name, merely the inscription 'Dai Buk Gung' 大伯公 (Great Grand Uncle) and is dated 1889. It has been said that no one was actually buried there and the stone is merely symbolic of a 'caretaker' of the burial ground whom the Chinese should honour. At least two other tombstones in the cemetery are dated 1889. One has no name, and the other is the grave of Kow Joe Pon (潘球祖) of Sun Tak county who died on 7 January 1889.

From the time the cemetery was laid out, separate sections were set aside for different religious sects as well as race groups. The Chinese maintained important aspects of their cultural traditions and continued to practise age-old burial rites. Reference to this is made by a newspaper columnist at the turn of the century:

> ...the heathen Chinese ... still observe the time-honoured custom of 'feeding the dead', a very interesting ceremony to those who have never witnessed it.[24]

The earliest Chinese grave in the Braamfontein cemetery in Johannesburg, is referred to as that of 'Dai Buk Gung' and dated 1889.

The legislation as it singled out Chinese and some of the petitions opposing and defending them will be covered in more detail later. The legislative measures outlined however reflect the extent of prevailing opposition to the continued presence of Asiatics in the ZAR and the persistence of attempts to limit their rights.

While Asiatic locations were established in at least 45 towns and villages of the Transvaal,[25] many Asiatics lived and traded outside locations and even owned fixed property by using the name of a White trustee. Such indirect ownership of land by Asiatics was common and this evasion of the law was countenanced and even assisted by government officials.[26] Those who urged the restriction of Asiatics to locations based their argument on 'sanitary grounds'. They often cited the 'loathsome' living standards of Asiatics which demanded their isolation away from the White population.

For the Chinese, Law 3 of 1885 had however formed the basis of legislation which would restrict their progress and exclude them from citizenship rights for more than the next 100 years.

APPEALS TO RESTRICT ASIATICS

The drive to exclude Asiatics from all sectors of the ZAR economy gained momentum towards the end of the 19th century. Anti-Asiatic sentiments were expressed in many petitions to the government and Chinese found their continued residence and trade increasingly threatened. Johannesburg's business community was the most vocal in its protests against the Asiatic presence in the Transvaal. In 1888 a petition from the Johannesburg Chamber of Commerce and traders appealed to the authorities not to grant any trading licences to Asiatics and to restrict them to a location away from the town.[27]

A year later some 6000 people signed another petition urging more stringent measures to prevent Asiatic entry into the republic. While most appeals were directed against Asiatics generally, this one focused on the Chinese and cited the problems caused in America and Australia by Chinese opium and gambling dens. The petitioners asked for 'Chineezen, Coolies en Arabieren' to be banished from the ZAR and denied any property rights.[28]

They also stated thousands of Johannesburg inhabitants, mainly British subjects, supported the exclusion of Asiatics and gave the following 'reasons' for their objections:

> ...the great injustice and difficulties under which the business portion of the White population are suffering from the unrestricted admission into this State of Chinese, Coolies, and other Asiatics, and also the dangers to which the whole community is exposed by the spread of leprosy, syphilis, and the like loathsome diseases engendered by the filthy habits and immoral practices of those people.[29]

The Chinese soon reacted to the barrage of criticism, appealing directly to the government for a fair deal. In a petition from all 121 Chinese resident in Johannesburg in 1890, and signed in Chinese characters, the new settlers asked for exemption from the £3 registration fee required of Asiatics and permission to remain in Ferreirastown, the western edge of early Johannesburg.

Their appeal, written in Dutch, was drawn up by lawyers who said the Chinese came from a nation civilized long before the birth of Christ, and should not be treated as 'wild and uncivilized barbarians'. The Chinese were willing to pay taxes, but did not wish to be moved to the 'koelielocatie' (Asiatic location) outside town. In their appeal, they differentiated themselves from the racial definitions of 'kleurlingen' (Coloureds) and 'koelies'. The State President and Executive Council did not respond favourably to their request.[30]

The administration of the £3 Asiatic registration fee was lax in some towns, but officials in outlying areas applied the letter of the law. When several Chinese entered the Transvaal through neighbouring Mocambique in 1893, railway officials at the Komatipoort border were instructed to ensure they paid their £3 levy.[31] Reiterating the objections raised in the Cape and Natal colonies, Transvaal editorial writers also painted lurid pictures of an Asiatic invasion and called for more stringent action to be taken by the government.

> ... The Asiatic is a steady drain on the resources of the country, while the European is a never-failing source of revenue ... The sympathy of all South Africans would be with the Transvaal Government if the example followed by Australia were followed here. £100 entrance fee and £100 for licence would soon stop the Asiatic invasion which has already nearly ruined Natal, and in time promises to ruin the mercantile community of the Transvaal. The Chinese corner groceries in Johannesburg are already doing half the local trade.[32]

In the last decade of the 19th century appeals to restrict Asiatic immigration and trade were frequent and vocal. Yet, between 1887 and 1899, the 'various resolutions of the Volksraad were carried out only partially and in a halfhearted manner.'[33]

SPECIAL CHINESE PASS

Although both the Indians and Chinese were classified as Asiatics, it is necessary to remember that Indians could, and did, claim the protection of the British government whenever new anti-Asiatic measures were proposed. Faced with persistent public demands to enforce existing laws and introduce even more stringent measures, Transvaal legislators were restrained to some extent by fears of British opposition. The majority of Chinese could not claim British citizenship so they provided a ready target for increasing anti-Asiatic agitation. Perhaps because legislators needed to reassure their constituents that they were seriously addressing the Asiatic problem, the Chinese were singled out for special discriminatory action.

On 8 September 1893, the governing Volksraad passed a resolution requiring each Chinese to pay £25 for a special pass to be in the ZAR. The pass had to be renewed every year and produced on demand from any government official. Penalties for not having the pass included a fine of up to £25, or up to one month in jail with or without hard labour, and deportation for repeated infringement of the law. The measure was to take effect from 1 January 1894.[34]

Considering that petitions before the Volksraad requested the payment of £150 to enter the Transvaal as well as a £100 annual tax, the levying of a 'mere' £25 could be regarded by some as light! Proposing the law, a government member Mr Jeppe said of Chinese and 'Coolies':

> They were nothing but pests. They were over-running Johannesburg, and underselling tradesmen. They lived on next to nothing, and could undersell respectable tradesmen which they were doing.[35]

Two Johannesburg Chinese, Lai Singfor and James Ahnow, promptly objected to the special pass requirement — using the same grounds which had afforded protection to British Indians. Stating they were British subjects, having been born in Hong Kong, they argued that the imposition of a special tax on the Chinese constituted a breach of the London Convention. The British High Commissioner in Cape Town took up their case and protracted correspondence with the ZAR government followed. It was eventually decided that only Chinese who were British subjects would be exempted from carrying the special pass.[36]

This Chinese claim to British intercession did not pass unnoticed. In a biting criticism, a local newspaper writer remarked:

> For some reason, with which I am not acquainted, Government are ... refusing to take the £25 head-money required of every John Chinaman who comes to dwell amongst us ... They do say that that fussy and foolish personage, the British Resident ... has lodged an objection to the differential treatment of Yellow Johnny on the ground that he is a British subject, and must have the same privileges as the rest of us on the Rand. It seems that all Chinamen come from Hong Kong ... I suppose even a Chinaman can lie sometimes; but the British Resident places an implicit reliance upon his word.[37]

Instructions on the administration of the special Chinese pass were issued in interdepartmental government circulars, but the requirement was not uniformly enforced. When officials at Volksrust, on the Transvaal border with Natal, imposed fines on Chinese who could not produce their special pass, it was, surprisingly enough, the shipping agents, King and Sons who objected.

Chinese refused to book passages to China through King and Sons because they were required to board ship at Port Natal and claimed they were fined between £10 and £25 at the Natal border. They preferred to board at a Cape port since the pass was not required nor was a fine imposed at Vereeniging on the Transvaal border. Fearing a substantial loss of business, a representative for the agents appealed to the State Secretary to clarify the matter.[38]

The issue was also taken up in Natal when the shipping agents appealed to the Colonial Secretary there to intervene since their steamers only called at Port Natal and not at Port Elizabeth in the Cape. After much correspondence between the Natal and Transvaal governments, it was pointed out that no general £25 fine was imposed on Chinese leaving the ZAR. Only those Chinese who had resided in the republic for a few years and who had not paid any registration fee were fined £10.[39] Nonetheless authorities tried, whenever possible, to enforce the special pass requirement and in 1898, six Chinese in Pretoria were fined £10 each for not being able to produce their passes.[40]

MOVE TO LOCATIONS

Much as the many opponents of Asiatics would have preferred a total prohibition on their entry into and residence in the ZAR, moving them to locations was the next best alternative. There they would be isolated from the generally 'White' business areas and would live and trade among themselves. Several attempts were made to carry out this resolve in Johannesburg, but the final removal date was postponed time and again.

A location was set aside to the west of Johannesburg in April 1889 and the sale of stands started in 1893. Stand holders were required to pay a licence fee of 10 shillings a month for small stands and 15 shillings for large stands, with the proviso that no one could own more than two stands nor could a White person buy stands.[41]

By 1894, the Mining Commissioner published a notice calling for applications for stands in 'the new Location for Kafirs and Coloured People ... [where] all Kafirs, Malays, Hindoos, Chinese, and other coloureds' had to move before 1 August 1894. The monthly licence fee was reduced to 7/6 per stand. Such an obviously unprofitable re-location away from their established businesses and regular customers was not appealing. Asiatics submitted numerous petitions against their removal, often supported by their many customers. Several Chinese appealed to the British High Commissioner in the Cape to intervene and the question was put to arbitration.[42]

The Johannesburg Chamber of Commerce was a persistent advocate for the removal of Asiatic traders. In 1893 it expressed strong objections to Chinese and Indians obtaining trading licences through the use of White nominees. The Chamber said the nominees were paid a monthly salary by the Asiatics, and they had found two nominees who had about 20 businesses registered in their names.[43]

They appealed for the practice to be stopped and submitted a list of 53 businesses, mostly Chinese, which were registered in the names of Whites. The businesses were concentrated in the city centre, Ferreirastown, Fordsburg and Braamfontein and were hired out at a monthly rental of between £2 and £15 to Chinese and Indians. To close up this loophole, the government enacted a measure requiring trade licence holders or their heirs to reside on their own property. In terms of this, a Chinese shopkeeper was evicted from Vrededorp to the west of Johannesburg because the area was 'a location for poor white people.'[44]

At least 65 Chinese shopkeepers were trading in Johannesburg in 1893, [45] and when a deputation of Chinese visited the State Secretary, they asked for an extension on their trading licences. By the end of 1895 the local Mining Commissioner stated the Chinese trading in Johannesburg's city centre were still refusing to move to the location.[46] Wholesalers and retailers in Johannesburg who earnestly desired the removal of Chinese reiterated the tried and trusted 'reasons' cited in the Natal and Cape colonies. One lengthy petition, signed by nearly 300 individuals, many representing companies, said the Chinese posed a threat to White businesses because

> they gave short weight goods, they would flock in from America and Australia to take over the most valuable properties, they were a menace to health and morals, they spent no money on schools and hospitals and did not contribute to charity.

They further added that North America enjoyed good wages and cheap food because

Chinese were not allowed to settle there whereas in Australia, where Chinese were permitted, wages were so low that White workmen had to emigrate.[47]

The continual postponement of the date for the removal of all Asiatics from the town was particularly trying for those wholesalers who wanted their cake and wanted to eat it. Writing to a local newspaper, one firm pointed out that they had spent five years advertising a particular brand of goods stocked by every Chinese shopkeeper. Since being told the Chinese would be moved to the locations and would no longer be trading, they had stopped orders from England, and consequently carried no more stocks of the goods in question. Should the Chinese, however, remain in town, and still require stocks, the wholesaler would lose the proceeds of all his advertising investment![48]

IN DEFENCE OF THE CHINESE

Although White businesses had a vested interest in the removal of Asiatic traders, not all sectors of the population supported them. The Chinese spoke up on their own behalf and their appeals were backed by many of their customers. In 1897, with the threat of removal to a location still imminent, nearly 420 Johannesburg Chinese asked the government to leave them in their existing businesses. They said some of them had been settled since 1886, they had always submitted to the laws of the ZAR and were eager to be regarded as loyal residents.

> Your petitioners came to this state solely with the purpose to carry on business on a small scale and because they only enjoy small profits, they hope that the poor inhabitants will benefit from this. That is why they ask that ... they would be awarded the same free right of trade and residence in this state that is given to all foreigners of all nationalities in China.[49]

A year later, in April 1898, 172 Chinese again petitioned the government to ease restrictions on them. In a plaintive appeal directed to State President S.J.P. Kruger and the Executive Committee of the ZAR, they asked only for the right to trade in the republic in their own names. They said it was well-known that the Chinese were 'an order-loving nation, always ready to obey the laws of the land that they reside in and also faithfully paying all taxes and never getting involved in politics ... [and] they therefore feel deeply the restrictions placed on them with regard to trade.'

In this document the names of several of the Chinese who played an important role in community affairs were featured. They included Lai Mun James, Lai Singfor and Leung Quinn (黎文占,黎勝和,梁佐鋆).[50] Several petitions to the government in 1897 and 1898 reflected the wish of ordinary citizens for the Chinese to be allowed to trade in White areas and to have licences in their own names. Many residents, particularly those living in the poorer quarters, said they were regular customers of the Chinese because of their reasonable prices.

On behalf of 1084 'arme inwoners' (poor residents) of Johannesburg, an appeal was made not to send the Chinese to locations since their customers had only limited means of subsistence and would be driven to poverty. They added that Whites were permitted to trade in China and asked for the same rights to be accorded Chinese in the ZAR.

Government officials transmitted a copy of this appeal to the local Mining

Commissioner J. L. van der Merwe, and asked for his comments. He said he could not support the petition since it was against the constitution to allow equality between Whites and Coloureds, it was also against the wishes of 'our people' and not in the interests of the White population. He also raised the following points:

> The Chinese live here as parasites ... they contribute *nothing* to the financial and moral development, growth and welfare of society. They do work hard, but spend practically nothing. They never learn the language of the country [landstaal — i.e. Dutch] while the poor Russians, Poles and German traders do all this. Why should a special case be made for the protection of Coloureds against the interests of a large class of White people?[51]

In the following year, White residents of the working class Johannesburg suburbs of Braamfontein, Vrededorp and Fordsburg submitted more petitions asking for Chinese traders not to be moved to locations. They said the Chinese sold goods more cheaply and in smaller quantities and were prepared to offer credit whereas White businesses would not. Since times were hard, the poor obtained better value from the Chinese.[52]

Petitions such as these offer a revealing glimpse of the day-to-day needs and concerns of ordinary residents in early Johannesburg.

> We sometimes have no more than one shilling; at the Chinese we can buy for example 3d bread, 3d cheese, 3d sugar and 3d coffee and this is for us poor people a great help. Then we can also buy all sorts of vegetables, wood, and in one word, everything that we need we can get from the Chinese. And when we have no money we are also assisted with credit by the Chinese. And for us who work away from home, if the Chinese were not there, it would have made it very difficult for our families to be provided for during the week.
>
> The markets in Johannesburg and Fordsburg would regret it if the Chinese were not there to buy wood, potatoes and other products on a large scale and then resell it to us at a tickey a time. If the Chinese were no longer here, we the poor would have to have at least 6d to buy at other shops ... By allowing the Chinese to live amongst us, we the poor will consider it a great concession by the government.[53]

The State Secretary replied that their request could not be granted since the government could not go against the law.

GENERAL DISCRIMINATORY MEASURES

From the earliest days, the Chinese tried to create a niche for themselves as an independent group who sought fair and equal treatment and did not wish simply to be 'lumped together' with other groups. In their early petitions to the authorities, they pointed out they were Chinese, not 'Coloureds' or 'coolies'.[54]

When a storekeeper, Mankam, was assaulted by a police constable at the Johannesburg Market in September 1891, 34 Chinese objected to his treatment in a petition to the State President.[55] They said he had simply been buying vegetables when the policeman kicked him and beat his ribs with a baton. In the court case which followed, the magistrate remarked the case had more to do with the Chinese trying to gain equal rights with the Whites than with any assault. In terms of a new decree,

Whites and 'kleurlingen' (Coloureds) had to make their purchases in separate sections of the market. The magistrate dismissed the charges saying the constable had only used the force necessary to move Mankam out of the part of the market reserved for Whites.

Discrimination on the basis of race was part of everyday life. Apart from the prohibition on citizenship and restrictions on residential and trading rights which were imposed on Asiatics, these are some of the limitations they faced at the turn of the century:

— they were not permitted to walk on footpaths and pavements;
— they were not permitted to drive in public carriages;
— they were only permitted to travel in third class compartments of trains;
— they were not permitted to buy or possess liquor.

In October 1897, a Johannesburg bottle-store keeper was fined for selling liquor to a Chinese, while all Asiatics were prohibited from entering the Johannesburg vegetable market and hawking on the streets after a smallpox outbreak occurred.[56] In February 1899, when bubonic plague broke out in Johannesburg, authorities prohibited travel by Coloureds and Asiatics within the four colonies of South Africa without special certificates from the State Secretary. Five Chinese on a visit to Johannesburg needed permission to return to Port Elizabeth, while another two, W.C. Lee and Liton, requested certificates to travel to Delagoa Bay where they planned to board ship for China.[57]

FLEDGLING CHINATOWN

The oldest part of Johannesburg was first known as Ferreira's Camp and later Ferreira's Township or Ferreirasdorp — an area bounded by Commissioner, Alexander, Ferreira's and Frederick streets.[58] From a motley assortment of tents, wagons and iron shacks, diggers ventured forth in search of gold and traders of every description gathered to supply their needs. It was here, on the western edge of town, that the majority of Chinese lived and worked, where they gathered socially and eventually established their first Chinese community organizations. They, like the Chinese in Kimberley and Port Elizabeth, also called the area 'Malaikam'. Although Johannesburg had its own Malay Camp, it was situated a few kilometres further north-west of Ferreirastown. By the turn of the century, many documents and press clippings referred to the western part of Ferreirastown as the 'Cantonese quarter.'

The Johannesburg Street Directory for 1893 refers to more than seven 'Chinaman's stores' in the midst of a score of bars, small houses, general stores, butchers, wagon builders' and stables in Ferreirastown.[59] That the Chinese did more than merely work in 'Malaikam' is shown by the arrest of 19 on gambling charges. On a Sunday evening in December 1897 they gathered in a house in Fox Street to play fan tan. When the police raided, they charged the men with contravening the gambling laws by playing a game of chance. Giving evidence in court, a policeman said the Chinese were playing in three different rooms and police found about 14 shillings on the tables. Ah Mong, the proprietor of the house, was fined £20, 13 players were fined £5 each and five were discharged.[60]

Although Chinese stores were scattered throughout Johannesburg and parts of the reef, fair numbers of Chinese made their home in 'Malaikam'. By 1904 the Medical Officer of Health for Johannesburg reported that there were between 400 and 500 Chinese working in about 177 general stores and a dozen laundries in the more densely populated parts of Johannesburg.

> These Chinese stores, etc., are, as a rule, fairly clean and well-kept, and their occupants give very little trouble to the sanitary inspectors.

His comments, however, on the Chinese 'dens' were not as complimentary. Stating that there were a number of places, consisting of about 40 rooms with 90 to 100 occupants, in the vicinity of Fox and Main streets, Ferreirastown, he remarked:

> The whole of this place is in an unsatisfactory state, and in many respects resembles an Indian 'warren'. The closets are not well kept, the inhabitants are not cleanly, and the rooms in question are a place of resort for the Chinese of the Town for opium smoking and gambling.

Although there were insufficient public health reasons for interfering with either the Chinese storekeepers or laundrymen, he said the Chinese dens were 'insanitary, undesirable, and should be relegated to the Asiatic Location'.[61]

IN THE PUBLIC EYE

Newspaper reports on the Chinese, although few and far between, inevitably reflected their occasional brushes with the law. Several incidents of Chinese being charged with gambling were featured, and being largely shopkeepers, the Chinese were also attractive targets for thieves. When three White men broke into a shop on the corner of Betty and Fawcus streets, Jeppestown, they shot the Chinese storekeeper, described in the report as 'a Celestial' and stole more than £10 as well as 'some of the delicacies of the store.'[62] In a rather brutal incident, a Chinese storekeeper named Ah Young, of Hanau Street, Jeppestown, was hacked to death by his Zulu servant.[63]

Occasionally some reports also offered insight into the occupations of early settlers, somewhat tinged by the writer's prejudices. A correspondent writing under the nom-de-plume 'The Vagrant' described his visits to Italian and Portuguese market gardens around Johannesburg, and concluded with this remark on Chinese:

> A number of Chinese have a garden on the way from Johannesburg to Fordsburg, every inch of which is under cultivation, but they are abominably dirty in their habits, and nothing in their opinion is too unclean for use on the young plants. There is no pleasure in a visit to their gardens ... But the Chinese are too cunning. They object to the hard work requisite to make a garden, preferring rather to wait until they see a chance of getting one already made, by a sharp deal and so in the meantime they attend to grocery stores and play fan tan. It's much lighter work and pays much better too. [64]

In another item, a newspaper letter writer reflected prevailing prejudices on the morality of Asiatics:

> As I was passing a certain Chinaman's shop last Saturday a number of little girls, varying in age from seven to four, came out with sweets in their hands, and I heard

Charge of Theft

**How Chinamen Swear –
an Interesting Sidelight**

Before the magistrate in 'B' Court today, Jon Tong, a Chinaman was brought up on a charge of stealing £31 13s. from a shopkeeper of the same nationality, carrying on business in Main Road, Fordsburg, and stabbing him with a knife. A preliminary examination was held.

Mr Walton, for the defence, asked that the witnesses might be sworn after the manner of their own country, namely, by cutting off a fowl's head, catching the blood in a saucer, breaking the latter, and blowing out a candle.

Mr Schuurman said the prosecution could hardly be expected to go to the expense of providing fowls for the purpose of administering the oath to all the witnesses in accordance with this alleged custom.

Mr Walton maintained that it was as necessary for Chinamen to be sworn in their own way as for Jews to swear with their hats on. The penalty, he added, when one of the former broke his oath, was that he was for ever excluded from returning to China.

In reply to the magistrate, Mr Walton said that a Chinaman who went home after swearing falsely would be arrested and instantly put to death by his own people. Mr Baines decided that the oath should be administered under the law of the country, and noted Mr Walton's application for the information of the Attorney-General.

The hearing of the evidence was then proceeded with, and subsequently the prisoner was committed for trial.[65]

> one little one remark to the others, 'Wasn't that Chinaman a nice man?' Now, Chinamen don't entice little girls into their shops and give them sweets without a purpose, and I warned the parents of the girls about these Chinamen; and I would like you to publish this letter as a warning to parents of the danger their little girls run of being enticed into shops by Asiatics.[66]

From time to time public attention was also focused on the agitation by White shopkeepers to enforce more strictly existing laws against Chinese trading in the towns of the Transvaal. They repeated claims of unfair competition against Indian and Chinese traders in Johannesburg, Krugersdorp, Potchefstroom, Klerksdorp, Makwassie Spruit, Eister Spruit and other districts.[67]

GROWTH OF SOCIAL ORGANIZATIONS

From the early days of Chinese settlement in the Transvaal, restrictive legislation contributed in large measure to bolstering awareness of the need for Chinese to work together as a group. Such united action was already evident in 1890 when all 121 Chinese in Johannesburg jointly petitioned the government to exempt them from a number of restrictions imposed by the Asiatic laws.[68]

At least two attempts were made in the 1890s to obtain land in Johannesburg for the erection of a Chinese temple. In November 1892, Lai Singfor, who played a prominent role in community affairs, appealed for a suitable site. Stating that he was the head and representative of the Chinese community, he submitted this appeal, written in Dutch:

> The Chinese in Johannesburg do not possess a proper place for the exercise of their extremely religious obligations ... the members of this Chinese community are loyal and obedient subjects of this State, but are not in a position to purchase a stand for the erection of a Chinese temple ... the community intends to request the honourable Government to donate to them a stand on which they can erect a proper temple for the execution of their religious practices.[69]

Lai Sing For (黎勝和)

Possibly the first community leader in Johannesburg was an enterprising young trader named Lai Sing For. At the age of 27 he had already established a business in Johannesburg, and made an attempt to secure land from the government for the erection of a Chinese temple.

For the remaining few years of his life he was active in community affairs, signing various petitions to ease restrictions on the Chinese. By the time the Anglo-Boer War broke out, he had a controlling interest in five shops around Johannesburg — all of which were managed by his nephew, Lai King.

According to a compensation claim he submitted for losses suffered during the war, he had been born in Mauritius, arrived in South Africa as a young boy and had lived for more than 20 years in the Cape and the Transvaal. He was naturalized as a British subject in Mauritius in 1898.

Lai Sing For died in June 1903, at the age of 38 years and is buried in the Braamfontein cemetery. His nephew, Lai King, continued to look after the businesses he had founded and the wholesale trading firm of Lai Sing For remained for many years one of the major Chinese firms in Johannesburg.[70]

The authorities refused his request advising the Chinese to purchase a stand in their own location for such a temple. Nothing seems to have materialized from this suggestion, and five years later some French-speaking Chinese, probably from Mauritius, again raised the subject. Appealing to the government on behalf of the Chinese residents in Johannesburg, the petitioners, Johnson Senquiy (or Sinquyi) and James Ah Non said:

> We are loyal artisans, having only for protection here the generosity of the Government of the country, the laws of which we have always obeyed. We are aware of the great qualities of the heart of the president, as well as his profound respect for all religion or belief, whatever it may be.
>
> ... we come to solicit the government to permit us to build on a terrain out of the town, a church, so that we may celebrate our religious ceremonies as all other believers do. We request the government either to lease us some land, within the conditions required by the law, or to allow us to buy this terrain.[71]

The authorities appeared to have no objection to Chinese buying land provided it was in the vicinity of the location. Whether or not the Chinese followed up on this matter is not known, but elderly community members have no recollection of the acquisition or building of any Chinese temple or church in Johannesburg.

The Case of the 'Troublesome Fellow'

A rather mysterious document in the Transvaal Archives poses more questions than it answers about the situation and concerns of the Chinese living in Johannesburg in 1898. It is a petition written in Dutch to the State President and signed by more than 100 Chinese.

We the undersigned Chinese living in Johannesburg, ZAR, have the honour to submit to you with humility the following so that if possible steps can be taken to help us. The reason for this memorial is the following:

1) There is living in Johannesburg for the last five or six years a certain Chinaman named Ah Mee who is a great burden because he constantly seeks to make the majority of the Chinese here dissatisfied with the regulations that the government has imposed on us.
2) That the aforementioned Ah Mee goes around and tries to influence all Chinese here to break the law by telling us that we do not need to keep a 'shop book', accounts of the shop etc, while we are convinced that we are according to law obliged to do so, and can be prosecuted for this omission.
3) The aforementioned Ah Mee keeps himself busy by advising many Chinese not to pay the £3 a year registration fee through which the government will suffer a great loss.
4) That the aforementioned Ah Mee keeps one or two rooms to serve as a house where gambling takes place at which he waits to entice his countrymen and there incites the spirit of dissatisfaction amongst them.
5) That Ah Mee is already known in China as a person of bad behaviour and service, as a result of which he was exiled from China.
6) That it is the earnest desire of your memorialists to obey all orders and laws of the state and to conduct themselves as respectable and orderly citizens but with such a bad character as Ah Mee in their midst it is nearly impossible to do so. Therefore it is the earnest request of your memorialists that steps be taken so that Ah Mee will be obliged to remove himself from our midst so that we can carry on our business in peace and quiet and in a lawful manner.
7) That Ah Mee has already been prosecuted for the running of the gambling house.
8) That it causes us great suffering to give this information against one of our own countrymen, but we regard it as our duty to make such facts known to the government so that an example can be made of such an agitator and can have a good result for all Chinese living here. Considering that we are only doing our duty. [72]

The petition was accompanied by 10 sworn affidavits stating that Ah Mee had been expelled from China for bad behaviour. Reviewing the petition, the public prosecutor remarked: 'He seems to be a somewhat troublesome fellow.' Before officials could take any action, it was found that Ah Mee had been fined £50 or 4 months' hard labour for an unspecified offence and had left the Transvaal.

Why did more than 100 Chinese go to such lengths to have Ah Mee removed? Was Ah Mee trying to organize some form of resistance to the restrictions Chinese faced?

Considering that the Chinese had always been careful not to attract undue attention to themselves, this petition indicated they were motivated by stronger fears. Perhaps they feared that one 'agitator' in their midst would provoke action against all Chinese, and so chose to take pre-emptive steps to prove their loyalty. Whatever the truth, there certainly seems more to this case than meets the eye.

CANTONESE CLUB

Johannesburg's first known Chinese 'community' organization was the 'Kwong Hok Tong', also called the Cantonese Club, which was formed on 1 June, 1898. While its English name implied it was exclusively for Cantonese-speakers, the club catered for all Chinese from the Kwangtung province (often also referred to as the Canton province) and included the Moiyeanese, who were and remained a minority among the Chinese in the Transvaal.

Within the first two years of its existence the 'Kwong Hok Tong' boasted a membership of nearly 150 men who gathered at the club's headquarters in Commissioner Street, Ferreirastown. Essentially a social club, its objectives were to keep members informed, to provide books and periodicals and to maintain a club house for meetings.

Such an organization also offered Chinese the support of a recognized body when dealing with officials. In August 1899, when two Chinese, L.M. Bodas and Lai Kam, wished to travel to Durban to board ship for China, the Kwong Hok Tong supplied them with a letter explaining the purpose of their journey. Since authorities had banned travel by Asiatics from one province to another (because of bubonic plague), the letter stated the required permission had been granted. It was marked with the club's rubber stamp and carried this description of the Kwong Hok Tong — 'Office of the Chinamen's Association, Johannesburg.' When asked for more particulars of the club, the chairman in 1903, Lai Mun James, wrote:

> The motives and purpose for which this above club has been instituted are varied. Firstly: For the education and information of our Cantonese people as also to bring about harmony and brotherhood amongst them which must tend to their welfare, and success of the country. Secondly: We are always in receipt of periodicals and other useful books, to which those people belonging to the Club can always have access to, and lastly, as there are very often meetings to be convened, and there is no other adaptable place more adapted for these people than the Club house ... Our people are very much given to Civilization, and want to see its cause promoted, and our ideas are similar to those of the Europeans, and we submit ourselves to the same laws and regulations as the Europeans do.

Investigating the facilities offered by the club, officials reported that the Commissioner Street clubhouse had two or three reception rooms, six bedrooms, a kitchen and latrine. Residents at the club paid £2 rent per month and rent on the

Lai Mun James (黎文占)

Although authorities were intent on restricting all Asiatics to locations, special exemptions were occasionally granted to individuals whose 'mode of living is in no way repugnant to European ideas'.[73] One such exception was the artist, photographer and co-owner of a mineral water factory, Lai Mun James.

To obtain his exemption, he had to provide detailed information on his life, his standard of living and his activities — all of which have left us with a comprehensive account of one of Johannesburg's early settlers. Born in Canton in 1875, he went to school there and continued his education in Calcutta. He studied drawing, oil painting and photography and worked in Calcutta for a year. He arrived in Johannesburg in May 1893 and worked as an artist and photographer until 1900 when he joined the firm of Alf Kan & Co., mineral water manufacturers, in Betty Street, Jeppestown.

He resided at the Cantonese Club in Ferreirastown and was the chairman of the club in 1903. In recommending his application, the Supervisor of Asiatics described Lai Mun James as a particularly well-educated man, of quiet disposition, good manners 'and to my mind a suitable person to obtain an exemption certificate.'

building amounted to £35 per month. It is interesting to note the remark an official made to the Colonial Secretary's office after seeing the club:

> I don't think we should do anything to encourage Chinese clubs. At starting they may be alright, but they are certain sooner or later to deteriorate into gambling houses.[74]

Renowned Indian leader, Mohandas Karamchand Gandhi, who would later as Mahatma Gandhi guide India to independence from Britain, was practising law in Johannesburg in the early 1900s and during that time had a number of dealings with the Chinese. He wrote of the Cantonese Club in 1905:

> Since the Chinese have no facilities for lodging, they have started a Cantonese Club which serves as a meeting place, a lodge and also as a library. They have acquired for the Club land on a long lease and have built on it a pucca one-storeyed building. There they all live in great cleanliness and do not stint themselves in the matter of living space; and seen within and from outside, it would look like some good European Club. They have in it separate rooms marked drawing, dining, meeting, committee room and the Secretary's room and the library, and do not use any room except for the purpose for which it is intended. Other rooms adjoining these are let out as bedrooms. It is such a fine and clean place that any Chinese gentleman visiting the town can be put up there. The entrance fee is £5, and the annual subscription varies according to the members' profession. The Club has about 150 members who meet every Sunday and amuse themselves with games. The members can avail themselves of Club facilities on week-days also.[75]

This description probably applied to the Cantonese Club headquarters which were permanently established on the corner of Fox and Alexander streets, Ferreirastown, and which remained the organization's property until the 1980s. By 1905 the Cantonese Club was a well-established organization with sufficient members to make it a key player in the protracted 'passive resistance campaign' which involved both the Indians and Chinese in the Transvaal between 1906 and 1911. These events are outlined in a later chapter.

The Cantonese Club building on the corner of Alexander and Fox streets boasted excellent facilities, including a billiards room and a sitting room.

THE SITTING-ROOM.

BILLIARD-ROOM.

CHEE KUNG TONG (致公堂)

Another organization which functioned as a loosely-knit 'club' prior to 1900 was the Chee Kung Tong, also called the Chinese Freemasons or Reform Club. Although little documentary evidence has been found to support its formal existence here prior to 1918, its very nature as a secret society would have limited knowledge of its activities to a select few.

Tracing its origins to underground triads formed after the Manchus seized power in China in the 17th century, the Chee Kung Tong aimed to oust the Ch'ing dynasty and restore China's former rulers, the Mings. When Chinese spread throughout the world, Chee Kung Tong branches were established in South East Asia, America, Canada and Australia.

From the 1890s, deteriorating political conditions in China led to the growth of radical idealism. Prominent among those intent on ridding China of its corrupt rulers was Dr Sun Yat Sen, the revolutionary who would later head the first Chinese republic, and who won substantial support from overseas Chinese for his campaign.

Although South Africa's Chinese were far from the shores of their homeland, their allegiance to China remained strong. It was most likely this support which encouraged one of Dr Sun's close collaborators, Yang Chu Yun, also known as Yeung Ku Wan, to visit this country. Fleeing Hong Kong after an abortive plot to capture Canton in 1895,

Members of the South African Branch of the Society to Restore China's prosperity, photographed in Johannesburg in 1897.

Yang travelled through South East Asia to spread the revolutionary ideals of a new China and then moved further southwards. Reaching Johannesburg at the end of 1896, Yang soon founded a branch of the Revive China Society (Hsing-chung hui — 興中會). How large or keen a following this new organization attracted locally is not known, but the regulations of the head office in China stipulated a minimum branch membership of 15. Furthermore branch offices were not to be used for gambling or social purposes, only to promote programmes to strengthen China.[76]

No community elders recall either the existence or the work of this secret revolutionary cell, but scattered references to the clandestine activities of the Chee Kung Tong which shared the aims of the Revive China Society imply, in Johannesburg at any rate, that they were one and the same organization. Whether it was through such societies or individually, the early Chinese would certainly have offered whatever material support they could muster for Dr Sun's cause.

ANGLO-BOER WAR

Britain's imperial designs on Africa as well as control of the immense wealth of the Witwatersrand were among the many factors leading to the outbreak of the Anglo-Boer War in October 1899. This culmination of long-simmering tensions between Boer and Briton turned into a protracted series of battles, lasting two years and eight months, eventually re-introducing British rule to the Transvaal and the Orange Free State.

As war became imminent, Chinese were torn between staying where they were and continuing to trade in a country under siege, or fleeing elsewhere. Those who could afford it either returned to China or made their way to Kimberley, Port Elizabeth and other parts of the Cape. Some simply boarded up their shops in the hopes their premises would remain unscathed while others continued trading in spite of the looming war.

Perhaps these circumstances were tailor-made for a bright opportunist. Just days before war broke out, a certain W.J. Pelser addressed an appeal to the government asking to be appointed as Agent or Commissioner for Chinese in Johannesburg. He claimed he had been approached by influential Chinese to represent them, adding that although it was not the time to appoint new officials, this was an important issue since it concerned a nation.

Indications that Pelser may have seen an opportunity to win a government appointment lay in the reasons he advanced for the necessity of an Agent. He stated the Chinese paid no tax and suggested they could contribute more to the treasury in this way. The government decided to postpone any decision on the matter.[77]

Throughout the first few months of the war, Johannesburg remained 'strangely peaceful' — Boer commandos strolled casually through the streets, residents had to observe a curfew and most gold mines closed down.[78] For ordinary people, there was still the business of living. In April 1900, the White women of Vrededorp, Burgersdorp and Fordsburg petitioned the government not to close the remaining Chinese stores in their area. Asking for the Chinese to be granted licences to continue trading during the war, they stated that their husbands were away on commando duty, they had no earnings and they were dependent on the Chinese shopkeepers for subsistence.[79]

Armed parties of Boer fighters waged war against British soldiers for more than two years from 1899 to 1901, eventually losing the second Anglo-Boer War and conceding control of the independent Boer Republics to the British.

Lawyers submitting this petition pointed out that the veldkornet (commandant) for Johannesburg supported the women's plea. But the war itself intervened and by early June 1900, British troops occupied both Johannesburg and the state capital, Pretoria. For some Chinese, this turn of events offered the fleeting hope that change was in the air, that perhaps they could, under British rule, look forward to a relaxation in the restrictions they faced. In many ways pragmatic, they prepared an illuminated address for the new High Commissioner, Sir Alfred Milner, accompanied by an assurance of their loyalty to the British government.

Here again the question of the appointment of a Chinese Representative reared its head. The presentation was submitted on behalf of the Chinese, on 17 May 1901 by a Johannesburg civil and mechanical engineer, J.Q. Braidwood. And within a week, Braidwood addressed another letter to authorities to obtain official recognition as the representative to act on behalf of the Chinese.

Saying he had had considerable experience with Chinese and knew their business habits, he supported his request with a letter signed by 21 Chinese who claimed they were unable to act without him. While officials were debating the question in interdepartmental memos, Braidwood applied for a concession for some Chinese traders to purchase goods, appending the title 'Chinese Representative' to his letter. This promptly raised the hackles of the Supervisor of Indian Immigrants who questioned the authority under which he had assumed the position.

Address to Lord Milner

This letter accompanied an illuminated address sent to the new British High Commissioner for the Transvaal Colony, Sir Alfred Milner, after the Anglo-Boer War. Although the sketches described have not been traced, the explanations given offer some insight into the expectations the Chinese held for British rule.

Your Excellency

The Chinese inhabitants of Johannesburg being anxious to show their loyalty to the British Government, have requested me to represent them, and present to you an illuminated address, they having no other person to represent them here. I have accepted the honour, trusting that however unworthy my fulfillment of this undertaking may be you will consider this attempt to convey to your Excellency a small item of appreciation and respect which have caused them to express themselves so strongly and to be thankful for whatever priviledges [sic] they have received at your hands.

The comparison between the late Government and your present administration is vividly impressed on their minds, and is better explained by the two sketches at the head of the Address, which convey their thoughts and which I will attempt to explain for your better information.

The first picture on the left represents a Chinese shop shut up on account of the War and being looted by the Boers, the Chinese having lost heavily in this manner.

The second picture on the right represents the same shop after the British Occupation, the shop being open, and business carried on under the protection afforded by the Military Police although still in time of War.

The third picture at the foot of the Address is meant as a tribute to the Brave Soldiers who fell in this War, of Liberty and they wish to express by this that the freedom from oppression which they now enjoy has been bought by the lives of hundreds of Brave Men which makes it the more valuable and have taken as the subject of the sketch a Lancer at Elandslaagte.

Again on behalf of the Chinese of Johannesburg I most respectfully ask your acceptance of this most humble tribute of respect from a people who but wish to live in peace under the British Flag under which many of them in various parts of the world have lived before and gladly become loyal subjects of our late Most Gracious Queen, and they humbly ask nothing more than the honour of becoming subjects of our most Noble King whose name is the symbol of Freedom and Just Governments.

I have the honour to remain

Your Excellency's humble servant

J.Q. Braidwood[80]

By the end of June 1901 the secretary to the Transvaal Administration addressed a curt reply to Braidwood stating 'that this Government is not prepared to recognize any person as representative of the Chinese in Johannesburg.'[81] Braidwood's name did not crop up again in any issues related to the Chinese.

PEACE PRESERVATION ORDINANCE

In May 1902, a peace treaty was signed and Britain took control of the Transvaal. Within months of the formal end to hostilities, the Peace Preservation Ordinance was passed to regulate the entry of returning refugees to the colony.[82] For the Asiatics, this constituted the first formal restriction on their immigration into the Transvaal, a restriction introduced not by the Boers, but by the British.

As the Registrar of Asiatics, Montfort Chamney noted:

> ... the Government has at least done what very few Governments would attempt unless backed by special legislation, namely has stopped all Asiatic immigration. None but refugees are allowed to come in and as these formed a part of the domiciled population, their return cannot be called 'immigration'. The Peace Preservation Act is the instrument employed to prevent the immigration of Asiatics ... The late Government imposed no restrictions whatever on Asiatic immigration...[83]

The law, which did not specifically refer to Asiatics, permitted entry only to those who had special permits, who could prove previous residence in the Transvaal or who were actually resident there at the end of the war. Because of the absence of records of registration certificates issued in terms of Law 3 of 1885, some Asiatics, either through bribery or fraudulently claiming previous residence, entered the Transvaal illegally.[84]

Once again the bogey of an 'Asiatic invasion' did the rounds. Asiatics were requested to register voluntarily and it was noted, by the end of 1903, that a total of 8121 Indians and 938 Chinese were registered to be in the Transvaal.[85] Unaware of the new legislation, numbers of Chinese who decided to return from Mauritius and China after the war found their entry prohibited. Without the relevant permits to enter the Transvaal, they were refused permission to disembark at Port Natal.

The situation caused sufficient consternation for one Chinese to write to the *Swatow Daily News*, a newspaper published in Kwangtung province in China. The correspondent, Leung Kwan (Quinn), would in the following years become an outspoken campaigner for rights for the Chinese in South Africa. In May 1903, however, he explained the significance of the new prohibition:

> Last year an Ordinance was passed in South Africa prohibiting Chinese Immigration. Upon the outbreak of war between Great Britain and the Boers, most of the Chinese in that place stopped business and returned to China. When peace had been restored some of these men left Mauritius with the object of returning to Africa, not knowing that such an Ordinance had come into force; but they were sent back in the same steamers as they came...[86]

Leung Quinn contacted Hong Kong officials who obtained details of the Peace Preservation Ordinance, and undertook to supply return permits for those who had

No. A 5564 AVAILABLE FOR ASIATICS ONLY.

PERMIT

TO ENTER AND RESIDE IN THE TRANSVAAL AND ORANGE RIVER COLONY.

Name (in full) Ah Nee

Nationality Chinese

Place of Birth Hong Kong

Occupation Store Asst

Last Address Joh'burg

District to which proceeding

Issuing Officer.

Place of Issue Joh'burg

Date of Issue 13/3/03

Authority for Issue

This Permit is not transferable, and any person making use of it, other than the original holder, will be liable to prosecution and to the penalties provided in Section 9 of Ordinance No. 5 of 1903. [SEE BACK]

Signature of Holder 金

Chinese paid three pounds sterling for permits entitling them to be in the Transvaal.

abandoned their businesses in South Africa at the outbreak of war. He requested returning Chinese to obtain their permits in Hong Kong before 10 June 1903.

Race was considered before nationality in determining the eligibility of any who wished to enter the Transvaal. A Chinese American, Jeong Shing, was arrested and imprisoned for six months with hard labour for being illegally in the colony. He had travelled from Diep River in the Cape to the Transvaal where he intended to open a Chinese merchandise store. The American Consulate was informed that Chinese, although naturalized in the USA, were deemed to be Asiatics, a definition which included persons belonging to any of the native races of Asia.[87]

Once they had overcome the problem of re-entering the Transvaal, the Chinese tried to re-establish their businesses. Several discovered their shops had been looted and applied to the British government for compensation. One of the many who suffered losses was Lai Singfor. He submitted a claim for £295 for goods commandeered from one of his five shops by the ZAR troops. As a British subject, he had left Johannesburg for East London in October 1899, returning on 24 June 1902. Three of his shops, all of which were in Bertrams and Jeppestown, were kept open for trade during most of the war by his nephew, Lai King. His claim was disallowed.[88]

Another general dealer, Martin Easton, claimed compensation of £198 for stock and furniture looted during the war. He said he had barricaded his shop on the corner of Marshall and Phillip streets and left the Transvaal for Kimberley in October 1899. On his return in May 1902, it had been 'looted of everything'. After a thorough investigation, he received compensation of £91.[89]

FORMATION OF TCA

British administration of the Asiatic laws initially ushered in few changes. The locations saga continued as municipalities and White businesses pressed for restrictions on Asiatic trading, and general measures such as those prohibiting Asiatics access to public transport or to purchase alcohol were enforced. But renewed agitation over the influx of Asiatics led the government, in April 1903, to announce its determination to enforce Law 3 of 1885 and to take positive steps to restrict Asiatic residence and trade to locations.[90]

Of Pavements and Trains *'Not First Class'*

Asiatics in the Zuid Afrikaansche Republiek (ZAR) were not permitted to walk on footpaths and pavements, to drive in public carriages or to use any but third class compartments of trains. By 1901, the new British administration of the Transvaal felt 'better class' Asiatics should be exempted from these provisions and granted special permits which stated they were 'entitled to walk on the sidewalks, drive in any public carriage or conveyance, and to travel on the Railway system, either 1st or second class in ordinary Railway carriages'.

When this permit was issued by the Military Governor's Office to four prominent Pretoria Indians, an official in the Native Affairs Office hastily despatched a private note objecting to one aspect of the permit.

> On Thursday last I saw the General and asked him if a little leniency might be shewn ... as regards the 'pavement question', as I thought at this critical moment when the Indian community was in such an agitative state it might be as well not to enforce this regulation too strictly as regards these men of better class...
>
> Well, to get to the point and the purport of this letter:
>
> I think in allowing them to travel *1st* class is granting them a little too much, and such a privilege I am sure will meet with the strong disapproval of the majority of white people. Is it too late to withdraw the 1st class and leave it at 2nd? I am of opinion such men might be allowed to travel 2nd in a country like this, where only the lower class of white people travel 2nd, but I think it is a great mistake to allow them the privilege of travelling 1st, for more reasons than one.[91]

The reference to 1st class was promptly deleted. It is not known whether any Chinese obtained such special permits, but this letter offers an interesting glimpse of 'petty apartheid' at the turn of the century.

Perhaps this was the trigger which prompted the Chinese to form a new organization, the Transvaal Chinese Association (TCA), some time in 1903. Like any group, the Chinese would have been motivated by what they perceived as a crisis and it was becoming abundantly clear that officials of the new regime would no longer be prepared to turn a blind eye to the continued presence of Asiatic traders in the towns.

Records in 1903 show increasing numbers of Chinese appealing against any removal to locations and officials' growing reluctance to allow traders to use White nominees as they had in the past.[92] Added to the awareness that their position was being threatened, the Chinese must have hoped that a formal association would offer them the best means of working collectively to stave off further restrictions.

In a court case, a judge offered the following description of the TCA's objectives:

> The Chinese Association, it appears, is a voluntary Association of individuals in Johannesburg, which was formed in the year 1903... apparently the Association had no written constitution, but it seems to have been formed for consultation, and for the protection of the joint interests of the members ...[93]

Given these aims, it is likely the TCA was the first 'politically' motivated Chinese organization in South Africa. To protect the interests of its members, it would have offered assistance in dealing with official channels and translating documents from English into Chinese. The association also probably played a role in community efforts in mid-1903 to dissuade Chinese from coming to work on the Witwatersrand gold mines.

Despite the lack of information on its early activities, a short newspaper report reveals that the organization in May 1905 provided rich pickings for enterprising burglars.

> Between 9 o'clock last night and 6 this morning the Chinese Association, 15 Bree Street, was broken into and the safe, containing £340 in gold and silver, besides numerous cheques and promissory notes, was taken away. An entrance was effected into the premises through the fanlight at the top of the front door, which was then opened on the inside and through which the safe was removed.[94]

The Transvaal Chinese Association moved its headquarters sometime in the next few years to Marshall Street, Ferreirastown. With the Cantonese Club, it was poised to play a key role in the dramatic events which would overtake the community of some 900 Chinese in the Transvaal in the following years.[95]

IMMINENT IMPORTATION OF CHINESE LABOURERS

Moves to import a mass of Chinese labourers to work on the Witwatersrand gold mines gained momentum in 1903. In the economic slump which was part of the aftermath of the Anglo-Boer War, mine owners argued the need for Chinese workers while labour movements and the public expressed strong opposition. The Transvaal was experiencing a 'shortage' of Black labour as the mines had reduced wage rates during the war and workers preferred alternative avenues of employment which had opened up in post-war reconstruction.

Inevitably, attitudes towards local Chinese surfaced in the controversy. One newspaper commented:

> We draw the attention of our readers to a letter written a day or two ago by a Rand Chinaman to a Rand daily, and who asks, in the name of his aggrieved countrymen, for 1) burgher rights; 2) full trading rights; 3) the right to hold fixed property. That shows what the aspiration of Chinamen will be if they come to this country.[96]

Claiming that the Chinese were already ruining White shopkeepers, opponents pointed out White artisans would also 'feel the pinch of the shoe' when Chinese artisans went into competition against them.[97]

The settled Chinese community in South Africa too was opposed to the importation of Chinese labourers and tried to discourage their compatriots in China from co-operating. Articles and letters published in Chinese newspapers outlined the discrimination Chinese encountered in South Africa and the restrictions Chinese labourers would face.

In May 1903, Johannesburg Chinese held a mass meeting at which they decided to warn fellow Chinese against emigrating to South Africa and to take steps to spread this warning throughout China. Commenting on this effort, the *Hong Kong Daily Press* said South Africa was determined to keep Chinese out of the country and added:

> ... these Celestials who have emigrated to the Transvaal are doubtless painfully experiencing the fact that they are not wanted and that things will be made uncomfortable for them if they remain. The Labour trouble has been a very real one in South Africa but it cannot be solved by the importation of Chinese.[98]

Other Chinese newspapers published in Kwangtung carried even stronger warnings from individuals and organizations who painted a grim picture of the conditions in mines in South Africa and listed the 'tyrannical measures' already applying to Chinese settlers. Here are just a few excerpts, translated from Chinese:

> These mines here are of a rocky nature running several hundred feet deep in the ground. Explosives have to be used to split up the rocks and when any explosions take place it sounds as if it were thundering and earthquake. It is not uncommon to see poor negroes while working in the cave are thus blown to death. Some losing their arms and feet and some with heads scald(ed) and burnt. The negroes are sometimes forced to work in the cave where the water never ceases to run and their feet thus immersed in the water for nights and days. Such hardships are unbearable even by oxen and horses. How is it possible for the Chinese to endure it? ...
>
> Nowadays the Chinese are poor and it is hard to get a living. On hearing that labourers are required for the gold mine many will avail themselves of the opportunity. If once got into the trap it is as entering into a living hell. Should he escape from being a ghost in the foreign land and finally return as survivor, it would be but a rare case. We, living in Africa ourselves, cannot bear to see the tragedy done to our race...[99]

Another newspaper highlighted the restrictions Chinese faced, stating:

> England has for long been known as a civilized country, but the Englishmen in that place (South Africa) have resorted to harsh measures like savages in the treatment of the Chinese. Is there no justice? ... there is no cheap Chinese labour throughout Africa. Why then have such a drastic law as the following:
>
> — that the Chinese are forbidden to walk under the verandahs,

— that they are forbidden to travel in first class carriages (trains),

— they are forbidden to drink wine,

— If they should go from one port to another en route for China, they are not allowed to land unless they can speak English ...[100]

It is likely this campaign contributed in some measure to the failure of recruiters to obtain sufficient Chinese labour from the southern province of Kwangtung. Those seeking labourers enjoyed far greater success in the northern provinces of China where poverty and unemployment had provided a more amenable and readily available pool of labour.

From 1904, nearly 64 000 Chinese labourers were imported to work on the mines of the Witwatersrand. Their presence heralded yet another chapter in the history of the Chinese in South Africa — one which catapulted them firmly into the limelight and shaped attitudes towards Chinese for generations.

5

On the Gold Mines

Why did South Africa have to import Chinese labour to work the Witwatersrand gold mines? What were the political, economic and social consequences of this 'experiment'? For local Chinese settlers, the controversial presence of over 60 000 labourers from 1904 to 1910 had far-reaching effects. This chapter examines the role of the British and Chinese governments, the conditions the Chinese labourers encountered, the repercussions of their stay and their compulsory repatriation to China.

The mass importation of more than 60 000 Chinese labourers to South Africa marked a brief and contentious episode in the country's history, one which had far-reaching consequences both for the Chinese community and South Africa. Not only did it exacerbate anti-Chinese racism and lead to the introduction of a Chinese Exclusion Act in the Cape, but it also contributed to the fall from power of the Conservative government in Britain. Although the negative effects of the Chinese labourers' stay have been longest remembered, it should not be forgotten that they revived the South African economy in the aftermath of the Anglo-Boer War by restoring the mines of the Witwatersrand to their position as the world's largest single producer of gold.[1]

One of the most enduring myths perpetuated by the labourers' presence is the belief that they were the forefathers of South Africa's Chinese population. Even currently published books repeat this erroneous information. In *Like it was : The Star 100 years in Johannesburg*, it is stated: 'Black recruiting began to pick up and the Chinese were repatriated. By 1910, only 2000 remained, and they never went home. About 1000 settled in Johannesburg, the nucleus of today's Chinese community.' How such a conclusion was reached is not known but could possibly have been a misinterpretation of a remark by Eric Rosenthal in his *Encyclopaedia of South Africa* which read: 'By 1910 most labourers had left the country, though a small number of Chinese, about 2000, live in the Republic ...'[2] It was commonly assumed that the Chinese community evolved in a similar way to that of the Indians who had arrived mainly as indentured labourers, and then settled in South Africa. The saga of the Chinese mine labourers however illustrated the lengths to which the British and Transvaal governments went to prohibit any further settlement of Asiatics in the country.

WHY CHINESE LABOUR?

The reasons behind the decision to import Chinese labour to work the gold mines were complex. The gold reefs of the Witwatersrand were characterized by the sheer size of their deposits (which covered a distance of approximately 40 miles), their depth and regularity.[3] Deep-level mining for low grade ore however required heavy financial outlay and the mines' profitability depended on a plentiful and cheap labour supply.[4]

At the end of the Anglo-Boer War in 1901, gold mines had virtually ceased operations except for a few which worked under government supervision. Gold production on the Witwatersrand was at its lowest since 1888, and wages which had been dramatically cut were well below the pre-war rate.[5] Unskilled Black labourers, dispersed by the war, did not return to the mines, preferring less hazardous and more congenial avenues of employment offered in post-war reconstruction such as railways, road-building and harbour improvement as well as agriculture. Apart from the low wages, discouraging factors in mine labour included the high mortality rate, poor transport, sleeping and medical facilities, a 30-day working month and dislike of compound life.[6] Labourers' discontent was further fuelled by the unpleasantness and dangers of underground work. Jail with hard labour was the penalty imposed on those who refused to work underground.[7]

Mine owners sought alternative labour sources since recruitment from southern and central Africa had not been successful.[8] Unskilled White labour was discounted because the Chamber of Mines feared Whites would drive up working costs by demanding higher wages, better food than 'labourers' meat' and 'maize', and they could not be housed in compounds with their families.[9]

A Select Committee recommended an investigation into the labour potential of the Far East, and in February 1903 the Chamber sent H. Ross Skinner and Herbert Noyes on a fact-finding mission to California, British Columbia, the East Indies and China to evaluate prospects for employing Asiatic labourers. In September 1903 Ross Skinner presented a comprehensive report in which he assessed the suitability of Chinese, Korean and Japanese labour and recommended the importation of Chinese, subject to strict controls. He emphasized that the 'grave objections' to the presence of Chinese in California and other parts of America were 'entirely due to the absence of restrictive legislation' when Chinese entered the country. Should the Transvaal adopt stringent legislation at the outset there was no reason for a Chinese presence to be harmful either to the State or to White workers.[10]

Southern vs. Northern Chinese

Officials seeking Chinese labour commented candidly on the differences between Chinese from southern and northern China. According to agent H. Ross Skinner, the following had to be considered:

> 'The Southern Chinese are, and have been for many years, accustomed to leave home, in many cases for far distant countries, and the idea of South Africa as a field of labour for surplus population will not be in the nature of an innovation. It is from Southern China that the labour will have to be obtained in the first instance, especially if it is wanted at short notice.
>
> In Northern China the idea of emigration to a far distance has to be brought home to the Coolie, but when this has been done (a process taking time and money) many fine men will be obtained from the North, especially from the province of Shantung.
>
> The Northern man is of an altogether larger and heavier build than the Southern; but he is reported to be duller in intellect. He appeared to me to be stronger constitutionally, but on this point I should hesitate to pronounce an opinion, as we saw the Southern man apparently as healthy in one climate as in the other — as healthy in British Columbia as in the Malay Peninsula.'[11]

Recruiters only managed to secure the services of some 2000 southern Chinese, so the majority of those who came to work on the Rand mines were from the northern areas of Chihli, Shantung and Honan.

To allow for the larger size of the Northerners, the initial rations apportioned to them were two and a half pounds of rice a day as opposed to one and a half pounds for the Southerners. Experience showed, however, that no one could consume two and a half pounds of rice, so the scale for the Southerners was later adopted as the standard.[12]

The Transvaal government, the Chamber of Mines and mine owners collaborated to turn public opinion in favour of Chinese importation. Although views among White miners fluctuated, it was politically important that the local population be seen to support the venture. The Transvaal Labour Commission was appointed in July 1903 to enquire into the labour situation and the possibility of obtaining adequate supplies from central and southern Africa. It found that there was a pressing labour shortage which could not be met locally.[13]

After the report's release, the pro-Chinese lobby became increasingly vociferous. Underhand methods allegedly used by the Chamber of Mines to 'educate' the public included victimizing anti-Chinese leaders, disrupting meetings or loading them with miners who risked losing their jobs if they did not vote for the employment of Chinese. Miners were given half-holidays to attend the meetings ... all in all, it was 'a situation which Chinese labour could only aggravate.'[14]

The public campaign to win support for importing Chinese labour began in March 1903 when Sir George Farrar, chairman of the Anglo-French Group, emphasized the shortage of labour in Africa and the need to look elsewhere:

> These mines are the largest gold producers in the world, and it is absolutely absurd to think that they should be crippled for want of labour. Surely common-sense says that if you cannot get labour in Africa, you must get it elsewhere and get to work.[15]

He did, however, make it clear that he did not envisage the Chinese being permitted to enter on the same terms as indentured Indians brought into the country earlier, saying: 'I have seen the evil of the Indians holding land and trading in competition with White people, and on no account whatever would I be a party to any legislation that permitted this.'[16]

Despite Farrar's assurances that skilled jobs at high wages would be reserved for White workers and that traders and farmers would be protected, his speech unleashed a storm of protest countrywide. When the government pressed ahead with the recruitment of Chinese labour in the face of widespread White unemployment in the Transvaal, the scene was set for virulent opposition from White trade unions and labour.[17] Protest meetings were held throughout the four colonies of South Africa. Organizations such as the African Labour League, the White League, the Witwatersrand Trades and Labour Council and the Black and Coloured communities expressed strong objections.[18]

The anti-Chinese lobby was strong and vocal, reflecting fear of reduced wages and competition, fear that the Chinese would not spend their money locally, fear that the restrictions and repatriation would break down, fear of unpleasant and alien customs, fear of the unknown.[19] The same objections which had been raised time and again in the 19th century towards Chinese entering the country were reiterated, with some of the venom being directed at the existing Chinese population. A deputation from the White League to Lord Alfred Milner, Governor of the Transvaal, insisted that the local Chinese be forced to pay £10 on entering the Colony, and that they should pay the annual tax of £25 provided by law. They complained that there were many Chinese shops, particularly in Jeppestown and Fordsburg, where the Chinese had secured corner positions, giving them an unfair advantage over White shopkeepers.[20]

Prominent lawyer and Indian community leader, M.K. Gandhi said the Chinese importation would indirectly prejudice the Indian cause since they were both treated as Asiatic. He criticized conditions such as compound life and said restricting the labourers to unskilled work was indefensible and unjust. His prophecy relating to the problems which would arise was remarkably astute and accurate.

> The pity of it all is that, after creating such an artificial situation, the Colonists would grumble if the 'Heathen Chinese', as he is called, turns out to be a moral leper, resorts to all kinds of make-shifts in order to throw off his yoke and by hook or by crook endeavours to make use of his abilities which he may have inherited from his ancestors. The mining industry is undoubtedly the mainstay of the Transvaal, but the Colonists may be buying its development too dearly.[21]

Opposition to the importation of Chinese labour was founded on a multitude of reasons, many completely contradictory.[22] In Britain trade unions orchestrated mass protests against the importation of Chinese labour which they described as 'Chinese slavery'. They charged that the Rand magnates were 'much more intent on obtaining cheap Chinese coolie labour than on paying high wages for British workers.'[23] Studies undertaken early in the 1900s showed that wealth was very unevenly distributed in Britain, one-third of the population living in chronic poverty.[24] Unemployment was high among the lower classes, with between three and a half to six percent of registered trade union members out of work between 1902-1908.[25]

White workers vociferously protested the importation of Chinese labour to the Witwatersrand.

At a demonstration in Hyde Park, attended by 80 000 people on 26 March 1904, the Parliamentary Committee of the Trade Union Congress passed the following resolution:

> That this meeting consisting of all classes of citizens of London, emphatically protests against the action of the Government in granting permission to import into South Africa indentured Chinese labour under conditions of slavery, and calls upon them to protect this new colony from the greed of capitalists and the Empire from degradation.[26]

Britain's involvement in the Chinese importation extended beyond having to give Royal assent to the scheme. The British government was the channel through which importation had to take place since the Chinese government refused to deal with any colonial authority and wished negotiations to be based on the Anglo-Chinese Convention of Peking drawn up some 44 years earlier in 1860.[27]

MEASURES TO RESTRICT CHINESE LABOUR

Importation of Chinese labour had never been intended to replace Black labour but was an experiment to supplement a temporary and fluctuating shortage.[28] As a solution to the Transvaal's post-war depression, Chinese labour had to be secured on terms acceptable to White vested interests. It was to be an unskilled labour force, brought in under government control, prohibited from trading, holding land or competing with Whites, indentured and finally, subject to repatriation.[29] In effect, Chinese labourers would be tolerated until the mines became operational and then sent back from whence they had come.

The official sanction of the British government was sought through the Labour Importation Ordinance (No. 17 of 1904) regulating the introduction of 'Unskilled Non-European Labourers' into the Transvaal. It did not refer specifically to Chinese to enable the door to remain open for the importation of labourers of other Non-White races. To appease White labour, a special schedule was inserted into the Ordinance listing 55 skilled occupations which the imported labourers would not be allowed to perform, such as blacksmiths, bricklayers, drivers of mechanical or electrical machinery, plumbers, masons, electricians and mechanics. This 'industrial colour-bar' was later extended to encompass all Black labour and was a striking example of the lengths to which the Transvaal Chamber of Mines went to legalize a racial definition for skilled trades.[30] In essence, legalized racial job reservation started when the Chinese were imported and remained a prominent feature of employment practice in South Africa for succeeding generations.

The Ordinance made the Chinese labourers 'captive' in many ways. They were restricted to unskilled labour in the exploitation of minerals in the Witwatersrand district, in other words, they could only work on the gold mines. After the end of a three-year contract or its renewal, they had to be repatriated at the expense of the importer to their country of origin. They had to live where they were employed, and could not leave without a permit which allowed an absence of a maximum of 48 hours. They were required to wear identification at all times, and had no choice in their place of employment. No liquor, mining, trading, general dealer's, importer's, hawker's or other licence whatever would be granted, nor could labourers acquire, lease or hold property.

Refusal to work, desertion, changing employer and conducting trade or business were not civil offences but became criminal charges, the penalties for which were fines, imprisonment or even deportation. The Ordinance required the appointment of a Superintendent to oversee its general administration, and inspectors to check conditions on the mines. It also stipulated the terms and conditions under which the labourers were to be imported, the keeping of registers, entering of bonds for repatriation, the reckoning of periods of service, medical care etc. The Foreign Labour Department was established to administer the importation of Chinese labourers.

The Transvaal's neighbours, the Cape and Natal, did not consider the Ordinance a sufficient safeguard against the influx of Chinese into their areas, and promulgated the Chinese Exclusion Act and the Transit Immigrants Act respectively. Both of these measures restricted the movements of all Chinese in the two colonies and had far-reaching effects on the local, 'free' Chinese.

Further afield, in Britain, Australia and New Zealand, opposition to the Ordinance was vociferous as labour movements said it 'sanctioned labour unfit for human beings.' The Chinese worker would be treated as a 'mere chattel or animated pickaxe.'[31]

NEGOTIATIONS WITH THE CHINESE GOVERNMENT

From the outset the Chinese government insisted on dealing directly with the British government. This insistence made negotiations more cumbersome and recruitment more costly, but the advantage was that the Transvaal, through Britain, was given access to Chinese labour for which demand exceeded supply.[32]

The Chinese Minister at the Legation in London, Chang Teh-Yih, conducted negotiations on behalf of his government from February to May 1904. He had no objections to the Labour Importation Ordinance, but wanted the regulations governing its application to 'be embodied in an Agreement to which His Majesty's Government themselves, and not merely a commercial agent from the Transvaal, nor even the Colonial Government, must be a party. The Chinese Government could not, for the purposes of an Agreement, take cognizance of any such person as the "importer" mentioned in the Ordinance.'[33]

Minister Chang proposed the appointment of consuls or consular agents to visit the mines, inspect the accommodation and make representations on the well-being of the labourers. He also proposed that no corporal punishment be inflicted on the labourers, that an 'importer' could not be a mere dealer or speculator in labour and that repatriation had to be to the port of embarkation, with only British ships being used for transport.[34] The Transvaal authorities, however, had strong objections to allowing a consul or consular agent to conduct inspections, especially if he was a local trader. They also felt corporal punishment was necessary for certain offences but it would only be inflicted after trial and sentencing by a magistrate or judge.[35]

The final agreement was the Anglo-Chinese Labour Convention, signed in London on 13 May 1904 by Chang Teh-Yih and Lord Lansdowne, British Secretary of State for Foreign Affairs. Drawn up to regulate employment of Chinese labour in British colonies and protectorates, it replaced the unratified regulations of 1866 and 1868. In some areas, however, this new Convention was less beneficial to labourers, for example Article X of the 1866 Convention restricted the working week to 6 days of nine and a half hours each, whereas no stipulation whatsoever was made in the new Convention.[36]

The terms of reference for the appointment of the first Chinese diplomatic representative to the Transvaal were contained in Article VI of the Convention:

> For the better protection of the emigrant, and of any other Chinese subject who may happen to be residing in the Colony or Protectorate to which the emigration is to take place, it shall be competent to the Emperor of China to appoint a Consul or Vice-Consul to watch over their interests and well-being, and such Consul or Vice-Consul shall have all the rights and privileges accorded to the Consuls of other nations.[37]

The First Chinese Consul-General

The first Chinese Consul-General in Johannesburg, Lew Yuk Lin, was a man of impeccable credentials. Born near Canton in 1862, he was the son of a diplomat, educated both in China and America and an accomplished linguist. Prior to his posting to the Transvaal, he served China in various capacities from consular official to Charge d' Affaires in New York, Washington, Singapore, London and Brussels.

When he arrived in Johannesburg on 14 May 1905, he was accompanied by his youngest daughter, as well as an entourage of officials, secretaries and servants. The Chinese Consulate was situated in a two-storey mansion, on the corner of Wilhelm and Wolmarans streets, Hospital Hill, Johannesburg,

> '... and, as might be expected in the residence of an aristocrat of an age-old land of quaint and appealing art, the interior is a jewel of Oriental elegance, veneering Occidental comfort in a harmony that bespeaks the cultured cosmopolitan.'[38]

Officials accompanying the Consul-General were: inspector Tong Sze Ku, secretary Liu Ngai, inspector Yang Kin San, writer Mew Wai Ching, servants Wong Sz and Ching Sing Ki and doorkeeper Chen Tim.[39]

The first Chinese Consul-General, Lew Yuk Lin, with his daughter and consular staff, photographed outside his residence at 95 Wolmarans Street, Hospital Hill, Johannesburg.

This enabled the Consul-General to intercede on behalf of the non-indentured or 'free' Chinese. Transvaal authorities wanted the consul to be an official of high rank, paid by the Chinese government, and to take up the Chinese point of view in matters of principle that might arise, but not to occupy himself with the conditions of the labourers on the mines. He would be given access to the records of the Transvaal government and the Chamber of Mines to avoid his office registering and enumerating labourers.[40]

Provision was made for the payment of a consular fee of $3 per man per annum to support the appointment of a Chinese Consulate-General in Johannesburg.[41] The Chamber of Mines converted this to six shillings for each indentured labourer, paying two-thirds of the amount to Chinese officials in Tientsin and one third to the consulate.[42] It was however to be the Superintendent of Foreign Labour, and not the Consul-General, who would have visiting rights on the mines. As a prominent mine labour recruitment official, F. Perry, stated: 'The last thing we want is a petty mandarin with an army of subordinates, registering the individual labourers and certainly blackmailing them in the process.'[43]

RECRUITMENT COMMENCES

Once the Labour Importation Ordinance and the Anglo-Chinese Labour Convention had been ratified, the Chamber of Mines Labour Importation Agency started work on the recruitment, embarkation and transportation of Chinese labourers at maximum cost efficiency. The Chinese government had insisted on the use of local Chinese recruiters with embarkation to take place only at designated treaty ports.[44]

Recruiting costs were high. In addition to the consular fee of $3 per labourer per annum, there were depot fees, recruiting licence fees, shipping fees, as well as transportation, food and salaries. The estimated cost of recruiting a Chinese labourer was £21-10-0, against a Black labourer's cost of £4-10-0. For the mine owners, three-year contracts gave them the shortest possible period for recovering these costs, particularly when considered with the capital outlay of the mines.[45]

Recruitment initially centred on Kwangtung (Guangdong) and Kwangsi (Guangxi) in south China but proved to be a dismal failure. Chinese in Johannesburg had waged a newspaper campaign in Hong Kong and Kwangtung to warn prospective recruits of the hazards of deep-level mining and the numerous discriminatory measures applied to Chinese in the Transvaal.[46] Not only was there bad publicity about conditions on the gold mines and intense competition in south-east Asia for the available labour supply, but there was also the open hostility of the Viceroy of the provinces towards indentured labour, so long regarded as 'buying and selling young pigs' (*mai-mai ch'u-ch'ai*). Ships with labourers were prohibited from leaving Canton for Hong Kong and some recruiters were arrested. The British firm of Butterfield and Swire, contracted as the South African agents for the southern areas, also ran foul of the authorities with damaging consequences for recruitment operations.

On 25 May 1904 the first shipment of Cantonese left Hong Kong aboard the S.S. *Tweeddale* with a disappointing number of 1055 men. The high incidence of beri-beri among the first two batches from south China led to the suspension of recruitment, and the sum total of labourers eventually distributed to mines from this area numbered a mere 2060.[47] That the Chamber of Mines had been overconfident about obtaining labour from south China was demonstrated by the fact that they had only secured the services of Cantonese-speaking staff for the Foreign Labour Department and to act as controllers on the mines.

Recruiters met with greater success in the populous northern provinces of Chihli (now Hebei), Shantung (Shandong) and Honan (Henan). Factors such as the Russo-Japanese War in 1904, economic stagnation and the collapse of the silk-spinning industry encouraged able-bodied men to sign up for work of any kind. Good road, rail and water links from the interior to the treaty port of Tientsin (Tianjin) and the embarkation port of Chefoo (now Yantai), facilitated the transport of labourers and recruitment was also aided by the support of the local Chinese authorities and British consular officials.[48]

No fewer than 62 000 of the 63 695 labourers eventually sent to South Africa came from the northern provinces.[49] As an incentive, recruiters offered advances of 30 Chinese dollars to ordinary labourers, and an additional $10 for higher positions such as cooks, policemen and headmen. These advances were particularly welcome at planting time or when food stocks were low, and recruiters were reimbursed by the labourers once they had been accepted for employment by the depots. Recruiters, however, lost money when their recruits were rejected as Chinese authorities required them to pay for the 'rejects' to return home. Labourers were also offered the incentive of having part of their wages paid directly to their families on a regular basis. This was probably the most important reason why such large numbers of labourers were recruited.

Whether or not the recruits understood the terms of their contract or the type of work they would be expected to perform was a moot point, as none of the Transvaal emigration agents either at Chefoo (Yantai) or Chingwantao (Qinhuangdao) could speak the northern dialects. This situation was only rectified in September 1906, three months before recruitment ceased.[50]

Prior to embarkation each recruit, on passing medical examinations, was issued with a metal disc with his number engraved on it, a passport, some clothing and a salary advance of about £2-10-0. He could also fill out an allotment book which allowed part of his salary to be paid to his relatives in China.[51] Non-indentured Chinese serving as interpreters and medical staff were employed for the voyage to South Africa. They were only permitted to accompany the labourers to Durban but could then be employed under special contracts which included repatriation.[52] With time on their hands and money in their pockets, the labourers relieved their boredom on the voyage by participating in gambling sessions. They were easy prey for 'squeezing' and racketeering by the more hardened gamblers and petty crooks, and quickly accumulated debts which would dog their footsteps while in southern Africa.[53]

ARRIVING IN SOUTH AFRICA

Between May 1904 and early 1907, a total of 34 shiploads with 63 695 Chinese labourers were despatched to South Africa. The journey from North China to the port of Durban took approximately 30 days by chartered steamship. In terms of the Anglo-Chinese Labour Convention, close attention was paid to the provision of wholesome food and water, sufficient space, sanitation, cleanliness and medical care on the journey. On arrival, recruits were given a medical examination and transported by train to the receiving depot five miles away at Jacob's Camp, a former British concentration camp used during the Anglo-Boer War, where they were fingerprinted and given brass badges bearing their number and employer's name. Another train journey of at least 27 hours took the labourers to one of 55 gold mines in the Transvaal, stretching from Randfontein on the West Rand to Springs on the East Rand.[54]

On arrival in Natal, Chinese labourers were kept at a special compound at Jacobs, just outside Durban, to prepare for transportation by train to the Transvaal mines.

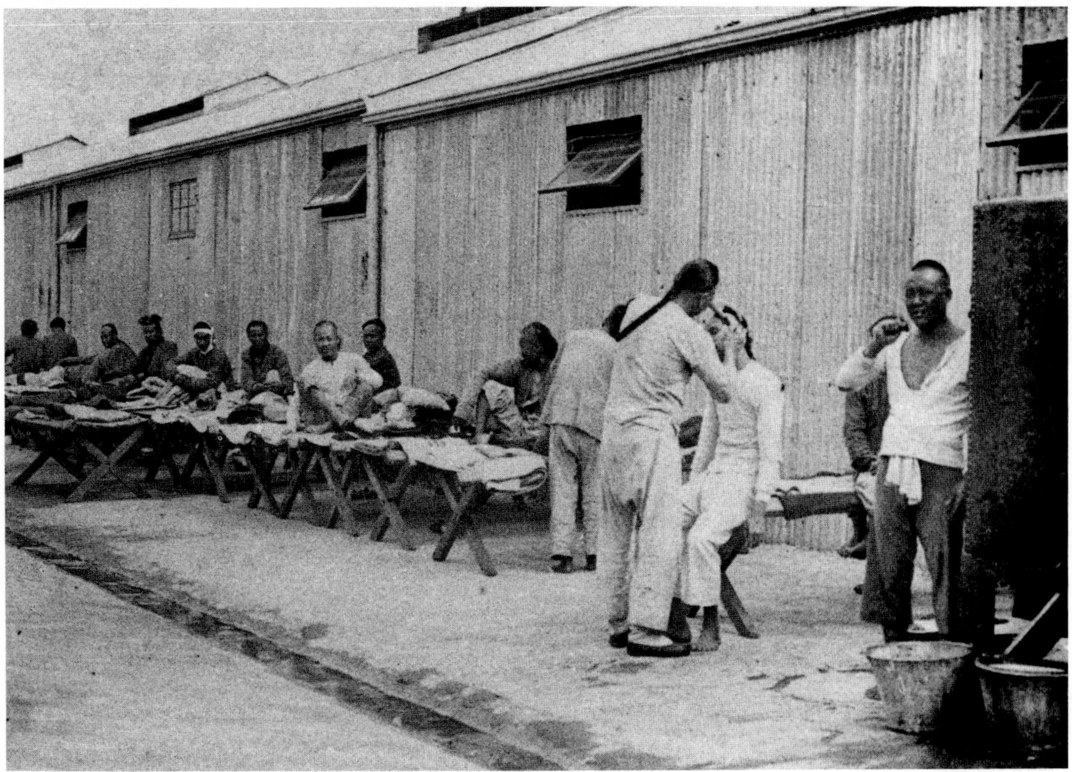

The first batch of Chinese mine labourers arrive at Randfontein in June 1906.

To contain costs as much as possible, mines provided accommodation for the labourers in compounds — large brick buildings enclosing a rectangular space. The buildings consisted of 'bunk rooms', many of which had been specially built for the Chinese. Accommodation varied from one compound to the next, with some labourers having low sleeping platforms divided by curtains and wire-mesh bunks[55] and others confined to rooms for 40 men, consisting of two tiers of concrete sleeping bunks. In some compounds the bunks had concrete sides and tops as well so that men could only enter them by crawling in at one end.[56] Communal bathrooms were generally found inside the buildings, while the latrines were outside so that pails could be removed daily.[57] Medical attention was good, with each mine having White and Chinese doctors, Chinese assistants and even Chinese medicine available.[58]

The terms of their indenture bound the Chinese labourers for a minimum period of three years to the mines and to compound life. They were only allowed to leave the compounds with a permit — a red permit allowed absence until sundown on the day of issue and a white permit allowed overnight leave or for a period not exceeding 48 hours.[59] The movements of the labourers were severely curtailed, and such 'compounding' had the psychological effect of dehumanizing them, reducing them to mere numbers.[60] Any labourer who wished to terminate his contract of service could do so, provided he

Bunk Room Remains

From *The Star*, 14 January 1975.

Perhaps the last vestige of the Chinese 'coolie' labour era on the Reef can be seen at the historic Simmer and Jack mine in Germiston.

At the mine's 'old compound', which once housed 1200 Chinese miners, a bunk room is still standing completely unchanged since the Chinese were repatriated in 1910.

The room, fitted with 40 concrete bunks, is believed to be the only mine quarters left on the Witwatersrand built especially for the Chinese.

The Chinese miners were subjected to grim living conditions if the Simmer and Jack bunk room is anything to go by. The bunks are 61 cm wide and 2.1 m long. They are in rows of 10s with the top layer a little over 91.5 cm above the lower one.

His bunk was bed and storing area to the Chinese. Apart from using the bunk to sleep on, his possessions had also to be kept on it. There were no cupboards or safe places to leave money and other valuables.

In recent years when excavations have been done around the mines in Germiston, gold coins and other treasures belonging to the coolie miners were discovered. The risk of leaving money or valuables in communal bunk rooms led many Chinese to bury these riches for safety. Sadly, many coolies never returned for their treasure.

Concrete bunks provided in sleeping quarters for Chinese mine labourers, circa 1906.

A Chinese 'police boy' enjoyed more luxurious quarters than the labourers.

repaid his employer the costs of bringing him to the Transvaal and returning him to his port of embarkation in China. This amounted to the considerable sum of £17-10-0, plus any advances made to his family.[61]

Meals were provided by Chinese cooks and were served in a large dining room on the mine. Daily food rations were:

one and half pounds of rice,
half pound of dried or fresh fish or meat,
half pound of vegetables,
half oz of tea,
half oz of nut oil,
salt.[62]

Those who exercised control over the labourers were in a position to cause much unhappiness. Each shipload had been accompanied by 'headmen', policemen (some appointed from the ranks of the labourers), Chinese-speaking Whites who would be Chinese Controllers at the mines, and interpreters.[63] Most of the compound managers or controllers had been employed because they were able to 'smatter' a few words in Chinese, but the majority could not communicate adequately with the labourers. Because labourers soon discovered the failings of controllers 'it was not long before bribes to wink at gambling, opium smoking, illicit trading and the like were offered and accepted.'

Compound police and interpreters too could use their position to withhold information, misrepresent facts and accept bribes.[64]

WORKING ON THE MINES

Most mines deployed Chinese labourers to underground work and supplemented with Black labour on the surface. Chinese were employed to the exclusion of Blacks by only three out of 54 mining companies. Because of the high costs involved in their recruitment, mines wanted to recoup this outlay rapidly by obtaining maximum productivity. Accordingly, they moved the Chinese to the most strategically productive jobs underground which simultaneously enabled them to avoid giving increases to Black labourers, since there was no minimum wage for surface work. Instead of breaking rocks with machine drills, mines were able to employ a high proportion of Chinese in hand-drilling on stopes.[65]

Inexperience contributed to many accidents, for example, labourers jumping into moving cages, drilling into unexploded charges and not knowing how to use explosives. Occupational hazards of mine work included such incidents as the snapping of cage-ropes, which occurred on the Simmer East mine and killed 23 Chinese.[66] It was estimated that 3192 Chinese labourers died on the Rand between 1904 and 1910, a mortality rate of nearly one in twenty. Of these, 986 died as a result of causes directly attributable to

Chinese mine labourers at work.

Many mines used Chinese labour for the most strategically productive jobs underground.

their conditions of work. A further 611 were partially or totally disabled, resulting in the repatriation of 523.[67] Major causes of death among the labourers included beri-beri, dysentery, phthisis, opium-poisoning, pneumonia, tuberculosis and other respiratory diseases, suicide and murder.[68]

Describing some of the problems the Chinese were encountering, a compound manager, Eugenio Bianchini, who also compiled an English-Mandarin dictionary, said in October 1905:

> It happens sometimes that a Chinaman is not physically strong enough to perform satisfactorily the work given to him, but simply because the Chinaman was, irrespective of his ability, allotted to a certain boss, he has to remain with him; and without consideration to his physique he has at times to perform a job which may be perhaps beyond his natural power to do.[69]

Misunderstandings also occurred about deductions made from labourers' pay. The issue of wages and pay for 'piece work' became highly contentious and led to numerous disputes. When labourers refused to work or were absent from work without leave, they were prosecuted for these 'crimes'. What proportion of the number of suicides and desertions was attributable to living and working conditions can only be surmised since the labourers were never given a forum to express their feelings. Even the Special Committee which met in 1906 to inquire into their 'control' did not interview any labourers or try to obtain first hand evidence from them.[70]

Language problems were at the root of many misunderstandings between the Chinese and White miners. Referring to the 'rough handling' of Chinese, the Foreign Labour Department reported that White miners often thought 'a blow or the application of a heavy boot ... to be the most efficient means of conveying to a coolie an idea of what his white boss wants.'[71] Such treatment often led to riots and work stoppages.

In the first six to eight months of the Chinese labourers' arrival, some 14 riots and disturbances took place on various mines.[72] The situation probably arose because of a lack of mediation which could have been offered by a Chinese consular officer as provided for in the 1904 Anglo-Chinese Labour Convention. The first Chinese Consul-General, Lew Yuk Lin, only arrived in Johannesburg in May 1905, nearly a year after the first labourers started work. Out of frustration and lack of recourse to appeal, many labourers resorted to desertion or took the law into their own hands.[73]

The Superintendent of the Foreign Labour Department, William Evans, attributed disturbances to ill-treatment and extortion on the part of the Chinese compound police, tactless treatment by some White miners and heavy gambling resulting in assaults and fights. In general, however, he was complimentary about their behaviour. In his Annual Report for 1904-5 he said:

> It is a matter of surprise — one may say of congratulation — that the tale is not longer, and it furnishes high testimony to the general good conduct of the majority of the Chinese labourers on the Rand. As a rule trouble breaks out owing to some slight misunderstanding or to some incident trivial in itself, and if the aggrieved parties once can command a following a serious situation may be created, as an angry mob of some two thousand men armed with crowbars and iron bedposts is not easy to parley with. Fortunately, however, after the first outburst the excitement gradually simmers down, and the men return to a reasonable frame of mind.

Procedures had been provided for labourers to submit grievances to the Foreign Labour Department, but because petition boxes were tampered with, or placed near the policemen's quarters, few labourers dared use them for fear of being victimized. In the second year of the labourers' presence, Evans noted that there had been virtually no 'disturbances' in the compounds, attributable 'to the fact that both employers and employed have got to know each other better.' The Foreign Labour Department itself had problems overseeing the registration and well-being of the labourers. It was understaffed, and its initial complement of staff, including Superintendent Evans, were Cantonese-speaking and had not expected the Northern Chinese to differ so much in 'ethnological descent, traditions, customs and language from those of South China, and that hence a different set of supervisors were required.'[74] The Chinese expression 'matching chickens and ducks' aptly described this situation, which was tailor-made for the unhappiness and misunderstanding which was to follow on both sides.

LABOURERS OFF DUTY

For local inhabitants of the Witwatersrand, the appearance of thousands of Chinese labourers in their midst excited much curiosity, not least because of their long, plaited pigtails. Stereotyped as strange, foreign and exotic, their presence gave rise to countless tales, repeated over the years, of their antics, their vices and their comings-and-goings.

Restricted to their compounds throughout the week, the Chinese were given Sundays off work and they made full use of the holiday to seek out entertainment or relaxation. Those labourers who were granted day or overnight permits to leave the compounds at weekends spent the time visiting friends on other compounds or window-shopping in the towns. They were often seen frequenting the Ferreirastown area of Johannesburg and riding rickshaws. Old-timers recollected the sight of Chinese labourers cycling at speed through the streets with their pigtails streaming in the wind. Bicycles became a popular means of transportation and many Chinese purchased these from the cycling agents, Shimwell Brothers. Contrary to predictions by those who opposed their importation, they did not hoard their money to take back to China but spent liberally to boost the local economy.[75]

For those who had to remain in the compounds, boredom was a key feature of life and there was little entertainment other than the sports days organized by the mine management. Black and Chinese workers competed against one another in various types of races, hurdles, tug-of-war and rock-drilling contests. There was no doubt that the participants had a good time, and such activities were often used for political propaganda to counter allegations that the Chinese were being treated as 'slaves'.[76]

Some 4200 Chinese labourers at the Simmer and Jack Mine. A total of 63 695 Chinese were recruited to work on the Witwatersrand mines between 1904 and 1910.

Other holidays given to the labourers included Christmas Day, Good Friday and three Chinese festivals, namely Chinese New Year, for which they had 3 days off work, the Dragon Boat Festival (1 day) and Winter Solstice (1 day).[77] On one occasion in 1908 when the management of the Simmer East Mines refused to allow the labourers a holiday for the Dragon Boat Festival, a riot broke out. Police and troopers were called in, but the labourers succeeded in securing their day off work.[78]

Although the Ordinance governing the labourers' importation made provision for them to be accompanied by wives and children, the terms of their indenture made it unattractive for them to exercise this option. Most labourers felt they could not afford to feed and clothe families on the wages they earned and, at that time, it was not usual for Chinese women to accompany their husbands overseas, particularly on short-term contracts. By February 1907 only two wives and twelve children were on the Rand.[79]

Elaborate Chinese theatre productions were a source of much pleasure and entertainment for the labourers, and on special occasions such as Chinese New Year, theatre shows ran for several days. Labourers from other compounds attended and there must have been great disappointment when theatre shows were banned sometime during 1906.[80] The reason for this was that the authorities felt the shows were a major source of male prostitution and crime.[81]

Chinese labourers enjoyed staging elaborate theatrical productions during their leisure time. Costumes were imported from China for shows which ran for several days, especially during celebrations such as Chinese New Year.

Chinese New Year 1906

The 3-day Chinese New Year celebration at the end of January 1906 was probably the gayest and most colourful ever seen on the Rand. By then the Chinese labourers had settled down and amassed sufficient money to plan some elaborate purchases including:

— collecting subscriptions from labourers on several mines to pay for procuring from China beautiful costumes, robes, umbrellas and banners for a three-day long grand opera;
— importing paper dragons, fireworks and foodstuffs for processions and feasts;
— decorating their rooms and compounds with colourful banners, lanterns and slogans to welcome the New Year.

The mine management, as usual, laid on the sports day and rock-drilling contests, and even these were participated in with zest.[82]

Critics of the Chinese labour importation scheme joined the outcry in 1905 against 'unnatural vice' which was said to be rife among the labourers. A one-man commission of enquiry was appointed to investigate the claims and the Bucknill Report, which was not made public, said allegations about sodomy and prostitution were true but exaggerated.[83] The Chamber of Mines was adamant that the Chinese were well-behaved and moral. Given the large numbers of males, the Superintendent of the Foreign Labour Department stressed that 'it should be particularly noted that not a single case of outrage on women has ever been proved.'[84] What really seemed to bother many critics was the thought of the labourers associating with white women, and even posing for photographs with them was considered as 'vice' and a 'public danger.'[85]

Sex Across the Colour Line

A police raid on a brothel in Ferreirastown, Johannesburg, attracted public attention to the somewhat contentious issue of sex across the colour line. Under the Immorality Ordinance no. 46 of 1903, it was forbidden for 'any White woman' to have 'unlawful carnal connection' with any 'Native'. The Ordinance made no mention of White men, so presumably this was allowed. 'Native' was defined as 'a person manifestly belonging to any of the native or Coloured races of Africa, Asia, America or St Helena.'

In a case before the Magistrate's Court in 1907, police described a raid on a brothel at No. 8 Fox Street where 'between two and three hundred Chinese Coolies were waiting in the back yard of the house, and were being admitted two at a time' by two White men to two White prostitutes.

The Chinese labourers in the rooms at the time were prosecuted, but one was acquitted as he was still fully dressed. The other was sentenced to twelve months' imprisonment with hard labour and a whipping of ten strokes. Both the White men and women were also found guilty and sentenced.

The Transvaal government was however so concerned about the case that they wanted to repatriate not only the guilty labourer but also the one who was acquitted. Action was even contemplated against the few hundred others who had been waiting in the yard, but reason prevailed when it was pointed out that 'there would be no chance of our being able to identify them now.'[86]

To cater for the few Christians among the labourers, several churches were allowed to distribute Bibles and tracts and to visit the mines on Sundays, Good Friday and Christmas Day.[87] Of those who followed religious practices, the majority were Buddhists, although several stated they were Mohammedans, Roman Catholics and Protestants.[88] In December 1905 a Johannesburg newspaper reported on the activities of a small Chinese congregation and the baptism of 10 converts in a mine dam.[89]

With a mine dump in the background, several Chinese, converted to Christianity, were baptized in a shallow dam on the Witwatersrand in December 1906.

FAIR PLAY

The major issues causing misunderstanding and tension between the mine managers and the Chinese labourers were rates of pay, what constituted a fair day's work and the operation of the western judicial system. Mines resisted increasing labourers' pay from 1s.0d per day to one 1s.6d after six months' work, despite contract stipulations, and calculated the average monthly rate of pay on 30 working days rather than 30 calendar days. The Chinese therefore earned less than Blacks and less than they had been led to expect. During 1905 the average wages were 37s.7d a month for Chinese and 51s.9d for Blacks.[90]

No minimum wage had been specified in the Ordinance relating to Chinese labour as this was deemed to be not 'desirable or necessary'.[91] Through the introduction of 'piece-work' the mines related payments to a fixed minimum of actual work, and were thus able to extract a great deal of free labour from the Chinese. As a rule, companies adopted a hole of 36 inches as the standard of a fair day's work — such holes had to be bored into rock by hand, using a hammer and chisel. Labourers were paid nothing for a hole of less than 24 inches. Equivalent scales were applied for other classes of work. Disputes broke out constantly over minimum-payment levels which gave rise to numerous confrontations between the labourers and mine owners.[92]

Mine managers were given the discretion to act as witness, prosecutor and judge in determining what work had been done and whether or not workers should be paid. All forms of protest, including peaceful meetings were banned and the Chinese had little recourse but to riot or desert.[93] Bonuses were paid for holes of 36 inches or more drilled in any one shift, an incentive which led to a high mortality rate when the Chinese drilled into unexploded or misfired holes from a previous blasting shift in an attempt to gain 'footage' and increase bonuses.[94]

Among the many complaints relating to pay were those of wages not being increased as stipulated in contracts, of families in China not receiving any money under the allotment scheme, of labourers not being given their tickets at the end of the shift to prove that they had worked, of payments being made to the wrong labourers and of short payments.[95] Many misunderstandings probably resulted from language difficulties and inadequate interpretation.

For the Chinese, South Africa's system of justice in which a guilty person could be discharged on a technicality made no sense. In the words of an observer at the time:

> The delays in the courts, the conviction of the innocent, the freeing of the guilty, imprisonment instead of the summary corporal punishment to which the coolie had been accustomed, and most of all the possibility of escaping punishment entirely, all encouraged crime.[96]

Congestion in the courts and the inadequate numbers of interpreters led to frequent remands with the Chinese being led from one government office to another, in what appeared to them an aimless manner, and finally being lodged in jail, convicted on charges which they did not understand. It was not uncommon for a prisoner on being discharged to state truthfully that he did not know on what grounds he had been confined, and confusion of identity occasionally led to prisoners being released prior to the expiry of their sentences, while others, whose sentences had expired, remained in custody. A feeling of bewildered helplessness was generated which often led to riots.

Inadequate interpretation was often at the root of the problem. According to the Superintendent of the Foreign Labour Department, the Chinese did not understand the British methods of judicial procedure. 'Guilty or not guilty', for instance, possessed no equivalent in the Chinese language and cross-examination bewildered Chinese prisoners and witnesses. White men who could speak Chinese were extremely rare and would not come to South Africa, while Chinese interpreters who did come were often acknowledged to be untrustworthy and open to bribery.[97]

FLOGGINGS

Flogging was one of the most contentious issues relating to the employment of the Chinese labourers and attracted much public attention both in the Transvaal and in Britain. Despite earlier assurances that corporal punishment would not be inflicted without legal recourse, compound managers ordered labourers to be flogged for various minor offences. Corporal punishment was used to circumvent legal proceedings because these were time-consuming and expensive.[98]

Horrifying reports and allegations of flogging and torture were given widespread publicity. Chinese who had deserted from mines claimed that if they had not drilled to depths of four hands (1 hand = 6 inches) they were kicked by their 'shift-bosses', not credited for the shift and sentenced to be flogged. Those who had been flogged claimed the types of whips used on them included strips of thick leather on the end of a 3-foot wooden handle, sjamboks, strips of rubber and short lengths of bamboo.

Press reports in the *Morning Leader* in Britain described some of the methods of 'torture' thus:

— To strip erring coolies absolutely naked, and leave them tied by their pigtails to a stake in the compound for two or three hours.

— To bind a coolie's left wrist with a piece of fine rope, which was then put through a ring in a beam about nine feet from the ground. This rope was then made taut so that the unhappy coolie, with his left arm pulled up perpendicularly, had to stand on his tip-toes.

— Being handcuffed to a horizontal beam which is so far from the floor that it is impossible for any but exceptionally tall men to sit while handcuffed. They must therefore squat, and for a change raise themselves in a semi-standing posture.[99]

The public outcry necessitated swift action. As criticism mounted, the Lieutenant Governor of the Transvaal stated that officials had only intended such punishment to apply to slight breaches of regulations, as was permitted in public institutions in England such as schools.

> From the facts which have been brought to my notice I have come to the conclusion that this permission to inflict slight corporal punishment has been abused both by the white mine officials and the Chinese police, and especially by the latter ... I must request you to be good enough to take immediate steps to put an end to this practice.[100]

Authorities believed flogging was a deterrent the Chinese would understand and said it was a punishment to which Chinese of the lower classes had been accustomed.[101] Flogging of labourers was discontinued in June 1905, but its occurrence in the Chinese labour experiment had a significant impact on the outcome of the British general election in 1906.

> ... When it was discovered in Britain that Chinese labourers were being flogged after all, a vote of censure was passed on Milner in the British House of Commons. He resigned as Governor in 1905. His fall — and the hullabaloo over 'Chinese slavery' — helped sweep CB [Campbell-Bannerman] and the Liberals to power in 1906.[102]

CRIME AND DESERTION

Although desertions from the mines started shortly after the Chinese labourers arrived in mid-1904, the Foreign Labour Department pointed out that the majority of the so-called deserters had simply been curious about their surroundings or neglected to obtain the necessary permits before leaving their compounds. Those who deserted intentionally had taken all their possessions and been arrested following railway lines in the hope of reaching the sea to return to China.[103]

Desertions however escalated in the following years, as did statistics for crime. It should be borne in mind that the authorities had defined as 'crime' a multitude of trivial offences including absence without leave or refusal to work. In the first year 21 205 cases of unlawful absence were reported from a working population which had not yet built up to 50 000.[104]

According to the Superintendent of the Foreign Labour Department,

> The great predisposing cause of all Chinese crime on the mines is gambling and its resultant debt, to a lesser degree supplemented by illicit traffic in opium ... The price of opium sold illicitly, which is largely adulterated prior to sale, being so much above the coolie's means, he borrows heavily to obtain it, and finding no means of paying such or other debts, he is compelled to desert, and after days of wandering becomes desperate through starvation and robs in order to live.[105]

Attempts to Return to China

Some Chinese labourers were so homesick or hated their conditions so much that they fell prey to charlatans in their midst. At one mine a wily labourer set himself up as a 'geographer', selling maps which ostensibly outlined the route back to China, via Tibet. His compatriots were told they would be able to 'reach that country in less than a couple of weeks.' [106]

There was also the case of a deserter from the Angelo Gold Mine who claimed to want to walk back to China. Arrested and charged with attempting to break into a house in Germiston, he told a court that he had left the mine with the intention of returning to China. He denied trying to enter any house and said he thought that if he followed the railway line he would 'get to China by and bye.' He was sentenced to two months imprisonment.[107]

Although opium was legally supplied to labourers who had obtained medical permits, illicit dealing made it freely available. Various church organizations advocated stricter controls of opium permits, complaining about the thousands of coolies who frequented opium dens in the Ferreirastown area.[108]

Virtually from the time the labourers boarded ship to sail to South Africa, advanced money in hand, gambling was the activity which occupied their free time.[109] Any unfortunate who accumulated debts he was unable to pay was ostracized, and could only commit suicide, desert, become a criminal or get himself jailed.[110] In several cases, defaulting debtors were pursued and murdered by those to whom they owed money.[111] According to the Foreign Labour Department heavy gambling was responsible for assaults and fights in compounds.[112]

Because gambling caused many other crimes, the Transvaal government promulgated special regulations in a sub-section of the 1906 Labour Importation Ordinance to ban all gambling or games of chance and prohibit the possession of gaming appliances by labourers whether in or outside any mine or compound.

> An instance has been quoted to us where a labourer has incurred a debt amounting to about £200 through gambling. This practically means that he has more than pledged the rest of his industrial existence in this country. Cases in which debts of this nature have reached amounts of £20 and £30 appear to be fairly numerous ...[113]

While acknowledging that some of the labourers were of a very bad class and included branded criminals, the Superintendent of the Foreign Labour Department pointed out that the majority were peasants and petty traders. Serious crimes for which Chinese were convicted between 1905 and 1906 included: escaping from custody (12), public violence (89), possession of dangerous weapons (40), common assault (630), murder (26), forgery (307), malicious injury to property (24), theft (207), robbery (8), housebreaking (220), fraud (19), possession of liquor (2) and gaming law (30).

> On these figures it may not unfairly be assumed that, taken as a whole, the large army of Chinese coolies employed on the Witwatersrand is law abiding ... [the coolie] has undoubtedly been guilty of acts, involving serious loss of life, calculated to cause righteous indignation and alarm, and these no one would seek to palliate. Still, in the case of white residents, robbery, not murder, has been his motive, and it was only when resistance on the part of the irate householder was offered that the latter came to an untimely end, and it should be particularly noted that not a single case of outrage on women has ever been proved. Deliberate murder of his fellow-countrymen, however, under aggravated circumstances of cruelty, is a charge of which he cannot be acquitted...[114]

The Foreign Labour Department recorded that the average number of labourers during 1905-1906 was 47 600 and the total convicted of offences was 13 532. Of these 11 754 were convicted of minor offences in terms of the Labour Importation Ordinance and cases of desertion numbered 1700. Referring to these statistics, an authority on the Chinese labour experiment, Peter Richardson said crime on this scale was 'indicative of a serious crisis of social control which was related to the totality of conditions under which the Chinese were forced to live and work ... the origin of so much unrest was to be sought not in the innate criminality of the Chinese, but in the structural conditions of life within the mine compound.'[115]

The ever-increasing scale of desertions and crimes committed by the Chinese labourers spread terror among residents of the Transvaal. After mass protest meetings and representations requesting the repatriation of the labourers, a virtual 'open season' was declared on Chinese and Whites were empowered to shoot or arrest any found outside the Witwatersrand.

Sensationalistic newspaper reports fuelled alarm and descriptions of Chinese deserters included many accounts such as this:

> ... hiding in dongas by day, slinking across the farms by night, dodging South African constabulary patrols, chivied by Boer farmers, chased by Kaffirs, stealing fowls, robbing lonely homesteads, barefooted, half-starved, desperate, with an Asiatic contempt of life in their blood and Chinese cruelty and callousness in their hearts. No one can understand them, they understand no one.[116]

Representations reflected the fear of residents on the Witwatersrand and included reports of farmers and their families leaving isolated homesteads at night to seek mutual protection with neighbours. To enable local residents to defend themselves from the Chinese, High Commissioner Lord Selborne issued instructions for a widespread distribution of arms and allowed summary powers of arrest.

> ... Any white man will be empowered to arrest without warrant any Chinese labourer found outside Witwatersrand district, and to hand him over to nearest Police Station. He will be refunded reasonable expense incurred in doing so ... I have authorized all farmers living in or near Witwatersrand district to possess firearms of any kind, except magazine rifles, and have made arrangements by which anyone who cannot afford to buy firearms can be lent a Martini-Henry rifle by the Government on application to the Resident Magistrate.[117]

Those who arrested Chinese deserters were paid on a sliding scale calculated according to the number of Chinese arrested and the distance travelled from the place of capture to the nearest charge office. According to the *Star Weekly Edition* of 14 October 1905, the rate was 1s.0d per mile for four labourers and 3s.0d per mile for eight or more.

To curb the level of crime and desertion, clauses of the Labour Importation Ordinance were made more stringent, opium and gambling were banned, theatre performances halted and a new permit system was introduced. Deserters inevitably faced a bleak future on the run. Compelled to steal to stay alive, they were readily recognizable as Chinese with their long pigtails and most were eventually captured or killed.

Chinese 'Pigtails' for Trophies

Among the most macabre stories of souvenir collecting from the Chinese labourers was this tale recounted by a prison official.

In an affidavit in 1906 he testified that Chinese prisoners had been scalped after they had been hanged. Their 'pigtails' were then appropriated by high-ranking officials in Pretoria jail as trophies and curiosities.

> At a later period two more Chinamen were hanged together. After the post mortem examination of the bodies, one of the Chinamen, whose pigtail was very small and had not been removed, was buried without being interfered with. The other Chinaman, who had a better pigtail, which also had not been removed before execution, was completely and entirely scalped. ...
>
> On coming out of gaol I went to the Chinese consul at his private house in Johannesburg. I told him the whole story as told in this affidavit. He said, 'I will not believe you; this is not an act of England, it is a barbarous act. Tell your story to the people of this country, and then it will be an international question....'[118]

POLITICAL REPERCUSSIONS

Issues arising from Chinese labour played a pivotal role in general elections both in Britain and the Transvaal. In January 1906 the British Liberal Party, collaborating closely with the Labour Party, ousted the Conservatives from power. Confronted by a range of concerns from protection versus free trade to school tax, the British electorate responded most readily to the election platform denouncing 'Chinese slavery', a charge which had excited emotional responses for more than two years.

Disclosures that Chinese labourers had been flogged strengthened the hand of opponents of the importation scheme and British voters showed their dissatisfaction with the ruling Conservative Party.

> Furthermore, the working man — and indeed the soldiers who had fought in South Africa — felt not only threatened but cheated. They had been promised South Africa as a new field for increased British employment, but saw — with the introduction of foreign workers — the percentage of British employed in the mines actually decrease ...[119]

The Liberals promised an immediate end to the importation scheme in the Transvaal and the repatriation of the Chinese labourers. Opposition by the mining industry however ensured that existing contracts were honoured and importation continued until November 1906. The view was held that:

> from the beginning the importation of Chinese labour was regarded as an experiment, and was accepted by H.M. late Government as necessary to meet a serious shortage of labour. Chinese labour was permitted as a supplement to, not as a substitute for, Kaffir labour, and it was necessary for H.M. Government to be assured that the numbers introduced were within the powers of supervision and control of the Transvaal Government ...[120]

Intent on removing abuses from the labour system, the new British government introduced a voluntary repatriation scheme offering free passage back to China for those who wished to return but did not have funds. Believing that many Chinese had not understood what mine labour entailed, they tried to ensure that no one was detained in South Africa against his will.[121] Mine owners feared they would lose many workers and objected strongly, delaying the publication of the terms of the scheme on the mines. No more than 830 Chinese successfully applied for repatriation in terms of this offer from May 1906 to December 1909.[122]

The political repercussions of Chinese labour were also significant in the Transvaal which was granted responsible government and held a general election in February 1907. United in their opposition to the continued importation, Afrikaners and British workmen joined forces against the interests of mine owners and those they regarded as capitalists. They voted into power the Het Volk party which had committed itself to ending importation and repatriating labourers when their contracts expired.[123]

Comparing the somewhat conflicting role played by the Chinese labour issue in the two election campaigns and the radically different attitudes towards the Chinese themselves, political commentator Joel Mervis said:

> In the best traditions of Chinese puzzles, the Chinese experiment exerted a crazy interplay of contradictory influences on the political fortunes of Het Volk and the British Liberal Party. On the face of it, those two groups were poles apart. Het Volk openly condemned the Chinese as heathens, murderers and thieves; the Liberals saw them as the innocent, suffering victims of oppression and slavery. Yet there were apparently no limits to the Chinese paradox. By putting the Liberals into power, which is precisely what the Chinese did, they also enhanced the prospects of their sworn enemies Het Volk.[124]

REPATRIATION

The stage had been set for the end of the Chinese labour experiment. In December 1906 the British government issued Letters Patent of the Transvaal Constitution and stipulated that no further recruitment of Chinese labour would be permitted nor would existing contracts be renewed. Provision was made for the repeal of the Labour Importation Ordinance, a step which could potentially turn the labourers into free men and would have allowed them to remain in South Africa. To close this loophole, the Indentured Labour Laws (Temporary Continuance) Act of 1907 was passed to allow sufficient time for contracts to run their course and to phase out Chinese labour over a period of two and a half years between June 1907 and February 1910.[125]

Chinese notices posted at the mines offered labourers the option of returning to China before their three-year contracts expired. Their compulsory repatriation started in June 1907 and by February 1910 the last group was shipped out of the country.

The imminent departure of the Chinese sparked a new round of protest, this time from those who wished them to stay. Not only were the mine owners loathe to let the Chinese go, but public organizations such as chambers of trade and municipalities argued that their departure would have disastrous consequences for South Africa.[126] With three years' experience, the Chinese had attained a high level of proficiency and competence as mine labourers. For the mine owners, who had brought them over at great expense and difficulty, compulsory repatriation represented the premature end to an anticipated long-term investment. As Chinese labour analyst Richardson pointed out:

> ... the full potential of this labour was never allowed to develop. The repatriation of the Chinese from mid-1907 onwards began ... at a time when they were approaching maximum efficiency.[127]

In a lengthy editorial published shortly before the repatriation began in mid-1907, the *Transvaal Leader* questioned the government's awareness of the 'dire consequences' of its actions. Pointing out the potential that had yet to be exploited with Chinese labour, it added:

> We have on these fields 50 000 Chinese — docile, industrious, and, as the comparative criminal statistics have shown, law-abiding workers. During their life on these mines the Chinese have acquired a high standard of efficiency in the performance of unskilled labour. Now, at the bidding of the people who have no real concern for the prosperity of this country, these labourers are to be sent away ...[128]

The Chinese too expressed great reluctance to leave. They submitted numerous requests to the Foreign Labour Department to be allowed to continue working on the mines. Many went so far as to draw up elaborately ornate petitions, one written on yellow satin, another measuring five feet in length and three feet in width, all containing thousands of signatures. The labourers appealed to the mine managers to intervene and repeatedly said they wanted to remain in South Africa because 'their hearts are in the country.'[129]

Increasing numbers of Black labourers had become available for employment on the mines after 1906, strengthening the hand of those pressing for the Chinese to be sent home. This availability lessened dependence on the Chinese but mines were also able to reduce Black wages based on what the Chinese were being paid. By the time the Chinese left, Black wages had stabilized and were lower than pre-war rates.[130]

As the three-year contracts of each batch of Chinese labourers expired, they were sent back to China. Repatriation, which began in June 1907, lasted until February 1910 and marked the closure of an experiment which had recruited a total of 63 695 labourers for the Witwatersrand gold mines. Confronted with the inevitable prospect of being loaded onto trains and then aboard ships, several Chinese went 'missing' from their compounds to avoid repatriation and then returned to the mines some time later in the hope of resuming work. The Superintendent of the Foreign Labour Department noted in May 1909 that 118 labourers absented themselves from their compounds just before a ship was due to sail, remaining away until it had departed. He therefore issued a proclamation stating that any who tried to evade repatriation would be fined up to ten pounds or imprisoned for up to three months.[131]

From: Transvaal Leader Weekly Edition

Randfontein Cremation
Oriental Customs

Tuesday Aug 6, 1907

For five hours today upwards of 100 Chinese were engaged in fulfilling the obligations laid on them by their deceased brethren, in that the bodies of the deceased should be cremated and their ashes conveyed to the land of their birth.

About 10 a.m. the coolies were seen making their way from the North Randfontein compound to a spot near the trim little cemetery which lies about three miles distant to the north-west of the property. They were all loaded with digging implements and inflammable materials, the latter of which included logs, timber roots, and large cases of paraffin. Some little distance from the boundary of the cemetery were rows of mounds, indicating the graves of 72 bodies who had succumbed to beri-beri and to accidents. From the first two rows 18 graves were selected by the coolies, and the men who had undertaken to unearth the remains were soon engaged in the work of exhumation. Within one hour the 18 coffins, which were in an excellent state of preservation, were removed under Municipal supervision with due regard for the regulation which will not admit of any removals taking place unless the graves have been in existence for 12 months or over. The removal of the coffins and contents was expeditiously carried out under the supervision of a stalwart Chinese police boy. Meanwhile, other coolies were engaged in making a line of primitive funeral pyres. In the majority of cases these were composed of a bed of stones, on which were placed wood roots and any inexpensive material which the men had gathered from the countryside. The lids of the coffins were deftly prized open, and after the preliminaries had been completed the structures were ignited. As the conflagrations grew, fanned as they were by a strong breeze, the heat became intense, but the Chinese did not relax their attention one instance, and late this afternoon the skeletons of the 18 coolies were reduced to ashes. Each pyre was denoted by small strips of red cloth tied to sticks, which bore what might be termed brief biographical sketches of the deceased. Bags about two feet square and gloves resembling in shape the ordinary flesh gloves, made of similar red cloth, were then brought into requisition. One of the five attendants who had assisted in each individual cremation, was deputed to gather the ashes. Placing the gloves over his hands, the man advanced to the smouldering remains, and carefully gathered the dust, which was placed in the bags and subsequently carried with great care to the compound, pending its final removal to China. The whole performance was effected without any ceremonial observances. Indeed, from the time of exhuming the bodies to the end of the work, the men had laboured in a most matter-of-fact and businesslike manner. A police boy, who had formerly served in the Wei-Hai-Wei regiment informed me that the ceremonies performed today were but an expression of the traditions to which the Chinese had clung so tenaciously throughout the ages. In China the belief exists that in a future sphere creature comforts may be enjoyed, and imitation money, and boats, and effigies of animals are burnt, with a view to transmitting them in company with the soul of the deceased for his service. The coffins burnt on this occasion contained pipes, cups, and the whole of the clothing and bedclothes of the deceased.[132]

Prior to the departure from the Transvaal, many labourers obtained permission to exhume and cremate the remains of their compatriots for transportation back to China.

Many departing labourers submitted urgent appeals to exhume and cremate the remains of their friends and relatives to take back to China. Local inhabitants of various West Rand towns such as Krugersdorp and Randfontein witnessed such mass cremations.[133]

The repatriation process posed some problems in the case of 40 prisoners who had been convicted of crimes such as robbery and murder and were serving sentences ranging from three to 12 years and even life with hard labour. Authorities pointed out their dates of discharge all varied and 'while by law they must be repatriated it is not practicable ... to charter a vessel to China for each man when he is due for discharge, there being no direct line to China.'[134] Attempts were made to ensure the interests of justice were served by transferring them to a jail in Singapore, pending the erection of a jail at Wei Hai Wei. But after months of debate, it was finally decided to remit their sentences and send them back to China with ten shillings each.[135]

Whether or not any of the indentured labourers succeeded in staying in South Africa is subject to speculation. Although all the Chinese should have been repatriated, elderly community members maintained that one managed to flee to Port Elizabeth where he started a business in Evatt Street. Author Hon Chong Wing King said everyone called the man 'Shantung Hung', but after marrying a White woman, he did not mix with local Chinese.[136] Another story is of two labourers who deserted to escape repatriation and worked on farms in the Transvaal. One died after years on the run and the other, called Ah Chong, found work with a Chinese family in Krugersdorp until, aged 70 or more, he returned to China in the 1950s.[137]

Belongings packed, Chinese labourers depart from the Rand mines.

LEGACY OF THE CHINESE LABOURERS

The Chinese presence on the Witwatersrand mines had far-reaching political, economic and social consequences. It played a significant role in toppling the ruling British government in 1906 and elevating to power the Het Volk coalition in the Transvaal. On the labour front, the Chinese 'experiment' legalized the industrial colour bar and contributed towards the lowering of wage rates for Black workers. Yet, in the space of just two years, it put South Africa's gold production firmly back in the lead internationally.[138]

The table below indicates the levels of gold production on the Witwatersrand prior to and for the duration of the Chinese labour experiment.

Levels of Gold Production

Year	*No. of mines*	*Gold output (fine ounces)*	*Total value £*
1898	77	4 295 608	15 141 376
1899 (Jan-Oct)	85	3 946 545	14 046 686
1899 (Nov)-1901(Apr)	12	574 043	2 024 278
1901 (May-Dec)	12	238 994	1 014 687
1902	45	1 690 100	7 179 074
1903	56	2 859 482	12 146 307
1904	62	3 658 241	15 539 219
1905	68	4 706 433	19 991 658
1906	66	5 559 534	23 615 400
1907	68	6 220 227	26 421 837
1908	74	6 782 538	28 810 393
1909	72	7 039 136	29 900 359
1910	63	7 228 311	30 703 912

(Extracted from Reports of the Chamber of Mines of the ZAR and the Transvaal Chamber of Mines, 1898-1910)

The hue and cry which accompanied tales of 'Chinese outrages' clouded public perceptions of the long-term contribution made to the country's prosperity. As author and journalist at that time, Hedley Chilvers remarked:

> It can hardly be denied that the Chinese saved Johannesburg, the Rand and South Africa, and that, as the salvation of the country had been from the first the prime consideration, the less admirable features of the experiment must be regarded as of secondary importance.[139]

From the time the first Chinese labourers arrived in 1904 to the departure of the last in 1910, gold output of the Witwatersrand doubled and its value increased from £12 million to more than £30 million. The number of mines worked reached a high of 74 in 1908 but dropped to 63 in 1910 when the repatriation process was completed.

Dramatic as these effects were on the country, the repercussions of the influx of nearly 64 000 indentured Chinese on the mere 2300 'free' Chinese scattered throughout the Transvaal, Cape and Natal colonies were different but noteworthy.[140] The most obvious consequence was the promulgation of the first and only specifically anti-Chinese legislation in South Africa. The Cape's Chinese Exclusion Act of 1904 emulated the 'insults of exclusion' which had been applied in the United States, Canada and Australasia as a result of Chinese labour importation.[141] Intended to prevent Chinese labourers imported for the mines from entering the Cape, the law effectively prohibited further male Chinese immigration and imposed strict controls over existing Chinese residents — a situation which lasted until 1933. In similar vein, the Natal Colony passed the Transit Immigrants Act of 1904 which confined the labourers to compounds in Natal and required 'free' Chinese to carry domicile certificates.

Within the Transvaal, the physical presence of thousands of foreigners who had been the subject of so much controversy readily exacerbated prevailing anti-Chinese sentiment. Local Chinese could not but be drawn into the verbal forays launched by editorial writers who 'probed oriental eccentricities as a fruitful source of news and comment.'[142] Sweeping generalizations on Chinese morality, attitudes and habits were made in countless press reports and long-standing fears of the economic threat posed by Chinese traders periodically surfaced. Such unwelcome publicity doubtless did little to aid local Chinese in their fight against anti-Asiatic legislation.

Another part of the legacy left by the Chinese labourers was the establishment of the Chinese Consulate-General in Johannesburg. From the outset, however, the Consul-General's involvement in the day-to-day activities of the labourers was deliberately kept to a minimum. He was consulted on broad policy matters but not allowed to inspect the mines, a constraint which inhibited his powers of intervention. While the Consul-General's brief was to safeguard the interests and well-being of the labourers, he was also given jurisdiction over 'any other Chinese subject who may happen to be residing in the Colony.'[143] It was in this sphere that the office of the Consul-General was to play an important role in the affairs of the Chinese throughout the Transvaal, Cape and Natal.

The mine labourers were not the forefathers of the Chinese who settled permanently in the country, but they had a significant impact on the fate of the community. It is difficult to assess the extent to which subsequent anti-Asiatic legislation was influenced by their advent, but it certainly retarded the growth and development of the Chinese community in the Cape.

The mass importation of labour was a short-lived episode in the story of the Chinese in South Africa. They came, they made their presence felt and then they left ... all within the space of six years from June 1904 to February 1910. That they made an indelible impression is undeniable and stories of their exploits continue to be passed from one generation to the next.

6

Passive Resistance and the Chinese

What made the Indians and Chinese resort to passive resistance in the Transvaal? Why did this cause a split in the Chinese community and riots in Johannesburg's Chinatown? This chapter describes the way in which the Transvaal authorities tried to curb the influx of Asiatics from 1906 with the imposition of stringent anti-Asiatic measures. Indians and Chinese rallied behind Mahatma Gandhi's campaign to resist compulsory registration, facing both imprisonment and deportation until 1911.

Note: *Much has already been written about the Indian community and its leaders during this eventful era in South African history. Since the numbers of the Chinese made them a mere fraction of the Asiatic population, their role has largely been overlooked. This outline focuses primarily on the attitudes and activities of the Chinese.*

Burning issues which aroused public passions, a clash of wills between ruler and ruled, differences of opinion which erupted into violence ... all these and more shaped the early years of the 20th century for the Transvaal's tiny 'free' Chinese population of some 1100 men.

The five years between 1906 and 1911 marked the most turbulent times in the history of the community and focused worldwide attention on a concept labelled 'passive resistance' or 'Satyagraha'.[1] Many people willingly went to jail, gave up their means of livelihood and even suffered deportation from the colony. From all parts of the Transvaal — Vereeniging, Pretoria, Potchefstroom, Germiston, Johannesburg — the 'free' Chinese, as distinguished from the indentured mine labourers, committed themselves to opposing a new Asiatic registration law which they considered degrading and humiliating.

The Transvaal Chinese Association, a political body formed in 1903, assumed leadership of the community until a bitter court struggle and riots in Chinatown destroyed its unity. Factions formed, old rivalries surfaced and for generations Chinese recounted tales of the rift.

CONCERN OVER ASIATIC INFLUX

After the Anglo-Boer War of 1899 – 1902, thousands of refugees returned to the Transvaal. Efforts were made to restrict the numbers of Asiatics to what they had been prior to the war, but since these records were incomplete, and many had been destroyed, the task proved impossible.

By June 1905, a total of 10 237 Indians and 1115 Chinese were registered as legally entitled to be in the Transvaal.[2] Many Whites however feared the actual numbers were far higher and appealed for measures to restrict Asiatic immigration. In a lengthy report on their admission and registration, the Protector and Registrar of Asiatics pointed to the loopholes in current legislation and the difficulties his office encountered in identifying those applying for permits. He said there were many Asiatics illegally in the colony, either without permits or with permits obtained fraudulently. To streamline administration, he recommended further legislation and the withdrawal of all current Asiatic permits, to be replaced by 'completely drafted documents ... bearing the full finger impressions of both hands'.[3]

These recommendations were in line with prevailing views on the need to control Asiatic immigration, and just a few months later, in August 1906, the authorities unveiled a measure requiring every Asiatic over the age of eight years to re-register.

The draft Asiatic Law Amendment Ordinance made it compulsory for Asiatics to surrender permits they already held, to obtain new registration certificates, to give all their fingerprints and to produce the certificate on demand. Only those with certificates would be granted trading licences and failure to comply was punishable by a fine, imprisonment or deportation. The Ordinance met with the immediate opposition of both the Indians and the Chinese.

ASIATICS PROTEST

In September 1906 Indians, who claimed British citizenship, held a mass meeting at the Empire Theatre in Johannesburg. They passed strongly worded resolutions objecting to the Ordinance and disputed that there had been a mass influx of Asiatics into the Transvaal. They said the Ordinance set up 'a system of passes and espionage unknown in any other British territory' and recognized no distinction between British and alien Asiatics.[4]

The meeting appointed a deputation to proceed to England and also passed the resolution which was to become the rallying call for the passive resistance movement the following year. They stated that should the Ordinance not be withdrawn,

> ... this mass meeting of British Indians here assembled, solemnly and regretfully resolves that, rather than submit to the galling, tyrannous and un-British requirements laid down in the above draft Ordinance, every British Indian in the Transvaal shall submit himself to imprisonment, and shall continue so to do until it shall please His Most Gracious Majesty the King Emperor to grant relief.[5]

The Chinese initially concentrated on the diplomatic channels open to them to voice their objections. The Transvaal Chinese Association (TCA) submitted a petition to the Imperial Chinese Consul-General for South Africa in Johannesburg to appeal for the protection of the vested rights of traders of long standing. It protested against the taking of fingerprints, stating that subjects of other nations merely signed their names and added the Ordinance would impose grave disabilities on all Chinese and inflict 'a degrading stigma on the subjects of a civilised nation.'[6]

This petition was signed by C. Cantin, acting chairman of the TCA, as well as Ho Ling, Wing Tongcheong, A.Q. Hooland, Leung Quinn, James Leo Wengsee, T. Emanuel, L. Howe and James Horn. Several of these men would feature prominently in the following years as leaders of and participants in the passive resistance campaign. At the request of the consulate, the petition was transmitted to the Governor of the Transvaal and the Colonial Office in London.

To emphasize their concern, the Chinese also appointed a special representative, Lai Mun James, to put their case to the Emperor of China's envoy in London. Accompanied by Consul-General Lew Yuk Lin, James travelled to the English capital to present another petition to the Chinese Minister. The petition stated that there was a daily increase in the 'oppressive and unjust laws' which affected the life, liberty and property of the Chinese. It objected to the injustice of the new Ordinance which applied only to Asiatics and particularly physical identification by fingerprinting which meant Chinese 'would be treated no better than criminals.' Repeated appeals by the Consul-General to improve conditions for the community had been to no avail 'owing to the anti-Chinese spirit which prevails here.'[7] Acting on this information, the Chinese Minister addressed a letter to the British Foreign Office Secretary stating the Chinese had a 'real grievance' and he felt the Ordinance would expose them to 'unnecessary hardships, inconvenience, and degradation.'[8]

Meanwhile, the delegation from the British Indian Association also called on officials in England and by early December 1906, the British government announced its decision not to proceed with the legislation. Any jubilation by Transvaal Asiatics on the successful 'hanging up' of the Ordinance was, however, to be short-lived.

The Transvaal was granted responsible government by Britain on 1 January 1907, held a general election on 20 February 1907 and constituted the Transvaal Parliament a month later. At the first sitting of this new legislature, the Asiatic Law Amendment Bill was introduced and passed its first, second and third readings within a mere 24 hours! In essence it was the same as the Ordinance which had aroused so much opposition just a few months earlier.

An obvious incentive for the speedy passage of the measure was the extensive support for it by the White population of the Transvaal, and particularly the business community. The Transvaal Municipal Association stated that 22 municipalities had expressed the wish for the Ordinance registering Asiatics to become law as soon as possible.[9] Elated supporters described the measure as 'the first step to stop what may mean the extinction of the white races in this country by immigration from the East.'[10] The new government's Colonial Secretary, General Jan Christian Smuts, said he had been gratified that the measure had been supported by opposing political parties in the legislature who had acted together to pass the law.[11]

The Asiatic Law Amendment Act, no. 2 of 1907, was promulgated on 5 April 1907 and simply needed royal sanction before being implemented. For the Asiatics, the time had come to act.

VOLUNTARY REGISTRATION OFFER

British Indians offered to re-register voluntarily and submit to necessary restrictions, provided the measure was repealed. Denying that there had been a mass, illegal influx of Asiatics into the Transvaal, they described their offer as a dignified way to resolve a difficult situation.[12]

Supporting this effort to stay the execution of the Asiatic Law Amendment Act, the TCA held a meeting on 14 April 1907 and echoed the Indian community's offer to re-register voluntarily. The chairman, L.T. Chue, appealed to the Colonial Secretary to accept the offer, saying the Chinese felt the legislation was unnecessary 'and wounds the feelings of the community.'[13]

A local newspaper, the *Rand Daily Mail*, said this appeal showed the united opposition of the Asiatic community to the law. It suggested the voluntary re-registration offer was as adequate a safeguard against illegal immigration as the law, 'and it is a pity that it was not suggested to the Government before the Ordinance went through, but this, it may be, was due to the fact that the progress of the Bill was unusually rapid.'[14]

Nonetheless, four weeks later, on 2 May 1907, the Asiatic Law Amendment Act was granted royal assent. Britain gave its approval since 'the Imperial Government had been greatly impressed by the unanimity of the people of the Transvaal in regard to the measure.'[15] Furthermore, it was pointed out that ... 'The Act which is now submitted has behind it a very different weight of authority. It has been introduced by the first responsible Ministry of the Colony, and has been passed unanimously by both Houses of the new Legislature.'[16]

M. K. Gandhi, honorary secretary of the British Indian Association expressed his bitterness at the 'trick played upon us' by the British government.[17] The man who would later achieve international renown as Mahatma Gandhi was an outspoken opponent of the new measure. As founder of the weekly newspaper, *Indian Opinion*, in 1903, he had to hand an influential medium of expression for the campaign to be waged against the new law.

The *Indian Opinion* greeted news of the royal approval of the act with a front page editorial on 11 May 1907 entitled 'To the Gaol!' Reprinting the text of the resolution taken the previous September, the paper said British Indians were now pledged to carry out their resolve to face imprisonment rather than submit to the law. The foundations for the passive resistance campaign were being laid.

CHINESE REACTION

The Transvaal Chinese Association called a community meeting at its headquarters in Marshall Street, Ferreirastown. The chairman of the Cantonese Club, Leung Quinn, presided and invited Gandhi to address the meeting. Gandhi pointed out the new law deprived Asiatics of their existing personal liberty, a position which 'no self-respecting subject of a civilised country could possibly accept.' He called on the Chinese to ignore the compulsory clauses to re-register and submit themselves to imprisonment.[18]

This meeting clearly spurred the TCA to commit the community to action. It immediately printed, published and distributed a lengthy pamphlet urging all Chinese in the colony 'to resist and oppose' the new law. Written in Chinese, it was dated the 33rd year, 4th moon in the reign of the Emperor Kwang Si — that is, May 1907. In the pamphlet, the TCA, under its Chinese name 'Chung Hua Hui Kuan', urged opposition to the law, gave a full account of Gandhi's address and spelled out what would happen to those who adopted passive resistance.

Stating that 'the heart of the white people is full of deadly poison', the pamphlet said the Chinese should be united, even at the risk of imprisonment, for submission to registration would confer on them 'the status of slaves'. It cited examples of Chinese heroes who had killed themselves or been imprisoned, and in highly descriptive prose outlined the consequences of registration.

> We see a great overflowing of tide and sea approaching and it makes our hearts sad at the sight of our countrymen being drowned in the engulfing water ... We would rather lose our heads than allow ourselves to be degraded .... rouse your energies and ... be ready for the fray, regardless of self and its interests. In this way you will attain the glory of imprisonment in gaol...
>
> If, by any chance you register under the Act, then be prepared to make your future homes in the location. Such a state of things will bring disgrace not only on oneself but on one's country. If this be the summit of your desires, then nothing more need be said. It lies in a man alone to establish his reputation and to make known his virtues...
>
> If there are any against us in this movement, we shall have nothing to do with them, either in private or business. If we can be unanimous in this matter, then all will be well, for, although the new Act is harsh and oppressive, yet we shall see it melt like so much ice. Brothers! Exert yourselves with all your strength to attain this end![19]

The pamphlet pointed out Gandhi had promised to appear in court, without charging any fee, on behalf of anyone arrested for non-compliance with the law. He had also urged the TCA to see to the maintenance of the families of any who were imprisoned and said if both the Indians and Chinese accepted imprisonment, there was some hope for a change in the law. It concluded:

> Alas! For the Chinese Community! ... There is every likelihood of the passage of further ordinances for our oppression. If we do not make up our minds to oppose the harsh measures against us, we shall lose our identity and will be wiped out from South Africa. Men of China! Arouse yourselves to Action![20]

This grassroots appeal to the community to resist the new law was also bolstered by what little diplomatic pressure the Chinese could bring to bear on the government. Early in June 1907, Consul-General Lew Yuk Lin visited Prime Minister Louis Botha to reiterate Chinese objections. He stated that the Chinese were prepared to 'suffer the extreme penalty of the law' and had offered to re-register voluntarily.[21] The Prime Minister said the Act was applicable to all Asiatics and did not distinguish against Chinese but aimed to provide for efficient identification.

> I regret to hear that the Chinese residents in the Transvaal are advocating the policy of setting the Act at defiance by refusing to submit to its requirements. The adoption of such a policy while it will certainly not in any way deter this Government from strictly enforcing the provisions of the Act will certainly deprive your fellow countrymen of all claim for consideration and I trust sincerely that your Excellency will exert all the great influence at your command to combat it.[22]

He went on to point out that had the Act not been passed, pressure would have been exerted 'to adopt still stronger measures to cope with the unauthorized immigration of Asiatics into the Transvaal.' The threat of defiance only entrenched official attitudes and it was clear the government would not withdraw the legislation.

Even individual Chinese expressed their feelings in the local newspapers. One P. Kimming of the TCA wrote that the Chinese objected to compulsion and wanted only fair play and fair treatment. He said the Chinese would 'fight for our right of freedom as bona fide residents, and fight we will to the bitter end.'[23]

RUN-UP TO RESISTANCE

By the end of June the contentious legislation was formally proclaimed and made effective from 1 July 1907. All Asiatics were to be registered and fingerprinted within four months, at stipulated times and places throughout the Transvaal.

The TCA called a community meeting addressed by the editor of the *Indian Opinion*, H.S.I. Polak. Commenting on the outcome, his newspaper stated:

> ... the Chinese are as fully determined to resist the law as the British Indians. They object to furnishing their pedigrees like Prize dogs. A paper is published by and circulated amongst them gratis, giving weekly reports of the position, and the Chinese are enthusiastic in their resolve to offer passive resistance to the objectionable law.[24]

To ensure the Chinese understood fully the implications of the new legislation, the TCA also translated and published the legislation in Chinese. The 50-page pamphlet showed 'the Chinese are fully alive to the dangers and insults of the new Act.'[25]

The Indians formed the Passive Resistance Association to co-ordinate their opposition to what had been dubbed the 'Black Act' and a mass open air meeting was held in Pretoria to reaffirm commitment to the resolution passed the previous year. One of the most emotive issues associated with the law was the compulsory taking of fingerprints. The Indians said this requirement presupposed all Asiatics were criminals, while the Chinese said in China the only people compelled to give fingerprints were illiterates and criminals.[26]

Although the Asiatic Law Amendment Act remained the focus of attention, another piece of legislation, the Immigrants Restriction Act (15 of 1907) was gazetted. This was closely connected to the provisions of the former law, and was to share the limelight as a target for attack by the Indians and the Chinese. Gandhi wrote several letters to Colonial Secretary Smuts suggesting amendments to both Acts, to no avail.

Leung Quinn

Leung Quinn was a shopkeeper who rose to prominence as a key participant in the passive resistance campaign in the Transvaal. Very little is known of his background other than that he was a native of Kwangtung province who arrived in the Transvaal in 1896 and soon became a partner in the firm of A. Kan & Co, mineral water manufacturers. He went back to China in 1901, but returned to Johannesburg in 1903 after appealing to Hong Kong authorities to assist Chinese to obtain permits to re-enter the Transvaal. By 1907 he was chairman of the Cantonese Club and acting chairman of the Transvaal Chinese Association.

Over the next five years, until 1912, he carved a name for himself as an articulate and outspoken crusader for the rights of the Chinese. With the support of his countrymen, he publicly committed the Chinese to passive resistance, gave numerous press interviews and appealed for the repeal the Asiatic Law Amendment Act. Although a colleague, M. K. Gandhi, assisted the Chinese in drafting several letters for submission to the authorities, Leung Quinn was sufficiently well versed in English to draw up many of his own petitions. He also translated relevant material into Chinese for the community.

He was jailed several times for his refusal to take out Asiatic registration papers and even deported from South Africa. Describing him as the heroic chairman of the Chinese Association in 1909, the *Indian Opinion* reported he had sold his stock and private furniture, leaving him with £30.

'Mr Quinn felt that he could not very well retain his possessions and his self-respect in a country like this. Mr Quinn was at one time one of the richest Chinese merchants, living on the fat of the land and enjoying all the nice things of modern life.'[27]

Although it is not known what happened to Leung Quinn after 1911, his impassioned stand against registration was a high point in the history of the Chinese. He believed surrender would humiliate the Chinese in the eyes of posterity ... and that by resistance 'our children might derive inspiration from the efforts and bitter experience of their fathers before them.'[28]

Leung Quinn, acting chairman of the Chinese Association of the Transvaal, 1907.

For the Chinese, Leung Quinn, acting chairman of the TCA, eloquently expressed their standpoint. In one of several petitions to the Chinese Minister in London, he summarized the reasons for their opposition saying, ' ... it is such legislation as can be accepted only by slaves, not free men.' Chinese realized passive resistance could lead to their financial ruin and deportation, but should their voluntary registration offer not be accepted, the Chinese Association felt strong representations should be made to the British government for the repatriation of all Chinese back to China, subject to full compensation being paid for deprivation of vested rights as to trade, residence, etc.[29]

In press interviews Leung Quinn emphasized the commitment of the community to passive resistance. He said the 'free' Chinese (as differentiated from the contracted mine labourers) in the Transvaal numbered some 1100, most of whom were storekeepers, as well as gardeners and laundrymen.

> We object to compulsion ... Every free Chinaman fully understands the condition offered to him, and more than nine hundred of these who are here have bound themselves in writing formally agreeing to the idea of passive resistance, and deciding that, as to any future action, they would be guided by the will of the majority of them. They are perfectly prepared to go to gaol for the sake of their principles.[30]

He pointed out the many different avenues the Chinese had explored in their efforts to have the legislation withdrawn. In addition to petitions to the Chinese Consul-General and the Chinese Minister in London, they had appealed to the Chinese Foreign Office in Peking as well as public bodies and chambers of commerce in China. The Chinese Students Association in Europe was considering the position, as was the Boycott Association which had been formed 'to safeguard the commercial interests of China in America.' Lai Mun James, the community's envoy to London the previous year, had already left for America 'to explain the position to the Chinese there, with a view to comparing the treatment accorded to Chinese in America and in South Africa.'[31]

Commenting on 31 August 1907, the *Indian Opinion* remarked that in the case of the Chinese the government was dealing not with British subjects, but with nationals of a foreign power.

> There is another aspect of the subject, too. Mr Quinn's reference to the Chinese Boycott Association has an ominous ring. Boycott is a very potent weapon, and, as a lever to move the Imperial Government through Manchester, it cannot conveniently be ignored. At all events, America has felt its effects and Great Britain will probably think twice before calling it into play.

The Chinese boycott on trade with America, from 1905 to 1907, cut US exports by nearly 50% and was widely supported by students and merchants in the major ports and trade centres of China.[32] This economic weapon, employed to further the interests of America's 90 000 Chinese, was however a futile hope for the Transvaal's mere 1100 Chinese.[33]

In the first months of the implementation of the law, the Asiatics' determination not to register became evident. Indian pickets patrolled the vicinity of the registration office in Pretoria to dissuade any last-minute waverers, and in Potchefstroom and Klerksdorp, registration officers were left twiddling their thumbs when no one came forward to take out new papers. Registration started in Johannesburg in October 1907 and volunteers picketed the Von Brandis Square registration office. Posters were also displayed asking Chinese to avoid the square during the registration period.[34]

Both Indian and Chinese picketers were instructed 'to observe absolute gentleness, never to go beyond argument' with those who might wish to register. Their duty was simply to warn people intending to register 'of the danger awaiting them.'[35] It was not long before the picketers ran foul of the law and two Chinese organizers were arrested and charged with obstructing the footpath in Pritchard Street, Johannesburg.[36]

By the end of October about 400 Indians and four Chinese had registered in terms of the new measure.[37] The majority, however, continued to express their opposition, and a newspaper columnist recounted the tale of a Chinese storekeeper in Pretoria who cancelled his lease, closed his store and moved when he discovered his Indian landlord had registered.[38] The government announced a month's extension to the registration deadline, making 30 November 1907 the final date for compliance with the law. But it was already clear the passive resistance movement had deterred the majority of Asiatics from registering.

Gandhi drew attention to the solidarity displayed by the Chinese in the early stages of the passive resistance campaign. He wrote:

Chinese Unity

'Messrs Harvin and Paterson, a prominent business firm here, have a large business with the Chinese. They supply them on credit goods worth about £5000 every month. The firm gave notice to the Chinese that further credit would be stopped if they did not take out the new registers. The Chinese, instead of being intimidated by this, became bolder. In reply, they asked the amount of the debit entries against them in the firm's books, offering immediate payment, and declining to do any further business with the firm.

Mr Harvin was silenced by this reply, apologized to the Chinese and agreed not to refer any more to the registers or to their accounts. Our merchants, when threatened by white merchants, get scared and become ready to take out registers as if they were slaves. They then forget the oath they had taken not to submit to the law.'[39]

DIFFERENCES BETWEEN INDIAN AND CHINESE APPEALS

From the outset the Indians and Chinese acted independently in their opposition to the legislation. Although both groups were classified 'Asiatic', they employed different grounds for objection and, to some extent, different tactics.

The Indians used their status as British subjects as the springboard for their appeals while the Chinese call for fair treatment was based on the international treaty obligations between two foreign powers. Gandhi said adversity had made the Indians and the Chinese 'strange bedfellows in this struggle'. Explaining the Indian case, he said he had tried to draw a line between British and non-British subjects and asked for a distinction to be made between the two types of Asiatics. In this way 'the Chinese fight was different to the British Indian fight.'[40]

Underlining the independence of the two groups, Gandhi wrote in later years:

> Still from first to last the activities of the two communities were not allowed to be mixed up. Each worked through its own independent organization. This arrangement produced the beneficent result that so long as both the communities stood to their guns, each would be a source of strength to the other. But if one of the two gave way, that would leave the morale of the other unaffected or at least the other would steer clear of the danger of a total collapse.[41]

Nonetheless, close collaboration was a marked feature of their relations, with members of the British Indian Association addressing Chinese meetings and Chinese being present at Indian gatherings. As Asiatics, they were united in the common cause of opposition to the law.

One Johannesburg newspaper asserted the whole passive resistance campaign was undoubtedly the result of the stand taken by the British Indian Association. It said the Chinese had at first 'expressed their willingness to register, but owing to the persuasion of the British Indian Association, they have now resolved to join the passive resistance movement.'[42]

Both the Indians and the Chinese took exception to this assumption. The British Indian Association denied that any persuasion had been exerted, and Leung Quinn pointed out that the Chinese Association had objected when the original Ordinance came out in 1906, going as far as sending a delegate to England.

> Naturally, the Chinese residents of the Transvaal would not have sanctioned so heavy an expenditure as was then made necessary, had they not from the beginning decided that, under no circumstances, would they accept a law which they regarded as humiliating and degrading in its tendency and effects. My Association has cordially agreed all through with the attitude adopted by the Transvaal British Indian Association, but it has acted from the commencement quite independently, and will continue to do so.[43]

A strongly worded petition, submitted by Leung Quinn to the Chinese Minister in London, supports this statement. He raised two arguments positioning the Chinese case differently from that of the Indians:

> ... the measure fails totally to recognise our ancient civilisation and the fact of our being an independent sovereign nation. It places Chinese subjects on the same level as British subjects coming from India. While it may be proper for the British Government to treat its Indian subjects as it pleases, Your Petitioner respectfully submits that subjects of the Chinese Empire should not be treated in a manner derogatory to the dignity of the Empire ... especially in view of the fact that China is a State in alliance with Great Britain and that the subjects of Great Britain receive the most favoured nation treatment in China.[44]

Comments on who was leading whom continued to make the rounds. When Colonial Secretary Smuts said the Chinese had initially been prepared to register through the office of the Chinese Consul-General, the TCA chairman decided it was necessary to assert the community's independence too from the consulate. Writing to the *Transvaal*

Leader on 9 January 1908, Leung Quinn said any offer by the Chinese Consul-General to register Chinese had not had the backing of the TCA.

> I beg to point out that the Chinese Consul-General, though we recognise his position as the representative of our Emperor, has no jurisdiction over non-indentured Chinese. The late Consul-General wrote to the local Government without any authority from the Chinese Association. It is possible that one or two of our community may have gone to him suggesting that if the registration took place at the Consul-General's office, the Chinese would raise no objection. I may state that this communication was never brought to the notice of my Association by the late Consul-General, from which I infer that the latter must have written on insufficient authority.

In view of the close co-operation between the consulate and the community, this public statement was surprising, but it did highlight the way in which the community perceived the consulate and its role.

REGISTRATION LEADS TO SUICIDE

As the November deadline for registration loomed, Chinese involvement in the passive resistance campaign was brought sharply into focus. Chan Tong, one of the few Chinese who had registered, returned his new papers to officials, saying he had made a 'terrible mistake' and the only way he could right this sin against his countrymen was to surrender his certificate and leave the country. He had traded in the Transvaal for 12 years, since 1895, and had registered because he feared losing his trading rights. His letter to the authorities concluded:

> In bidding goodbye, therefore, to this inhospitable country, the only regret I have is that, perforce, I must leave my brave countrymen to fight the cause of freedom and humanity, and that I cannot take part in it because I was advised that the Asiatic certificate, which is truly described as the badge of slavery, once granted cannot be forfeited by its owner.[45]

But for another Chinese who had taken out the new registration papers, suicide seemed the only solution. Chow Kwai For, a 24-year-old servant, hanged himself on 11 November 1907 in his employer's home in Derby Street, Bertrams, Johannesburg. He explained his reasons in a suicide letter to the Chinese Association. At Chow's funeral, Leung Quinn expressed the community's outrage and dismissed suggestions that Chow had been threatened in any way.

> But what is the moral of this, to us, tremendous tragedy? I must call a spade a spade. This is not an occasion when I can possibly use soft words: and I do deliberately charge the Transvaal Government with the murder of an innocent man, and this only because he was an Asiatic. The Asiatic Act has already begun to tell upon us materially. It has now exacted blood.[46]

The first casualty of the new law attracted more than passing attention from quarters outside the Asiatic communities. The Bloemfontein *Friend* newspaper commented that for Whites who saw Asiatics as 'callous and soulless', the recent suicide would come as a shock:

Chow Kwai For

The story of how Chow Kwai For met his end in Johannesburg began in London in November 1903. Dr F.C. Sutherland, a medical practitioner, of Blenheim Crescent, Kensington, London, wrote to the Assistant Colonial Secretary in Pretoria stating that he wished to move to Johannesburg 'and I wish to take out with me my Chinese servant, he is at present here with me in England.' A year later, in October 1904, Chow, whose full name was also written as 'Quai Wah' arrived in Durban, aboard the *S.S. Saxon*. He was granted a special pass to journey by train through Natal to Johannesburg's Park Station.

From 1904 to 1907, Chow worked for Dr Sutherland who had taken up residence at 20 Derby Road, Bertrams. Originally from Hoi Nan (Hainan) Island which lies south of the Chinese mainland, he spoke a different dialect to that of the mainly Cantonese Chinese in Johannesburg. This would have made it difficult for him to communicate with and mix freely among the local Chinese — a fact he mentioned in his suicide letter.

At the inquest into Chow's death in November 1907, Dr Sutherland testified that Chow had worked for him as a domestic servant for seven years. Dr Sutherland had taken Chow to register in terms of the new law two weeks previously and thought Chow had hanged himself because of this.

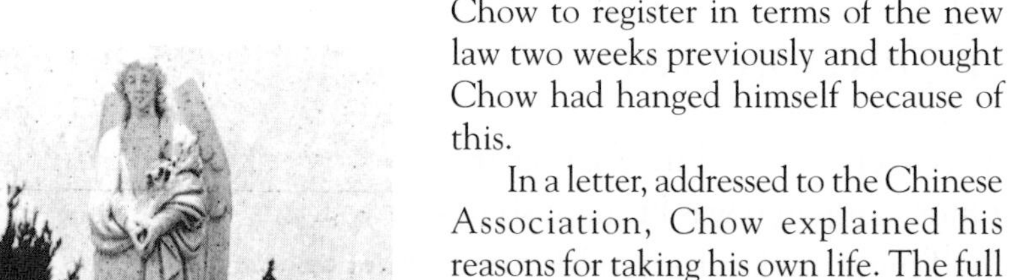

The Chinese community paid £200 for this tombstone in the Braamfontein cemetery, Johannesburg, to honour Chow Kwai For 'who committed suicide for conscience sake'.

In a letter, addressed to the Chinese Association, Chow explained his reasons for taking his own life. The full text is reproduced in Chinese on his tombstone. It read:

> 'I am going to leave the world, but I must give a public explanation why I intend to commit suicide. Therefore, I address this letter to my countrymen. Since I came to South Africa, I have only been in domestic service. My dialect is quite different from that of my countrymen, with whom I have very seldom associated. I am always in the house of my employer, who had advised me to re-register. At first I refused to do so, but I was informed that I would be dismissed from my employment. I thought that I should have to lose my situation. Therefore, I was obliged to re-register, but I did not know the degradation that

would follow until my friend talked to me about the registration matter and showed me the translation of the law. I found that I would be treated as a slave, which would be a disgrace to myself and my nation. I was not aware of all this before. Now it is too late for me to repent. I cannot look my countrymen in the face. I hope all my countrymen will take warning by my error.'[47]

The simplicity and finality of Chow's last words added impetus to the mood of resistance. For his funeral the Chinese Association organized a traditional memorial service. Chinese inscriptions were hung on the walls of the TCA headquarters, and a portrait of Chow, painted on silk, was prominently placed over an altar of flowers and burning sandalwood.[48]

Describing the occasion, Gandhi wrote:

'No one present ... could help feeling admiration for the Chinese. Their beautiful hall was adorned with black cloth. On one side in the hall there was a photograph of the Chinaman who had died. In the centre were standing all those who had served as pickets. Surrounding them on all sides were chairs which were occupied by invitees. About a thousand Chinese, with flowers in their hands, gently passed by the photograph, praying for the soul of the departed one and went out through the door opposite. Then they sang dirges in Chinese ... Their unity, neatness and courage — all these three things deserve to be emulated by us.'[49]

A year after Chow's death, the Chinese community paid for the erection of the tombstone on his grave. At that time, two large statues of sleeping lions were placed at the foot of the stone, but these were either removed or stolen sometime in the next 80 years. Some Chinese have said the lions were not a good omen which could possibly explain their removal.

> The man we refer to was known as Chow Kwai For, a name which from its uncouthness, as also its connotation of a yellow and barbarous humanity, few Europeans could hear pronounced without smiling contemptuously. Chow Kwai For had in him, however, as the event proved, that stoical sense of honour which has extorted through the centuries the admiration of Christian readers for the great Roman suicides. He thought life not worth keeping if emptied of self respect.[50]

The *Transvaal Weekly Illustrated* on 16 November 1907 interpreted the suicide as a peculiarly Oriental means of 'saving face', and said:

> To those who understand the tortuous workings of the Oriental mind there is nothing peculiar in this rehabilitation by suicide, and, in fact, an authority on Chinese and their ways predicted some time ago that if there were any registrations among them they would very likely be followed by suicide as soon as they ascertained that they had 'lost face'. The Chinese ethics of suicide are certainly incomprehensible to the European.

Leung Quinn promptly repudiated these comments saying as a Chinese he was not aware of suicide being common in China. The Chinese regarded human life as valuable and only ended it 'when they are driven to desperation by much the same causes as induce suicides amongst Europeans.'[51]

ARRESTS AND IMPRISONMENTS

The final deadline for registration arrived and Asiatics waited for the government to take action. General Smuts however stood firmly against any repeal of the law. He said about 5000 Asiatics had already left the Transvaal from 'sheer fright', and that firm but fair measures had to be taken against those who refused to register. He cited three courses of action — the refusal of trading licences, imprisonment and deportation.[52]

Defending his call to passive resistance, Gandhi said he wished to promote the welfare of the country, but maintained that 'the method of passive resistance adopted to combat the mischief is the cleanest and safest, because, if the cause is not true, it is the resisters, and they alone, who suffer.'[53]

Meanwhile, the Immigrants Restriction Act was granted the royal assent. This allowed for those who had not registered to be declared prohibited immigrants, to be prevented from acquiring trading licences and from owning and leasing property. At the same time orders were issued for the arrest of Asiatics who did not hold registration certificates.

The first three Chinese charged were Leung Quinn, Martin Easton and John Fortoen who appeared in court with many Indians, including Gandhi. Passing sentence, magistrate H. H. Jordan pointed out the law allowed him to order them to leave the colony, failing which they faced varying jail terms. He said he hoped

> that a little common sense would be shown in these matters, and that the Asiatic population of the Colony would realise that they could not trifle and play with the Government. If they did they would find that when an individual set himself up against the will of the State, the State was stronger than the individual, and the individual suffered and not the State.[54]

Martin Easton said he objected to registration 'because it was too degrading and was against his religion.'[55] As a Taoist, he was not permitted to give his fingerprints. He was ordered to leave the colony within 48 hours. John Fortoen, aged 21, told the court he arrived in the Transvaal as a child and lived there for 13 years before going to study at the Hankey Institution, near Humansdorp in the Cape. He was ordered to leave the Transvaal within seven days. Leung Quinn told the court he had been expecting prosecution, had made all his preparations and was content to be given 48 hours notice to leave. The magistrate ordered him to leave the colony within 14 days.

Since none of the passive resisters intended to follow the court's orders, namely to leave the colony, the stage was set for them to follow through their resolve and face imprisonment. Both the British Indians and Chinese held mass meetings to rally their supporters and also to examine the implications of the Immigrants Restriction Act, described as 'the new phase of the struggle'.[56]

Throughout January 1908 more arrests followed. The acting chairman of the TCA, J.L. Wengsee, was arrested with Ho Ling, Lu Chin and 13 other Chinese and charged with being in the Transvaal without a permit. They were all ordered to leave the colony within 14 days. In Pretoria three Chinese pickets, F. Foote, Affan and Tamsen, were arrested outside the Registry for Asiatics in Pretorius Street. Another eight — Ah Sing, Tay Sing, Kwang Chow, Ho Ford, Ah On, Ah Chew, Ho Wing Sun and Pun San Wing — were charged with not having registration certificates.[57]

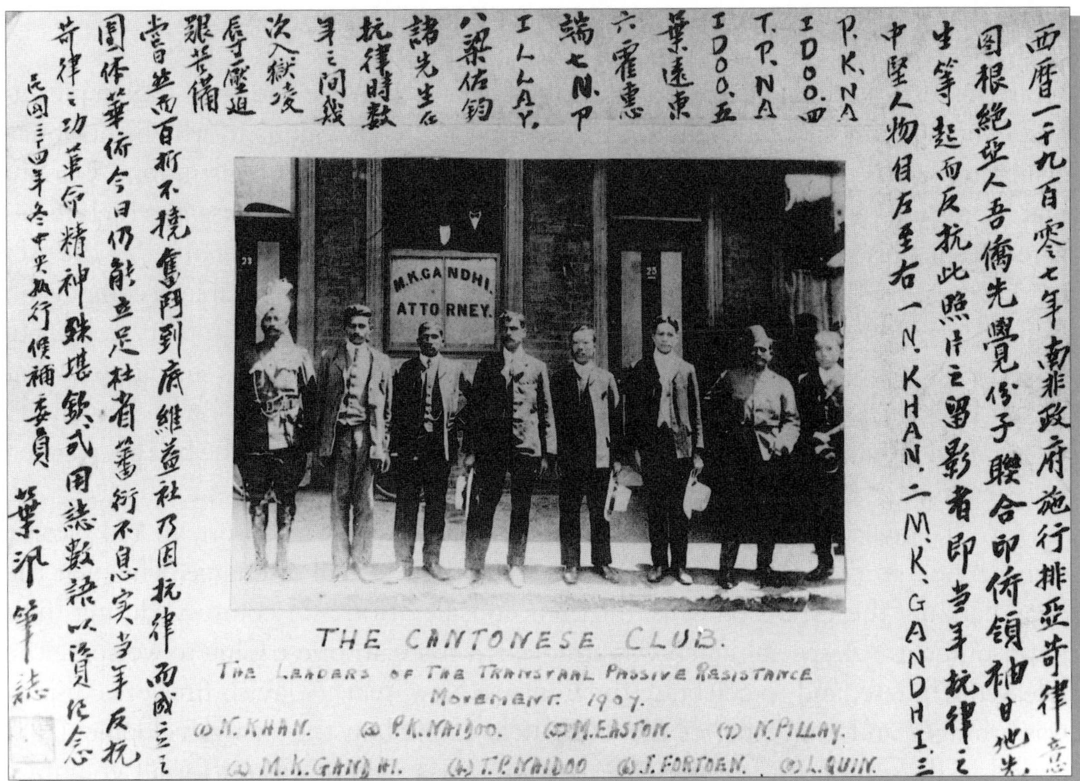

A large framed copy of this photograph hung in the Cantonese Club premises in Ferreirastown, Johannesburg, for many years but has since been lost. The Chinese inscription states:

'In 1907 the Transvaal government proclaimed the Anti-Asiatic law, aimed to exterminate Asiatics. We Chinese, with enough foresight, joined the Indian leaders to oppose the law. This photograph is a memento of the time and the core of the people who started this campaign. They are, from left to right, N. Khan, M.K. Gandhi, P.K. Naidoo, T.P. Naidoo, M. Easton (Yip Yan Dung), J. Fortoen (Fok Why Toen), N. Pillay and L. Quin (Leong Dzo Quan).

During the resistance period, they went to jail many times. Even though humiliated, they were not defeated. The Cantonese Club was established because of this resistance stance. The community today can still hold its head up in the Transvaal because of the stand taken by these people. We must recognize and respect their spirit and these few words pay tribute to their memory.'

Dated Winter, 34th year of the Republic of China (1945).

This was signed by Yip Sin who was a teacher and secretary of the Kuomintang in Johannesburg.

Those who had already been ordered to leave were jailed for refusing to obey the court's orders. Leung Quinn, Martin Easton and John Fortoen were each sentenced to two months' imprisonment with hard labour, as was Gandhi. Asiatic traders went about their businesses without trading licences since only those who had registered qualified for these documents.

The situation had reached an impasse. As one observer has noted:

> The conscious breaking of the law by a whole community and the demand by the transgressors that they be allowed to pay the maximum penalty was so novel and foreign to the bureaucratic mind that it tended to produce panic.[58]

COMPROMISE AND VOLUNTARY REGISTRATION

From the Johannesburg jail, Gandhi, Thami Naidoo, who was the chief Indian picket, and Leung Quinn addressed a letter to Colonial Secretary Smuts in which they once again proposed the concept of voluntary as opposed to compulsory registration.[59] Gandhi met Smuts in Pretoria and the result of the meeting was a compromise in which it was agreed that those who registered voluntarily would not have the penalties of the Act enforced against them. The compromise therefore removed the principle of compulsion from registration and allowed for educated persons, merchants and property holders to give their signatures rather than fingerprints. Much controversy has surrounded what in fact happened at this meeting since Gandhi later claimed he had offered voluntary registration provided the hated Act was repealed. Smuts denied that he had ever agreed to repealing the Act.

On 31 January 1908, after spending just over two weeks in prison, all 153 passive resisters held in the Johannesburg Fort received their formal discharge. They left the jail, thanking the prison officials 'for their consideration and courtesy' during their imprisonment.[60] A special lunch was arranged at the Cantonese Club to welcome the released Chinese, and to celebrate the Chinese New Year. A lavish fireworks display was arranged and a meeting of the TCA held to explain the new developments. A period of three months, from 10 February to 10 May 1908, was set for all voluntary registrations.

Asiatics were, however, not unanimous in their attitude towards voluntary registration. Many Mohammedans objected to fingerprinting and the Chinese too refused to compromise on this point. The chief Chinese picket, Yam Chow, said he had 80 pickets who were determined not to offer separate impressions of each finger and thumb. He stipulated:

> As soon as the Government decide to accept two thumb impressions ... we will register, but not before.[61]

Describing the Chinese as holding aloof, a newspaper remarked the situation was rather delicate. It said fewer than 10 Chinese could claim exemption from the fingerprint requirements of the law on the grounds of their education.[62] Gandhi himself regarded the Chinese stand on fingerprints as unnecessary. He said, 'The more the Chinese persist in such childish obstinacy, the more they lose their good name'.[63]

For the authorities the Chinese objections were merely a minor obstacle and their attitude reflects the extent to which the size of the community has nearly always limited its political bargaining position. Governor of the Transvaal, Selborne, stated:

> Some trouble is being experienced through the unwillingness of the Chinese residents of Johannesburg to accept the agreement made with the Government, but I do not anticipate that this trouble will be of long duration, and in any case, their numbers are not sufficiently large to render their obstinacy a cause of very serious embarrassment.[64]

The Chinese Consul-General, Liu Ngai, with Leung Quinn and others petitioned the government to accept two thumb prints from Chinese. The government conceded the point, and a meeting of the community was held where it was decided to issue placards urging everyone to register without delay.[65]

Registration officials suddenly found themselves inundated with work. Several were sent to the TCA headquarters to carry out the registration of Chinese there.[66] By the end of February 1908 practically all the Chinese had registered in terms of the compromise and 946 applications had been submitted to the registrar.

When the three-month deadline for voluntary registrations expired, a total of 9158 of the estimated 10 000 to 12 000 Indians had registered voluntarily. Now Asiatics anxiously awaited the repeal of the Asiatic Law Amendment Act. Their hopes were, however, not to be fulfilled. Instead, only amendments legalizing voluntary registration were included in the original Act and the law itself remained in force. Asiatics were incensed by what they regarded as a breach of faith on the part of the government. The situation was aptly summarized thus:

> Without the repeal of Act 2, the mailed fist was too apparent behind the velvet glove, and the thin veil of self-respect provided by the concept of a totally voluntary registration was forfeited. [67]

PASSIVE RESISTANCE RESUMED

Indians and Chinese who had registered voluntarily requested the return of their application forms. They pointed out the compromise had been based on an understanding that the registration act would be repealed. Gandhi accepted personal responsibility for the position which had once again necessitated the revival of passive resistance, 'to undergo the same measure of suffering, only far more bitterly.' He said:

> I am responsible for it, responsible because I had too great faith in the statesmanship of General Smuts, in his honesty, and in his integrity ... they gauge me by the result of my action, the result of having foisted the compromise on the whole of the Indian community, and I include also the Chinese community, because although there were two other gentlemen [Leung Quinn and Naidoo] who signed the letter that was addressed to General Smuts, they did so fully believing in my own good faith, fully believing that what I was doing was what they were all working for, namely the repeal of the Act not only in word but in deed ...[68]

Colonial Secretary Smuts said he wanted to meet the Asiatics as far as possible, provided this did not conflict with the essential objects of the Act. Many Asiatics were, however, still entering the colony illegally, and on Gandhi's promise to revive passive resistance, Smuts concluded:

> I have however good grounds for believing that in this fresh phase of his agitation he will not have the same degree of support as previously. The Mahommedan community especially appear to be weary of him and think that he is looking after his personal aggrandisement and his pocket more than after their interests.[69]

Indians took to hawking without licences to court arrest, and Leung Quinn with members of the TCA executive followed the same line of action.[70] On 16 August 1908 a mass meeting of more than 3000 Indians was held at the Hamidia Mosque in

Johannesburg. Leung Quinn and another dozen Chinese sat grim-faced in a front row. All those who held voluntary registration certificates ceremonially placed them in a huge cauldron which was then doused with paraffin and set alight. In a front page report on the meeting, the *Indian Opinion* stated:

> The ceremony of burning the certificates has been described as a soul-stirring event. The enthusiasm of the people was unbounded ... Passive resistance has not been unknown to Indians or to the Chinese, though the application of it in the Transvaal is certainly new, but we think that the struggle has assumed this particular form because the races who are engaged in it are submissive ... They have no voice in, or control over the legislation affecting them. In such circumstances they have adopted a weapon worthy of any submissive race.[71]

The compromise was over and this time the passive resistance campaign was directed not only at the refusal of the government to repeal the Asiatic Law Amendment Act, but also against the Immigrants Restriction Act.

Asiatics gathered to burn their voluntary registration certificates in a huge cauldron (top right) after the government refused to repeal the hated Asiatic Law Amendment Act.

SPLIT IN CHINESE COMMUNITY

For the Chinese, however, the call to resume resistance split the community. Two factions emerged from the ranks of the TCA — 'some being in favour of acquiescing in the Act, while others advocated a continuance of the policy of opposition to the Act and of passive resistance.'[72]

At a meeting on 23 August 1908, a week after the public declaration by the Indians to continue with passive resistance, some TCA members challenged Leung Quinn's right to speak on behalf of the community. They claimed he had defied a majority decision to comply with the law. It was finally agreed that neither those for nor against passive resistance could use the association's funds until the dispute was settled.

Four months later, on 20 December 1908, three TCA office bearers, the treasurer Ho Ling, vice treasurer Tam Hung and secretary Wing Tong Cheong called a meeting at which they and members present objected to allowing funds to be used for appeals under the registration law. They passed a resolution to apply for trading licences in January 1909, to donate £400 to the Johannesburg Hospital for the erection of a special ward for the Chinese community and to send £480 to a hospital in Hong Kong for the relief of floods in Canton. The following day Leung Quinn and Foo Kimson applied for and obtained a rule nisi in the High Court preventing such disposal of the TCA's funds. A court battle followed in which the opposing parties each presented their claims to the funds totalling just over £900.

To identify the groups, one was called the 'Passive Resistance Party' and the other the 'Party of Compliance.' Leung Quinn claimed the 'Passive Resistance Party' had the support of 33 TCA members who, with others, had contributed more than £1000 to the association's funds. In papers before the court he stated the funds were for specific objects which included: the repeal of Act 2 of 1907; the relaxation of laws adversely affecting the Chinese status and securing recognition by the Transvaal government of the Chinese as members of a civilized community.

He claimed the Party of Compliance wished to dispose of the funds for purposes other than those for which the money had been donated. Defending the action, the Party of Compliance stated that the funds contributed to passive resistance were for an illegal object and as such was 'tainted money.'[73] They claimed Leung Quinn had ceased to be a member of the TCA in August 1908 and was therefore not in a position to bring the action.

Furthermore, the TCA's funds were dealt with in terms of resolutions of the members, and the decision to send money to the Chinese Hospital in Hong Kong for the relief of floods in Canton was within the objects of the association to spend money for public benefit. Denying that individual members had control over funds in the name of the association, they said the TCA was a purely social and charitable body which did not create legal obligations between it and its members.[74] In his judgment, Sir William Solomon froze the funds of the organization. He upheld the Passive Resistance Party's claims and ruled that office bearers be restrained from disposing of any part of the funds.

Sweet Revenge

Whether they were trying to make a point or merely to aid the less fortunate, the Chinese decided early in 1908 to donate a sum of 100 guineas to the Rand Aid Association 'to alleviate the distress amongst the white population of Johannesburg'.[75] Announcing the contribution, the chairman of the Transvaal Chinese Association, Leung Quinn, added that if further help was required, another donation would be made.

Commenting on this incident, a newspaper in England remarked:

> 'A piquant feature of the Asiatic question in the Transvaal was a gift recently of 100 gns. by the Chinese community there to the association formed for relief of the unemployed white population — that is to say, for the citizens who are insistently clamouring for the exclusion from the colony of all races and classes of Asiatics. The Chinese are ill to beat in diplomacy.'[76]

This donation set a precedent for another group of White workers who promptly approached the Chinese for assistance in their 'hour of need'. Stating that they intended marching to Pretoria to request minimum pay scales for Whites, members of the 'Unemployed Organization' paid a call on Leung Quinn. It is not known whether or not a donation was made to their cause, but Leung Quinn paid for the convoy waggon which transported them to the meeting.[77]

RIOTS IN CHINATOWN

The temporary court victory for the passive resisters sparked off a violent escalation of the dispute just two days later. On Sunday, 18 April 1909 a pitched battle erupted between the resisters and non-resisters in the Chinese quarter of Ferreirastown, Johannesburg. Armed with revolvers, knives, sticks, stones and iron bars, the opposing factions attacked each other, inflicting wounds which left four Chinese in hospital and led to 29 arrests.

Under the colourful headlines, 'Riot with Revolvers — Chinese 'Passive Resisters' Run Amok ... A Chase over Roofs', the *Rand Daily Mail* described how between 40 and 50 Chinese engaged in a fierce gun battle.

> The leaders on either side exchanged a few words ... and then the revolvers leapt from their pockets and the shooting began.[78]

According to the police, a group of 24 Cantonese was celebrating a national feast at the TCA headquarters at 2, Marshall Street when they were told that another group was approaching from the Cantonese Club in Alexander Street to attack them.

> They sallied forth, some with firearms, others with stones and sticks. The opposing force was met somewhere near 6, Alexander Street, another Cantonese Club, and here, with very little parley a battle royal commenced in real earnest...[79]

In this vein newspapers gave graphic descriptions of the riots, saying it was clear that the Chinese community was not short of revolvers.

> During the melee... something like 50 revolver shots were indiscriminately fired ... For nearly half an hour the streets in which the Cantonese clubs abound presented a very wild appearance...[80]

Hundreds of spectators gathered, attracted by the hubbub and confusion. The police were alerted and amid the piercing shriek of whistles, charged through the crowds. The scenes are best recaptured in various newspaper reports. The *Rand Daily Mail* said:

> Firing ceased immediately the alarm of the approaching police reached the ears of the combatants, and with remarkable celerity the yellow men disappeared among the houses on either side of the street. The police threw a cordon round the premises, and a quick search was organised. Soon the scrambling, falling figures of a couple of Chinamen appeared above the roof of a house. Others began to try the same method of escape, but the active police had little difficulty in securing them.[81]

The *Transvaal Weekly Illustrated* added:

> Even on the appearance of the officers some of the most desperate ... kept up the fire, one even going so far as to point his revolver at an officer and fire ... Some scenes of an extraordinarily lively character were witnessed during the rounding-up of the combatants. For instance, Constable Franzin tackled a couple of Cantonese on the first-floor verandah of one of the clubs, and during the fierce struggle which ensued the railing of the verandah gave way, and the unfortunate constable was precipitated into the roadway. Fortunately, however, he escaped with only a shaking.[82]

Whichever side was to blame, at least four Chinese were taken to hospital and several more probably declined to report their injuries.[83] Those with gunshot wounds were Ton Kai, Man Haing, Quan To and Wong Shan Cheong. The police arrested 29 Chinese, and patrolled Ferreirastown to keep a close watch for further disturbances. The following morning another scuffle broke out in a yard between Fox and Main streets.[84]

While in custody at the Johannesburg Fort, those arrested for involvement in the disturbances were confronted with demands that they register in terms of the hated 'Black Act.' In an incident described as 'something singularly like foul play', an inspector of the Asiatic Registration Department visited the prisoners to register them. All except one refused which led to them being charged under the registration act, as well as taking part in the disturbances. The registration charges were later dropped. Commenting that the police showed antipathy towards the passive resisters, the *Indian Opinion* reported five resisters were on bail of £500 and others on £100 whereas members of the party of compliance had been released on bail ranging from £5 to £50.[85]

TRIAL, CONVICTIONS AND COMPROMISE

In the trial which followed, the judge described the evidence given by both the resisters and non-resisters as 'absolutely incredible'. He said even if the riot had been started by the non-resisters, 'people were not entitled to have a pitched battle in the streets because they had a quarrel to settle.'[86]

Twenty-six Chinese, all supporters of passive resistance, were charged in the High

Court with public violence. Addressing the jury, the judge said they should remember that all the evidence against the accused was brought by the non-resisters who had told a remarkable story.

> They said they had been to a peaceful feast of 'Ho' and were returning to their homes or the Cantonese Club when suddenly the resisters came upon them with revolvers and began firing at them without any provocation whatever. He thought it was an absolutely incredible story. On the other hand the story told by the defence was equally incredible, that the accused should have locked themselves in their rooms without taking any note of what was going on outside. It was for the jury to decide whether they could believe the prisoners or the evidence of the Chinese witnesses. Those witnesses never saw one of the non-resisters fire a shot, a fact which he thought made their testimony extremely doubtful...
>
> ... it was quite clear to him that the non-resisters had been a good deal smarter than the other side. That they had got on the side of the police and got the police to arrest the other side. Not a single non-resister apparently was taken into custody until a special complaint had been made. It seemed to be that having regard to the strong feeling between the parties it would be dangerous to rely on the evidence of people hostile to the accused for their conviction.[87]

The jury found 17 guilty, and 9 not guilty. Passing sentence, the judge said those found guilty had committed a serious offence, injuring two people and firing on the

Press reports provided dramatic coverage of the 1908 riot in Ferreirastown when Chinese in favour of and others opposed to passive resistance fought gun battles in the streets.

RIOT WITH REVOLVERS.

CHINESE "PASSIVE RESISTERS" RUN AMOK.

5 PERSONS WOUNDED.

A CHASE OVER ROOFS.

Between five and six afternoon forty to fifty in a fight with revolv Street. four of them while a Jew who was received a bullet wou present there are offenders lodged in pected that further before the matte courts.

During the riot were attracted the police we

RAND POLICE COURTS.

THE CHINESE RIOT.

PASSIVE RESISTERS PUZZLED.

...CE COURT PROCEEDINGS.

...liminary enquiry into the ...s of the Ferreirastown a number of Chinese revolvers

THE CHINESE RIOT.

The locality of the Chinese riot Sunday evening — Ferreirastown larger number of po

DISCONTENTED CHINESE.

Riot in Ferreirastown.

Four Men Wounded.

A quarrel which has been simmering for some time between sections of the Cantonese community in Ferreirastown brought to a head meeting of a lar of each

THE TRANSVAAL WEE...

CANTONESE RIOT

SCENE IN FERREIRASTOWN

REVOLVERS FIRED FREELY

WHITE MAN AND FOUR CANTONESE INJURED

THIRTY-ONE ARRESTS MADE

THE CHINESE RIOT.

"KNIVES AND REVOLVERS."

The preliminary examination into the charge against 29 Chinamen of rioting in Ferreirastown on Sunday last was resumed before Mr. Van den Berg in "A" Court yesterday. Mr. Samuels prosecuted and Mr. Benson defended.

police. Although he had made allowance for their feelings being 'much excited', he had to impose severe punishment. Seven were sentenced to prison terms ranging from nine months to seven years with hard labour, while ten were fined £15 each or two months' imprisonment with hard labour.

Commenting on the case, the *Indian Opinion* described the sentences as appalling and said they seemed to be 'altogether out of proportion' to the offences. Reviewing the judge's remarks, the paper said it was difficult to prove the guilt of the accused and the question arose whether those most actively involved were in fact arrested.[88] Claims that the police had taken the side of the non-resisters continued to surface. Since the judge had himself pointed out that the non-resisters 'had got on the side of the police', it is interesting to compare how the non-resisters fared for their part in the disturbances.

Of 13 arrested, only 5 were eventually charged in a magistrate's court, not with public violence, but on a lesser count of breach of the peace. And, 'after warning them all to be good boys, and not to do it again, the Magistrate, in his discretion, sent them away free to their homes'.[89]

This was the description offered by Advocate Alex S. Benson who had represented the passive resisters in their trial. In a lengthy letter to the daily newspaper, the *Transvaal Leader*, he stated the handling of the two cases showed a new method in the administration of justice. Although it was not for him to say who started the fighting, he suggested, on the day of the riot, the party of compliance 'were probably smarting under a sense of defeat' after the passive resisters' victory in the civil courts over the use of the TCA's funds. Nearly all the passive resisters charged had been 'pointed out for arrest to the police by members of the party of compliance.' Only after sworn affidavits had been made by victims or eyewitnesses were 13 members of the party of compliance arrested.

Benson questioned why the two groups had been tried separately since 'whatever crime each party had committed had been committed under exactly the same conditions.' He also pointed out the passive resisters' trial judge had expressed regret that the police had not seen fit to collect evidence from both sides in connection with the riot.[90]

The dispute over the TCA's funds, frozen by the High Court order, was resolved by a settlement between the two parties. It was agreed that of the association's funds totalling £936-18-0, a sum of £400 would be handed over to Rev J.J. Doke, Rev Charles Phillips and Liu Ngai, Acting Chinese Consul-General for British South Africa, for establishing a Chinese ward in the Johannesburg Hospital. Arrear rents on the TCA's premises at 2 Marshall Street and the caretaker's wages would be paid. The balance would be jointly controlled by Ho Ling, representing the party of compliance, and Fok Shau Tsun, representing the passive resistance party, with payments only being made by resolutions passed at meetings of both parties. It was further agreed each party would pay its own costs in the High Court litigation. Leung Quinn and Foo Kimson represented the passive resistance party while Wing Tong Cheong, Ho Ling, Ah Kie and L. T. Chue represented the party of compliance. The agreement was made an order of court on 21 July 1909.[91]

PASSIVE RESISTERS CONTINUE STRUGGLE

Leung Quinn and his followers continued to ally themselves with Gandhi and the efforts of the British Indian Association to obtain the repeal of Act 2 of 1907 and a number of other concessions relating to Asiatic immigration. Both the Indians and Chinese pointed out they did not wish to have unrestricted Asiatic immigration into the Transvaal.[92] In February 1909 Leung Quinn was arrested for failing to produce a registration certificate. Faced with a £50 fine or three months in jail with hard labour, he opted for imprisonment. Leadership of the Chinese passive resisters was taken over by Chion Fan James Frank, a Chinese from Vereeniging.

Presiding over an enthusiastic meeting of more than 200 Chinese on 10 March 1909, James Frank congratulated both Gandhi and Leung Quinn for going to jail 'for the sake of conscience and honour' and confirmed the determination of the Chinese 'to continue this struggle, till the bitter end.' He said the Chinese had not borne the brunt of the struggle because they represented a minority of the Asiatic population, but their hearts were as much in it as their fellow Asiatics. Quite independent of the British Indians, they were nevertheless 'united in a common struggle for existence.'[93] James Frank also objected to an agreement with Portuguese authorities allowing for deportations from the Transvaal via Mocambique, directly to India and China. Claiming this was contrary to the spirit of treaty rights, he said the Chinese passive resisters would cable their protest to the Chinese Minister in London.[94] By March 1909, the Registrar of Asiatics had on file the names of at least 32 Chinese under sentence of deportation from the colony.[95]

Government statistics on the numbers of Asiatics in jail did not differentiate between passive resisters and other prisoners. For the Chinese therefore, the numbers are inordinately high, but these would obviously have included prisoners among the Chinese indentured labourers working on the Reef gold mines from 1904.

Average numbers of Indians and Chinese confined in Transvaal jails from 1902 to 1908:

	Indian Males	Chinese Males
1902-3	19.3	—
1903-4	Statistics not available	
1904-5	40.2	202.3
1905-6	41.1	1089.0
1906-7	54.3	1206.5
1907-8	64.9	885.5

(Source: Cd. 4564)[96]

To add to their problems the passive resisters also had to contend with the animosity of fellow Chinese who kept authorities informed of the names and addresses of those who had burned their registration certificates.[97] James Frank represented the Chinese passive resisters at public meetings, under the name of a new organization the 'Chinese Reform Union.'[98] Like Leung Quinn, he too took advantage of the press to express his

This photograph, published in a Johannesburg newspaper in 1908, was captioned: 'The recalcitrant Chinese of Pretoria and Johannesburg, who recently went to prison for refusing to register under the Asiatic Registration Act. Mr Leong Quin (President of the Chinese Association) in the centre.'

Some of the Chinese Passive Resisters

Among the many Chinese who appeared in court in Johannesburg to answer charges for not producing registration certificates were:

Martin Easton, John Fortoen, J L Wengsee, Ming Loo Chu, Yok Chu, Chan Narn, Hoi Ling, Pook Tim, Leary Kang, Chan Pak Wah, Sang Kai Yuen, Fook Tim, Leong Chin, Lo Tim, Sing For, Fook Ding, Sam Chu, A Tong, Lung Too, Cha Yok Chea, Cha Narm, Hoo Sing.

Chinese arrested for picketing or not producing certificates in Pretoria were: F. Foote, Affan, Tam Sen, Ah Sing, Tay Sing, Kwang Chow, Ho Ford, Ah On, Ah Chew, Ho Wing Sun, Pun San Wing.

Over the next years Chinese who were jailed or deported included: A. Yee, T. Foolee, L. Johnson, Leong King, Lawson, Leong Sing, Leon Wan, Ah Young, Lam Sing, Leong Long, Leung Tun, Mah Hoy, Chan Chue, Hok Loe Hin, Chan Soo, Shum Ki, Joseph Cowhee, Ah Fook, Martin Easton, Ah San, Leong Tchu, Ah Hung, Leong Yung, Wo Tung, Ah Chan, Ah Ching, Ah How, Wong Ying, Luk Nan, Lai Tomai, Law Pa, Chu Fat, Ho Long, Hong Kong, Ah Yong.

Chinese passive resisters arrested and sentenced to hard labour at either the Fort or Diepkloof prisons on or after 18 March 1911, included:

C.F.J. Frank, Lee Kong, Luk Nan Dickson, Ho Low, Sam You, Chong Ah Kie, Wo Kim, Ah Wy.

opinions and challenged the government to act against the passive resisters. Claiming the government was apparently afraid to arrest the leaders of the Chinese who were free and were known to the authorities, he said his members were prepared to come forward and would be 'glad to receive the highest penalty that the Law can impose, even though it mean absolute financial ruin and deportation from the Colony.'[99]

His letter was written as acting chairman of the Transvaal Chinese Passive Resisters and was countersigned by the secretary, C. Canteen and three committee members — F. Kimson, Martin Easton and H.K. Lee. In the following months, Chinese passive resisters continued to submit to imprisonment. In Vereeniging, James Frank was 're-consigned to prison for six weeks with hard labour', both Martin Easton and John Fortoen took advantage of the government's hospitality, as did at least another 40 Chinese.[100]

When 9 Chinese were arrested in the Cantonese Club at the end of August 1909, another 100 offered themselves up for arrest. The *Indian Opinion* reported the occurrence under the heading 'Our Friends the Chinese':

> We note with pleasure that our staunch friends, the Chinese Passive Resisters, are again to the front. When nine were arrested last week, at least a hundred offered themselves to the police, and were disappointed that their company as prisoners was not required. We congratulate Mr Leung Quinn and his compatriots on this fresh proof of their loyalty to the cause.[101]

Prison Diet

The most unpalatable part of imprisonment for Chinese passive resisters was the food they were given in jail. They were fed the standard daily prison diet for Blacks which consisted of mealie meal porridge for breakfast, mealie meal porridge or beans on alternate days for lunch and crushed mealies with fat for supper. Indian prisoners were permitted rice and ghee (clarified butter) instead of crushed mealies.

Gandhi said that neither Chinese nor Indians were used to eating mealie porridge, especially without milk or sugar. For most prisoners the diet meant 'practically starvation' and even when it was eaten resulted either in constipation or diarrhoea. He added the Chinese fared worse because they had no rice at all.[102]

The Chinese themselves complained that the mealie meal porridge diet was 'calculated to induce sickness among Chinese' and appealed for it to be substituted by rice and bread.[103] Leung Quinn conveyed this request to Acting Chinese Consul-General, Liu Ngai, saying:

> 'If therefore, Cantonese prisoners are condemned to exist upon a diet which is in every sense of the word repugnant to them — a diet which no other civilised country in the world would force upon them — a diet which is actually detrimental to their physical wellbeing, then imprisonment of hard labour must of necessity mean an intrinsically heavier punishment to the Chinese and other Asiatics than it does to the other races of mankind who may suffer imprisonment in Transvaal gaols.'[104]

Liu Ngai wrote to the Attorney-General of the Transvaal describing the passive resisters as 'political prisoners' and appealing for a diet which was more in accord with Chinese habits and customs. He was informed that Chinese could choose between the Black or Indian diet.[105]

Leung Quinn called a meeting attended by about 300 supporters who passed resolutions reaffirming their commitment to passive resistance and congratulated those 'who have obtained the opportunity of going to gaol rather than prostitute their manhood to the demands of an unjust legislation.' The meeting also expressed concern over prison conditions and the prison diet and requested that Chinese prisoners be given rice and bread instead of mealie meal porridge.[106]

IN AND OUT OF JAIL

Arrests of passive resisters continued with 27 Chinese being detained at the end of August 1909 and another 80 in a mass arrest in mid-September. Describing this as the first time such a large number of passive resisters had been arrested in one place and at the same time, Gandhi said government actions had only served to strengthen the Asiatics' resolve.[107]

Leung Quinn was among this group which had been arrested en masse on the Cantonese Club premises. They promptly challenged the legality of the search warrant and the police action. A magistrate ruled, three weeks later, that they had been unlawfully arrested on private premises. Defending the Chinese decision not simply to submit to arrest, Leung Quinn said the Chinese were quite willing to suffer imprisonment but objected to the illegal methods used by the police. He stated these methods brought 'discredit on the Chinese, by making it appear as though they are criminals and need to be surprised in order to be caught.'

He added that the arrests had not awakened fear and cowardice in the community, but had 'only served to strengthen us.' Since the arrests, he said, another 100 Chinese had joined the passive resisters. The Chinese once again addressed an appeal to their compatriots internationally and passed a resolution calling on the Chinese Students Association in Europe 'to help their brethren in South Africa in this hour of need.'[108] When a Jeppe storekeeper, Ho Si, was arrested and sentenced to three months' imprisonment, he charged the police with trespass for climbing over a fence to enter his shop. The case was first dismissed in a magistrate's court, but Ho Si persisted, appealing to the Supreme Court where he won his case.[109]

Chinese continued to shuttle back and forth from prison. The *Indian Opinion's* pages reflected the steady stream daily being jailed or released for 'the usual offence', and remarked the frequent imprisonments had changed attitudes towards jail.

> In days gone by, it brought shame, humiliation and the criminal taint with it. Men edged away from the person who had 'done time' while the family of such a man felt keenly the degradation. Now the glory of heroism rests like a halo upon it — and in the Transvaal the man who has not been to gaol is the questionable character.[110]

In mid-December 1909, James Frank was released from Vereeniging Prison after serving practically six months of continuous imprisonment. He was met by the new acting chairman of the Chinese passive resisters, Lai Koen. He was admitted to hospital for treatment shortly afterwards, but less than a month later, was again arrested. Of him, the *Indian Opinion* wrote:

> Mr Frank is yet far from well. He says that he would rather die in gaol suffering for his countrymen than as a discharged prisoner in a hospital. Mr Frank is perfectly ready to go to gaol as often as the Government would take him. As he remarks, his body is at the disposal of the Government so that he might hold his soul free.[111]

Leung Quinn was released from Diepkloof jail at the end of January 1910 after serving yet another three-month prison term. He was described as looking quite cheerful, stating firmly 'there was to be no rest for him until the end was gained.'[112] Remarking on the attitude of the Chinese, the *Indian Opinion* said:

> The Chinese friends are 'going strong'. Five more went to gaol last Friday. I understand that nearly 150 will find themselves in that haven of liberty at Diepkloof. The enthusiasm our Chinese friends are showing is simply wonderful.[113]

Since being arrested had become 'socially acceptable', a Chinese man held on a gambling charge claimed he too was a passive resister. James Frank had to deny that Ah Tow was part of the passive resisters or a member of the Cantonese Club.[114]

Vernonism

The word 'Vernonism' was coined by the *Indian Opinion* newspaper to convey the vigour and enthusiasm with which the local Asiatic Department's police officer, Superintendent John G. Vernon, sought out Asiatics for arrest in terms of the registration laws. He was reprimanded by a magistrate for saying of Asiatics: 'I think it is a white man's duty to hunt these people out of the country.'[115]

Among Vernon's more publicized exploits were the mass arrest of some 80 Chinese at the Cantonese Club in terms of an illegal search warrant and breaking into a shopkeeper's locked premises on the pretext of searching for Asiatics without registration certificates. In an appeal in the Supreme Court, the Chief Justice ruled that Superintendent Vernon had been guilty of trespass and had used an invalid warrant which subverted elementary rights of freedom.[116]

Another controversial case involving Vernon was the incident in which one of his constables arrested a Chinese passive resister and paraded him through the streets of Vrededorp in handcuffs. The *Indian Opinion* commented that presumably the constable was merely putting into practice his superior's belief in the 'white man's duty'.[117]

Asiatics protested that it was not right for them to be placed at the mercy of such a police officer and repeatedly accused the superintendent of high-handedness in the pursuit of his duties.

DEPORTATIONS

The protracted passive resistance struggle entered a new phase when more of those arrested were placed under deportation orders instead of simply being jailed. This became for many the true test of their commitment to resistance. As Gandhi remarked, 'Not all could overcome the fear of being deported. Many more fell away and only the real fighters remained.'[118]

Chinese and Indian passive resisters on their release from the Johannesburg Fort — three Chinese on the left are John Fortoen, Martin Easton and Leung Quinn.

From June 1908, nearly 200 Asiatics were expelled — with 29 being sent to India.[119] Under order of deportation, Leung Quinn addressed a petition in April 1910 to the Chinese Ambassador in London. He appealed for the ambassador's intervention with the British government to repeal 'the obnoxious law', to secure the rights of Chinese to enter the Transvaal on the same basis as Whites and to prevent further imprisonments and deportations.

He outlined the passive resistance struggle over the previous three years, saying that out of a possible population of 900 Chinese, over 150 had already suffered imprisonment, and that 20 were now facing deportation. He added that the government had a secret agreement with the neighbouring Portuguese authorities and handed over Chinese to be deported through Lourenco Marques.[120] The government contended that only those deportees who were not entitled to residence in other colonies of South Africa were shipped abroad.[121]

In May 1910 Leung Quinn and 25 other Chinese were deported to India. After landing in Colombo in early June 1910, he travelled to Rangoon 'to collect funds amongst the Chinese community there' while the 25 others went to Bombay to join compatriots.[122] He maintained his opposition to the repressive laws stating 'before we are Chinese, we are men, and we claim to be treated as men and to have our manhood recognised.' Justifying continued passive resistance, Leung Quinn said surrender would humiliate the Chinese in the eyes of posterity.

> It is often urged against us that we are a people who live in the past and that we worship our ancestors. But whilst that may be true, it is not all the truth, for we live in the present for the sake of the future ... so we ... felt that the duty of maintaining the honour of the great Asiatic nation, China, had been imposed upon us, that by accepting it courageously and worthily performing it, our children might derive inspiration from the efforts and bitter experience of their fathers before them.[123]

By the end of September 1910, many of the deported passive resisters returned to South Africa on board the *S.S. Sultan* and attempted to land at Durban. They included 22 Chinese, of whom only Martin Easton passed the educational test allowing him to land. Another two, Ho Tung and Lai Tomai, were given visiting passes but the remaining 19 were turned back to Delagoa Bay and then Bombay.[124] At the request of Consul-General Liu Ngai, a Durban Chinese storekeeper, J.L. Fontbin went on board to take provisions to the passive resisters and to speak to them.[125] The two Chinese who had successfully obtained visiting passes to be in Natal tested their rights to re-enter the Transvaal and were promptly arrested. Lai Tomai was held at Volksrust and fined £25 or six weeks' hard labour, while Ho Tung, also referred to as Ho Yong, was sentenced to three months' imprisonment with hard labour for crossing the Transvaal border at Vereeniging.[126]

In November 1910 Chinese passive resisters in Johannesburg held a meeting at the Cantonese Club to honour *Indian Opinion* editor, H. Polak, and another supporter of the campaign, L.W. Ritch.[127] When Polak undertook a journey to the Cape, the president of the Chinese Association in Port Elizabeth, W. Singson, and members of the Chinese community attended a meeting to welcome and thank him. Singson also appealed for unity among all the Asiatics in the country.[128]

By the end of December 1910, Leung Quinn too was due to return to South Africa, and the passive resisters engaged lawyers to ensure he and Leong Tung would be permitted to land in Natal.[129] To mark the occasion, the *Indian Opinion* published Leung Quinn's photograph on its front page under the headline 'Chinese Courage'.[130] After his absence of eight months, he boarded a train for the Transvaal, was arrested at the border town of Volksrust and sentenced to three months' imprisonment with hard labour for entering the Transvaal without a registration certificate.

Other passive resisters continued to court arrest for not producing registration certificates. Seventeen Chinese, who had earlier tried to land in Durban, returned aboard the *S.S. Somali* and were permitted to land on 19 February 1911. Consul-General Liu Ngai requested assistance to be given to Martin Easton who would meet the ship and pay the deposits required for the Chinese passengers' visiting passes. This time he called on the services of another Durban Chinese, S.L. Chowson, of Point Road, to pass his request on to the authorities.[131]

Leong Tung, the deportee who had returned to South Africa with Leung Quinn, accompanied Martin Easton to Natal where they welcomed the passive resisters and set off back to the Transvaal. Predictably, at Volksrust, the newly returned resisters were arrested. Imprisonment and deportations continued to be a pattern — in March 1911, James Frank was again arrested and sentenced to three months' jail with hard labour while Ah Koon, a Krugersdorp storekeeper, was deported.

PASSIVE RESISTANCE SUBSIDES

Efforts to resolve the Asiatic question continued and in February 1911 the government tabled a new Bill to consolidate the Union's immigration policy. As the new acting chairman of the TCA, Martin Easton telegraphed the Minister of the Interior stating that the Chinese, with the Indians, wanted the removal of any colour or racial bar in the new Bill, and protection to be given to the wives and children of legal residents. Furthermore the Chinese hoped the government would allow a few 'cultured Chinese' to enter the country and not to be restricted by the Chinese Exclusion Act which was enforced in the Cape.[132]

Gandhi and Smuts negotiated the suspension of the passive resistance campaign, reaching a settlement in May 1911. The terms included the repeal of Act 2 of 1907, the right of passive resisters to register and the maintenance of the existing rights of Asiatics. Chinese supported the settlement, and Gandhi asked for them to be granted the same protection as the Indians. He added: 'There are now, I think, more Chinese than Indian passive resisters in gaol.'[133] He named eight Chinese among the ten passive resisters still in jail. They were C.F.J. Frank, Lee Kong, Luk Nan Dickson, Ho Lon, Sam You, Chong Ah Kie, Wo Kui and Ah Wy.[134]

APPEAL FOR CLEMENCY

One issue the Chinese sought to resolve was the imprisonment of those convicted for public violence after the riots in Ferreirastown three years previously, in April 1908. According to the *Indian Opinion*,

> The one very satisfactory result, so far as the Chinese are concerned, that has been achieved is that the two parties into which they were unhappily divided after the renewal of the struggle in the middle of 1908 have now been re-united.[135]

Saying four Chinese were still in prison as a result of the fight between the two factions, Gandhi appealed for General Smuts to recommend the favourable consideration of an appeal for clemency.[136] Leung Quinn also addressed an appeal to the Governor-General of South Africa for the release of the prisoners. In a petition, signed by 354 Chinese in May 1911, he outlined circumstances leading up to the disturbances and said the proposed settlement had reunited the Chinese and enabled them to bury past differences.[137]

The Chinese offered to put up financial security to guarantee the future good conduct of the prisoners — Ho Yong, Leong Toy Dai, Cheong Wai and Ho Si — all being held at Diepkloof prison. The Minister of Justice said he was unable to recommend a remission of sentence on the grounds raised in the petition, and pointed out that Ho Si who had been sentenced to a two year and three month term had already been released on probation. By the end of 1911, however, the remaining three prisoners were also released.

WHAT DID PASSIVE RESISTANCE ACHIEVE?

For the Chinese, the passive resistance campaign was at an end and they were left to deal with its aftermath. The TCA maintained its nominal role as the community's representative body, but the differences which had emerged within its ranks remained alive. Despite public statements to the contrary, those who had opposed passive resistance and those who supported it parted ways, organizing themselves into separate and mutually exclusive social clubs.

The Transvaal Chinese United Club (聯衛會所)was formed in 1909, by members of the 'party of compliance' and, for at least the next 70 years, no one from the Cantonese Club (維益社)— home base of the passive resisters — was accepted as a member, or even permitted to set foot in the United Club's premises. The rift was further consolidated along ethnic lines. Since most Moiyeanese belonged to the Cantonese Club, no Moiyeanese (Hakka) was accepted as a member of the United Club.

As far as the Indians were concerned, the settlement proved to be temporary, and passive resistance was renewed two years later, in 1913, to appeal for the recognition of Indian marriages and to have the government waive a £3 tax imposed on indentured labourers in Natal. It has been said that the Chinese did not join in the renewed campaign since the issues involved were of concern only to the Indians.[138] Recalling the role of the Chinese and their leader, Leung Quinn, in later years, Gandhi however wrote:

> Many of the Chinese eventually fell away as their leader played them false. He did not indeed submit to the obnoxious law, but one morning someone came and told me that the Chinese leader had fled alway [sic] without handing over charge of the books and moneys of the Chinese Association in his possession. It is always difficult for followers to sustain a conflict in the absence of their leader, and the shock is all the greater when the leader has disgraced himself ... For some time at any rate Mr Quinn put in very useful work.[139]

Whether or not Leung Quinn betrayed the trust of the Chinese, he disappeared without trace after 1911. No Chinese in the 1990s recalled what happened to him. It is nevertheless unlikely that his 'departure' alone led to the non-participation of the Chinese in further passive resistance. One could speculate that the Chinese came to realize how little they had in fact achieved by resorting to such methods. Perhaps too the enthusiasm generated by the early, heady days of resistance had, after five years, simply burned itself out. The authorities certainly granted concessions and even repealed the contentious 'Black Act' — but, beyond winning 'moral victories', Asiatics in South Africa remained second class citizens.[140]

7

Discrimination in the Union of South Africa

How did the formation of the Union of South Africa affect the tiny Chinese population scattered around the country? What role did the Consul-General of China play in community life? From the country's unification in 1910, Chinese found themselves becoming part of an increasingly race-conscious society in which a network of laws limited their entry and restricted their place of residence and choice of occupation.

In 1910 the four self-governing British colonies of the Cape, Natal, Transvaal and Orange River were amalgamated to form the Union of South Africa under a central government. It was an alliance born of economic and political compromises to unite Boer and Briton and entrench the dominance of Whites over non-Whites.

Unification was seen as a solution to problems arising from the rapidly disintegrating system of trade relations, railway and customs tariffs between the colonies and the need for a uniform 'native policy' to secure Whites against Black uprisings.[1] Despite conflicting regional and racial concerns, representatives of each colony attended a National Convention to negotiate the terms of Union. They emerged with a unitary constitution in the British mould which converted the existing colonies into four new provinces retaining the same names except for the Orange River Colony which reverted to the Orange Free State.[2]

Distribution of power was the Convention's prime concern and, without the participation of any Blacks, Coloureds or Asiatics, it drew up a blueprint for government which limited the political rights of non-Whites and balanced the interests of rural and urban Whites.[3] Although the Cape had long extended a qualified franchise to all races and its delegates pressed for equal rights for all civilized men, the Transvaal and Orange River Colony (former Boer republics which had been annexed after the Anglo-Boer War ended in 1902) only allowed the franchise to White males. Their delegates 'insisted that there would be no union at all were the non-white vote to be extended northwards and seats in Parliament open to others than Europeans'.[4] As a compromise the Convention agreed to maintain the existing franchise laws in each province, to exclude anyone who was not of 'European descent' from Parliament and to protect non-Whites in the Cape from disenfranchisement by entrenching a two-thirds majority constitutional safeguard.[5]

The same constitutional protection was afforded to maintaining the status of English and Dutch as equal official languages. Afrikaners had long feared the erosion of their culture by anglicization and the preservation of the language was seen as vital for their survival as a distinctive national group. The burgeoning sense of Afrikaner nationalism remained a crucial element in the political mix with Afrikaners constituting well over 50% of the country's White population at the time of Union.[6] The Convention also compromised on the choice of a capital for the Union, and eventually agreed that the legislative capital would be in Cape Town, the administrative capital in Pretoria and the judicial capital in Bloemfontein.

The British Parliament passed the South Africa Act of 1909 which embodied the constitution of the Union of South Africa, and on 31 May 1910 the country became a self-governing dominion of the British Empire. The significance of the formation of Union is aptly summed up by historian Leonard Thompson:

> Any final assessment of the achievement of an imperial power must depend largely upon the sort of society it left behind when it withdrew. In withdrawing from South Africa, Great Britain left behind a caste-like society, dominated by its white minority. The price of unity and conciliation was the institutionalization of white supremacy.[7]

Legal differentiation on racial grounds remained part of the fabric of South African society affecting all groups to a greater or lesser extent. Although post-Union legislation tended to introduce uniformity in the application of laws, it generally pegged the existing state of affairs. The Natives Land Act of 1913 created a uniform policy for ownership and occupation of land by Blacks, demarcated reserves for their occupation and maintained the status quo by prohibiting Blacks from acquiring land outside the reserves. Blacks were also subject to special 'pass' laws restricting their freedom of movement. Asiatics in the Union were prohibited from moving between the provinces, except by special permit.[8]

For the Chinese the country's network of racially-based legislation affected virtually every aspect of life. From their entry into South Africa to where and how they could live and work, they faced laws which restricted their development and kept them on the fringes of the country's economic, social and political strata. Although the Chinese as a group never again resorted to the militancy displayed in their opposition to the Asiatic Law Amendment Act, they channelled political expression through the offices of the Chinese Consulate-General and the strengthening of community organizations.

The business of survival was paramount, fuelled increasingly by a desire to secure the future. In the first decades of the 20th century men who had established themselves returned to China to fetch their wives and children. Others went back to find brides to join them. And new concerns confronted these people, many of whom were no longer sojourners, but settlers ... how to ensure their livelihood, how to educate their children, how to retain their Chinese heritage yet also become part of a society essentially western, and often as alien to them as they were to it. This chapter outlines the most significant legislative measures affecting Chinese immigration and land tenure as well as the varied occupational fields in which the evolving community found its niche.

ROLE OF CONSUL-GENERAL

The office of Chinese Consul-General was just one of the legacies left by the indentured Chinese mine labourers to the local community. Certainly the minuscule size of the community would not have warranted the presence of an official Chinese government envoy in South Africa. Why the consulate-general was maintained after the labourers left is unclear, but it is likely that the first two consuls-general were sufficiently concerned about the situation of the Chinese to encourage the retention of this office in South Africa.

Although community organizations had been formed in virtually all centres where Chinese settled, no unified countrywide organization emerged to address the community's concerns until the 1950s. Until then it was largely through the Chinese Consulate-General that community leaders channelled appeals for the relaxation of restrictions they encountered.

The first Chinese Consul-General to British South Africa, Lew Yuk Lin, arrived in Johannesburg in May 1905, and took up residence in a stately home secured for him by the Chamber of Mines. Although his official stay was brief, a mere two years, he soon involved himself in petitions to the authorities on behalf of the Chinese community.[9]

He travelled to London with community representative, Lai Mun James, in October 1906 to outline to the Chinese Minister there the grievances of the

The residence of the first Imperial Consul-General for China to South Africa in 1905. The gracious home, called 'Amerden' stood at No. 95 Wolmarans Street, corner Wilhelm Street (later renamed King George Street), in Hospital Hill, Johannesburg.

Consul-General Liu Ngai (centre) photographed with members of the Cantonist United Benefit Society in Port Elizabeth in 1921.

community. Often glowingly described in newspaper interviews as a man of culture and education who spoke excellent English, the Consul-General was recalled to Peking (Beijing) and left South Africa in August 1907. Just a few years later he was appointed Chinese Minister in London, from which position he continued to advocate better treatment for the Chinese in South Africa.

The second Consul-General, Liu Ngai, was initially English secretary to Consul-General Lew before assuming the more elevated office of diplomatic representative. He served two extended terms of office, first as Acting Imperial Chinese Consul-General, from 1907 to 1911 and later as Consul-General from 1919 to 1930 — a total period of 15 years. His determination to effect changes to discriminatory laws is reflected in the mass of official communication he addressed to the authorities, and by 1910 he drew sharp censure from both the British and South African governments.

When he persistently requested the repeal of the Chinese Exclusion Act in the Cape, the Governor-General, Lord Gladstone, wrote to the Minister of the Interior, General Smuts:

> ... Mr Liu Ngai seems to me to have passed beyond the legitimate sphere of his Consular functions and to be assuming the role of a diplomatic agent ... Personally I have refrained from taking any official action in this matter ... but I may perhaps be permitted to suggest that it would be well in future to discountenance any direct correspondence with Consular Officers on questions of policy.[10]

Britain held that representations on general political questions should be handled at government level through the Foreign Office and that consuls were only permitted to raise matters connected with the personal welfare of their nationals, as individuals. Liu Ngai's repeated attempts to intercede on behalf of the community were clearly considered a breach a diplomatic protocol, as Smuts pointed out:

> ... When his first letter reached me I was very much inclined to tell him that he was overstepping the mark in writing to me at all on the subject ... besides writing to me he attempted repeatedly to have an interview with me which I would under no circumstances grant him.
>
> His second letter was an even greater breach of the proprieties than his first ...
>
> I fully concur with Your Excellency as to the desirability of not allowing Consuls to arrogate to themselves positions to which they are not entitled.[11]

Although no official complaint seems to have been lodged about Liu Ngai's activities, just four months later he was recalled to China on a leave of absence. An American consul, Edwin N. Gunsaulus, was appointed acting Consul-General of China at Johannesburg on 1 April 1911.[12]

The year 1911 was a turning point for China. Led by Dr Sun Yat Sen, revolutionary groups overthrew the Ch'ing rulers who had controlled China for more than 250 years and founded a republic in October 1911. In the formative years of the new republic, the situation of the Chinese in far-off South Africa would have been of minimal concern and the American consulate retained charge of Chinese interests in South Africa for seven years until 1919.

Several factors may have led to the official re-opening of the Chinese consulate in South Africa after the end of World War I. Despite the continuing decrease in the size of the Chinese population [from 2292 in 1904 to 1828 in 1921], the community maintained close contacts with their families in China and may well have urged the need for diplomatic representation. It is probable too that the first Consul-General, Lew Yuk Lin, exerted influence as Chinese Minister in London and his successor, Liu Ngai, may have indicated a willingness to resume the position.

Liu Ngai returned to South Africa in October 1919 and was officially recognized as Chinese Consul-General for South Africa, including Basutoland, Swaziland, Bechuanaland Protectorate and Rhodesia.[13] It was, however, not long before he again ran foul of the authorities for requesting a relaxation in the restrictions facing Chinese. He addressed an appeal to the Governor-General stating many laws affected the rights and privileges of Chinese and requested the removal of such disabilities. Officials noted that the Consul-General was *again* exceeding his consular functions! In a terse reply, he was informed that it would be more appropriate to make his representations through the usual diplomatic channels.[14]

Confronted with such reminders that diplomatic recognition offered limited leeway for action, Liu Ngai involved community representatives more directly in his approaches to the authorities. He established close contacts with Chinese in all centres of South Africa and continued making representations on their behalf, often allying these with petitions and letters from Chinese organizations.

When the Chinese consulate was first established in 1905, its running costs were covered by the Chamber of Mines who paid a \$3 (six shillings) levy for every Chinese mine labourer. In 1910 the repatriation of the labourers shut off this source of revenue. It is not known whether or not the Chinese government or local community made any contribution towards the American Consulate for maintaining an acting Chinese Consul-General. By the early 1920s however, Consul-General Liu Ngai was largely dependent on funds from the South African Chinese community to cover his official expenses.[15]

Evidence of this funding has been traced in correspondence between the Uitenhage Chinese Association and the consulate. In letters to the association between 1923 and 1926, Consul-General Liu Ngai requested the registration of all Chinese merchants.

He said his office was in dire need of funds since the Chinese government had not sent any money to maintain him. Everyone who registered was to pay a fee, and only those who were unemployed could be registered without charge. Consular registration books were issued to the association and the stubs, with the fees, were to be returned to the consulate.

The average registration fee was £2 per person, although it seems those who could not afford this paid between five and ten shillings. The registration took place annually and was probably conducted by Chinese associations throughout South Africa. Over a period of four years the small Chinese population of Uitenhage in the eastern Cape alone contributed a total of £100-15-0 in registration fees to the consulate.

When this registration system was instituted, what its original purpose was and how long it was maintained is not known. As early as 1913 however the American consul in charge of Chinese interests issued certificates of registration stating the name, age, marital status, origin, occupation and address of individual Chinese. It should be noted these consular registration certificates were not the same as those required by law for Chinese to reside in the different provinces of South Africa. Perhaps the consular certificates offered some means of identification for those who did not have other documentation, or they may simply have enabled the consulate to maintain a check on the numbers of Chinese in the country. Many elderly Chinese still have copies of consular registration certificates which were issued well into the 1940s.

In addition to paying registration fees, local Chinese also offered other financial assistance to the consulate. The Transvaal Chinese United Club periodically lent Consul-General Liu Ngai sums of between £500 and £600, and also spent £300 on a motor car for him in 1920.[16] Liu Ngai was recalled in May 1930 and was followed in quick succession by various representatives of the Chinese government, each of whom, until 1948, held office for no more than three years.

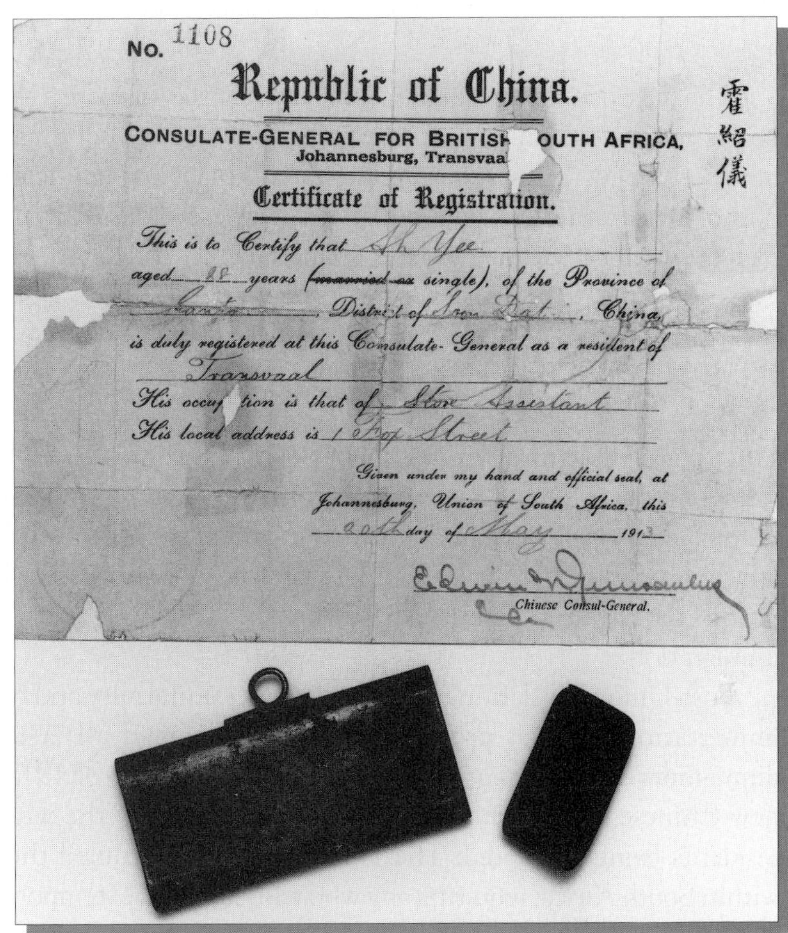
No. 1108

Republic of China.

霍紹儀

CONSULATE-GENERAL FOR BRITISH SOUTH AFRICA,
Johannesburg, Transvaal

Certificate of Registration.

This is to Certify that Ah Yee
aged 28 years (~~married or~~ single), of the Province of Canton, District of Sun Tai, China,
is duly registered at this Consulate-General as a resident of Transvaal
His occupation is that of Stor Assistant
His local address is 1 Fox Street

Given under my hand and official seal, at Johannesburg, Union of South Africa, this 20th day of May 1913

Chinese Consul-General.

One certificate was kept by its owner in a small metal case which could be hung on a chain around his neck.

An example of a certificate of registration issued to Chinese by the Consulate-General in Johannesburg.

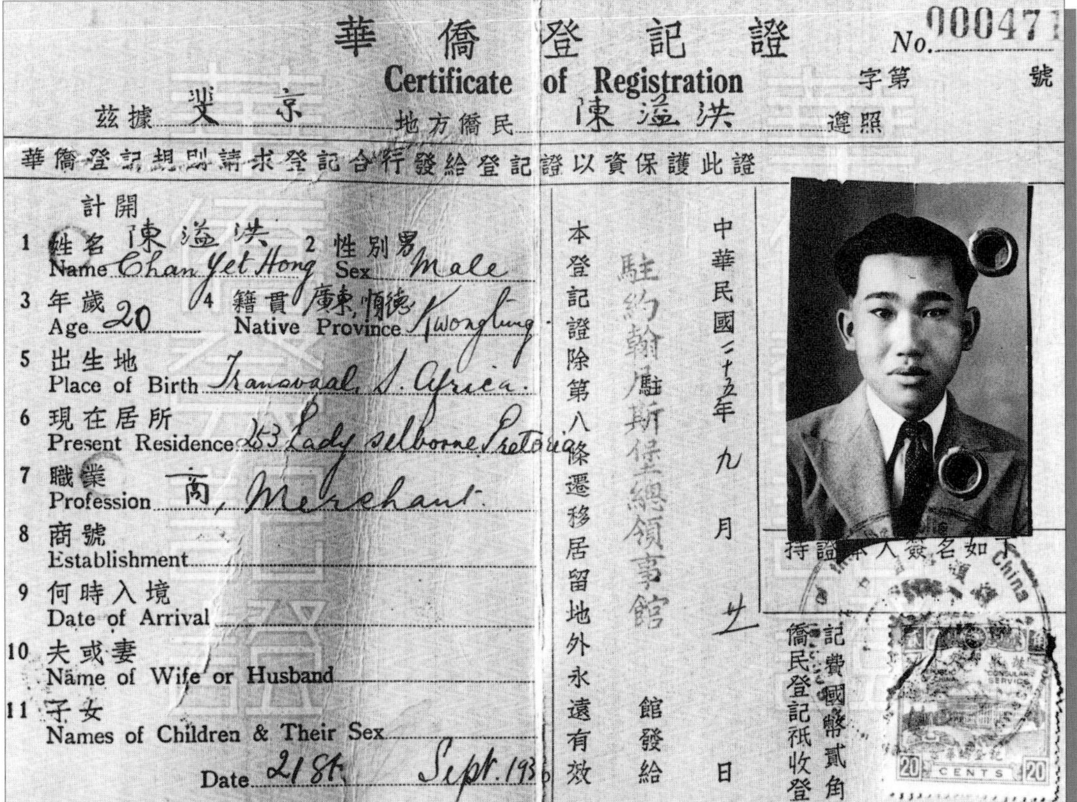
華僑登記證 No. 00047

Certificate of Registration 字第 號

茲據 艾京 地方僑民 陳溢洪 遵照

華僑登記規則請求登記合行發給登記證以資保護此證

計開

1 姓名 Name 陳溢洪 Chan Yet Hong 2 性別 Sex 男 Male

3 年歲 Age 20 4 籍貫 Native Province 廣東順德 Kwongtung

5 出生地 Place of Birth Transvaal, S. Africa.

6 現在居所 Present Residence 253 Lady selborne Pretoria

7 職業 Profession 商, Merchant

8 商號 Establishment

9 何時入境 Date of Arrival

10 夫或妻 Name of Wife or Husband

11 子女 Names of Children & Their Sex

Date 21st Sept. 1936

本登記證除第八條遷移居留地外永遠有效

駐約翰尼斯堡總領事館 館發給

中華民國二十五年九月廿一日

持證本人簽名如下

記費國幣貳角 僑民登記祇收登

20 CENTS 20

The presence of a consulate-general offered the Chinese a formal avenue of approach to the South African Government, at the same time serving as a link to their far-off homeland. Several consular representatives played a significant role in addressing the host of legal restrictions imposed on the Chinese and their involvement in community concerns will be outlined in later chapters.

IMMIGRATION

Entry by Chinese into any colony of South Africa was severely restricted prior to the formation of Union in 1910. In Natal only those who could pass an education test in a European language were allowed entry and the Cape's Chinese Exclusion Act prevented any immigration except by Chinese of British nationality. The Orange Free State prohibited all Asiatic entry while in the Transvaal a barrage of laws restricted immigration.

Post-Union legislation introduced greater uniformity and by 1913 a comprehensive immigration law was promulgated which deemed all Asiatics to be 'prohibited immigrants'. The Immigrants Regulation Act, no. 22 of 1913, shut the door on any new Chinese immigration to South Africa, with only the wives and children of legal residents being exempted. The law furthermore curtailed the movement of Asiatics within South Africa, requiring any who wished to travel temporarily to another province to apply for visiting permits. Chinese who were absent from the Union for a period of three years or longer lost all domicile rights.

In his capacity as Minister at the Chinese Legation in London, Lew Yuk Lin despatched a strong letter of objection to the Secretary of State for the Colonies. Describing the treatment of Chinese as shameful, he drew attention to the new immigration law as well as the many residential and trade restrictions enforced in the different provinces. He appealed for the removal of 'all such invidious discriminations' and concluded the letter:

> Unless some remedy can be found for these grievances, their existence, if persisted in, must, it is to be feared, sooner or later, impair the good relations which exist between the peoples of our two countries.[17]

The Secretary of State noted that this sentence was 'rather curious' and referred the letter to South African Prime Minister, Louis Botha, who pointed out that it was 'obviously impossible to give to Chinese any greater rights, either of immigration or in other directions ... than are accorded to His Majesty's Indian subjects'.[18]

International relations between China and Great Britain may not have contributed towards improving the position of the Chinese in South Africa, but, between the first and second world wars, they offered the community some hope that external influence could be exerted on their behalf.

Wives and Children

The fact that Chinese wives and children were not, until the 1950s, barred from entering the country had a profound effect on the establishment of a truly Chinese community in South Africa. Not only did wives increase the numbers of Chinese, but their presence fostered the retention of Chinese language, culture and values in succeeding generations.

In the first two decades of this century, restrictive immigration legislation had however whittled down the overall numbers of the Chinese in South Africa. The following table reflects this decline as well as the increase in the number of wives permitted to join their husbands. Only by 1936 did more women and a natural population growth substantially swell community ranks.

South African Chinese Population, 1904 - 1936

		1904	1911	1921	1936
NATAL					
	Males	161	161	75	46
	Females	4	11	33	36
CAPE					
	Males	1366	804	584	782
	Females	14	19	148	462
TRANSVAAL					
	Males	907	905	828	1054
	Females	5	5	160	564
	TOTAL:	2457	1905	1828	2944

Source: South Africa. Office of Census and Statistics.[19]

While the 1904 and 1911 censuses recorded the presence of a mere handful of women, it should also be remembered that these included non-Chinese women, married to Chinese and therefore counted as part of that race group. Although the 1913 immigration law allowed for the entry of wives and children (under the age of 16), for the Chinese this provision was fraught with problems.

Firstly, there was the question of the recognition of Chinese marriages. Although Chinese law, prior to 1930, permitted men to have several wives simultaneously, such polygamous unions were not regarded as legal in South Africa, and therefore 'the wives and children of Chinese are ipso facto prohibited immigrants'.[20] Secondly, obtaining documentary proof of marriages and the birth of children in rural China was next to impossible. Immigration authorities were well aware that most Chinese hailed from villages which did not have resident magistrates empowered to supply them with official certificates.

From 1915, community leaders with the American consul responsible for Chinese interests and the Chinese Legation in London addressed numerous letters and petitions to officials in attempts to reach a compromise.[21] The British consul in Canton temporarily issued certificates to intending emigrants but pointed out he was unable to verify claims on marriages. While an administrative order was issued to treat Chinese on the same lines as Indians, many individuals tried for years, without success, to obtain permission to bring either a wife or child into the country. In practice, Chinese men with more than one wife tended to leave the first wife in China to care for the family home and bring a younger wife to work with them in South Africa.

Records on Chinese which had been kept since the introduction of the Peace Preservation Ordinance in the Transvaal

The Tam Tims were one of the first Chinese couples to marry in Johannesburg. They signed the marriage register at a Black church in Langlaagte in 1916. The bride from Canton was aged 16.

Young brides who left China in the late 1920s to settle with their husbands in Mauritius and Cape Town, South Africa.

in 1902 enabled officials to maintain a close check on any claim by a man to introduce his dependants as immigrants. Some who had neglected to state that they had families in China when they initially took out Asiatic registration certificates paid dearly for this omission in later years.

One such case was that of a Johannesburg trader, Leong Hoi, who tried for more than two years between 1916 and 1918 to bring his son, Sam Hue, into the country. When the boy, aged 14, arrived, he was promptly deported to Lourenco Marques where he remained for months before being sent back to China. Despite appeals by the Transvaal Chinese Association and the presentation of various certificates by the father, officials pointed out Leong had not previously stated he was married. Their records also showed the dates when he was in the Transvaal and they held that he had not returned to China at the time when he claimed to have been married, therefore the boy would not be permitted entry.[22]

To ensure that their marriage, formalized in China, would be recognized in South Africa, many Chinese re-married in Mauritius to obtain official papers.

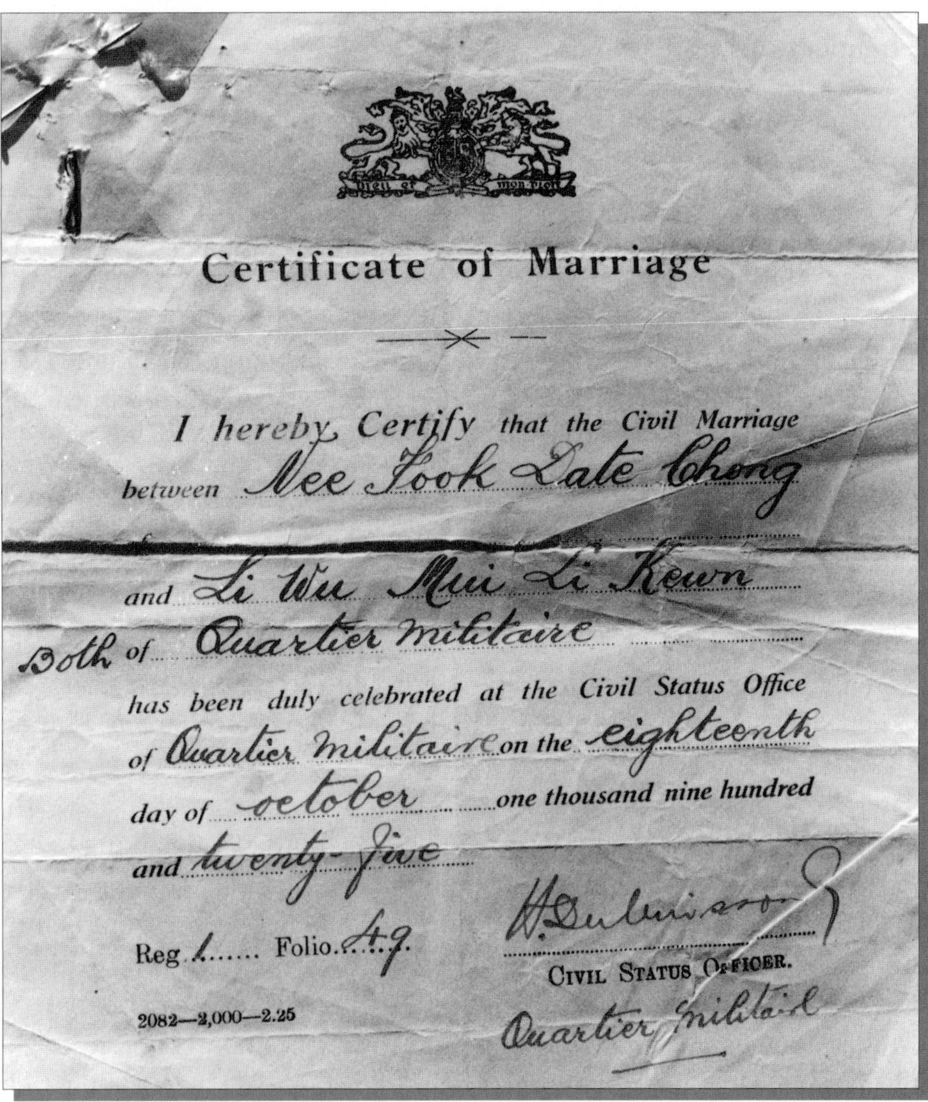

Certificate of Marriage

I hereby Certify that the Civil Marriage between Vee Fook Date Chong and Li Wu Mui Li Kewn Both of Quartier Militaire has been duly celebrated at the Civil Status Office of Quartier Militaire on the eighteenth day of October one thousand nine hundred and twenty-five

Reg. 1 Folio 49

Civil Status Officer.
Quartier Militaire

2082—2,000—2.25

By the end of 1918 agreement was reached on the documentation required of men who wished to introduce their families. The authorities also emphasized that no consideration would be given to any boys aged 16 or more on arrival in South Africa.[23] In later years officials exercised discretion in admitting women on temporary permits pending their marriage to legal Chinese residents. To avoid the possibility of their fiancees being turned away, several men travelled to Mauritius to marry before returning with their brides to the country. In the Cape where the Chinese Exclusion Act operated in conjunction with the 1913 immigration law, children up to the age of 18 were permitted entry. Between 1913 and 1928 a total of 165 boys and eight girls were admitted to the province.[24]

By 1927 immigration legislation required all minors to be accompanied by their mothers and in 1930 the Immigration Quota Act limited the number of Chinese dependants permitted to enter South Africa to a maximum of 50 per year. A later immigration law, the Aliens Act of 1937, reaffirmed the position that Asiatics were considered prohibited immigrants and maintained a check on the growth of the Chinese population.

Illegal Immigration

Illegal immigration was a hotly debated issue and White fears about an 'Asiatic invasion' led to strong support for stringent legislation in the first decades of this century. Since any who entered South Africa illegally obviously tried to steer well clear of the authorities, official records only contain accounts of those who were either discovered or who confessed to their illicit entry.

The eastern borders of the Transvaal were subjected to particular scrutiny and authorities maintained checks on the railway routes from Lourenco Marques (Maputo) in Mocambique and Port Natal. In 1906 the Protector of Asiatics warned police of methods used by those seeking to enter undetected:

> ... I think it might be expedient to warn your officers, especially at Volksrust, that both Indians and Chinese appear to be dressing themselves up as fine gentlemen for the journey, travelling first class and hoping through these means to escape scrutiny.[25]

The police pointed out all permits were thoroughly checked, and the only way Chinese could perhaps smuggle themselves in would be on board the trains carrying Chinese mine labourers. No evidence has been found to suggest that any Chinese ever took advantage of this means of entry.

In later years however several Chinese entered the Transvaal illegally through Lourenco Marques. Some travelled part of the way by train, disembarking to cross the border on foot and then boarding another train to Johannesburg. Others paid drivers to smuggle them by car across the border. While one can only speculate on their reasons for running the risks of illegal entry, for most the prospect of earning some form of living was more appealing than the certain poverty of their homes in China.

Most illegal immigrants joined relatives already in the country and through them were able to obtain employment, either for a minimal rate of pay or simply to have a

Motorcycle Getaway!

An elderly Chinese man, suspected of being an illegal immigrant, made a hasty getaway on a motorcycle after 'disappearing' through a cellar when police and immigration authorities arrived to search a shop in Sophiatown, Johannesburg.

Responding to reports that some Chinese men who had entered South Africa illegally were hidden in Chinese shops in Sophiatown, two detectives and an immigration official set out on 23 February 1933 to investigate. They arrived at a shop on the corner of Gibson Street and Edward Road where they found five Chinese men. One was the shopkeeper, Lee Why, three others were known to the police and the fifth was 'an elderly Chinaman who appeared to be known to the shopkeeper'.

When they questioned the elderly man, the shopkeeper offered to fetch his permit, but first went outside and started his motorcycle. The elderly man went into what police thought was a bedroom.

> '... as this adjoining room was previously inspected by us and found to have only the one door and the one window barred, we thought that the suspect would be quite safe...'

But the man did not return, so a thorough search was launched. It was discovered that a trapdoor led from the room into a cellar which 'was clearly in use as a living room and also as a place of concealment for several persons'. No trace was found of any exit from the cellar, but neither was there any sign of the elderly man. In the police account of the incident, it was reported:

> 'I am almost certain that the fifth Chinaman was a prohibited immigrant and the Police were rather cleverly bluffed by the shopkeeper, Lee Why, in order to permit him to escape. The Chinese who are here without the necessary permits work for their own nationality for practically nothing more than their food. If they ask for more they are threatened with exposure. There is therefore a strong inducement for Chinese traders to protect such persons.'[26]

roof over their heads. In 1924 a number confessed their illegal entry to the authorities and applied for temporary permits to enable them to save up enough money to return to China.[27]

The constant fear of discovery which dogged illegal immigrants exposed them to blackmail by business competitors and made them the target of anonymous tip-offs to immigration authorities. By 1933 the Chinese consulate tried to intervene, stating that Chinese storekeepers had been harassed and suffered many hardships through regular police raids and searches for illegal immigrants. The Commissioner for Immigration and Asiatic Affairs pointed out the authorities had to check all information received.[28]

The age limit of 16 for the admission of children imposed a pressing time constraint on all who tried to unravel the red tape restricting immigration. Those unable to secure the necessary papers within the deadline found their sons were indefinitely prohibited from joining their fathers in South Africa. In the Chinese family tradition, sons to carry on the lineage were considered of prime importance, and it is known some parents resorted to smuggling their children, without papers, into the country.

Members of the Chinese Youth Club, formed in Port Elizabeth in 1939. One of its functions was to dissuade Chinese from reporting illegal immigrants to the authorities. Long-serving teacher at the Chinese School, Wong Pan Ngian is seated second from the left in the front row.

'Paper Sons'

The expression 'paper sons' has been widely used to describe those Chinese emigrants, to America and elsewhere, who posed as other men's children by adopting false names in order to enter a country. Men, legally entitled to be in South Africa, who reported after a visit to China the birth of any children were usually allowed to bring them in at some future date, provided they had not reached the age of 16. Some whose children did not use these papers, or others who had reported fictitious children, were then in a position to bring relatives into the country or to sell these valuable entry documents.

The 'paper son' would have to be as close in age as possible to that of the child whose papers he used, and would have to spend his life in the country under the assumed name. All who used such papers ran the same risk of exposure and deportation as those without any documents. Nevertheless this option offered some opportunity for those desperate to introduce either children or relatives into the country.

Chinese Exclusion Act

The 1904 Chinese Exclusion Act consisted of 36 sections relating to the immigration, movement and rights of Chinese in the Cape Colony and the community soon dubbed it 'the 36 unjust laws'. In their many attempts to have the law amended or repealed, Chinese objected to the fact that the legislation distinguished between them and other alien groups, placing upon them 'the stigma of inferiority and colour'.[29]

From the outset, the Exclusion Act effected a 'steady diminution' in the numbers of Chinese in the Cape. Statistics compiled annually showed the numbers who registered, who left the colony or died and those who had been deported. By 1906, the number of Chinese men decreased from 1393 to 1102. The administrative officer reported that the majority of these Chinese congregated in the four urban centres of the colony, namely Cape Town, Port Elizabeth, Kimberley and East London, and remarked this was 'a fact truly indicative of the Chinaman's habits and position in a country not his own.'[30]

Cape Town Chinese photographed in the early 1930s with Consul-General Ho Tsang outside the Chinese Republic United Association headquarters in Loop Street.

The formation of Union in 1910, coinciding with the mass repatriation of the Chinese mine labourers whose arrival had first 'necessitated' the Exclusion Act, gave the Chinese some hope of an improvement in their position. In two petitions signed by 107 Chinese in Port Elizabeth and 36 in Uitenhage, the Governor-General of South Africa was asked to consider the repeal of the law which imposed 'an unnecessary and heavy burden' on the Chinese in the Cape. The receipt of these appeals was acknowledged, but no action followed.[31]

Acting Chinese Consul-General Liu Ngai pursued the matter, writing to both the Union government and the Governor-General and pointing out that since the Chinese indentured labourers had left, the necessity for the law no longer existed. He described the law as 'harsh, unreasonable and ... absolutely uncalled for', adding that 'so far as I am aware the provisions of this Act are without a parallel in the civilized world'. The authorities took umbrage, considering Liu Ngai to have overstepped the bounds of his diplomatic duties, and merely acknowledged receipt of his letters.[32]

The provisions of the Exclusion Act prohibited relatives or friends from even visiting Chinese residing in the Cape. In August 1919, Chinese in Johannesburg appealed for a relaxation in this restriction and were told visiting permits for holiday purposes would be issued on payment of a deposit. Just a few months later, however, this concession was revoked.[33]

During the 1920s Chinese associations and the Consul-General pleaded, with almost monotonous regularity, for the repeal of the Exclusion Act. By 1928, immigration officials themselves recommended its repeal stating that as little distinction as possible should be drawn between Chinese and Indian immigrants. Nevertheless the authorities seemed loathe to dispense entirely with a system which enabled them to keep a check on the numbers of Chinese in the Cape and draft legislation was drawn up for a Chinese Registration Act in 1929. This draft was never implemented and the Exclusion Act remained in place.[34]

The passage of time, however, gave rise to a new problem in the administration of the law — race classification. When the Act was first introduced, it had been relatively simple to identify a Chinese person. But more than 20 years later, with restrictions on the entry of unmarried Chinese women into the country, several men had married local women and officials faced the problem of whether the children of such unions were or were not Chinese for the purposes of the law.

Legal advisers pointed out the main factors determining race were appearance, genealogy and the habits and associations of the people concerned. They said it was impossible to apply any hard and fast rules, but the law stipulated '... the Court, Judge or Magistrate may decide upon their own view or judgment whether any person produced before them is a Chinaman'. Officials were advised to register such children in terms of the law and to leave further investigation on what constituted a Chinese to cases which were appealed.[35]

By 1932, a year before the Exclusion Act was repealed, a total of 77 Chinese had been deported from the Cape for various contraventions of the law, and the number of registered Chinese totalled 623 men over the age of 18, fewer than half the number first recorded in 1904.[36]

ENTRENCHING SEGREGATION IN LAW

Class Areas Bill

The Transvaal's land laws had long determined areas in which Chinese could trade and reside, but by 1924 another piece of legislation was drawn up to provide for the segregation of certain racial groups throughout the country. Euphemistically called the Class Areas Bill, it was intended primarily to enable the government to proclaim separate residential and trading areas for Asiatics.[37] The fact that such enforced segregation would deprive them of their means of making a living prompted Asiatics to oppose the measure.

Proponents of the measure pointed out there was in South Africa a 'predominating majority of the European people who are not willing to share their political privileges with the people of the Asiatic race or even the civilized members of some races of South Africa'. Given the prevailing public sentiment, the Minister of the Interior, Patrick Duncan, said 'some measure of segregation in urban areas was inevitable'.[38]

The proposed law's object was 'to make provision for the reservation of residential and trading areas in urban areas for persons other than natives, having racial characteristics in common'. It allowed local authorities to decide whether or not to proclaim a separate area for a specific class of people. The government would then appoint a commission to investigate the suitability of the area, the availability of necessary services and related issues. If an area was proclaimed, only the class for whom it was set aside could live, trade and purchase property there.[39]

Indians reacted angrily, holding meetings throughout the country and despatching a deputation from the South African Indian Congress to protest.[40] Chinese too feared the implications of the Bill for their future and within days of the publication of the proposed law, letters flew fast and furiously between Consul-General Liu Ngai and Chinese organizations countrywide. In notices to community leaders, the Consul-General outlined the provisions of the proposed law, asked for their views and said he would travel to Cape Town to make representations on their behalf. Opposition to the measure was unanimous and, in both the Eastern Cape and the Transvaal, Chinese formed new organizations to tackle the issue. Encouraging Liu Ngai to do whatever he thought necessary to oppose the promulgation of the law, the Port Elizabeth Chinese Association wrote:

> We understand this law for separate areas will drive all Chinese into a corner and put a stop to our livelihood. Chinese are Asiatics and if we do not take urgent action now, how will we be able to avoid the future reach of the law? We Chinese number only a couple of thousand, and there will be no way to make a living. This is even more severe than the past 36 unjust laws [Chinese Exclusion Act]. It is unthinkable ... We shall form an Anti-Law Committee to support you.[41]

The 'Port Elizabeth and Uitenhage Anti Bill Joint Committee' was formed, and in Johannesburg the 'Transvaal Chinese Anti New Law United Association' came into being. They raised funds, sent a petition to the Chinese Minister in London and despatched representatives to Cape Town to assist the Consul-General in efforts to have Chinese exempted from the measure.

Although the Bill had primarily been directed against Asiatics, its general wording as a 'Class Areas' measure also encompassed other groups such as the Jews since legislators held that people of any nationality had common racial characteristics.[42] Whether it was this realization or the spate of opposition from Asiatics which influenced events, the government did not proceed with the promulgation of the law.

Two years later, in 1926, a revised version of the same Bill, this time called the 'Areas Reservation and Immigration and Registration (Further Provision) Bill' was proposed. The Chinese again raised objections, and in a letter to the Consul-General, the Prime Minister offered the assurance that owing to 'the peculiar conditions obtaining with the Chinese community in the Union,' the relevant provisions of the measure would not be applied to them.[43] The Bill itself was referred to a Select Committee, after which consideration on it was postponed.

Segregation as a policy was, however, certainly not intended to die an unceremonious death. If such a measure could not be implemented nationally, there was still opportunity in the Transvaal where numerous laws were already in force to prohibit Asiatic ownership and occupation of land. So it was in the Transvaal that further segregationary land legislation was promulgated.

Transvaal Asiatic Land Tenure Act

In the years following the formation of the Union, failure on the part of authorities to enforce all statutory land restrictions led to many Asiatics and Coloured people contravening the law by illegally living and trading in prohibited areas. Parliamentary select committees recommended steps to prevent the further spread of Asiatics into restricted areas as defined in the 1908 Gold Law.[44]

In 1932 the Asiatic Land Tenure Act was passed to consolidate and extend existing legislation. The law protected the acquired occupational rights of all Coloured people and included a provision for the exemption of consular officials. At the same time a Commission of Enquiry was appointed, under the chairmanship of Mr Justice R. Feetham, to investigate the extent to which the laws had been contravened, to compile a register of those in legal and illegal occupation of land and to make relevant recommendations.

The Chinese immediately objected to the provisions of the new law. They submitted petitions to both the Minister of Justice, Oswald Pirow, and the Governor-General, the Earl of Clarendon. Stating that they were a small, law-abiding community which would be deprived of the means of earning a livelihood, they asked to be exempted from the application of the law.[45]

In addition to expressing their own views, the Chinese enlisted the support of 'European members of the commercial, financial and industrial community and registered voters of Johannesburg'.[46] Armed with more than 10 000 signatures to another petition, the chairman of the Transvaal Chinese Association, Ho Tong, flew to Cape Town to present the appeal to the Minister of the Interior, Dr D. F. Malan and members of Parliament.

Signatories vouched for the integrity and honesty of the Chinese in business, saying insolvency among them was rare. They pointed out Chinese freedom to trade was very limited, and the law would further curtail this. The petition requested that Chinese be permitted to retain rights they had held prior to the passing of the law and that they be excluded from the definition of the term 'Asiatic'.[47]

Meanwhile, the Feetham Commission commenced its investigation and the Transvaal Chinese Association, represented by Ho Tong and secretary Y.K. Akin, submitted a lengthy memorandum in which they asked for the 'just grievances' of the Chinese to be addressed. They summarized the historical position of the community in the Transvaal, China's standing in the League of Nations and their fears for the future. These extracts from their memorandum reflect the moderate approach which community leaders countrywide adopted in all their appeals to the authorities:

> The Chinese in the Transvaal number in all some two thousand people, men, women and children, of whom approximately three hundred are traders in Johannesburg and its suburbs ... [They trade] mainly amongst the Poor Whites, Coloured people and Natives. These people deal with Chinese storekeepers because our prices are low — we give reasonable credit and do not press our debtors unduly. It is an almost unheard of thing for a Chinese storekeeper to sue his debtor for money.
>
> We claim to be law-abiding and we take a pride in being self-supporting. Many of the Chinese nationals have been long years in the Transvaal, and look on it as their home; their interest is the future welfare of this land; they have grown up here, have all their interests here and will die here ... Many of the Chinese traders here have families. The Government has given them a domicile and it should now allow them to live without interference ... We cannot help expressing the view that the reason behind this legislation is not based on any real fear of a Chinese menace but to enable the European to enjoy an advantage over us and is a real interference with what little liberty remains to us. Though we have referred to ourselves herein as citizens of the Chinese Republic it is the desire of most, if not all, of us to settle here and regard this as our home; and even though we may never be granted full rights of citizenship, in so far as it involves the granting of the franchise, we must nevertheless in our own interest — to put it on its lowest basis — work for the good of the country as a whole, and the greater our rights in the country, the greater our interest, and consequently the greater our endeavour for the good of the land of our adoption. We desire, as the citizens of a friendly civilized nation, to be treated with justice and humanity by a friendly civilized nation.[48]

When the Feetham Commission presented its report it stated that appeals such as had been submitted by the Transvaal Chinese Association for exemption from the law were beyond its terms of reference and it had therefore 'felt bound to ignore them'. Statements on 'the good character of the Chinese trader, and the manner in which he conducts his business' were however borne out and police evidence too constituted 'a striking tribute to his honesty, and his success in inspiring confidence in his customers.' The report added:

> The only special point made against Chinese traders as a class is that some of them indulge in fah-fee, and other gambling games of that description, and demoralise their customers by appealing to and gratifying their gambling instincts.[49]

The Feetham Commission sat for more than four years, turning into one of the most expensive enquiries yet held in South Africa.[50] It released its report in eight volumes, much of which was embodied in the Transvaal Asiatic Land Tenure

Amendment Act (Act No. 30 of 1936) and the Asiatic Transvaal Land Tenure Further Amendment Act (Act No. 32 of 1937). These laid out procedures for implementing segregation in the Transvaal, but also conceded rights to Asiatics and Coloured people to own property in specific areas, subject to parliamentary approval.

In an extensive analysis of the legal status of Chinese, a keen observer of the times, Tung Miao wrote of the Commission:

> Its ultimate end is obviously stricter and more effective enforcement of the Gold Law provisions against any further contravention by Asiatics by setting apart certain special areas within proclaimed land and compiling a Coloured occupation register — thus far and no farther.[51]

Slum clearances also provided opportunities for the authorities to expropriate and demolish Asiatic occupied properties. Many Chinese trading in Prospect Township on the outskirts of Johannesburg in 1937 were removed from their businesses in terms of such a clearance. Chinese continued to protest in vain against the operation of the law on their livelihood. In the following years restrictions on Asiatic ownership and occupation of land as well as trading licences were further extended through a series of 'Pegging' Acts which affected both Transvaal and Natal Asiatics.[52] In 1949 Transvaal and Natal Chinese organizations again pointed to the minuscule size of the community which politically and economically made it 'of no consequence' and appealed for just and equitable treatment in pursuit of legitimate trading rights.[53]

LIQUOR LEGISLATION

Although the bulk of representations Chinese made to authorities concerned issues affecting their livelihood, one subject raised time and again related surprisingly enough to liquor. Perhaps more than most discriminatory measures, liquor restrictions epitomized the social stigma cast on Chinese and as such were particularly galling, more so since the Chinese, generally, did not even consume alcoholic beverages on a regular basis.

Neither the Cape nor Natal barred Chinese from access to alcohol, but in the Transvaal all 'Coloured persons' had been, from 1902, prohibited from purchasing or possessing any intoxicating liquor, defined as spirit containing more than two percent alcohol.[54] Both the Transvaal Chinese Association (TCA) and the Cantonese Club applied for special permission to serve wine at Chinese festivals.[55]

When a Select Committee sat to consider the Transvaal liquor laws in 1918, evidence was given by a TCA deputation consisting of Martin Easton, Lai Ky (Lai King), Chiong Fan James Frank and David Kan, assisted by legal adviser, Alexander Stanley Benson. They summarized Chinese objections to the law and said the granting of liquor privileges 'would relieve the community from the stigma at present laid upon them'. In their lengthy submission, repeated references were made to the Chinese simply wishing to be allowed privileges generally extended to all civilized nations and their protest against differential legislation.[56]

The TCA also appealed for the intervention of the Chinese Legation in London.[57] When the Select Committee recommended a concession to allow non-Whites to purchase malt beer and wine, the Chinese objected that they were not concerned with various grades of liquor but the status which was accorded their race. TCA chairman D. Kan stated:

> It is common knowledge throughout the civilised world that there is no more abstemious or temperate race than the Chinese and it is an insult to our national character that we should be pilloried in any legislative enactment as persons who are incapable of making a proper use of alcoholic stimulants.
>
> It is an equally wellknown fact that alcohol in all its varied forms plays an important part in all social and religious Chinese ceremonies, and the liquor law as at present existing in the Transvaal debars us, unless we choose to break the law of the land in which we live, from carrying out any ceremonial in accordance with our national rights and customs.[58]

Consul-General and Liquor

No changes to the liquor legislation were effected and in the following years the Chinese and the Consul-General continued their campaign against the restrictions.[59] An interesting aspect of the liquor question is the extent to which the Consul-General assisted the community in avoiding prosecution for any infringements of the law. As a representative of a foreign country in South Africa, he was exempt from restrictions on the purchase of liquor and could therefore offer alcohol to Chinese guests at any community functions he hosted.

During the early 1920s, Consul-General Liu Ngai ordered liquor to be delivered to Chinese clubs in Ferreirastown for various community celebrations. Despite his diplomatic status, he had on each occasion to obtain permission from the Criminal Investigation Department of the South African Police and be present at the club concerned when the alcohol was delivered.[60]

Diplomatic privilege did not always shield consular personnel from exposure to embarrassing situations. The Minister of Lands, Deneys Reitz recounted the following incident in a letter to his colleague, the Minister of Justice:

> I may say that recently when I was invited by the Chinese Consular Staff to a dinner at the French Club, Johannesburg, the anomalous position arose that I was permitted to order wine whereas the Consul-General and his staff could not be served.[61]

When a new liquor law enacted in 1928 exempted Japanese from the definition of 'Asiatics', Chinese asked for the same exemption. They protested against the law distinguishing between Chinese and Japanese and said it was a question of national honour.[62] The law also introduced more stringent restrictions on the availability of liquor to Chinese in Natal, and the local community objected vocally, submitting several petitions to the authorities.[63]

The Commissioner of Police compared the positions of the Chinese and Japanese in each province and recommended individual Chinese be permitted to apply for permits to purchase liquor once an investigation into their style of living had been conducted. He objected to exempting the Chinese as a whole from the definition of Asiatic citing these reasons:

Drinking a toast at a Double Ten celebration in East London ... not a simple matter for Chinese, outside the Cape, who needed special permission to purchase alcohol. From left: Wally Fong Chong, the Mayor of East London, George Mason, John Louis Fontbin and Y.S. Lee Sun.

> Although the Chinese are members of an ancient civilisation, and at the present time struggling to re-gain some of their former prestige, they are not to be compared with the Japanese, who are to-day a recognised world power, and who are both from an educational and mode of living point of view superior to the Chinese.
>
> In the light of the foregoing, I strongly oppose that the Chinese be afforded the same concession as that granted to the Japanese, because the danger to my mind, if they were excluded, would be that although they may be a sober race themselves they would have facilities — open to easy abuse — for obtaining liquor for prohibited persons.[64]

The fear that Chinese would sell liquor to others was substantiated in later years when several shopkeepers ran foul of the law for this offence in Sophiatown and neighbouring western areas of Johannesburg.

Chinese Consul Recalled

During the 1930s, several individual Chinese in the Transvaal successfully obtained permits, renewable annually, to purchase liquor for their own use. Consular representatives too were granted similar exemption. By 1936 however, police uncovered evidence that Consul Ping Yang Lei, also called Lai, 'was abusing the courtesy extended to him' by ordering liquor and then passing it on to 'trusted members of the Chinese community'.[65]

It was found that his monthly liquor bill was between £10 and £15, but this increased gradually and, in the first four months of 1936, he spent more than £500 on alcohol. Asked to explain, Lei said he had ordered liquor for a number of Chinese festivals in the early part of the year. Police then questioned other Chinese and arrested a boarding house proprietor who claimed he had obtained seven bottles of brandy and two bottles of vermouth from the Chinese consulate.

Steps were immediately taken to have the consul, who was acting Chinese Consul-General in Johannesburg, recalled to China. The Minister of External Affairs, J.B.M. Hertzog outlined South African liquor restrictions to the British Ambassador in Peking and stated Lei had violated these laws. He pointed out that only 12 Chinese in Johannesburg had been granted exemption from the prohibition in force, and concluded:

> It will be appreciated that the Union Government cannot but take a serious view of this abuse of his privileges by Mr Ping Yang Lei, not only because of its gravity, but also because this is not the first time that His Majesty's Government in the Union have had reason to view the activities of the Chinese Consulate's personnel in Johannesburg with suspicion.[66]

The issue did not end with Lei's recall. Several Chinese supplied the Department of Justice with the names of five community members in Johannesburg and Pretoria, claiming they were dealing in liquor and asking for them to be deported. Within two weeks, police raided the offices of the *Chinese Consular Gazette* newspaper, confiscated 25 bottles of wine and a pistol and arrested the paper's editor, Che Leong. They later returned and also removed the newspaper printing press.

In a strong letter to the Secretary for External Affairs, the then acting Consul-General T.C. Chow registered his protest 'against the manner in which this raid was conducted and also against the insulting attitude taken up by the police'. He demanded the return of the confiscated articles which were all the property of the consulate and asked for the police involved to be reprimanded. He was peremptorily informed that the Department of External Affairs would not interfere in any action legitimately taken by the police. Despite an explanation that the wine was what remained of supplies ordered for the New Year celebrations by the consul who had been deported, the editor Che Leong was convicted for possessing liquor as well as an unlicensed firearm and fined a total of £20 or four months' hard labour.[67]

Efforts continued to have liquor restrictions on Chinese lifted, and from 1939, Consul-General Fartsan T. Sung despatched many letters to officials and even appealed to Prime Minister J.C. Smuts. In April 1940, the arrest of 102 Chinese at a 'tomb festival' banquet precipitated a compromise and the Consul-General was granted special permission to supply liquor to Chinese guests at specified places. This meant Chinese would have access to alcohol provided the functions were hosted by the Consul-General.[68] For many years representatives of the Consulate-General were asked to act as nominal hosts for functions such as weddings to enable guests to enjoy the not unreasonable pleasure of toasting a bridal couple.

In Natal Consul-General Sung suggested that the chairman of the Natal Chinese Association, J.L. Fontbin, be permitted to host celebrations in the same way for the province's 110 Chinese. After consultation with the police who described the Chinese

102 Chinese Arrested

The Chinese community in South Africa continues to observe the annual 'hang cheng' or 'ching ming' tomb festival which is an occasion to visit cemeteries and commemorate the dead. Various clan groups and clubs usually arrange a dinner for the occasion, and on the evening of 7 April 1940, more than 100 Chinese gathered at the Chinese United Club premises in Commissioner Street, Ferreirastown, for just such a celebration.

No sooner had they seated themselves when a squad of detectives raided the club and arrested all present. They were transported to police headquarters at Marshall Square, charged with being in possession of liquor and released on bail of 10s.0d each. All 102 were to appear in the Johannesburg Magistrate's Court the following day.[69]

Consul-General F. T. Sung immediately took up the matter with the Minister of Justice. In a lengthy letter explaining the significance of the festival as a 'national day for ancestor worship', he said he had personally invited the Chinese to the memorial banquet and had previously informed the police of the dates of Chinese national festivals. Consul-General Sung added that he and the community were 'deeply aggrieved and hurt by the action of the Police on this occasion'.[70]

> 'The day in question is set aside for the carrying out of the most sacred rites of the Chinese. On this day all Chinese, old and young, visit the cemetries [sic] and clean the graveyards and offer wreaths and sacrificial wines to the ancestral spirits ...
>
> ... The one hundred and two Chinese after suffering the humiliation of being arrested, and being herded to the Police Station like cattle, were charged with being in possession of liquor. The liquor that was found on the premises was liquor which was provided by me for the gathering, and which was essential for the religious side of the ceremony. The liquor in question was used as a sacrifice to the dead, and not as a treat for the living.'

Police pointed out that they had not been notified of the celebration, but the Minister of Justice decided to withdraw the charges against the 102 Chinese. Thereafter the authorities granted the Consul-General special permission to provide Chinese guests with liquor, a concession which was exercised well into the 1960s.[71]

as 'very law-abiding', the Department of Justice agreed to permit Chinese in Natal access to alcohol under the same conditions as those in the Transvaal.[72]

Chinese were officially excluded from the definition of Asiatic in the Liquor Act in September 1943.[73] Restrictions were, however, later re-imposed as Chinese shopkeepers, particularly in the western areas of Johannesburg, were involved in selling liquor illegally to Coloureds and Blacks. The issue of liquor and the Chinese continued to remain contentious and confusing up until the late 1970s.

WORKING IN SOUTH AFRICA

For the Chinese who had secured a foothold in the country, earning a living was their prime consideration. Originating from rural China, most of the first generation of settlers were not of the educated class and were initially drawn into occupations which enabled them to make an independent living, without necessarily having a command of either English or Dutch.

Most survived as traders, laundrymen and market gardeners, living where they worked, in tin shanties or brick dwellings which served as shops, or renting rooms in the vicinity of the Malaikams in Kimberley, Port Elizabeth and Johannesburg. How and where they made their living was largely affected by the laws relating to property, trade and residence in each province, as well as the understandable inclination on the part of new settlers to congregate among their own on a social and kinship level.

In Natal and the Cape, Chinese were permitted to buy fixed property relatively freely. Those who had saved up enough capital, and who were able to find a property owner prepared to sell to them, took advantage of this opportunity to secure their families' livelihood and future. From 1922 however ordinances enacted in Natal enabled town councils to restrict the ownership and occupation of land to specific racial groups.[74] Although there were no statutory prohibitions on the sale of property to Chinese in the Cape, township contracts usually precluded occupation by 'Coloureds' and both the Port Elizabeth and Cape Town municipalities could and did hinder the transfer of property to Chinese.[75]

In the Transvaal, on the other hand, Chinese were subject to the whims of landlords and generally relegated to trading in locations or so-called exempted areas. A formidable array of legislation, in force from the days of the Boer Republic, prohibited the ownership of land except in specially set aside areas. In 1908, a Precious and Base Metals Act (No. 35 of 1908), often referred to as the Gold Law, prevented any person of colour from residing on or occupying any proclaimed land. This measure effectively barred Chinese from trading in the mining areas which constituted the most populated and prosperous parts of the Witwatersrand. The community and consulate registered objections to the law, to no avail.[76] The Townships Amendment Act (No. 34 of 1908) prescribed areas in which Chinese could live, and in later years even more legislation was added to the mass of restrictions on the landowning, residence and trading rights of Asiatics in the Transvaal.

In terms of employment in various trades, Chinese had, from the time the mine labourers were imported, been barred from undertaking any skilled labour.[77] This prohibition was further extended by the Mines and Works Act, no. 12 of 1911, which allowed discrimination on racial grounds and a later amendment in 1926, often called the 'Colour Bar Act', distinguished different racial groups and prohibited Asiatics from handling any machinery.[78]

Racial discrimination was very much part of everyday life throughout the country. Traders were often refused licences because they were Chinese. Trams, trains and public amenities were segregated. Yet, whenever possible, the Chinese used channels open to them to try to redress inequalities. They appealed to Chinese officials, to local authorities and some even took their cases to the courts.

Occupations of Chinese: 1905/1906

	Cape	*Transvaal*
Store keepers and assistants	729	861
Laundrymen	263	39
Gardeners etc.	46	69
Cooks	28	42
Artisans and labourers	21	20
Miscellaneous (including interpreters, bakers, hawkers and agents)	15	28
TOTAL	1102	1059

Source: documents of various government departments.[79]

The table above reflects the occupations of the Chinese in the Cape and the Transvaal early this century. Similar statistics for Natal have not been found, but the majority of the 165 Chinese there in 1904 were small traders, interspersed with a handful of laundrymen.

Shopkeepers

More than 70 percent of Chinese were small traders. In tiny stores, situated ideally on corner stands to attract passing custom from several directions, they sold everyday necessities in penny and tickey quantities, often giving credit when asked. Since the outlay of some capital was necessary to stock even the most basic shop, many relied on relatives for loans or took advantage of the 'fee' or 'hui' lending scheme, run by clan or community associations, to raise funds.

Laws restricting trading hours effectively prevented those prepared to work long hours from doing so.[80] Control of trading licences was in the hands of local authorities whose decisions generally were not subject to appeal. In the face of persistent calls to restrict Asiatic trade, licences were often refused purely on the grounds that the applicants were Chinese. Even transfers of licences, should the holder wish to move to larger premises or sell his business, were fraught with difficulty.

Several Chinese overcame such obstacles by trading under the names of White nominees. When residents in Newlands and Albertsville, Johannesburg appealed in 1904 for this practice to stop, the authorities discovered that some traders had resorted to subterfuge to disguise the fact that they were Chinese. One Ah Yong changed his name to Albert Young to try to secure a trading licence and officials noted that another licence had been issued since 'it did not occur to the Revenue authorities that Charles Canteen was a Chinaman'.[81]

Two Durban Chinese, Gumption and Wing, were refused permission to transfer their retail licence from 4th Avenue to Umbilo Road. The licensing officer said he

A Chinese general dealer's store in Dassiekraal, Port Elizabeth, circa 1920.

East London Chinese store, circa 1930.

An established Chinese business in Kingwilliamstown — this imposing stone building was bought by E.H. Kingston in 1930.

The interior of a Chinese shop in Port Elizabeth in the 1930s.

refused the transfer because the applicants were Asiatics and it 'was common knowledge in the Umbilo district that Asiatics were not wanted'.[82] In 1910, White traders in Port Elizabeth argued that Asiatic business was a serious menace and appealed for more legislation to 'eliminate the evil'.[83] The Chief Sanitary Inspector reported that the majority of grocery businesses in Port Elizabeth were run by Chinese — 94 Chinese grocers compared with 52 'Britishers' and 16 Indians in 1909. He particularly criticized Chinese traders for the common practice of giving 'm'basela' or 'pasella' — small presents of fruit or sweets to children making purchases. He pointed out that children generally frequented Chinese and Indian stores because of this practice.[84]

An interesting sociological point raised was the Chief Sanitary Inspector's view that Chinese grocers were only successful if they remained single.

> ... I can put my hand on four Chinamen in Port Elizabeth who were once in a fairly decent way as grocers while they were unmarried, but as soon as they took unto themselves wives the profits of their business were not sufficient to sustain them, so they gradually went to the wall, and to-day are living in town doing odd jobs... the married Chinaman has very little chance of competing with the unmarried one, and what shall we say for the European, with his higher standard of civilization and his greater responsibilities to his town and the State. The 84 unmarried Chinese grocers in Port Elizabeth carry on a tremendous trade under altogether unfair economical conditions.[85]

Chinese in Pretoria became the focus of public attention in September 1913 when the local Civic Association objected to the granting of licences to 27 traders. Stating that a total of 657 licences had already been issued to Asiatics, the association claimed

Those Fingerprints Again!

In the Transvaal, the issue of trade licences was inextricably linked with that of Asiatic registration and the thorny question of fingerprinting. When 27 Chinese in Pretoria applied for storekeepers' licences in 1913, they were required to submit proof of their identity. Eleven who refused to give their fingerprints were promptly arrested.

The lawyer appearing on their behalf, Alex Benson, wrote to the Governor-General of South Africa, Viscount Gladstone, to object to actions taken by the licensing authorities and to point out that Asiatics could not be compelled to give fingerprints if they could sign their names in English. He said his clients had been laughed at when they offered to sign their names.

> 'If this matter is allowed to go further, everyone of my clients will go to gaol, but the trouble will not end there. They feel ... that their trust has been most grossly and unlawfully abused...'[86]

Referring to the refusal of the Chinese to give fingerprints, the Registrar of Asiatics said he had been at the licensing proceedings but that he was 'only met with insolence and obstruction by the Chinese, most of whom had not the courtesy to remove their hats'.[87]

Although all the Chinese later submitted their registration certificates as proof of identity, eleven were prosecuted for refusing to give their fingerprints to an authorized official and convicted. Three were given warnings and the rest fined sums between £1 and £10.

this was too many and objected on health and general grounds to the Chinese obtaining licences.[88]

The *Pretoria News* took the opportunity to urge more stringent legislation to limit licences and to reiterate rumours concerning Chinese trade:

> It is said that the Chinese trade illicitly and that their cunning and ingenuity is such as to enable them to evade detection at the hands of the police and to carry on a nefarious traffic in drugs and forbidden stimulants...
>
> It is said that the Chinese traders cut down prices, that they sell well-known lines such, for instance, as Flag Cigarettes at a loss and that that loss can only be made good in some illegitimate manner.[89]

When the Germiston Town Council refused a grocer's licence to Lo Ko Lee, he appealed the case and the Mayor and town councillors were summoned to give evidence in court.[90] The renewal of licences to Chinese traders, particularly in the Transvaal, remained a contentious issue. By 1929, it became the subject of extensive correspondence between the Chinese and British governments. After a court decision to expel an Indian trader from Braamfontein, the Johannesburg City Council decided to suspend all applications from Asiatics and Coloured people for licences in 19 townships — practically prohibiting trade in all districts where Chinese had worked for decades. The affected areas included Albertskroon, Braamfontein, Burgersdorp, City and Suburban, Denver, Fordsburg, Ferreiras, Jeppestown, Johannesburg, Marshalls, Mayfair, Malvern, Norwood, Kenilworth and Booysens.[91]

In appeals to the British government to intervene, the Chinese Charge d'Affaires in London stated that 'societies had been formed ... for the purpose of expelling Chinese merchants from the country'. The Chinese Minister for Foreign Affairs in Nanking also expressed his concern 'that the lives and property of Chinese emigrants are in imminent danger' and pointed out 'that the expulsion for no reason of Chinese residents ... is greatly opposed to justice and equity'. The British Foreign Office replied that the areas from which Chinese were excluded were private townships in which the title deeds expressly prohibited occupation by Asiatics. Despite this restriction, Asiatics had illegally occupied and traded on such stands.[92]

In the following year, 1930, a Select Committee was appointed to inquire into the position of Asiatics in the Transvaal. Two representatives of the Transvaal Chinese Association, Dr L.N. Liang and Lai King, appeared to plead the case for the Chinese. Dr Liang, who played a prominent role in community affairs for more than 30 years, appealed for Chinese to be given equal rights and permission to trade without restriction.

In a lengthy submission in which he referred to laws affecting the Chinese, their standard of living and trading practices, he said the Chinese only asked that 'common justice and fairplay be dealt to us without racial discrimination'. Most Chinese in the Transvaal had resided in the country for 20 to 30 years and as permanent residents had earned rights of domicile and unrestricted trade. He said China was an independent nation and the status of the Chinese was different from that of other Asiatic communities.[93]

A report by the Johannesburg Municipality's Licensing Department to the Select Committee showed that 262 licences had been granted to Chinese traders and 57 held over in 1929. In the following years repeated appeals by the Chinese to be exempted from the restrictive provisions of land laws were to no avail.

Laundrymen

Laundries offered Chinese an independent avenue of employment in which sheer hard work was the chief requirement for survival. While there were more than six times the number of Chinese laundrymen in the Cape than in the Transvaal, as was to be expected, their presence sparked more controversy in the former Boer Republic than elsewhere. In the last decade of the 19th century, Zulu washermen, called the AmaWasha, held sway over Johannesburg's laundry business but their eventual, enforced removal out of the city cleared the way for other entrepreneurs to enter the market. Small hand-washing businesses, run by Chinese, increased dramatically in number from about a dozen in 1904 to over 40 in 1907.

Concentrated in central Johannesburg as well as in the suburbs of Fordsburg and Jeppe, Chinese laundries soon became the focus of agitation against their employment of poor White women. For some middle class sections of White Johannesburg, 'what truly horrified them were those cases in which such women workers developed intimate relationships with their employers — hardly the most surprising turn of events given the fact that the local Chinese community was almost exclusively male'.[94]

Moves were made to launch public wash-houses to provide employment for poor Whites and also to remove women from Chinese laundries. Speculating on the reasons for the widespread employment of White women in these laundries, one newspaper said:

> ... several white girls are employed in Chinese laundries — eight to my knowledge. They receive 6s. [shillings] a day: better pay than they could get from most European laundries.[95]

Another referred to the economic depression of the times:

> The Chinese have found it to their advantage to engage white girls, and in some instances they send them round to solicit washing. From the point of interest of the white girls the association can be nothing but degrading ... Quite a large number of the girls who have sought to earn the means of existence in Chinese laundries are of Dutch extraction, and their relatives unfortunately live in a state of penuriousness in Vrededorp ... Their environment has been against them. They have been compelled to take any employment offered, and the Chinese laundries offered an open door.[96]

Why customers chose to use Chinese instead of White laundries was vigorously debated in newspaper letter columns and one customer of the former offered these reasons for her patronage:

> Perhaps I can say why some people prefer coolies or Chinamen to do their washing ... I have tried many 'white' laundries, and their work and prices are disgraceful ... At least I can instruct coolies or Chinamen what to do. The white men in the laundries are content to let the black men do their work, and apparently forget to pass on instructions given...[97]

Public wash-house schemes for Johannesburg did not materialize and Chinese laundries remained in business, numbering some 46 by 1914.[98] As for the rest of the country, Chinese laundrymen went about their business without attracting undue attention. Random references have been uncovered to the existence of Chinese laundries in the major centres but few details on their activities.

Two Durban laundries, both owned by a man called Ah York, were the Sunlight Laundry and the British Laundry in Point Road in 1907. Other laundrymen in the city included Monson whose business was situated on the corner of Stamford Hill and Harvey roads, Joseph Ayock of Umbilo Road, and Leong Ding, also known as Chong Handson, who ran a laundry for many years at 66 Broad Street until his death in 1936.[99]

Port Elizabeth too had its fair share of laundries. In 1911, the city's laundry business was entirely in the hands of Asiatics and divided between 14 Chinese and six Indian businesses.[100] The Chinese laundries included the following: Chinese Laundry, Military Road; Foley, 49 Clyde Street; Hop Lee, Evatt Street; Long Tong, Hartman Road; Man Lee, 48 Walmer Road; Quang Chong, 80 Westbourne Road; Sing Lee, 1 Robson Street; Tong Look Laundry, Evatt Street and Wingson, 23 Green Street.[101] By 1925 the number of Chinese laundries had dwindled to eight businesses employing 27 people and serving just over 400 customers.[102]

East London had in 1912 at least three Chinese laundries. Low Bun and Man Lee, trading under the name 'F. Dickson' lived and worked in a wood and iron dwelling at No. 1 Wolseley Street where they starched and ironed clothing after washing them at the municipal wash houses. Ah Fat married a Miss M. A. Fetting, of 37 Rhodes Street, where he lived with her family and ran a laundry. A Chinese known as John Day worked in a business called 'The American Laundry'.[103]

One of the first Chinese laundry businesses in Cape Town which developed into perhaps the largest and most successful in the 1920s and 1930s was Sam Lee's. Established at 48 Pine Road, Woodstock in the late 19th century, it expanded into a large operation with about 30 branches throughout Cape Town.[104] By 1924 the success of Sam Lee's hand laundry led to his decision to modernize and the Woodstock premises were converted into a steam laundry.[105] Another Chinese laundry was run at a house called 'Seaford' in Main Road, Sea Point, by Lam Young and Ah Kim in 1922.[106]

Eating Houses and the 'Chinese Concoction'

Between 1905 and the early 1920s, numbers of Chinese in Johannesburg were involved in the 'kaffir eating house' trade, a label commonly used for establishments supplying food and drink to Black workers. Eating houses run by Chinese were particularly popular because of their sales of a heady, intoxicating brew, variously known as hopana, hop beer, ginger pop or the Chinese concoction.[107]

Although the number of businesses legally registered in the names of Chinese was small, they were among 'the most significant and most controversial participants in the early eating house trade'. From 1905, the Johannesburg municipality adopted a policy of refusing eating house licences to Chinese and even tried to prevent Chinese from being employed in eating houses.

At least two Chinese took local authorities to court to challenge their refusal to grant them eating house licences. In 1908 Lai Wing successfully appealed his case against the Johannesburg Public Health Committee and secured his licence.[108] A year later, a Roodepoort magistrate ordered the local Municipal Licensing Committee to grant Ah Shi an eating house licence. In his judgment, the magistrate said:

> It appeared ... the fact that the appellant was a Chinaman was the guiding reason which prompted the refusal ... It was for the Council to satisfy the Court that the principle of free competition in the licensing of Kafir eating houses would be contrary or prejudicial to the interests or rights of the community, of public interest, or of a class thereof ... as far as the natives themselves were concerned, the more competitors there were the better, and it was more likely that increased competition would mean a better food supply. The laws of supply and demand would ... apply as well to that class of business as any other.[109]

And it was the law of supply and demand which drew increasing numbers of Chinese into the eating house trade, especially their ability to brew the much sought-after drink, hopana. Eating houses generally were closely connected with illicit liquor sales, but hopana, although intoxicating, was usually found to contain less than two percent alcohol which did not contravene existing liquor laws.

Business boomed and the popularity of hopana grew. Reputed to be a traditional Chinese drink, it was made according to the individual recipes of its many brewers. Nevertheless its prime ingredients were hops, until the use of this was banned, or a combination of quassia chips, mixed spice, nutmeg, ginger, black sugar, liquorice as well as tulip root and dagga (marijuana).

Although the maximum number of eating house licences issued to Chinese in Johannesburg was 19 in 1919, many ran businesses licensed to Whites or even operated without licences. After numerous objections to the authorities about the manufacture of hopana and the effects of this on Black workers, eating houses were prohibited from selling the brew. Gradually the numbers of Chinese involved in eating houses tailed off, and by 1924 only eight premises were licensed to them.[110]

Interpreters

No more than a handful of Chinese countrywide had the necessary language skills to act as interpreters in court cases. Nevertheless the few references to Chinese interpreters in official documents highlight their unique position as well as the ongoing disputes they had with authorities over payment for their services.

As early as 1898, W.C. Lee, probably the first Chinese interpreter in Johannesburg, appealed to the State Secretary to secure his fees for interpreting in a case heard before the circuit court.[111] Others who worked part time as interpreters in Johannesburg's law courts included Leung Quinn and Martin Easton, two active participants in the passive resistance campaign.[112] Easton even applied to the Chief Justice for a permanent appointment as Cantonese interpreter for the Transvaal in 1908. Stating that he spoke several Chinese dialects and had a thorough knowledge of English, he said there were more than 1000 Cantonese in Johannesburg and no competent interpreter. The Law

Reprinted from *Transvaal Weekly Illustrated*, 2 October 1909.

The art of Interpreting

An episode with which frequenters of the Johannesburg Police Courts will be familiar in some form or another:

A Chinaman was called as a witness in the police court in the case of a driver who had run over a dog. The magistrate asked him what time it was when he saw the man run over the dog.

'Me no sabe,' replies the witness.

'I say,' replies the judge, 'what time was it when you saw this man run over the dog!'

'Me no sabe,' repeats John, smiling blandly.

'We shall have to have an interpreter,' comments his worship, as he realizes that the witness does not understand English; and accordingly another Chinaman is haled into court to act as interpreter. 'Ask the witness,' commands the magistrate, 'when he saw this man run over the dog.'

The interpreter turns to his fellow countryman and says: 'We chung lo, ho me choo lung wow, e-ho me no chow chee, loo know so-loo bing gong ton yit ben.'

To which the witness replies: 'Wong lin kee, wo hoo, wing chong lung yue lee, kin sing, choy yoke coey ying lung ding wha, sling suey way san yick ling toy bing coey bow taue, po tong po gou hung mow kim quong po tong po gou hung mow kim quong yuen lee chow you ben tong.'

The interpreter then turns to the magistrate and says: 'Him say "Two o'clock".'

Department informed him that there was no vacancy to which he could be appointed.[113]

In mid-1914 the wheels of justice ground to a halt when court cases involving Chinese had to be abandoned or postponed because of a 'strike' by Chinese interpreters in Johannesburg and Pretoria. Unwilling to work for 5s.0d per hour (the Law Department's stipulated casual rate of pay), all available interpreters demanded 7s.6d an hour and refused to undertake any interpreting until this was granted.[114]

Under the headline 'Chinese laughing at the Law', a local newspaper said justice was going astray and described a case in which charges against a Chinese shopkeeper had to be withdrawn after the accused insisted he could not speak English. It quoted an official saying

> ... with the present deadlock unbroken, any Chinaman charged with a crime cannot be adequately tried. It is a disgraceful way of going on, and the Government will have to do something, for justice is being laughed at by Chinatown.[115]

Officials approached the Acting Chinese Consul-General, Edwin Gunsaulus, requesting him to recommend a Cantonese interpreter willing to work for seven shillings an hour. Gunsaulus pointed out no qualified interpreter was willing to work for such a rate because of 'the irregularity of the time required for such services and ... the person undertaking to interpret must hold himself in readiness to appear at the Court's pleasure'.

Over the next few years men such as James Frank and John Fortoen, also earlier involved in the Reef's passive resistance campaign, worked as casual interpreters in Johannesburg and Pretoria at seven shillings an hour. Interestingly enough, by 1930 the Department of Justice's official tariff of fees for casual interpreters ('Indians and other Asiatics') still stood at the 1914 rate of 5s.0d per hour, to a maximum of 30s.0d per day.[116]

At least two Chinese interpreters worked in the Cape early this century. The Kimberley resident magistrate described M.W. Manshon, a general dealer, as the only reliable Chinese interpreter in the town. In 1908 Manshon too protested against the going rate of 4s.6d an hour, with a maximum of 10s.0d a day, saying this was not adequate compensation for his loss of business while working at court. The Cape Law Department agreed he could be paid a maximum of £1 a day.[117] Interpreter Law Yen Woon was employed to collect income tax from Chinese living in the Cape Peninsula in 1909 and 1910. For his services he was paid a total of £15.[118]

SOCIAL AMENITIES

On a day-to-day basis, the Chinese were primarily concerned with making a living. What there was of a social life was concentrated on family, clan and community activities. But it was impossible to remain totally removed from the wider society, and Chinese, like all other non-White groups in the country, were segregated in their use of public facilities such as trains, trams and hospitals.

In 1905, when the Chinese mine labourers were making their presence felt on the Witwatersrand, railways limited Chinese to travelling in third class compartments. Ticket sellers, however, had the discretion to decide whether or not to sell first and second class tickets to Chinese of a more 'respectable class'.[119] Train carriages were set aside for different race groups, and in later years Chinese were required to obtain letters from the Consulate-General to testify they were persons 'of good behaviour and high social standing' to enable them to travel in a separate compartment of a carriage reserved for Whites.[120]

From 1902 Johannesburg's traffic bye-laws placed racial restrictions on cabs and rickshas, and after electric trams started running in 1906, provision was also made for segregated travel. Conductors were empowered to evict anyone who was not White from trams, or who did not have a special exemption to be aboard. One of those exempted was the Chinese Consul-General, but other Chinese too tried to obtain permission to use trams, without success. From 1927, Coloureds, Indians and Chinese were permitted aboard trams, provided they used only the upstairs seats, positioned outside without cover.[121]

Throughout South Africa Chinese organizations made a point of sending regular donations to their local hospitals. After the 1909 court case on the Transvaal Chinese Association's funds, discussed in the previous chapter, an amount of £400 was set aside for the provision of a Chinese ward at the Johannesburg Hospital in 1912. The superintendent of the hospital, however, said that since no funds were available for a 'new Native hospital', a separate ward could not be provided for Chinese patients.

> I am, however, prepared to partition off four beds at the West end of the Kaffir Surgical Ward, which would give privacy and a separate entrance for Chinese patients.[122]

The cost of supplying this partitioned off section amounted to £13-15-0 and by 1913 was available to the Chinese. Local Chinese clubs supported the ward financially, replacing equipment and bedding when necessary.

On a more general level, Chinese in the Transvaal were prohibited from carrying firearms[123] and on a personal level, in common with all persons of colour, were not permitted to marry White women.[124]

Opium-smoking and gambling

Stereotypes often associated with Chinese in the public mind were opium-smoking and gambling. In the mass of documentation accumulated on the concerns of the community, references to these activities are, relatively speaking, few and far between. During the 19th century opium-smoking was a fashionable English habit, even indulged in by Conan Doyle's creation Sherlock Holmes. In China, however, its use had been banned from 1729, but British and American merchants launched a lucrative opium-smuggling trade, as a result of which millions of Chinese became addicted to the narcotic drug.

In South Africa, quite a few early Chinese settlers, men who lived alone without wives and families, sought temporary refuge from their day-to-day struggles in the euphoria of opium-smoking. Never widespread, the habit was catered for in tiny dens in the various 'Malaikams' throughout the country. From 1906, all importation of opium, except for medicinal purposes, was prohibited. While customs officials kept a sharp lookout for the smuggling of opium, attention was particularly focused on the problem when the Chinese mine labourers were on the Witwatersrand.[125]

In the Transvaal, an Opium Trade Regulation Ordinance (No. 25 of 1906) allowed individuals to purchase a maximum of two pounds of opium a month provided a medical prescription was produced and a magistrate issued a permit. Permits were not readily given, but officials were nevertheless concerned about reports that doctors prescribed opium too freely, thus allowing non-smokers to buy it for re-sale to addicts.[126]

By July 1908, Acting Chinese Consul-General Liu Ngai addressed a plea to the Prime Minister of the Cape Colony for further legislation to eradicate opium-smoking. He said the Imperial Chinese government had directed him 'to suppress the habit' among Chinese in South Africa and asked for opium-smoking to be made illegal. Included among his suggestions were gradual reduction in the prescribed amount of opium permitted to a smoker and the prohibition of all opium dens. The Prime Minister, John X. Merriman, assured him the government was addressing the issue, but because of budget constraints was unable to take any immediate steps.[127]

In the Transvaal church organizations launched a campaign to ban opium, citing the existence of more than 20 opium dens in Ferreirastown which were patronized by some 300 addicts, mainly Chinese, but also including Coloureds and Whites. The Transvaal Chinese Association allied itself with moves to prohibit opium importation

Evatt Street Opium Den

In the 1930s, Evatt Street, just beyond Port Elizabeth's city centre, was the hub of Chinese social life. Referred to as 'Malaikim', it was the place where Chinese bought provisions, met for meals, gathered at various clubs and where some frequented the opium den situated on the floor above the bean curd shop.

Under the watchful eye of the owner, known as 'Fa Tai Buk', between six to eight men at a time reclined on makeshift beds to take long puffs at pipes of the sweet-smelling opium. Midst clouds of smoke they sunk into reverie, talking for hours of their memories and experiences.

Harry Simpson recalled visiting the den as a child to listen to the stories told by the opium smokers.

> 'I used to enjoy smelling the opium ... it was so sweet, like being in a chocolate factory. First they used to roast the opium over a flame ... it was wet like a sticky goo and then they put it into the hole in the opium pipe to smoke. They would blow out this huge cloud of smoke. I tell you, it smelled fantastic. And then they talked about their old days in China, what they did, how naughty they were as children ... it was fascinating.'[128]

Edmund Quat, whose father ran the Chinese medicine shop in Evatt Street for many years, also recollected the opium den:

> 'It was in a double-storey building. When I was a young boy, out of curiosity I went upstairs and there I saw the people smoking opium. They were lounging on their sides ... the opium smelt sweet. I will always remember that smell.'[129]

and in a letter to the Colonial Secretary said the continued availability of opium 'had caused very great moral and physical evil'.[130]

By June 1909 new legislative measures were introduced to curb opium-smoking,[131] and in the following years isolated references were found to elderly Chinese, unable to give up the habit, who continued patronizing a few opium dens, in Ferreirastown, Johannesburg, and in Evatt Street, Port Elizabeth.

Gambling was a popular pastime among local Chinese who generally viewed it as a social activity and not a vice. This perspective and legal prohibitions on games of chance led to quite a few trials and convictions. Chinese have often been described as gamblers at heart, and many indulged in gambling 'as an antidote to boredom and loneliness', in search of quick fortune, but for just as many, resulted in inevitable ruin.[132] Chinese usually gambled among themselves, playing games such as fan tan, poker and mahjong. In later years the popularity of numbers games or lotteries such as puck-apu and fah fee extended to other sectors of the population who took part in draws organized by Chinese.

Newspaper reports and official documents show that Chinese were convicted of gambling in all major towns where they had settled — Kimberley, Port Elizabeth, Cape Town and Johannesburg. Police often used 'traps' to uncover illegal gambling activities and were able to produce in court all the paraphernalia for such games as poker, fan tan and tin gau (dominoes).

When three Cape Town laundrymen were found guilty of running a gambling house in 1905, they were each fined £100 or four months' jail and the 33 Chinese present on their premises were each fined £5.[133] The Cape's Chinese Exclusion Act, however, imposed additional penalties on those who indulged in gambling. It stipulated that a Chinese twice convicted of gambling would be deported to China after serving whatever sentence had been imposed for the crime.

Social clubs formed by Chinese in the first half of the century usually included some form of gambling as a recreational amenity for members. By levying a commission on the different games played, many clubs were able to raise substantial sums of money for charitable activities and relief work.

By the time the Union of South Africa came into being in 1910, Chinese had settled in three of the country's four provinces. More stringent immigration legislation limited any substantial growth in their numbers, but the gradual influx of wives and children contributed towards the development of a compact, closely-knit community of no more than 3000 people in 1936. In many respects the labyrinth of laws which confronted the Chinese at every turn encouraged the formation of a multitude of community organizations countrywide. How such organizations reflected community needs and aspirations is fully examined in the next chapter.

8

Community Organizations Flourish

What organizations did the Chinese form to give themselves a group identity? How did such support structures reflect the diverse nature and needs of this evolving community? Covering the period 1906 to 1948, this chapter outlines the development of a strong community spirit in various parts of the country and the formation of different types of Chinese organizations to express political, economic, social and cultural aspirations.

In the first few decades of this century, the Chinese formed a community united largely through adversity. Distinguished on the grounds of race, nationality and language, they pooled resources among themselves and fostered a community spirit through the establishment of a variety of social and political organizations.

Constituting a virtually negligible minority group, they nonetheless concentrated on improving their position in South African society. The slow but steady immigration of Chinese women changed the nature of community life as greater emphasis was placed on the family unit, and particularly the future security of children born in South Africa.

The first generations of settlers retained firm ties with their homeland, some dreaming of returning there one day, but all hoping that China could regain its prestige as a strong and independent country. Many who had ventured abroad believed the discrimination they encountered was closely tied to the world's perception of China, at the turn of the century, as weak, corrupt and powerless.

China itself was undergoing dramatic changes. In 1911, after prolonged skirmishes with rebel groups, the imperial Ch'ing dynasty was toppled and revolutionaries established the Republic of China. The fledgling years of the new republic were difficult and China remained a country ruled by feudal warlords and split into factional groups. Both the first president, Dr Sun Yat Sen, and later his successor, Chiang Kai Shek, aimed to unite the country under the control of the Kuomintang (Nationalist Party). The 1920s, however, saw the gradual rise of communism and in the 1930s China was pitched into war with long-time rival, Japan.

All these events were of concern to the Chinese in far-off South Africa. They mustered what financial support they could to assist the nationalist movement and formed branches of the Kuomintang around the country. Several young Chinese were fired up with dreams of going to China to help build the nation and to assist in the war against Japan. But for most Chinese organizations, the immediate needs of the developing community in South Africa remained priorities.

Several organizations were working in major centres before and after the formation of the Union of South Africa in 1910. These offered settlers a support system, a network of compatriots who spoke a common dialect and who shared the same experiences in trying to fit into a foreign land. Although most community organizations directed their attention to the restrictions imposed on Chinese, several were purely social in character. Such organizations offered a variety of recreational facilities and the opportunity to meet for a game of billiards or mahjong, read Chinese newspapers or ask a more educated compatriot to write Chinese letters to send home. Several clubs and clan groups also organized burials, arranged for inscriptions on tombstones or simply offered a monthly venue for the draw of the 'fee' or 'hui' money-lending scheme.

A significant aspect of census statistics on the Chinese is that they excluded the Chinese mine labourers, as the 1904 census was held before they arrived and the 1911 census after their repatriation. The numbers of Chinese in South Africa declined between 1904 and 1921 as some returned to China, others died and the Cape's Chinese Exclusion Act as well as the Union's 1913 Immigrants Regulation Act took its toll. The increased immigration of women, however, coupled with births in the country, contributed towards a steady growth in the community's size in the following years. The graph below reflects the total number of Chinese men and women as recorded in the relevant official censuses and the community's distribution in the Cape, Natal and the Transvaal.

Chinese in South Africa

	1904	*1921*	*1936*	*1946*
Males	2434	1487	1882	2463
Females	23	341	1062	1877
Total	2457	1828	2944	4340
Distribution				
Cape	1380	732	1244	
Natal	165	108	82	
Transvaal	912	988	1618	

Source: South Africa. Office of Census and Statistics.[1]

Chinese in South Africa

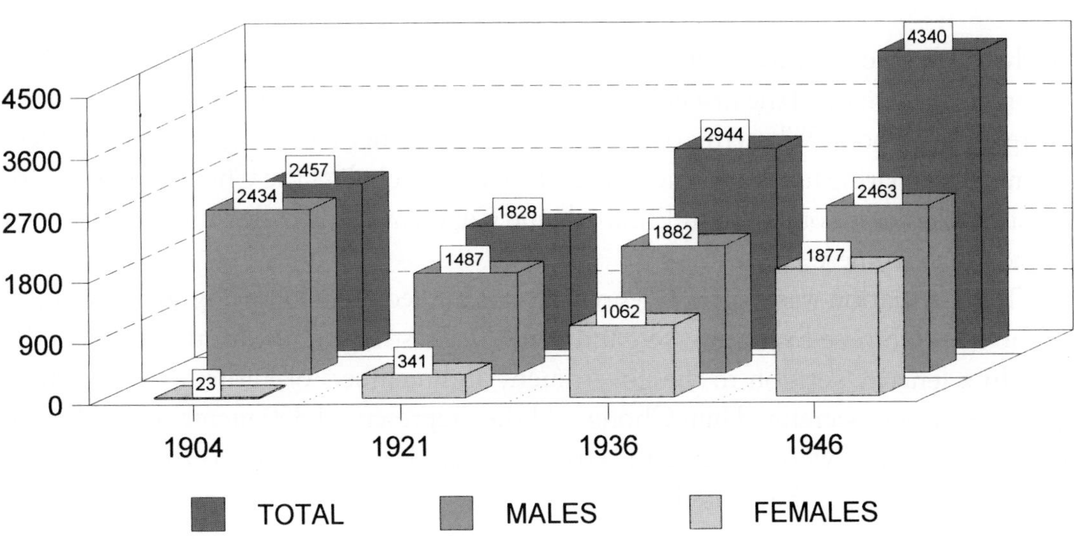

Census figures for 1921, 1936 and 1946 also tabulated the numbers of Asiatics born in China. Since immigration was prohibited (except for wives and children) and only a handful of Chinese in the country were born elsewhere, it would be fair to assume that the balance of Chinese recorded in the total figures were born in South Africa. From the table below, it is interesting to note therefore that more than half of the Chinese population in 1946 was South African-born.

Birthplace

	1921	*1936*	*1946*
Total No. of Chinese	1828	2944	4340
Born in China	1409	1648	1878
Presumed born in South Africa	419	1296	2462

Source: South Africa. Office of Census and Statistics.

This chapter covers the interests of the many formal and informal community organizations established before 1948, and outlines aspects of general community life, excluding activities relating to the Sino-Japanese War (1937– 1945), which follow in the next chapter. Closely interwoven with the growth of community organizations was the concern of parents for the education of their children. Community groups therefore not only addressed the current social, business and political needs of the Chinese, but also turned their attention to the formation of Chinese schools. Because of the importance of this issue to the overall development of the community, the subject of education will be dealt with separately.

EARLIEST BROAD-BASED CHINESE ASSOCIATION

In the Cape, the early formation of the Cape Colony Chinese Association — shortly before 1906 — marked the first effort by scattered community groups to create a broader representative body. When this organization gave evidence before a government Select Committee relating to Asiatic grievances, it spoke on behalf of the Chinese associations of Kimberley, East London, Port Elizabeth and Cape Town and called itself the 'Cape of Good Hope Chinese Association'.

The association was most active in the years immediately following the imposition of the 1904 Chinese Exclusion Act, and by 1920 was still pleading for the repeal of the law. In a lengthy petition to the government and members of Parliament, chairman Leong Song and secretary Hum Chong said they represented 850 members resident in the Cape, most of whom wished to settle and regard South Africa as their home. Of Chinese aspirations, they stated:

> ... And even though they may never be granted the full rights of citizenship, in so far as it involved the granting of the franchise, they must nevertheless, in their own interest, put it on its lowest basis — work for the good of the country as a whole and the greater their rights in the country, the greater their interest and consequently the greater their endeavours for the good of the land they have adopted.

They also pointed out the Chinese labourers, against whom the Chinese Exclusion Act had originally been directed, had long since been repatriated.[2] No further documentation on the organization has been found. The obvious communication difficulties in maintaining such a broadly based grouping, the strengthening of local organizations in each town as well as the increasing involvement of the Consul-General in community affairs may have contributed to its demise.

Its existence nevertheless foreshadowed later drives to unite all the scattered Chinese 'communities' in the country under a national umbrella body. The first such attempt took place at an All South Africa Chinese Conference held in Johannesburg in August 1930, but it would take yet another twenty years before a formally constituted, national organization emerged in the 1950s to represent the Chinese in South Africa as a whole.

Prior to 1948, a diverse array of organizations developed in each region where Chinese had settled, particularly in the eastern Cape and the Transvaal where the population was most concentrated. To reflect the extent of their activities, each area will be covered geographically.

NATAL

The numbers of Chinese in Natal dwindled from 165 in 1904 to fewer than 100 in 1936.[3] The majority lived in Durban, with a mere handful in Pietermaritzburg. Making up the smallest group of Chinese in the country, they nevertheless formed a loosely-knit community and, by 1909, were represented by an organization called 'The Chinese Association'.

According to a printed letterhead lodged in the Pietermaritzburg Archives, the association was based at 500 West Street, Durban. Nothing is known of its social activities, if any, but from the outset the organization certainly reflected concern for the welfare of Chinese in Natal. In a letter to the Chief Immigration Officer, the association's chairman, L. Mundon, said:

> I have been informed that, for some time past, Chinese who have applied for Domicile Certificates or other documents, have been asked to take their boots off when standing for the measurement of their height. This, besides being an arrogance, is considered an indignity by the Chinese in having to take off their boots.
>
> May I ask you to be so good to dispense with this method in measuring the height of any Chinese who may in future apply for Domicile Certificate or Visiting Permit. This is a special favour which I beg to ask of you on behalf of my countrymen, and which, I trust, will receive your favourable consideration.

The request was dismissed on the grounds that official documents required correct personal descriptions of the holders, including their height and that 'correct height is not ascertainable if the person measured is standing in his boots.' The Principal Immigration Restriction Officer also made the following observation on Mundon's request:

> At the same time I have to point out to you that as there is no compulsion on any person to take out a certificate of Domicile, the persons who object to removing their boots are entirely at liberty to avoid the objectionable process.[4]

Domicile certificates were required to prove residence in Natal and Chinese leaving the colony were not permitted to re-enter without this document.

By the 1920s and 1930s, chairmanship of the organization alternated between James Louis Fontbin and Lee Rennie Chapson, both established traders in Durban. They maintained contact with the Chinese Consulate-General in Johannesburg, using this office to voice their concerns about discrimination encountered as far as schooling, hospitals and access to liquor were concerned.

In 1928, at the tender age of 16, Bertram Lee was co-opted onto the Chinese association committee because of his English language skills. Having been born in Durban in 1912, the young man was asked to interpret in court, and to handle English correspondence for the organization. He said:

> The association was run by the older members, and it was always Chinese policy to keep a low profile. We were never aggressive in any way ... and we merely dealt with any incident that occurred. The association was formed to present unity. The community was very scattered and isolated, and with the association we were at least together.[5]

When South Africa's liquor laws were changed in 1928, preventing Natal Chinese from purchasing alcohol, a petition was circulated in the community to voice objections. Signed by 30 members of families in Durban and Pietermaritzburg, the petition appealed for exemption to be granted to Chinese.[6]

Socially, the Durban Chinese kept very much to themselves, avoiding public amenities wherever possible, even the city's beaches. The 'colour bar' was accepted as part of life and social activities consisted of picnics or boating trips, including games of mahjong.[7]

As the nearest South African port to the Transvaal for embarkation onto major shipping lines to the east, Durban was an essential stop-over point for many Chinese from the interior. Wary of public hotels which would refuse them accommodation, many Chinese made use of a 'boarding house' run by the Song family in Point Road. For £1 a night, they were able to share a room with four beds. More affluent Chinese, however, stayed in the most expensive hotels which did not raise objections to their patronage.[8]

During World War II the increased sea traffic through Durban's harbour and the arrival of scores of Chinese seamen caused an upsurge in community activity which will be outlined in the next chapter.

KIMBERLEY

No records remain of the early activities of the Kimberley Chinese Association beyond references to its support for the work of the Cape Colony Chinese Association in 1908. Perhaps it was no more than a name adopted by the city's Chinese for the purposes of presenting a united front against Cape legislation. Nevertheless, the 'Kaiyin Fee Gon', established in 1895, and also known as the Chinese Benevolent Society, continued to be the social hub of the community. Chinese met socially at its headquarters in the Malay Camp over weekends to gamble, to draw the monthly 'fee' or to visit the Guan Ti shrine housed there.

By 1920, another Chinese club was established in Coghlan Street, also in the Malay Camp. According to community elders, this was the headquarters of the Chinese Nationalist party, the Kuomintang (KMT), which in 1922 had a membership of 40 people.[9] The KMT club served as a general community meeting place for recreation and gambling. It promoted the welfare of the Chinese homeland, periodically raising money from the local community for relief work after floods or droughts in China.[10]

Both these clubs played a key role in forging a close-knit community in Kimberley numbering, in 1936, a total of 140 people — 94 males and 46 females.[11] By the mid-1940s, however, the Malay Camp became the target of an extensive slum clearance programme to make way for Kimberley's new civic centre. Over the years the area had become increasingly overcrowded and was often described as 'one of the worst slums in South Africa.'[12] Leases were terminated and buildings throughout the Malay Camp demolished, including the two Chinese clubs.

For the Kimberley Chinese, the loss of these venues did not mean social activity and interaction dwindled. Instead, the community entered a new phase in which the younger generation came into its own. The Kimberley Chinese Association was formed sometime in the late 1930s or early 1940s, with the objective of establishing a Chinese school. Funds were raised from Chinese throughout the country and, combined with the proceeds received from the expropriation of the 'Kai Yin Fee Gon' building in the Malay Camp, used to purchase an old hotel in York Street.[13]

This building was renovated and in 1945 became the headquarters of the Kimberley Chinese Association, as well as the new site of the Guan Ti shrine. Chinese language classes were offered for a year or two, but difficulties in funding and running a fully-fledged Chinese school led to the venture being stopped. The association, whose first chairman was Wai Sing Chan Yan, concerned itself with general issues affecting the Chinese and participated in the wider Kimberley community's fund-raising efforts during World War II.

As part of the resurgence in community activity, young Chinese decided, in 1943, to establish the Kimberley Chinese Recreation Club (KCRC). Unlike previous social clubs for the older generation which offered gambling and opportunities to reminisce on days gone by in China, KCRC members in their teens and twenties organized a host of sports and social activities reflecting the changing interests and lifestyles of the new generation.

They played cricket, soccer and softball. Using the York Street headquarters of the Kimberley Chinese Association, they ran ballroom dancing classes, film shows, concerts and plays and organized regular table tennis and badminton matches. Every Christmas they organized sports matches, followed by a dance through the night which was rounded off with an all-day picnic along the banks of the Modder River. 'Watermelon fights' were highlights of the occasion and transport for all was provided courtesy of a lorry belonging to the Chinese owner of a local brickfields![14]

The young Chinese of Kimberley, as well as those in East London, had the advantages of being part of a particularly close-knit community, but with sufficient numbers to enable them to organize group activities. Elsewhere, in Durban and Cape Town, the Chinese were too dispersed to make the most of the interests of a specific age group. In Port Elizabeth and Johannesburg on the other hand, the Chinese communities were more diversified and less united. Although their numbers enabled them to form a variety of Chinese organizations, few matched the simple, high-spirited pleasures of the KCRC in the course of the 1940s.

CAPE TOWN

The Cape Town Chinese Association was already active in 1902 and concentrated its efforts on obtaining the repeal of the Cape's Chinese Exclusion Act.[15] Court records show that the organization either owned or rented property which it used as headquarters. In March 1908, a man called Tang Hang was sentenced to 10 days' imprisonment for 'damage to property in the Chinese Association.'[16] The location of the association's premises was however not stated.

By April 1921 a constitution was drawn up and the association was formally named the Chinese Republic United Association. Open to all Chinese, it stipulated a monthly membership fee of 10 shillings. Its headquarters were situated at Nos. 168, 170 and 172 Loop Street — property purchased on behalf of the association whose trustees were Tim Fat, Hum Chung, Charles Edward Kow, Tam Hingwoo, Ah Foo, Young Kee, Nean Son, Coo Wan and C. Johns. At least two of these trustees, Hum Chung and Tam Hingwoo, also acted as representatives of the umbrella body, the Cape Colony Chinese Association.

By naming their organization the Chinese Republic United Association, Cape Town's community reflected their allegiance to China as their homeland and their support for the newly formed republic. The stated objects of the association however were 'to constitute and provide a place for meeting and recreation of members.'[17]

Poultry was kept in the yard behind the association's headquarters, and probably provided some of the meals when members met socially over weekends. The organization was run by a committee of 20 members who were required to meet every month, and to hold a general meeting of all members annually.

The association constitution also provided for the fining, suspension and expulsion of members convicted of 'crimes against the laws of the country on the Association's premises.' This provision may have been intended to prevent gambling at the association's headquarters, but it is likely the community, as in other centres, also enjoyed regular games of mahjong and fan tan, and organized a 'fee' or 'hui' to assist one another.

No minutes of meetings have been traced to reflect the association's activities, but it is known that the chairman in 1922 was Tin Fat. The Chinese Republic United Association's premises were used for community celebrations such as weddings and also served as accommodation for representatives from other parts of the country who visited Cape Town to object to proposed Class Areas legislation in 1924.

The headquarters of the Chinese Republic United Association in Loop Street, Cape Town in the 1930s.

Members of the Chinese Republic United Association in 1943.

By the 1930s, the association organized regular gatherings of the community to celebrate major festivals such as Chinese New Year and the Double Ten, so called because it was held on the 10th day of the 10th month to mark the anniversary of the founding of the Republic of China on 10 October 1911. In 1936 the Chinese population of Cape Town and its suburbs was 102, being 64 men and 38 women.[18]

The war years greatly increased sea traffic around the Cape and the local community faced the need to accommodate and assist the hundreds of Chinese sailors stationed aboard ships temporarily in dock. This aspect of their activities will be outlined later. In the 1940s, the Chinese Republic United Association moved from its Loop Street premises, first to a house in Palmyra Road, Claremont in 1943, and then to another two-storey house in Avenue Road, Mowbray.[19]

By 1945 the Chinese association had 61 adult male members[20] and embarked on plans to build a hall on the Mowbray site to accommodate 800 people. Several of the younger Chinese played tennis and table-tennis at the association's premises, and in later years also formed sports clubs. Reflecting on the aims of the organization during this period, elderly community members said it was important to unite the different Cantonese and Moiyeanese sections of the community as well as to ensure the young retained an awareness of their Chinese heritage.

'The whole point of the association really was to keep our community together, to instill Chinese thoughts into our young people and to establish a good school with Chinese included in the curriculum. But because of our small numbers, the school was never a success ... We had to carry on simply because other schools were closed to us,' said Bertram Lee, who had moved to Cape Town from Durban and served for many years as the organization's English-language secretary.

Many of Cape Town's established Chinese families moved there from Port Elizabeth, citing difficulties in obtaining business licences in the eastern Cape as a reason. The freer, more cosmopolitan nature of Cape Town enabled the Chinese to trade in White, Coloured and Black areas with fewer restrictions.

EAST LONDON

Beyond its stalwart protests against the Chinese Exclusion Act in 1905, little is known of the activities of the East London Chinese Association prior to 1930. Community elders believe the first chairman may have been Tan Pak Fah, a Chinese trader from Singapore who adopted the name Bernard Brown in East London.[21]

When the Chinese community countrywide was up in arms over the proposed Class Areas Bill in 1924, the East London Chinese Association agreed to support any action suggested by their compatriots in Port Elizabeth.[22] It organized a regular 'fee' or 'hui' to give their fellow Chinese access to capital at a low interest rate and functioned as a social organization. Perhaps some of the old people also met to smoke opium and to share reminiscences of their homes in China.

By 1931, Yung Mason was chairman of the association and John Louis Fontbin the vice chairman. Without permanent premises, members held monthly meetings to draw the 'fee' in the barn behind a shop belonging to Wong Kee, who also used the surname 'Green', in St John's Road, North End. Lee Sing Gen took over the chairmanship of the organization and, with men such as Mason, Wong Chong, Tup Chong and Wong Kun, purchased premises in St Peter's Road to enable them to establish a Chinese school sometime in the mid-1930s.[23]

The support of Chinese in other parts of the country was enlisted as association members travelled widely to raise funds. A major motivation to strengthen the Chinese Association and start a school was to ensure the future of the new generation. Lee Sing Gen, who remained active on the association for more than three decades said:

> We were thinking of the younger generation, worrying about them. When they grew up, we wanted them to read Chinese as well as they read English and so on.

The Chinese Association addressed the problems faced by the community and levied subscription fees on members of between 10s.0d and £1. In 1936, the East London

Chinese population totalled 117 people, made up of 78 males and 39 females.[24] A handful of Chinese living in Kingwilliamstown and Queenstown also took part in the East London Chinese Association's activities.

By late 1946, idealistic and enthusiastic young members of the community formed the Chinese Youth Society to promote sporting and cultural activities. Through the medium of a regular newsletter called 'New China', written by Aubrey Wong On, the youth group outlined its aim to unite the community and adopted the motto 'one for all and all for one'. It organized monthly meetings as well as picnics, dances, bazaars and tennis tournaments.

The first office bearers of the society were L. Fontbin, F. Mason, A. Wong On and H. Lee Sun. Committee members were also appointed to organise entertainment, sport, physical culture, music and art. As in Port Elizabeth, the group also formed its own band which was called the 'Rose Room Orchestra'. Consisting of a tenor sax, an alto sax, a clarinet, drums, base and piano, the orchestra was a popular attraction at social functions.[25]

East London's Chinese Youth Society was very much part of the new breed of Chinese organizations which would mushroom throughout the country in the following years. Usually formed by the first generation of university-educated Chinese, they expressed more vocally the changed aspirations of the young who had been born in South Africa but who also grappled with the problem of what it meant to be Chinese in a 'foreign' country.

PORT ELIZABETH AND ENVIRONS

Although only the second largest settlement, Port Elizabeth's community constituted the highest density of Chinese in South Africa. And with settlers from neighbouring towns, they formed a variety of political, social and business organizations. No doubt some existed for a year or two then disappeared without trace. Informal clan organizations of people who shared the same surname met either to operate a loan club (fee / hui) (會) or to arrange communal visits to cemeteries.

Prejudices from their homeland remained strong and separate organizations were formed for Moiyeanese and Cantonese. Not all the bodies were however mutually exclusive, and members active in one organization often played key roles in other community groups.

When the Spanish Flu Epidemic of 1918 took its toll on lives throughout South Africa, Chinese were among the more than 2000 people in the vicinity of Port Elizabeth who died between October and December that year.[26] A row of cement topped graves, many without headstones, in the Chinese section of the North End cemetery offers mute testimony to the impact of the epidemic on the community. At least a dozen children and women in their twenties and thirties died suddenly and community elders still recount how the city turned into a ghost town as the influenza spread. By 1936 Chinese in Port Elizabeth and suburbs numbered 705 people — 419 males and 286 females.[27]

A handful of Chinese settled in the more outlying areas of the Eastern Cape such as Somerset East, Grahamstown, Cradock, Elliot and Aliwal North. Far too few in number to create any formal organizations, they became self-contained family units which kept very much to themselves and only dealt with other race groups in their small general trading stores. In both Somerset East and Grahamstown where there were a few families, young Chinese formed small tennis clubs in the 1940s to compete among themselves.

Chinese Association

The first chairman of the Port Elizabeth Chinese Association was probably W. Singson. He was described as president of the association in 1905 when he asked the Natal authorities to clarify restrictions on the immigration of Chinese.[28] Also allied to the Cape Colony Chinese Association, the Port Elizabeth organization collected funds from community members in 1906 to pay for a representative to travel to London to appeal against the Chinese Exclusion Act.[29]

The Chinese Association aimed to unite the Chinese, promote their interests and improve their conditions. Strapped for funds, it was unable to establish permanent headquarters and rented premises for its meetings.[30] Membership was open to both Moiyeanese and Cantonese, and when a reorganized constitution was drawn up in 1919, special provision was made to ensure the executive committee consisted of an equal number of Moiyeanese and Cantonese.[31]

At that time the association did not limit its jurisdiction to Port Elizabeth alone and membership was open to any Chinese, even those temporarily resident in the Union of South Africa. Subscriptions required were substantially lower than the 10s.0d.

When Helen Ah Yui arrived in the eastern Cape as the young bride of Ignatius Ah Yui in the early 1920s, she walked some 15 miles to reach her new home. The couple travelled by train from Port Elizabeth, disembarking at Cookhouse, the nearest station to the town of Somerset East. Assuming that villages were as closely situated as in her home county of Canton, she suggested they walk ... only to find it was a long journey on foot, laden with baggage. They nonetheless settled happily in Somerset East where Mrs Ah Yui gave birth to 13 children.

per month asked of members of the Cape Town association — owners and employees in any profession, business or trade paid 1s.0d. a month, and shops, laundries, cafes or market gardens a sum of 2s.0d. a month. Apart from outlining the duties of various committee members, the constitution also allowed the association to make loans of up to £50 to members.

The chairman of the association in 1919 was Chong Lawson and committee members included Lai Green and L. Chu Lum. The revised constitution was drafted in Chinese and translated into English by the general secretary, Lo Pong, a self-educated man who remained active in community affairs for many years in Port Elizabeth, Uitenhage and Queenstown.

In his preface to the constitution Lo Pong urged unity within the community and summarized the purpose of the association:

> What we desire is that each and every member shall do his share towards making this Association a success and a source of interest and benefit to all our fellow countrymen. We desire that you shall rise above all evil passions and cultivate the best part of human nature with lofty ambition, striving always to climb up the ladder of knowledge, progress and peace.[32]

In 1922, the Chinese Association established its base in a building belonging to the Moi Yean Commercial Association at 162 Queen Street, where it remained for at least thirteen years, paying rent of up to £60 per year for use of the premises.[33] The association maintained close contact with Consul-General Liu Ngai, and in 1924 urged him to oppose the promulgation of the Class Areas Bill, a measure providing for the residential and trading segregation of Asiatics. With Chinese in Uitenhage, they formed the 'Port Elizabeth and Uitenhage Anti Bill Joint Committee' and raised over £200, more than half of which was used for the Consul-General's travelling expenses.

Chong Lawson was succeeded as chairman of the association by L.S. Johnson and later by Lo Yang in 1930. The association addressed problems confronting Chinese generally, and in June 1935 compiled a comprehensive report on the position of the Chinese for observers despatched to South Africa by China's Foreign Ministry in Nanking.

Written by the Chinese secretary, Yuen Whiteley, the report recounted the history of Chinese settlement, the legal restraints on immigration and trade, and included the following observations on life for the Chinese in Port Elizabeth:

> We ... are affected by harsh restrictions and suffer racial discrimination. The situation is so unbearable, it is as though we live through the fire of hell ... Overseas Chinese here exist in the most atrocious conditions, belittled by others ... they are in no better a position than that of stateless Blacks ...
>
> There are a total of 658 Chinese here — 267 men, 179 women and the rest children ... A few men have married local women ... Besides traders, some Chinese are laundrymen and farmers. Those unemployed are not small in number ...
>
> There are 162 shops — other than about 10 fruit shops and cafes, they are mostly grocery stores. Many of us came empty handed, forced by circumstances. To raise capital, we borrowed from relatives and friends ... only a handful of Chinese shops are profitable ... the rest eke out a mere existence.[34]

Discussing the activities of the Chinese Association, the report deplored the lack of unity in the community and said the formation of cliques had led to a loss in confidence in the association.

> More often than not, matters are not carried out according to resolutions passed ... We have no special power to force others to comply ... They not only ignore the resolutions passed, they refuse to pay annual subscriptions. When one person takes the lead, many others follow.

Such periodic divisions in the ranks plagued virtually every Chinese organization, but the association, then under the chairmanship of Foong Chong, survived and in 1937, accumulated sufficient funds to move out of its rented premises and erect its own headquarters at 64 Evatt Street.[35] The new building was just a few minutes' walk away from the Moi Yean Commercial Association and situated in the heart of 'Malaikim', the social centre for community activities in the first half of this century.

Disunity within the community, fuelled perhaps by clan rivalries, personality clashes, as well as the classic divide between the old and the young, led to changes in the Chinese Association in the late 1930s. After a hotly contested election, a new committee was installed, first with Choo King and then Lo Yank as chairmen. In 1940, Walter Sout Chong Wing King, then only 24 years old, was elected chairman of the Eastern Province Chinese Association, a position he held for 24 years until his death in 1964.

The headquarters of the Eastern Province Chinese Association, at No. 64 Evatt Street, Port Elizabeth, erected in 1937.

Walter Sout Chong Wing King

Dedicated, untiring, selfless, a man of vision who sought only to improve the lot of the Chinese people of South Africa — these are just some of the many descriptions given by friends and family of Walter Sout Chong Wing King. Born in Port Elizabeth in 1915, the third son of Lim Wing King, who left Moiyean (Meixian) in south China at the turn of the century, he was to become an influential and highly respected community leader both in his home city and throughout South Africa.

Walter Sout Chong Wing King, chairman of the E.P. Chinese Association.

As a three-year-old boy, he was sent to China after the death of his mother in the Influenza Epidemic of 1918, returning at the age of 14 to work in his father's shop. He became chairman of the Eastern Province Chinese Association at the relatively tender age of 24 in 1940. In this capacity, until his death in 1964, he worked to unite the Chinese community and to improve educational standards with the foundation of the Chinese High School in Port Elizabeth.

Wing King believed the wider community needed to see that Chinese people were their equals and encouraged active participation in fund-raising during World War II as well as in Port Elizabeth's various charitable drives. Despite the responsibilities of running a general dealer's business in Walmer and supporting six children, he sacrificed much time to his community activities.

Reflecting on the reasons for the impact he made on the community, his English tutor, Mrs Amy Heard, wrote in 1964 that it had been 'the fine quality of his character — his honesty, sincerity, sympathy, and "Do unto others as you would they should do unto you" attitude...' Wing King died at the age of 48 from cancer, and in a moving tribute to him, Mrs Heard added:

> '... I felt that Walter's life had been a great success, he had raised the status of his people, increased their educational facilities, set his children a wonderful example and earned the respect of the world in which he lived, and like St Paul "Had fought the good fight and finished his course".'[36]

Early in 1942 the association approached the Minister of the Interior to grant it recognition as the official representative body for Chinese in Port Elizabeth, Uitenhage, Grahamstown, Somerset East and Cradock. Offering to mediate on behalf of the community with the authorities, the association pointed out it had assisted in matters relating to Chinese immigration and wished to ensure that the Chinese did not 'in any way act unfavourably towards the Administration.'[37] The Commissioner for Asiatic Affairs objected to any official standing being accorded the association, stating:

> ... there can be no question of the official recognition of a purely private Chinese Organization to act as an intermediary between the Government and the Chinese Community. It is considered that the Chinese Consul-General is obviously the only person who should deal with the Government on general questions affecting the nationals of his country who are in the Union.[38]

In the following years, the association became integrally involved in matters affecting the education of the young as well as general issues relating to the community's welfare.

Moi Yean Commercial Association

Said by some community elders to be the oldest Chinese organization in Port Elizabeth, the Moi Yean Commercial Association was formed early this century to serve the interests of Moiyeanese traders and to strengthen ties with their home county of Moi Yean (Meixian) in south China. The holding of a monthly loan club meeting ('fee' 會) was most likely its chief activity and members assisted each other with advice and guidance in commercial matters.

The Moi Yean Commercial Association was formally reconstituted as an organization in 1918 after it purchased property at Number 162 Queen Street for its headquarters. By that time it had already accumulated assets in excess of $100 000 (Chinese dollars) and established a branch in Moi Yean, China, where it was planning to erect a five-storey building.[39]

The amended constitution stated that the organization had been formed by Moiyeanese businessmen to 'foster better relations, to extend business activities and also to establish a Chinese School for the benefit of the Moi Yean community.' While these objectives were for the benefit of Chinese settled in Port Elizabeth, the Moi Yean Commercial Association clearly intended to forge close links with 'home', as evidenced by these reminders to members:

> The members of the association have a duty to assist in charitable affairs in Moi Yean (China) and to publicize and promote such activities.
>
> The members should endeavour to promote business enterprises or investments in Moi Yean, whether in partnership or on a shareholding basis to show our remembrance of our origins.
>
> This association strives to unite and assist the Moi Yean community in their efforts in business and industry which will be for the benefit of all members.

Its trustees in 1918 were Chong Lawson, Wong Singmin and Martin Sin Hidge and the organization was run by a committee of 19 members, elected by secret ballot. Membership was only open to Moiyeanese, each of whom was required to invest a minimum of £1 in the association. This was not a subscription, but gave the member a share in the association and the right to dividends from investments made. When the constitution was amended, the names of all members and the amounts they had invested were recorded. On the death of a member, the eldest son was entitled to claim his father's shares.

Among the benefits of being a member was the right to use the association's hall in Port Elizabeth for weddings and funerals without charge and to stay in its premises in

Headquarters of the Moi Yean Commercial Association, in Queen Street, Port Elizabeth, erected in 1918. The building was decorated to celebrate VJ Day (Victory over Japan) in 1945.

Members of the Moi Yean Commercial Association with chairman Chong Lawson (centre, wearing spectacles) , photographed in the 1920s.

Moi Yean, China. When a loan club was run at the association, ten percent of the amounts tendered was charged for the use of the hall.

The organization's 1918 constitution stated that the Moi Yean Commercial Association had taken over the Toong Teh Tong Association which had a total of 64 members. Beyond this reference, nothing is known of the Toong Teh Tong or its activities, but it is likely it functioned primarily as a loan club.

The Moi Yean Commercial Association building became an integral part of community life in Port Elizabeth. It housed the country's first Chinese school from about 1920 until the early 1950s and was a popular venue for weddings, community functions and sports activities. In later years, however, the association encountered financial difficulties in maintaining the building and paying the rates and taxes. The property was eventually sold in the late 1980s.

Cantonist United Benefit Society

Although the number of Cantonese in Port Elizabeth was substantially smaller than Moiyeanese, on 1 January 1918 they formed an organization called the Cantonist United Benefit Society. Probably intended as a parallel group to the Moi Yean Commercial Association, the society aimed to unite all 'Cantonists' and also ran a loan club on the first Sunday of each month.

Its constitution laid down regulations for the loan club, limiting loans to a maximum of £40 and stipulating terms of repayment. The society shared the rented premises of the Chinese Association, and included among its aims the establishment of a library as well as a debating society. Members were required to pay an entrance fee of ten shillings, a deposit of £2, as well as a monthly subscription of sixpence or one shilling, depending on whether they owned businesses or were employees.

Although constitutions are generally dry documents reflecting the duties of committee members and the conditions under which meetings may be held, this society's rules and regulations offer some interesting insights into the intentions of its founders. After stipulating that financial transactions should first be concluded at each monthly meeting, the regulations state:

> On the termination of these affairs, any subject worthy of interest may be brought up for discussion, whether it be an address or the latest news concerning our country or a debatable subject. This will greatly improve our humanity, intellect and morals.[40]

Furthermore, channels were created for settling disputes. A complainant had to explain the matter to the secretary and pay ten shillings to cover expenses. The chairman and secretary would then cross-examine those involved and the committee would act as a jury to decide on a verdict.

> The Committee shall give their vote for or against the complainant or defendant by means of the black and white bean method. Each Office-bearer shall be given two beans, one black bean denoting guilt and the white bean indicating innocence. If an Office-bearer thinks the defendant guilty, he shall put the black bean into the box and the remaining bean shall be handed back to the President. If the

The opening ceremony of the Cantonist United Benefit Society on 1 January 1918.

> number of black beans in the box is in the majority, the person shall be found guilty and if the number of white beans in the box is in the majority the person shall be found innocent.

After the verdict was delivered in a case, the chairman was empowered to fine the guilty party up to £5, and expel him from the society should he not pay the fine.

Although the constitution does not record the names of the first office bearers of the society, by 1923 Warson James was the president and Lo Pong the general secretary. It is uncertain whether or not the organization remained active since community elders maintain the only Cantonese organization in Port Elizabeth in the 1930s was known as the 'Gwong Sook Gung Chai Hui' or the 'Sa Jya'.

Perhaps the dwindling numbers of Cantonese in Port Elizabeth led members to concentrate more on social welfare rather than the loan club function of the society. When the Chinese Association erected headquarters in Evatt Street in 1937, the 'Sa Jya' rented rooms close by and offered free accommodation to any destitute, elderly Chinese. The rooms housed up to 20 people and included a kitchen. In later years, the Cantonese became fully involved with the Chinese Association and any separate Cantonese organization ceased to exist.[41]

Uitenhage Chinese Association

Chinese settled in Uitenhage, just over 30 km away from Port Elizabeth, well before the turn of the century. Although they numbered only 88 men and 2 women in 1904, they were a closely-knit community and are said to have formed their own Chinese association sometime before 1911.[42] Perhaps this too was an informal organization catering for local social and business activities. Yet, by 1923, the Uitenhage Chinese Association had been formally constituted and was participating actively in attempts to improve the position of the Chinese in South Africa.

Correspondence of the association, dated from 1923 to 1926, was kept for many years by one of its last chairmen, Y.S. Manlee.[43] It is a unique collection of documents, virtually all in Chinese, which mirror the activities and concerns of the community at that time. Not only did the association conduct an annual registration of residents to provide funds for the Consul-General, it also subscribed to newspapers and government publications to keep members abreast of developments in China as well as in South Africa. It established links with Chinese organizations throughout the Cape and Transvaal and made a point of sending regular donations to the local Uitenhage hospital.

The association's letterhead featured the five-colour, striped flag of the first Chinese Republic, and its notices to members indicate that it held meetings in a club house where rooms were also hired out to tenants. This may have been rented property at Number 64 John Street which in later years was used for social functions and housed a Chinese school.

Most voluntary organizations reflect the personalities of the people behind them, individuals whose motives and intentions give groups their driving force. One such personality was the chairman of the Uitenhage Chinese Association from 1923 to 1926, Lo Pong. Just a few years earlier he had been general secretary to the Chinese Association in Port Elizabeth, as well as the Cantonist Benefit Society, and also held office as the chairman of the Cape Province branch of the Kuomintang party. Working with him were committee members such as Out Kong, Chan Harry, Chan Pensley and Lee Sun, all prominent traders in Uitenhage.

In 1924 the Uitenhage Chinese Association played an active role in opposing the Class Areas Bill. Lo Pong and a representative from the Chinese Association in Port Elizabeth, Yap Dze Dong, travelled to Cape Town to assist Consul-General Liu Ngai with appeals against the Bill.

Apart from its involvement in South African politics, the association also sent funds to China for relief aid. When Chinese students were killed in protests against the British presence in Shanghai in the mid-1920s, Lo Pong wrote to the Canton/Hong Kong Strike Committee on behalf of the Uitenhage Chinese Association and the Port Elizabeth Relief Committee:

> The foreigners' massacre of Chinese in Shanghai, Canton and Hong Kong is heartbreaking. Our government is not doing much. Thank heavens students and labour unions are active. This is our national pride, which imperialist hegemony cannot end. We hope you struggle to the end ... We overseas Chinese far away are ashamed that we cannot participate and we have collected £198-3-6 to send to you ...

The cultural side of life was as important as the political. Apart from paying twice yearly visits to the cemetery for the spring and autumn festivals, several Chinese in Uitenhage gathered regularly to play traditional Chinese music. After the association purchased property for its headquarters in John Street in 1939, a substantial collection of old string and wind musical instruments was kept on display, and sometimes played during celebrations.

As in other areas, the association provided local Chinese with a place to gather socially, to read Chinese newspapers and play card games. A small and close-knit community, they celebrated Chinese New Year and the Double Ten each year. By the late 1940s, young people formed the Flying Ball Tennis Club and eventually developed a full-fledged youth group called the Uitenhage Chinese Youth Society which organized a variety of sports and social activities within the community. Although the official censuses in 1936 and 1946 did not offer a breakdown of the number of Chinese in Uitenhage, community members estimate the population numbered at least 150 by the late 1940s.[44]

General Social Activities

Port Elizabeth too saw its fair share of sports and social activities in the 1930s and 1940s. The second generation of Chinese, many born in South Africa from 1910 onwards, were making their mark and engaging in pastimes little dreamed of by their parents such as tennis, boxing and big band music.

A tennis club, called the Chinese United Club was formed in the early 1930s and organized twice-weekly tennis games for about 20 members. Players raised funds to build two tennis courts in Victoria Park, Southend, a site rented to them by the municipality.[45]

By 1939, the Port Elizabeth Chinese Boxing Club was already an active organization with over 30 members. Its chairman was Archie Pow Chong, secretary Aubrey Wong On and treasurer Sidney Kim Sing. The Starlight Dance Orchestra, begun by a group of enthusiastic Chinese musicians in 1945 or 1946, became sought-after entertainers on the Port Elizabeth social circuit. The band leader was Hyman Li Green with various band members including James Affat, Kinyun Lee, Louis Wong, Alvin Wong, Wing Lee Son Kee, Edwin Jack Kee, Kingson Peacock and Lo Chong Low Kum.

Young Chinese also formed their own unit of St John's Ambulance Brigade to learn the rudiments of first aid. The group lasted for three or four years in the 1940s, but disbanded after they were told Chinese were not permitted to wear the same uniforms as their White counterparts.[46] By the late 1940s the Chung Wah Country Club was established to offer sports and social activities for the community. A group of young Chinese bought a large property in Kragga Kamma, renovated the two-storey thatched house and built two tennis courts. The club became a popular venue for parties and weddings. Members also gathered there most weekends to play sports, but after seven or eight years the club eventually lost support.[47]

Much in demand on the social circuit in Port Elizabeth, the Starlight Dance Orchestra was formed by enthusiastic musicians in the 1940s.

Port Elizabeth's 'Malaikim'

Although only a miniature version of Chinatowns elsewhere in the world, Port Elizabeth's 'Malaikim' in Evatt Street was the place where the Chinese met and mingled in the first half of this century. During its heyday in the 1930s, the area was sometimes also called 'Chinese Street'. It was a cosmopolitan little enclave where people of all races lived and traded, where three or four restaurants served Chinese delicacies and where curious passers-by could sometimes catch a whiff of the sweetish odour of opium.

One of the landmarks was a two-storey building known as Singer & Co which is said to have been started as a herbalist store by a runaway Chinese mine labourer sometime after 1910.[48] The labourer was originally from Shantung province in north China, the area from which the majority of mine labourers were recruited to work on the Witwatersrand. A long-time resident of Port Elizabeth, Mrs Nee Fook Date Chong, who arrived in the city in 1925, aged 20 years said:

> Singer was the first herbalist, and when he came he had a pigtail, but the government later sent him away because he had no residence rights. That is what I was told.

In the 1920s, a group of Chinese bought shares in Singer & Co which was then trading as a wholesaler. The company eventually went bankrupt, but the ground floor of the premises remained in use for many years as a popular 'gambling den'. There patrons indulged in games of tin gau or teu gwat (a form of dominoes), mahjong and poker. Upstairs in the same building, Wong Fah Quat ran a busy Chinese medicine store from which he dispensed herbal treatments for all kinds of ailments. His son, Edmund Quat, described how people came from far afield to seek advice.

> I don't know how he learned to make up Chinese medicines, but he often helped when western doctors said there was no hope ... He had many books and most treatments were so simple and inexpensive. He also sold carved ivory curios and gave advice to people on what herbs they could use, what mushrooms they could and couldn't eat.[49]

Another often-frequented place was the opium den, right next door to Singer & Co. Sundays were the busiest days in 'Malaikim'. Many Chinese who shut their own stores elsewhere went to Evatt Street to buy Chinese specialities such as roast pork, dumplings and bean curd or to have a meal of thick rice soup at one of the small restaurants. Chinese groceries were obtainable from Warson James, a corner grocery store which imported its own supplies and distributed Chinese goods to outlying areas.[50]

After 1937, the headquarters of the Chinese Association too became a popular meeting place. Many elderly Chinese lived in rooms behind the association building, in a place called the 'Sin Seh' or 'Sa Jya'. Nearby traders and residents often took food to them and Chinese Association members assisted by supplying Chinese herbal medicines.[51]

TRANSVAAL

After the formation of Union, the Transvaal's community constituted the largest settlement of Chinese in the country and the diversity of organizations they formed reflected their multiplicity of concerns and interests. From political and social organizations to sports and cultural groups, they also often divided themselves along ethnic or clan lines. Far more Cantonese than Moiyeanese, however, settled in the Transvaal.

Although Chinese were scattered throughout the Witwatersrand and in outlying areas, Johannesburg remained the focal point for communal activity. Every weekend people congregated in 'Malaikam', Ferreirastown, drawn by its assortment of Chinese clubs, restaurants and shops. From the 1930s, Chinese in Pretoria formed their own organizations and in later years local groups were established in most towns where Chinese settled.

The Transvaal's plethora of restrictive legislation was a fact of life which several organizations tried to address, both independently and through the offices of the Consul-General. Unlike their counterparts in the Cape, Chinese organizations faced formidable barriers in acquiring property for their headquarters. Since Chinese ownership of land was largely prohibited, only a handful succeeded in establishing some kind of permanent base. Several small groups served the specific interests of their members, focusing on social or business activities. As was common practice elsewhere, clan organizations arranged visits to cemeteries while other groups organized loan clubs (the 'fee' or 'hui').

In reviewing the activities of Chinese organizations, it should be remembered that very few functioned continuously over the decades. As is the case with most voluntary groups, organizations were only as strong and active as their core membership, and when that handful lost interest, the group became defunct. Several organizations experienced a stop-start existence, only becoming active when some crisis arose in the community.

In 1936, the Chinese in the Transvaal numbered 1618 people — 1054 males and 564 females. By far the majority however settled in Johannesburg and its suburbs (1122) while the remainder were scattered in Pretoria (227), Krugersdorp (35), Roodepoort (13) Germiston (33), Boksburg (18), Benoni (37), Springs (37), Nigel (4) and other areas such as Vereeniging and Lydenburg.[52]

Transvaal Chinese Association (南非杜省中華公會)

The passive resistance campaign in the early years of this century took its toll on the unity of community organizations in the Transvaal. After a brief few years as the major representative body for the Chinese, the Transvaal Chinese Association split into factions which channelled their energies into the strengthening of two separate clubs — the Cantonese Club and the Transvaal Chinese United Club.

First formed in 1903 and at its peak in 1908, the Transvaal Chinese Association was virtually a spent force when passive resistance came to an end for the Chinese in 1911. Perhaps it had been linked too closely to the turbulence which had split the community, for even its office-bearers such as the last chairman Martin Easton, as well as members, James Frank and John Fortoen, used the name of the Cantonese Club when dealing with authorities in the following years.

By 1917, however, the need for an organization to promote the interests of the community as a whole, rather than separate sections, led to its reconstitution. In June 1917, the honorary secretary, James Frank, wrote to the Department of the Interior stating that representatives of the Chinese had decided to form an organization called the Chinese Association of the Transvaal.[53]

Its constitution stipulated its objects as the advancement and protection of the interests of the Chinese in the Transvaal. Run by a committee of 15, all members were required to pay a monthly subscription of two shillings. The chairman was David Kan, the vice chairman Lai King, the treasurers S. Wing Sui and Luk Tow and the secretaries J. Frank and Chohing. Over the years the association drew into its ranks many prominent members who served as spokesmen for the community.

One of its first actions was the submission of a petition to the American consul in charge of Chinese interests to appeal against provisions of the liquor law in the Transvaal.[54] It also assisted Chinese who encountered problems with bringing either their wives or children into the country and sent letters to the authorities testifying to the good standing of individuals and appealing for relief in the stringency of the immigration laws.[55]

Concerned as it was with broader political issues, the Transvaal Chinese Association (TCA) concentrated on efforts to improve the position of the Chinese as a whole. In December 1924, it submitted a petition to the government asking for restrictions on the Chinese to be removed. The document was signed by H. Fahy of Pretoria as chairman, C.P. Yenson as secretary and Ah Kie, as treasurer. They said the Chinese saw South Africa as their home, wished to work for its good and only desired 'to be treated with justice and humanity.'[56]

When the government appointed a Select Committee to investigate the position of Asiatics, in March 1930, the TCA was represented by Dr L.N. Liang, the first Chinese doctor in the community, and Lai King, long-time resident and community leader. They appealed for Chinese to be given rights by virtue of their length of residence in South Africa and answered a host of questions on the laws affecting Chinese, their business practices, mode of living and related issues.

Dr Liang argued eloquently for Chinese to be given 'equal rights and unrestricted rights to trade', citing the community's standard of living as well as China's 5000-year-old civilization which made the Chinese the equal of any western culture. He pointed out that other Asiatic races such as the Assyrians, the Persians, the Turks and the Greeks had been exempted from the definition of Asiatic and asked that the Chinese too be treated similarly.[57] No changes in the position of the Chinese were however effected.

The Transvaal Chinese Association never established permanent headquarters, but seems to have served as a loosely-knit alliance for various Chinese groups to represent the community as a whole. When the Asiatic Land Tenure Act was promulgated in 1932, a number of petitions were submitted to the authorities in the name of the TCA. Signatories to the appeals included chairman Ho Tong, secretary Y.K. Akin as well as H. Shang, L. Kan, A. Kai and C.P. Law. A few of these men were active in the Transvaal Chinese United Club and C.P. Law was a prominent figure in Pretoria's Chinese organizations.[58] The organization continued to pursue legal channels to express opposition to the legislation and, in 1937, appointed Johannesburg lawyer, Alec Oshry, its honorary legal advisor.

Describing his work for the TCA, Oshry said his primary role was to assist in drawing up memoranda relating to the Land Tenure Act as well as other discriminatory legislation.

> The Chinese were chiefly concerned with rights ... the right to trade, not to be discriminated against. I never heard of them asking for voting rights. They were apolitical as far as that was concerned.[59]

Oshry said the TCA directed its appeals through the offices of the Consulate-General since the community felt these representatives had the ear of the government. Between 1938 and 1940, Consul-General F.T. Sung played a significant role in assisting the community to obtain relief from the liquor restrictions.

In the following years the organization again went into a decline, and by early 1946 community representatives reconstituted and reorganized a new Transvaal Chinese Association. Spokemen described it as a move to unite the community in the Transvaal against the strictures of the Asiatic Land Tenure Act, pointing out that the previous political organization had become inactive.[60]

Several hundred Chinese attended a community meeting at which the new TCA's constitution was passed and an executive committee sworn in to hold office for one year.[61] The new TCA addressed problems such as the eviction of a Chinese tenant from property affected by the Land Tenure Act and the presence in the country of illegal Chinese immigrants. Men such as Dr L.N. Liang, Ho Kawa, A. York, C.P. Law and Lai Kan were elected to the executive committee and remained integrally involved in the many political events which would overtake the Chinese community in the 1950s.

Cantonese Club (維益社)

Called the Kwong Hok Tong before the turn of the century, the Cantonese Club is the oldest known Chinese organization in Johannesburg. It was based in the heart of 'Malaikam' where club members erected a two-storey building on the corner of Fox and Alexander streets, Ferreirastown, in 1905. Leung Quinn, a prominent participant in the passive resistance campaign, was chairman for a number of years and in 1906 the acting Chinese Consul-General Liu Ngai described himself as the club's vice president.[62]

Membership certificates issued in later years, however, stated that the club was only formed three years before the Chinese Republic — namely 1908. It is likely this date was selected to mark the rift with other members of the TCA who had formed the Transvaal Chinese United Club, and also to ally the Cantonese Club firmly with the passive resistance movement. New members were notified the club 'was formed to resist the unjust law',[63] and its core consisted of members who were known as the 'passive resistance party'.

An early membership certificate for the Cantonese Club, Johannesburg.

CANTONESE CLUB

INCORPORATED WITH THE CANTON TRUST LTD.

南斐洲 杜蘭士哇省 維益社 股票 約翰斯堡埠

P.O. Box 5927.
Phone 2777.

CANTONESE CLUB BUILDINGS,
1, FOX STREET, JOHANNESBURG,
TRANSVAAL, S.A.

No. 200

This is to Certify that *Ah Chung Esq.* of *24/12/19* has this day been admitted as a member of the Cantonese Club, Johannesburg.

EXTRACTS FROM THE CLUB RULES.

1. Every member of the Club shall be entitled to rank as an equal shareholder in all the assets of the Club.
2. Every member of the Club shall be entitled to one (1) vote at all meetings of the Club in any matters pertaining to the Club.
3. Every member shall be entitled, so long as he remains a member, to participate in the yearly distribution of the Club's profits.
4. This Certificate of Membership is under no circumstances transferable, and the benefits conferred by membership in the Club will only apply to the holder of a Certificate of Membership duly signed by the members of the Governing Body, and registered in the books of the Club.
5. The Club does not recognise nor hold itself liable to pay to any person other than the person named hereon any sum or sums which may accrue to such person by virtue of his or her membership.
6. The dividends in each case should be declared between October 1st and 15th, and the Transfer Books of the Company will be closed on those dates, both dates inclusive.

Chairman.

Director of Canton Trust, Ltd.

Secretary.

M. Easton
Treasurer.

L. Kemp.
Assist Treasurer.

此券證明陳元長先生為南斐洲金山之維益社社員本社始於
民國紀元前三年因抗苛例集合而成迨民國二年苛例告一結束從
此銖積寸累至民國六年成立廣東有限公司營業部買受本社
樓宇地基一座今後如各社員仍屬本社社員所有本社及營業部
一切本息得永遠平等享受平等均分特製此股票授與本社社員
陳元長先生存執
股票凡例附後

維益社主席 書記
營業部總理 理財

民國八年十二月廿四日發給

Members of the Cantonese Club, photographed in Johannesburg in 1934. No women were admitted as club members.

Apart from its social activities, the Cantonese Club was concerned about the facilities set aside for Chinese at the Johannesburg Hospital. In 1916, its secretary, John Fortoen, enquired whether the Chinese ward required any new equipment, and was given a list by the hospital superintendent which included: 3 pairs of pyjamas, one table, six feather pillows, 12 pillowslips, three mattresses, 3 feeding cups, 3 urinals and two bedpans.[64]

The past remained ever present for club members who often harked back to the passive resistance campaign, refusing to allow entry to anyone belonging to the opposing Transvaal Chinese United Club. Membership of the Cantonese Club was only open to males, over the age of 18, but did include both Cantonese and Moiyeanese-speaking Chinese. The majority of Moiyeanese in Johannesburg were members of the Cantonese Club, a fact not quite as contradictory as it sounds. Community elders point out that the adjective 'Cantonese' in earlier days referred not only to those originating from the city of Canton (Guangzhou) but also to the province of Kwangtung (Guangdong). Since Moiyean (Meixian) is part of that province, Moiyeanese qualify as 'Cantonese' in a geographical sense.[65]

Gambling was a popular pursuit among Chinese and the club harnessed this activity to raise funds. Rights to organize gambling were auctioned to the highest bidder among members and the club took ten percent of all bets placed. By 1918, members had raised sufficient money to purchase the property on which the club was built. Because of legislation prohibiting landownership by Asiatics, however, the club formed a company named The Canton Trust Limited to conclude the transaction.[66] Members became shareholders of the club's assets and entitled to receive annual dividends from profits. Office-bearers in 1919 included Hall Fisher as chairman, Chu Yenson as director of Canton Trust Limited, H. Dantje as secretary with M. Easton and L. Kemp as treasurers.

During the 1922 Rand Revolt when thousands of miners went on strike, scores of Chinese from Fordsburg — the suburb at the eye of the storm — took refuge at the Cantonese Club to escape hostilities.[67] Community elders also claim the club purchased property in Canton (Guangzhou) to offer accommodation to members visiting China.

The club's facilities which included a large hall as well as various games rooms made it a social centre for community gatherings. Members organized parties, weddings and funerals there and numbers of individuals rented rooms at the club. In the late 1940s, a fire destroyed much of the club's building, contents and records. Major renovations were undertaken and the headquarters modernized to cater for community functions and provide better accommodation. The Cantonese Club remained a focal point in 'Malaikam' until the early 1980s when the building was eventually demolished.

Transvaal Chinese United Club (聯衛會所)

The Transvaal Chinese United Club was established in 1909 by a faction of the Transvaal Chinese Association who were called 'the party of compliance'. Opposed to moves to involve the Chinese in a renewed passive resistance campaign in late 1908, they formed a new social organization which had its headquarters two blocks away from the Cantonese Club, on the corner of Wolhuter and Commissioner streets, Ferreirastown.

Minutes of the club's early meetings, recorded in Chinese in an impressive leather bound volume, were retained by community elder, Fok Yu Kam, and offered fascinating glimpses of the concerns of the club's founders. They collected donations to cover the hospital costs of members wounded in gun fights with opposing Cantonese Club members in April 1909, and even sent £100 to a newspaper in China to publish a repudiation of reports about the activities of Leung Quinn.[68]

Because of the high level of tension between community factions, notice was issued to members staying at the club premises that the doors would be locked at 1 o'clock every night.

> All members please be home before then. Members returning late, please lock the doors after you. Those who knock to be let in, please wait a little ... someone will get up to open. Don't make a noise. Now is a troublesome period and we must be careful.[69]

The constitution stated it was a social club which aimed to assist and uplift the community. After members approved the constitution in April 1909, it was sent to the Chinese government to register the club as an official Chinese organization. From the outset the club concentrated on charitable activities, assisting the elderly and disabled, erecting tombstones and supporting worthy causes in China. It subscribed to a variety of Chinese newspapers and regularly ordered Chinese books. Not all its activities were serious — the club even donated money to organize a bicycle race in October 1909 for its members' entertainment!

From mid-1916, the club organized gambling on a regular basis to raise funds and by June 1917 was able to purchase the property on which the club building stood. A maximum of £3000 was budgeted for this purpose. To sidestep restrictions on Asiatic ownership of land, the club took out registration as a company and appointed seven trustees as the shareholders — Ah Kie, Ah Sun, D. Kan, Tong King, Ho Forley, Loo Ching and Lai King.[70]

Firmly established and flourishing in 1917, the United Club passed a resolution restricting membership only to those who had 'genuine Chinese mothers and fathers'. Although membership of the club could be passed from one generation to the next, children who were not 'pure' Chinese were not permitted to inherit this privilege. It also excluded 'anyone who distributed pamphlets to give fingerprints' — a reference to the voluntary registration phase of the passive resistance campaign. When the 1918 influenza epidemic broke out countrywide, many Chinese gathered at the United Club to drink a special herbal brew to ward off illness. Community elders say proof of the remedy lay in the fact that only one Johannesburg Chinese, who refused the drink, died during the epidemic![71]

That the Transvaal Chinese United Club was highly successful and reasonably wealthy can be seen by its payment of monthly salaries of £12 to its Chinese-language secretary and £11 to its English-language secretary, as well as its many donations to various causes. By 1918, the club's property in Ferreirastown was insured for £4000 and just five years later, in 1923, it allocated a sum of £2000 for the erection of a United Club Building in Canton, China.

The Transvaal Chinese United Club premises, in Commissioner Street, Ferreirastown, photographed in the 1940s.

P.O. Box 4266. 15 DEC 1921 TELEPHONE 2251.

TRANSVAAL CHINESE UNITED CLUB.

10, Commissioner Street.
Johannesburg
South Africa.

branch
Canton, China.

This is to Certify

that Mr Quan Moon

In terms of the rules of the above Club, We the undersigned hereby certify that bearer is registered as a Member of the above Club and remains such, so long as he pays his Annual Subscription and subject to the rules of the Said Club.

This certificate is the property of the Member and is not transferable except to the lawful heirs of such member.

President

Secretaries H. Forley

Treasurer

杜蘭士哇省

南斐洲華僑聯衛會所 股票

烏乃斯堡埠

No. 673

此券證明關新滿先生為南斐洲杜省華僑聯衛會所會員因聯合積資買受本會所樓宇地基一座及在廣州市長堤建築南斐洲杜省華僑聯衛會所分會樓宇地基一座此後如再有擴充利益仍屬各會員所有一切權利永遠平等均分特設此股票授與本會所會員

廣東省廣州府南海縣吉利堡吉利鄉

關新滿先生收執為據 股票例附列於後

主席
西書記 鄭聯
中書記 陳逸堂
理財

中華民國拾年十二月十五日 發給

An early membership certificate for the Transvaal Chinese United Club, Johannesburg.

It donated money on several occasions to the Transvaal Chinese Association to petition the authorities on trading licences and liquor restrictions. With the Cantonese Club, it supported the provision of facilities at the Johannesburg Hospital for Chinese and made donations for the purchase of equipment and clothing.

Even Consul-General Liu Ngai turned to the United Club for assistance. They bought him a motor car for £300 in 1920, and several times advanced him double this amount for the running expenses of his office. When the Consul-General called on the club's members to take out registration at the consulate, the club donated lump sums of between £20 and £150 towards the registration fees.

Most of the club's funds were obtained from its gambling activities since a percentage of all transactions on the club premises went into its coffers. Members shared in annual dividends and the club regularly hosted Chinese New Year and the Double Ten celebrations. Like every organization, the United Club also had its share of scandal. In January 1930 the club's records tersely noted the disappearance of the Chinese secretary, Lo Sec Ham, with an undisclosed amount of the club's money. After a week, he was expelled and club members resolved to circulate monthly balance sheets to maintain tighter control of funds.

The Transvaal Chinese United Club continued to grow and prosper, becoming one of the most successful Chinese organizations in the country. It maintained its property in Canton (Guangzhou) to offer accommodation to members visiting relatives in China, and in the late 1940s acquired the property adjoining its club buildings. There it erected a five-storey block of flats which can still be seen in Ferreirastown today.

Chee Kung Tong Society (Reform Club) (致公堂)

Probably the earliest Chinese 'secret society' active in South Africa, the Chee Kung Tong only formally proclaimed its existence in 1918. The society formed a company called the Chee Kung Tong Trust Limited to purchase property on the corner of Wolhuter and Commissioner streets, diagonally opposite the headquarters of the Transvaal Chinese United Club.

Because of its connections with the revolutionary movements involved in the overthrow of the last dynasty in China, the Chee Kung Tong's activities were shrouded in mystery and it has been described as a secret society, chiefly concerned with Chinese politics. When the society formed a trust company in 1918, its shareholders were listed as Chong Bong Achim, Tam Tim, Hoe Law, Leong Ping, Ho Piaw and Loo Kee, all general dealers residing in Johannesburg who had deposited amounts of between £300 and £500 each for their shares.[72]

In September 1919, the Chee Kung Tong arranged a lavish opening ceremony to which they invited various Chinese organizations, as well as members of the already established Chee Kung Tong in Lourenco Marques.[73] These representatives were, however, refused permission to enter South Africa despite repeated appeals and an offer of the society's title deeds as security that the visitors would return to Lourenco Marques.

Club secretary, John Fortoen, supported his petition for the men to be allowed entry with this description of the origins of the society:

> They are not merely coming for a visit but they come as delegates for the opening ceremony of the Chinese political society here. This Chee Kung Tong (Chinese society or party) was established more or less 250 years ago and its establishment was to overthrow the late Manchu dynasty. Before the Chinese Republic this was a secret society in China but after the annihilation of the Manchu throne this was a formal society or party in the Chinese political affairs.[74]

The opening ceremony was, however, attended by members of the United Club who decided that gifts taken to the function should not be in excess of £15 — still a princely sum in 1919.[75]

The Chee Kung Tong was, in later years, also called the Reform Club. It functioned chiefly as a social and welfare organization and raised funds by organizing gambling on the club's premises. It offered accommodation to members, organized and paid for burials and erected tombstones in cemeteries.

The club building housed an altar, inscribed with the names of the five Buddhist monks who founded the Chee Kung Tong in China as well as all deceased members. Incense was burnt there every day to honour the spirits of the departed. New members were required to undergo an initiation ceremony, learning secret signs which would identify them to fellow members. Part of the ceremony involved burning yellow paper and chopping off a chicken's head, symbolizing the fate of any who 'defected' from the society.[76] It is likely such rituals gave rise to the description of society members as Chinese Freemasons.

Membership was open to all Chinese. Those involved in the organization in later years said the Chee Kung Tong, unlike the Cantonese and United clubs, was willing to accept illegal immigrants and Chinese of mixed parentage as members.[77] In addition to welfare work among the elderly, the function for which the society became best known, it celebrated major Chinese festivals, particularly the spring and autumn cemetery days when all members were required to pay tribute at the graves of the deceased.

Other Special-Interest Groups

The diversity of the Chinese population in Johannesburg was further underlined by the formation of several other groups catering for specific interests or causes. While several more may well have existed prior to 1948, references to the following have been uncovered:

- Sometime in the 1920s shopkeepers pooled resources to form an organization called the 'Transvaal Chinese Traders Association'. Intended to further the interests of Chinese traders and protect their rights, the organization levied a membership fee of 10 shillings, and an additional 10 shillings for each shop run by a member. In a 15-page printed constitution, the rights and duties of members were outlined and control of the organization was vested in a 15-member committee.[78] This organization addressed the issue of licences for Chinese traders and assisted with legal costs for shopkeepers who appealed against licensing decisions in court.[79]
- Periodic floods, droughts and natural disasters in China prompted the community to contribute whatever funds they could for relief work. In the 1920s the 'Cantonese Flood Relief Fund' was established as a channel for the transmission of such funds.[80] Donations were collected from local traders, and in later years similar charitable work was undertaken by clan groups and organizations such as the Tong Yet Relief Society.
- On the cultural front, several Chinese formed an opera group in Ferreirastown during the mid-1920s. A handful of members played Chinese musical instruments and practised singing for their own entertainment.[81] During the late 1920s and early 1930s, visiting troupes of entertainers — musicians and actors — from China were invited to Johannesburg by a few of the larger clubs which sponsored their stay. They gave concerts in 'Malaikam' and several of the women in these troupes married local Chinese and remained in South Africa.[82]
- In 1930 Consul-General Ho Tsang suggested the formation of an organization to promote activities for overseas Chinese far from their homeland. To meet this aim, a cultural group called the Young Chinese Culture League was formed. It held meetings in Johannesburg each Wednesday and Sunday and levied a monthly membership fee of 5s.0d.[83] Consisting of 30 or 40 members, mostly in their twenties, the league organized sports activities such as tennis and held regular night classes for members to study English.[84]

- A social club catering only for Moiyeanese was operating in Johannesburg before 1933. Said to have had its headquarters in a two- storey house on the eastern side of Market Street, close to End Street, the club opened on Wednesday afternoons and over weekends for members to play cards, mingle socially and listen to music. The club was called Tai Poong and also offered accommodation to members.[85] This was probably the forerunner of the Moiyeanese Club, a loosely-knit group whose membership overlapped with that of the Cantonese Club. A major function of the Moiyeanese Club was the organization of twice-yearly visits to the cemeteries.
- By the late 1930s, younger Chinese in Johannesburg formed their own sports clubs. A handful who lived in Bezuidenhout Valley played tennis on a regular basis, and in the early 1940s formally named their group the Transvaal Chinese Tennis Club which organized games at courts in Ophirton.[86]

Johannesburg's 'Malaikam'

Johannesburg's Chinatown or 'Malaikam' remained the social hub of community activity. Situated to the south-west of the city centre in Ferreirastown, the area was densely populated by all racial groups and consisted of a motley assortment of shops, wood and iron houses, tenement rooms, schools, churches and a handful of more solidly constructed brick buildings.

Commonly referred to as the Chinese quarter, 'Malaikam' was the site of most Chinese social clubs, the community's two schools and, from 1931, the only Chinese language press in Africa which produced a thrice-weekly newspaper.[87] Small shops and restaurants catered mainly for the Chinese, selling essential groceries, medicines and herbs and producing specialities such as roast pork, roast duck and steamed buns.

Consul-General Lo Ming Yuan and community members outside the Chiao Sheng Pao offices in Ferreirastown. Seen in the inset is Dang Sui Wah, a former editor.

Chiao Sheng Pao

Far away from their homeland, the first generation of settlers felt keenly the lack of news, published in Chinese, about events in China as well as information relevant to their lives in their adopted country. Most had little education in English and this concern prompted the All South Africa Chinese Conference to resolve to establish a Chinese medium of communication within the community.

The *Chiao Sheng Pao* started publication on 1 June 1931. A company was formed and shares sold to the community to raise the necessary capital for its launch. The majority of shares totalling £1001 were bought by local community member, Leong Gin Shin. After purchasing machinery and office equipment, the newspaper was already in debt for an additional £80 — a sum lent to them by another community member, Hok Sun Kai.

The newspaper's English name was the *Chinese Consular Gazette* 'in order to obtain facilities for printing otherwise difficult for non-Europeans to obtain in the Union'.[88] By the 1940s, the newspaper appeared three times a week, in Chinese only, and covered local and international news of interest to the Chinese.

The paper's first premises were at the Kuomintang offices at 30 Fox Street, Ferreirastown, where the newspaper was accommodated rent-free for its first six months. One of the teachers at the Chinese school, Mr Wei, was the newspaper's first editor. It later moved to Becker Street then to Number 13 Alexander Street where it remained until the late 1960s when it moved to the Chinese Kuo Ting School premises in Doornfontein.

Extensive fund-raising within the community was undertaken in 1962 when Consul-General Wei Yu Sun launched plans to reorganize the *Chiao Sheng Pao*, to introduce a pictorial supplement and to print an English-language version of the newspaper. These plans were however shelved when Consul-General Wei left South Africa and by 1965 there was still uncertainty over what would happen to the funds. The Eastern Province Chinese Association requested the return of their donation, but was advised by Consul-General Chen Yi Yuan that the Taiwan government had instructed him to retain control of the funds.[89]

A house at Number 93 Gordon Road, Bertrams, Johannesburg was eventually purchased by the Consulate-General to house the newspaper. The *Chiao Sheng Pao's* English name was changed from *Consular Gazette* to *Overseas Chinese Newspaper* and control of the publication was taken over entirely by the Taiwan government.

Weekends were the busiest times as the Chinese gathered to socialize and catch up on community news. A variety of small clubs with names such as the Far East Club, Wah Nam and the Sui Tung Kung were scattered among the established premises of the Cantonese Club and the Transvaal Chinese United Club. Most of these provided gathering places and venues for gambling, running such games as poker, fan tan, dice and mahjong.

Several 'puck-apu' shops were situated in Commissioner Street and offered gamblers the opportunity to win substantial sums. These shops distributed ornately printed sheets consisting of 80-character Chinese poems and took bets on selected words. Punters had to predict correctly which 10 words were chosen each day, their winnings being determined by the size of their bets and the number of correct words.[90]

On major festive occasions such as Chinese New Year or the Double Ten, the community gathered in 'Malaikam' to set off fireworks and enjoy lavish meals. Other social functions such as the twice-yearly 'tomb sweeping' festivals as well as weddings were also held in the various clubs.

Pretoria Chinese Organizations

Chinese settled in Pretoria, some 60 kilometres north of Johannesburg, before the turn of the century. Too few in number to constitute a separate community, they participated in the activities of the clubs in Johannesburg, and several Pretoria Chinese were known to have been prominent in the passive resistance campaign as well as in the activities of both the Transvaal Chinese Association and the Transvaal Chinese United Club right up to the 1950s.

Ferreirastown, Johannesburg, in 1955 — with a view of Bezuidenhout and Fox streets.

Alexander Street, Ferreirastown, in the 1950s.

The Pretoria Chinese Association was formed in 1931 by a small group of men who met to discuss the issues of the day in a sorghum beer factory in Barber Street, Pretoria.[91] Among its founders were Foley (Ho Woo Lai), T. Foote, C.P. Law, Lew Wai Fung and How Shone. Members initially met socially to draw a 'fee' and perhaps from this grew the idea to establish an organization to address the political problems Chinese faced.[92] In the 1930s and 1940s however the association functioned as part of the Transvaal Chinese Association, which represented the community throughout the province.

On the social level, the Pretoria Chinese Association regularly hosted community celebrations such as the Double Ten. Gatherings were held at the Fung family's sorghum beer factory where community members prepared roast suckling pigs and a variety of Chinese delicacies. When a Chinese school was established in Pretoria in the mid-1930s, the association moved its headquarters to the same premises at Number 191 Boom Street.

Another Chinese organization was, however, the focal point for community activity in Pretoria. The Young Chinese Cultural League was established in October 1932 and aimed 'to promote the culture and character of the Overseas Chinese Community, to overcome the political injustices prevailing over our community and to assist the Motherland.'[93] Its first task was to find headquarters, and despite objections from White neighbours, the organization secured a large house on the corner of Boom and Bosman streets, on the edge of the city centre. Among those opposed to the presence of Chinese in the area was a city councillor, who also happened to trade with Chinese shopkeepers. The Chinese boycotted his company, and went ahead with plans to buy the property. Because of legislation prohibiting Chinese property ownership in the Transvaal, the league approached Consul-General Feng Wang whose diplomatic position enabled him to have the property registered in his name.

The Young Chinese Cultural League headquarters, in Boom Street, Pretoria, where the Chinese School was later established.

The Young Chinese Cultural League paid £2000 for the property, a sum raised by subscriptions, donations and a generous interest-free loan offered by member Lee Dak Loi. Other prominent Pretoria Chinese involved in the league included C.P. Law, How Shone, Fung Ngok and Hau Yoon.

Gambling of any kind was prohibited at the league's headquarters. Determined to stay on the right side of the law, the league was 'rather particular about who they accepted as members' and any who did not hold legal papers to be in South Africa were refused entry.[94]

By 1936 the Pretoria Chinese numbered 227 people. In 1944 young Chinese formed the Pretoria Chinese Tennis Club and in later years extended their activities to other sports, developing a strong local spirit within a close-knit community.

KUOMINTANG

Pressing as immediate local issues were to the South African Chinese, many nonetheless retained a strong allegiance to China and concern for political developments there. Before the 1911 uprising which toppled the Ch'ing dynasty, several Chinese made substantial donations to revolutionary movements and 'some even sold their own shops to join the revolution.'[95]

The Chinese Nationalist Party, the Kuomintang (KMT), started as a revolutionary league in China. A year after the founding of the Chinese Republic, the KMT became a political party which took part in the formation of the first Chinese parliament.[96] Chaos however overtook the new republic, forcing the KMT to work underground and in subsequent years the party leader, Dr Sun Yat Sen, tried valiantly to unite the southern provinces of China with the north, run by feudal warlords. Only by 1928 was most of China joined under the control of the KMT and Chiang Kai Shek, the man who eventually assumed the party leadership after Dr Sun's death in 1925.

In South Africa, branches of the KMT were established from 1920 onwards in such centres as Johannesburg, Kimberley, Cape Town and Port Elizabeth. Focusing primarily on issues affecting China, the party attracted an influential following among local leaders. Included in the KMT's aims and objects were the following:

— to foster and protect the constitution of the Republic, morally and physically,
— to support democracy and suppress autocracy,

Headquarters of the Kuomintang (Nationalist Party) in Ferreirastown, which housed Johannesburg's first Chinese school from 1928.

— to promote socialism, uplift the masses, redistribute wealth and nationalize the natural resources of the country,
— to obtain international recognition and justice for the smaller and weaker powers,
— to introduce compulsory State education, technical and practical.[97]

In Johannesburg, C.P. Yenson was appointed director of the KMT in 1922, and by 1928 the party rented headquarters in Fox Street, Ferreirastown, where it also established a Chinese school. In Kimberley the KMT headquarters were situated in Coghlan Street, in the Malay Camp and claimed a membership of about 40 people in 1922.[98]

The Kuomintang branch in Port Elizabeth was launched with an impressive inauguration ceremony at its headquarters in Evatt Street on 31 May 1921. In an elaborately decorated hall, flying both the Union Jack and the flag of the Chinese republic, delegates from all parts of southern Africa gathered to toast 'the re-awakening of Chinese nationalism and patriotism'.[99]

Chairman of the new branch Lo Pong, assisted by his vice chairman, Tup Chong, welcomed representatives from Chinese organizations and outlined the aims of the party. He also made an appeal for the establishment of a governing body or grand council to act on behalf of all KMT districts in southern Africa.

Fervent speeches were made by many present, including C.P. Yenson and Lai Chuen of the KMT in Johannesburg; Low Ah Kee and Chan Whiteley of the Chinese Association of Port Elizabeth; Quan Hong of the Cantonist United Benefit Society, C. Chu Lum of the Chinese Charities Society and Chong Lawson of the Moi Yean Commercial Association. Other organizations represented were the Transvaal Chinese United Club, the KMT in Cape Town and the KMT in Lourenco Marques.

The speeches reflected the strong patriotism of KMT members who urged unswerving support to President Sun Yat Sen in his attempt to reunite China into a single, world power. Delegates were called upon to swear allegiance to the republic and to offer for the cause their lives and property. The opening ceremony, reported at length in a local English newspaper, concluded with a banquet.

Chinese who had settled away from their homeland were often referred to as the 'overseas' Chinese or *huach'iao (hua qiao)*. They not only gave moral but also substantial material support to Dr Sun's cause. From 1911 onwards, vast sums were collected for various campaigns, military equipment and publications. In 1922, records of funds received at KMT headquarters in Shanghai show the South African Chinese sent donations totalling several hundred dollars.[100]

After Dr Sun's death, the KMT's Cape Province branch hosted a special memorial service in Port Elizabeth. Obituary notices were sent out by the chairman Lo Pong inviting members to a service in Evatt Street on Sunday, 12 April 1925.

It was the outbreak of war in China which stoked a strong nationalistic fervour within the community. The second Sino-Japanese War, from 1937 to 1945, united the South African Chinese in a new spirit of patriotism and desire to help China defeat Japan. Throughout the war years Chinese, young and old, were caught up in unprecedented fund-raising activities as they sought to show support for their far-off motherland.

9

War in China: The Community Responds

Why were Japanese given better treatment than Chinese in South Africa? How did the Chinese community contribute to the worldwide fund-raising efforts for the Sino-Japanese War from 1937 to 1945? This chapter compares the status of Japanese and Chinese, describes the nationalistic fervour of the community during those turbulent years and their futile expectations of obtaining equal rights after World War II.

Within the ranks of Asiatics in South Africa, the tiny Japanese population constituted an anomaly. Also treated as prohibited immigrants from 1913, they were nonetheless accorded privileges denied other 'non-Whites'. By 1928, the 'improved' status of the Japanese was formally written into law and the Chinese vigorously protested against such differentiation, arguing that on the international front, Chinese were placed on the same footing as Japanese.

Over the next twenty years the status of Chinese became the subject of much discussion, both within the community and publicly. A major community conference in 1930 raised the issue, but the Sino-Japanese War and World War II also focused the attention of South Africans on the position of Chinese. Both South Africa and China were allied with the major western powers during World War II, and in the course of the 1940s, thousands of South Africans supported drives to raise funds for China. A heightened awareness of the Chinese as comrades-in-arms led to calls for the community to be given equal rights, but more stringent restrictions were in store when 1948 saw the rise to power of the Nationalist Party in South Africa.

This chapter covers developments affecting the South African Chinese between 1920 and 1948, with particular emphasis on community activities and concerns during the turbulent years of war.

THE JAPANESE ISSUE

In the early years of 20th century South Africa, Japanese faced the same restrictions as all Asiatics as far as immigration, freedom of movement and property rights were concerned. Instances occurred of Japanese being refused permits to enter or trade in the Transvaal, and although various individuals objected to these restrictions, the authorities applied the laws universally to all Asiatics.[1] The Japanese were, however, not regarded as 'ordinary' Asiatics, a fact highlighted by efforts to introduce special exemptions for them soon after the Union of South Africa was formed.

Pointing to treaty obligations between Great Britain and Japan, the Secretary of State enquired, in August 1910, whether amendments could not be made to the legislation restricting Japanese subjects in the Transvaal and Orange Free State. Prime Minister Louis Botha expressed the government's regrets that it could not comply with the request.[2] Although no official change in the status of the Japanese was formally proclaimed, in the following years a distinct differentiation in treatment became evident.

A glimpse at the trading relationship between South Africa and Japan offers a possible reason for the softening of official attitudes. Between 1910 and 1920 Japan had become the second largest export market for South African goods, after the United Kingdom — its purchases having climbed from a mere £45 pounds to a staggering £6 million. By 1933 Japan had joined the ranks of the six major suppliers of goods to the Union.[3]

Although Asiatics were classified as prohibited immigrants in terms of the 1913 Immigrants Regulation Act, special administrative concessions permitted the admission of Japanese. As early as 1915, on the recommendation of Japanese Consul Feruja, temporary permits were granted to 'Japanese subjects entering the Union for the purpose of business'. Such permits were valid for a year, renewable for five years.[4]

Efforts to increase South African trade with Japan prompted a further relaxation of the arrangement between the two governments. In 1921 the number of Japanese permitted entry was restricted to 30 each year, but by 1922 even this limit was withdrawn. A much smaller group than the Chinese, the Japanese in South Africa in 1921 numbered 54 people — 39 men and 15 women.[5]

More Rights

In 1928, however, the distinction between Japanese and other Asiatics was elevated from mere practice to law. The 1928 Liquor Act exempted Japanese from the definition of Asiatic, giving them the same rights as Whites in terms of possession of alcohol and admission to public bars. Official reasons for this decision were that there were very few Japanese in South Africa (approximately 100) and that no harm would come to such a group if the protection of the law designed for Asiatics was withdrawn.[6]

Consul-General Liu Ngai requested the same privilege be granted to Chinese, stating that the question had now become one of national honour. Natal Chinese pointed out their standard of civilization and living was equal to that of the Japanese and they were 'equally deserving of favourable consideration'.[7] Authorities turned down these appeals, stating that the decision to exempt the Japanese had not been motivated 'by any desire to differentiate between that nation and the Chinese ... [but by the] substantial considerations of the well-being of the community ...'. It was further argued that the greater size of the Chinese population, 'their numbers approximate 5000', included many whom the liquor law was designed to protect.[8] (It is interesting to note that the official census, some eight years later, in 1936, recorded the number of Chinese as fewer than 3000 countrywide.)[9]

Gentlemen's Agreement

Nevertheless, in 1930, the unique status of the Japanese was further underlined by the conclusion of a 'Gentlemen's Agreement' between the South African and Japanese governments. The agreement simply formalized the situation which had already existed for years as far as the admission of Japanese was concerned.

In an exchange of notes between the two governments, it was agreed that all Japanese tourists, students and merchants recommended by the Consul would be allowed to enter the country for one year, with renewable permits. Such people would, however, not be entitled to live, trade or farm in the Orange Free State, nor would any children born to temporary permit holders be entitled to South African nationality.[10]

Newspapers greeted the development with shock, using headlines such as 'SA at grips with peril ... Asiatic Flood Feared, Astonishing powers given to Consul.' It was pointed out that the relatively free influx of Japanese wholesale merchants would threaten White businesses and the country's immigration laws had become null and void as far as Japanese were concerned.

Representatives of commerce and industry viewed the agreement with suspicion arguing that the country would be flooded with cheap Japanese goods. Labelling the agreement as a case of 'slapdash diplomacy', one newspaper editorial pointed out it was 'bound to provoke resentment in other Oriental countries to which similar facilities are not extended.'[11]

The Consul for Japan, S. Yamasaki, pointed out that provision had been made to restrict the admission of wholesale merchants and buyers to a reasonable limit, and expressed his satisfaction with the agreement.

> Now that the stain on Japan has been removed by this agreement the highway to trade of benefit to both our countries has been opened. It is just a friendly gentleman's agreement, and I see no harm in it. We will observe its spirit to the letter. Its results will not follow in a day or a month, but I am sure, they will be beneficial ...
>
> Sentiment influences trade in a remarkable degree. For a long time Japanese merchants refused to have anything to do with South Africa, which treated them so dishonourably ...[12]

Consul Yamasaki said Japan imported about 1000 tons of wattle bark from South Africa each month, as well as manganese and scrap iron, but wool would be considered and he was investigating the possibility of maize as a poultry feed.

During heated parliamentary exchanges the government was sharply criticized for concluding the agreement. Prime Minister Hertzog defended the move on the grounds that it would be a means of promoting the expansion of South Africa's export trade, and said South Africa had a glut of unsaleable agricultural products. Colonel Deneys Reitz, MP for Barberton, declared that the government was 'in fact conferring on the Japanese merchant who had never been in the country far greater benefits than on the Chinese merchant who had been in the Union for many years.' Furthermore, he added, if the agreement was as good as had been made out, 'why debar the Free State from its benefits?'[13] Government speakers pointed out that other Commonwealth countries such as Australia, New Zealand and Canada had similar agreements with Japan and that South Africa's trade would expand in wool and maize.[14]

The agreement remained in effect although periodic rumours of Japanese expansion into local markets continued to do the rounds. In mid-1931 the Acting Japanese Consul, T. Hongo, vehemently denied that any Japanese warehouses had been established and said it was 'really ridiculous to talk about a "Japanese Trade Menace".' South Africa's markets were neither big enough nor profitable enough to warrant such fears and he dismissed allegations of cheap labour costs in Japan.

> The low price of Japanese goods is due to good management, excellent organisation of industries, efficient machinery and the application of scientific methods, and a system of mass production. For the current low price of Japanese goods in this country, I think that South African businessmen ought to shoulder part of the responsibility, as there is a great deal of unnecessary competition among themselves ... I would like to urge that we desire nothing more than to promote the benefit and prosperity of both countries,' Mr Hongo said.[15]

A key feature of Japanese 'settlement' in South Africa was that it was temporary. By 1936 there were 146 Japanese in the country, only a handful of whom had been resident for longer than five years. Interestingly enough, the census of 1936 showed that one Japanese man had entered South Africa as early as 1881 and a Japanese woman sometime between 1891 and 1896.[16]

STATUS OF CHINESE IN THE UNION

The noticeable elevation of the Japanese as a group highlighted the position of the Chinese in South Africa. Throughout 1929, press reports reflected the concern Chinese felt about their status and the fruitless attempts by Consul-General Liu Ngai to obtain full and equal citizenship rights for the community. At the beginning of the year, a commissioner of the Overseas Bureau of the Chinese Foreign Office in Nanking, C.N. Mok, was sent to investigate the conditions under which Chinese settlers in South and East Africa lived.

During his visit to Johannesburg he said the Chinese were 'greatly dissatisfied with the restrictions which are imposed upon them as Asiatics'. He pointed out that when the Kuomintang (Nationalist Party) assumed control of China in 1928, one of its first actions had been to institute the enquiry into overseas Chinese worldwide. Patriotism among Chinese was growing, he added, because they felt China had an important contribution to make to civilization.

> All we ask of the Western peoples is to give us a chance and to show us by their treatment of our nationals settled in their respective countries that they sympathise with China's national hopes and aspirations.[17]

As a result of Mok's visit, Consul-General Liu Ngai campaigned for an improvement in the status of the Chinese, not only leading a delegation to the Minister of the Interior in Cape Town, but also publicizing his appeals in local newspapers. He asked for Chinese to be given recognition on the same basis as other foreign nationals.[18]

The Consul-General's appeal was prominently featured in the *Canton Gazette* in China, which highlighted the fact that Chinese paid the same taxes as others, yet had no voice in municipal affairs. An editorial in the Chinese paper also added the following barbed comment:

> The world's most famous scientists have failed to discover any characteristics of the Mongolian race that could in any way show any inferiority to the white race ... and it would, indeed, be educative to have Johannesburg law-makers tell us just exactly how they have arrived at their conclusions attributing the Chinese to a lower social order.[19]

Community members have claimed that the South African government was prepared to offer the Chinese a 'gentleman's agreement' similar to that concluded with the Japanese. The community, however, was uncertain of its terms, some saying an immigration quota would only benefit a few 'educated' individuals while others speculated it would elevate the status of the Chinese as a whole. Although no official documentation has been traced to substantiate the existence of such an offer, it is quite likely that the outcry over immigration concessions granted to the Japanese would have forced the authorities to retract any such offer.[20]

A 'Typical' Chinese

To 'explain' the Chinese to the public, a local resident and community leader, Dr L.N. Liang wrote an article for *The Star* in which he said the 'colossal lack of sympathy for the Chinese' was due to ignorance and it was time to make facts about the community better known. He outlined the way of life of a 'typical' Chinese in Johannesburg, explaining how such a man lived, dressed, ate, did business and gave to charity. He attributed the success of Chinese shopkeepers to sheer hard work and generalized to convey his community as one worthy of high regard. Dr Liang explained the social structure of families in which filial piety remained strong and said the Chinese did not give ready expression to emotions ...

> They are so given to thought and reflection that not only are they slow to leap, but they are inclined to look so long that they never leap at all. This is a great drawback, as when circumstances require action the Chinese are in danger of not acting, and when they finally decide to act it is perhaps too late. The Chinese when confronted

Dr L. N. Liang

Community leader, Dr Luke Nain Liang.

The first Chinese doctor in South Africa, Luke Nain Liang, was born in Moiyean (Meixian), China, in 1901. Arriving in South Africa at the age of nine, he attended a Coloured school on the corner of Market and Becker streets in Ferreirastown, Johannesburg. His father's untimely death in 1918 left the teenager with the responsibility of a small shop.

Running foul of the law for buying sugar through the 'back door', he was placed in the charge of a social worker who recognized his talents and assisted him to pursue an education overseas. Although a medical school had opened in Johannesburg in 1919, the admission of non-Whites had not been considered at the time and proved to be a highly contentious issue in later years.

For the student abroad, finances were a struggle. He obtained money to pay his passage by bidding for the Moiyeanese 'fee' (hui) and was also assisted financially by members of the Cantonese Club, as well as Hall Fisher and Mr Mason. After completing his studies in England, Scotland and Ireland, Dr Liang practised in Johannesburg where he established a reputation for the treatment of rheumatoid arthritis with 'gold injections'. He married Patricia Wong Chapson of Port Elizabeth and had three children, Peggy Yu-Lan, David Youn-Sen and Shireen Fey-Lan.

For nearly 40 years he played an active role in Chinese community affairs, becoming the first chairman of the Central Chinese Association of South Africa in the 1950s. Being fluent in Hakka, Cantonese, Mandarin and English, he was unusually well-equipped to serve as a community leader. He died in 1964 at the age of 63.

> with quarrels and disputes will always seek peaceful means of settlement rather than the aggressive method of combat for the outlet of his emotions.[21]

In letters to the government, Consul-General Liu Ngai repeatedly raised the issue of the status of Chinese and told a newspaper the Chinese would never be satisfied until they were treated as a friendly nation, in the same way as the French and Americans were.[22]

> I am in no way demanding what the Chinese are not entitled to as a friendly people and lawful citizens, but just exactly what South Africans would demand if they were subjected to such conditions in any foreign country as the Chinese in South Africa have suffered under in the past and are suffering at present.[23]

ALL SOUTH AFRICA CHINESE CONFERENCE

The year 1930 marked a significant shift in the state of Chinese politics in South Africa. Scattered as the people were in different and distant provinces, subjected to varying restrictions, they had nonetheless, over a period of some fifty years, grown into a readily identifiable community. Despite some internal divisions, the Chinese recognized the need for unity, for separate groups to work together to address the common problems they faced.

A new Consul-General, Ho Tsang, assumed office in May 1930, and within months of his arrival played a key role in convening a major meeting of Chinese organizations throughout the country. At the end of August 1930, more than 100 representatives from the Cape, Natal and the Transvaal gathered in Johannesburg for the first All South Africa Chinese Conference.

Representatives who attended the All South Africa Chinese Conference called by Consul-General Ho Tsang in Johannesburg in August 1930.

They met, over two weekends, at the Kuomintang headquarters at 30 Fox Street, Ferreirastown, in rooms decorated with Chinese scrolls and tapestries. The conference was presided over by Consul-General Ho Tsang, assisted by vice-consul Ting Shao. Among the subjects discussed were education, trade restrictions in the Transvaal, the Quota Act, the Liquor Act, the establishment of a Chinese newspaper, the appointment of more consuls and a trade treaty between South Africa and China.[24]

Interestingly enough, the conference was reported in local English-language newspapers which covered the views the Chinese held and quoted extensively from statements, specially made in English for the benefit of the press, by one community representative, Dr L.N. Liang.[25] Not only did Dr Liang use the opportunity to reiterate appeals Chinese had made time and again for equal treatment, he also expressed their fears for the future.

Pointing out that it was the Chinese mine labourers who had saved the Witwatersrand's economy, and therefore South Africa's, he questioned why the community 'should now suffer from so many laws and unfair discriminations against them'.[26] Impending legislation, in the form of the Asiatic Land Tenure Bill would, Dr Liang said, worsen the position of the Chinese since its aim was 'to exterminate existing lawful Chinese interests in a course of a few years'.[27]

When the conference ended on 7 September 1930, the Chinese attitude was best expressed in the statement made by conference delegate, D. Summ:

> We feel that we have an equal claim in this country ... for apart from the existence of treaties, we have helped towards building South Africa. Above all, the Chinese here have always scrupulously observed law and order, are self-respecting and have been generous to the poor. We are well qualified as citizens of this country.[28]

Describing the importance of the conference for the Chinese, one observer of the times and participant in community affairs, W. King wrote:

> Very few people paid attention to ways of opposing the unjust laws, but this changed when they could not go back to the mother country. They realised this country was where they would grow old and that it was not right to be looked down upon. So the Chinese came together and worked out what to do ... Consul-General Ho and Vice-Consul Shao were responsible for an historic event for South African Chinese. The Chinese representative meeting was very successful ... There were a few resolutions to form a South African Chinese Association, to form a company selling shares to start a Chinese newspaper and to make changes to the Chinese school. Although the formation of the broad Chinese Association failed, the start of the company to found a newspaper was successful.[29]

It was unrealistic to imagine that one conference would alter the course of legislation determined by provincial and national authorities. But among the Chinese themselves, various reorganization measures were undertaken at the KMT's Chinese school in Johannesburg and plans were set in motion to launch a Chinese newspaper. The conference marked a key development in community terms, bringing together individuals with a common purpose and paving the way for the later formation of a national representative body for the Chinese. For the next twenty years, however, developments in China itself occupied centre stage in the community's awareness with the outbreak first of the Sino-Japanese War and then World War II.

SINO-JAPANESE WAR

Japan's invasion of Manchuria in 1931 marked the start of an undeclared war during which she steadily extended her occupation of north China. Despite appeals to the League of Nations and economic boycotts of Japanese goods, China was unable to prevent the establishment of the independent state of Manchukuo under Japanese control in 1932 and further territorial encroachments.

Bitter civil strife between the Kuomintang (Nationalists) and the Communists weakened China's resistance to Japan. Under fire from the Nationalists, the Red Army undertook the Long March in late 1934, eventually to establish its stronghold at Yenan in north western China. Only by 1936 did the two sides declare an armed truce to establish the semblance of a united front against the Japanese threat.

On 7 July 1937 a clash between Chinese and Japanese troops on the Lukouchiao bridge (the Marco Polo bridge incident) outside Peiping, precipitated the outbreak of full-scale hostilities. China faced the problems of a lack of industrial expertise to wage modern warfare, inadequate transportation and military supplies, a small airforce and virtually no navy. Within months the superior Japanese military machine launched relentless bombing raids, capturing both Shanghai and the capital of Nanking, 'amid scenes of wholesale rape and the slaughter of helpless prisoners and civilians, which shocked the civilized world.'[30]

The toll in lives was estimated at over 200 000 in Nanking alone,[31] and descriptions of the massacre reflect unspeakable horrors and brutality. A floodtide of refugees, ordinary Chinese men, women and children took to the roads ahead of the inexorable Japanese invasion and nearly two million lost their homes in 11 cities and 4000 villages which were flooded out when Chinese authorities dynamited the dams of the Yellow River to slow the Japanese advance.[32]

By the end of 1938 Japan had conquered the coast of China and occupied key economic centres, including the port city of Canton (Guangzhou). The Chinese government under Generalissimo Chiang Kai Shek moved its headquarters to Chungking to rally the forces of 'free' China in the south west. There, industrial plants, arsenals and a communication network were established to enable the Chinese to fight a long war, while behind the front lines, in 'occupied' China, Communist guerrillas under Mao Tse Tung (Mao Zedong) harassed the Japanese.

When the Japanese bombing of Pearl Harbour in 1941 drew the Americans into World War II, the Sino-Japanese conflict became part of an international struggle. On 8 December 1941 America, Great Britain, Australia, New Zealand, the Netherlands as well as other European and South American countries declared war on Japan while China declared war on Germany, Italy and Japan.[33]

Recounting the key features of the Sino-Japanese War is complicated by the widely differing interpretations of the roles played by the Kuomintang forces and the Communists, and the effectiveness of their respective strategies for waging war. Observers have cited many factors influencing the course of events, including Chiang Kai Shek's perception of the Communists as his major enemy rather than the Japanese, as well as factionalism, corruption and inflation. Nonetheless, the Chinese people as a nation were committed to resistance and, with the Allied Nations, eventually claimed victory over Japan in 1945.

War in China had a major impact on the Chinese in South Africa. Not only did it stoke up a fiercely nationalistic spirit and a sense of patriotism towards China, it also unified the community in efforts to do all they could to aid their motherland. Many maintained that only when China was perceived as a strong country would it be able to exert influence on behalf of Chinese abroad. Living as they had for years on the edge of South African society, the Chinese responded with alacrity to the opportunity to 'belong' in some way to a struggle in far-off China.

A COMMUNITY MOBILIZED

The war years, although austere, ushered in a period of unprecedented community activity on many fronts. For the first time Chinese women came into their own, new organizations sprouted countrywide and Chinese were treated as welcome allies by South Africans in general.

Within the community, scores of social functions, Chinese operas, variety concerts and bazaars became the order of the day. Everyone was urged to boycott Japanese goods and even schoolchildren were reminded to 'save their pennies for Madame Chiang'.[34] Chinese women formed groups to raise funds, Kuomintang members and other patriotic Chinese sold war bonds and throughout the country the appeal to 'save China' made people dig deep into their pockets.

Elderly community members have said, time and again, Chinese government authorities acknowledged that the South African Chinese donated more money per capita to the war relief effort than any other overseas Chinese community. Although no documents have been traced to substantiate this, by 1943 the community — numbering fewer than 3000 men, women and children — had already sent at least £90 000 in cash to China.[35] A great deal more was represented by donations in kind of valuables such as jewellery and individual investments in China's war bond issues.

In Port Elizabeth a Chinese women's auxiliary group collected old jewellery to support the war effort. Women were asked to donate their gold and diamond earrings, rings and bracelets, a sacrifice willingly made by many.[36] Women's groups were also formed in East London, Durban, Cape Town and Johannesburg. Their exhaustive fund-raising efforts included the collection of groceries from shopkeepers and wholesalers for resale at bazaars. Because of wartime shortages, many essential foodstuffs such as butter, sugar, flour and rice were sought-after commodities.

Chinese even harnessed the pastime of gambling to support the relief cause. In Pretoria, a club known as the Nan Tung Hui was formed to aid war orphans. They met regularly over gambling sessions in a shop in the Asiatic Bazaar, handing over their winnings to the needy in China.[37] For the duration of the war, the Eastern Province Chinese Association ran a 'gaming club' in its Evatt Street headquarters, levying a charge on all games of 'tin gau'. Other gambling dens sent their customers to the association to ensure the war fund-raising was fully supported.[38]

Members of the Chinese Women's Relief Fund Committee in Johannesburg who launched numerous fund-raising efforts during the Sino-Japanese War.

Celebrating their 10th anniversary on 14 September 1947, members of the Chinese Women's Relief Fund Committee gathered at their headquarters at No. 4 Fox Street, Ferreirastown.

In Johannesburg, a young teacher, Leong Pak Seong, organized teams of Chinese school pupils to form the 'Old Students Club' with the aim of raising enough money to buy 10 000 cotton vests for soldiers in China. In November 1938, they distributed a pamphlet calling on all Chinese, in the words made famous by a Sung dynasty general, to 'sacrifice yourself for your country'. The club was able to send nearly 4000 Chinese dollars from its winter clothing collection drive to the Bank of China.[39]

Community elder and long-time teacher at the Chinese school, Fok Yu Kam, recalled the contribution of children to the war effort. 'The children were very good. Every day the class leader would go around and collect money, a penny, a tickey ... to help save their country. They were giving up their tuckshop money.'

Minor problems relating to the country's liquor laws surfaced. When the Chinese ran a stall at the Allies Fair in Turffontein, Johannesburg in September 1941, Consul-General Dekien Toung had to request a special exemption to enable Chinese to patronize the restaurant where liquor would be served. He also referred to the fact that Japanese were exempted from such laws and expressed the growing indignation of the Chinese who felt 'the Union Government of South Africa is according a better treatment towards the people of an enemy country rather than the people of an Allied Nation.'[40]

Although community members throughout South Africa recall with some nostalgia the commitment of all to the war effort, particular mention should be made of two organizations whose members kept records of their work during those active years. They were the Chinese Women's Relief Fund Committee in Johannesburg and the Eastern Province Chinese Association in Port Elizabeth.

Chinese Women's Relief Fund Committee

The Chinese Women's Relief Fund Committee was formed in late 1937 by teacher, Miss Daisy Lai, with the involvement of well-known ladies such as Mrs Chan Fee Foong and Mrs Leong Suk Jan. In its heyday, the group had more than 100 active members who campaigned vigorously for donations to aid China.

Members paid monthly subscription fees for the privilege of working for war relief. They held meetings every Sunday in their rented headquarters, a small house at Number 4 Fox Street, Ferreirastown. There they examined every avenue for persuading people to part with their money, starting with straightforward collections and appeals to staging plays and full-scale Chinese operas.

A member and later treasurer for the committee, Mrs Ivy Leong, described the enthusiasm with which the women tackled fund-raising.

> There was a great deal of pride in belonging to the association. For us the most important thing was to help China win the war ... Sometimes we went for a week or two with no sleep. We had to practise for the opera, and then go out and sell tickets, door to door. From early morning whenever someone had time to drive us ... then late at night, go to the treasurer's house to write receipts for the money ... We were like beggars, asking people all the time to give money.

The operas, held in the Chinese school hall or a nearby cinema in 'Chinatown', proved to be social occasions for the community who turned out in large numbers. To ensure sufficient variety, members changed their programme each month and drew on the talents of some musicians and singers who had been part of performing troupes.[41]

The organization published annual accounts detailing its many fund-raising drives and listing the names and contributions of each donor, as well as the role played by individuals whether it was providing meals or giving lifts to collectors to outlying towns. Apart from visiting shops and homes throughout Johannesburg, the women travelled as far afield as Krugersdorp, Potchefstroom, Springs and Vereeniging. In 1941 alone, they raised nearly £1500 from collections for wounded soldiers and refugees, for winter clothes and for gas masks.[42] All funds collected by the women were sent directly to the Bank of China, initially in Nanking and later in Chungking, and copies of receipts obtained were also published.[43]

Enthusiasm for the war effort never flagged. In July 1943, to mark the sixth anniversary of the Double Seventh (the seventh day of the seventh month), the start of the Sino-Japanese War, the women, with the Old Students Club and other organizations mounted a stage show and held an American auction. Admission alone

A Chinese farmer from Mafeking donated these giant winter melons which were auctioned in aid of war relief in Johannesburg in the early 1940s.

Johannesburg Chinese produced lavish operatic productions to raise funds during the war years.

raised more than £500.[44] Even Chinese market gardeners contributed giant winter melons to auction in aid of the fund-raising.

The Chinese Women's Relief Fund Committee did not limit its focus to the Sino-Japanese War alone and also participated in general fund-raising for the whole Allied cause. Young Chinese women joined the scores of street collectors on Johannesburg streets during such drives and also took part in the city's Liberty Cavalcade, resplendent in traditional Chinese *cheongsams*.

This organization thrived throughout the war and celebrated its 10th anniversary on 14 September 1947. Madame Chiang Kai Shek, wife of the Chinese leader, sent the group a citation commending their sterling fund-raising efforts. Reiterating the claim by Chinese throughout the country, Ivy Leong added:

> Madame Chiang recognized the work we did and she said the South African Chinese women, per capita, raised the most money of all overseas Chinese for the war effort.

By the late 1940s however the Chinese Women's Relief Fund Committee became defunct and was replaced by another, more socially oriented women's group. This group, run by Mrs Muriel Whyte, played an important role in aiding other charitable causes and raised funds for the building of a new Chinese school in the late 1940s.

Eastern Province Chinese Association

Anti-Japanese feeling ran high in the Eastern Cape. In December 1937, the Eastern Province Chinese Association, supported by 600 Chinese, launched a boycott of Japanese goods, announcing their drive in a parade through the streets of Port Elizabeth. About 30 cars carried huge banners inscribed with the slogans 'Boycott Japanese Goods! Buy British!'[45]

The association went even further by organizing a collection of donations each month from all Chinese to support the war effort. The following report by long-time Chinese secretary, Yuen Whiteley, best described the commitment of the Port Elizabeth community to the war effort:

> These are just some words concerning the Eastern Province Chinese in the 7 July War of Resistance and the happenings of that time. During the war, in the cities of Port Elizabeth, Uitenhage, Somerset East and Cradock, the community responded to the central government's call. Have money, donate money. Have strength, donate strength. Resist greedy Japan. After calling a meeting, the community established an 'Aid China Association'.
>
> Because we live far away overseas, we can only assist with money. Therefore, under the chairmanship of Lau Hwei Chun, every Chinese must contribute. The Eastern Province Chinese all promised to make monthly donations. The business people naturally did their utmost. Even ordinary shop workers subscribed a portion of their wages to express their national citizen's duty.
>
> At that time different districts elected responsible people to collect the monthly pledges. These were then handed over to the treasurer, Chan Tze Gin, to send to the Consul-General in Johannesburg for remittance to the central government. For eight years these collections have continued.
>
> There was a senior community member, Liu Foe Tse. Because of his age, he could not continue running his business and it was not convenient for him to make donations each month. So he sold his property and gave it all, the total sum of £2000. This was a generous act which should be publicised. Also, when it came to buying war bonds, the community was very generous.[46]

Since the majority of Port Elizabeth's Chinese ran small grocery shops, they were regularly approached to donate goods for fund-raising bazaars. As did Chinese elsewhere in the country, they too co-operated with other organizations to support the overall Allied fund-raising effort.

Vereeniging

More outlying towns which did not have large Chinese communities also pledged commitment to China's war relief. In an industrial area some 80 km south west of Johannesburg, the Vereeniging Chinese Relief Fund Committee was formed in the late 1930s. Supported by the 15 Chinese families in the area, they collected donations to send directly to China and also contributed the sum of £126 to the China War Relief Fund in 1943.

When the demands of the war faded, the group was reconstituted to form the Vereeniging Chinese Association. In November 1946 the Overseas Chinese Affairs Commission of the Republic of China issued a certificate to the Vereeniging Chinese

Relief Fund Committee acknowledging its loyalty and support during the war years. Long-time resident and past chairman of the association, Sun Hing, said funds were raised by dinners and collections.[47]

RELIEF FUNDS

Not only did the Chinese tap their own resources, but for the first time they were also drawn into the wider South African community. After South Africa entered World War II and China was acknowledged as one of the Allied forces, public concern was extended to focus on the war in China. The Chinese were hailed as comrades-in-arms and throughout the country, China War Relief Funds were established, 'China Week' fund-raising drives launched and South Africans from all sectors of society demonstrated their concern.

War catapulted the Chinese into the limelight. Numerous publications were devoted to outlining conditions in China and South Africa's leading citizens paid tribute to China's 'heroic resistance' and 'magnificent stand against Japanese aggression'.[48] In cities and towns countrywide, Chinese were invited to participate on fund-raising committees, to provide entertainment for functions and to work with their fellow South Africans for a common cause.

The lists of patrons and executive committees of various China War Relief Funds read like a South African 'Who's Who'. They included cabinet ministers, diplomats, bishops, mayors, city councillors, academics, the country's most prominent business people and ladies whose names featured regularly in every newspaper's society columns. All exerted their considerable influence to encourage support for China and to aid the war relief effort.

Students at various South African universities established a Chinese Universities' Relief Fund in 1938. They expressed concern for students and staff at Chinese universities, pointing out that 'Japanese aggression has been largely directed against centres of higher education, which have, in many instances, been completely destroyed.' The Students Representative Councils at both the University of the Witwatersrand and the University of Natal organized fund-raising drives for this cause.[49]

Johannesburg

The China War Relief Fund was inaugurated in November 1942 by the Reverend A.S. Moore Anderson, a minister who had worked in China and Malaya for many years. Fund chairman, Dr J.B. Robertson, reported that more than £7000 had been raised in the first few months of operation, but that a 'China Week' had been arranged to increase 'this token of our sympathy with China's millions and our unity with them'.[50] Large-scale 'China Week' fund-raising drives were held in Johannesburg in April 1943 and October 1944. The extensive programmes of activities included film shows, art exhibitions, talks on Chinese culture and philosophy, a street collection, morning market, puppet shows, concerts and dinner dances. Local Chinese contributed by performing in plays at the Kuo Ting School in Alexander Street and children also gave demonstrations of traditional Chinese dancing. School teacher Fok Yu Kam, co-organized the 1944 procession in which ladies from the Chinese Women's Relief Fund Committee joined hundreds of fund-raisers rattling collection cans through the streets of the city.

To focus attention on their campaign, the Johannesburg China War Relief Fund organizers produced stirring publications such as *China at War*, *Salute to China* and *South Africa and China*.[51] These not only reported on conditions in China and featured appeals by Madame Chiang Kai Shek for aid, but also recorded the contributions in cash and kind from hundreds of businesses, voluntary groups, schools and individuals. Fund-raising efforts during the 1944 China Week in Johannesburg realized the sum of a further £7500.

Cape Town

The 'Help for Free China Fund', under the chairmanship of Sir Herbert Stanley, hosted a China Week in Cape Town in February 1943. In addition to an exhibition of Chinese art, the fund organized prayer services in churches and synagogues, an auction, film show, street collection and a 'mile of money' drive in the city centre.

Reporting on the planned activities, the local *Cape Times* correspondent remarked on 4 February 1943: 'While the Chinese Exhibition is on, real Chinese children from their school at Claremont will perform on stage and will, I am told, sing national songs in their own language.' No doubt many Capetonians took advantage of the rare opportunity to see 'real' Chinese children! The handsome sum of of £8750 was collected during China Week.

To thank the fund-raisers for their efforts, the Cape Town Chinese Association hosted a Chinese banquet at the Woodstock town hall. Maria Liu, daughter of the Chinese charge d'affaires in Kubishev, Russia, addressed the gathering in Chinese, guests took to the dance floor and the function ended with the playing of the Chinese national anthem and 'God Save the King'.[52]

In October 1943 the 'Help for Free China Fund' organized a further round of activities to mark the Chinese national day, culminating in a lavish ball in the city hall with the theme, 'A Night in Cathay'. The Cape Town Chinese community continued to play an active role in the fund-raising, organizing a dinner dance and an exhibition of Chinese war pictures.[53]

As part of the Liberty Cavalcade in Cape Town, the Chinese ran a restaurant, an exhibition and a stall selling Chinese objets d'art.[54] Many different countries were represented, and those responsible for the China section were chairman George Ming, treasurer S.F.C. Hunt and secretary L.A. Ying with the committee of the Chinese Association.[55]

Salute to China

MADAME CHIANG'S APPEAL TO THE RAND

TO all friends of Johannesburg, who have so generously demonstrated their interest in the welfare of the people of China during the past seven years of our continued resistance against Japanese aggression, I wish to express my heartfelt thanks.

In spite of the broad programme of relief work being undertaken by our national Government, much misery still exists. To try to alleviate this suffering, the women of China have put their shoulders behind this heavy task and have striven to contribute their strength and spirit to lighten the yoke which an invaded country inevitably bears. The projects which would most interest you are the Homes for the care of War Orphans, now commonly called Warphanages Centres, of maimed soldiers; and factories for the families of recruits. In these projects we have aimed to train the children, the maimed, and the womenfolk of the men fighting at the front, to become a part of our national life, to inspire in them the feeling that in the days of peace they have yet a contribution to make to the reconstructed world, and that in the case of the wounded soldiers in the present days of travail they should, insofar as possible, make themselves selfsupporting and develop within themselves an inner citadel of steadfastness and unswerving initiative, so that when their convalescence is complete they will face the world again as normal and useful citizens.

I wish to express again our heartfelt appreciation of the practical sympathy which the good people of Johannesburg have continuously shown to us during these troublous times.

MADAME CHIANG KAI SHEK.

Received 3rd March, 1944.

CHINA'S INSPIRATION

SMUTS PAYS TRIBUTE TO GALLANT CHINA

"Now is Your Opportunity for Financial Sacrifice"

LONG before we felt a direct Axis threat to our national and personal freedom, the Chinese were fighting with desperate bravery to withstand Japanese militarism. For nearly seven years they have faced repeated onslaughts by this highly integrated military power, which has had the advantage of guns, ships and supplies. Under the command of that remarkable man, Marshal Chiang Kai Shek, undisputed leader of more than 400,000,000 people, the Chinese have refused to allow the Japanese to subdue them. And these people—devoted, brave, patient—are our Allies.

But the Chinese have been fighting for a long time. Their losses in manpower and material have been enormous. They need every possible help that can be given to them now. I appeal to you, therefore, to give to this great cause, and to give generously. Without her heroic resistance, Japan might at once have had her hands and forces free and free access for the attack on our and Allied territories. Think of the danger at that time that might have resulted to our cause.

Now is your opportunity to prove by your financial sacrifice that you really understand and appreciate what the Chinese have done; what they have dared against every chance. She has not merely waged a good fight. She has fought—and is still fighting—a great historic fight against Imperialist domination and for the preservation of everything that is best in humanity.

MADAME CHIANG'S PLAN FOR THE NEW CHINA

MADAME CHIANG KAI SHEK is the first woman in China. She is more than that. She is probably the most amazing woman in the world. Physically, mentally and spiritually she is a tower of strength. Her beauty, that willow-like beauty of the Chinese woman, cannot be surpassed.

It is well-known now that were it not for Madame Chiang the Generalissimo would have found his colossal task almost impossible. She has been his inspiration. She has shared his heartbreak over the rape of China by the Japanese. She has buoyed up his courage in the long, cruel battle for freedom. She has urged on his vision for the new China when the aggressors are driven from the land.

She said recently that in her country a new kind of Chinese Socialism based on democratic principles is evolving. Its principles are a nationalism which is quite distinct from imperialism, the rights of the people to freedom, and freedom from want for all the people.

Defining Democracy, she said "To my mind Democracy means a representative government, and by representative I mean representative of the steadfast and settled will of the people, as opposed to irresponsible and spellbinding slogans of political hawkers. Furthermore, in a democracy, minority parties should not be left out of consideration."

Govern a nation as you would cook a small fish.

She belives that the valiant struggle of her people has brought China for the first time abreast of the Great Powers.

And she asks: "Cannot we in the new day whose dawn is approaching, strive together to gain supremacy in the peaceful arts of government and administration that will secure lasting happiness for the people of all races, and thus create a world vitalised by new hopes and worshipping more a Christlike ideal?"

Some of the many publications produced in South Africa to highlight fund-raising activities for the Sino-Japanese War effort during the 1940s.

Cape Archives

— OFFICIAL PROGRAMME FOR CHINA WEEK —

THE... China Week News

13TH TO 18TH DECEMBER, 1943.

Published by China War Relief Fund. EAST LONDON Price 3d.

MARSHAL CHIANG KAI-SHEK

DON'T PASS THIS PAPER TO YOUR FRIENDS—TELL THEM TO BUY ONE.

CONSUL-GENERAL FOR CHINA SPEAKS TO SOUTH AFRICA.

Mr. Dekien Toung, Consul-General for China, speaking in Johannesburg to a crowded public meeting, said:—

"This world war which has so cruelly struck all of us, but which has so closely united us, began by the Japanese invasion of Manchuria on September 18th, 1931. Since then, Italy started her conquest of Abyssinia; Germany tore up the Treaty of Peace; Hitler and Mussolini plotted together a civil war in Spain; and Japan, when her turn came again, launched all her armies against China on the fateful date of July 7th, 1937. Then the Third Reich successfully annexed Austria and Czechoslovakia until its invasion of Poland. Who can deny to-day that this series of tragic events in Europe, Africa and Asia did not come directly from the Japanese aggression at Moukden, and that the invasion of Poland in 1939 was not an inevitable consequence? It is since 1931 that China fought our common enemy. In these eleven long years of bitter resistance we have lost nearly nine rich provinces and nearly six million soldiers and civilians, but we have also inflicted more than two million casualties on the invaders, and are still tying down more than a million of them on a front of two thousand miles. To Japan the annihilation and immobilization of three million soldiers mean a telling effect. It was impossible for the militarists of Tokyo to send more than a tenth of their army in December, 1941, for the invasion of the countries in the South-western Pacific.

China has been constantly warning the democratic powers that a world war was coming to all of us if they did not try to nip aggression in the bud. I can now say that, without the several years warning from China, the surprises of the sudden invasion of Poland and the sudden attack on Pearl Harbour, would have been much more cruel and perhaps even fatal to Democracy and the civilisation of mankind.

The leaders of the United Nations admit that without the concurrence of China they can hardly strike the death blow against Japan; we must say also that without the collaboration of our allies, China alone will have great difficulty in destroying the Japanese war machine. Speaking about the importance of co-operation between our two countries, I should point out that China has prevented Japan from attacking the Union of South Africa so that the Union could disregard the menace on its Eastern flank and send all its brave Springboks to the North in order to gain the great victory. Our South African allies have kept open the last sea route for supplying China and have helped in clearing the Japanese submarines in the Indian Ocean by the occupation of Madagascar. That is why mutual friendship, esteem and sympathy naturally arose.

If we are the first victims of the Axis powers, we are proud to be the first defenders of Liberty. One knows the heroism of our troops at the front but one knows little of the heroism of our guerillas in the rear of the enemy who have been struggling for eleven years against a barbarous foe. One knows the loss and the sufferings of our army, but one knows little about the loss and sufferings of our old men, our women and our children in the occupied regions. In these eleven years of struggle, incredible misery reigned in a large part of China to such a degree that I can say without the least exaggeration that it has been ten times worse than Europe under Hitler. But our immense sacrifices will not be in vain; we will continue to make such sacrifices until all the peoples of the world will be free.

CHINA WEEK PROGRAMME

13th to 19th DECEMBER, 1943.

MONDAY 13th:
CHINESE CONCERT, City Hall, 7.30 p.m.

TUESDAY, 14th:
OPEN-AIR CARNIVAL and DANCE, Marine Park, Esplanade, 7 p.m.

WEDNESDAY, 15th:
CARNIVAL and DANCE, Marine Park, Esplanade, 7 p.m.

THURSDAY, 16th (DINGAAN'S DAY):
ALL-DAY CARNIVAL IN MARINE PARK—10 a.m. to 10 p.m. 3rd Battery Band. Dancing Displays. Tug-of-War. Songs. Lucky Dips. Chinese Restaurant. Games of Skill. Refreshments. Beer Garden. Gypsies. Dancing from 7 p.m.

FRIDAY, 17th:
BAZAAR at St. Peter's Hall, Hood Street, West Bank, at 7.30 p.m. (Gifts accepted during afternoon).
CARNIVAL AND DANCE, 7 p.m., at Marine Park.

SATURDAY, 18th:
BEWARE OF THE SUNSHINE GIRLS.
CARNIVAL AND DANCE, 7 p.m., Marine Park.

SUNDAY, 19th:
CONCERT, 20th Century Theatre 7.15 p.m.

CARNIVAL IS HERE!

LET YOURSELVES GO!

BREAK AWAY FROM WARTIME DULLNESS AND HELP CHINA WAR RELIEF.

HASTEN VICTORY BY HELPING OUR CHINESE ALLIES DURING CHINA WEEK.

— GIVE GENEROUSLY DURING CHINA WEEK —

Young and old were drawn into activities to aid the 'Help for Free China Fund'. Pupils from the Cape Town Chinese school, photographed in 1943.

Port Elizabeth

'China War Week' was inaugurated in Port Elizabeth with a cocktail function at the Chinese School in Queen Street on 7 September 1943. Hosted by the chairman of the China War Relief committee, Mr Justice A. Schauder, it marked the start of a round of activities in which organizers pursued imaginative avenues to persuade people to donate money.

Community elder, Edward Jack Kee said women visited shops throughout the city to collect groceries in short supply and then sold them at fund-raising bazaars.

> 'People wanted goods that were rationed, like butter and rice, so that raised money. We also had a Chinese restaurant and organized games and things like that. We even hired the city hall and the Feathermarket Hall for dances and bazaars,' he said.

Miss M. Whiteley recalled the frenetic pace of activity during the fund-raising effort:

> I worked myself to a standstill because I was alone in my shop and I also had to run this flower stall at the Feathermarket Hall. My friends went to the market to collect flowers for me to sell ... We made a lot of money in those days, and we even sold buttonholes for £1! Of course, we also gave donations every month.

Under the chairmanship of Sout Chong Wing King, the Eastern Province Chinese Association also assisted in the organization of the Liberty Cavalcade in Port Elizabeth, an effort which realized over £10 000.[56] Although fund-raising efforts focused on the Sino-Japanese War relief effort, the community also supported general war drives. In June 1945 the Chinese Association hosted 'A Merry Party' in aid of Air Force Drive Week, at the Chinese school hall.

Chinese women outside the Feathermarket Hall in Port Elizabeth during their war relief fund-raising.

Queenstown

The Queenstown Aid-To-China Committee raised the sum of £3200 during March 1944. Reporting on the enthusiasm with which residents supported the fund, organizers said: 'Almost every money raising avenue was successfully explored, and some of our public bodies even went so far as to protest at not being asked to help!'[57]

Activities included a grand carnival, a police 'braaivleis' (barbecue), a race meeting as well as raffles and Chinese dinners. Particular tribute was paid to the Chinese community's generosity and assistance. The local newspaper noted that Mr Ah Chee, Mr Hwang and Mr and Mrs Easton donated furniture, a camphor chest, vases and pictures for competitions. Lo Pong virtually constituted a fund-raising drive on his own while the Yankee family were generous supporters at every function.

In a report on their activities, the Queenstown organizers wrote:

> There are only four Chinese families in Queenstown, and they raised more money and gave more money than almost everyone else put together ... Indeed, the enthusiasm and hard work of the Chinese themselves during the drive revealed on a smaller scale the same high spirit and the same worthiness to be helped as is shown by China herself today. The European members of the Committee were emphatic in asserting that they had never been more pleased to assist anyone, and had never worked in such a happy atmosphere.[58]

East London

East London's citizens were urged, cajoled and entertained into giving generously. *The China Week News*, published on the occasion of China Week from 14 to 18 December 1943, carried the appeal on its front page: 'Don't pass this paper to your friends — tell them to buy one'.

Urging support for the fund, Clive Gilbert, editor of the pamphlet, said both South Africa and China had played vital parts in the war. 'Destiny has fated the two countries to be friends. It is now our privilege to show our friendship in a positive and active manner; and also to think of China not as an Asiatic power, but as a working partner in the United Nations of the world.'

Noting the contribution of the Chinese community, the pamphlet pointed out that Chinese in East London had already donated £6000 for war relief while the Chinese in South Africa as a whole had sent more than £90 000 to China. The East London branch of the China War Relief Fund was formed by more than 50 of the city's prominent residents, under the chairmanship of M.T. Flemmer, and included on its committee were the chairman of the East London Chinese Association, Lee Sing Gen, as well as Yung Mason and a Mr Green. Fund-raising activities consisted of a Chinese concert, several carnivals and dances as well as a bazaar.

An active Chinese women's organization, run by Mrs Y. Mason, played an important role in community fund-raising. The group levied subscriptions on its members and participated in activities such as running food stalls for the war effort.

East London Chinese participated in the China Week effort at Marina Glen in the 1940s.

Durban

The China War Relief Fund (Medical Aid) was the name of the Durban organization which hosted a China Week from 22 to 28 August 1944 and netted the sum of £5500. Included among its patrons were leading citizens as well as the High Commissioner for India, Sir Shaffa'at Ahmed Khan, and the Council of Natal Jewry.

Fund-raising activities included the production of a concert called 'Tonic for the Blues', film showings, an American auction of a Kruger sovereign, a mayoral reception as well as a street collection. Well-known Chinese community members were closely involved with the fund's activities. Both Lee Rennie Chapson, chairman of the Natal Chinese Association, and Thomas Wong Lunking, served on the fund's committee which was chaired by the superintendent of the McCord Hospital, Dr Alan B. Taylor. To mark the China Week fund-raising, a subcommittee produced an eight-page tabloid brochure called '*China Today*'.[59]

As in other parts of the country, Natal produced an active Chinese women's association which played a key role in the war relief fund-raising. Organized by Mrs Wong Hoption, a prominent personality in the community, the women's association involved itself in welfare work for seamen as well as many social functions. Durban Chinese also participated in the Liberty Cavalcade, manning a stall to sell Chinese food and running a tombola stall offering groceries as prizes.

Kimberley

Not to be outdone by the other centres, Kimberley was equally active in fund-raising. Community elder, Wai Sing Chan Yan, said the China Week activities raised at least £3000. Working with other residents of the city, the community helped to organize a ball as well as the first Chinese dinner at the Constance Hall. Local shopkeepers and wholesalers also donated goods for a fund-raising fete.

Throughout the country, enthusiasm for the China War Relief effort ran high. The close co-operation between the Chinese community and other South Africans concerned for the welfare of another Allied nation marked a memorable, but brief, few years in the community's history.

SEAMEN'S ASSOCIATIONS

The increased sea traffic of Allied supply ships around the coast of South Africa led to large numbers of Chinese seamen spending some time in the country's port cities. Among the more colourful incidents during the war years were several involving Chinese seamen. Being sailors and unused to the kinds of restrictions imposed on Chinese, they reacted strongly and often violently to being refused admission to tearooms, bars and hotels.

Community members in the ports of Cape Town, Port Elizabeth, East London and Durban recount with some awe stories of seamen running amok and engaging in fisticuffs with the police. As Sam Chong put it:

> They said they were in the war to fight for these people, but they couldn't even have a cup of tea. The Chinese seamen just smashed up tearooms which refused to serve Chinese.

Another Cape Town resident, Les Hoy, recalled:

> I remember the police came in droves to pick up one of the seamen ... but he was a kung fu expert ... so he and other sailors just got involved in a big fight with the police ... even the shop owner couldn't tell which ones had smashed up his shop because they all looked alike.

A Chinese Seamen's Association was formed in Cape Town in the 1940s to assist the many seamen who were temporarily stationed in the port.

Because of language difficulties, as well as a shortage of accommodation, shipping companies approached the local Chinese communities to assist in housing and caring for the seamen. Families took them into their homes, the chain of Sam Lee laundries in Cape Town offered a welcome refuge while several families in Durban accommodated seamen in laundries, sheds and on a large farm. Shipping companies paid up to £10 per month for the maintenance of each seaman.

After the fall of Hong Kong in December 1941 and the consequent difficulty of repatriating seamen there, their numbers grew. Community members estimate there may have been as many as 300 Chinese seamen at times in both Durban and Cape Town. These included men whose contracts had expired, who required hospital treatment or were survivors off sunken vessels. A report by the social welfare officer in Cape Town highlighted some of the problems officials perceived in the seamen's sojourn:

> Chinese Seamen in proportion to their number have caused more trouble in this port than any other group. There are to date still 113 Chinese Seamen in Cape Town. They are comfortably housed in the Chinese Club, at Hum Hoy's laundry in Woodstock, in a garage in Long Street, and a small number is in Newlands. They cook their own food in liberal quantities, dress well and are in no hurry to leave such luscious pastures. Every opportunity for repatriation and every billet offered is most minutely examined, and they invariably succeed in detecting some undesirable aspect sufficiently serious to warrant a polite, yet firm refusal. Resistance, however, is by no means always passive as the free fight in Hum Hoy's laundry proved, when it became necessary to select 14 Chinamen for repatriation. In the end they did not go. The ship left with 14 unoccupied berths.[60]

The Chinese seamen's escapades also drew attention to the country's restrictive liquor laws. In a letter to the Minister of Justice, Consul-General Dekien Toung pointed to the incidence of brawls when Chinese seamen had been refused service in bars in Durban and Cape Town. He said even a magistrate had remarked on the anomaly of a situation which permitted the Japanese to obtain liquor while the Chinese could not. Such humiliating and discriminatory laws against the Chinese stood in the way of close collaboration and harmony and the Consul-General appealed for a change to the law.[61]

To centralize the organization of accommodation for the seamen and to cater for their needs, Chinese seamen's associations were formed in both Durban and Cape Town.

The Chinese Seamen's Association in Natal was established in August 1942, with its headquarters at 280 Berea Road, Durban. Its chairman and trustee was Durban resident, Alfred Lunking. Membership was open to anyone of Chinese descent, on payment of an entrance fee and monthly subscriptions. The association aimed to improve relations among Chinese seamen, to unite them in achieving a speedy end to the war and to provide social activities while they were on leave in Durban. The organization operated for three years, until 1945, when the trust was wound up and assets of about £80 handed over to the China Relief Fund.[62]

Durban community members recall the seamen's association being run by a sailor, Wong Lung Sin, who lived with a Durban Chinese family for years during the war. A highly educated man, Wong also taught Mandarin to children and young people in the community. He married a White woman in South Africa before returning to China.[63]

The prime mover behind the formation of the Chinese Seamen's Association in Cape Town was community elder, Lam Al Ying. As secretary for the Cape Town Chinese Association, he was assigned to assisting the seamen and acting as an interpreter for them. With the steadily growing numbers of seamen, the makeshift facilities at Sam Lee's laundries proved insufficient.[64]

By May 1943, Ying hired a building to provide accommodation as well as recreational facilities for between 30 and 40 men. The site was a two-storey building at Number 5,

Bree Street, Cape Town. Enlisting the support of the Chinese Consul-General Dekien Toung, Ying approached shipping companies for donations to furnish the club.[65]

Officially known as the Chinese Seamen's Association (Cape Town branch), it was empowered by the Consulate-General of the Republic of China to 'represent the interests of all Chinese Seamen sojourning at or passing through Cape Town'. Its chairman in 1944 and 1945 was seaman, Lee Chiu.[66]

The association's headquarters were well used for four to five years, but eventually closed in the late 1940s when the numbers of seamen in the port diminished. During their stay however the seamen participated in the local Chinese community's activities and assisted with fund-raising efforts for China's war relief.

WAR BONDS

A key source of funding for the Sino-Japanese War was the Chinese government's sale of war bonds, or 'Liberty Bonds'. These were issued in several series called 'aviation bonds', 'establishment fund bonds' and 'save the country' bonds. Extensively promoted among overseas Chinese communities, they were sold in American, French and Chinese currencies, and in denominations ranging from \$5 to \$10 000.[67] Printed in English and Chinese, each bond contained 33 coupons which promised 4% interest, payable at the end of August every year from 1938 until 1970. The face value of the bonds was to be redeemed by 1971. For many South African Chinese, the Liberty Bonds represented another opportunity to aid China while simultaneously investing their savings.

Throughout the country, Chinese organizations and individuals, particularly members of the Kuomintang Party, promoted the sale of the war bonds and channelled payment through the offices of the Chinese Consul-General in Johannesburg. The fact that none of the war bonds was redeemed and investors effectively lost all the money they had contributed has remained a bone of contention in the community. Long-time member of the KMT, Lew Johnson, said:

> I don't know how many war bonds I sold. It must have been more than £25 000. The consulate gave me books where I filled in people's names and the amounts, and then the bonds were sent to them from China. I was a travelling salesman and visited so many people all round Johannesburg to sell the bonds. Today, people blame me because they haven't got their money back and all those bonds are worthless.

Although only a boy at the time, Port Elizabeth community leader, Gordon Loyson, recalled the sacrifices people made to buy war bonds:

> 'My mother mortgaged our shop for £2000 to buy bonds. We had a big pile of the bonds. And many other people used up their savings. For a small community, Port Elizabeth was very generous.'

Underlining this view, Port Elizabeth-born David Low Kum said:

> I remember my father buying a lot of war bonds ... I believe it was £10 a month for the duration of the war from 1937 to 1946. We had a small grocery shop then and £1200 was a lot of money considering that one could buy a new American car for £300 at that time.[68]

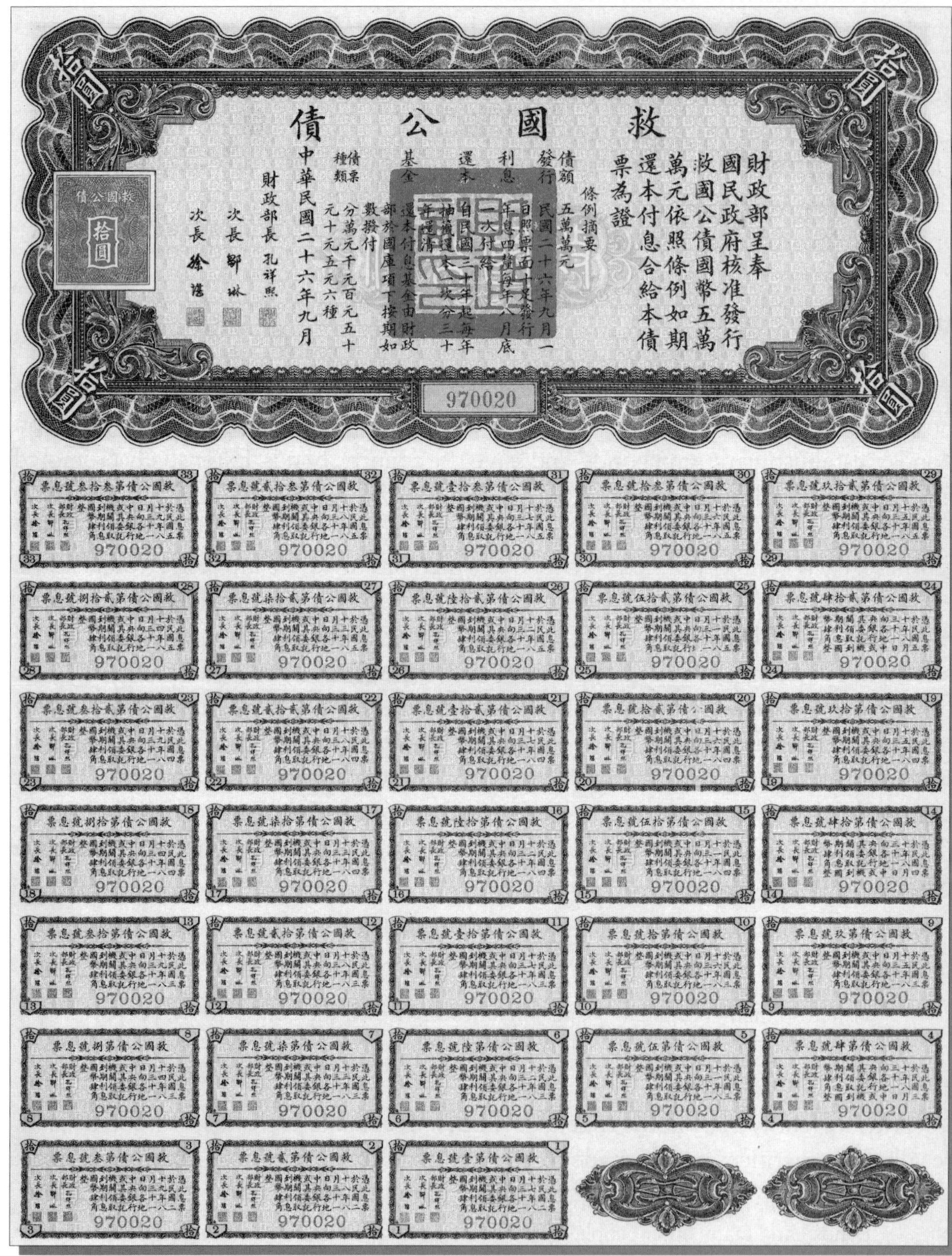

拾圓

救國公債

財政部呈奉
國民政府核准發行
救國公債國幣五萬
萬元依照條例如期
還本付息合給本債
票為證

條例摘要
債額 五萬萬元
發行 民國二十六年九月一日照票面十足發行
利息 年息四釐每年八月底一次付給
還本 自民國三十年起每年抽籤還本一次分三十年還清
基金 還本付息基金由財政部於國庫項下按期如數撥付
債票種類 分萬元千元百元五十元十元五元六種

中華民國二十六年九月

財政部長 孔祥熙
次長 鄒琳
次長 徐堪

救國公債 拾圓

970020

An example of the war bond issued by the Chinese government during the 1940s. Many South African Chinese still hold sheafs of these bonds which have not been repaid.

Community elder and chairman of the East London Chinese Association for more than thirty years, Harry Wong, explained how many patriotic Chinese invested all their savings in the war bonds.

> You know, a lot of old people lost everything with those bonds. They bought the bonds because the piece of paper said they would get so much interest every year. Then after so many years, they would get their money back and wouldn't have to work anymore. They put up all their money ... and lost it all.
>
> There are no more old people to fight for their money. If they're still alive, I think they can demand that. I'm still owed a lot of money ... I have a whole lot of bonds from my father. The Taiwan government is so rich, they can afford to pay us now .... they should pay it back.

Although the purchase of war bonds was supposedly a redeemable investment, it nevertheless represented substantial and tangible support for China's cash-strapped economy during the war years. Very few, if any, investors ever received interest or repayment on their bonds. Many elderly community members still hold sheafs of the bonds, issued by the Ministry of Finance of the National Government of the Republic of China.

Despite China's eventual victory in the Sino-Japanese War, the subsequent civil war led to the takeover by the Communist Party of the Chinese mainland, and the retreat of the Kuomintang government to the island of Taiwan in 1949. Since then attempts by individuals to secure the redemption of the bonds have been unsuccessful.

Exactly how much money was invested in war bonds by the South African Chinese is not known, but it no doubt ran into hundreds of thousands of pounds sterling. In America, the National Chinese Welfare Council reported on fruitless efforts to obtain repayment of the bonds in 1990. The official response from the government of the Republic of China on Taiwan was 'we will take it up when we return to the mainland.'[69]

CHANGED PERCEPTIONS OF CHINESE

War had, for the Chinese, the rather novel effect of focusing more widespread public attention than previously on their position in South Africa. From 1942 journal articles raised the question of Chinese rights in the light of China's status as an allied nation in the war and a campaign was launched to win sympathy for this cause.

In an article entitled *The Chinese allies we insult*, the minister who started the China War Relief Fund in Johannesburg, the Rev. A.S. Moore Anderson, paid tribute to the generous hospitality of South Africans but remarked that he was amazed this was only given to White people. Pointing out that Britain and the United States had recognized China as both an ally and an equal power, he questioned whether it would not be 'a just and happy gesture on the part of South Africa now to extend more 'equal' treatment to Chinese living here'.

He highlighted social as well as legal disabilities facing Chinese and described his experiences while travelling with a Chinese student:

> In Durban it was impossible to get a meal at an hotel: no European hairdresser

The following article appeared in the journal *The Forum* on 9 August 1941:

COLOUR BAR
Sharp Reproof From Chinese

Weighty reproof from four Chinese of high distinction has been levelled against Durban on the score of colour prejudice. They are Dr T.C. Ooi, Advocate J.H. Ho, Mr H.B. Lin and Mr L.N. Yuan, all visitors to Natal.

Dr Ooi has a string of letters after his name, including M.A., B.M., B.Th. (Oxon.), B.T.M. (Liverpool) and L.M. (Dublin). Advocate Ho is a Barrister-at-Law, Middle Temple, London, and once represented China in the Davis Cup Tournament. Mr Yuan has an English D.Sc. degree.

The four Chinese visitors complain of marked prejudice against members of their race. Apart from 'distinctions drawn against the Chinese in various phases of social life,' one of them was refused refreshments in a well-known establishment.

In a joint letter to the press, the Chinese visitors write:

'We resent the treatment meted out to the Chinese as no doubt all people of culture must resent the pernicious theory of racial superiority as championed by the Nazis. But our personal resentment is as nothing compared with our disapproval of the discourtesy extended to our countrymen as a whole. Our disapproval is intensified by the realisation that the Japanese are given preference over the Chinese, and are accorded the full courtesy of a privileged race.'

* Particularly forceful was this concluding paragraph: 'That such a barbarous practice as the colour-bar should exist may be due to long years of purblindedness which have rendered those responsible insensible to the rudimentary principles of justice.'

> would cut my friend's hair. We had to travel in a coupe on the train, and though, as a special concession, we had our meals in the restaurant car, a screen was erected round us in one corner lest we should be seen![70]

In a lengthy account of the discriminatory measures imposed on Chinese in all areas of life, another writer, A.J. Friedgut, pointed out that of the total of 2944 Chinese in South Africa, over 40% had been born in the country. They had, however, no political rights and were restricted in trade, education, public transport, property rights, freedom of movement, hospitalization and the like.

> Taken all in all, this anti-Chinese discrimination is a big blot on a none-too-clean South African slate. There is no doubt whatsoever that if Japan had not had to keep large forces on its Chinese flank, the Mikado would have sent his fleet and troopcarriers to South Africa. China has thus helped considerably to save the Union from invasion. Now, then, is the time for our country to show its gratitude. Let it remove restrictions on the Chinese.[71]

Whether or not such sentiments were widely shared, they gave the Chinese hope for change in the not-too-distant future. In 1944 an organization called the 'Chinese Association of South Africa' launched a campaign to win public support for more rights for Chinese. In a four-page pamphlet outlining the anomalies in the treatment accorded

Chinese and Japanese, an impassioned appeal was made to South African citizens to show their support for the Chinese.

> The Chinese in South Africa ask nothing but to be allowed their rights as equal citizens. But as a means to this end they need you, the South African public, to insist on action wherever you can influence action, and co-operation in any way in which you can give it. Your indignation against their oppression is the weapon which they need to overcome it.[72]

A form at the end of the pamphlet requested signatures to the following pledge: 'I, a citizen of South Africa, am sympathetic to your cause.' The number of those who responded to this plea, if any, is not known, and the organization itself ceased to function. It had been an attempt to unite the Chinese countrywide by the creation of a national representative association, but failed to survive beyond a few months.

POST-WAR COMMUNITY

Victory over Japan, officially observed as VJ Day by the Allies on 15 August 1945, was a cause for great celebration. The Kimberley Chinese Association bedecked their newly acquired headquarters in York Street with flags and bunting and hosted a VJ day cocktail party for the city's dignitaries. After eight years' intensive community effort in support of war relief, the South African Chinese held onto hopes that a stronger China would emerge.

As soon as sea routes to China reopened, scores paid visits 'back home' to resume family contacts or to contract marriages and return with their new brides. Children who had been sent to China for their education before war broke out were able to return home as young men and women, while in South Africa, educated young Chinese

Children at the Chinese school in Ferreirastown, Johannesburg, celebrate VJ Day in August 1945.

Premises of the Kimberley Chinese Association in York Street, Kimberley, were festively decorated for VJ Day.

were encouraged to help in the reconstruction of China. Newly graduated doctor, Ted Wong Hoption recalled:

> Consul-General Shih wanted me to go and serve the mother country, and arranged a post for me at a Nanking hospital in 1947 ... I went to Hong Kong and then Moiyean (Meixian), but my family were worried about the political situation so I didn't go to Nanking, but worked in Hong Kong for a few years.

A spate of publications by young Chinese surfaced with names such as *New China*, *New Youth*, *South Wind* and *New Dawn*, all reflecting a renewed pride in their Chinese heritage and a determination to forge a strong united Chinese community in South Africa. Chinese youth organizations — primarily geared towards social and sports activities — were formed in Kimberley, East London, Pretoria, Durban and Port Elizabeth.

Between 1945 and 1949, the civil war in China between the Kuomintang and the Communists continued to focus community attention on developments in their motherland. Still harbouring the dream that a strong China was the answer to many of their disabilities, the Chinese awaited the outcome of the struggle with trepidation. The eventual retreat of Chiang Kai Shek's troops to Formosa (Taiwan) and the declaration of the People's Republic of China by the Communists signified the 'closing off' of China. Visits back home ceased and even communication by letter became erratic.

For the 'overseas' Chinese worldwide and the South African Chinese particularly, China became inaccessible. No longer could wives be 'imported', or children sent back for a Chinese education. Further immigration restrictions introduced in South Africa in 1953 prohibited the entry of all Chinese. This physical severing of contact with the mainland underlined sharply the realization for the Chinese who lived in South Africa that they were there to stay.

World War II had ushered in significant changes for Chinese in other parts of the world. In both America and Canada, restrictions on immigration were eased with the repeal of those countries' Chinese exclusion laws in 1943 and 1947 respectively. The way was being paved for greater civil rights for Chinese, and in the aftermath and euphoria of the war, it seemed reasonable for the Chinese in South Africa too to anticipate an improvement in their lot. But a change in government in South Africa in 1948 and the implementation of a policy called 'apartheid' soon put paid to such hopes.

As new generations were born, the vital question of education had come to the fore and community efforts were harnessed to establish schools which could keep the young in touch with their roots as Chinese, but also offer them the means to survive and succeed in a land which barred them from equal opportunities.

World War II had ushered in significant changes for Chinese in other parts of the world. In both America and Canada, restrictions on immigration were eased with the repeal of those countries' Chinese exclusion laws in 1943 and 1947 respectively. The way was being paved for greater civil rights for Chinese, and in the aftermath and euphoria of the war, it seemed reasonable for the Chinese in South Africa too to anticipate an improvement in their lot. But a change in government in South Africa in 1948 and the implementation of a policy called 'apartheid' soon put paid to such hopes.

As new generations were born the vital question of education had come to the fore and community efforts were harnessed to establish schools which could keep the young in touch with their roots as Chinese, but also offer them the means to survive and succeed in a land which barred them from equal opportunities.

10

Education: From Shops to Universities

How did parents try to maintain Chinese language and identity in their South African-born children? Why did their aspirations for their children undergo a transformation in the 1950s? This chapter explores the significance of education within the community and the establishment of Chinese schools countrywide from 1918. It covers the way in which parents' views on education evolved, their emphasis on the necessity for attaining a tertiary qualification and their drive to use education to better the position of the Chinese.

The dilemma of a community tied by origin to China, yet having to cope with life in an alien environment, is typified in the Chinese approach to education in the first few decades of this century. Children were given whatever Chinese teaching parents could arrange while at the same time they were sent to 'Western' schools for a year or two to learn some basic English and Afrikaans. The wish to ensure that children learned Chinese yet were still able to make a living in a foreign country resulted in most children in the first decades of this century having an incomplete, somewhat mixed education, neither fully Chinese, nor fully Western. Only when travelling to and from China became difficult, and the imposition of further discriminatory legislation in the late 1940s threatened the community's future in South Africa, did the Chinese attitude to education undergo a transformation.

As in every other aspect of life in South Africa, education too was segregated and this account reflects the ways in which the Chinese tried to circumvent prevailing race barriers, to maintain their Chinese identity and eventually to diversify from small businesses into the professions.

In the first half of the 20th century schooling was free and compulsory only for White children. The Union constitution had given control of elementary and secondary education to provincial authorities, each of which enforced strict separation between the races.[1] In the Cape, schools for non-Whites were generally managed by religious denominations since practically no public schools were provided and in Natal no child could be admitted to a White government school unless the principal was satisfied 'that the child is of pure European ancestry for three generations on both sides.'[2] Chinese were allowed admission to Coloured and Indian schools, but the parents of pupils at these schools were liable for tuition fees since schooling for non-Whites was not fully subsidized. In Durban and Kimberley particularly, Chinese children who attended Coloured schools achieved notable success to become the community's first crop of university graduates in the 1940s.

Access to tertiary education was limited for non-Whites. The industrial colour bar kept them from competing with White workers as artisans and technicians, and the technical colleges which provided such training excluded them from admission. At university level, non-Whites could study theology, education and law at the University of Fort Hare and the University of South Africa — but the only medical schools were at the University of the Witwatersrand and the University of Cape Town, both of which restricted non-White admissions prior to World War II.[3]

As the numbers of Chinese children in the community increased, parents became ever more concerned about the younger generation retaining its cultural heritage and the ability to speak, read and write Chinese. During the 1920s and 1930s, those parents who could afford it made a point of sending their children back to their 'home' villages in China for a few years' education. Elderly Chinese even recount stories of men who had married either Black or Coloured women and then sent both their wives and children back to China to learn Chinese. From 1918, however, private Chinese schools were established, despite many difficulties, by Chinese organizations countrywide. The development of Chinese schools in the 1930s and 1940s also coincided with rising Chinese nationalism, inculcating into children a patriotism towards China, Dr Sun Yat Sen's teachings, and the Kuomintang.[4]

The spread of Christianity within the South African Chinese community, particularly Catholicism and Anglicanism, can in large measure be attributed to the substantial role played by both denominations in the provision of education for the Chinese. Anglican and Catholic mission sisters assisted Chinese organizations in establishing several Chinese schools and these religious orders were the first to admit Chinese pupils to their privately-run White schools in the late 1930s and early 1940s.

This chapter outlines the development and spread of Chinese schools and traces the role played by the Anglican and Catholic churches both in the provision of education and within the community. It examines the later emphasis placed on tertiary education with the entry of Chinese to universities in the 1940s and 1950s and the extent to which the community strove to become a 'professional' class.

CHINESE SCHOOLS

For many parents, Chinese schools fulfilled the dual role of providing education with a Chinese content as well as limiting contact with children in Coloured and Indian schools who often teased the Chinese and subjected them to racial slurs.[5] Between 1918 and 1955, some 12 Chinese schools were established, with a greater or lesser degree of success, in virtually every city and town of South Africa where more than a hundred Chinese had settled.

Just as the schools themselves became a focal point for local community activities, the establishment of new schools became a strong unifying force for the Chinese nationally. From the 1930s, teams of volunteers travelled the country soliciting donations from Chinese in all centres — for the Pretoria school, for one in Lourenco Marques, then a new school in Port Elizabeth, as well as in Cape Town, East London and Johannesburg. People learned of activities in other areas and donated generously to fund the various schools.

Perennial problems which plagued the Chinese school committees included the provision of suitable premises, fund-raising to cover the costs of running a private school

Which Chinese to Teach?

In a 'mixed' Chinese community consisting of Hakka and Cantonese, the formation of a Chinese school inevitably raised the question of which Chinese dialect to teach — Moiyeanese (Hakka), Cantonese or the national language, Mandarin. Schools usually opted for the dialect predominantly used in the local community, but were also restricted by which dialect the Chinese teacher employed there was able to teach.

Although Mandarin seemed to be an obvious choice because it would be acceptable to both Moiyeanese and Cantonese, the disadvantage was that parents did not use the language at home and thus were unable to communicate with or help their children. Describing this dilemma, Mr Y. Whiteley, long-time secretary of the Eastern Province Chinese Association, said: 'We had trouble with deciding which Chinese language to teach in order to keep the Cantonese and Moiyeanese happy.' So although Chinese teaching in Port Elizabeth started off in Moiyeanese, pupils were taught Mandarin by the mid-1930s.

Up to the 1950s in Johannesburg both Cantonese and Mandarin were taught in different classes, but a strong stand taken by some Cantonese parents led to Mandarin teaching being stopped. It was noticeable then that very few Moiyeanese attended the Kuo Ting Chinese School. Only from the early 1970s was Mandarin reintroduced.

Because of immigration restrictions, schools experienced great difficulty in obtaining the services of suitable Chinese teachers. The quality of Chinese teaching was therefore erratic, some teachers having to cope with dialects in which they themselves were not always proficient. Teachers often moved from one school to another and throughout the 1940s one finds the names of the same teachers having worked in Lourenco Marques (Maputo), Johannesburg, Port Elizabeth and Pretoria.

and recruiting suitable teachers, especially for Chinese language teaching. Furthermore, in selecting which Chinese dialect to teach, the persistent Cantonese versus Moiyeanese division was compounded by the introduction of Mandarin as the national language of China in 1923. Several Chinese schools also exercised their own form of discrimination, barring from admission children who were not 'pure' Chinese or whose parents were not accepted or classified as Chinese.

Education was a particularly emotive issue in Port Elizabeth which witnessed the founding of several 'rival' Chinese schools. In Johannesburg too, two Chinese schools operated simultaneously for a short time. The small number of Chinese in places like Durban did not warrant their own school, although parents in Queenstown and Kingwilliamstown arranged informal Chinese classes for children in their homes. Even children in their teens who had to work in their parents' shops during the day were able to attend night school for a basic grounding in Chinese or to maintain the level of Chinese they already knew. In Port Elizabeth, Johannesburg and Pretoria special classes were arranged for a few years in the 1930s by teachers and members of the Chinese consulate.[6]

In Port Elizabeth, pupils at the night school organized their own sports activities and ran a popular boxing club for several years. They were mainly older children who had to work in their parents' shops during the day or attended Coloured schools and learned Chinese in the evenings.

According to Chinese scholars, overseas Chinese retained a 'strong China-oriented identity' because of a sense of nationalism, the threat of a Japanese invasion of their motherland and discrimination in the countries where they had settled. Through the Kuomintang's (KMT) branch parties and organizations, Chinese schools were made part of a campaign of nationalist indoctrination which taught allegiance to the KMT and its leaders, and required children to learn Dr Sun Yat Sen's Three Principles of the People, to salute the flag and sing the national anthem.[7] Elements of such teachings made up part of the syllabus of most of the Chinese schools established in South Africa.

Children who attended Chinese schools not only learned to speak, read and write Chinese, enabling them to mix more readily with their Chinese elders, but were also taught about Chinese cultural traditions. It was from these schools that young Chinese forged sporting links, lasting friendships and even marriages which served to unite an already closely-knit community.

While pursuing the goal of securing a Chinese education for their children, parents also realized, living in a Western country, that their children needed to become proficient in English. They coined a somewhat philosophical expression to describe the situation of children caught between the two worlds:

> The Chinese always say you're eight ounces and half a pound — in other words you know a little Chinese, but not very much. You also know a little English, but not very much. So it balances out.[8]

This combination of insufficient Chinese and not-enough English was to prove a drawback in later years for children who wished to pursue a higher education. The children particularly affected were those who arrived in South Africa as teenagers and those whose western schooling was 'interrupted' by being sent back to China for a few years. Those who had the opportunity to continue their schooling at secondary level, either at Coloured schools or private White schools, were best placed to move into the professions.

From the 1950s, however, the establishment of Chinese high schools enabled more pupils to extend the length of their school careers, and eventually to pursue a tertiary education. The necessity for children to be adequately equipped to make a living other than as shopkeepers also prompted schools to re-evaluate the Chinese content of their curricula. Time spent on learning Chinese was gradually reduced as pupils reached higher classes and inevitably younger generations lost the ability to read and write Chinese.[9]

PORT ELIZABETH

South Africa's first and longest surviving Chinese school started with eight pupils in a tiny room in a mission house in Port Elizabeth. A joint venture by the Moi Yean Commercial Association and sisters of St Marks Anglican Mission, the school officially opened on Monday, 4 February 1918[10] at the mission in Queen Street (now called Main Street), on a site later owned by Castle Breweries. Numbers soon doubled to sixteen and the school moved across the road, into the newly purchased headquarters of the Moi Yean Commercial Association. It was this organization which collected school fees and paid the school principal, a mission sister.

The history of the Chinese Mission School is interwoven with the spread of Anglicanism within the community. While parents were eager to obtain the services of the sisters to teach their children English, the Church was equally keen to establish a Chinese mission. Within four months of the school's opening, nine pupils were baptized and as numbers increased, a corresponding growth in conversions to Christianity took place, among both children and their parents.

A classroom, known as the 'Upper Room' served for ordinary schooling during the week, religious classes on Sunday and was turned into a 'church' for services every third Sunday of the month. The altar had to be enclosed by a cupboard when the room reverted to a school during weekdays![11]

Community elders took the view that Christianity was one means by which Chinese could strengthen their claims to remaining in South Africa. According to Archie Pow Chong, born in Port Elizabeth in the 1920s,

> ...There was a lot of talk among the senior Chinese who said, look, we are from China and we're in a foreign land. You have a child born here, registered in the book of births, but becoming baptized, the church gave you a baptism certificate. And the future of your child is made much easier, because now he's got two documents to prove who he is and that stood him in good stead. If there are any complications, he has two certificates.[12]

Proof of identity and particularly residence was of importance in terms of the 1904 Chinese Exclusion Act which regulated the movement of Chinese into and out of the Cape Province. By 1921 the school boasted 33 pupils, including two married women sent by their husbands to learn English. Numbers continued to grow, peaking at 212 in the 1940s, despite fluctuations caused by some children being sent back to China for further education.[13]

Throughout the first 20 years of the school's existence, parents struggled to introduce and maintain Chinese language tuition. In September 1923, Yip Siow Chun arrived from China to give two-hour classes each afternoon. He stayed for five years, but thereafter no teacher could be found to replace him.[14]

Visiting Port Elizabeth in 1932, Consul-General Ho Tsang and Vice-Consul Ting Shao expressed their disappointment at the lack of Chinese teaching. They launched a fund-raising drive and the 18 office bearers of the Port Elizabeth Chinese Association set an example by each donating £5. Appeals were directed to Chinese in other parts of the country to contribute, and the Consulate-General also levied a £1 education fee on all passports issued for travel to China.

A consular official, Ho Wai Yuen, was seconded from his diplomatic post to teach Chinese at a salary of £20 a month. He also offered night classes for older children who had to work in their parents' businesses during the day. Classes, however, ceased when donations dried up. After some months of fund-raising, the School Affairs Committee and parents managed to employ Chu Pak Nga from Portuguese East Africa (Mocambique) to restart lessons in January 1934. As was to be expected, it was less than a year before funds again dwindled. Chu took a drop in salary and stayed on for a few more months before leaving the school in 1935.[15]

Some anti-church sentiment within the community led to the Anglican Church giving up its role of providing staff for the school at the end of 1932. A School Affairs Committee was formed to manage the 'Chinese Primary School', under the sole control

Pupils at the Chinese Mission School in Port Elizabeth in the 1920s. The school was housed in the premises of the Moi Yean Commercial Association in Queen Street.

Jack Kee, chairman of the Chinese School Board in Port Elizabeth, died in 1921 — just three years after the school was formally launched.

of the Moi Yean Commercial Association.[16] Although the shortage of funds periodically led to fears that the school would have to close, by June 1936 the school had two English teachers and secured the services of Wong Pan Ngian who settled in Port Elizabeth and taught Chinese for more than 20 years.[17]

In 1939 another school was started in opposition to the Chinese Primary School, which was often referred to as the Queen Street school. The reasons for its establishment were complex, including political in-fighting within the Port Elizabeth Chinese Association and a controversial election campaign. The Eastern Province Chinese Primary School or 'breakaway' school, as it was dubbed by many members of the community, was started by a dissident group within the Chinese Association who claimed that existing standards of Chinese education were inadequate.

The founders were Lee Simpson, Wong Foong Chong, Gordon Alfred (Kin Yat) and Yan Long Lee Son. They purchased some property on the farm Nooitgedacht in Kabega, some 30 km from the Port Elizabeth city centre, which they donated for the building of a new school.[18] To raise funds, the group travelled as far as Johannesburg, Pretoria and even Lourenco Marques appealing to the Chinese communities to support their venture.[19] The school, however, only ran until about 1948 before financial difficulties forced its closure.

Attending local Coloured schools remained the only viable option for children who needed a high school education and in Port Elizabeth several generations of Chinese

The 'Breakaway' School

The Eastern Province Chinese Primary School started in late 1939 with Chinese classes for about nine children at the headquarters of the Chinese Association in Evatt Street. It moved to Cape Road, Kabega, where new premises had been erected and at a formal opening ceremony on 12 September 1942, attended by the Mayor of Port Elizabeth, the school's four founders each planted a tree outside the school building.

Because the school was far from the city, where most families lived, Wong Foong Chong used a delivery van to transport local children. By the mid-1940s, more than 40 children attended the school which also offered boarding facilities to attract pupils from outlying areas such as Grahamstown, Queenstown, Cradock, Somerset East, Aliwal North and De Aar as well as a few from the Transvaal. Nearly half of the school's pupils were boarders. Children slept in dormitories and a Chinese cook provided meals.

The school placed great emphasis on Chinese teaching and offered subjects such as arithmetic and history in Mandarin. The Chinese teachers included Chang Lo Chiao and Hwang Chih Wu. Former pupils described the school as almost military in approach, with strong discipline being exercised and children being required to wear khaki uniforms and learn Chinese slogans.[20]

After the school closed down in the late 1940s, the property stood empty for a few years, until the E.P. Chinese Association agreed to take over its outstanding debts and mortgage payments. In 1951, the E.P. Chinese High School was established there.

successfully passed through the doors of the Patterson High School. The Moi Yean Commercial Association continued to run the Chinese Primary School until 1950 when control was handed over to the Eastern Province Chinese Association. To obtain funding to support the school, the association sought assistance from the Anglican Church and gained recognition by the Cape Education Department for the school as an 'Anglican Mission School'.[21] From 1951, teachers' salaries were paid by the education department, and the school remained in Queen Street until 1973 when it relocated to new premises in the Chinese group area of Kabega Park.

High Schools

Port Elizabeth witnessed the founding of two Chinese high schools in the early 1950s. Some opposition by White parents to the presence of three Chinese girls at the Priory Convent in Walmer in 1949 caused their parents to remove them from the school, despite appeals by Catholic Bishop Hugh Boyle for them to remain. The Bishop promptly set about establishing a school for the Chinese, with the assistance of the Catholic sisters who had been involved in a Chinese school in East London. The Chinese Educational Institute which was later renamed the Assumption Chinese College was situated in the predominantly Coloured suburb of Schauderville where substantial numbers of Chinese had their shops and homes. It opened its doors in 1950 with eight pupils, rapidly increasing its intake until it reached a peak of 120 pupils in 1956.

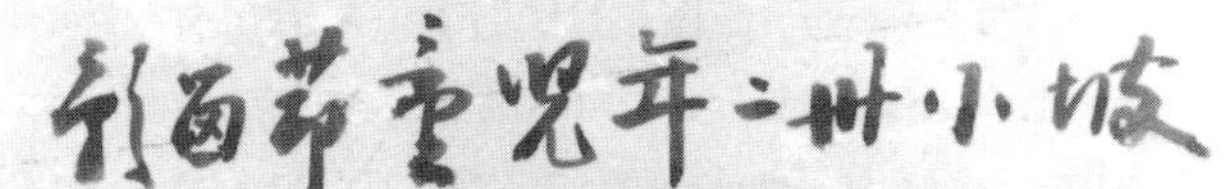

Some of the Port Elizabeth youngsters who attended the Chinese Primary School in the 1940s.

Nursery school children in Port Elizabeth — 1950s.

But just as the foundation of the 'breakaway' school had caused rifts in the community, so was the establishment of the new college accompanied by its share of controversy. Father Ignatius Ou, the Chinese priest who came to South Africa to teach at the school, recalled:

> It was very discouraging. All along the Chinese had supported the Anglicans, and there was a campaign telling parents not to support the school because it was in a Coloured area and it was a Catholic school ... afterwards parents saw the school offered a good education and then they didn't care about the area.

The college thrived throughout the 1950s, but as the Group Areas Act took effect in the 1960s, pupil numbers dropped. Gradually Chinese moved out of Schauderville and after twenty years' existence, the college finally closed in 1970. Fr Ou said the school accomplished what it had set out to achieve in that it had equipped many young people to go on to university and to qualify in diverse fields such as medicine, engineering and even the priesthood.

Another high school, known as the Chinese High School was started by the Eastern Province Chinese Association in 1951. Using the abandoned premises of the 'breakaway' school in Kabega Park, the school was funded privately and staffed by three teachers, Aubrey Wong On, Lee Tao Min and Mrs D. Schoultz. By 1957, school enrolment was approximately 90 pupils. In the mid-1950s the possible amalgamation of the Chinese High School with the Assumption Chinese College was discussed, but issues such as teachers, control and religion were not resolved and the two remained separate.

Perennial funding difficulties in maintaining premises, paying teachers' salaries and obtaining new equipment eventually led the Association to apply to the Cape Education Department to take over the school in 1958. While this meant that the school would have to follow the syllabus and requirements set down for government schools, the authorities permitted the continued teaching of Chinese for 35 minutes each day. Because teachers' salaries were scaled at the Coloured rate which was lower than the White rate, the school education committee continued fund-raising activities to make up the difference and also to pay the Chinese teachers whose salaries were not covered by the Cape authorities.

On 1 July 1973 the Chinese Primary and Chinese High amalgamated into one school and moved into new premises in Topaz Road, Parson's Vlei, centrally situated for the growing numbers of families who had settled in the Chinese area of Kabega Park.

JOHANNESBURG

In the early years of this century, Chinese children attended Coloured schools in the 'Malaikam' area of Ferreirastown, the best known being the school on the corner of Market and Becker streets. Most were several years older than their Coloured classmates and generally only stayed for a year or two before starting work in their parents' shops.[22]

Overseas Chinese School

Johannesburg's first Chinese school, called the Overseas Chinese School or the Johannesburg Chinese School, was established by the South African branch of the Kuomintang (KMT) in 1928. Situated at Number 30 Fox Street, Ferreirastown, the KMT headquarters consisted of an office, a hall and stables previously belonging to a horsecart transport company. About 30 pupils attended classes held in the hall, while the stables were first used for lodgings and later to house the offices of the *Chiao Sheng Pao* newspaper.[23]

When this property was expropriated in the early 1930s for the construction of Johannesburg's magistrates courts, the school and the newspaper moved to rented premises at Number 2 Fox Street. There, in a two-storey house, the activities of the school and its pupils were vividly recounted by a writer, Allister Macmillan, who published a book on Johannesburg in the early 1930s. He wrote:

> The girls are all dressed in navy blue gyms and the boys wear navy blue shorts and blazers ... The school at present numbers about fifty children, but there were seventy-eight pupils the term before. The staff now consists of four teachers, while formerly there were six. The school is State-aided and is run by a Board, who have to find the funds not supplied by the Government. The syllabus is modelled on that recommended by the Chinese Educational Board in China; and among other subjects, the children study modern history. They learn both English and Chinese ... The blackboards are covered with English and Chinese characters. Arabic figures are used in teaching arithmetic, for they are easier than the Chinese symbols ...
>
> A large photograph of Dr Sun Yat Sen, the first President of China, adorns the hall, which is used both as a meeting place and a classroom. His famous words,

> framed, may be read round the walls. The room is decorated with flags, and with beautiful silk panels, embroidered in blossoms.[24]

When the KMT purchased property at Number 13 Alexander Street, on the corner of Marshall Street, for its headquarters, the school again moved. Because Chinese were not legally permitted to buy property in the Transvaal, it was necessary for the acting Chinese Consul-General, Feng Wang, stationed in Johannesburg until 1934, to have the property registered in his name. This technicality was to have repercussions on the school just a few years later. The new KMT headquarters were extensively used by members who met there regularly to exchange news, have letters from home read to them and to enjoy twice-weekly dinners provided on Wednesdays and Sundays.[25]

Teachers at the school in the 1930s included well-known community members such as Huang Cheong Kuan, known as Oliver Young, W. King, Chu Pak Nga, Fok Yu Kam and Leong Pak Seong. The latter two, as enthusiastic sportsmen, organized sports activities for the school children and in early 1939 cleared space on top of a mine dump to turn it into a basketball field. By mid-June the pupils were able to field a Johannesburg team called '629' to play against Pretoria.[26]

In the same year however the school became embroiled in a dispute between Consul-General Fartsan Sung and the school principal, Fok Ling Kien. Bitter and controversial, the wrangle saw school pupils demonstrating outside the consulate offices and led to the deportation of Fok Ling Kien from South Africa as well as the formation of an 'opposition' Chinese school.

Pupils at the Johannesburg Chinese School, Alexander Street, Ferreirastown, 1935.

Differing accounts have been given for the causes of the quarrel, some attributing it to local 'politics' and the principal's role on the Transvaal Chinese Association, while others claiming it was the school's refusal to admit 'half-Chinese' children. Writing about events of the time, another former school principal W. King said of the incident:

> The history of the Chinese school changed course ... At a meeting, the Chinese Association discussed a matter that Consul-General Sung was not happy about, so he sent Consul Dzong to the school to fetch the minute books. Mr Fok was only the secretary [of the TCA] and he had no right to hand the books over. So the two had an argument ... Consul-General Sung was angry and reported Mr Fok to the immigration office to cancel his immigration permit ... Because of this, Teacher Fok had to leave ...[27]

To support this interpretation, W. King reproduced, in Chinese, copies of two letters sent by the Consul-General to the authorities to request the teacher's deportation. The same letters are retained in official correspondence files in the government archives and make mention of numerous issues relating to the school principal and his activities.

Addressing the Minister of the Interior, Consul-General Sung complained about Fok Ling Kien's performance both as a teacher and member of the TCA, saying these activities were endangering the interests of the community. Claiming that the school had been established primarily through the efforts of the consulate, the Consul-General said because the pupils were Chinese subjects, they were under his jurisdiction.

> Acting upon instructions from my National Government it was the expressed policy of this Consulate-General to see to it that the school accepted children whose mothers were Union Nationals, but, notwithstanding the instructions to this effect, the School Committee has, as a result of the interference of Mr Fok Ling Kian, repeatedly spurned and ignored such instructions ...
>
> As a result of these subversive activities ... numerous complaints have been received from that section of the community wherein the fathers are Chinese and the mothers are Union Nationals, and who have children of school-going age. These children number approximately 50.[28]

The Consul-General also alleged that Principal Fok had mismanaged the finances of the school and said his role on the TCA had made him a leading spirit in fomenting discord and disturbance. He was unhappy that the school committee no longer consisted of the people whom the consulate had appointed and expressed his displeasure at an incident at the school on 14 June 1939 when a group of pupils shouted 'Down with the Consul'.[29]

The authorities withdrew Principal Fok's temporary residence permit and instructed him to leave South Africa by August 1939. The news of this imminent deportation caused upheaval at the school. Groups of schoolchildren picketed the Chinese consulate premises in Commissioner Street, Johannesburg. They carried protest placards in English and Chinese objecting to the consulate's interference in the school's affairs.[30]

School teacher Fok Yu Kam recounted the incident saying that the children had waited all day outside the consulate to see the Consul-General, who refused to meet them.

> The Consul-General came from Batavia where the consulate was used to oppressing the Chinese, and he thought he could do the same to us here.

Members of the school committee and more than 30 parents also submitted a petition to the Minister of Interior to reconsider the decision. They said Fok Ling Kien had worked at the school for over two years, had given 'every satisfaction' and they knew of no circumstances which rendered him undesirable. Pointing out that the school would not function properly until another teacher could be employed from China, they said the number of pupils already stood at 120.

> The School enjoys the benefit of a government grant of £148 per annum. Beyond this Government grant the School is entirely financed privately by the Chinese community. It is quite independent of the Chinese Government and receives no assistance from such Government, nor is it in any way subject to control by the Consular representative of the Chinese Government. There have been differences of opinion between the Consul and the Committee of the School, and the Consul intimated that he desired to place one of the Consular staff as a teacher at the School. The Committee gave the matter their consideration and considered the proposed appointment was unsuitable.[31]

Faced with these conflicting requests, the departments of the Interior and Immigration decided to stand by their earlier decision to revoke Fok's residence permit. Noting that a delegation from the school had spoken highly of the headmaster, the Commissioner for Immigration and Asiatic Affairs made the following observation:

> It is evident that there are two distinct factions in the Chinese Community, one of which is headed by the Chinese Consul-General. The Department has decided upon a course of action, after consideration of the representations of the Consul-General ... and it would seem that the Department should not now deviate from that course. If it did, the position of the Consul-General in the country would become untenable.[32]

The principal duly left South Africa, but the turmoil had not come to an end and the school was soon reminded of the obligations incurred by past 'assistance' from the consulate in registering the KMT school property. In his account of the school's history, former principal, W. King wrote:

> Consul-General Sung was still not satisfied. He wanted to manage the school himself and he threatened the school. Although the property belonged to the Kuomintang, it was registered in the name of the previous Consul-General, Feng Wang. If the school did not comply with his wishes, it would be evicted. The school did not submit, and therefore moved out and sought another place next door, in an old church hall to continue lessons. Consul-General Sung then asked vice consul Chan Kuei Miao to start the Kuo Ting School at No. 13 Alexander Street.[33]

Kuo Ting School

So a 'second' Chinese school opened its doors in Ferreirastown on 8 August 1940. Called the Kuo Ting School, meaning 'stability of the nation' or 'established by the nation', it started off with some 30 pupils and a school board appointed by the Consul-General. Meanwhile, the original KMT school, the Johannesburg Chinese School, continued its activities in nearby premises at Number 7 Alexander Street, taking with it most of the existing pupils.

A special farewell for Principal Fok Ling Kien, whose deportation from South Africa in 1939 caused a split in the community and the formation of two Chinese schools in Johannesburg.

Johannesburg Chinese School principal Fok Ling Kien (left) with teacher, Fok Yu Kam.

Morale at the new Kuo Ting school was high. A student's association was formed to promote competitive activities, games, concerts and even cleaning up the classrooms. Children assisted various organizations with fund-raising and contributed towards the Sino-Japanese War effort. The school produced a special brochure for a Children's Day celebration on 4 April 1942 featuring photographs of the staff of seven teachers and many of the school's 128 pupils.[34]

The continued existence of two 'rival' schools was, however, not only financially draining but also contributed to dividing an already small community. By early 1943, some two and a half years after the formation of Kuo Ting, the new Consul-General in Johannesburg, Dekien Toung, began efforts to amalgamate the schools. After a number of meetings between the two school committees, agreement was reached and the names of both schools were combined to form the Johannesburg Chinese Kuo Ting School.[35]

Two Schools Combine

Within a few months of amalgamation, in July 1943, the school boasted an enrolment of 218 pupils.[36] Wong Chuk Wu was appointed principal and a new school committee was constituted. Classes continued in premises scattered along Alexander Street, at numbers 7, 13 and 15. Finding a permanent and more suitable site for the school had become a priority and a building committee was formed to raise funds for this project. With its first appeal in September 1943, the committee managed to raise £8000 in a week!

Enthusiasm for fund-raising ran high until tragedy struck in February 1944. Returning from Pretoria after an official visit to appeal for property for the school, two members of the building committee were killed in a car accident. Percy Whyte and Ah Quy died while their companions, Consul Tsong and Sam Sun Yet were seriously injured. Burial services, featuring flower bedecked motorcades wending their way through Ferreirastown, were attended by well over a thousand people who came out to pay tribute to the men who had died in the course of service to the community.

Little progress was made over the next few years until the Johannesburg City Council agreed to make some land available for the school's new premises on the corner of Market and Siemert streets, Doornfontein. Situated on the eastern side of the city centre, the half-acre site gave rise to controversy. Some community members felt it was too far from Ferreirastown, involving children in unnecessary travel, while others objected to spending money to build on leased land which would not belong to the community. Because of the Land Tenure Act which restricted Chinese occupation in certain areas, it was 'reluctantly' decided to accept the land on lease for 50 years at a nominal rental of £1 per year.[37]

By the end of 1947 plans were drawn up by architect, Kouang-Chien Toung, and the school committee embarked on an extensive fund-raising drive for the estimated £33 000 to cover the building costs. Efforts were made, without success, to obtain a loan of £10 000 from both the Johannesburg City Council and the Transvaal Provincial authorities.[38] Drawing yet again on community resources, organizations such as the Chinese Literature and Arts Society and the Chinese Women's Association organized

Percy Whyte

The two school board members who were killed in a motor accident on official work for the Johannesburg Chinese Kuo Ting School on 3 February 1944. Both were buried in the Newclare Cemetery in Johannesburg.

Ah Quy

Johannesburg Chinese Kuo Ting School building, erected in 1949. The site was used as a Chinese Cultural Centre from the 1980s.

The Chinese Kuo Ting School Board, 1956.

concerts and dances. A pedigreed dog was raffled and two sailors caught cheating at gambling promptly had the £90 in their possession confiscated for school building funds![39]

On 4 December 1949, the school's new premises were officially opened by the deputy mayor of Johannesburg, Dr C. Becker. School started on 17 January 1950 with 360 pupils in classes spanning grade 1 to Standard 8 and a staff of eight English and five Chinese teachers.[40] The premises served the school for the next 30 years until its proximity to the city centre, noise and traffic congestion eventually forced a move to Brampton Park, some 20 km away, in 1981.

Respected teachers who served as principals of the Kuo Ting School for many years were Seu Lau Fok and Doreen Tim. Both graduates of the University of the Witwatersrand, they established the school on a sound footing to make it an integral part of the Chinese community.

Kliptown

Two major accidents on the routes between Johannesburg and Kliptown, a suburb nearly 20 km south-west of the city centre, prompted the formation of the Kliptown Chinese School in 1948. Although no Chinese were involved in either the train or bus accident, parents feared the daily risks their children took in travelling to Johannesburg and pooled their resources to start a small school.

About 20 children and a few teachers began classes in a rented house in East Road, now called Boundary Road, Kliptown. The move was not without controversy as older community members accused Kliptown parents of 'stealing' pupils from the existing Chinese school in Johannesburg.[41] Nonetheless, the parents persevered, calling on the services of any willing volunteers to teach, and sought grants to maintain the school.

Chairman of the school board for more than 20 years, Lew Johnson, recalled how parents contributed money to buy desks and equipment and also paid school fees of about £10 per child. Former teacher, Oscar Kwan gave Cantonese classes three times a week after he arrived in South Africa in 1949. As difficulties in maintaining the school continued, the school board approached the Catholic Church for assistance and two Dominican sisters were seconded to run the school. At its peak, enrolment reached 90 pupils and a large prefabricated hall was added to the house to extend the school's facilities. Among the teachers who taught at the school during its 25 years' existence were Sr Bonaventura, Sr Flora and Sr Bathildis, all warmly remembered by their pupils for their dedication and discipline.

Although only offering tuition at primary level, the Kliptown school attracted pupils from all parts of Johannesburg because of its association with the Catholic Church. Many parents believed this connection would give their children easier entree to private White Catholic high schools which had during the 1950s and 1960s started more readily admitting Chinese pupils. The Kliptown school eventually closed in the early 1970s.

A founder member of the Pretoria Chinese School, C.P. Law devoted his energies to raising funds for its etablishment.

PRETORIA

The Pretoria Chinese School was the first school to be established with money collected from Chinese communities throughout South Africa, and the success of this venture set the precedent for fund-raisers from other schools. In the course of 1933 members of the Young Chinese Cultural League (YCCL) traversed far-flung towns of the Transvaal, Natal and the Cape to solicit funds, explaining that their new school would cater for scholars throughout southern Africa by providing boarding facilities. The persistent fund-raisers, who included prominent community leaders C.P. Law, W. Kwan and H.P. Ho, amassed a total of £934-2-0 in their travels over some 5000 miles.[42]

Plans were drawn up to erect a two-storey building next to the YCCL headquarters at 191 Boom Street, Pretoria. The school officially opened in September 1934 with Lum Yang (Hon Chong Wing King) from Port Elizabeth as the first teacher and 34 pupils. Three years later provision was made for additional classrooms and boarding facilities as well as a school hall which also served as a centre for community use.[43]

The school's boarding facilities for boys attracted pupils from outlying areas of the Cape and Transvaal and as far afield as Southern Rhodesia (Zimbabwe), many of whom forged lasting friendships during their school days in Pretoria.[44] By July 1943, the school boasted an enrolment of 53 pupils[45] and reached a peak of 150 pupils in 1958.

During the late 1940s a fund-raising drive was launched to build a new school and a sum of about £9000 was raised.[46] The project was however shelved when a dispute arose over the siting of the school and the Group Areas legislation of the 1950s imposed further restrictions on its location. Although numbers at the Pretoria Chinese School remained in the vicinity of 50 to 100, it continued to be maintained by parents and the Pretoria community. New premises were built for the school in Wingate Park, Pretoria, in 1993 and it has remained the only privately run and funded Chinese school in South Africa.

CAPE PROVINCE SCHOOLS

Chinese schools were also established in other parts of the country — in Kimberley, Uitenhage, East London and Cape Town — serving the local communities for between two and forty years. But dwindling numbers and the relaxation of admission restrictions at other schools eventually took their toll and by 1980 the last of these schools had shut its doors.

The Pretoria Chinese School Board, photographed in October 1934, shortly after the opening of the original school in Boom Street, Pretoria.

In centres where there were too few Chinese to support a school, attempts were made to offer Chinese language classes. Private tutors were hired for the children in Kingwilliamstown, and in Queenstown, a Chinese teacher, Mrs Chang Seu Lau, gave afternoon lessons to some 17 young children at the home of the Lo Pong family in the mid-1950s.

In 1945 the Kimberley Chinese pooled funds from the Moiyean and Kuomintang clubs to buy a two-storey house in York Street to establish a school. Donations were also solicited from other parts of the country and a teacher recruited to give Cantonese lessons. Classes were held in the afternoons but only lasted for a year or two.[47] Local Chinese children continued to attend the well-known Coloured schools of New Main Street Primary, William Pescod High and Perseverance High and established a reputation as high achievers.

Uitenhage's small community consisting of some 30 families started a primary school in about 1944 at the Chinese Association premises at Number 64 John Street. Between 16 and 20 children attended Chinese classes given by Mrs Sam Yuk Sin from Grahamstown, and English classes conducted by a Mrs Haines and later a Mrs Armstrong. All the pupils of varying ages were taught in one class, but difficulties were encountered in finding teachers and by 1949 the school had closed.[48]

East London

Efforts by East London parents to educate their children in Chinese dated back to the early 1920s when informal lessons were held at the Chinese Association premises in North End. Community elders said a Chinese teacher was employed for some time, but the school closed prior to 1926.[49] In the late 1920s however a group of children were given daily lessons at the 'Miss MacKay school' on the West Bank, run by the four MacKay sisters, one of whom had taught at a local high school. The sisters owned property rented by Chinese and agreed to give classes for their tenants' children. The 'school' operated in a wood and iron outbuilding on the sisters' property for some five years and the children were taught standard school subjects, for which their parents paid school fees of about £1-10-0 a month.[50]

By the early 1940s, however, the community finally succeeded in establishing a fully fledged school called the East London Chinese School. Also funded with donations collected from Chinese countrywide, the school was situated at Number 52 St Peter's Road, Southernwood, a property originally purchased by community leaders, Lee Sing Gen and Yung Mason. The school was run with the assistance of Catholic Dominican sisters and offered a comprehensive curriculum including Chinese language classes. Chinese teachers were recruited from Mauritius and taught for two-year periods.

East London's Chinese School was situated at No. 52 St Peter's Road, Southernwood.

Pupils at the East London Chinese School in the 1940s.

On 4 April 1946 the foundation stone for a large hall was laid by Consul-General Chao Ying Shih. The hall, situated behind the school, became a focal point for community activities and was regularly used for weddings and other gatherings. Between 70 and 80 children were enrolled at the school during the 1940s and 1950s.[51]

The East London Chinese Association was financially responsible for the school and the salaries of the Chinese teachers. Because school fees were usually insufficient to cover costs, the association launched numerous fund-raising activities, including illegal bingo games. For nearly four years the association, working with the Arrows sports club, organized Saturday evening bingo games, attracting up to 400 players, mainly from outside the Chinese community.

Long-time chairman of the association, Harry Wong said:

> You see, we called it a 'tea club' and everyone had to carry a membership — and we did give them tea and a biscuit. Business was so good we had to refuse members. Every Saturday night we had bingo, but then, we went too big ... other people went to ask the police to run bingo games, and said the Chinese were doing it ... then the police came and raided the school ... and confiscated all the money. They also wanted to arrest everyone, but taking the names of 300 or 400 people was not easy ...

Several bingo players paid admission-of-guilt fines and after some negotiation the confiscated takings were returned to the school. The bingo came to an end and fund-raising followed more traditional avenues such as 'kung fu' film shows, which also proved extremely popular and lucrative. As other schools opened their doors to Chinese, the numbers of children attending the East London Chinese School dropped. By the mid-1960s, with fewer than 20 children aged between 6 and 12, it was decided to close the school.

Cape Town

The Cape Town Chinese School started with between 24 and 30 pupils in a house in Palmyra Road, Claremont, in 1943. Also the headquarters of the Chinese Association, the premises were purchased to replace a dilapidated building previously used in Loop Street. The numbers of pupils grew and within two years it was necessary for both the school and the association to move.

A public auction of the Claremont property only raised about half of the £7500 required to purchase the gracious two-storey mansion in Mowbray that community leaders wanted. So, following the precedent set by Chinese in other parts of the country, fund-raisers went on the road to collect donations. The chairman of the Cape Town Chinese Association, Leong Sean, and his committee, which included Lam Al Ying, George Ming, Mouly Chong, Bertram Lee, Kay Chong and S.F.C. Hunt, embarked on a month-long drive in 1945 to solicit funds, travelling as far afield as Durban and Johannesburg. According to the Chinese secretary at the time, Lam Al Ying:

Pupils at the Chinese school in Mowbray, Cape Town, 1960.

> We paid £7500 to buy the building in those days. And that building does not belong to the Cape Town Chinese alone. It belongs to all of the South African Chinese who helped us.[52]

For the next 35 years the school experienced the inevitable ups and downs of a community-run institution. Tuition was mainly offered at primary school level, after which children went on to Coloured high schools or private White schools. When suitable Chinese teachers could be hired, Chinese teaching was given but by the 1970s, numbers declined to an all-time low and by 1980 the school ceased to operate. The title deeds of the Mowbray property were registered in the name of the Chinese Republic United Association, the predecessor of the Western Province Chinese Association, and the premises were maintained for use by the local community and Chinese seamen passing through the port.

Durban

Because the Durban Chinese community was made up of only a handful of families, no Chinese school was ever established there. Durban did, however, produce a significant proportion of the first Chinese students at the University of the Witwatersrand in the 1940s, most of whom had attended Coloured schools such as St Augustine's, Albert Street, Malvern Road and Umbilo Road.

PRIVATE CHURCH SCHOOLS

Both the Catholic and Anglican churches played an important role in providing education in South Africa outside the framework of state-run schools. They established mission schools for various race groups, including private White schools which offered a standard of education generally considered superior to state-run or government schools.

By the mid-1930s and early 1940s, a handful of wealthier Chinese parents sought and obtained admission for their children to some of the most select private White schools in the country. Probably the first Chinese to be admitted to a White school was Kouang-Chien Toung, a nephew of Consul-General Dekien Toung, who enrolled at Marist Brothers College in Observatory, Johannesburg, in 1933. Four years later, the college boasted two Chinese matriculants, H. Chei and R.H. King.[53] From 1937, community leader Dr L.N. Liang sent his daughter, Peggy, to Belgravia Convent, End Street Convent, Redhill and then Kingsmead while his son, David, attended Marist Brothers College in Koch Street, Johannesburg.[54] Pretoria businessman Walter Kwaan secured admission for Chinese to exclusive Anglican schools such as Park Town School, the Ridge and St John's in Johannesburg, St Andrew's in Grahamstown as well as Michaelhouse in Natal.

Since segregated schooling remained integral to the social fabric, the admission of Chinese to such private schools was very much a privilege, dependent on the goodwill or willingness of each school's principal or governing board to 'bend the rules'. Limited openings and costly school fees also served to keep this option beyond the reach of most parents. A private school education was however regarded as the best way of ensuring a child's entry to university and many parents made substantial financial sacrifices to send their children to such schools.

In the following decades several hundred Chinese attended private Catholic and Anglican schools with many from outlying areas enrolling as boarders. Some of the schools operated an informal quota system accepting only a limited number of Chinese pupils each year. From an early age children were constantly reminded that it was a privilege to be at such schools and of the necessity always to be on their best behaviour. A premium was placed on academic success with both parents and teachers exerting pressure on children to perform. One former pupil recalled: 'I remember the pressure put on me to succeed was enormous and nothing was allowed to interfere with success at school.'[55]

Clampdown on Admissions

As legislation enforcing segregation mounted during the 1950s, private schools too faced pressures to enforce strict separation. An account of the stand taken by Catholic schools over the admission of Chinese pupils is most lucidly given by Fr Michael Tuohy, an Irish priest who became closely involved with the community and its concerns from the mid-1950s.

> There was a crisis in the late 1950s ... in Witbank there were four Chinese at the Dominican convent and some vicious individual reported them and the sisters were told to get rid of the children. The Department of Education said if the children did not go, they would rescind the school's registration. There were very serious problems facing the schools at that time ... it showed apartheid at its ugliest.
>
> Bishop Hugh Boyle had long supported the Chinese people and when he was pressured over this issue, he sent a memo to all the school principals saying 'to refuse admission to a Chinese child would be to incur a responsibility ... Before God I would have nothing to do with it.' It was an awful time, a time of anxiety. From the Church's point of view, the Catholic Church has always taught that Catholic parents have a right to educate their children as they wish and that the State may not interfere and this was a right that the State was trying to take away. Bishop Boyle was adamant as regards the Chinese, that they had to be accepted. You had one or two exceptions — but one could speak about them at the expense of those schools that did stand up for the Chinese. I think we had about 22 Catholic schools at one stage where Chinese children went. It all eventually subsided, but then parents had to apply for permits for their children to go to private schools. They had to say why their children could not go to the Chinese school, how far the school was from their homes and so on.
>
> A school is just a human institution ... I don't deny that at some there was also this hard racial attitude. I remember one school where I applied for a Chinese child to go and the principal, a South African, said to me 'We can't take her. We don't have a permit.' I said Sister, you can get a permit, you can apply. 'Why does she want to come here anyway ... If she wants to come here, that means others will want to come too.' Looking back on that it was completely unchristian, racialistic, but that did not reflect in general.
>
> Around the time of the 1959 crisis, there was Sr Mary Clare, a small little person. When she was told the Chinese children had to go, she said 'over my dead body' — and I think we owe a lot to educationists like that. The King Dominicans,

Fr Michael Tuohy, who served the Chinese community for nearly 40 years until his death in 1994.

> the Mercy sisters ... had well over 100 Chinese children during those times. Also Marist Brothers ... the Catholic schools played a very big part in bringing Chinese children into the faith but also in giving them an education and helping them to have something that they might otherwise not have got.[56]

Admission to private schools run by religious denominations was often dependent on the child or its parents belonging to that particular faith. The spread of Catholicism among the Chinese, particularly in the Johannesburg area, can largely be attributed to their admission to Catholic schools as well as the role played by Catholic sisters at the Kliptown Chinese school. As Fr Tuohy pointed out:

> It is true that a number of Chinese became Catholics in order to go to school. It was an unfortunate situation where ... one could say it was a forced conversion ... Not every school made it a condition ... Mayfair accepted non-Catholics ... Of all those who became Catholic for that reason and then fell away, I would say they're in a minority. I myself never baptized anybody for that reason. I told them straight I'll help you, I'll do all I can to get you into a Catholic school but I won't do that.
>
> The schools played a very big part in bringing the Chinese into the Catholic faith. I won't say completely, but a big part. Many who did become Catholics then are very good Catholics today. God can work in various ways and maybe this is one way he chose. I know many who became Catholics when their children were at school. Those who were forced would be a small number. The human element is there ... nobody would find fault with those who did become Catholic to go to school. And to classify these as insincere would be unfair.

Throughout the 1950s and 1960s Chinese parents continued to seek out openings for their children at private schools. In Cape Town, Chinese were admitted to Anglican schools such as St Cyprian's for girls and St George's for boys from the early 1960s,[57] at about the same time that Catholic schools in Durban opened their doors.

A handful of Chinese children also attended non-denominational private schools such as the Auckland Park Preparatory School, established by the ratepayers of that suburb of Johannesburg. As early as 1943, the school admitted five Chinese pupils. Fearing however that the school might become inundated with Chinese, the governing body resolved to limit Chinese admissions to seven and a half percent of the total number of children attending the school, a decision which prevailed for some 15 years. In the face of objections by the Transvaal Education Department which requested in early 1957 that Chinese be 'forthwith excluded', the school appealed for special consideration to be given to allow children already enrolled to finish their schooling. No further action was taken.[58]

The high costs of a private school education imposed a financial burden on many parents who continued to seek entree for their children to White government schools where education was fully state-sponsored. Although at least two Chinese attended a White Afrikaans high school in the Transvaal town of Heidelberg in the mid-1940s, this case was very much an exception.[59] Only by 1971 were special concessions secured for Chinese children to attend government schools first in Queenstown,[60] then in Kimberley, and by the late 1970s Chinese children were generally admitted to White government schools.

PREPARATION FOR THE FUTURE

Up to 1940 the education of Chinese children could best be described as an erratic, part-Chinese, part-Western combination which did not prepare many for professional careers in South Africa. Those born in China usually arrived in South Africa as teenagers who only spent a year or two in classes with much younger children to learn some basic English. Those born in South Africa started their elementary schooling in English but were often sent back to China (to learn Chinese) for several years at a crucial stage in their academic development. Others who remained in local Chinese schools only studied up to primary school level because no Chinese high schools had been established prior to 1950. Virtually all these children were put to work in their parents' or relatives' shops.

From the 1950s as more Chinese were admitted to private church schools, the shaping of the younger generation took a new course. The totally western European emphasis of the education offered by private White schools, and Coloured schools, meant children never learned Chinese formally. And except for those parents or grandparents who ensured their children at least spoke some Chinese at home, the majority of these children did not learn to read and write Chinese characters. In as much as speaking Chinese can be considered necessary to retaining a Chinese identity, most of the pupils at such schools became increasingly westernized, often using English as a home language and mixing socially with non-Chinese.

As far as the first generation of Chinese university graduates in the 1940s was concerned, virtually all were products of Coloured schools or private White schools. It would appear that the insistence of parents that their children receive a 'Chinese' education to a large extent left those offspring ill-equipped for a 'Western' academic career. It was only years later, by the early 1960s, that pupils from Chinese high schools joined the ranks of those attending universities.

TERTIARY EDUCATION

Prior to World War II tertiary education for people of colour was virtually inaccessible in South Africa. Not only did technical colleges exclude them from training for any skilled occupations, but the majority of universities were exclusively for Whites. Although courses in theology, education and law were offered to non-Whites through the University of Fort Hare and the University of South Africa, only a handful had also, prior to 1939, been admitted to the two so-called 'open' universities, the University of the Witwatersrand (Wits) and the University of Cape Town (UCT).[61]

Non-Whites who wished to pursue an education beyond high school, particularly in the field of medicine, had to do so overseas. In 1920, when a young Johannesburg Chinese decided to become a doctor, he enrolled at Edinburgh University in Scotland. Despite financial hardships, Dr Luke Nain Liang graduated in 1927 before returning home to set up a medical practice and become a leading figure in South African Chinese community affairs.

It was in their medical schools — the only two in South Africa — that the 'open' universities faced the most trying tests of their admissions policies. In a study of the history of Wits, Bruce Murray stated that at its inception 'Wits very much reflected the prejudices of the society to which it belonged.' Non-Whites were only slowly admitted, and not in any substantial numbers until the outbreak of World War II made it impossible for them to pursue professional studies overseas. It was the government itself which wanted Wits to train non-White medical students, even making scholarships available for the purpose. The numbers of such students rose from 4 in 1939 to 87 by 1945.[62]

The first recorded case of a non-White being allowed to register at the Transvaal Technical Institute (later to become the University of the Witwatersrand) was that of a Chinese student, recommended by the Consul-General, in 1906. It appears that the student did not however take up the opportunity. Only in 1926 did Wits agree to enrol a Coloured medical student, whereas UCT five years earlier had persuaded an Indian applicant to study medicine elsewhere.

Two young Chinese, Hop Hee Dunne and her brother were reported to be the first Chinese admitted to study at the Technical College in Johannesburg in the late 1930s. During the war they both went to America where Miss Dunne achieved distinction by becoming one of the very few Chinese women pilots.[63] During the 1950s, appeals were made for technical and artisan training facilities to enable Chinese to become electricians, motor mechanics, plumbers, fitters and carpenters.[64] Those interested in the trades had to study by correspondence, and also faced difficulties in finding employers willing to take them on as apprentices. It was only by the early 1970s that Chinese were permitted to enrol at technical training colleges.

Universities

The drive towards a university-level education started with several Durban Chinese, including Thomas Lunking, Joyce Kolling and Michael Pakshong, who read for Bachelors degrees at the Sastri College, a tertiary education institution for Indians in the early

1940s. The first Chinese to be admitted to the University of the Witwatersrand in 1941 was Ted Wong Hoption, also from Durban, who enrolled in the medical faculty. He had initially been accepted by a university in Hong Kong, but the spread of the Sino-Japanese War prevented his departure. His application to Wits was submitted on an 'off-chance', and he was accepted.

> I think it was probably because they didn't realize with my surname that I was Chinese ... at medical school there were five or six Africans and Indians in my class. We were segregated as far as which patients we could treat were concerned. When I arrived at the residence, they were quite gracious and said they did not expect me to be Chinese but that I could have a couple of weeks to find another place to stay. I didn't try too hard. Braamfontein was an Afrikaans area and I didn't want to be rebuffed. And eventually I just stayed on ...
>
> ... I joined the South African armed forces in 1942 and worked part time in the SA Medical Corps because some of my colleagues at residence did ... I didn't expect to be accepted. We did weekend training and during July winter holidays we camped out at Zonderwater.[65]

In 1942, Kouang-Chien Toung who had been the first Chinese at Marist Brothers College, Observatory, enrolled at Wits for architecture. He was soon followed by students who included Fine Jackson (Port Elizabeth, medicine); Albert Fontbin (Durban, engineering); Sidney Lunking (Durban, engineering); Ralph Pakshong (Durban, engineering); George Changfoot (Kimberley, science); Henry Leetion (East London, engineering); Frank Leetion (East London, medicine); Francis Lunking (Durban, medicine) and Jack Mason (East London, medicine).

Women, though far fewer in number, were also among the first crop of Chinese university students in the 1940s. Honey Wong from Johannesburg enrolled for an arts degree in 1945 and was followed two years later by Irene Pakshong and Joyce Kolling, both from Durban, who subsequently studied for medical degrees. It was only from 1948 that more Johannesburg students joined the Chinese ranks at Wits. They included Edward Yenson (medicine), Dennis Hangchi (medicine), Arthur Wong (science) and Peggy Liang (arts).

The initial intake of Chinese university students at Wits was predominantly Moiyeanese (Hakka) and second or third generation South Africans. Virtually all had attended Coloured high schools and came from the smaller Chinese communities, primarily Durban as well as East London, Kimberley and Port Elizabeth. The majority enrolled for medicine, with engineering following a close second.

South Africa's other 'open' university, the University of Cape Town admitted its first Chinese student for an arts degree in 1942. He was Aubrey Wong On, from Port Elizabeth. Others including Sam Hing and Tony Hoe Easton enrolled soon afterwards for medicine. Several Chinese also attended the non-White University College of Fort Hare, in Alice in the eastern Cape. One of these was Edgar Ah Shene of Port Elizabeth who took his science degree there in the late 1940s and then completed a teacher's diploma at Stellenbosch College in 1952.

It should be noted that although the two 'open' universities admitted non-White students on a basis of academic equality, they certainly did not extend this to social equality. The official policy at Wits was one of 'academic non-segregation and social segregation'.[66]

Medical Training

Entering the medical profession was fraught with difficulties for the Chinese in the 1950s. They were not permitted to enrol for dentistry, nor could they train in areas such as occupational therapy, physiotherapy or logopaedics [speech therapy] because these disciplines required them to work in hospitals which did not permit non-Whites to attend to Whites. Those who wished to become nurses or radiographers generally had to do so overseas.

Access to the medical school at the University of the Witwatersrand was also strictly curtailed from 1953 when it was announced that only 6 of the 23 non-White students who had passed first year would be allowed to proceed to second year. By the end of 1953 the Wits University Council adopted a permanent quota system which limited non-White admissions to the first year to eight, and reserved another twelve places in the second year for recognized scholarship holders transferring from Fort Hare and B.Sc graduates.[67]

Responding to objections that many more non-White students could be admitted than the new quota system allowed, the Principal, Professor W.G. Sutton asserted: 'the University could not face a situation, under present conditions, where a considerable number of European applicants of desirable quality would have to be turned away, to allow of places being allotted to an increasing number of non-Europeans.'[68]

Recalling his experiences at Wits medical school in the early 1960s, one Chinese graduate, Dr Norman Yenson said: 'We were five so-called non-Whites — two Indians, two Chinese and one Black — and in 3rd year pathology we had to cut up cadavers. If it was a White body, we weren't allowed to go in. In the first session the body was cut up and the organs were taken out. Once the body was cut up, then we were allowed to go in ... so we really felt discriminated against. That actually carried on for a good many years after I left. As far as the hospitals were concerned, we weren't allowed to go to the White hospitals ... Even when our training was finished, our wages were about 60 to 70 percent of the White scale.'[69]

One of the first Chinese women to study medicine at Wits in 1947, Irene Pakshong, had to complete her studies abroad because of the numerous difficulties she encountered in finding transport at odd hours to the non-White Baragwanath hospital, some 20 km from Johannesburg.

Changes in Direction

The attitude of Chinese parents towards the need for tertiary education for their children underwent a rapid change when the National Party government came to power in 1948. For a community which had essentially only consisted of small shopkeepers in South Africa, the implementation of the Group Areas Act in 1950 threatened this form of livelihood. Its objective to separate the various racial groups into their own areas meant most Chinese could lose their shops and their children would no longer be certain of a future in the family business.

Increasing numbers of parents realized that higher education was the only way in which their children would be equipped to move beyond shop counters into other occupations. The radically changed political situation in China — with the Communist

Teacher, Aubrey Wong On

Aubrey Wong On

Aubrey Vernon Wong On was born in Port Elizabeth in February 1920 of a Chinese father and an Irish South African mother. The first Chinese student to enrol at the University of Cape Town in 1942, he had attended the Chinese Mission School in Queen Street, then St Marks and Patterson High School.

Highly strung and sensitive, he did not stay to complete his degree but later continued studying through the University of South Africa, obtaining his B.A., then B.A. (Hons) and finally his M.A. in 1947. He enrolled at Fort Hare University College where he completed a teaching diploma in 1948. In the course of his studies he taught English for several months at the E.P. Chinese Primary School in Cape Road and spent a year in East London where he played a crucial role in the formation of the Chinese Youth Society.

Conscious of not being fully Chinese in appearance, he however took pains to learn to speak and write Mandarin, described himself as 'South Africa's first Chinese writer' and often quoted from the works of Dr Sun Yat Sen. Through his involvement in publications such as *New Dawn*, *New China* and *Blue Banner*, he urged young Chinese to make full use of limited educational opportunities. He emphasized the need for a high school for Chinese in Port Elizabeth and served as principal of the Chinese High School from its inception in 1951 until 1962.

Highly regarded by his pupils as a dedicated teacher, he was however replaced as principal when the school was taken over by the Cape Education Department. In the following years he suffered severe emotional problems, spending more than a decade in an institution. Despite bouts of depression throughout his life, he achieved notable academic success and left behind writings and poetry which reflect the trials and triumphs of his own experiences. He died in 1987 at the age of 67.

Party taking control of the mainland in 1949 — also meant children could no longer be sent back there. Perhaps it was only then that the Chinese became fully aware of the pressing need to equip themselves for living permanently outside China, whether that future was in South Africa or in another Western country.

Chinese high schools had opened in both Johannesburg and Port Elizabeth and parents pushed children to achieve academically. Diversifying into technical training was not possible because of the difficulties in being apprenticed and finding employment. As for those who were employed by larger commercial concerns, they often discovered that employers were reluctant to hire them for positions which could, at some stage, give them supervisory authority over Whites. The numbers of Chinese students at universities increased in the 1950s at the same time as the possibility of universities closing their doors to students of colour loomed large.

In December 1953, Prime Minister D.F. Malan stated that the mingling of Whites and non-Whites at two of the largest universities in South Africa would have to be eliminated as speedily as possible and that, provided proper provision was made for the

The imminent Government clampdown on the mingling of Whites and non-Whites at 'open' universities sparked vigorous opposition. Chinese medical students, (from left) Victor Sam, Herbert Wong and Richard Hung were among the many Wits students who mounted a placard demonstration outside the Johannesburg City Hall on 22 May 1957.

needs of both sections, this would not be unjust.[70] Staff and students at both Wits and UCT protested vigorously at the imposition of racial separation in university education and interference in their autonomy. Despite protests, mass meetings and demonstrations over a period of six years, the Extension of University Education Act, no. 45 of 1959, was passed to put an end to 'open' universities and academic freedom. For the Chinese this meant that they needed to apply to the Minister of Education, Arts and Science for permission to attend a particular university or study a particular course.[71] The need to obtain permits for study remained in force until the early 1980s.

Young Chinese themselves questioned the anomalies of a situation in which parents were insistent on their children obtaining a university education. Pointing to the fact that the percentage of Chinese students at universities was particularly high in relation to the community's numbers, a student Maureen Kim Sing concluded that there were many who should not be there.

> Partly the problem is political, and partly parental ... the Chinese are forced to seek fields of employment other than retail business, and since some channels are closed to us the choice is say, sales representative, clerk, shorthand typist and little else. ... Many parents unconsciously force their own aspirations onto their perhaps less talented, less ambitious children ... Everyone wants doctors and lawyers ... what price mechanics and plumbers?[72]

Student Activities

The Chinese Consul-General, Shih Chao Yin, encouraged the formation of an organization for Chinese students at Wits in 1944. Basically a social group, it organized talks and gatherings to include high-school and university students.[73] By September 1948, however, students formalized the objectives for the Chinese Students Society (CSS) and elected Francis Lunking as their chairman.

From the outset, the CSS reflected its concern with social issues. Open to university students as well as pupils in their final years of high school, the society had among its aims the promotion of 'friendliness, understanding and co-operation', cultural interests and involvement in the social problems of the Chinese community. Prominent in its description of its work was concern for anticipated academic segregation of Chinese, segregation of Chinese in hospitals and upliftment of the status of the Chinese community.

The society tackled relief work, visiting Chinese patients at Baragwanath hospital with food parcels and started negotiations with the university to have Chinese exempted from segregation legislation. Included on its agenda for activities in 1949 was the organizing of a study circle for learning Chinese, sports events such as tennis and softball competitions as well as social gatherings.[74]

The Cape Town Chinese Students Society was formed in the late 1950s and published a contentious student magazine called *Spectrum*. When Chinese were admitted to Rhodes University in Grahamstown from the late 1950s, they also formed a society to serve as a support group. At all the universities the Chinese participated in the usual student activities such as building floats, fund-raising for Rag and playing sports. They also played an active role in the local Chinese communities, organizing social activities and bringing new life to political debates.

Chinese students at the University of the Witwatersrand participated in the annual Rag Procession, building their own 'Slow Boat from China', circa 1950.

SIGNIFICANCE OF EDUCATION

Educating children outside of China confronted parents with complex choices, not least of which were decisions on what constituted the best education and whether or not there was a conflict between an education geared for occupational success and one which ensured the retention of a Chinese identity.

Those children who spent some time in China were equipped with the essential Chinese language skills of reading, writing and speaking whereas those who attended local Chinese schools only learned the basics. The majority of those whose education had been 'interrupted' by their sojourn in China rarely continued studying in South Africa after their return, either because their English was too limited or they were very much older than the children at whose level they were placed. It was to be expected that the first Chinese who were qualified to attend universities in the 1940s came from non-Chinese schools.

On the subject of Chinese children studying among non-Chinese, scholars have said that if children studied in the same schools, the educational and cultural values imparted should lead to integration or even assimilation. Whether it did or not depended on the numbers of Chinese, government attitudes and racial factors. In Southeast Asia, Chinese studying among non-Chinese benefitted by acquiring 'foreign language skills, access to a more modern education which stresses skills and professionalism, and a better understanding of the countries in which they have chosen to settle.'[75] As far as Chinese in South Africa were concerned, most who went to non-Chinese schools lost fluency in spoken Chinese and did not learn to read and write it.

The desire of parents to secure a 'good' education for their children necessitated many financial sacrifices. For most, however, tertiary education was regarded as a vital investment in their children's future. By the 1960s the Chinese had achieved an enviable graduate rate, but it was to be these very professionals who led the exodus of many Chinese from South Africa as the policy of *apartheid* — implemented by the National Party government from 1948 — reached new heights.

11
Grand Apartheid

What did apartheid mean for the Chinese? Where did this tiny minority fit into South Africa's complicated new race classification system? Why did the Group Areas Act in particular cause consternation among the Chinese? This chapter probes the far-reaching consequences of this and other 'colour bar' laws affecting access to public facilities, immigration, the franchise and mixed marriages, spanning the time period from 1948 to the 1970s.

APARTHEID: THE CONCEPT

South African society had long been segregated on racial lines, but from 1948 more laws were promulgated to entrench differentiation among the various race groups. The rise to power that year of the National Party, with its strong commitment to the principle of Afrikaner nationalism, marked the official implementation of the policy of 'apartheid'. An Afrikaans word, it can be translated as separateness, separation, apartness, aparthood or differentiation.[1] Apartheid was not limited to racism as a set of values, ideas and political structures, but also incorporated racially repressive mechanisms.[2] Essentially it took the practice of segregation to new levels of sophistication.

As the policy evolved, it also became known as separate development and theoretically was intended to preserve the separate identities and cultures of the many ethnic groups in the country, allowing each to develop along parallel lines. In practice however the policy led to a horizontally rather than vertically stratified society in which Whites dominated politically, socially and economically as the only group with the franchise and free access to land. Laws were promulgated to classify people by colour and regulate virtually every sphere of life and activity by race.

The cornerstone of this policy was the stringent racial classification of the population, in terms of the Population Registration Act, no. 30 of 1950, into one of three groups, namely 'European', 'Native' or 'Coloured'. Only the latter two groups were further sub-divided into ethnic groups, and were commonly referred to as 'non-Europeans'. Over the years terminology changed from 'Europeans' to Whites, and from 'Natives' to Bantu, Africans or Blacks. The term 'Coloureds' encompassed everyone who was neither White nor Black, and included people of mixed blood, Griquas, Malays, Indians and Chinese.

The 1951 census reflected the total population of South Africa in excess of 12.6 million — comprising 8.5 million Africans, 2.6 million Whites, 1.1 million Coloureds and 366 000 Asiatics (of whom fewer than 5000 were Chinese).

The array of laws introduced to implement the policy of apartheid was extensive and far-reaching. Their combined effect was the further compartmentalization of a society in which people were racially divided in every sphere of life. Separation was the norm and governed whether or not people could buy land, where they lived, who they mixed with or married, how they gave voice to political aspirations, where and what they could study, the work they did and even where they could eat, drink or dance. The laws, to name but a few, included:

Prohibition of Mixed Marriages Act, no. 55 of 1949;
Immorality Amendment Act, no. 21 of 1950 and no. 23 of 1957;
Population Registration Act, no. 30 of 1950;
Group Areas Act, no. 41 of 1950;
Suppression of Communism Act, no. 44 of 1950;
Separate Representation of Voters Act, no. 46 of 1951 and no. 30 of 1956;
Immigrants Regulation Amendment Act, no. 43 of 1953;
Reservation of Separate Amenities Act, no. 49 of 1953;
Industrial Conciliation Act, no. 28 of 1956;
Extension of University Education Act, no. 45 of 1959;
Community Development Act, no. 3 of 1966;
Prohibition of Political Interference Act, no. 51 of 1968.

An ambitious experiment in social engineering, the National Party's policy was described as a determination 'to refashion South African society according to Afrikaner ideals of racial purity and segregation and at the same time to end once and for all any possibility that the country might ever move towards an extension of economic and political rights for blacks at white expense.'[3] Apartheid entrenched the White group in a position of superiority, with rights and privileges denied to people of colour. Because basic rights in South African terms equalled White rights, Non-Whites naturally sought to attain 'White' rights.

Non-Whites were stripped of all representation in Parliament, leaving political power exclusively in the hands of the White minority. Laws prohibited social intermingling and enforced residential segregation, depriving many of their homes and livelihoods. The excluded groups, relegated to second-class status, were left to compete with each other for access to opportunities. By 1970, the Study Project on Christianity in Apartheid Society (SPROCAS) summarized the position as follows:

> South Africa is a plural society. Its diversity is expressed in terms of race, nationalism, culture and tribalism. Group identity and legally enforced discriminatory norms determine the patterns of social and personal relationships. There is an economic cleavage on racial lines, with the White group representing the 'haves' and the other racial groups, particularly the African group, representing the 'have nots'.[4]

POSITION OF THE CHINESE

As second and third generation descendants of free traders who had settled in South Africa from the 1870s onwards, the Chinese, in the late 1940s, numbered 4340 men, women and children — a minuscule minority in a population of more than eleven million.[5] They were concentrated in urban areas — on the Witwatersrand goldfields with Johannesburg at its centre, the capital of Pretoria, the diamond city Kimberley, and the coastal centres of Port Elizabeth, Cape Town, East London and Durban. Although laws differed from one province to another, the Chinese had historically been subjected to restrictions which prohibited adult male immigration and, in the Transvaal, prevented them from buying property, trading freely or even settling where they wished.[6]

Prior to 1950 Chinese were included in the broad category of 'Asiatic' for the implementation of laws relating to immigration, acquisition of property, employment and the like. With the racial classification of all South Africans in terms of the 1950 Population Registration Act, the Chinese were placed in the Coloured group and later defined as follows:

> In the Chinese Group shall be included any person who in fact is, or is generally accepted as a member of a race or tribe whose national home is in China.[7]

As a system of race classification, the law used the criteria of appearance or general acceptance for belonging to a specific group and provided for a population register and the issuing of identity cards. Although the bulk of the population could be readily classified, there were numerous 'borderline' cases which required investigation, often leading to hardship and causing humiliation and resentment.[8] Race classification boards had to decide into which category such people should be placed, giving rise to some cases in which members of the same family were classified as belonging to different groups.

In March 1962 the country's race classification system was challenged by a Chinese man, who successfully applied to be reclassified White on the grounds that he associated with Whites and was 'generally accepted' as White. As was to be expected, the anomaly of the situation excited widespread media attention, prompting questions to be asked about the viability of the Population Registration Act, first promulgated 12 years previously.

> The implications are now such as to present the Government with a major problem. The Act appears to be open for any Coloured or Asian to be declared White, provided he can bring evidence to show he is accepted as White.[9]

Newspapers described the case as highlighting the absurdity and hypocrisy of South Africa's race laws.

> Under the kind of legislation which allows an admitted Chinese, born in Canton, to be declared a White South African anything can happen. These humiliating quibbles become necessary when a government attempts to define the undefinable. There is no accepted scientific system of race classification, so all attempts to draw such frontiers must be artificial and subject to endless dispute.[10]

Nonetheless, just two months after David Song's reclassification from Chinese to White, amending legislation was promulgated to tighten up the definition of White, and applicants had to be White in appearance *as well as* be accepted as such.[11] Prior to the closure of this loophole in the law, it appears that several more Chinese had applied to be reclassified White in order to retain their businesses in White areas.[12]

One's racial classification was particularly significant for the simple reason that it affected one's rights, liberty and privileges. Racial provisions in the laws had a greater impact in some areas than in others, being profound as far as politics and the constitution were concerned and in terms of an individual's personal rights, such as marriage, choice of residence, employment and business opportunities.[13] A person's racial group determined where he could own property, whether he could participate in collective bargaining with employers, what pension and compensation benefits he received, and most importantly, his race decided his 'rights as a citizen of the state.'[14]

The classification of parents was the prime factor in determining the race of children and problems arose when parents belonged to different groups. The overwhelming majority of applications for reclassification came from individuals of such mixed descent and from people who had or were marrying across the colour line.

From the 1980s the Department of Internal Affairs adopted a more pragmatic approach to reclassification cases after courts ruled that the principle of *general acceptance* by a community was of more relevance than descent. Before an individual was reclassified into a particular group, he had to provide proof of a *substantial connection* with that group such as living among them, mixing socially, playing sport, schooling etc. Inspectors were sent out to speak to the applicant's neighbours and friends and make recommendations on the case.[15]

Between 1974 and 1990 a total of 183 adults and minor children were classified into and out of the Chinese group — Chinese were reclassified White, Cape Coloured, Malay and Indian and members from these groups were reclassified Chinese. The Population Registration Act of 1950 and its amendments were repealed by the Population Registration Act Repeal Act 114 of 1991. From 28 June 1990, race was no longer indicated on South Africans' birth, marriage and death certificates.

APARTHEID LAWS AFFECTING THE CHINESE

In a society where the issue of race had become paramount, the Chinese were readily identifiable, but their small numbers made it difficult to accommodate them in terms of the 'apartheid' structures. They lived and traded on the fringes of all race groups, having

Reclassifications: From 1972 to 1990

Statistics extracted from Department of Interior, later Home Affairs, Annual Reports

	Coloured to White	White to Coloured	Indian to Malay	Malay to Indian	Malay to White	Cape Col to Indian	Indian to Cape Col.	Indian to White	Cape Col to Chinese	Chinese to Cape Col.	Chinese to White	White to Chinese
1972	26	7	8	3	-	2	13	-	1	-	-	-
1973	20	12	12	3	-	3	20	-	1	1	-	-
1974	33	10	8	13	-	24	26	-	-	2	2	-
1975	24	14	18	11	-	21	26	-	-	-	2	-
1976	62	8	13	11	-	9	23	-	-	1	3	2
1977	44	9	3	22	-	3	16	-	-	-	-	-
1978	150	10	6	2	-	3	10	1	2	-	-	3
1979	101	2	4	10	-	10	11	-	3	2	1	6
1980	133	1	1	3	-	6	4	-	-	-	-	3
1981	153	1	-	-	1	-	-	-	-	-	5	1
1982	722	3	19	16	4	39	34	1	4	-	7	15
1983	462	4	15	26	2	37	31	-	8	-	9	4
1984	325	8	11	18	1	33	39	-	2	-	2	-
1985	495	17	14	28	5	41	55	-	8	1	10	2
1986	463	6	27	33	3	52	60	-	7	-	4	-
1987	438	10	42	50	21	85	87	-	12	2	17	1
1988	347	13	47	25	11	63	52	-	1	3	3	-
1989	261	7	9	-	6	26	34	9	7	1	-	2
1990	138	12	-	-	5	-	-	-	2	-	2	-

Notes:

a) In 1990, one (1) Chinese was reclassified Indian. Three (3) Chinese were reclassified Malay in 1973, 1976 and 1990. Two (2) Malays were reclassified Chinese in 1984 and 1990.

b) Several categories of reclassification which first appeared in the departmental reports in the 1980s (e.g. White to Malay, Other Asian to Coloured, Black to Coloured, etc.) have not been tabulated.

c) The department notes that the Immorality and Prohibition of Mixed Marriages Amendment Act, 1985, provided that marriages solemnized contrary to the provisions of the Prohibition of Mixed Marriages Act, 1949, may on application be declared valid. In 1987, 101 such marriages were declared valid. In the same year, of the 181 697 marriages solemnized, 413 were between a White and Non-White person.

d) The Population Registration Act of 1950 was repealed with effect from 28 June 1991. Race groups were thereafter not indicated on birth, marriage or death certificates.

South Africa's First 'White' Chinese

The David Song case was a landmark in the annals of race classification, precipitating a change in the country's Population Registration legislation. In March 1962 a Durban Chinese businessman, David Song, applied to be reclassified and was officially declared White by the Race Classification Board. He used the legal argument that, although he was Chinese, he could be classified as White on the grounds that he associated with Whites and was generally accepted as White. Witnesses were called to testify that they accepted him as White.[16]

For the Song family however, the reclassification gave rise to unforeseen repercussions. Because he had only applied for reclassification for himself, his wife and children remained 'non-White'. Parliamentarians questioned whether or not he and his wife were entitled to live together in terms of the country's Mixed Marriages and Immorality laws.[17]

Appealing for his family to be reclassified White on compassionate grounds, Progressive Party MP, Helen Suzman, told Parliament it would be disastrous if his family were not included in his classification. In a letter substantiating his appeal to the MP, David Song wrote:

'I beg of you to view the position of my family with compassion. In view of the Group Areas Act and other legislation I shall fall foul of the law merely by living with my own family. It would also mean that my family cannot occupy my property in Point Road. Where are they to go? They are dependent on me for their livelihood. ... I and my family know of no other home except the Republic of South Africa, and, being law-abiding citizens, we humbly pray and request that the position of my family be reviewed and reclassified as members of the White Group.[18]

In the Senate, Senator Fagan, a former Chief Justice, said the Race Classification Board had made a mistake in reclassifying Song and said there was a difference between acceptance as a White person and treatment as a White person. He maintained that the board had confused acceptance as a social equal with acceptance as a White person.[19]

None of the remaining members of the Song family was reclassified, and in the following years they encountered increasing problems with Group Areas legislation. They repeatedly applied for extensions to permits to occupy their own premises in the White area of Point Road, where Song had lived for over 40 years. Although several other Chinese lived in the area, only the Songs were prosecuted in late 1966 for living there illegally.

Again the Song case was raised in Parliament when the Minister of Community Development was asked why a man with a White identity card could not live in a White area. He replied that in terms of the Group Areas Act, 'a person with a White identity card who is married to a person belonging to another racial group must move to the group area of the other person'. Although there had been no complaint about the Songs' presence, the Minister said his department had drawn the attention of the police to the family who had been repeatedly told that if they wished to remain in Durban, they had to move to the Norse Street area where Chinese occupation was permitted.[20]

The 'elevated' status of White did not appear to hold advantages for Song and the family eventually left Durban.

established good working relationships with their customers. Being neither 'White' nor 'Black', and variously categorized as either 'Asiatic' or 'Coloured', the Chinese felt compelled to safeguard their own culture and identity by obtaining classification as a group in their own right.

In the aftermath of World War II during which China had participated as one of the Allied powers, the social position of Chinese in South Africa had gradually improved. Many hoped their legal status would undergo a similar change as experienced by Chinese in North America who were granted the franchise and exempted from long-standing exclusion laws in the 1940s.

By the 1950s the Chinese found themselves 'trapped' in an increasingly hostile South Africa. Not only were more discriminatory laws being promulgated to implement apartheid, but the takeover of the Chinese mainland by the Communists made the option of returning there virtually impossible. They needed to secure their own future in South Africa, no matter how bleak it appeared.

The introduction of the controversial Group Areas Bill in 1950 was the catalyst which mobilized the Chinese community countrywide into co-operating with one another. Threatened with the loss of their homes and their businesses, they turned to their local community associations for leadership and assistance. The Chinese did not have the vote and were numerically too small and too scattered to become a viable pressure group. Nonetheless they realized the necessity for organizing themselves, for creating a national representative body to articulate their views and to present a unified viewpoint to the authorities.

CHINESE FORM A UNITED FRONT

The concept of a single, united Chinese organization had been raised prior to 1950 and an attempt had even been made in April 1947 to form such a body. Meetings were held in Johannesburg with representatives from various regions and agreement reached on a structure which would work for social rights, lobby for an end to discriminatory practices and assist in China's reconstruction.[21] Pretoria delegate, C.P. Law, was elected chairman, with Fok Yuk Ho as vice chairman and Lim Hon Dzong as secretary.[22] Unfortunately the new organization did not last long and only when confronted with the Group Areas Bill did the Chinese re-group to establish a functioning national body.

In June 1950, representatives from Chinese organizations in Port Elizabeth and East London flew to Johannesburg to hold urgent consultations with Consul-General Li Chao and other organizations. Within days, delegates were summoned from all parts of the country to form a new, national Chinese organization. Despite deep differences over how such a body should function, the majority agreed on the need to present a united front to the government. A central body would enable the various regions to monitor developments countrywide and to co-ordinate a national strategy. To fund this work, a £10 fee was levied on every Chinese shop.[23]

Two months later, in August 1950, representatives met again to structure the as-yet unnamed organization. Durban initially decided not to participate in the new body, but

The executive committee of the Central Chinese Association of South Africa, photographed in 1956.

Representatives from various parts of South Africa who attended a special meeting convened by Consul-General Tsung Han Liu in 1960.

all other regions confirmed their support. A driving force behind the formation of the organization was the chairman of the Eastern Province Chinese Association, Sout Chong Wing King. He was, however, not elected to the first executive committee because of a unanimous decision that all office-bearers should be from the Transvaal where the Chinese Consul-General was based. In early correspondence, the organization called itself the 'Chinese Association of South Africa', but by April 1954 formally adopted the name 'Central Chinese Association of South Africa'.[24]

Constituting a nationally representative association proved to be no mean feat. Confronted with diverse views and groups from each centre, the association struggled to reach consensus. Over a period of twenty years, its constitution was amended several times to reflect changes both within the organization and the community. At the outset the Central Chinese Association (Central) declared its independence of all official organizations, either inside or outside South Africa and pledged its commitment to the welfare and legitimate interests of the Chinese community in the country.[25]

It is interesting to note how Central's thrust evolved over the years. Its first constitution was the direct result of the immediate crisis faced by the community in the

Central Chinese Association Preamble and Aims — 1960

Preamble:

Within recent years, there has come upon the Chinese scene in South Africa an increasing need for the formation of a corporate body which may speak with one voice for the Chinese people. It is felt that the privileges and trading interests, built up by sweat and honest toil over many years, require protection. This realization gave birth to the Central Chinese Association of South Africa.

The Association has also dedicated itself to realize these ideals: that every Chinese in this land may live a life of usefulness to himself, his family and his community; that his life may be one of happiness, peace, equality, justice and freedom from legislative discrimination.

The Association owes no allegiance to any organization; neither will it accept any direction from any body in- or outside the Union of South Africa. It is subservient to none, nor does it subscribe to any political ideology.[26]

Aims:

- to preserve the Chinese national and cultural identity;
- to strive for freedom of trade, residence and movement and to remove the disabilities to which the Chinese are subject;
- to solve all difficulties by peaceful representation and negotiation;
- to protect all interests of the Chinese people in South Africa;
- to co-ordinate the functions and activities of the constituent member bodies;
- to encourage education and to provide better facilities for higher education;
- to promote and assist the cultural growth of the Chinese people in South Africa;
- to cause proper health and welfare services to be provided for the Chinese in South Africa;
- to foster harmony and goodwill among the Chinese people and to promote and maintain good relationships with other racial groups.

Group Areas Act and was directed towards self-preservation and the protection of the community's interests. By 1960 the association focused more on the role of Chinese in the wider society, and emphasized the need to promote and maintain good relationships with other racial groups.[27]

Composition of Central

From the outset, the concept of proportional representation was used as the basis for drawing as many Chinese organizations as possible into Central. The aim was to build a strong, united body with representatives from every existing organization, who would then not only be able to spread word of Central's activities to their individual members, but also facilitate the more efficient collection of funds.

The association was made up of a 'general conference' which consisted of representatives from all member organizations, an 'executive committee' representing different regions and a 'standing committee' of office bearers. Each member of the association was formally required to sign an oath declaring his commitment to serving the cause of the Chinese people and following the aims and ideals of the constitution. The Consul-General played an important role in calling together community representatives to form the central body and in assisting with representations to the government. Because of the many different interest groups within the community, his office was in a position to act as arbiter. By the early 1960s however members of Central felt it was better not to have diplomatic personnel directly involved in the association's decision-making.

Central's Work

Prompted by a sense of urgency and increasing fear of the impact of the Group Areas legislation, the newly formed united organization mobilized the community countrywide. In a submission to the Minister of the Interior, in February 1951, the association appealed for Chinese to be accorded the same treatment as a 'friendly nation' in the international community and to be permitted to buy residential and business property. Pointing out that the Chinese had never been considered on their own merits, as a group, the memorandum stated:

> Due to the small number of Chinese traders in South Africa, the exemplary manner in which they conduct their business, their high standard of living, their pacific temperament and along with their background of a high cultural attainment, the Chinese would make model citizens in South Africa if freedom from restrictive measures is given them.[28]

Central persevered in co-ordinating problems encountered in different regions and developing a national strategy. Office-bearers held meetings with government officials on a regular basis, even managing to arrange interviews over the years with South Africa's Prime Ministers. While the focus of Central's work in its formative years was the Group Areas legislation, it also addressed issues such as the status of the Chinese, immigration, travel restrictions, tertiary education, employment opportunities and social amenities.

The organization was, however, continually racked with dissension. Lack of unity, with accusations of individuals meddling in negotiations with the government, bedevilled Central. Personality differences and power plays were often allowed to become more significant than the real issues. Differences of opinion and approach between the older and younger generation became increasingly evident — a crucial issue being whether the Chinese owed their primary loyalty to China or to South Africa.[29] By 1967 Central effectively ceased to function and organizations in each region were left to deal with their own affairs. Nevertheless, the part it played in addressing issues confronting the Chinese will be outlined in this chapter.

The Dr Wei Incident

The controversial and premature transfer of Consul-General Wei Yu Sun from South Africa to Italy in April 1964 highlighted deep divisions among Chinese organizations in South Africa.

Dr Wei, a graduate from Cambridge University in England, was posted to South Africa as Consul-General in July 1962. Among the first projects he initiated was the launch of fund-raising efforts to reorganize the Chinese newspaper, *Chiao Sheng Pao*. In correspondence with the Eastern Province Chinese Association he also reflected concern over numerous restrictive measures which adversely affected the Chinese such as inheritance of property in the Cape in terms of Group Areas legislation, acquisition of firearm licences and permission to teach at private schools.[30] Some have also credited him with playing a crucial role in obtaining concessions for the Chinese to be admitted to White hospitals and schools.[31]

When Dr Wei was transferred to Rome, having served only two years of the usual three-year term of a Consul-General, a number of Chinese associations sent cables to the Foreign Minister in Taiwan expressing support and requesting him not to be transferred if this action was the result of 'false representations'. It transpired that the Transvaal Chinese Association had published a letter in a Hong Kong magazine (Tian Hsia — 天下) levelling accusations against Dr Wei and describing him with words such as 'avaricious' and 'corrupt'. The letter stated that evidence of the Consul-General's activities had been submitted to the 'Government of Free China' and asked for his recall.

Ten Chinese associations[32] rejected the 'disgraceful allegations' against Consul-General Wei, whom they said was loyal, honest and wholeheartedly anti-Communist, and objected to the 'lamentable action' of the Transvaal Chinese Association in publishing such a letter. The E.P. Chinese Association also distributed a confidential circular with a full English translation of the original TCA letter and in separate letters called for support from more than 30 Chinese organizations throughout South Africa, the then Southern Rhodesia (Zimbabwe) and Mocambique.[33]

The Consul-General's transfer was, however, not rescinded. Although no direct connection can be proved between the TCA's published allegations and the Taiwan government's decision to remove him from South Africa, the dissension it sparked between the TCA and many other regional associations rankled for years.

Role of Regional Associations

Existing regional associations negotiated directly with the authorities and the Consulate-General on problems encountered in their areas, such as Group Areas proclamations and permits, access to public facilities and education. Among the more established regional bodies were those in Cape Town, Kimberley, Eastern Province, East London, Durban, Pretoria and Transvaal. They arranged social functions over Chinese New Year and the Double Ten and participated in charitable fund-raising activities for the wider community. While still maintaining a low profile politically, virtually all the organizations recognized the need to make the Chinese better known to others in South Africa and to win social acceptability.

One regional association which was perhaps more active than others was the Eastern Province Chinese Association (EPCA). Being geographically far removed from the Consulate-General in Johannesburg, the association became virtually self-sufficient in coping with community matters. Judging by the meticulous records they kept — from minute books dating back to 1934 and extensive files of correspondence, press clippings and documents — the EPCA dealt with a wide range of issues. They made numerous representations to the Department of Community Development to protect the trading interests of their community and pressed repeatedly for access to technical training for Chinese. Co-operating closely with their Chinese School committees, they handled thorny problems relating to the admission of Chinese teachers into the country, the maintenance of standards and fund-raising.

THE GROUP AREAS ACT

Cumbersome, contentious and far-reaching, the Group Areas Act of 1950 was the legislation which wrought the most upheaval, hardship and insecurity in the lives of the South African Chinese. The law provided for the separation of races into areas where each group would live and work, removed as far as possible from contact with other races. Introducing the Bill in 1950, the Prime Minister, Dr D.F. Malan, said it embodied 'the essence of the apartheid policy.'[34] The government determined where people of different races should live and control was imposed on all interracial changes in the ownership and occupation of property throughout the country. Allowance was made for the removal of people of the 'wrong colour' from areas not set aside for them.[35]

Residential segregation as a concept was not new to South Africa and had been implemented from the 19th century with the demarcation of separate areas for Blacks as well as restrictions on Asiatics and Coloureds, particularly in the Orange Free State and Transvaal. From the 1940s legislation was passed to regulate Asiatic ownership and occupation of property in Natal. What differentiated the Group Areas Act was the scope of its application. Not only did it impose racial criteria for residence and trade in specific areas, but in the course of its numerous amendments it evolved to encompass admission to and use of places such as hotels, halls and sports facilities, and also applied to conditions of employment.

Justifying the law's enactment, the government stated that it was desirable on the grounds of cultural and political differences, maintenance of Western civilization and avoidance of racial contact which might lead to racial conflict.[36] Political observers were more scathing in their assessments, and an English newspaper editor commented:

> The Group Areas Act 'was passed in the first flush of Nationalist enthusiasm for the policy of apartheid and the mood of the governing party demanded that sacrificial offerings should be made to the new god. Accordingly, the provisions of the Act were made to operate as harshly as possible ... against the Indian and other non-European groups.'[37]

By setting aside areas for the exclusive occupation of a single race group, the Group Areas Act set up artificial barriers between races, compartmentalizing the entire population. The stringent application of territorial separation and the 'total purification' of each area would eventually create a totally new pattern of distribution for the different races.[38]

Chinese in the Cape and Natal had enjoyed relative freedom to buy fixed property, but in the Transvaal, legislation such as Law 3 of 1885, the 'Gold Law'[39] and subsequent measures either prohibited or severely restricted their rights to own land or live in certain areas. The promulgation of the Group Areas Act, however, placed all Chinese countrywide on the same precarious footing. Those who owned property faced probable expropriation and relocation; those who did not own land but occupied rented premises also faced the threat of enforced removal to their own group area.

The proclamation of a 'Chinese' group area as well as the non-proclamation of an area would have an equally profound impact on the community. In the first instance everyone would have to move to their demarcated area; in the second instance they would have nowhere to live or trade. As small traders who had lived and worked for decades among all races, the Chinese perceived the law as the death blow to their livelihood. Describing themselves, they said:

> The Chinese people on the whole are in a state of intense depression. They feel they are up against a stone wall ... The provisions of the Group Areas Act, which, if they are strictly applied, must inevitably spell doom and dissolution for them in so far as trading activity is concerned.[40]

Operating in tandem with the Group Areas Act was the Community Development Act. Because people had to be moved and resettled in areas set aside for them, the development of townships or the provision of housing and municipal services was required. Community Development focused on property affected by the Group Areas Act and controlled the disposal of such property, by purchase or expropriation. The Community Development Board had far-reaching powers, over the heads of local authorities, to terminate leases, expropriate property and close businesses with compensation for goodwill being 'entirely at its discretion'.[41]

Community Response

Throughout the 1950s and early 1960s, the Central Chinese Association (Central) strived for a united approach in representations to the authorities. Fearing that precedents set in one area could have an adverse effect elsewhere, appeals were made to regions to conform to agreed policy and to consult Central when negotiating with local authorities.[42] Many letters, memoranda and submissions were directed to all persons of influence and deputations appeared at Land Tenure Board and later Group Areas Board hearings to appeal for the Chinese to be left where they were.

Within the community, every attempt was made to ensure that all Chinese were made aware of the significance of the legislation. The Chinese Literature and Arts Society in Johannesburg painstakingly translated the entire Group Areas Bill into Chinese and distributed copies countrywide.

Community leaders repeatedly argued that the size of the community did not warrant their own separate areas. Furthermore, they could not survive by trading among themselves if they were all confined to one area. The Chinese wanted the flexibility to live and trade in all areas and to have the right to purchase property freely. Realizing this 'freedom' was beyond the scope of the law, they sought relief from the provisions of law through exemptions and permits. Their prime concern was the retention of existing trading rights, and to safeguard these, they asked the authorities to separate 'residential' rights from 'business' rights in applying the law.

Summarizing the community's approach, Central chairman, Dr L.N. Liang said the Chinese requested the following:

- to be allowed to continue to trade under a system of permits;
- to have Group Areas proclaimed for them only for the purpose of residence; and
- that the granting of property rights be reviewed to ensure some security of tenure to traders.[43]

The Chinese adopted a non-confrontational approach in their dealings with the authorities, negotiating for differential treatment for the Chinese as a minority group. They justified their requests for special consideration on the basis of their small numbers, their general acceptance within society, their record as a quiet, law-abiding community and their standard of living.

> The Chinese people are all agreed that the solution of all our difficulties lies in South Africa by peaceful representation and negotiation with the Union Government, and as a community our people will make the declaration that the employment of violence and the use of subtle propaganda against the good name of South Africa in our effort to obtain relief to some of our difficulties, is hereby totally rejected by us.[44]

The Consul-General of the Republic of China on Taiwan played a key role in representations to the authorities, accompanying representatives of Central to meetings and co-signing memoranda. Not only did his diplomatic status give him standing in the community, but it also provided entree to high level government officials. It was only in later years that questions were raised about the continued involvement of the Consulate-General in local Chinese affairs.

Copies of the Cape of Good Hope magazine, produced by the Chinese Literature and Arts Society in the 1950s.

Chinese Literature and Arts Society

Among the many organizations which flourished in the 1950s was the Chinese Literature and Arts Society. Formed in early 1950, its object was to promote Chinese cultural awareness and an interest in Chinese writing and literature. One of its first accomplishments however was of a more pressing, practical nature — conveying to the community the full import of the government's Group Areas Bill.

Within weeks of the Bill's first reading in April 1950, the society prepared a detailed Chinese translation, which ran to 30 pages in neatly handwritten characters, roneoed approximately 4000 copies and distributed them countrywide. In a preface it was stated that the translation had been undertaken because of the grave threat posed to the interests and status of the Chinese community. Unless the Chinese were fully aware of the significance of the measure, they would not be in a position to take action. The translators apologized for any shortcomings in their work and asked the community to point out any errors to them. The Group Areas Bill passed through three readings in Parliament in record time to become law just three months later on 7 July 1950.[45]

At its peak, in the mid-1950s, the Chinese Literature and Arts Society had about 50 members who met monthly. People drawn to its ranks were mainly those who had been educated in China or Lourenco Marques (Maputo) and who sought to establish a Chinese intellectual circle. Society members celebrated 4th May as the day marking the renaissance of Chinese literature, and produced two issues of a Chinese magazine called *Good Hope* in February and May 1953.

The society also organized a Chinese photographic exhibition which was displayed in Johannesburg's city centre and mounted stage shows to collect funds for the Kuo Ting Chinese School. Among the many well-known Chinese involved in the Literature and Arts Society were: Lau Wing Sun, Dang Sui Wah, Stanley May, Wellington Ford, Leong Pak Seong, Kin Mun Kew, Jack Lau King, Joe Foar and Fok Yu Kam. By the late 1950s, however, interest in its activities waned, and the society ceased to function.[46]

Regional Developments

Special administrative boards were established by the government to colour in the map of South Africa by zoning areas for each racial group. Chinese in each part of the country were affected differently by the implementation of the law. Only one Chinese group area was proclaimed in the Transvaal, whereas three were proclaimed in the Cape. Although authorities and officials in several cities lent a sympathetic ear to appeals by the Chinese, others went about their task zealously to ensure strict adherence to the letter of the law.

TRANSVAAL

From the earliest days, Transvaal legislation, particularly Law 3 of 1885, enforced residential segregation by prohibiting Asiatics from owning or occupying fixed property except in a limited number of designated areas. Chinese and Indians were therefore compelled to live and work predominantly in mixed areas, Asiatic bazaars and Black townships.

Of the more than 3000 Chinese in the Transvaal in the early 1950s, about 2500 were concentrated in Johannesburg, 600 in Pretoria, and no more than 300 scattered in the vicinity of nearby towns such as Springs, Benoni, Germiston, Vereeniging, Nigel and Krugersdorp.[47] Several towns hoped to avoid the problem of declaring separate Chinese areas for their relatively insignificant numbers of Chinese by recommending to the Group Areas Board the idea of a single large area to house all Chinese on the Reef and Pretoria.[48] Other towns tried to settle the Indians, Chinese and Coloureds in one collective area.[49] Most of the Vereeniging Chinese of about 80 people lost their businesses when the Black population of the Top Location were moved to Sharpeville in the late 1950s.

PRETORIA

Chinese numbered 600 of the estimated 350 000 people who lived in the capital city of Pretoria in the early 1950s. The Pretoria City Council was vocal in promoting the creation of a single area for all Asiatics on the Reef and in Pretoria,[50] and in February 1961 proclaimed a Chinese group area on vacant land to the north of the Indian area at Laudium, south west of Pretoria.[51] According to press reports, the Pretoria City Council 'had originally taken the view that the Chinese were too small a community for their own area, but had since suggested a site should a group area be found necessary.'[52]

The Pretoria Chinese Association employed the services of an advocate to plead the case for the community which was scattered throughout the city centre, Lady Selborne, Claremont and in the Asiatic Bazaar. In August 1965 the Minister of Community Development, P.W. Botha, ordered the speedy development of the Chinese area to move all the Chinese from the city within 18 months 'regardless of their protests and opposition'.[53] Priority would be given to moving Chinese from Lady Selborne and Prinsloo Street which were earmarked for White occupation.

Fear and uncertainty dogged the community in the following months as periodic press reports focused on the redevelopment of the Asiatic bazaar and highlighted their tenuous position.[54] By February 1967 the Pretoria City Council abandoned the plan to move the Chinese because their demarcated area was needed for the expansion of the Indian area at Laudium.[55] Although the proclamation of another Chinese area was suggested, nothing materialized.

JOHANNESBURG

South Africa's largest city, Johannesburg, developed rapidly and haphazardly in the hectic years following the discovery of gold in 1886. By the 1950s it had a total population in excess of one million as well as a serious housing shortage, particularly for non-Whites. Residential segregation combined with overcrowding had resulted in slum conditions for the multitude of non-Whites who lived in areas such as Pageview, Burgersdorp, Sophiatown, Martindale, Newclare and Alexandra township.

Western Areas Removal Scheme

Although the Johannesburg City Council intended to clear the slums in the Western Areas (Sophiatown, Martindale and Newclare) in the 1930s, its plans were suspended during World War II. Group Areas and the Natives Resettlement Act (No. 19 of 1954) empowered the Nationalist government to override the city council's plans and proceed with the systematic removal of all non-Whites from what was described as a 'black spot' in the city. The Western Areas Removal Scheme precipitated a crisis for the Chinese, a substantial number of whom had established businesses there, living in a few rooms behind their shops.

Of the 2500 Chinese scattered around the city, nearly 1000 were estimated to live in Sophiatown and Martindale which were earmarked for slum clearance. By 1956 more than 170 Chinese families faced the loss of their shops, eviction from their homes and little or no prospect of making a living elsewhere. Licences for Chinese to trade in other parts of Johannesburg were refused and finding alternative accommodation was virtually impossible.[56]

As early as April 1950 the Chinese formed the Western Areas Chinese Association to protect the interests of Chinese shopkeepers. It worked with the larger community organizations to draw attention to the hardships Chinese would face with any enforced removal. Living and working within the Coloured and Black community in the area, Chinese traders had built up good relations with their neighbours. When the Defiance Campaign, a national civil disobedience drive defying apartheid laws, was being planned in early 1952, members of the African National Congress approached the Chinese for support. Several Chinese students were involved in the campaign, and community elder, Stanley May, recalled how the Western Areas Chinese Association met with Nelson Mandela, then national president of the ANC Youth League, and made donations to the organization.[57] In the Pretoria suburb of Lady Selborne, Chinese traders also gave financial asistance to the local ANC branch.[58]

Chinese shops in Sophiatown and Newclare, established from the 1930s and 1940s.

In May 1953 a committee of the Johannesburg City Council approved in principle the allocation of a portion of Ferreirastown, bounded by Fox, Commissioner and Wolhuter streets as well as an area on the farm Langlaagte for Chinese occupation. It was also recommended that those Chinese trading and residing in areas set aside for Whites be allowed to remain under permit.[59] When the first 14 Chinese families in Sophiatown were given notice to vacate their premises by the end of 1956, Central took up the case. In a lengthy memorandum to the Group Areas Board on the desperate position of families awaiting eviction, chairman Dr Liang wrote: 'Their dilemma is that they have no place to go.' Central requested the speedy consideration of trading permit applications (which often took in excess of 18 months), priority treatment for Chinese from Sophiatown and Martindale, and also suggested a site for the establishment of a Chinese residential area.

The memorandum stated:

> The irreconcilable and unhappy position of the Chinese people in the Western areas where approximately 1000 people, women and children included, will soon become homeless and dislocated, calls to my mind the question of an early allocation of a suitable residential site for these and other Chinese people in the Transvaal so as to offset the acute housing shortage.

Dr Liang said the community had been offered land on a portion of the old Langlaagte Mine, near Main Reef Road, Industria and that his association was 'very favourably impressed that both the locality and the character of the surrounding area is in every way ideally suited for the proclamation of this area as a Chinese Township for residential purposes.'[60]

Evictions

The fear, uncertainty and despair of families evicted from their homes in Sophiatown was vividly portrayed in numerous newspaper reports throughout April and May 1957. Headlines such as 'Chinese will not know where to sleep tonight' and 'Evicted Chinese families facing hunger' drew sufficient public attention for questions to be asked in Parliament.

After Sophiatown was declared a White group area in 1955, the Natives Resettlement Board moved landowners and tenants out of the area. Despite receiving eviction notices, two Chinese families, the Ah Hungs and the Hoy Icks, refused to leave their shops and homes saying they had nowhere to go since the Chinese had no area and they would lose their livelihood. Temporary alternative accommodation was offered to them in dilapidated shacks, without water or electricity.

The Ah Hungs who had traded in Sophiatown for 20 years defied their eviction order until the authorities threatened to demolish their home around them. The Hoy Ick family were, however, repeatedly granted reprieves from removal to enable Mrs Hoy Ick to recover from an operation following the birth of a baby.

The daily newspaper coverage focusing on the near-destitution of evicted families prompted readers to donate money to the Ah Hungs and Hoy Icks, with the *Rand Daily Mail* reporting that it had received over £80.[61]

The government was, however, unwilling to distinguish between trading and residential rights[62] and the Chinese community thereafter voiced its strong opposition both to Langlaagte and all subsequent proposals for Chinese areas in Johannesburg. Arguing again that the community was too small to be self-sufficient, the Transvaal Chinese Association pointed out that there were, in Johannesburg, about 600 traders, 25 market gardeners, four Chinese clubs in Ferreirastown owning immovable property worth £250 000 and a Chinese school building worth £45 000. It asked for the retention of existing rights, permission to purchase immovable property and permits to expand into other areas.[63]

Alan Paton's View

Renowned South African writer, Alan Paton, author of *Cry the Beloved Country* highlighted many of the racial problems of his homeland. In a 44-page booklet entitled, *The People Wept ...*, he attacked the Group Areas Act 'as a callous and cruel piece of legislation'. Outlining its implications, he recounted the stories of many individuals, and wrote of the Chinese:

> 'There are only 2500 Chinese people in Johannesburg, most of them dependent on trading. Some of them have had shops for many years in white suburbs, have served the community faithfully, and have kept very much to themselves. For us as children the Chinese shops were romantic places; it never occurred to us that we would live to see the day when their presence would be thought intolerable, and their owners be moved without regard to their happiness or security.
>
> The day before Good Friday 1957 (the holiest day of the Christian year) 30 days' notice was served on Mr H.*, a Chinese shop keeper of Sophiatown, to vacate his shop which was then due for demolition. This took place under the Natives Resettlement Act, not the Group Areas Act, but in cruelty they are identical. The 30 days' notice is in itself a cruelty.
>
> But Mr H. was not merely losing his premises, he was also losing his business. He was allowed to occupy temporarily a vacated house, but there was no question of his getting a licence for a business in what was now to be a white area. He asked the officials, as so many have done before, and as so many must yet do, what he must now do, and he heard, as so many have heard and must yet hear, that it was not their business.
>
> So there he is, he and his wife and his children, with no place to go, and with his home and his business destroyed; and the authority who is directly responsible for it, washes its hands of him and his troubles.
>
> I have seen Mr H. He has lost his home, he has lost his business. And it looks as though he is losing his mind too.[64]

The situation of the Western Areas Chinese was quietly resolved in December 1960 through an 'understanding' reached with the Group Areas Board. They were allowed, under permit, to move into parts of Denver, Jeppe, City and Suburban, Doornfontein, Ophirton and Fordsburg. Accepting the 'unique position' of the Chinese, the Board gave an undertaking that they would not, for the time being, press for the proclamation of a Chinese area and that the present occupants of trading and residential premises would be left undisturbed except where slum areas were cleared.[65]

During the course of the 1960s suggestions on possible areas for Chinese in Johannesburg continued to surface. In March 1967 the Group Areas Board earmarked a site at Willowdene, nine miles to the south west of Johannesburg, for Chinese occupation.[66] Objections were lodged by the Chinese, by Whites living on smallholdings in Willowdene as well as by the Johannesburg City Council and less than a year later, the plan was dropped.[67] Talk was also rife in the community about the possibility of an apartment building called 'Octavia Hill' in Fordsburg being set aside for the Chinese.

By the mid-1960s Chinese were concentrated in the city's semi-industrial and less desirable areas such as Doornfontein, Bertrams, Jeppe, Mayfair, Fordsburg, Turffontein and Rosettenville. Even there, their tenure was insecure. If any neighbours complained about their presence in a declared White area, the authorities were forced to take some action and several Chinese were prosecuted and evicted from their homes. Faced with an acute shortage of rented accommodation, some resorted to buying homes either by using White nominees or forming companies.

Chinatown Proposal

From 1970 attention was focused on the proposed development of 'Chinatown', the few city blocks in Ferreirastown to the west of Johannesburg. The government sought to obtain the co-operation of Chinese businessmen to build large blocks of flats and provide amenities for schooling and recreation. Outlining the government's policy, the Minister of Community Development, Blaar Coetzee, said no further group areas would be proclaimed for Chinese, but that where there were no areas, provision would be made for Chinese 'to form their own ethnic concentrations'.

> It is in conformity with this general policy that I am anxious to see the development of 'China Town' in Johannesburg. A large concentration of the Chinese community is already to be found there and it is ideally situated to create a central core which can accommodate many of the Chinese families. While all possible help in the development of the area will be rendered through the medium of the Community Development Board, it is desirable that the Chinese themselves should initiate such development.[68]

Although permits for the Chinese to reside elsewhere would continue to be considered on merit while the development was taking place, the Minister emphasized that the policy of concentrating ethnic groups in their own areas would have to be implemented. His department requested the formation of an action committee of Chinese leaders to start on the project, but by September 1971 it became clear that the community's objectives in supporting the development conflicted with those of the government.

The Chinese had been under the impression that the development was primarily to house, on a voluntary basis, those who were in 'desperate need' of accommodation and that property owners would have the flexibility to invest either in 'high class' or sub-economic buildings. They also thought that Chinese already residing in other areas would be allowed to remain where they were and no one would be forced to live in the newly developed Chinatown.[69]

In a peremptory reply, the Minister pointed out that the terms of the development had been fully explained to the Consul-General and stated that unless the Chinese community continued to play their part, the development would be taken over by his department and the necessary land expropriated. He further reiterated that 'China Town is in fact an area where Chinese people will have to be concentrated since this is the only possible area where housing can be provided for them in the near future.'[70] This overt intention to create an informal group area deterred the Chinese from collaborating further on the project, and the matter was shelved.[71]

Johannesburg's Chinatown is possibly the smallest in the world because of the Group Areas Act. The awareness of the dangers of grouping themselves and having an area imposed on them made the Chinese repress the tendency shown in Chinatowns elsewhere to move into a vicinity where they could socialize with other Chinese. Little was done to develop or expand the area and long established clubs moved out or closed down. It was only from the 1980s, with the influx of new immigrants from Taiwan and Hong Kong, that 'Chinatown' has developed a more vibrant character to become an attraction in the city.

CAPE PROVINCE

The impact of the Group Areas Act was in some respects more far-reaching for Chinese who lived in the Cape Province. Unlike their compatriots in the Transvaal, they had long enjoyed relative freedom to purchase property. When areas in which they lived or traded were set aside for other groups, many faced financial hardship by being forced to close down established businesses and to sell property well below market value. Most encountered great difficulty in obtaining permits either to live or trade elsewhere. In addition, the law precluded them from further purchases of property, unless it was in their own designated area.[72]

In both Cape Town and East London, group areas for Chinese were proposed, but not proclaimed. No Chinese area was set aside in Grahamstown, but although Chinese areas were proclaimed in both Kimberley and Uitenhage, they were not developed. The only Chinese group area proclaimed and developed in the 40 years' existence of the law in South Africa was Kabega in Port Elizabeth.

CAPE TOWN

As the longest established city in the country, Cape Town was home to over half a million people in the 1950s. Over the centuries the homes of non-Whites had become interspersed with those of Whites and their geographical separation entailed 'removing' many thousands of families to their own group areas. No more than 300 Chinese lived in the vicinity of Cape Town and in July 1955 a group area was proposed for them in Fraserdale, straddling the Klipfontein Road, near Rondebosch Common and Athlone.

Chinese community leaders in the Cape

Harry Wong, East London

Yuen Whiteley, Port Elizabeth

Y.S. Manlee, Uitenhage

Leong Sean, Cape Town

Sidney Kim Sing, Port Elizabeth

Local residents of the area objected and the South African Institute of Race Relations pointed out that the selection of the area was 'particularly arbitrary' since no Chinese lived there whereas many Coloured families did.[73]

Other Chinese areas were proposed in the Heatherly Estate or the Mosman Road area in Lansdowne in November 1960.[74] The Chinese Association of Cape Town objected on the grounds that both sites were far away from their established businesses as well as the Chinese school in Mowbray. They reiterated appeals that the size of the community did not warrant a separate area and that as shopkeepers, the Chinese would not be able to make a living trading among themselves. Pointing out that they had never agitated against or stirred up racial feelings against government policy, they asked for sympathetic consideration of their position.[75] No group area was set aside for Chinese in Cape Town but several established Chinese businesses in areas proclaimed for other groups were forced to move.[76]

EAST LONDON

In the busy sea port of East London, on the south eastern coast of the country, the Chinese population consisted of 45 families, numbering about 265 people in the early 1950s. When a Chinese area, off Kimberley Road, behind the Indian area, was proposed, the local newspaper argued that the few Chinese in the city should be 'left to continue the service they have long rendered the European community, without danger to the principles embodied in the Act'.[77]

The East London Chinese Association said a separate area for the Chinese would lead to the 'economic ruin' of the community, the majority of whom were general dealers. Their businesses were scattered throughout East London and after years of trading and living in the city 'we venture to assert that we are not regarded as outcasts of human society nor are we ostracized by our European fellow citizens'.[78] No Chinese group area was proclaimed, and most Chinese continued to live and work where they had been established for years.

KIMBERLEY

The first Chinese group area in South Africa was proclaimed in the diamond city of Kimberley on 31 July 1959.[79] Intended to accommodate a community estimated to number 200 people, it was an undeveloped site situated more than two miles from the city centre to the south west of Mint Village, bounded by the railway line and Transvaal Road. Assessing the implications of the proclamation, the South African Institute of Race Relations pointed out the enforced removal of homes and businesses to the area would deprive the Chinese, all of whom were traders, of their means of livelihood.[80]

The Kimberley Chinese Association appealed for the community to be left where they were and stated that the allocated site was too close to the abattoir and sewage disposal works. Their appeals became even more urgent when, nine years later, attempts were made to start developing the area for occupation. Association chairman, Meng

Chan Yan, told the city council it would be 'wasting its money' since the local Chinese numbers had dropped to 146, and were continually decreasing as young people left Kimberley in search of better employment opportunities. He appealed for the indefinite suspension of plans to develop the Chinese area and asked the authorities to issue permits to Chinese for housing or business purposes.[81]

By 1970 only two Chinese families had built houses in the area.[82] The Kimberley City Council was sympathetic to the appeals lodged and submitted an application, finalized in 1973, for the deproclamation of the site as a Chinese group area.[83]

UITENHAGE

In Uitenhage, a town some 30 km away from Port Elizabeth, the tiny Chinese community of 130 people were allocated a group area in the vicinity of Baines Road and Lower Caledon Street, in October 1967. The local Chinese association had earlier asked for the Chinese to be left where they were, but if the authorities insisted, they suggested a residential area on undeveloped land where their occupation would not antagonize other race groups.[84] Most Chinese did not move into the area, and it was deproclaimed in 1979.[85]

PORT ELIZABETH

As South Africa's only fully established Chinese group area, Kabega's proclamation and development is shrouded in controversy, suspicion and accusation. Not only have fingers been pointed at community leaders for 'accepting' the group area and potentially jeopardizing the Chinese position in other cities, but insinuations have also been made that individuals exploited the situation for financial gain. Force of circumstance in the community's historical development, however, served to create 'ideal' conditions for the development of the Chinese group area in Kabega, some 12 km from the city centre. Not only had a Chinese school and a Chinese-owned township already been established there, but the community had also to deal with an active Group Areas Board, City Council and the reality of slum clearance projects.

Of all the Chinese communities in South Africa, that of Port Elizabeth appears to have been placed under sustained pressure from the early days of the Group Areas Act's implementation. Whether or not the Chinese community wanted an area was not at issue, it was simply a question of where the area would be situated. In the mid-1950s, the approximately 1500 Chinese, of a total population of no more than 250 000[86] in the city, constituted the highest density Chinese community in the country although numerically it ranked second to Johannesburg.

Led by Sout Chong Wing King and Sidney Kim Sing, the Eastern Province Chinese Association (EPCA) played an active role in monitoring town planning and group area developments. They made a detailed study of the legal implications, securing the services of lawyers and senior counsel to write memoranda and make representations to the authorities. Aware of the need to argue their case with sound evidence, the association compiled comprehensive statistics on all businesses, residences and families.

The Chinese were scattered throughout Port Elizabeth, particularly in the city centre, Sidwell, Korsten, South End, Sydenham, Perkin Street and Dassiekraal. Many owned the properties on which their businesses and homes were situated and the racial zoning of any area meant they would not only have to be relocated if they were not of the race group to which the area was allocated, but they would also lose long-held property rights.

The development of a Chinese group area in Port Elizabeth is closely tied up with the history of the Chinese schools. At the turn of the century, community organizations established their headquarters in the centrally located Evatt Street area, known as 'Malaikim', and it was in this vicinity that the first Chinese school put down its roots. When the rival E.P. Chinese Primary School was formed in the early 1940s, its founders purchased land off Cape Road in Kabega. Although the school closed after a few years, its premises were taken over by the EPCA to house the Chinese High School in 1951. Situated in the midst of farms and residential areas populated by Whites, the school's geographical position was to become one of the determinants in the eventual decision to allocate that area to Chinese.

A Chinese shop in central Port Elizabeth.

Objections and Counter-proposals

When the Port Elizabeth City Council published its provisional town planning scheme in December 1952, areas were zoned for White and non-White residence, business and industrial use. The Chinese were allotted a residential area near Korsten, adjoining the Malay and Cape Coloured areas.[87] The EPCA objected on the grounds that nearly half of all Chinese businesses in the city, about 97 shops, would have to be moved to conform with the scheme and that the whole community's residence would be affected.

Submitting that the Group Areas Act had not been passed 'to destroy any particular Group, but to alleviate racial tension', the EPCA suggested that 'where a group was too small to form a Group Area ... it should be allowed to maintain its present position in so far as it does not constitute an economic, social or cultural threat to any other Group so as to cause racial tension'. Throughout the lengthy memorandum which also listed all affected businesses, repeated requests were made for Chinese to be allowed to remain where they were. The proposed Chinese residential area was described as too small to absorb the numbers of Chinese who would have to live there or to accommodate any natural increase.

> It is suggested that for those Chinese families which may be displaced as a result of the Town Planning Scheme, and for the purpose of accommodating the natural increase of the Chinese community, the council should set aside a *residential* area for occupation by the Chinese in the vicinity of the Chinese school in Cape Road.

The memorandum concluded with an objection to the zoning as 'European', of the area on which the EPCA's then headquarters, Number 64 Evatt Street, were situated. It was stated that the association wished to sell the site provided they were allowed to erect their headquarters on the school site in Cape Road, Kabega.[88]

The city council's planning scheme incorporated free trade areas for all race groups, a concept which ran counter to the aim of the Group Areas law. Furthermore Group Areas did not distinguish between residential areas and business areas, but aimed to compartmentalize the different race groups totally. Although the plan was modified, no agreement was reached with the authorities and four years later, in 1956, the Group Areas Board conducted public hearings to prepare submissions for the delimitation of areas in Port Elizabeth.

By this stage, the group area under consideration for the Chinese had changed to that on Cape Road in the vicinity of the Chinese high school. The EPCA again reiterated its strong objection to the establishment of any Chinese Group Area and was given an assurance that the City Council opposed the application of the Group Areas Act to the Chinese community and did not want them to lose any of the rights and privileges they then enjoyed.[89]

It should be noted that the community drew a clear distinction between a *residential* area being set aside for the Chinese and a *group area* as defined by the law (which intended a designated area to serve all a group's needs, segregating them both residentially and economically). The EPCA employed an advocate to put its case before the Group Areas Board. It stated its opposition to a group area for Chinese in Cape Road because the establishment would mean the removal of Chinese traders from their customers, with the consequential effect of depriving the Chinese of plying their trade as general dealers.

> This will ultimately force them to become a burden on the Government instead of a valuable commercial asset. The establishment of a group area for the Chinese would have a catastrophic effect upon the Chinese community in Port Elizabeth.[90]

Property owners in Linton Grange and Bramhope Township, close to the proposed Chinese group area, also submitted objections stating that the Chinese area in the midst of White areas was contrary to the spirit of the Act. The attorney appearing for a White farmer who owned land in the proposed area said there was no necessity for creating a separate Chinese area for a community of only 240 families and they should be left where they were.[91]

Uncertainty hung over the community as group areas were steadily proclaimed in other parts of the country. By May 1961 it was Port Elizabeth's turn and Proclamation 144 of 1961 demarcated areas for the occupation and ownership of Whites, Chinese, Coloureds and Indians. The area set aside for Chinese was in the vicinity of the Chinese School, in the locality known as Kabega, bounded by Parsons Vlei and Cape Road.[92] Significant too was the concession that existing Chinese businesses could remain in those areas where they were already established.

What Constituted 'Acceptance'?

In the following years, accusations were levelled, both in Port Elizabeth and by Chinese in other parts of the country, that community leaders had 'accepted' the Chinese group area. Yet the proclamation was no different from those which set aside Chinese areas in Kimberley, Pretoria and Uitenhage. What then differentiated Kabega?

Chinese had owned property in the area since 1942 when the Eastern Province Chinese Primary School, the 'breakaway' school, was established there. The school's four trustees jointly purchased a large tract of land and donated a portion to the school. Disagreements arose over the division of the remaining land and Lee Simpson bought out the other trustees to acquire the entire property. Although this school only lasted for a few years, the EPCA took over the property to establish the Chinese High School there in 1951. By the time Kabega was proclaimed, the school had been in existence for some 10 years, which meant that children were regularly commuting to and from the area.

Original premises of the Eastern Province Chinese Primary School, established in Kabega in 1942.

In anticipation of Kabega being set aside either for Whites or Chinese, property owners had begun the development of a township by providing electricity and water and subdividing the land into plots. Property transactions were however frozen in the uncertain years between the Group Areas Board sitting in 1956 and Kabega's proclamation in 1961.

On the often-repeated assertion that the Port Elizabeth Chinese 'accepted' the area, those closely associated with the leaders of the day maintain that the story has been twisted to imply that the community wanted an area. Ernest Wing King, son of the then EPCA chairman, Sout Chong Wing King said:

> It was very simple. The government of the day could have done anything it wanted. That's how powerful they were. They wanted to implement their Group Areas Act which is one of the pillars of apartheid ... I'm absolutely certain that PE was chosen by the Government as the trial for the Chinese.
>
> What they did leave open to us was that we could negotiate where we wanted it, but we were going to get it regardless. So the point was, if we had to have it, then the ideal residential group area would be at the school ... then there's no commuting. We objected totally to Group Areas — but if we had to accept anything as a compromise, we would take a residential one, because that would also improve the standard of living ... The residential and business rights were two different things and my father was fighting to keep the businesses where they were, because that was our livelihood.[93]

Another long-time member of the EPCA whose family had lived in Kabega since the 1940s, Harry Simpson, said:

> We said in writing that we were opposed to any group area for Chinese in Port Elizabeth, but if we are forced to have a group area we would rather have it in Cape Road, because our school is here and it is a better area ... and they turned it around and said we asked for it, to have a group area ...

Unlike other cities in which Chinese group areas were proclaimed, notably Kimberley and Pretoria, it was not possible for the Port Elizabeth Chinese to refuse to move there or to 'boycott' the area. Simpson added:

> We were here already — our school was here. When my family established the township, some of the people had already bought about five or six plots. We semi-started our area on our own, before the Group Areas came in. That's what it amounted to ...[94]

Although community leaders had objected strongly to the principle of implementing group areas for Chinese throughout the 1950s, there is no evidence that when Kabega was proclaimed in May 1961 an official objection was lodged. This silence probably contributed to the lingering accusations that the Chinese community of Port Elizabeth 'accepted' their area. Whether or not to object to the proclamation placed community leaders in a 'no-win' situation. Repeated objections had been to no avail, while the area eventually allocated did represent a concession in that businesses would not be affected. The possible negative repercussions of objecting after the proclamation may have been the allocation of another, less convenient area, and a change in attitude by officials towards the retention of existing business rights.

Several Chinese speculators started buying land soon after the area was proclaimed, although it was some years before most families moved, with great reluctance, into the area. It could perhaps be said that moving in to Kabega was tantamount to 'acceptance', but many Chinese were compelled to do so when they received eviction notices from their homes in other parts of the city. Another factor which accelerated the community's settlement there was the erection of flats (apartments) both by Chinese individuals and the Department of Community Development in the late 1960s.

Town planning schemes and slum clearance projects in areas such as South End, Korsten, Walmer, Fairview and Salisbury Park from the mid-1960s resulted in the expropriation of properties and the eviction of many Chinese families. This required them to seek new business premises, for which they would have to apply for permits, and to move to the proclaimed Chinese residential area. A proposal by the Department of Community Development for the relocation of Chinese businesses was the erection of segregated shopping centres either in Kabega, Kempston Road or Perl Road, sites which were all vigorously opposed by the EPCA.[95]

As the stark reality of the Group Areas Act became evident, Chinese reassessed their future in South Africa. For many, emigration was seen as the only option to escape the ever-confining effects of apartheid and Port Elizabeth's Chinese community was particularly affected by the departure for Canada and Australia of many families who had lived in the city for generations.

Development of Kabega

Once proclaimed and established however, the group area brought in its wake new problems for the Port Elizabeth Chinese. Although some 20 families had settled in Kabega by 1967,[96] urban development projects throughout the city displaced ever-increasing numbers who had no option but to seek accommodation there. The large scale erection of houses and flats by the Department of Community Development and individuals also prompted fears that Chinese then living in other parts of the city would be forcibly relocated.

The implementation of group areas affected the rights of families to inherit property which was situated in areas set aside for other groups. Throughout the 1960s, the EPCA was involved in lengthy correspondence with officials in attempts to stave off demands for the immediate sale of property after the death of the head of a household. Furthermore, those who purchased property in Kabega knew that their 'investment' was not subject to normal economic forces. Because they would only be permitted to sell to Chinese, potential buyers were limited and it was said that sellers often struggled to recoup what they had spent.[97]

During the 1970s group areas restrictions on Chinese in other parts of the country had gradually begun to ease as permits were granted to enable them to buy property in White areas. In a memorandum to the Minister of Community Development in September 1974, the EPCA appealed for the deproclamation of Kabega and asked that Port Elizabeth Chinese be given the same concessions as those granted Chinese in other cities.

Chinese Beach and Fishing Pier

The Chinese of Port Elizabeth not only had their own group area in the city, they also had a separate beach and their own portion of a fishing pier.

The Chinese beach, allocated by Port Elizabeth's Separate Beach Amenities Committee in 1966, was situated on the Marine Drive Lands, in an area known as Schoenmakers.[98] It consisted of a rocky beach frontage, pool and picnic site as well as men's and women's changerooms, complete with Chinese signage. The community contributed towards the cost of erecting the changerooms, and frequented the beach in large numbers, particularly on weekends and public holidays.

Access to the sea was also segregated for fishermen. In the late 1950s, W. J. Pow Chong, Archie Pow Chong and Kee Son formed a fishing club to secure a spot for local anglers. They were granted a portion of a fishing pier, positioned between the Whites and the Coloureds. Describing it, S.S. Pow Chong said:

> On the jetty, there were the Europeans who had the best part over the deep sea ... we didn't have a very bad spot because we were in the middle and the Coloureds were further in, almost fishing on the land. The sections were marked out on the jetty and we all fished in our own positions.[99]

The PE Chinese Angling Society applied for fishing permits for their members each year. The society held regular competitions and was actively supported for three to four years, but eventually disbanded in the early 1960s.

A fishing permit issued to the Port Elizabeth Chinese Angling Club.

S.A.R. (HARBOURS)
PORT ELIZABETH HARBOUR

This permit is
not transferable

NON-EUROPEANS AND CHINESE
YEARLY ANGLING PERMIT 8/4
YEAR 1959

> The fact that there is a proclaimed Chinese Group Area here means the Government officials are obliged to enforce the provisions of the Act with resulting hardship to our Chinese Community ... We are frequently told by senior Government officers, 'It is my job to move you into the mixed trading area and into the Chinese Group Area.[100]

It was also pointed out that the Department of Community Development was building 47 houses and 48 flats in the area, 'far in excess of the number of Chinese families actually displaced by urban redevelopment'. The EPCA said officials had taken income surveys, using housing application forms which they insisted that community members complete. Despite an assurance to the EPCA that these were only to survey income, the number of houses and flats being erected was based on the assumption that all completed forms were in fact applications for housing in the Chinese area.

Preliminary steps were taken to proclaim a further area for Chinese in 1976, but after some negotiations and yet another appeal from the EPCA for the deproclamation of the existing area, the matter was shelved.[101] The EPCA submitted that the present area was sufficient to provide housing for at least 10 to 15 years. It also pointed out that of the 1400 Chinese in Port Elizabeth, only 71 families were not settled in Kabega by 1976.[102] Just three years earlier the Chinese Primary and High schools had been amalgamated and moved to new buildings with sportsfields in Topaz Road, Kabega.

For many, life in the Chinese area did have its compensations, not least of which was a substantial improvement in living conditions. No longer confined to a few rooms behind or on top of shops, many Chinese built comfortable to lavish homes while others were accommodated in sub-economic houses and flats, built by the Department of Community Development. The proximity of the Chinese school and the establishment of community institutions such as the EPCA headquarters and the St Francis Xavier Church in the area further contributed towards the moulding of a tightly knit community. Kabega was officially deproclaimed as a Chinese area on 5 July 1984, giving the community the freedom to choose where they wished to live and enabling non-Chinese to purchase property in the area.

DURBAN – NATAL

Affected in much the same way as the Chinese in the Cape who had previously held landownership rights, the Chinese in Natal numbered about 160 people in the mid-1960s. Group Areas officials made efforts to move them into Norse Street, on the outskirts of Overport, where some Chinese from Johannesburg had settled a few years earlier.[103]

In Parliament, the Minister of Community Development said there were six houses of 'superior quality' in the Norse Street area which were available for purchase by Chinese. They were priced between R14 000 and R20 000.[104] Those who owned properties and businesses in other parts of Durban were obviously loathe to move and continued to apply for permits which, with some difficulty, they obtained. Four members of a Chinese family who lived in Point Road, Durban, were prosecuted for remaining in the proclaimed White area in late 1966. The Minister of Community Development said as disqualified persons, the family should have vacated the area in June 1959 but had 'made no attempt of their own accord to leave the area'. Permission had been granted to them to stay 'with the warning that if they wished to remain in Durban, they had to move to the Norse Street area'.[105] The authorities did not pursue attempts to group the community and the majority of Durban Chinese were largely left to continue living and trading where they had long been established.

IMPACT OF GROUP AREAS

Fear that they would lose their livelihood as small shopkeepers was the driving force behind the Chinese community's opposition to Group Areas. Community leaders vigorously opposed the proclamation of any Group Areas for the Chinese, and although four were set aside, only the one in Port Elizabeth was eventually developed. Even in this case, the Chinese secured the significant concession from the authorities to separate business rights from residential rights. The impact of the law was such that all Chinese throughout South Africa felt its effects, whether or not separate group areas were proclaimed for them.

Proclaimed Chinese Group Areas

	Date proclaimed	*Developed*	*Deproclaimed*
Kimberley	31 July 1959	No	1973
Pretoria	February 1961	No	± 1967
Port Elizabeth	May 1961	Yes	1984
Uitenhage	October 1967	No	1979

Not having an area gave rise to its own problems, perhaps causing even more hardship for many Chinese. For some 20 years between 1955 and 1975, their position in terms of the Group Areas Act turned them into 'displaced' persons, a community 'living in a twilight zone where their rights are blurred and undefined ... for whom no accommodation is available within the law'.[106]

Prohibited from owning property, the Chinese had to rent homes and businesses, which made them dependent on the goodwill of landlords and neighbours. It was a precarious situation, exposing them to exploitation as well as eviction and prosecution for living in areas set aside for other groups. Families were forced to settle for inferior housing, often at exorbitant rents, and could be ordered to vacate the premises at short notice. Some were known to have spent large sums renovating houses to make them habitable, only to have their rent increased or be told to make way for tenants prepared to pay more. A Chinese who faced eviction from Doornfontein, Johannesburg, said this of his predicament:

> We are sometimes exploited by landlords who know that we are desperate for accommodation. They offer us accommodation at grossly inflated rates — hoping that in our desperation, we will pay.[107]

In Johannesburg, Durban and Cape Town, a number of Chinese were prosecuted and sentenced for living illegally in White areas although the courts were told that no areas had been set aside for them. The obvious inequity of the situation led one courageous magistrate to caution and discharge three Chinese found guilty of living in Jeppestown. Passing sentence, magistrate T.R. Maxted said:

> One cannot expect Chinese people born in this country to live in the air. They must have some place to base their family life ... Until such time as alternative accommodation is available, I will not pass an unfair sentence.[108]

Many Chinese lost their businesses and homes when the areas in which they had long been established were set aside for other groups, while others were plagued with uncertainty over when their turn would come. For nearly three decades the Chinese persisted in their objections to the application of the Group Areas Act, managing to secure some concessions from the authorities in the 1960s and 1970s.

Although the legislation was not uniformly applied throughout the country, it had a major impact on the community as a whole. By 1970, a total of 899 Chinese families had become 'disqualified' in terms of various proclamations.[109] By 1975, the Minister of Community Development reported that 142 Chinese families had been moved, while 1092 had still to be moved since the implementation of the Group Areas Act.[110] These figures probably do not include families who lost their homes in terms of slum clearance, township development and the Natives Resettlement Act.

Some Chinese tried to circumvent the prohibitions on buying property by using nominees or by forming companies. Nominees were chosen because they belonged to the correct race group for the area in which the property was situated and Chinese purchasers had to depend totally on their trustworthiness. Since the property deeds were registered in the nominees' names, the Chinese had no recourse to the law. Several people lost homes and businesses when nominees later claimed ownership of their properties.

From 1971 the Department of Community Development began to issue permits allowing Chinese to purchase property in White areas, with the proviso that none of the immediate neighbours objected. This initially required the Chinese to undertake the humiliating task of asking all those who lived alongside and opposite the house they intended to purchase whether or not they had objections to a Chinese family living there. A single objection was all that was needed for the family not to be granted a permit. In time this requirement prior to the issue of a permit to Chinese was eventually dropped.

The necessity first to obtain a permit served to delay many property transactions and sometimes led to the loss of a prospective purchase. Property prices too were affected by the implementation of group areas. Within a Chinese group area, the market for potential buyers was limited. In the 'open' market, many Chinese found themselves buying at inflated prices because estate agents knew of the restrictions they faced.[111]

By the late 1970s the granting of permits for Chinese to live in White areas became a formality, although the community in Port Elizabeth still encountered problems until their existing group area was deproclaimed in 1984. Officials kept a close eye on the racial classification of Chinese and their spouses seeking permits, occasionally refusing permits in cases of intermarriage.

When a special commission investigated the application of the Group Areas Act and other legislation in 1983, it recommended that the Chinese 'in respect of ownership and occupation of land be granted the same rights as members of the White group but with the same disqualifications on marriage or cohabitation with a member of another population group'.[112] On 30 May 1985 this amendment was officially promulgated, enabling the Chinese to acquire, hold or occupy property in White areas without permits. In parliamentary discussion it was pointed out that the Chinese lived in White areas and made use of White facilities on a daily basis and that the Bill was 'a small step to reform and in many ways it is just making *de jure* something which is *de facto* in South Africa'.[113]

The Group Areas Act as a whole was repealed on 28 June 1991 when State President F.W. de Klerk signed the Abolition of Racially Based Land Measures Act which abolished racial discrimination in respect of land.[114]

IMMIGRATION

While barriers to Chinese immigration to North America were lowered during and after World War II, the door was totally shut on Chinese entry into South Africa in 1953. Long-standing prohibitions on non-White immigration had already curtailed the growth of the Chinese community by excluding all adult male immigration and only permitting entry to some wives and children.

Hardship in China drove emigrants to seek new lives abroad, particularly the upheaval following the founding of the People's Republic of China in 1949. Despite the restrictive barriers applied to people of colour, South Africa remained attractive to those escaping poverty in search of new lives and better opportunities. No adult Chinese men could enter the country, and the few who did had to use illegal means. Although only a handful of wives and children arrived during the war, post-war statistics reflect a substantial increase before 1953. Of particular note was the number of new brides who were brought into the country from China in the years immediately following the end of the war.

The Immigrants Regulation Amendment Act (No. 43 of 1953) closed off this last avenue of influx, restricting the already small Chinese community to natural increase to swell its numbers. The Central Chinese Association described the Act as a hardship which would affect the community for years and appealed for it not to be applied to the Chinese.

> It will also vitally affect the composition and character of the Chinese population in South Africa. Hitherto the Chinese people in South Africa is a homogeneous community of pure stock. Very few mixed marriages have been contracted by our people. Under the stress of the above restriction however where the choice of a mate is confined in a small community, mixed marriages of an undesirable kind is more likely to occur.[115]

This appeal for the maintenance of racial purity, in keeping with the essential elements of apartheid, no doubt appealed to government officials who readily reassured the Chinese their position would be unchanged. The Secretary for External Affairs stated:

> It should be pointed out that the latest amendment in 1953 to the Immigrants Regulation Act, 1913, does not affect the Chinese people. Their position is still the same as it was under the original Act of 1913, and the Amending Act of 1953 was introduced to cancel the preferential treatment accorded in this respect to the Indian people under prior legislation. The Minister concerned will, however, use the discretionary powers conferred upon him ... in such a manner as to avoid undue hardship in deserving cases. Each case will be treated on its merits ...[116]

The assurance, however, proved to be hollow. Four years after the law was promulgated, Central pointed out that although many applications had been made on behalf of Chinese wives, none had been approved. Despite numerous appeals by organizations and individuals, the situation remained unchanged and schools wishing to employ Chinese teachers encountered many difficulties in obtaining permits for them to enter the country.[117]

More than 20 years later Chinese organizations were still appealing for a relaxation in the immigration restrictions. Wives and children remained excluded, as did any other Chinese immigrants, despite attempts by many local restaurants to 'import' qualified Chinese chefs to cope with the growing demand for Chinese cuisine. In isolated cases, some of these chefs were permitted entry on temporary permits. The Minister of Immigration told Parliament in July 1970 that only White immigrants were permitted to settle in the country; their descent was traced and the application form asked for confirmation that they were 'pure White'.[118]

Strife in neighbouring countries, Mocambique and Rhodesia (Zimbabwe), prompted numerous appeals by community members for their relatives to be admitted into South Africa as refugees. In 1975 the Transvaal Chinese Association asked the government to grant permanent residence to between 80 and 90 families from Lourenco Marques (Maputo), but the majority were refused.[119] These Chinese were forced to seek asylum farther afield in Portugal or South America, although their existing family ties with the local community would have eased their plight and aided their resettlement.

Interprovincial Travel

Chinese repeatedly raised objections to the barriers on interprovincial movement imposed on Asiatics since 1913. This prohibited Chinese from moving freely from one province to another. In an appeal to the Prime Minister in 1954, Consul-General Ting Shao and the Central Chinese Association of South Africa stated:

> We must confess that the Chinese people are quite unable to comprehend the meaning of the inter-provincial barrier to free movement and exchange of residence or trade ... If this restriction is done away with, it will greatly help our people in the pursuit of useful employment amongst themselves and the production of greater unity and identity of interests in the organization of the Chinese people throughout the Union.[120]

The government pointed out that the Chinese as Asiatics were prohibited from moving freely from one province to another.

> The Government regret that they cannot see their way to removing the provincial barriers from the Chinese as a class, but are prepared to consider applications by individual members of the Chinese community who wish to move from one province to another. Obviously the number of moves by any one person that will be considered will be strictly limited and applications based purely on mercenary considerations will not be entertained.[121]

Although it was not strictly enforced, the requirement for Chinese to obtain permits to move to another province, whether for residence, study or merely visiting, applied until the late 1970s.

Illegal Immigration

Chinese organizations periodically had to deal with the thorny issue of illegal immigration, appealing for leniency on humanitarian grounds. Asking for illegal Chinese immigrants to be treated as refugees in 1954, Consul-General Ting Shao and Central said:

> We have collected enough evidence to show that the number of Chinese illegal immigrants spread over the course of the last half century is under 200 ... We can only say that the position of these floating and unsettled people is an unhappy one. Owing to their illegal status their salary scale is always very much below that of other persons in similar employment. They live in a state of perpetual fear and insecurity. They can never hope to establish any state of settled existence ... Wherefore we suggest that the presence of these people in the country be accepted either by having their temporary permits indefinitely renewed or that special permits be issued to them on the basis of refugees.[122]

The government showed sympathy for this appeal, pointing out they had records of 125 Chinese, of whom 107 had confessed illegal entry when they registered in terms of the Aliens Registration Act of 1939. Most of these people had been in the country for 15 to 35 years, had married and raised families and would suffer hardship by being deported. Provided they did not have a criminal record, the government was prepared to allow those who had confessed in 1939 to remain in the country. Those who had entered subsequent to 1939 would have to leave, although officials remarked: 'One must not lose sight of the fact also that at the present moment they cannot be deported owing to the state of affairs in China.' The government said they hoped that Formosa (Taiwan) would co-operate in receiving the remaining illegal immigrants.[123]

Over the following years, illegal immigrants persisted in attempts to join family members in South Africa, often stowing away on ships which docked at Lourenco Marques and Durban. By the mid-1960s, the issue assumed grave proportions for the Chinese community as a whole. Community members said after the assassination of Prime Minister Hendrik Verwoerd in September 1966, police launched a thorough investigation into illegal immigration because of false documentation discovered in the assassin's possession.

The South African government was vocal in its opposition to communism, enacting stringent legislation to enable it to prosecute those deemed to be furthering the doctrine. Illegal immigrants from mainland China were generally assumed to be 'communists'. In May 1967, the Minister of Justice told Parliament that several hundred Chinese who entered South Africa illegally were brought in by methods that were the same as those used by communists to infiltrate agents into other lands.[124] South Africa had maintained diplomatic relations with China from 1905 and after the Communist Party gained control of mainland China in 1949, the Chinese Consulate-General, based in Johannesburg, continued to represent the Nationalist Kuomintang government of the Republic of China which had moved to Taiwan.

Over several months at the end of 1966 and the beginning of 1967, nearly 400 Chinese were questioned in connection with the smuggling of people into the country from China. Of these, 21 from Pretoria, Johannesburg and Durban were held under

Illegal Immigrants Petition

When more than 100 Chinese confessed to being illegal immigrants in 1939, they would have been deported but for the outbreak of World War II. By 1945, immigration officials were still adamant that the authorities should not allow 'the accident of war' nor claims that the immigrants had been in the country from 15 to 30 years to influence their decision.

> 'To be lenient is simply to put a premium on illegal entry, the argument being that if illegal entrants can only succeed in keeping underground for a sufficiently long period the Government will allow them to remain in the Union.'[125]

The authorities stated they were aware that illegal immigrants had been brought into the country 'with the connivance of a former Chinese Consul-General who ... introduced them as typesetters on the Chinese Gazette, a quasi-Consular publication. Others, of course, made their way into the Union surreptitiously across the Portuguese East African border.'[126] Officials felt this involvement by the Consulate had prejudiced sympathetic consideration for all the illegal immigrants.

The immigrants themselves had formed an organization called the Illegal Entrants Society to enable them to work together to stave off their anticipated deportation. Ah York, a member of the Transvaal Chinese Association, was asked to act as chairman for the organization and to address appeals to the relevant authorities. In February 1947 he visited Cape Town to raise the subject with influential members of government and also addressed petitions both to the Prime Minister as well as King George VI who was visiting South Africa on a royal tour with his family.

The petition to the King, signed by 115 Chinese, appealed for his intervention to prevent their deportation. Pointing out that the government was granting amnesty to long-term prisoners on the occasion of the royal visit, they asked that their illegal entry be condoned.

> 'Your Petitioners pray His Majesty will sympathetically consider our unfortunate position, and that in view of the number of illegal entrants in the Union is just a small figure as compared with the very large number of European Emigrants who are shortly to arrive in the Union at the invitation of the Union Government, Your Petitioners ask most humbly that His Majesty may recommend free-pardon and grant us the necessary permission to enable us to remain the the Union ... '

They said they had made South Africa their home and although illegal entrants, they had not committed any crimes in the country and had lived 'respectably, harmless and law-abiding'.[127] Whether or not the King made any recommendation is not known, but the case remained unresolved for several more years until the authorities, in the mid-1950s, permitted them to remain in South Africa.

South Africa's 180-day detention laws which allowed detainees to be seen only by a magistrate and State officials.[128] Two of the detainees, however, died while they were being held by police. Although relatives questioned the circumstances in which they died, inquests returned findings that the official causes of the deaths of Leong Pin, 50,

Chinese die in Detention

Of the 21 Chinese held for questioning in connection with illegal immigration at the end of 1966, two died in detention and at least one was known to have attempted suicide.

Leong Yen Pin, 50, a Chinese cook employed at the Ming Saan Restaurant in central Johannesburg, was arrested on 18 November 1966 and detained at the Leeuwkop prison in terms of the 180-day detention clause. On the following day he was found dead, hanging by his shirt. Although community members have questioned the circumstances surrounding his death, an official inquest returned a finding of suicide by hanging.[129]

Ah Yan, 63, a Chinese general dealer arrested on 30 November 1966, was found hanged in the cell which he shared with three other Chinese at the Silverton police station in Pretoria on 5 January 1967. According to evidence given at his inquest, a policeman said the detainee had tied a sock around his neck and used socks to hang himself from a water pipe in a shower cubicle. The District Surgeon of Pretoria testified that the only marks on Ah Yan's body were those around his neck and it was not possible for anyone else to have hanged him otherwise there would have been marks from a struggle.

The attorney representing Ah Yan's family asked the court to call for evidence from detainees to establish what had happened in the cell prior to the hanging. The prosecutor opposed the suggestion saying the State had done all in its power to meet the requests of the family and the Consul-General, and had also allowed a doctor representing the family to be present at the post-mortem. He said two of the detainees in the cell were asleep when the third discovered Ah Yan's body in the shower cubicle.

The court returned a finding that Ah Yan had died as a result of hanging and that 'no one was to blame'.[130]

a cook from Johannesburg, and Ah Yan, 63, a general dealer from Pretoria, were suicide by hanging.[131]

In urgent negotiations with the police, Consul-General Lo Ming Yuan, was asked to co-operate in calling for the voluntary surrender of all illegal Chinese immigrants in the community. These included any who held false birth certificates, identity cards and residence papers and those who had no residence documents. In turn, Consul-General Lo asked that all who surrendered voluntarily would not be detained, that no bail would be required and that they would be issued with 'emergency' residence documents. He also asked for the immediate release of those in detention. The police said those who surrendered voluntarily would not be detained, but had to provide information on when and how they entered the country and would have to stand trial. The Department of the Interior eventually agreed to allow the Consul-General to issue special temporary residence documents until the immigrants were tried in court. In early January 1967 Consul-General Lo wrote to Chinese associations outlining the situation and stating that the decision on whether or not to surrender rested on each individual.[132]

As the investigations continued, fear spread throughout the community. Threats were relayed that the police were prepared to raid every Chinese home countrywide and squads would surround areas where Chinese congregated to search and detain suspects.[133] Community members were closely questioned and government officials in Port Elizabeth visited cemeteries collecting information from tombstones to compare with papers produced by Chinese suspected of being illegal immigrants. Both the Consulate-General and Central issued circulars in Chinese warning the community of the consequences if illegal immigrants did not come forward to give themselves up.

After a meeting with the head of police in Johannesburg in February 1967, the acting chairman of Central, Dr Norman Yenson, issued a circular saying he had been asked to convey the following message to the community:

> The police chief showed sympathy for the Chinese, including the difficulties experienced by escapees from Red China. Those who had surrendered were issued with temporary residence papers and were allowed to return home.
>
> Many illegals had however not surrendered despite this sympathetic attitude and this was a disappointment. If there was no increase in the number of surrenders, the police would investigate the entire Chinese community — person by person, house by house — which would be unpleasant for all the Chinese. Whether the Chinese volunteered or the police had to arrest them, ultimately all illegals would be found. Their fate depended on the authorities and they could not be guaranteed rights to remain in South Africa.
>
> Illegals who surrendered and made satisfactory statements would not be detained but would be given temporary permits, renewable monthly. Later when decisions were made on their future, their degree of co-operation would be considered.
>
> Illegals who did not surrender would be detained and could not expect sympathetic treatment. They could expect to be deported.
>
> South African born Chinese who resisted or obstructed investigations would reap far-reaching consequences. Those who harboured illegals would be arrested too. The Chinese in South Africa would suffer unfavourable repercussions, especially in the field of White public opinion. Therefore the Chinese had to be fully aware. From the police standpoint, whichever method was employed, the end results would be the same. Chinese had to investigate and pick out the illegals as this matter affected their future in South Africa. Time was limited and the threatened police action might soon be taken.[134]

Consul-General Lo also reported that the police were not satisfied with the number of illegal immigrants who had surrendered by mid-February 1967. They had told him that those who hoped to escape detection were deluding themselves. Because leniency had already been shown, the Consul-General could not protest against further police action which might include surrounding areas where Chinese congregated.

The situation was further exacerbated as police began searching Chinese homes in the Kliptown area of Johannesburg. Teams of young Chinese volunteers in Johannesburg visited homes every night to distribute appeals to the illegal immigrants to surrender and to ensure the message reached the community.[135] Police had also started checking from shop to shop in Port Elizabeth, Uitenhage and Grahamstown where they took statements from Chinese which were compared with immigration files.[136]

In April 1967, a Chinese man from Pretoria was tried and imprisoned for three years after he was found guilty on 17 charges of forging false identity cards and birth certificates. In the following month an official of the Department of Immigration was sentenced to nine years and nine months' imprisonment after he was convicted on 36 charges of accepting bribes to issue identity documents for illegal Chinese immigrants.

Between 1960 and 1966 he had received more than R36 000. The judge said because Chinese who entered the country illegally could not be deported since China refused to take them back, the accused had placed the State in a grave quandary.[137]

The publicity accompanying the court cases further highlighted fears of the spread of communism as reports referred to hundreds of 'Red Chinese' who had entered the country illegally because of corruption in the Department of Internal Affairs. The Minister of Justice said statements had been taken from 400 witnesses, the majority of whom had come from 'Red China' and of these police had detained 21. A major Afrikaans newspaper pointed out that the question had been raised in various quarters whether it could be assumed that the immigrants were bona fide refugees from Red China or whether the presence of some of them in the long term could be regarded as a danger to internal security.[138]

Fears of the repercussions that such speculation could have on the entire Chinese community prompted the acting chairman of Central, Dr Yenson, to call an immediate press conference. Appealing for sympathy to be shown to the illegal immigrants, he denied that any were communist spies and said they were in fact refugees from the tyranny of communism who had desperately tried to reach the security of a country like South Africa. He asked that they be allowed to stay in South Africa and said that the 400 refugees included men, women and children, most of whom were settled in productive work and had entered the country at great hardship.

> They face an uncertain future, and they are strongly anti-Communist like the Chinese in South Africa, who have a good record for this and have first hand knowledge of Communism through contacts with their own relatives who have fled from Communism.[139]

Dr Yenson said to his knowledge not one single communist plant had been found among them. It was realized that illegal immigration was an international problem and the government could not ignore it, but he wanted the public to realize that the South African Chinese were avowed anti-communists.[140]

Consul-General Lo Ming Yuan too worked strenuously to clear the illegal immigrants from suspicion of communist affiliations. Community members repeatedly tell how he reassured the authorities by staking his personal reputation on their good standing. Former chairman of the Pretoria Chinese Association, Shiang Chum, said: 'If Mr Lo had not been here, many Chinese would have been in jail. He put his neck out to say they were not communists ... he guaranteed he would stand security for them.'[141] In mid-1967 press speculation and further potentially damaging publicity on communism within the Chinese community came to an end.

Consul-General Lo continued negotiations with the authorities and urged affected Chinese to form an organization to plead their case. He called a public meeting at the Chinese School in Johannesburg to appeal again to those with false papers or without papers to surrender to the police. Approximately 380 members joined a newly formed organization, simply named The Chinese Club, which worked closely with the Consul-General over the next few years to legalize their residence. Initially they were given temporary residence permits, renewable every few months, then permanent residence and eventually citizenship.

Lo Ming Yuan

One of the Consuls-General who left a lasting impression on the Chinese community in South Africa was Lo Ming Yuan. His insight into their concerns and his willingness to take up the cudgels on their behalf, combined with his ability to communicate in Cantonese, enabled him to build up an exceptionally close relationship with the local community.

Born in Shanghai in 1922, Lo Ming Yuan completed his schooling in Chungking before joining the foreign service and completing his university studies in Malaysia. Recalled to the foreign ministry in China while the government was on the retreat from the communist forces, he described how officials were forced to move from Canton to Chungking, on to Chengdu, then to Hainan island and finally Taiwan by December 1949. He was part of the Republic of China's (ROC) mission to the United Nations Congress in Paris before being posted to South Africa in 1953 as a consul to work with Consul-General Ting Shao.

Angered by his early encounters with petty apartheid, he soon became a tireless campaigner for better treatment for Chinese.

> 'When the Consul-General and I went to Pretoria on business, there was nowhere for us even to have a cup of tea or a simple lunch. Twice we were chased out of restaurants ... When I protested to the protocol department, they told us we had to give them 24 hours' notice and they would make advance arrangements with a restaurant... We decided rather than do this, or take a flask of tea in the car with us, we visited Chinese friends in Pretoria ... mostly Mr C.P. Law, and the Winchiu family who were very kind to us.
>
> We heard from people about all the places Chinese could not go ... and whenever I heard of Chinese being insulted or humiliated, I asked them for all the details and I took up the matter. I went to the banks, the post office, railway station, hotels, Department of Interior to talk to them to see what could be done.'[142]

During three extended postings to South Africa for a total period of 11 years, from the 1950s to the 1980s, Consul-General Lo played a significant role in the many issues which confronted the Chinese, not least of which was the 'illegal immigrants' crisis in the late 1960s. Many community members spoke highly of his integrity and commitment and described him as the finest diplomat to have worked with the Chinese in South Africa. He served the ROC as Ambassador to African states such as Swaziland, Lesotho and Malawi and has held high office in the Ministry of Foreign Affairs.

The Chinese Club chairman, Ignatius King, spoke highly of the role played by Consul-General Lo, saying 'If it wasn't for all that Mr Lo did, I don't know what would have happened.'[143] He said the Consul-General assisted the club in making many representations to various government departments, including an appeal to the Prime Minister. Out of gratitude to Consul-General Lo, the communities of Johannesburg and Pretoria raised more than R20 000 to establish the Lo Ming Yuan Scholarship in 1967. Up to nine scholarships were offered annually to university students on the basis of academic merit.[144]

Curbs on Chinese immigration were relaxed from the late 1970s when investors from the Republic of China on Taiwan (ROC/Taiwan) were granted special permission to enter the country. As the relationship between ROC/Taiwan and South Africa warmed, Chinese immigrants were even permitted to establish themselves in the Orange Free State, the province from which Asiatics had been barred since 1891.[145]

SOCIAL AMENITIES

Distinction was generally drawn between *grand* apartheid and *petty* apartheid to separate the fundamental tenets of the policy from those which were essentially cosmetic. Social segregation in the provision of separate public facilities and amenities was usually described as *petty* apartheid since it functioned on a superficial rather than intrinsic level. For non-Whites however such segregationary measures constituted daily, humiliating pin-pricks, instances in which 'even piffling laws could have a severe impact'.[146]

Cinemas, theatres, hotels, restaurants, buses, trains, hospitals and such public amenities had customarily been segregated, but with the implementation of the Reservation of Separate Amenities Act (No. 49 of 1953) a uniform 'colour bar' was imposed on all public premises and vehicles. Through this legislation, apartheid was extended to parks, libraries, beaches, civic halls and the like, bringing in its wake separate entrances, queues, counters, toilets and those ubiquitous signs saying 'Whites Only/ Slegs Blankes' and 'Non-Whites only/Slegs Nie-Blankes'. By equating 'colour' with 'class', the law effectively reserved the best facilities for Whites, regardless of their class, and relegated whatever was left to all non-Whites.

It defined *public premises* as

> any land, enclosure, building, structure, hall, room, office or convenience to which the public had access, whether on the payment of an admission fee or not but does not include a public road or street;

and *public vehicle* as

> any train, tram, bus, vessel or aircraft used for the conveyance for reward or otherwise of members of the public.

The law reserved such public premises and vehicles 'or any counter, bench, seat or other amenity or contrivance in or on such premises or vehicle, for the exclusive use of persons belonging to a particular race or class'. A fine of not more than £50 and/or imprisonment of not more than three months was laid down for those wilfully using facilities not set aside for them. Representatives of foreign governments were exempted from these restrictions. The law further stipulated that the provision of such separate facilities, 'whether past or future, could not be ruled invalid on the grounds that provision had not been made for all races, or that the separate facilities provided for the various groups were not substantially equal'.[147]

Apartheid signs made it clear which race was entitled to use which public facilities.

Chinese men at East London station use the bench reserved for 'non-Europeans'. The benches under cover are reserved for 'Europeans only'.

Chinese Position

Applying the Reservation of Separate Amenities Act to the Chinese proved to be particularly problematic, highlighting as it did their ambiguous position in the indistinct no-man's land between White and Black. By the end of World War II, a few informal social privileges had been extended to the Chinese. They were permitted to use some White amenities such as cinemas and public transport, particularly in the more cosmopolitan cities, such as Johannesburg, Durban and Cape Town.

In March 1954, the Central Chinese Association appealed for the Chinese to be exempted from the new law, pointing out that differential treatment had in the past been accorded to them and its application was therefore unjustified. The government replied that the legislation was primarily an enabling act, applied by various authorities, and it was therefore not possible to grant the Chinese a general exemption. Sympathetic consideration of the Chinese would be given, within the limits permitted by law.[148]

Because officials and entrepreneurs in all walks of life could enforce the colour bar, there were many discrepancies in its application countrywide. Some cinemas admitted Chinese, just as did some restaurants. The uncertainty of whether or not they would be allowed admission, hesitancy over which queue or entrance they should be using and overall fear of embarrassment led many Chinese to avoid frequenting public facilities. When incidents occurred, Chinese associations in each area took up individual cases with local authorities and also worked through the Consulate-General to secure some concessions through quiet diplomacy and the cultivation of a wide network of contacts.

In early 1960 the Kimberley Chinese Association, through the efforts of its chairman, Meng Chan Yan, obtained permission for Chinese to be admitted to White provincial hospitals in the Cape Province. The Director of Hospital Services said admission would be left to the discretion of medical superintendents who would decide on suitable accommodation for Chinese patients, based on local circumstances. Whenever practicable, Chinese patients should be kept in separate rooms and attended to by White nurses.[149]

In the Transvaal, however, the strict segregation of hospital treatment had potentially dangerous consequences. Johannesburg couple, Terry and Mary Lai King vividly described the night they were involved in a motor car accident in the early 1960s as the most humiliating experience of their lives in South Africa. Mary Lai King suffered a double fracture of the pelvis and her husband cuts to the face, but when they were wheeled into the casualty ward of the Johannesburg General Hospital, they were 'literally chased out'.

> The superintendent took one look at us and said 'Chinese! They can't come in here. This ward is for Whites only. They must go to the non-White section.' So we were carried back out to the ambulance and driven to the non-White hospital where it was dark and packed with people, sleeping on concrete slabs and on the floor. Then a nurse came along and said: 'We can't attend to you. You must call your house doctor because there is no doctor here.'

Their house doctor arrived several hours later and arranged for their admission to a private White hospital, together with their injured companions, Kenneth and Edith Whyte.[150]

Representations to the authorities, extending as far as the Prime Minister, Dr Hendrik Verwoerd, were unsuccessful in securing permission for a Chinese girl to undergo nursing training at a White hospital. In 1962 and 1963, Catholic priest, Fr Michael Tuohy, wrote numerous letters on behalf of June Ho to the South African Nursing Council, the Department of Community Development, the Minister of Health and finally the Prime Minister. The barrier to her training was the proviso in the Nursing Act that hospitals would commit an offence by allowing any White person to be under the supervision of someone who was not White. As a Chinese trainee who would eventually attain seniority over those who entered training after her, she would have to supervise juniors — a situation which was not legally permitted.

The Nursing Council pointed out that as a Chinese, Miss Ho was deemed to be Coloured. In his reply, the Prime Minister said although the government had a high opinion of the Chinese ...'This does not make solutions in individual cases easier, since the more general implications of any decision must be overriding. After careful investigation and consideration it has become quite clear that the legal position cannot be altered to meet single cases, and that training at a European Hospital would not be possible.'[151] June Ho did not train as a nurse and eventually followed another career path. Generally, employers feared the consequences of allowing Chinese to hold supervisory positions over Whites, a situation which denied many the opportunity to advance their careers.

Appealing to the government for a reappraisal of the Chinese position in early 1962, Central enumerated facilities at which Chinese were accepted with Whites. Problems had generally not been encountered with theatres, cinemas, restaurants, hotels, private hospitals, trains, post offices, ladies' hairdressers and public conveniences. Chinese in Johannesburg and Pretoria were not admitted to provincial hospitals or municipal health clinics, and only in Port Elizabeth and Durban were Chinese permitted to use railway buses. Only a few gents' hairdressers in most cities would accept Chinese customers. As far as sporting activities were concerned, up to 1962, Chinese belonged to White sports clubs, played on their teams and also represented their provinces and universities in sports such as basketball, badminton, table tennis and softball.[152]

From 1957, in terms of proclamations prohibiting mixed audiences in cinemas, theatres, civic halls and at sporting events, permits were required for multiracial gatherings and only granted if separate entrances, seating, toilets and facilities for refreshments were available. The Chinese were particularly affected by a proclamation passed in early 1965 which stipulated that a public hall in a group area proclaimed for one racial group could not be hired by members of any other racial group.[153] In Kimberley, the Annual Chinese Dinner Dance had to be cancelled after a permit was refused for Chinese to use the Constance Hall in the city centre. The charitable fund-raising event was a highlight on the city's social calendar and widely supported by non-Chinese officials and businessmen.[154] In Boksburg in the Transvaal, Chinese were turned away from a school dance at which Chinese food was served.[155]

In addition to general restrictions relating to separate amenities, no provision was made for Chinese to be given social pensions or disability grants from the State. From the mid-1960s organizations and individuals appealed for such aid for Chinese who needed it.[156] By 1972 parliamentarians were told that a total of nine Chinese countrywide were receiving old age pensions of a maximum of R216 per annum (R18 per month).[157] Whites received a basic pension of R38 per month, Indians a maximum of R17 and Coloureds an average of R16 per month.[158] Questioned on whether the gaps between the amounts paid to the various race groups would be narrowed, the Minister of Social Welfare and Pensions replied that different Ministers prescribed amounts for each group. His department handled grants to Whites only 'and can reduce the gaps between such pensions and grants and those payable to the other population groups only by reducing the pensions and grants payable to Whites. Such a step is not contemplated.'[159]

Unwelcome Publicity

The ambivalent position of the Chinese provided countless opportunities for newspapers to highlight the inconsistencies in apartheid. Throughout the 1960s, the community was mortified to see reports on Chinese sportsmen being barred from competitions, professionals being refused employment, an accident victim denied hospital treatment and racegoers turned away from White enclosures at turf clubs.[160] Special concessions granted to the Japanese in late 1961 added further fuel to the fire as newspapers focused on the absurdity of differentiating between the two groups.

In February 1962, railways spokesmen said Chinese who held diplomatic identity cards 'were treated as Whites in all respects'. Ordinary Chinese required 'letters of exemption issued by the Consul-General for Nationalist China' to enable them to use White coaches on long distance trains, but were not allowed into dining cars.

> They are booked in the first coupe or compartment of a White coach either behind or in front of a reserved (non-White) coach and refreshments and meals are served to them in the compartment. On suburban lines, they make use of the facilities provided for Whites.[161]

The letter of reference from the Consul-General testified to a community member's social standing and was required at least until the mid-1970s before Chinese could purchase train tickets.

Despite assurances that diplomatic representatives were exempted from segregationary measures, the Chinese Consul-General was 'slighted' in an incident at South Africa's largest airport in the late 1950s. Although offering no details on this incident, an Afrikaans newspaper columnist described the humiliating treatment of foreign visitors to the country as an unforgiveable error of judgement.[162] In practice, the handful of non-Whites who used the country's national airline were seated separately from other passengers, either to the front or rear of aeroplanes.[163]

Group Areas Again!

The tentacles of the Group Areas Act reached out to encroach upon the domain of the Reservation of Separate Amenities Act. Provisions of one law impinged upon the other, but in practical terms, the effects were a complexity of restrictions on people of colour. Permits were required to use the facilities set aside for a specific group and Chinese

From *The Star*, 18 June 1965.

'A Chinese Gesture ...'

Almost all the Chinese who were turned away from the dinner-dance given by the Parents and Past Pupils Association of St Dominic's Convent, Boksburg, last Friday have refused to accept a refund of money they paid for their tickets.

The Chinese were turned away because the association, when it applied for a mixed audience permit under the new segregation laws, was only allowed to have parents of Chinese pupils at the dance.

These parents did not attend in sympathy with about 50 other couples who had bought tickets, but could not attend.

Mrs M.A. Donnell, chairman of the association said the action of the Chinese people in not accepting refunds was a fine gesture, especially as most of them did not come from Boksburg.

As a result, the organizers made a profit.

The dinner-dance was held to raise money for additions to the convent school.

Chinese food was eaten.

were prevented from frequenting hotels where liquor was served, from renting public halls for social functions and even from writing examinations in the same room as fellow White students.[164]

The Cape Ways Boy Scouts, a Chinese troop formed in Port Elizabeth in 1968, had no problems participating in gatherings with other scouts if they met on private grounds. When Lady Baden-Powell, wife of the founder of the Boy Scouts movement, visited

Boy scouts and girl guides in Port Elizabeth, late 1960s.

the city, the Chinese scouts were not permitted to take part in the processions and displays because the gathering was held on municipal grounds. Instead, they were asked to attend merely as spectators.[165]

Colour zoning also extended to employment opportunities. The Group Areas Act required companies to provide separate canteens and restrooms for employees, a proviso which enabled employers to turn down Chinese applicants on these grounds. Despite a shortage of medical practitioners, a Chinese doctor was refused permission to open a practice in a Coloured area in Boksburg in 1967.[166]

A Chinese motor mechanic was told by the Department of Labour in Port Elizabeth that he had to work in a separate area of the workshop from his White colleagues, and a non-White women's toilet had to be reserved for his exclusive use. On the other hand, a young White apprentice was barred from working for a Chinese journeyman.[167] Even in the field of entertainment, an East London pop group whose lead guitarist was a Chinese had to give up playing at a city hotel in the late 1960s.[168]

Publicity Reaches Fever Pitch

The year 1970 was particularly embarrassing for the Chinese. As officials insisted on the strict application of the laws, the Chinese once again found themselves caught up in controversy. Unprecedented publicity followed numerous incidents where Chinese were barred from a variety of events and places.

There was the case of Rhodes University student, Ava Junkin, who suddenly withdrew from the finals of the Rag Queen contest in Grahamstown after pressure was exerted on her family by university authorities. A fellow Chinese student said her parents feared the repercussions on the community and the possibility that Chinese would not be given permits to attend the university.[169] Then there was the teenager, Patricia Tam, who was barred from participating in an inter-school tennis tournament in the town of Aliwal North in April 1970. A complaint was lodged about her participation and the police intervened, informing organizers they should have obtained a permit for her to compete against White children.[170]

In Port Elizabeth, owners of beachfront amenities which included a putt-putt course and an ice-skating rink were told they were liable to prosecution if they continued admitting Chinese. Billiards and snooker saloons too were off-limits and Chinese were restricted to attending the Port Elizabeth Agricultural Show on one day a week, with other non-White visitors.[171]

In May 1970 a rugby tour of South Africa was called off by a Rhodesian (now Zimbabwean) club which was unofficially told its Chinese scrumhalf would 'not be accepted'.[172] And a month later the University of the Witwatersrand in Johannesburg withdrew from the inter-varsity weight-lifting championships in Bloemfontein after the Rector of the Orange Free State University said he 'could not possibly allow' participation by two Chinese team members, Ernest Ling and John Lam. He asked: 'How can I accept a team which does not consist of White members only?' and added that Asiatics were only permitted to stay in the Free State for 24 hours.[173]

One of the most notable incidents was the expulsion of Chinese schoolboys from

SUNDAY TRIBUNE. AUGUST 2, 1970

CHINESE AND WHITE GIRLS TOLD: 'YOU CAN'T HAVE A GAME OF NETBALL'

Now petty apartheid hits schoolchildren

Staff Reporter

saloons to bar Chinese

Chinese must get permit or quit

STAFF REPORTER

Situation of Chinese still obscure

Chinese toddlers must quit creche

Publicity on the invidious position of the Chinese reached fever pitch in 1970. After numerous incidents in which ridicule was directed at government policy, the Chinese were permitted to mix on a social and sporting level with Whites.

Prime Minister B.J. Vorster's apartheid policy was made the butt of this cartoon when a Chinese girl was barred from playing in a tennis match against Whites.

an aptitude test in Johannesburg on the grounds that it had been designed for Whites only and results from Chinese would be unreliable. Questioned about the matter in Parliament, the Minister of Labour maintained that his department had no tests which were standardized for a group with a 'Chinese cultural background'. Opposition politicians greeted the remarks with 'howls of derision' and psychologists were drawn into a public debate on the cultural adaptability of tests.[174]

Reviewing the position of the Chinese, a journalist wrote:

> The Chinese are back in the news again — and how they hate to be there. To be written about is to invite attention and for Non-Whites who generally manage to stay on the White side of the line, attention is never welcome.[175]

The Nationalist Sunday newspaper, *Dagbreek*, appealed to politicians and left-wing groups to leave the Chinese alone and not to use them to further their political ends. An editorial asked 'how many blows the tiny Chinese community can endure before losing their dignity and silent acquiescence'.[176] That the 'Chinese issue' was evoking more than its share of attention was commented upon by another newspaper editor who wrote:

> It seems paradoxical that one of South Africa's smallest ethnic minorities — the Chinese community of 8000 — is dealing some of the heaviest blows to the crumbling wall of applied apartheid. Soul-searching in Nationalist intellectual circles has, possibly, been more evident over the Chinese question than with any other problem of racial segregation.[177]

The national furore which erupted over eight Chinese toddlers at a White creche in Port Elizabeth however seems to have been the final straw. The children were threatened with expulsion after an anonymous complaint about their presence in the White group area of Newton Park in July 1970. Newspapers reported the incident under emotional headlines such as 'Tears over creche bar on Chinese' and 'Babies' fate is up to Cabinet now'. Politicians criticized the Department of Community Development for heeding complaints, pointing out that the publicity harmed South Africa's reputation throughout the world.[178] Although the necessary permit for the creche owner to care for the children was initially turned down, it was later granted by the Minister of Community Development, Blaar Coetzee.[179]

Chinese 'Exemption'

Under siege in both the press and Parliament, the Minister had to be seen to be taking action. Within days of allowing the children to remain at the creche, Coetzee announced that a blanket exemption would be granted for Chinese to mix freely with Whites at sport and social gatherings. He told Parliament that permits would no longer be necesssary to allow Chinese and Whites to mix socially and at sporting gatherings, and he would personally deal with any problems which arose.

> I also want to make it quite clear to everybody that I will definitely not take any notice of crackpot objectors and isolated trouble makers.

The Minister stated that although the Chinese were a separate racial group with a separate identity, they were too small a group to be given separate facilities. They would therefore be allowed to attach themselves to one or another group and if there were no complaints, the government would not take exception.[180]

Progressive Party Member of Parliament, Helen Suzman, questioned what sort of civilization there was in South Africa 'when people are only left in peace provided no bigoted crackpot has made a complaint'.[181] Editorial writers were quick to point out

The Argus newspaper of 4 July 1970 summarized the anomalous position of the Chinese in the following news item:

Scourge of Apartheid Spreading

From weight-lifters to beauty queens. From ice-skaters to national all-star basketball championships. From nursery school children to university students. No Chinese can escape the escalating scourge of petty apartheid.

The alarming increase in the number of 'disgraceful' incidents of discrimination against Chinese will be a talking point at the next session of Parliament.

Mr Hendrik van Zyl Cillie – 'new boy' – in the United Party Parliamentary team, will be seeking 'justice and clarity' for the hopelessly confused Chinese in the Eastern Cape.

Mr van Zyl Cillie freely admits an allegiance with the city's Chinese community.

His narrow victory over Nationalist Willie Delport in the marginal Central constituency here was attributed in part to voters' 'seething discontent' at the treatment suffered by the city's Chinese community.

Now this treatment is continuing and Mr van Zyl Cillie has stated that he will demand justice be done.

'For years the Chinese have enjoyed equal rights with Europeans — voting rights included — why the devil must they now suffer this inhumane and unjust treatment?' he asked.

In recent months the blacklist of incidents involving the Chinese community has grown.

BANNED — from ice-skating on the city's seafront ice-rink
BANNED — from a primary school tennis tournament in Aliwal North
BANNED — from a university rag queen competition
BANNED — from the basketball league after 16 years
BANNED — from an inter-varsity weight-lifting competition at Orange Free State University

The normally publicity-shy Chinese, reluctant to cause conflict, have welcomed the offer of help from Mr van Zyl Cillie.

Mr Gordon Loyson (chairman of the Eastern Province Chinese Association) said this week he was pleased someone had taken his people's interests to heart.

'Our community once numbered about 2000 — now following the Group Areas Act delimitation at least 200 Chinese have left the city for London and Canada,' he said.

'Normally I would not comment on the way we are treated — that should be left to our consul in Johannesburg.

'I cannot help but say how happy I am that someone is fighting our cause,' he added.

that the Minister's exemption merely restored the status quo by which Chinese had been accepted for years at sporting events and in places of entertainment and placed them in the same position as they were prior to the intervention by members of his department.[182]

Isolated incidents involving the Chinese continued to surface in the next few years, the majority relating to the application of the Group Areas Act. On the sports front, students from the University of Port Elizabeth were forbidden to play against a Rhodes University basketball team in mid-1971 because it included Chinese players. Although the game later went ahead, the Chinese were not allowed to attend a post-match function, so the whole Rhodes team boycotted the occasion.[183]

In December 1979, many restrictions on the multiracial use of facilities were relaxed with 'blanket exemption permits' in terms of the Group Areas Act. Among the facilities desegregated were: libraries, private hospitals, theatres and halls, conferences, private clubs, exhibitions and fetes, drive in cinemas, circuses, cafes and restaurants.[184] Finally, in June 1990, the Reservation of Separate Amenities Act of 1953 was repealed by the Discriminatory Legislation regarding Public Amenities Repeal Act.

OTHER APARTHEID LAWS AFFECTING CHINESE

Numerous other segregationary laws affected the Chinese to a greater or lesser extent. This section deals with the Chinese position in relation to political rights and marriages across the colour line, commonly called mixed marriages.

The Franchise

Chinese had never had any political rights in South Africa except for a handful of male property owners who could vote in the Cape Province prior to 1956. With the passing of the Separate Representation of Voters Amendment Act (No. 30 of 1956), all Coloured and Asian men in the Cape were removed from the common voters roll and only given indirect representation in Parliament. In 1968 separate councils were established to give the Coloured and Indian groups authority over their own affairs, but the Chinese position was not given any consideration.

From the mid-1970s, public attention was increasingly focused on the status of the Chinese. Journalists predicted that Chinese could become 'the first "disqualified" group to gain all White privileges' and United Party politicians proposed 'the full inclusion of the Chinese into the White group' arguing that they should not be denied the franchise.[185]

In early 1978 a Member of Parliament tabled a motion calling on the government to give Chinese South Africans 'the same legal status as white South Africans' and full voting rights on a common roll with Whites.[186] The motion was, however, withdrawn when the Chinese objected, pointing out that they did not want to be classified as Whites. In the Catholic Chinese newsletter, *Inter Nos*, Fr Ignatius Ou stated:

> As Christians, it should certainly not be our objective to seek to be elevated merely to lord over any less fortunate groups than ourselves, but rather to seek to achieve

> equal status whilst at the same time retaining our identities as Chinese and always fostering our rich Chinese culture of which we should be justifiably proud ... our aim should not be to protect an ideal of separate development and discrimination but to strive for the fundamental equality of all South African Citizens.[187]

The Prime Minister, B.J. Vorster, told Parliament in April 1978 that the government had good contact with the Chinese who had never expressed political ambitions.

> They are a law-abiding group of people with no political ambitions whatsoever. We would be doing them a disservice to drag them into the political maelstrom of South Africa; they do not want to be involved in it.
>
> Through the years, not one of them has made representations to me in that regard. In my view, we have a case here where we should allow those people to decide on their own future and that we should not force the issue.[188]

Chinese political involvement, however, became a contentious issue with the formation of the President's Council in 1980. This subject is explored in the next chapter.

Mixed Marriages

One of the first laws passed by the National Party government in 1949 was the prohibition of any marriage between Whites and members of other racial groups. Prior to the promulgation of the Prohibition of Mixed Marriages Act (No. 55 of 1949), several marriages between Chinese and Whites had taken place in the Cape Province, and remained legal. Couples from these two races could not even choose to live together as they faced prosecution in terms of Section 16 of the Immorality Amendment Act (No. 21 of 1950). Other marriages across the colour line, among Non-Whites, were legal and several Chinese married Coloureds, Indians and Blacks.

A number of Chinese were forced to leave South Africa as a result of these laws although others took the risk of remaining in the country. Some Chinese legalized their marriages in neighbouring countries or overseas, although the law expressly stated that such marriages were null and void in South Africa.[189] Police zealously followed up reports of any 'mixed' relationships and for people caught up in such a situation, life was fraught with the fear of discovery.

Johannesburg Catholic priest, Fr Michael Tuohy, told how he solemnized at least 19 marriages between Chinese and Whites while the law was still enforced.

> My attitude was that you can't prevent people of different racial groups falling in love and they have a natural right to marry. It's not for the State to determine who may or may not marry ... These people were Catholic and they had a right to the services of the Catholic Church ... I was a bit nervous in the beginning because if I was found out, I would lose my licence as a marriage officer. I could even have been deported. In the beginning, about 1968, I performed the services behind closed doors. Later I said it was ridiculous and performed them openly. It wasn't in any sense bravado or done to defy anybody. My conscience said these people were Catholic ... their marriage was binding before God.
>
> The reason why most of these marriages have succeeded is that they had so much prejudice to overcome. If they didn't love each other, it would have broken up before ... their love was proved. I did suggest that they go elsewhere to have their civic marriage formalized, so that should they emigrate, they'd have some legal papers.[190]

In Port Elizabeth, Catholic priest Father Ignatius Ou said he had also blessed a handful of mixed marriages. Because White spouses had to be reclassified for the marriage to be legalized, Fr Ou was asked to provide certificates stating that the spouse was accepted by the Chinese community. 'I have to give this certificate to them, because we didn't want any apartheid ... I gave certificates for quite a few marriages.'[191]

Marriage across the White/non-White colour line affected all race groups. To legalize such unions, without compromising the tenets of apartheid, the White partner had to move 'downwards', taking on the classification of his or her spouse. For the purposes of the Group Areas Act, a White man marrying a Chinese woman became part of the Chinese group, while a woman of any group marrying a Chinese man became Chinese. A Chinese woman however who married outside of the White or Chinese group was excluded from the definition of Chinese.[192]

In later years, 'general acceptance' was more widely used as a basis for classification and allowed individuals or families to be reclassified into the group with which they most associated. The increase in the number of reclassifications in the 1980s reflects the easing of the stringent administration of the Population Registration Act, as more non-Whites, including Chinese, were reclassified 'upwards' into the White group.

According to the Department of Home Affairs, most of the reclassifications of Chinese to other groups resulted from intermarriage. In administering the law in the 1980s, due consideration was given to the group into which someone was assimilated and the best interests of children born of a marriage.[193]

Generally, the Chinese had reservations about marriages across the colour line, especially because of problems children from such unions would have in being assimilated into the Chinese community. The thorny issue of racial purity came increasingly to the fore as the Chinese gained exemptions from legislation. In a society in which race determined all aspects of life, Chinese leaders had to confront sensitive issues such as whether or not such children should be admitted into Chinese schools in Port Elizabeth and Johannesburg.

The Immorality and Prohibition of Mixed Marriages Amendment Act, no. 72 of 1985, provided for the recognition of previously illegal marriages across the colour line, and repealed all the provisions of the Prohibition of Mixed Marriages Act.[194]

CONCLUSION

The combined effect of the apartheid laws was to instill a pervading sense of insecurity within the Chinese community. Group Areas legislation made an impact on their livelihood, deprived many of their homes and left them fearing for their future. Throughout the 41 years of this law's existence, the community opposed the setting aside of any separate Chinese area.

Immigration restrictions had long curbed the growth of the population and, in the 30 years after 1953, fewer than 100 Chinese were admitted into South Africa. Uncertainty in terms of what they were or were not permitted to do moulded a community that became increasingly introverted and newspapers during the mid-1960s had this to say:

> Today, the position of the Chinese in South Africa is as invidious as ever. They are the forgotten minority group, the Cinderella people of the Group Areas Act,

while another editorial remarked:

> Suddenly, the pendulum has swung back for them. For 50 years they were the silent community, politely going about their business, avoiding all action that might draw attention to their existence.
>
> Until now they have sometimes been honorary Whites, but only because of a kind of official 'blind eye'... Sometimes they have been plain non-White; the Immorality Act makes this clear.
>
> But, mostly, their status has been surrounded by confusion and uncertainty.[195]

The Chinese way of clarifying the uncertainty was not to protest or campaign publicly. Quietly yet persistently, they appealed for special consideration to be given to their minority status. They sought to improve their position, not at the expense of other groups, but in their own right as Chinese who had made South Africa their home.

12
Seeking Some Concessions

Why did the 'honorary White' status of Japanese affect the Chinese? How did the Chinese adapt to apartheid? How did apartheid help to forge a closely-knit Chinese community? From the formation of the Republic of South Africa in 1961, this chapter explores the position of the Chinese, the anomalous status of the Japanese and the use of the 'permit system' to ease restrictions on Chinese. It outlines too the further expansion of Chinese-only organizations and the way in which sport fostered close ties within the community.

SOUTH AFRICA BECOMES A REPUBLIC

Throughout the 1950s and 1960s, the Chinese had to come to terms with the day-to-day aspects of segregation. Averse to confrontation, they chose the path of negotiation to try to secure some amelioration from discriminatory legislation. Through the efforts of the various regional community organizations, the Central Chinese Association of South Africa (Central), and the Consulate-General, continual representations were made to the authorities to ease restrictions or obtain concessions.[1]

From 1960 the Chinese felt increasingly concerned by the possibility that their position would deteriorate should South Africa became a republic and withdraw from the Commonwealth. Fearing that the country's racial policies would become even more restrictive, they sought to secure their status in the country's new constitution. A deputation from Central met the Minister of the Interior, Tom Naude, and pointed out that the Chinese were loyal, law-abiding citizens and wished to be recognized as an integral and permanent part of South Africa. They asked the government 'to consider making certain provisions in the new Constitution exempting Chinese from the discriminatory laws, and to raise the Chinese to a status equal to those at least of the Lebanese and Turks in South Africa.'[2] Both these groups had previously been treated as non-Whites.

The Minister reassured the delegation that the Chinese were known to be law-abiding and said the government would make concessions in the application of the Group Areas Act to the Chinese. He told them that racially discriminatory laws had been in operation in South Africa for over half a century and it was not possible to alter these overnight. It was also not feasible to make specific mention of the Chinese in the Constitution at that stage. In discussions with the Group Areas Board, the delegation was assured that the Board would not press for the proclamation of Chinese areas and that permits would be given for Chinese to live in parts of Johannesburg, south of the railway line.[3]

On 31 May 1961 South Africa became a republic, severing its ties with the British Crown and Commonwealth. In a referendum limited to the country's White population, a narrow majority had opted for the republic — 52.1% in favour and 47.4% against.[4] The government's commitment to apartheid however set the country on a course which led increasingly to its international isolation. Although an insignificant minority, the Chinese were nonetheless caught up in some of the 'crossfire' from United Nations debates seeking to condemn or sanction South Africa for its policies of racial discrimination.

EXTERNAL PRESSURES: UNITED NATIONS

Faced with restrictions jeopardising their livelihood in South Africa, the Chinese also had to contend with public perceptions of themselves as 'foreigners', a readily identifiable minority who 'belonged' elsewhere. In the early 1960s the Chinese were acutely aware of their vulnerable position and were made to feel answerable for the actions and attitudes adopted by the Republic of China on Taiwan (ROC/Taiwan) towards South Africa. At that time the ROC/Taiwan (also called Nationalist China) was still recognized internationally and held a permanent seat on the United Nations Security Council.

The international community became increasingly critical of South Africa's apartheid policy in the wake of the Sharpeville disturbances of March 1960. When the United Nations Security Council was called upon for the first time to consider South Africa's internal policies as a possible threat to world peace, the ROC/Taiwan voted in favour of a resolution deploring the country's policies. In South Africa, several Chinese questioned the possible repercussions of this action on the local community.

Prominent Kuomintang member, C.P. Yenson wrote to the Minister of Foreign Affairs of the ROC/Taiwan in May 1960 pointing out that the actions of the UN delegate potentially jeopardized the privileges and concessions the Chinese had obtained in South Africa. He also contended that South Africa had in the past staunchly opposed the admission of Red China (the People's Republic of China or PRC) into the United Nations. Should the ROC/Taiwan continue to vote against South Africa, it could lose South Africa's support in future.[5]

At the UN, an increasing number of members supported diplomatic and economic sanctions against South Africa and in 1962 an overwhelming majority in the General Assembly voted for sanctions including the breaking off of diplomatic relations, the closing of ports, the boycotting of South African goods and an embargo on exports including arms and ammunition.[6] Japan was one of 16 countries which opposed the resolution while the ROC/Taiwan supported it.

Chinese community leaders met with Prime Minister Dr Hendrik Verwoerd in November 1962 to discuss the issue. After an hour-long meeting, representatives of Central issued a statement saying that they had, on behalf of the Chinese community, expressed 'deep concern and regret at the unnecessary action of the Chinese delegation to the United Nations in voting for sanctions against South Africa. The community is at a loss to understand this deviation from previous policy. The delegation has now voted against a State with whom China has always been on friendly and cordial terms.' Central also sent telegrams to President Chiang Kai Shek and the Chinese delegation at the UN expressing these sentiments.

Association secretary, Norman Song added: 'We told Dr Verwoerd that we regarded ourselves as South Africans and for that reason we were siding with the government in this matter.'[7] Central chairman, Wellington Ford said Dr Verwoerd had told the delegation that the government was 'very bitter' about the action taken by the ROC/Taiwan government. While individuals could eventually forget such actions, it would not be easy for a government to forget. With the publicity the sanctions vote had been given, it was possible that Afrikaners would harbour ill feelings towards the local Chinese. Ford said Central had emphasized that most community members had been born in South Africa and regarded it as their country.

This incident highlighted the invidious position of the Chinese. Having chosen to work quietly behind the scenes and establish contact with the authorities, they suddenly found themselves having to bear the brunt of the government's ire. In trying to explain the actions of the ROC/Taiwan and protect themselves, they found they had to 'defend' apartheid by declaring loyalty to South Africa.

Several years later the South African Chinese again became involved in a controversial United Nations decision. The anticipated admission of the PRC to the UN in place of the ROC/Taiwan prompted representatives of 285 Chinese organizations worldwide to express their opposition. In a full page advertisement in the *New York Times* of 21 November 1967, they said 17-million overseas Chinese opposed the 'admission of Red China into U.N.' They deplored the lawlessness and wanton destruction of the Cultural Revolution and were 'particularly disturbed by the threat of extinction faced by Chinese culture and tradition on the mainland'. Signatories from South Africa were the Central Chinese Association of South Africa, the Transvaal Chinese Association, the Eastern Province Chinese Association and the Pretoria Chinese Association.

The participation of local Chinese in this drive to exclude PRC from the UN was most likely prompted by the need to show the South African government that they were anti-communist. It was in 1967 that the 'communist witch hunt' in the Chinese community reached its height as hundreds of illegal immigrants were investigated. In

Representatives from the Transvaal Chinese Association arranged meetings with several South African leaders. Seen with Prime Minister Dr Hendrik Verwoerd ...

... and Prime Minister B.J. Vorster.

THE NEW YORK TIMES, TUESDAY, NOVEMBER 21, 1967

ADVERTISEMENT ADVERTISEMENT ADVERTISEMENT ADVERTISEMENT

全僑關切大陸動亂

反對中共入聯合國

17,000,000 Overseas Chinese Oppose Admission of Red China Into U.N.

As representatives of 285 overseas Chinese organizations in 47 countries and territories, we declare once again our opposition to the admission of Red China into the United Nations.

Events of the past year have proved beyond a doubt that the Chinese Communist regime, split in the turmoil of the "Great Proletarian Cultural Revolution," is facing insurmountable difficulties on the mainland. So far, Mao Tse-tung and his followers have "seized control" of only six out of 26 provinces, plus Peking and Shanghai. Tanks and guns have been employed by Maoists and anti-Maoists against each other in Wuhan, Canton and other major cities. Both government and party structures have become increasingly paralyzed. Economic and social order has been disrupted beyond repair. The damage to education from the closing of all schools for 18 months is incalculable.

Driven by xenophobic fury, the Chinese Communists have blindly attacked friends and foes alike. Half of the foreign missions in Peking have been targets of Red Guard demonstrations; two were completely sacked. There were attempts to export the "Cultural Revolution" to Asian and African countries. The recent wave of terrorism in Hongkong is an extension of the lawlessness and wanton destruction from the mainland.

The Chinese Communist regime is not as firmly rooted and stable as it pretends, or as some have described it to be. It has never enjoyed the support of the Chinese people. And because of its desperation, the regime today is more dangerous to world peace and security than ever before. Now it is trying to brandish its crude and limited nuclear weapons for international blackmail.

We represent 17,000,000 overseas Chinese living in every part of the world. While most of us are loyal and peace-loving citizens of the countries in which we live, we cannot view the momentous events now taking place in the land of our ancestors without serious concern. We are particularly disturbed by the threat of extinction faced by Chinese culture and tradition on the mainland.

We urge all Americans to heed the warning sounded by Vice President Hubert H. Humphrey on October 15 that: "The threat to world peace is militant, aggressive Asian communism, with its headquarters in Peking."

We urge the United Nations General Assembly to defeat once and for all the move to bring the Chinese Communist regime into the world body.

At this critical juncture, the Free World must refrain from giving aid and comfort to Mao Tse-tung and his cohorts, for such help will be tantamount to prolonging this tyranny and foreclosing the chance for the enslaved millions on the Chinese mainland to regain their freedom.

The above statement has been signed by 285 overseas Chinese organizations in 47 countries and territories. Their names follow:

Argentina

Yutang Li, Chairman
Chinese Association in Argentina

Australia

Dick Boon, President
Chinese Citizens Society, Victoria

Chao Yut Poh, Chairman
Chinese Chamber of Commerce, Victoria

Kwong Yick, President

Colombia (Continued)

Antonio Ching Yi, Presidente
Fraternidad de Anticomunistas Chinos, Barranquilla

Carlos Fong, Presidente
Centro Social de la Colonia China, Buenaventura

Pun Yi Chow, Presidente
Centro Social de la Colonia China, Santa Marta

Costa Rica

Jamaica

Chen Kung Yee, Chung Koon Pen, Willie Lyn, Executive Members
Chinese Benevolent Association, Jamaica

Chang Hong Gin, Editor-in-Chief
Chung San News

Japan

Lin I-wen, President

Malagasy Republic

Choi Ah-ying, Chairman
Federation pour la Reconquete de la Chine Continentale, Section Mananara-Nord

Lo Tai-yin, Chairman
Federation pour la Reconquete de la Chine Continentale, Section Maroantsetra

Chan Wong, Chairman
Federation pour la Reconquete de la Chine Continentale, Section

Netherlands

Chen Tso Shu, President
Chinese Vereniging Nederland

New Zealand

J. C. Kum, President
New Zealand Chinese Anti-Communist Union

Rev. Y. S. Chau, President
Auckland Chinese Anti-Communist

South Africa

Fok Yue Fun, Acting Chairman
Central Chinese Association of South Africa

Fok Yue Fun, Chairman
Transvaal Chinese Association

Sidney Kim Sing, Chairman
Eastern Province Chinese Association

T. J. Sheng, Chairman
Pretoria Chinese Association

United States (Continued)

Richard C. Moy, Wing-Poy Chan
Co-Presidents
On Leong Chinese Merchants Association, Chicago

Jou Wing, Yin P. Moy, Co-Chairmen
Hip Sing Association, Chicago

You-Mow Mui, Gin H. Wong
Co-Chairmen, Chicago Lodge, Chinese American Citizens Alliance

Mrs. Jean Eng, Mrs. Wayman Wong

United States (Continued)

William F. Mah, President
Chinese Consolidated Benevolent Association
President, Ho-Sun Ning Yung Benevolent Association

Steve M. Jeong, Co-President
Chinese Consolidated Benevolent Association
President, Soo Hing Benevolent Association

Pow Sam Yee, Co-President

The advertisement in the *New York Times* of 21 November 1967 which reflected opposition to the People's Republic of China's admission to the United Nations.

addition, the community had long-standing links with the ROC/Taiwan and an especially close relationship with its Consulate-General in Johannesburg.

THE JAPANESE ANOMALY

In the first year of the new republic, the status of another minority group focused attention on the position of the Chinese. The Japanese who numbered approximately 50 people were granted some 'White' privileges — a special exemption which prompted much comment when it was publicized towards the end of 1961. Newspapers questioned the disparity in treatment between the Japanese and Chinese, two groups which could not be readily differentiated on racial and physical grounds.

South Africa's withdrawal from the Commonwealth and a significant decrease in trade with countries such as Britain and Canada opened up opportunities for other nations to move into the market. Japan's growing need for industrial raw materials had led to the substantial strengthening of trade links with South Africa after World War II. Between 1955 and 1961 Japan almost doubled its exports to South Africa, becoming the country's fourth largest trading partner. In 1961 Japan imported material worth £25.6 million, and exported products amounting to £17.9 million to South Africa.[8]

The maintenance of this trading relationship was widely considered to be the reason for the South African government's decision to grant special concessions to the Japanese as a racial group. As early as 1910, the Japanese had been differentiated from Chinese and Indians in South Africa, enjoying exemptions from liquor restrictions and immigration laws. In April 1961, replying to a question in Parliament, the Minister of the Interior stated that the Japanese were regarded and treated as White for the purposes of the Group Areas Act.[9] This proviso encompassed most aspects of day-to-day life, enabling them to live and work among Whites, to acquire property in White areas and to use facilities such as White restaurants and hotels.

The special status accorded Japanese only seemed to have become more widely known towards the end of 1961 when several newspapers reported a senior government official as confirming that Japanese had been classed as Whites.[10] One of the trade agreements which was often cited with reference to the status of the Japanese was the conclusion of a R180 million deal for Japan to buy pig-iron ore from South Africa in the early 1960s. Inevitably pundits came out with comments such as 'pig-iron and not pigment' counted in South Africa, and even Prime Minister, Dr Hendrik Verwoerd accused opponents of ridiculing the government by their stating one could 'buy Whiteness' with pig-iron.[11]

Explaining the decision made on the Japanese, the Minister of the Interior told Parliament it was in the 'best interests of the country', and added:

> There is a very small number of Japanese here. They visit this country for the purposes of trade (which is to our advantage) and these people are exempt from the Group Areas Act because we do not want to cause them unnecessary trouble and because we want to make things easy for them.[12]

'Making things easy' in fact caused more than a few problems for the Japanese and also exposed inconsistencies in South Africa's complicated apartheid scheme. Although the Japanese were White in terms of the Group Areas Act, they were 'Coloured' for all other laws. The country's fundamental race classification law, the Population Registration Act, was not applied to temporary residents, as most Japanese were, but it did provide for Japanese to be classified ethnically as 'Coloured — sub-section Other Asiatic'. Confusion surrounded their status in terms of laws such as the Reservation of Separate Amenities Act, the Mixed Marriages Act, the Immorality Act and the Census Act. Both government spokesmen and the Press contradicted themselves at various times stating that the Japanese were White and then non-White in terms of these laws.

'Honorary Whites'

Newspapers dubbed the Japanese 'honorary Whites', a condescending contradiction which at once stated that they were privileged yet were not really Whites. The bitingly accurate description was repeatedly used to mock the government and its policies, and to underline the unique status of the Japanese. It was also claimed that South Africa's stance had a historical precedent since Nazi Germany had in 1935 recognized the Japanese as 'honorary Aryans'.[13]

In the first few months of 1962 a series of incidents focused widespread attention on the preferential position of the Japanese. Heated debate among councillors accompanied the decision by the Pretoria City Council to allow Japanese gymnasts to take part in a competition in a municipal hall.[14] But two weeks later the same Council refused permission for a touring team of Japanese swimmers to use a municipal swimming bath. As one supporter of the ban was reported to have stated: 'The Japanese may be civilised but nobody can tell me that they are White'.[15] A flurry of newspaper reports questioned the potential repercussions of this decision on South Africa's relations with Japan as well as the government's stated policy that Japanese should be treated as Whites. Questions were asked of the government and within days the Council rescinded the ban on the swimming bath in the light of 'additional information that has become available'.[16] Town councils in many parts of the country were questioned about their policy on admitting Japanese and Chinese to swimming baths and reflected divergent approaches.

Special consideration for the Japanese was fraught with problems for the simple reason that most people could not tell the difference between Chinese and Japanese. In February 1962 a Pretoria bus driver precipitated a diplomatic incident when he refused to allow a Japanese to board his bus. The Japanese Consul-General lodged a complaint because the man belonged to the consular staff and after a disciplinary hearing, the driver was strongly reprimanded. Both the driver and the city transport department apologized to the Japanese Consul-General.[17] All bus drivers had been instructed to pick up the staff of both the Japanese and Chinese consulates, but not to permit other Chinese on their buses.

Newspapers continued to ridicule the absurdity of differentiating between the Japanese and Chinese and headlines such as 'Confucion' and 'Japanese are in a Chinese puzzle' pinpointed anomalies in their treatment.[18] Anthropologists were questioned on the anatomical differences between Chinese and Japanese, stating categorically that both were Mongoloid and neither were European or Caucasian.[19] An editorial in the *Rand Daily Mail* summed up the approach thus:

> So once again we have this queer logic: the Japanese must be allowed to swim with Whites because they are important commercial allies. The Chinese must be admitted because it is hard to tell the difference between them. And apartheid, they say, is a matter of principle.[20]

Questions were repeatedly asked in Parliament on the status of the Japanese and by May 1962, the Minister of the Interior, Senator Jan de Klerk felt impelled to spell out the government's policy. He criticized Opposition politicians for taking the same approach as the anti-government press in ridiculing the government, saying:

From *The Star*, 13 February 1962.

Honourable bus

There seems to be only one solution for the dilemma in which the bus drivers of Pretoria find themselves. The Municipality of Pretoria will have to establish a School of Oriental Languages as a subsidiary of its transport department.

The situation, as we understand it, is that a bus driver is required to pick up a Japanese or a Chinese if he is a consular official. Ordinary Chinese are required to travel in non-white buses. The position of ordinary Japanese, who may be wool buyers from Tokyo, is a little vague unless they are on their way to a swimming-bath.

Would it be too much to ask visiting Japanese to carry, and wave, a little bale of wool coloured with cherry blossom? As for Chinese of consular status, perhaps they could be persuaded to wear little number plates marked 'C.D.' (which bus drivers would recognize as meaning 'Corps Diplomatique').

It is difficult to imagine Confucius driving a bus in Pretoria but if that grand old man had ever been required to deal with such a problem he would undoubtedly have said: 'Better warm seats in bus than cold hearts outside it.'

> ... they continuously emphasize the discrimination in favour of the Japanese, in an attempt to make all the other non-Whites feel hurt, particularly the Chinese, with the object of destroying good relations ...[21]

Pointing out that the government was not yielding to 'the progressive undermining of its policy of apartheid', the Minister said the Japanese in South Africa were not permanent or numerous, and any measures affecting them would not endanger the continued separate existence of different racial groups.

> From this it follows that it is not necessary to declare them to be Whites, or to classify them as Whites, or to grant them the status of Whites, as various people have alleged, inter alia, in order not to humiliate them ...
>
> No Japanese has therefore been declared White, and no Japanese has been humiliated by our not doing so. Just as little has the dignity of any Chinese been hurt by not declaring him White ...
>
> All that has therefore happened is ... in 1961 it was decided, for purposes of the Group Areas Act, to treat them in the same way as Whites, but that does not justify any ridicule to the effect they have now been declared White. In fact, it only confirmed the practice which had existed for many years, also under previous governments, in terms of which they have always been allowed access to various places together with Whites ...
>
> In the case of Indians and Chinese, the position is quite different from that of the Japanese. The Chinese, who constitute a very peace-loving community of high standing, nevertheless consist of more than 6000 persons who are mainly located in a few centres as settled communities. They cannot, and do not want to, be assimilated, and when taking any action in regard to them the precedent it may set in regard to larger settled communities must be borne in mind ...[22]

The Minister's 'clarification' made sense only to those steeped in the intricacies of the Group Areas Act. Most people did not understand what it meant to be White only in terms of Group Areas Act, and the ensuing confusion created embarrassing situations not only for the government but also for the Japanese and the Chinese. Newspapers were quick to point out that the legal position of the Japanese remained 'as tangled as a Chinese puzzle'.[23]

Throughout the 1960s and early 1970s the Japanese found their 'honorary White' status attracted unwelcome publicity, and was little protection from racial slights. They were turned away from restaurants, refused houses to rent and in 1970 a Japanese jockey was refused a visa to race in South Africa. A prominent Japanese businessman told of his experiences aboard the country's national airline, South African Airways, saying 'SAA had tried to issue him its Non-White ticket — sitting in the front if it is a Viscount and at the back if it is a Boeing'.[24] Japanese seamen were arrested for contravening the country's Immorality Act, which forbade sexual relations between Whites and non-Whites, but were released after the Attorney-General decided they were to be regarded as Whites.[25]

By 1974 the Japanese temporarily resident in South Africa numbered approximately 600. They established a Japanese school near Emmarentia, a select Johannesburg suburb, holding classes for pupils aged between six and 15 years to prepare them for their return to Japan. A monthly newspaper in Japanese was produced by members of the Nippon Club of South Africa, an organization sponsored by 52 Japanese corporations to promote the welfare of Japanese, friendship between South Africa and Japan and to encourage trade.[26]

As the international sanctions campaign against South Africa gained momentum from 1985, Japan found itself in the somewhat unenviable position of being South Africa's biggest trading partner, with exports in excess of 114 million yen in the first half of 1988. A Japanese diplomatic source said there was great concern over the trade figures which could be incorrectly interpreted as an indication that Japan supported apartheid.[27] The Japanese government promptly started moves to limit trade with South Africa. Sanctions had earlier been imposed on airlinks, the purchase of Krugerrands, iron and steel, agricultural products, computer equipment, nuclear technology, new investments and government loans.[28] It was only in the 1990s that Japan resumed normal trade relations with South Africa.

CHINESE REITERATE APPEAL FOR CONCESSIONS

As soon as it became widely known in late 1961 that specific concessions had been granted to the Japanese, Central called a special executive meeting to prepare new representations to the authorities. It was decided to brief lawyers for the task and accordingly an extensive 15-page document including statistics on the community and its disabilities was drawn up for submission to the Ministers of Community Development and the Interior.

After summarizing the origins, distribution and position of the Chinese in South Africa, the memorandum appealed for reconsideration of specific aspects of the Group

From *The Argus*, 2 May 1962

Japanese Question as Tangled as Chinese Puzzle

The legal position of Japanese in this country remains as tangled as a Chinese puzzle — in spite of efforts by the Minister of the Interior, Mr J. de Klerk, to clarify the position once and for all in the Assembly last night.

Japanese are treated as White under one law, as non-White under at least three other laws and, under a fourth law, they might be treated as White and non-White.

This is how some M.P.s, poring over their law books, saw the position to-day. But there may be other Acts and by-laws which they have not taken into account.

They point out too, that the main legislation governing Japanese — the Group Areas Act — is so complicated after all its amendments, that not even all legal experts fully understand it.

It seems probable that in practice a Japanese will be treated as White in all his day-to-day affairs — provided he is not mistaken, by those ignorant of oriental cultures, for Chinese.

For a Japanese with a legal mind, however, these possibilities arise:

- Under the Group Areas Act he is White and may occupy a house in a White area.
- Under the Population Registration Act he is classified as 'another Asiatic' and must behave as a non-White.
- Under the Separate Amenities Act, people in charge or control of premises or vehicles can set aside 'any counter, bench, seat, amenity or contrivance' for the exclusive use of Whites or non-Whites or other groups.

WHITES ONLY

Exclusive use, say for Europeans only, can be set aside on any land (including sea or seashore), building, hall, enclosure, room, office or convenience. The law says this must not apply to a public street.

Thus a Japanese, who is in no way classified a European, could find himself legally excluded from swimming pools, park benches, beaches, restaurants and even business offices reserved for Europeans.

Under the Group Areas Act, however, he has access to many of these things. He may attend cocktail parties and dances.

IMMORALITY ACT

A Nationalist M.P. said in Parliament this week a Japanese is non-White in terms of the Immorality Act. A Japanese is also non-White in terms of the Mixed Marriages Act.

Not only do there appear to be enough legal contradictions to confuse Confucius, but political contradictions have also arisen over the government's policy on Japanese.

Mr de Klerk told Parliament yesterday that it was incorrect to suggest that Japanese were treated as White in the interests of trade. It was simply because there were so few of them. (Because there are many Chinese, they are treated as non-White).

But Mr P.C. Pelser (Nat, Klerksdorp) said the previous day that although there were few Japanese in the country, many Japanese visitors came on visits mainly concerned with trade matters.

In view of this it was for the benefit of a country that there should be as few obstacles as possible during their stay, he said.

Areas legislation. It was pointed out that the treatment of Japanese as Whites 'has created new problems for the leaders of the Chinese community and has, in fact, created a situation in which the government should reappraise the position of the Chinese community.'[29]

The Chinese conceded that the Japanese community was small and transient, and that the government could grant them special treatment 'without the same socio-political repercussions that would result from similar treatment of the Chinese'. Nonetheless, the government had, in all justice, to consider and recognize the implications of such action. To maintain the authority of the leaders of the community, the government had to make a substantial concession to Chinese who wished their leaders to press for similar treatment as the Japanese. Furthermore, the memorandum said from historical association and national pride, the Chinese disliked a situation in which the Japanese were more favourably treated as a group. It added that the Chinese government in Formosa (ROC/Taiwan) could perhaps 'be favourably influenced by practical concessions to the Chinese'. The memorandum specifically focused on the Group Areas restrictions Chinese encountered, and a strong appeal was also made for the opening up of educational facilities.[30]

Throughout the 1960s and early 1970s opposition party politicians and the press persistently questioned why the Chinese could not be granted the same privileges as the Japanese. Dr Verwoerd pointed out there were between 6000 and 8000 Chinese who were permanently resident in South Africa and added:

> Even if their standard of living and standard of development is equal to that of the Japanese, one cannot treat them differently from other permanent population groups. If one did that one would be asked to offer the same concessions to the Indians and to the Coloured people.[31]

The publicity was not appreciated by the community and led the chairman of the Kimberley Chinese Association, Meng Chan Yan, to write in a community magazine:

> We also agreed at the Central Association meeting that the English press was doing us more harm than good by pointing out the anomaly in our position and that of the Japanese. We all agreed that this was intended more to embarrass the Government than to help the Chinese.[32]

Community leaders persisted in adopting a low-profile, diplomatic approach to bring about improvements in their position. It was generally held that whatever had been achieved by the Chinese had been through their being 'inconspicuous' and this remained their best course of action.[33] Regional associations took up problems encountered in their areas, and in many cases succeeded in securing sympathetic consideration from the authorities.

The channel through which concessions were granted was the permit system. Although the law laid down prohibitions, permits allowed exemptions, and in the 1960s and 1970s such permits enabled the Chinese to live, trade and eventually buy property in areas for other racial groups, to give receptions and parties for mixed groups in civic halls, to travel from one province to another, to use the railways, to attend universities and technical colleges, to enrol at White private schools (and later government schools), to attend pre-school creches, to frequent cinemas and public swimming pools, and even to participate in recreational activities such as sports, miniature golf, billiards and horse-racing.

As concessions, permits represented 'privileges' rather than rights. Often dependent on the sympathy, understanding or whim of officials in different parts of the country, permits were granted on an ad hoc basis which meant the Chinese never really knew where they stood. By the same token, other South Africans were equally uncertain of the Chinese position and through a process which could be likened to trial and error, Chinese initially tested the waters with trepidation, tending mainly to frequent places where they knew the owners would admit them. According to one Chinese:

> The Chinese have no rights — only privileges. 'Privileges' is a concept which makes me angry, cynical and confused; those privileges are not in the statute-book and can be withdrawn at any time; so where do we stand? We are told that we can go into restaurants and hotels, but there is always the chance that we will be asked to leave.[34]

The community fostered good relationships with other racial groups, donating money to charities and worthwhile causes and building up a reputation as a quiet, law-abiding and hard-working section of South African society. By the mid-1970s Chinese were admitted to White state schools and technical training colleges. A sociological study in the late 1970s concluded that the Chinese had become largely accepted by and assimilated into White society, with the younger generation diversifying into the professions and generally regarded as upwardly mobile and economically secure.[35] Such general acceptance led to many officials turning a 'blind eye' to the necessity for Chinese to apply for permits on a social level.

Granting 'honorary White' status to the Japanese was arguably the beginning of the end of the rigid White and non-White divide on which apartheid was based. Not only was the government exposed to biting derision for more than 15 years, but it was also forced to defend what was essentially a contradiction in terms. Critics were quick to point out that the government had 'sold' White status for trade and had compromised the principle of apartheid.

The incident in which a Japanese diplomat was refused permission to board a municipal bus in Pretoria in 1962 has often been cited as a turning point in the authorities' treatment of the Chinese. Given the glare of publicity and the ridicule which accompanied each case of 'mistaken identity', the authorities were forced to realize that the man-in-the-street had real difficulty in telling the difference between Japanese and Chinese. Perhaps in attempting to shield the Japanese from embarrassment, they became less rigid in their application of discriminatory laws to the Chinese.

PROMOTING THE CHINESE

Although the community studiously avoided press publicity relating to its position, it sought out other opportunities to promote an understanding of the Chinese. Many community organizations believed the more the general public knew of the Chinese culturally, the easier it would be for the community to win social acceptance. From the 1940s they had already forged friendships with the many South Africans who had supported fund-raising efforts for the Sino-Japanese War. They willingly responded to all invitations to participate in festivals and charitable functions where they sold Chinese food, displayed Chinese wares and performed traditional dances.

At the 1960 Union Festival, Chinese ran a restaurant and a gift shop and built a colourful float for a procession through the streets of Johannesburg. In Port Elizabeth, Chinese involvement in the local community carnival and other fund-raising activities raised large sums for the P.E. Community Chest. The Pretoria Chinese ran a restaurant called the *Rice Bowl* at the annual agricultural show for five to six years, and Cape Town Chinese often hosted fund-raising dinners.

Because October 10th happened to be a public holiday in South Africa, the community was able to celebrate the Chinese National Day of Double Ten every year. Regional Chinese associations often used the occasion to introduce the Chinese community to influential people from all sectors of society. For the Chinese themselves, Double Ten provided the ideal opportunity for an annual get-together, whether it was a tea-party, picnic or cultural festival. In Johannesburg the Blue and White Sports Club organized a Double Ten dance from the 1950s. It was a glamorous occasion at which Miss Double Ten was crowned, and the dance remained an annual social highlight in the community.

Johannesburg's Chinese participated in the 1960 Union Festival celebrations, parading this float through the city streets.

The stand manned by Chinese at the 1960 Union Festival celebrations, at Zoo Lake, Johannesburg.

Perhaps the most ambitious project to promote the Chinese was their participation in the 1960s in the Rand Easter Show, the largest agricultural and trade show in the country. Staged annually in Johannesburg, the show attracted hundreds of thousands of visitors and, in keeping with South African practice, it was open on certain days to Whites and other days to non-Whites. Major countries exhibited their products and innovations at the show, and community leaders believed a Chinese pavilion would provide the opportunity to present the Chinese as a cultured and advanced part of the international community. The promotion of trade between ROC/Taiwan and South Africa, in line with the precedent set by the Japanese, was seen as a means of improving the position of the Chinese.

The driving force behind the project was Consul-General Lo Ming Yuan who appealed to Chinese to become involved in the venture which was intended 'to elevate the status of local Chinese, to increase trade and to strengthen ties between the governments of our two countries'.[36] Funds were needed for leasing a pavilion, importing goods from ROC/Taiwan and paying for the staff from the China External Trade Development Council. Consul-General Lo called a meeting of community leaders throughout the country in 1967 to form the Sino-South African Trade Promotion Committee which would be responsible for fund-raising and managing the pavilion.

To exhibit at the show was a bold step since it involved the community and consulate in taking out a five-year lease on the pavilion and ensuring that large sums were raised each year to cover expenses. Although some people felt hesitant about such a long-term commitment, they nonetheless gave their support out of loyalty to Consul-General Lo who had played such a significant role in resolving the 'illegal immigrant' crisis in the community earlier that year. A sum of NT $1.5 million was donated by the ROC/Taiwan government for the show while nearly R9 000 had been raised from the Chinese community by July 1967 to host a trade mission from Taiwan and to support the show.[37]

Enthusiasm for the venture ran high in the community and there were many volunteers to model clothes, guide visitors through the exhibits and generally assist wherever needed. Guests stepped through an ornate Chinese archway, flanked by one-ton stone lions, into the two-storey pavilion which housed an extensive array of products from Chinese furniture and handicrafts to textiles, televisions, motorcycles and even a motor car. Local Chinese folk dancers and musicians provided insights into Chinese culture, complemented by an impressive display of Chinese bronzes and pottery. The Chinese pavilion proved to be a major attraction at the show and during its five years — from 1968 to 1972 — won several medals and awards.

As far as promoting the image of the Chinese was concerned, the pavilion at the Rand Easter Show was an achievement. At a time when South Africa did not yet have television, visitors were surprised and impressed at the range of products produced by Taiwan. The show enabled the community to feel a sense of pride in being Chinese and secured for them one concession from petty apartheid — they were allowed to attend the Rand Show on all days.

Controversy surrounded the decision not to renew the lease on the pavilion in 1973. According to Consul-General Wei-Min Lee, who replaced Consul-General Lo in 1970, the ROC/Taiwan had not taken 'a single order' from its exhibition in 1972 and, after five years, 'we have not even been able to get the authorities to allow Chinese people at the show to use the White lavatories'. The show authorities denied that the latter had ever been a problem and 'the reason for Taiwan's withdrawal was political'.[38] The community itself disagreed with the Consul-General's statement and was unhappy over his unilateral action. Since the community had also been responsible for setting up the pavilion, it felt strongly that the Consul-General should have held consultations before ceasing participation.[39]

COPING WITH APARTHEID

Life under apartheid essentially offered the Chinese three courses of action — to resist, to adjust or to escape.[40] Although community leaders avoided the first option, some Chinese did join resistance movements to voice their opposition to the government's actions. Adjustment, compromise and making the best of the situation was considered the only viable choice for the majority, and escape by emigration from the 1960s became an option for those with qualifications or means, and who were unwilling to adapt to life in South Africa.

In the 1940s and early 1950s a handful of young Chinese were closely involved with political organizations such as the Communist Party, the African National Congress and the Indian Youth Congress. Ley Changfoot who had been born in Kimberley in

Some of the many community volunteers who assisted at the Chinese pavilion at the Rand Easter Show in 1968.

One of the highlights of the Chinese pavilion at the Rand Easter Show was a fashion show featuring Chinese models.

1916 was sent to China as a child and became involved in the Chinese Communist Party's activities. Returning to South Africa in the 1930s, he helped establish a Communist Party branch in Kimberley and in East London before the Party was banned in 1950. His name was however well-known to police and he was rounded up in the wake of arrests after the Sharpeville shootings in 1960, and held for six weeks in terms of South Africa's detention without trial laws.[41]

Several Chinese participated in the Defiance Campaign in June 1952, attending mass meetings and joining the civil disobedience drive to defy laws which enforced segregation. One participant, George Changfoot, said he became involved in politics while studying medicine at the University of the Witwatersrand.

> It was a time of tremendous ferment and ideas ... There were only a few Chinese involved, because the community leaders were very pro-Kuomintang, and concerned about action against the Chinese if we took part. I remember attending this mass meeting where Fr Trevor Huddleston addressed about 50 000 people in Alexandra township ... I also gave speeches ... the police would come at 4 in the morning and raid the apartment where I was staying with Indian friends, and strip search us.[42]

Other Chinese who were involved included Douglas Lai, an interpreter at the Johannesburg magistrates' courts and a young medical student, Keem Lau Kee, nicknamed 'Tojo', of Pretoria. Refused admission to a South African university, he studied for a few years in Vermont, USA, before returning home to become actively involved in resistance politics. During the Defiance Campaign, he drove as many as 50 or 60 Blacks in a truck to places such as the Pretoria railway station where they would then use the entrances reserved for Whites in order to defy the law and court arrest.[43]

In adjusting to changing circumstances from the 1950s, the Chinese showed their resourcefulness by diversifying into new occupations, pursuing educational opportunities and forming a host of exclusively Chinese organizations for sport, social and cultural activities. These aspects of the community's life, its aspirations and its quest for an identity will be explored in depth in the remainder of this chapter.

OCCUPATIONAL DIVERSITY

Group Areas legislation made the Chinese realize their vulnerability as a 'community of shopkeepers' and prompted increasing numbers of families to seek out more secure avenues of employment for themselves and their children. In the 1950s only some displaced shopkeepers succeeded in finding alternative premises to reopen shops while the rest had to move into other spheres of activity. No longer self-employed, some started working for others, as storemen and representatives for wholesale companies and as clerks in offices. A number of Chinese made a lucrative living by illegally selling liquor and running lotteries, known in South Africa as 'fah-fee'. This form of gambling was popularized by Chinese in many parts of the world and worked on a system of 36 numbers, each of which had a designated symbol.[44] Its appeal to the poorer classes lay in the fact that fah-fee bankers accepted very small bets and that the game was steeped in dreams and superstition.

Taking part in these illegal activities exposed the Chinese to police raids, prosecution, heavy fines and sometimes imprisonment. Nonetheless, those who had no formal Western education and were unable to read and write English, were restricted to such occupations. Justifying the Chinese position in the mid-1950s, the Central Chinese Association told the Minister of the Interior:

> The Chinese people have often been accused of having dealt in illicit liquor and the promotion of gambling. Superficially such an indictment, of course, is serious enough to exclude us from any sympathy from the Government. And while we do not wish to condone any such practices, we should like to point out that the root causes arose directly from a hostile environment in which every avenue to make a decent honest livelihood is closed to them. In most cases it is through compulsion and not from choice that such people embark on their illegal activity.[45]

A Johannesburg attorney, Alec Oshry, who defended many Chinese on fah-fee and liquor-selling charges from the 1950s, endorsed the view that restrictive conditions and a lack of education caused Chinese to turn to illegal activities.

> Basically the Chinese are law-abiding and were hardly ever involved in serious crime. In Sophiatown, Martindale and Newclare they could only augment their living by selling liquor ... it was the same with fah-fee. I had numerous cases and I would say in 90% of them, I managed to get them off on technicalities. But as the younger people became better educated, it mostly died out.[46]

A better education involved high school and university since technical education was barred. Proportionate to the community's size, the Chinese had an exceptionally high university enrolment rate in the 1950s and 1960s. Many, to avoid problems with finding employment later, entered professions which offered them a measure of independence, for example, medicine, architecture, accountancy and engineering.

The range of job opportunities open was however limited. Community leaders repeatedly appealed for Chinese to be given access to technical colleges to enable young people to become mechanics, electricians, fitters, plumbers etc.[47] Other occupational avenues such as nursing and radiography were closed and employers were reluctant to employ Chinese for positions which could, at some stage, give them supervisory authority over Whites. Chinese receptionists, clerks and office workers were often sought by employers who described them as hardworking and loyal, although there was one obvious advantage for the employer in that Chinese workers were paid less than White workers.

Once qualified, Chinese professionals nonetheless continued to encounter race restrictions. Chinese doctors were not permitted to work in White hospitals until the 1970s and their pay scale was substantially lower than that of their White counterparts.[48] Many young Chinese found difficulties in obtaining employment and although no reasons were given, they were convinced their rejection was due to racial bias.

Had technical and vocational education not been closed to Chinese prior to the 1970s, the community may well have had a more balanced occupational profile. Many parents sent their children to university, whether or not they had the aptitude or inclination to be there. Those who did not succeed at this level had no viable career path and even many who did graduate found themselves in careers they would not have chosen for themselves.

Employment Problems

More than a few qualified Chinese professionals encountered problems in finding employment in South Africa in the 1950s and 1960s.

- I went to university in the USA and majored in electrical and mechanical engineering, with a minor in business administration. I married in 1950, and my wife and I came back to South Africa. I spent about a year looking for a job in Port Elizabeth, could not find one and ended up working in my father's shop. I applied to Ford Motors, General Motors, the SA Railways, and an English cable company. The latter two did not even want to talk to me. I knew at that time a lot of companies wanted qualified people, but I soon got the message that I was not wanted, and went back to San Francisco. (David Low Kum)
- Cecil Date Chong was recommended by the Health Committee of the Port Elizabeth City Council for appointment to the post of analytical chemist and bacteriologist at the municipal laboratories. He had all the necessary qualifications, but was turned down by the government. No reason was given for the decision, and the post had to be readvertised.[49]
- In Johannesburg in the 1960s there were only a few companies that were prepared to accept Chinese employees. Among these were the tobacco companies like L. Suzman, Capital Tobacco and L. Feldman. The Chinese liked to work together because there was safety in numbers. (George Leong)
- I think you had employers who exploited Chinese. Some Chinese never stood up to demand their rights. It was an ugly time. Often in those days, people friendly to the Chinese were very few and far between. I don't blame those who left either. To go to some other place where their dignity would be respected. That early part of the 1960s was the worst part. That's what gave impetus to the emigration. (Father M. Tuohy)

'BRAIN DRAIN'

From 1960 South Africa's internal policies led to the exodus of numbers of non-Whites, either as political refugees in the wake of the country's state of emergency and the banning of political organizations or as emigrants, particularly to Commonwealth countries. Whites were also leaving and concern was expressed in the mid-1960s that South Africa was losing many of its leading scientists, university professors, medical practitioners and experts in various fields.[50]

As the Chinese community felt the impact of discriminatory laws, they too reviewed their future in South Africa. The South African Institute of Race Relations described the uncertainty and insecurity generated by their 'fringe' status in 1966:

> No group is treated so inconsistently under South Africa's race legislation. Under the Immorality Act they are Non-White. The Group Areas Act says they are Coloured, subsection Chinese ... They are frequently mistaken for Japanese in public and have generally used White buses, hotels, cinemas and restaurants. But in Pretoria, only the consul-general's staff may use White buses ... Their future

> appears insecure and unstable. Because of past and present misery under South African laws, and what seems like more to come in the future, many Chinese are emigrating. Like many Coloured people who are leaving the country, they seem to favour Canada.
>
> Through humiliation and statutory discrimination South Africa is frustrating and alienating what should be a prized community.[51]

The more the Chinese moved up the educational and occupational ladder, the more they resented the inequalities imposed on them as second-class citizens. Unlike their forbears, many had either attained the educational qualifications or the financial means to enable them to escape life in South Africa. Increasing numbers of Chinese sought a new future in countries such as England, Canada, America, Singapore and later, Australia. South Africa's withdrawal from the Commonwealth after it became a republic in 1961 prompted fears that the doors to emigration would be shut, and those who wished to settle in Britain left as soon as they could.

By 1967 it was estimated that 30% to 40% of Chinese graduates had emigrated in search of greater professional freedom and the number was steadily growing. Uncertainty over the future and resentment against apartheid were cited as the main reasons for substantial numbers in Port Elizabeth pulling up roots and settling elsewhere. Describing the Chinese as proportionately among the most literate and highly educated groups in the country, the acting chairman of Central, Dr Norman Yenson, appealed to university graduates to remain in South Africa to help improve conditions for the community. He said emigration amounted to a 'brain drain' which could only impoverish South Africa.[52]

The exodus continued as traders and their families joined the ranks of departing professionals. Assessing the reasons for their emigration, one Chinese wrote to a newspaper in Port Elizabeth:

> What then are the basic causes of dissatisfaction? They are the lack of respect for human dignity, the denial of equality of opportunities, rewards and justice in this land of our birth ... because of the basic desire to live in a harmonious society where merit alone and not colour is the criteria for acceptance.[53]

Despite the easing of restrictions on the Chinese in the 1970s through the granting of permits for housing and social amenities, the Chinese knew these represented concessions rather than rights. The Catholic priest who had worked among the Chinese for many years, Fr Michael Tuohy explained:

> ... I do not see what loyalty they could have for a place where they have no rights. While a greater proportion of professional people are steadily leaving, I feel many more would go if emigration were easier. Leaving is their top priority. They are not prepared to live on the crumbs of privilege as they must do here.[54]

Increasing political instability in South Africa after the Soweto riots of 1976 also contributed towards the outflow of people of all races. Economists have deplored particularly the loss of university graduates, pointing out that emigration had a cumulative effect in 'stripping South Africa of layer after layer of its sum total of talent'.[55]

Much has been written on the patterns of Chinese migration worldwide being an initial exodus from China in the 19th century and, from the 1950s, an outflow from south-east Asia to western countries. The South African example is interesting in that it reflects a second wave of emigration, this time not from China but from South Africa, of locally born and educated Chinese, to other western countries.

Although there are no statistics on the numbers of Chinese emigrants from the 1960s, there is no doubt that they ran into many hundreds. In the medical field alone, the majority of doctors who qualified in South Africa emigrated. Between 1947 and 1987, a total of 80 Chinese doctors graduated from the University of the Witwatersrand.[56] From all accounts, despite initial difficulties, most established themselves in their chosen professions abroad. Many of those who emigrated in the 1950s and 1960s especially went on to achieve a level of success and recognition which would have been withheld from them in South Africa.

For the South African Chinese the departure of such a substantial segment of the community created a void and represented the loss of talent and leadership which could have altered the course of its development.

STRENGTHENING COMMUNITY TIES

Exclusively Chinese organizations had long been a feature of the community's social life in South Africa and from the 1950s these became increasingly evident. Mixing with other Chinese who shared the same background and customs offered a sense of security and identity. Even among the younger generation, born and raised in the country, more fluent in English and Afrikaans than Chinese, many new Chinese-only clubs were formed. Generally reticent, most Chinese saw these as a means of avoiding embarrassment or being rebuffed by non-Chinese clubs. Racially restrictive legislation, discouraging the intermingling of different groups, further contributed towards the development of a marked cohesiveness in the community.

The proliferation of sporting, cultural and social organizations reflected the growing diversity among Chinese countrywide. Leisure-time activities expanded beyond mahjong parties to include a variety of outdoor pursuits and hobbies such as fishing and photography. Groups were formed for Catholics, students, music lovers, cinema-goers as well as followers of virtually every sport. And the publications which issued from these organizations' ranks reflected not only the changing concerns of the 1960s and 1970s, but also the soul-searching quest for an identity among young Chinese who questioned how they could be described as 'South Africans' in a country where their race set them apart.

SPORT

Throughout the country, Chinese sports clubs of every kind mushroomed. The most popular sports were basketball, soccer, table tennis, softball, tennis and badminton, played by clubs with such motivational names as Lightning, Comets, Leos, Golden Dragons and South China. Matches were initially played between local clubs, but the competitive spirit soon extended to challenging Chinese from other centres. In 1948,

Durban Chinese fielded a soccer team to play against the Blue and White Sports Club in Johannesburg, while the Kimberley Chinese Recreation Club invited teams from Port Elizabeth and Johannesburg to play cricket, softball and table tennis over the Christmas holidays.

Lack of sporting facilities was a problem in most areas. The Institute of Race Relations reported in 1949 that there were virtually no recreation facilities for the Chinese except for one basketball field in Main Street, Johannesburg. 'Two boys' and two girls' teams occasionally compete against Bantu teams. Two Chinese soccer teams in Johannesburg play against Coloured teams using the Coloured sports grounds in Natalspruit whenever they are available.'[57]

Group Areas and the Reservation of Separate Amenities legislation prevented Chinese from participating in many sports with other race groups. In areas such as Johannesburg and Port Elizabeth, Chinese players ran their own leagues from the 1950s to provide competition, to promote social contact and to avoid the possibility of becoming the focus of racial incidents. Problems for Chinese sportsmen arose when they were selected to play for provincial teams, when they used municipal facilities or when they tried to play in White leagues.

In the 1960s and early 1970s numerous incidents involving Chinese received widespread publicity. In February 1962 six Chinese women chosen for the Border provincial team, were barred from the South African Softball Championships when the Pretoria City Council refused to allow them to use the municipal grounds. Then, three years later, the Western Province Basketball Association sought permission from the Minister of Community Development, P.W. Botha, before selecting Chinese players for the provincial side. The Minister stated categorically that the government did not wish to have mixed sport in South Africa.[58]

In Port Elizabeth, Chinese players participated freely in White basketball, badminton and table tennis leagues as well as in many other sports. By 1970 the unprecedented attention focused on the position of the Chinese caused sports bodies to apply for permits, and Chinese participation was promptly suspended. Only when the Minister of Community Development intervened was a blanket exemption granted for Chinese to take part in sports activities with Whites.[59]

Sport proved to be the ideal means of forging links among Chinese throughout southern Africa, and teams from neighbouring countries, Mocambique and Rhodesia (Zimbabwe), often participated in local tournaments. When the Tje-Lig (meaning self-strength) team from Lourenco Marques (Maputo) made a clean sweep in the 1954 Easter knock-out basketball tournament in Johannesburg, crowds flocked to watch the visitors' more modern style of play and precision-like teamwork.[60]

Port Elizabeth hosted the country's first South African Chinese Softball Tournament on 26 and 27 December 1954. Organized by the Chinese Youth Club (CYC), visitors included Swallows, Comets and the Johannesburg Chinese Youth Society, all from Johannesburg; Arrows from East London and the Cape Town Chinese Recreation Club. Welcoming the participants and spectators, CYC chairman, Gordon Loyson, said it was hoped that other centres would organize similar gatherings annually to foster a closer relationship among all Chinese in the country.[61]

Members of the Arrows Chinese Softball team from East London wing their way to a sporting event in Johannesburg. Six of their team were barred from taking part in the South African Softball Championships in Pretoria in 1962.

The committee of the Chinese Youth Club in the 1950s who organized one of the first national sports events for young Chinese.

This hope materialized just a few years later when the Easter Tournament became a national sports gathering for teams selected on a regional rather than club basis. From 1960, the tournament was held every year, over the Easter weekend, and hosted in centres such as Port Elizabeth, Beira, East London, Lourenco Marques, Cape Town, Pretoria and Johannesburg. A national co-ordinating body, the Southern Africa Chinese Sports Association (SACSA) was formed in 1969 to promote amateur sports among Chinese and to standardize the rules governing the various sports. Among the many sportsmen and women who played a significant role in managing SACSA were Kenneth Whyte, Cecil Kamson, Dick Kee-Son and Shirleen Man.

Political changes in southern Africa since the 1970s wrought many changes in the nature of the Easter Tournament. Teams from Mocambique and Zimbabwe ceased to participate and emigration depleted the numbers of competitors from smaller centres. From the late 1980s, the immigration of Taiwanese introduced new teams from areas such as the Orange Free State and Natal, and from the 1990s teams from Reunion and Zimbabwe again joined the tournament.

The annual Easter Tournament offered Chinese the opportunity to test their skills against each other, and many excelled sufficiently to win wider recognition on both a provincial and national level in South African sport. The first Chinese to win their Springbok colours in basketball were Terence Date Chong of Port Elizabeth and Sonia Ho Tong of Pretoria.

Sport more than any other activity was the means by which the community became more closely knit, locally and nationally. Not only did it allow young people to socialize in their own towns, but it enabled them to extend their circle of friends to Chinese throughout the country. Most clubs' activities were not limited purely to sports. From the 1950s many organized variety concerts, held parties, arranged dances, raised funds and provided all the social opportunities for the community to become truly cohesive.

SOCIAL AND CULTURAL ACTIVITIES

Just as sport played a vital role in uniting the community, so social and cultural occasions served to strengthen ties among Chinese. Traditional Chinese celebrations remained an important feature of family and community life — from month-old parties for babies and lavish nine-course wedding dinners to the annual Chinese New Year and Double Ten festivities. Clan organizations continued to arrange the customary twice yearly visits to the cemeteries followed by communal dinners.

From the late 1940s, Chinese operas and concerts were regularly staged and many organizations screened Chinese films to raise funds for their activities. The Consulate-General usually assisted in obtaining and distributing such films. Among the groups which played an important role in maintaining an awareness and appreciation of Chinese music and dance were the Chinese Musical Society and the Lion Dance Club. In March 1963, a Transvaal Chinese Women's Association was formed to foster friendship among Chinese women. The group disbanded a year later when Madame Wei Yu Sun, wife of the Consul-General and driving force behind the group, left South Africa.

The Bright Stars soccer team, Johannesburg, 1960s.

Cape Town Chinese cricket team, 1960s.

Softball was a popular sport among young Chinese ... seen here are Southern Transvaal and Border teams who competed against each other at an Easter Tournament in the 1960s.

Blue and White basketball team, Johannesburg, 1954.

Lightning basketball team, Port Elizabeth, 1950s.

Large crowds support the Easter Tournament, the annual sporting highlight in the Chinese community.

Community dances were festive occasions ... and young Chinese entered into the spirit of fancy dress affairs. Taken in Johannesburg, 1950s.

One creative pastime which gained an enthusiastic following from the 1950s was photography. The Chinese Camera Club was formed in Johannesburg in 1952 to promote the advancement of photography. It held monthly meetings and organized an exhibition of members' works at the Johannesburg City Hall. The Chinese Photographic Society was formed in Port Elizabeth in 1969 after Chinese were turned away from the city's White camera club and refused admission to the technical college's course.

Past pupils of the Chinese schools in Johannesburg and Pretoria formed societies to maintain contact with each other and to assist their school. The Kuo Ting Former Students Association, founded in July 1961, published a newsletter, participated in sports, arranged ballroom dancing lessons and many social functions. The Pretoria Chinese School Former Students Association, established in March 1963, was actively involved in fund-raising, published the *Feiking Bulletin* and formed the Northern Transvaal Chinese Red Cross and Home Nursing units to provide aid at sports gatherings.

WELFARE AND RELIGIOUS ORGANIZATIONS

By the early 1960s a substantial proportion of Chinese in South Africa were Christian, mainly Anglicans and Catholics. The influence of these churches in the community had been extended through the education of children by Anglican sisters in the Chinese

Mission School in Port Elizabeth from 1918 and by the opening of private Catholic and Anglican schools to Chinese from the 1930s.

In Port Elizabeth, Chinese Anglicans were fully involved in the activities of the St Francis Xavier Church, the first Chinese church in the country. Initially occupying a room in the premises of the Moi Yean Commercial Association, the church was formally housed in Brassel Street, North End, in 1954. The interior of the church reflected the Chinese character of its ministry, featuring a marble altar embossed with Chinese characters and statues with Chinese features.[62] The removal of many families to the Chinese group area in Kabega eventually necessitated the building of a new church, and in March 1980 the St Francis Xavier Church was consecrated in Agate Road, Kabega. Community members participated actively in fund-raising for the church, in taking office as church council members and wardens and teaching Sunday school classes. Fr Gutsch was a driving force behind the church for many years and long-serving churchwardens included Cecil Date Chong and David Low Ah Kee.

In Johannesburg, the Catholic Chinese Association was formed in 1961 to work for the welfare of the community, to unite Catholic Chinese and to promote Chinese culture. It organized a variety of social functions such as picnics and talks, and also offered financial assistance to those in need, launching an annual Debutantes Ball in 1965 for young ladies to raise funds for charity and offering a bursary for university students from 1971.

Chinese Anglican Church, Brassel Street, Port Elizabeth, 1950s.

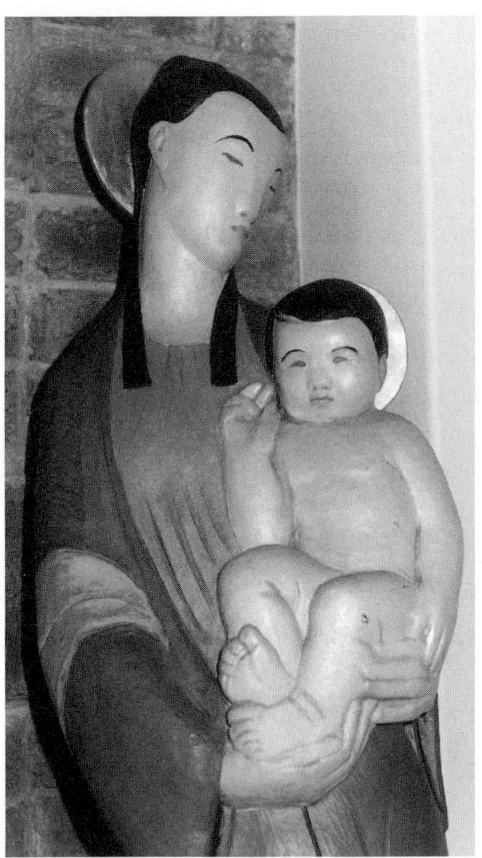

Mother and child statue in St Francis Xavier Church, Kabega.

Fr Ignatius Ou, Port Elizabeth

Chinese-style rosewood altar in Chinese Catholic Centre, Sherwood Street, Port Elizabeth.

The Catholic Chinese Association started publishing a newsletter in the mid-1960s which was eventually named *Vinculum* in 1967. Although many of its issues dealt with religious topics, it also provided information on subjects such as the meaning of Double Ten and Chinese opera. For many years it filled a vital communication gap in the community, relaying news on Group Areas developments and commenting on concerns in the community. In *Vinculum*, its then editor, Veronica Chokie, first mooted the idea of a Chinese old age home in 1972. Aware of the dire circumstances in which some elderly Chinese without families were living, she invited the community to respond to the idea of establishing a home for the aged.

Undeterred by the lack of interest and even opposition from those who argued that it ran counter to Chinese precepts that children had a duty to care for their parents, Miss Chokie and members of the Catholic Chinese Association pursued the objective. An attempt to establish the home with a group from another church was abandoned after pre-conditions for intended residents were laid down such as no gambling, no drinking and no swearing. An anonymous donor contributed R10 000 towards the establishment of the home, provided no restrictions were imposed to make it an institution. A standing committee was formed and finally, after years spent untangling red tape and obtaining registration as a welfare organization, the Hong Ning Chinese Aged Home officially opened its doors on 25 January 1981.

Several South African Chinese followed a religious vocation, becoming priests and nuns. Most active in the Chinese community was Sister Lily Lee Sun, who originally took her vows as Sister Paul.

The Chinese Baptist Church grew out of student meetings organized by a teacher, Mrs A.S. Rabie, at the Johannesburg Chinese Kuo Ting School from 1952. It ministered to members of the community under this name for more than 25 years, acquiring its own church premises in 1975 and was officially renamed the Southdale Baptist Church in 1978. Its then-minister, the Reverend Arthur Song, recommended the adoption of a non-ethnic name for the church which however retained a Chinese character.[63] An active welfare group stemming from this church was Christian Care for Elderly Chinese. Providing assistance for the aged who lived with their families or on their own, it was run by Seu Lau Fok, Timothy Sam and Inmie Brown. Its activities included driving the elderly to church services and hospital, organizing social gatherings and raising funds to assist the needy.

Other active Chinese churches in Johannesburg were the Chinese Christian Fellowship, begun in 1973, by Mrs J. Lee and her son Eddie, from Cape Town and the Chinese Assembly of God, established in 1976 by missionary, Sonja Botha. The latter church evolved from the formation of the Happiness Chinese Creche in 1964 to cater for the toddlers of Chinese working mothers in the eastern suburbs of Johannesburg.

The Port Elizabeth Catholic Chinese Association, formed in March 1976, raised funds to establish a parish community centre and administered the Ou Te-Lung Jubilee Fund to provide financial assistance for students to the priesthood. The fund, named after Chinese priest, Fr Ignatius Ou, who had worked in the community since the mid-1950s, also supported the study of Chinese language as well as religious and cultural activities in the community.

Hong Ning Chinese Aged Home, Belgravia, Johannesburg.

COMMUNITY PUBLICATIONS

From the 1950s different publications were produced by Chinese organizations to reflect their developing interests, to provide a forum for community news and to articulate publicly their concerns about their position in South Africa. Although most were short-lived ventures, they created the basis of a communication network which served to keep the community informed.

The only continuous medium of communication had been the *Chiao Sheng Pao* or *Chinese Consular Gazette*, established in 1931. Published three times a week, the newspaper's influence was limited to those able to read Chinese. In 1962 the Consulate-General raised funds to improve the paper and to publish in both English and Chinese, but it remained an exclusively Chinese language paper, under the control of the Consulate-General and later the Embassy of the ROC/Taiwan.

In Port Elizabeth, a newsletter called *South Wind* was published between September 1949 and December 1950 to keep the community abreast of the changing political situation in China. Produced exclusively in Chinese, it also included translations of press reports in South African newspapers, lengthy coverage of the impending Group

Areas legislation, news on the community in various centres, poetry and essays. Volunteers were called in to handwrite and print stencils, staple the pages together and then post the newsletter to some 200 Chinese individuals and organizations.[64] Politics too was a primary concern behind the publication of the newsletter *New Youth* in Kimberley from 1953. Written by George Changfoot and Frank Wong Fatt, it aimed to make Chinese more politically aware, exhorting them to support the communist struggle in China and to become involved in demands by non-Whites for equal rights in South Africa. Regarded as a radical leaflet by the community, it disappeared after a year or two.[65]

It was also in Port Elizabeth that the first national, dual medium English/Chinese magazine, the *E.P. Chinese Review*, made its appearance in April 1964. Its opening editorial stated that there was no effective means of communication among Chinese countrywide and their aim was to reach the younger generation who could not read Chinese. Encouraging young leaders to become involved in community organizations, EPCA chairman, Sidney Kim Sing suggested the new magazine could serve as a vehicle for the exchange of ideas. He wrote:

> We have become Chinese South Africans. We live in South Africa and most of us must find our adjustment here, while trying to maintain our cultural identity. This will not be easy, but it can be done, provided that we have imagination and initiative in leadership supported by the close unity of our people.[66]

The *E.P. Chinese Review* contained an assortment of articles from the political and cultural to the philosophical and practical. It expressed views on controversial issues, relayed general community news and also provided practical information for Chinese travellers and those interested in the export market. Among those responsible for its publication were Wally Ah Now, L. Ou Tim, Trevor Gin, Yuen Whiteley and Percy Date Chong. Originally intended to appear bi-monthly and to be distributed throughout the country free of charge, the magazine soon encountered financial problems and was published irregularly. Despite appeals for donations, only seven issues appear to have been published, and the magazine's production ceased sometime after December 1965.

Two years later another magazine made its appearance to focus community attention on pressing concerns of the day. Aptly named *The Voice of South African Chinese*, it was an independent, monthly publication. Written in English and Chinese, the magazine consisted of between 10 and 24 pages per issue. Although its lifespan was short — from July 1967 to April 1968 — it nonetheless provided a unique national forum for the exchange of ideas among Chinese.

The magazine was produced by an editorial board which affirmed its independence and non-affiliation to any Chinese organization. Its editor was Alan Ma Sing, an arts graduate of Wits University, assisted by numerous community members including Lorraine Leong, Jackson Leong, Sidney Kim Sing, Cecil Leong, Norman Yenson, Kenneth Winchiu, Rodney Leong Man and Arthur Song.

In an appeal to the community to support the magazine financially, its editorial board gave the following synopsis of its standpoint:

> From many quarters we have heard praise for our sincere attempt to create a greater awareness in our community of our responsibilities as South Africans of Chinese descent, of our right to claim a full share in the life of the civilized groups in this country, and of the privilege we enjoy as inheritors of one of the world's greatest and oldest cultures.
>
> The few critics we have are concerned that South African Chinese should be giving their loyalty to South Africa instead of to another country. To such people we would point out that the Government of Free China has repeatedly urged that Chinese expatriate communities must give their total loyalty to the country in which they reside. We are glad to support such a far-sighted policy.[67]

That the opinions aired in *The Voice* evoked controversy and much heated debate is evidenced by the many readers' letters submitted to the magazine for publication. As strongly as the editorial board expressed its views, so too did its readers raise 'hot' issues such as in-fighting among community organizations, the maintenance of Chinese racial purity and corruption by those who wanted payment to help fellow Chinese.

The Voice's contribution to public debate was significant in that it took a clear, often unequivocal, stand on vital issues. Its content was mixed, ranging from the political and cultural to women's features and sport, but it distinguished itself as a publication which fearlessly addressed concerns previously unseen in print in the Chinese community.

Prior to the publication of both the *E.P. Chinese Review* and *The Voice*, sports, student and religious groups produced newsletters to reflect activities in their own circles. Probably the earliest was the *Weekend Review*, published between 1953 and 1957, which commented each week on sports events and social activities. From the mid-1950s, the Chinese Students Society at the University of the Witwatersrand issued an irregular newsletter called the *SA Chinese Student*, later *The Chinese Student*, and from about 1961, the University of Cape Town's Chinese students produced *Spectrum*. Past pupils of Chinese schools in Johannesburg and Pretoria too released publications such as the *Kuo Ting Review* and the *Feiking Bulletin* from the early 1960s.

The Catholic Chinese associations in Port Elizabeth and Johannesburg circulated the *Inter Nos* and *Vinculum* magazines, from the mid-1960s. Both publications still appear regularly. From 1981 the Transvaal Chinese Association published a bi-monthly newsletter, in English and Chinese, which was distributed nationally. Featuring topical items on community activities, the *TCA Newsletter* remained the major means of bilingual communication among Chinese throughout the 1980s and early 1990s.

IDENTITY CRISIS

Just as the emergence of many new Chinese organizations reflected a need to share similar interests, so the consciousness of a common identity stimulated intense discussion on the community's life in limbo. Virtually all publications produced by the Chinese throughout the 1960s and 1970s debated their role and place in South African society. Obviously differentiated by race, but settled for two and more generations, younger people in particular questioned how 'Chinese' they still were and where they belonged. Loathe to describe themselves as South Africans since they were neither accepted nor treated as citizens, they nonetheless questioned the sense of owing 'loyalty' to a far-off homeland, either mainland China or Taiwan.

Up to the 1960s, many South African Chinese would have conformed in most respects to the definition of overseas Chinese contained in the label *hua-ch'iao (huaqiao)*. The epitome of this term for all Chinese living outside China was '... a sojourner who enjoyed the protection of the Chinese government (through its embassies or consulates), and who lived in spirit in China, politically, culturally and emotionally attached to his mother country,' according to author, Lynn Pan.[68]

Technically citizens of South Africa by birth, many Chinese nonetheless regarded the Consul-General of the 'Republic of China' in exile on Taiwan as their representative, and their support for Chinese nationalism and the Kuomintang demonstrated their attachment to China as 'home'. For the older generation particularly the celebration of the Chinese National Day, the Double Ten, served to display their loyalty and pride in being Chinese. Younger people however were more concerned about their own role and future in South Africa. They questioned the part played by the Consul-General in representations on behalf of the community, pointing out that this perpetuated the view that South African Chinese were foreigners. They argued that the community should use its own representative bodies to express its aspirations.[69]

By the 1960s the community's new crop of young leaders was emerging. Most were products of a wholly western education, able to speak some Chinese, but unable to read or write it. They asked what it meant to be Chinese and how proud could they be of a Chinese identity when it carried the label of 'second-class citizen'.

Articles in community publications confronted these issues. In 1965, Maureen Kim Sing asserted: 'The fear of most minority groups is of losing their identity — apartheid will preserve ours.'[70] Others however felt the process of westernization had already robbed the Chinese of their identity. In the *E.P. Chinese Review,* Ernest Wing King said the majority of Chinese spoke English in their homes, were influenced by their education and environment and, if they were not confronted with separate development, 'at least 80% of us would have no hesitation in calling ourselves pure and simply South Africans'.[71]

Even harsher in his assessment, Trevor Gin asked whether old moral values associated with Chinese civilization still existed.

> The Chinese in SA are roller-coasting down a cultural cul-de-sac. The only recent 'cultural' activity of note in PE for example has been ... a rock-'n-roll championship!

He argued that community leaders had failed to realize that living in South Africa they could not 'smugly sit back and expect correct Chinese attitudes to take root and flourish in the minds of children who are receiving practically a one-hundred per cent Western education'.[72] *Spectrum* highlighted the 'perfect paradox that most youth can hardly read and write Chinese, but the one newspaper specifically serving the Chinese community is printed only in Chinese'.[73]

The same theme was taken up in the following years as community members questioned whether they had become 'cultural outcasts', Chinese in appearance and no more. Many urged that efforts should be made to reawaken pride in a cultural heritage

A Double Ten celebration at Johannesburg's Langham Hotel, 1950s.

and consciousness of being Chinese to avert the danger of the total loss of identity.[74] On the religious level, minister Arthur Song stated that Chinese Christians faced a conflict between their faith and traditional cultural rites, which could be interpreted as ancestor worship.[75]

The dilemma of a South African-born Chinese was further explored as *Vinculum* questioned in 1972 how significant 'national' days such as the Double Ten, Overseas Chinese Day and President Chiang Kai Shek's birthday were for the community.

> We are born and bred in South Africa, and the fact that our skins are yellow does not alter the fact that this is the only place we know. What are our memories of the fatherland, the National Party, her glories and ideals? — Nil, absolutely nil! Whatever we know about them is from what our fathers and perhaps grandfathers have told us and from our history lessons. We are not citizens of Nationalist China but citizens, perhaps even second class, of South Africa. Our dreams, rather not our dreams, but our future, lies in this country and not in the island of Taiwan or even the mainland of China. For many of us South Africa will be the only country that we will know and for this reason this is where we should build our future.[76]

Arguing that public perceptions of the Chinese as inscrutable, mysterious people whom Westerners could never know in fact worked to the detriment of the community, the magazine said the Chinese sought rights basic to the dignity of human beings, without encroaching on the rights of others.

> We have only one life to live. And we want to live that life in peace and dignity. But not at the expense of apologising for what we are. That would be our death-knell.[77]

Many South African Chinese families continue to follow traditional wedding customs. Lynette Man serving tea to her new in-laws, Johannesburg, 1975.

Whether or not individual Chinese followed traditional practices depended on their home environment and the presence of one or both grandparents. Many did retain customs connected with major events, especially births, marriages and deaths. Over the years these practices were simplified to suit the occasion, often resulting in a combination of East and West. For example, a typical bride wore a white wedding gown instead of red, but still followed all the rites of the traditional tea ceremony for the groom's family.

According to Linda Human, who conducted sociological research on the Chinese in the late 1970s, the community had become more assimilated into White society than many other overseas Chinese communities. This assimilation was illustrated by their involvement in the professions, their high level of education and standard of living, the fact that they competed in the White labour market and shared the same aspirations as Whites in seeking upward mobility and economic security.

Despite the fact that many had given up cultural customs relating to festivals, religion and associations, she found they held onto certain Chinese values in terms of family life, education and occupation.

> ...it would appear that a distinction has to be made between values and practices; although Chinese people in general, and young Chinese people in particular, may, in many respects, be extremely Westernized in their practices, many retain a value-system which is, to all intents and purposes, quite traditionally Chinese. Moreover, even if the Chinese were granted equal status with Whites, they would always attempt to retain an identity that is specifically Chinese.

Linda Human added that equality and cultural pride were two separate issues, although the Chinese saw these as wanting 'the best of both worlds'. It was a sad fact of life in South Africa that race distinctions had left many people ashamed of their cultural heritage, but the Chinese, unlike other non-Whites, were unwilling to recognize the so-called 'superiority' of White culture.[78]

The quest for social acceptance led the Chinese to seek out as many ways of 'belonging' as they could. Through the process of westernization, they became more assimilated but at the same time alienated themselves from their Chinese heritage and lost the use of the Chinese language. The experience of South Africa's Chinese was aptly summed up in this description by prominent Chinese scholar, Wang Gungwu, of the new breed of Chinese in Southeast Asia: 'They are often too Western to be comfortably Chinese and yet too Chinese to accept conditions where Chineseness is being penalized.'[79]

For a minority, the Chinese, who numbered approximately 6000 in the early 1960s, attracted far more than their share of public attention. Their uncertain status, somewhere between White, Japanese and non-White, provided opposition politicians and journalists with a convenient means of taking potshots at the government and its apartheid policy. Little wonder that the Chinese felt they were being used as a 'political football'.

Through negotiation and social acceptance, they had obtained many privileges which gave them social and economic mobility, but not the rights to secure them. When the process of reform started in 1979, the National Party government considered the possibility of political representation for groups other than Whites. It was then that the Chinese were once again pushed into the limelight, to begin yet another phase in their search for rights and recognition as South African citizens.

13
The End of an Era

Why was the Chinese Association of South Africa (CASA) formed in 1981? Why did South Africa allow investors from Taiwan to settle in the country while no Chinese immigration was officially permitted? This final chapter outlines the appointment of a Chinese to the President's Council, the relations between South Africa and the Republic of China on Taiwan, South Africa's political reforms and the country's first, all-race elections in 1994. As the new millennium approaches, the Chinese community's make-up is changing and it confronts new challenges not least of which are the tensions wrought by the 'two Chinas' debate.

South Africa in the late 1970s was a country under siege. International pressures against its apartheid policies continued to mount, armed conflict raged in neighbouring Rhodesia, South West Africa, Angola and Mozambique and riots erupted in Black townships countrywide after the initial outbreak in Soweto in June 1976. Its growing isolation from the world community was underlined as emigration increased and investors departed. When the government of Prime Minister B.J. Vorster imposed a massive security clampdown in October 1977, following the death in detention of Black activist Steve Biko, the UN Security Council imposed a mandatory arms embargo against South Africa.[1]

The new Prime Minister P.W. Botha took office in September 1978 when South Africa was under threat of more wide-ranging economic sanctions from the West. Described as a man who viewed the world in military-strategic terms, he propounded the concept of 'total onslaught' against South Africa and devised a 12-point national strategy to combat communist subversion. Among these was the option of forging alliances with other countries 'outcast' from the international community such as Israel and Taiwan.[2] On the domestic front however it was Botha's government which set in motion the process of constitutional reform in South Africa.

PRESIDENT'S COUNCIL

In 1979 investigations began into a new parliamentary system to extend decision-making power to groups other than Whites in South Africa. The Schlebusch Commission of Inquiry was appointed to inquire into the introduction of a new constitution and, in May 1980, included among its recommendations the appointment of a President's Council. This body would serve in an advisory capacity to the State President, who would select 60 White, Coloured, Indian and Chinese nominees, recognized by their respective communities as leaders as well as nationally acknowledged experts in their respective fields.

The implementation of this recommendation sparked widespread criticism because of the exclusion of Blacks from the President's Council. Opponents objected to the fact that the Council had been created by Whites only and that it was merely an advisory body. Although a separate Black council had been proposed, the concept had been rejected. Leaders of the Black 'homeland' territories (which had been earmarked for eventual independence in terms of the grand apartheid scheme) said the exclusion of Blacks entrenched apartheid and would not solve South Africa's race problems. It was also pointed out that Coloureds and Indians would 'be reluctant to serve on the council ... because it would be perceived as an attempt to draw them into a confrontation with Africans'.[3] The official Opposition, the Progressive Federal Party, said the President's Council was a creation of apartheid because it retained a racial basis for representation, reported to an exclusively White Parliament and was 'a body which excludes 70% of the population while giving a place to the 10 000 Chinese'.[4]

The specific mention of the Chinese in the context of the President's Council was unexpected because the community had never been involved in any government-created political structures. The Coloureds and Indians, on the other hand, had been allocated a nominal form of representation on advisory councils from the early 1960s. The inclusion of the Chinese appears to have been a direct result of a state visit to South Africa in March 1980 by the Republic of China on Taiwan's premier, Sun Yun-Suan. Constitutional commission chairman, Alwyn Schlebusch said at the time the government had undertaken to look into the position of the Chinese and he would investigate the question of their political rights.[5] Relations between South Africa and the ROC/Taiwan had warmed considerably during the 1970s as both countries faced international isolation.

The public debate on the President's Council and its structure once again put the Chinese in the spotlight as political analysts pointed to the obvious disparity of according a place to the smallest minority, yet leaving out the vast majority of the population. Reporters sought reactions from 'spokesmen' for the Chinese community only to discover there were as many views as there were people.

Chinese throughout the country were concerned about the implications of Chinese participation on the President's Council and how it would be perceived by other groups. Once again it required a crisis to mobilize the community. They realized the need for a united, national organization to decide whether or not to participate on the President's Council and to have a say in who, if anyone, should represent the Chinese. The previous body, the Central Chinese Association of South Africa, had effectively ceased to function after 1967.

In September 1980 three regional associations from Port Elizabeth, Johannesburg and Pretoria convened a conference of Chinese organizations countrywide. Their agenda was to discuss representation on the President's Council and the formation of a national body to represent the Chinese. In lengthy debate over two days, views expressed included the following: participation would identify the Chinese as a separate group; all racial groups should be represented; the Chinese should first be given full rights; and the government intended to nominate a Chinese whether or not the community approved. Delegates asked how other race groups would react, saying participation could possibly jeopardize the existing position of the Chinese.[6]

The meeting passed motions opposing Chinese representation on the President's Council, saying the Chinese wished to be excluded from participation and anyone who would be or had been appointed should be informed of these views. It was also resolved to form a steering committee to draft a constitution for a national Chinese organization. To the surprise of all involved, two weeks later, newspapers reported that Kenneth Winchiu, of Pretoria, who had been present at the meeting, had accepted nomination as the first Chinese to serve on the President's Council.[7]

Shiang Chum, who had chaired the national meeting of Chinese organizations in mid-September, expressed shock at the news saying that as a member of the Pretoria Chinese Association committee, Kenneth Winchiu was 'fully aware of the facts but he nevertheless took it upon himself to take up this appointment'.[8] In a press statement later, Chum also announced that Winchiu had been expelled from the Pretoria Chinese Association because his acceptance was contrary to the wishes of the association and the Chinese community. He said Winchiu did not command the support of the community 'and will in future be regarded as an individual acting only in his personal capacity.'[9]

Winchiu said he had accepted the nomination because as a non-political individual and as the first Chinese to be nominated, this was more a responsibility than a privilege. Later he refused to comment on whether or not he would represent the Chinese community but said he hoped he would be able to reflect their feelings. A wealthy handicrafts businessman, Winchiu said in spite of his expulsion and the opposition to the President's Council, he would still serve on it as he believed it could have a role to play in shaping South Africa's future.[10]

Analyzing the Chinese position in relation to the President's Council, *Sunday Times* political correspondent Ivor Wilkins said:

> Unhappily for many Chinese their willy-nilly inclusion on the President's Council has reinforced their separateness from the White society, in which they had so nearly been assimilated. It has pushed them once more into their own racial box, spotlighting them as a 'problem' for whom political 'solutions' will now have to be found.[11]

FORMATION OF CHINESE ASSOCIATION OF SOUTH AFRICA

In March 1981 the steering committee, appointed by the conference of Chinese organizations in September 1980, called another meeting to constitute the Chinese Association of South Africa (CASA). Eighteen Chinese organizations attended the meeting which accepted a constitution based on regional representation. CASA's aims included the attainment of full rights for the Chinese, the preservation of the Chinese cultural identity, safeguarding and promoting the interests of the Chinese and assisting the community in overcoming difficulties. It also aimed to foster harmony and goodwill among Chinese and promote good relations with all other communities.[12]

TCA *Rejuvenated*

Moves to form a national body to represent the Chinese prompted the revival of the Transvaal Chinese Association (TCA), the Johannesburg-based community organization which had not held elections in more than a decade. After canvassing the community to encourage them to vote, a new executive committee was elected and took office in November 1980.

One of their first priorities was to inform the community of their plans, but because the organization had no funds, each committee member had to contribute ten Rand to print and post their first news bulletin! They embarked on a wide range of activities, organizing community celebrations, calling report-back meetings and addressing problems such as admission to schools and disability grants. The TCA also undertook the major function of certifying the identities of community members who wished to reclaim properties, confiscated by the authorities since 1949, in mainland China. Half the TCA's committee served on the executive of the Chinese Association of South Africa, formed in March 1981.

One of the TCA's first and most ambitious projects was the organization of a Chinese Week Festival in October 1982. Intended to introduce the Chinese community to their fellow South Africans, it involved hundreds of volunteers who undertook everything from decorating an exhibition hall to cooking in the Chinese restaurant. The festival was opened by South Africa's Vice State President, Alwyn Schlebusch and ran for five days. It offered visitors displays of traditional Chinese folk dancing and martial arts, exhibitions of Chinese paintings and artefacts, various handicraft stalls as well as cookery demonstrations by the renowned Fu Pei Mei, author of several books on Chinese cuisine. Included too was a photographic display on the history of the Chinese in South Africa which marked the beginning of what would develop into the South African Chinese History Project. Financially the success of the festival placed the TCA on a sufficiently sound footing to function independently.

Through its involvement in CASA, the organization participated in decisions on issues of concern to the Chinese community as a whole and continued the publication of its national newsletter in English and Chinese. Through this medium it launched numerous fund-raising drives for causes including flood relief in China and drew the community's attention to issues such as the incidence of hepatitis B among Chinese. The TCA also extended its activities to plan for the development of a country club or community centre to serve the needs of the growing Chinese population.

One of the founding organizations of the Chinese Association of South Africa (CASA) was the Transvaal Chinese Association. The 1980–1982 TCA executive committee comprised: [Seated, from left] Terry Lai King, Cecil Leong, Rodney Man, Eric Yenson, Stanley May, {Standing} Mario Lee, Basil Song, Leslie Leong, Melanie Yap, Cecil Kamson, Kaye Luk and Colin Song.

Unlike its predecessor, the Central Chinese Association of South Africa, the new organization drastically limited the number of member organizations. It had six founder members, each being regionally based and given voting powers based on the number of Chinese it represented. The six associations were: the Transvaal Chinese Association (6 votes), the Eastern Province Chinese Association (3 votes), Pretoria Chinese Association (2 votes), Cape Town Chinese Association (1 vote), East London Chinese Association (1 vote) and Kimberley Chinese Association (1 vote). When new Chinese settled in other areas such as the Orange Free State and Natal, CASA accordingly extended membership to them, with one vote each based on their initial estimated numbers of permanent residents.

Welcoming the formation of CASA, the Ambassador for the Republic of China on Taiwan, H.K. Yang said his embassy had served as a link between the government and the Chinese community, but it was time the South African Chinese reflected their own views about their interests and their role as useful citizens of the country. The new CASA chairman, Rodney Leong Man, endorsed this view, stating:

> We recognise that first and foremost the diplomats must serve their own country. Where that benefits us as well, that is fantastic. But when it comes to the push, they will look after their own interests. We accept that we must stand on our own feet.[13]

CASA notified government departments of its formation and met with Cabinet

Ambassador H.K. Yang and Rodney Man.

Ministers to discuss the community's concerns. Among the issues the new organization addressed were the continued impact of the Group Areas Act, the Community Development Act, the Population Registration Act, restrictions on Chinese immigration, various laws governing education and labour legislation. One of the problems it faced was the reclassification of Chinese of mixed origin, since member associations were receiving requests for affidavits that these people were accepted by the community as Chinese. A detailed study was made of the numerous laws affecting the Chinese to establish how changes could be sought within the framework of the existing laws.

Communication was a priority which CASA addressed through the *Transvaal Chinese Association Newsletter*. The publication, written in English and Chinese, appeared approximately every two months and was distributed free of charge to Chinese families nationally. Since its inception in 1981, it featured news on local events, matters of concern to the community and reports on CASA's activities and views.

REFORM GAINS MOMENTUM

In 1984 South Africa adopted a new constitution which provided for a tricameral parliamentary system for Whites, Coloureds and Indians and enabled each of these race groups to vote for representatives in its own separate parliament.[14] The nebulous position of the Chinese in the country's colour spectrum again became evident when this tiny minority could not be readily slotted into any of the three tiers. The community's unique position was described by member of Parliament, J.J. Lloyd, thus:

> These people are citizens of South Africa but they do not have the vote in South Africa. Everyone in South Africa can vote: The Black people can vote, the Whites can vote, the Coloureds can vote and the Indians can vote. However the Chinese, who are citizens of the country just as I am, cannot do so.[15]

In terms of South Africa's 'homeland' government policy, Blacks were technically citizens of various homelands and had the right to vote for legislatures in these areas. The Chinese therefore were the only racial group without any form of franchise, however nominal.

This lack of representation again gave Opposition politicians and the press the opportunity to point to the community as a forgotten minority and to urge that they be given full rights. Answering criticism in Parliament, the Minister of Internal Affairs,

F.W. de Klerk pointed out that the community's small size and countrywide dispersal necessitated a special approach to their situation. He gave the assurance that the Chinese would be fully involved in the political decision-making process and that this would be done in consultation with them.[16]

Commenting on this promise, an editorial in the *Eastern Province Herald* stated:

> In arguing for the incorporation of the Chinese community in white society, one is forced to talk — distasteful though it may be — in racial terms. That is because politically and socially South Africa is structured according to race; because the new Constitution is governed by race and because race is the argument that directs the Government ...
>
> Their numbers are so small (about 10 000) that none but the most obtuse can say — to employ Government ideology — that they threaten white identity. In fact the reverse. The Chinese community worries about its *own* identity. The Chinese are not rushing around trying to become white.[17]

CASA maintained contact with the Ministry of Constitutional Development and Planning, submitting memoranda and reiterating the community's wish to be consulted before any decision was taken on its political future. In view of previous sensitivity regarding the appointment of a Chinese person to the President's Council, CASA pointed out that the community wished to avoid a recurrence of the situation and would accept a decision not to appoint another Chinese.[18]

Intense newspaper speculation focused on the Chinese being integrated into the White chamber of Parliament, especially after the Group Areas Act was amended allowing Chinese the same rights as Whites in early 1985.[19] The position of the Chinese remained unresolved although various suggestions were made about the community exercising constitutional rights by voluntary association, that is, individuals would be free to choose the group with which they wished to associate to exercise their political rights.[20]

Widespread protest action had greeted the introduction of the new constitution in 1984 and by 1988 South Africa was under extreme pressure, internally and externally. A state of emergency was in effect as political violence escalated with school boycotts and worker strikes. Internationally the country's enforced isolation was extended as economic sanctions were imposed by the European Community in 1985 and the United States passed its Comprehensive Anti-Apartheid Act of 1986. Despite criticism that the process of political reform was too slow, the government pressed ahead with the repeal of discriminatory legislation and in October 1988 scheduled the country's first nationwide municipal elections, involving voters of all races. They were however voting on separate rolls, for separate institutions.[21] Again, the 'voteless' Chinese attracted attention.

During the municipal election campaign, Progressive Federal Party candidate, Clive Gilbert, described the Chinese as the only group in South Africa which was totally disenfranchised. Saying the Chinese were treated as Whites, he appealed for the immediate registration of the Chinese as voters, 'not as a token of good faith because we trade with the Far East, but as a matter of common decency to a neglected group'.[22]

CASA chairman, Rodney Man said the Chinese wanted rights but did not want to be labelled. From the community's point of view, the vote was not a 'pressure point'. He added:

> If one takes a wider view of the issues in South Africa, then there are much more fundamental challenges ahead, such as drawing all people together into a political structure acceptable to all.[23]

The possible extension of political rights to the Chinese was the subject of community meetings countrywide as CASA member associations sought to establish a consensus of opinion. Diverse views were expressed, from acceptance — because the vote represented what the community had always strived for — to rejection, because the racial basis of the constitution amounted to 'approval' of apartheid. A majority supported a 'middle of the road' approach allowing the Chinese to exercise constitutional rights by voluntary association in the areas where they lived. Community members pointed out that a distinction had to be drawn between *full rights* and *White rights*, saying the community wanted full rights, but not as *Whites*.

Intertwined with the issue of the vote was concern that Chinese men of 18 and over would become subject to compulsory military conscription as were all Whites. Although some community members argued that they did not want their sons to fight for a country in which they had always been 'second class' citizens, others pointed out rights carried responsibilities. Young men stated they would willingly go to the army if the Chinese had full rights. Should the issue of military service arise, CASA intended to ask for the Chinese to be given the same options as other groups, namely that it be introduced on a voluntary basis, followed by a ballot system and finally by compulsory conscription.

After much discussion and debate, it was agreed that CASA would send a letter to the State President expressing the community's wish that consideration of its position be delayed until a constitutional solution acceptable to all South Africans was found. It said the issue of a vote for the Chinese could not take priority when South Africa needed to address more fundamental issues. Should the government however decide to grant the franchise to Chinese, the community supported the option of exercising these rights by voluntary association.[24] What had also emerged in community discussions was the concern that the Chinese should avoid any situation in which its position could be 'used' to score political points.

RELATIONS BETWEEN SOUTH AFRICA AND ROC/TAIWAN

It was in the 1970s that both South Africa and Republic of China on Taiwan found themselves increasingly isolated from the international community. South Africa faced intensified and vociferous condemnation of its racial policies in the United Nations. Trade embargoes were taking their toll economically and the country's sports teams were shunned globally. The Soweto riots of 1976, sparked by Black opposition to compulsory teaching in Afrikaans, had once again highlighted the deep divisions in South African society. ROC/Taiwan in turn had lost its seat as a permanent member of the United Nations Security Council when it was replaced by the People's Republic of China (PRC) in 1971 and was gradually losing its diplomatic links as countries accorded recognition to the PRC.

South Africa opened a consulate in Taipei, Taiwan, in 1967 and a few years later, in 1972, the ROC/Taiwan, in addition to its existing Consulate-General in Johannesburg, opened a consulate in Cape Town mainly to assist Chinese seamen passing through the port. The warming of relations between the two countries, both avowedly anti-communist, was demonstrated by a rapid increase in bilateral trade, visits by trade missions and the exchange of visits by Cabinet Ministers. Interestingly enough, when ROC/Taiwan had been a member of the UN it had supported the anti-South Africa lobby and voted in favour of sanctions.

Back to the Days of the Dynasty

Diplomatic contact between South Africa and China started in the days of the imperial Ch'ing dynasty when the first Chinese Consul-General, Lew Yuk Lin, was posted to Johannesburg in May 1905. His prime function was to monitor the situation of the more than 60 000 Chinese labourers contracted to work on the Reef gold mines. Even after his recall in 1907, one of his staff, Liu Ngai, was appointed acting Consul-General to serve until the repatriation of the last of the labourers in 1910.

The American consulate in Johannesburg handled matters relating to Chinese interests in South Africa during the tumultuous years following the overthrow of the imperial government and the founding of the Republic of China (ROC) in 1911. It was only nine years later, in 1920, that Liu Ngai returned to South Africa as 'Consul-General in South Africa including Basutoland, Swaziland, Bechuanaland Protectorate and Rhodesia'.[25] Since then consular representation by ROC in South Africa has been continuous. Local Chinese leaders were at times appointed to honorary consular positions to assist the Consul-General.[26] The community was also occasionally called upon to support the consulate financially, especially when funds could not be transmitted from China.

Although South Africa had no reciprocal representation in China, the Chinese consulate-general in Johannesburg was maintained throughout World War II, civil upheaval in China in the 1940s and the establishment of the People's Republic of China (PRC) on the mainland in 1949.

After the government of ROC moved to Taiwan, it retained international recognition and its seat as a permanent member of the United Nations Security Council for more than 20 years until it was replaced by PRC in 1971.

South Africa opened a consulate in Taipei, Taiwan, in 1967 and in 1972, the ROC/Taiwan opened another consulate in Cape Town. In May 1976 the two countries exchanged ambassadors to cement their ties and to reflect the closeness of their relationship. Growing commercial interests and the increase in numbers of Taiwanese industrialists in the Orange Free State and kwaZulu Natal prompted the opening of another consulate in Durban in July 1993.

In the 1990s contact was, however, also established between South Africa and the People's Republic of China. In March 1992 South Africa opened an informal interest office in Beijing and the PRC established a similar office in Pretoria under the name Chinese Centre for South African Studies. Representatives in both offices carry out consular functions and have diplomatic status.

In foreign policy terms, Prime Minister P.W. Botha had identified the forging of alliances with other 'outcast' or 'pariah' countries as one of the strategic options open to South Africa. Although this was realized to be a 'hazardous enterprise', South Africa had cultivated close ties with two such states, Israel and Taiwan.[27] According to political analyst Deon Geldenhuys there were economic, technological and military benefits in these ties.

> South Africa's 'pariah' partners, in turn, no doubt also derive material advantages from their relationships with the Republic. But apart from considerations of material self-interest, 'pariahs' characteristically also perceive other common interests, such as being small or middle-rank powers faced with a serious external, usually communist or communist-inspired threat.[28]

By May 1976 South Africa and ROC/Taiwan raised their diplomatic representation in each other's countries to ambassadorial level. Both Prime Ministers made reciprocal state visits in 1980 to strengthen trade, scientific and technological ties and to conclude agreements in various fields. Apart from boosting trade, the visits also gave rise to press speculation that the position of the South African Chinese would be reviewed. Prime Minister Botha said the government was 'already working on a better deal for the local Chinese'.[29]

INFLUX OF TAIWANESE INVESTORS

One of the significant effects of the warm relationship between the ROC/Taiwan and South Africa was the steady influx of Taiwanese industrialists into the country in the 1980s. South Africa's long-standing prohibition on non-White immigration had to be waived to accommodate them and investors from Taiwan were initially permitted entry on temporary permits.

Two of the first industrialists to settle in southern Africa were brothers, Chung-Nan (John) Aou and Andrew Aou who started a knitwear factory in Swaziland in 1972. They later moved to Transkei and Ciskei where they established the first of several factories in 1977. From knitwear, they moved into the production of cutlery, plastics and shoes.

By mid-1981, the start of an influx from Taiwan became evident from three questions raised in Parliament about conditions governing their entry and residence. The Minister of Internal affairs said visas were required of citizens from Taiwan who sought temporary residence for industrial or commercial investment. They were then granted temporary residence permits, but were not classified in terms of the Population Registration Act. It was also confirmed that although they were subject to the Group Areas Act, they were free to apply to any school for the admission of their children.[30]

Ironically enough, the new Chinese immigrants were also permitted to establish businesses in the Orange Free State, the only one of the country's four provinces in which Asiatic settlement was completely prohibited. An official blind-eye was turned to the 1891 law which stipulated that 'No Arab, "Chinaman", Coolie, or other Asiatic Coloured person ... may settle ... for the purpose of carrying on a commercial

Chinese Immigration to South Africa from 1961 - 1995

The following statistics, obtained from the Department of Home Affairs, reflect the number of Chinese who have been granted permanent residence in South Africa.

Year	Number
1961 - 1975	69
1976	2
1977	1
1978	4
1979	3
1980	4
1981	1
1982	2
1983	-
1984	4
1985	1
1986	7
1987	133
1988	301
1989	483
1990	1422
1991	1981
1992	275
1993	1971
1994	869
1995 (Jan to 31 Oct.)	350
Total No. of Chinese granted Permanent residence between 1961 and 1995	7 883

Note: The breakdown, by country of citizenship, for new permanent residents in 1994 and 1995 was as follows:

	1994	**1995 (to 31 Oct)**
Republic of China/Taiwan	596	232
People's Republic of China	252	102
Hong Kong	21	16
	869	350

business ...'[31] South African-born Chinese who tried to work in the Free State town of Welkom however continued to face problems. Nevertheless the extension of the 'privilege' of being in the province was not without incident for new immigrants.

In August 1983, a young Chinese girl was refused permission to enrol at the Harrismith Primary School and was sent to board at a private school in Johannesburg, more than 300 km away from her family's business.[32] Investors encountered difficulties in renting accommodation in Bloemfontein and no Chinese were permitted to purchase property in the province until the ordinance prohibiting Asiatic settlement was eventually repealed in 1986. The same amending Act, Matters concerning Admission to and Residence in the Republic Amendment Act, no. 53 of 1986, placed all immigration on a merit basis and enabled new immigrants to become permanent residents.[33]

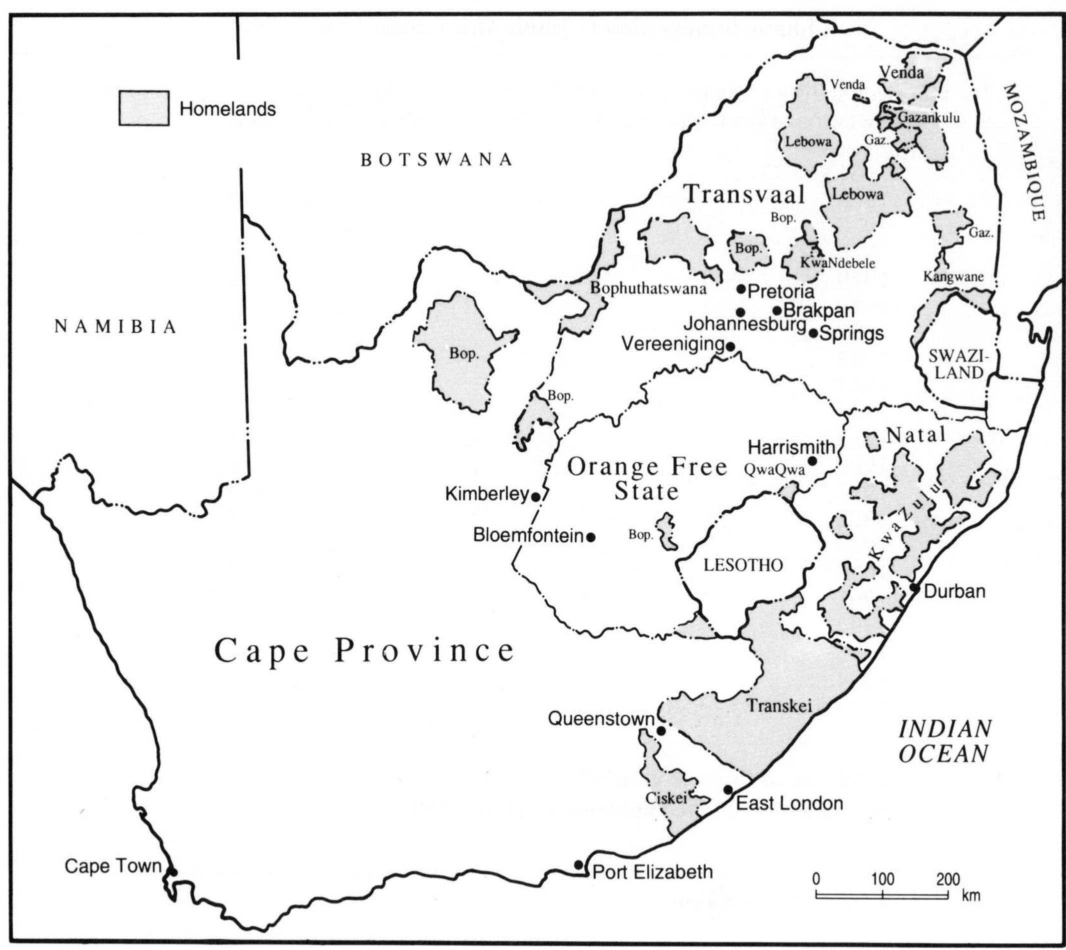

Many new Chinese immigrants to South Africa in the 1980s settled in the Black "homeland" areas of South Africa where they established small factories.

INDUSTRIALISTS SETTLE IN

During the mid-1980s the immigration of investors and their families from ROC/Taiwan and Hong Kong gained momentum in the face of the growing international sanctions campaign against South Africa. They were encouraged, with generous South African government incentives, to invest in border industrial areas in or near the 'homelands'. The intention was to develop labour-intensive concerns providing employment for Blacks who had been resettled in the underdeveloped homelands and to stimulate the economies of these areas.[34]

In July 1986 the investors formed an organization called the Association of ROC Industrialists, under the chairmanship of former Consul-General Lo Ming Yuan. Its intention was to foster unity, protect the interests of industrialists and assist them in establishing themselves. Several years later it decided to broaden its base and renamed itself the Association of Chinese Industrialists in Southern Africa. Its Chinese name however still made it clear that it was allied to ROC/Taiwan.

By 1988, it was estimated that nearly 2500 immigrants from Taiwan had arrived. They settled in remote parts of the country, in Transkei, Ciskei, Bophuthatswana, Venda, Lebowa, Gazankulu, kwaZulu and Qwa Qwa, with several establishing themselves in Newcastle. Financial incentives for investors included relocation costs, subsidizing wages for seven years and rent for 10 years. Perks also included the cheap transport of goods to urban areas and housing loans.[35] These incentives, as well as the favourable exchange rate offered by the Financial Rand, also attracted Chinese investors from Hong Kong, a handful from South America and the local Chinese community.

By 1989 the industrialists were reported to have established nearly 150 factories, with investment capital of some US$300 million, manufacturing products such as clothing, plastic, giftware and electronics. In the following year the number of factories had doubled to 300, but just two years later, in 1992, it dropped to 276, a reflection of the economic recession, political instability, labour problems and insufficient market research. According to the Association of Chinese Industrialists, investors from ROC/Taiwan had created over 40 000 jobs and invested capital of some one billion Rand by 1992.[36]

Starting a business in a foreign environment was difficult at the best of times, but there were particular problems in the South African context. Outlining some of the difficulties investors faced, Charles Liao, secretary of the association in 1991, said too many promises had been made to Chinese investors and that both the governments of the ROC/Taiwan and South Africa could have offered industrialists more assistance. Not only did Chinese investors struggle to speak some English, but they had to do so with rural Blacks, many of whom themselves spoke little or no English. The result was sign language, misunderstanding and often costly mistakes on expensive machinery.

From densely populated Taiwan to the rural undeveloped countryside of the border areas, the new settlers found themselves isolated, far from city amenities, without a place of worship for Buddhists, Taoists or Confucianists and unable to purchase Chinese provisions. At the operational level, there was an inadequate infrastructure in terms of power supply and telecommunications. Insufficient research sometimes led to the establishment of factories producing goods for which there was no market.[37]

The most pressing problems the industrialists faced were labour-related. Setting up took much longer than anticipated, with several industrialists stating it was at least three years before they showed any profit. In addition to low productivity, unrest, stayaways, industrial disputes and theft, they found themselves having repeatedly to train unskilled rural labourers when their experienced workforce moved to better-paying jobs in the cities. The shortage of middle-level managers also inhibited the growth of the factories, their major drawback in attracting such staff being their remoteness from urban areas.

The greatest fear of investors was the depreciation in the value of the Rand and its effect on their capital investments. Investor Lawrence Ting said the industrialists initially had problems raising finance as they were not known to the South African banks and by providing most of the capital themselves, they were at the mercy of South Africa's exchange control regulations. To cater for investments by ROC/Taiwan nationals, the state-owned Bank of Taiwan opened an office in Johannesburg in April 1992, becoming the first Asian bank to establish itself in South Africa.[38]

Chinese garment factory in Dimbaza, Ciskei – 1987.

Andrew and John (Chung Nan) Aou, who emigrated from Taiwan to southern Africa in the 1970s.

Association chairman, C.C. Kan said in July 1992:

> In the past three years, partly due to the opening arms of other countries, Taiwanese industrialists invested more in Southeast Asia and mainland China, and less in Southern Africa. Although the incentives for investment offered by the South African government are still better than those by any other country, the rising labour cost and political uncertainty here deter many potential investors.

By the end of 1994, only nine more Chinese factories had opened their doors, (bringing the total number to 285) — a reflection of the wariness of investors and the drastic reduction in incentives offered. Many investors from ROC/Taiwan also entered South Africa as entrepreneurs, opening import and export firms, restaurants and small businesses. Based in South Africa's larger cities, there were approximately 300 such companies in 1994.[39]

As the numbers of new immigrants grew and they were given permanent residence, they formed a variety of business organizations as well as social, cultural and sports clubs. Because ROC/Taiwan permitted dual citizenship, many immigrants exercised the option to become naturalized South Africans after five years' permanent residence. To cater for their spiritual beliefs, the first Buddhist temple in the country was built in the Transvaal town of Bronkhorstspruit in 1993.

'CHINATOWNS' — GROUP AREAS REVISITED

Speculators, property developers and town councils sought to attract investment capital by encouraging the immigration of Chinese investors from Hong Kong as well as ROC/Taiwan. Among the 'incentives' offered was the creation of exclusive 'Chinatowns' for the immigrants to live among fellow Chinese, to establish their own communal facilities and not be confronted with language problems in a foreign country.

From 1990, various proposals for the development of 'Chinatowns' surfaced in towns such as Queenstown, Springs, Brakpan, Bronkhorstspruit, Verwoerdburg and in an outlying part of Johannesburg as well as in the Western Cape. Included in some of the proposals was the idea to develop such settlements into tourist attractions, with Chinese-style architecture, shops and restaurants.

While welcoming the settlement of Chinese from Hong Kong and Taiwan, the Chinese Association of South Africa (CASA) nonetheless expressed its opposition to the development of 'Chinatowns'. In a statement, CASA said:

> The community has fought long and hard over the previous decades against problems associated with the discriminatory provisions of the Group Areas Act, and cannot therefore tolerate any exclusive grouping, whether this be voluntary, or enforced.
>
> It is hoped that promoters and developers of such schemes as well as all authorities — central as well as local government — take note of the feelings of the Chinese community in this regard.[40]

The councils of Bronkhorstpruit, which set aside a residential and industrial area for Chinese from ROC/Taiwan, and Verwoerdburg which aimed to attract Hong Kong investors, both assured CASA that their developments would not be limited to Chinese occupation. When a developer requested that 60% of stands in Liefde en Vrede township, on the outskirts of Johannesburg, be reserved for Hong Kong immigrants, CASA said this was effectively a quota system based on race.[41] Although groupings of Chinese formed in various parts of the country, no exclusively Chinese townships had been developed by the mid-1990s.

'TWO CHINAS' POSE NEW PROBLEMS

From the 1990s, the dismantling of apartheid opened South Africa to contact with countries previously regarded as taboo because of their communist ideology. In March 1992 South Africa established links with the People's Republic of China (PRC) by opening an informal interest office in Peking (Beijing). The PRC reciprocated by establishing an unofficial presence in Pretoria, under the name Chinese Centre for South African Studies. Personnel in both offices carried diplomatic status, issued visas and effectively acted as consular offices.

This situation in the face of South Africa's formal recognition of the Republic of China on Taiwan gave rise to new tensions in the community, many of whom still had relatives in mainland China, but had historically and often ideologically supported the Kuomintang and ROC/Taiwan. Local organizations were subjected to pressure from ROC/Taiwan officials not to have any contact with the new PRC office and visiting dignitaries. Both CASA and the Transvaal Chinese Association had maintained some contact with PRC authorities in China and the embassy in neighbouring Botswana for a number of years to assist the community with reclaiming property on the mainland and to obtain visas to visit their families.

CASA called a special general conference on 1 March 1992 to formulate a policy stance and issued the following statement on future relations with the PRC and the ROC/Taiwan.

> The Chinese Association of South Africa is committed to serving the best interests of all Chinese in this country and believes it is inevitable and desirable that there be formal contact between CASA and PRC, with due regard being paid to the sensitivities of the community and the ROC. Such contact will mainly be on practical issues, and on social, cultural and trade levels. Contact of any other nature will first be referred to CASA's member associations. The Chinese Association of South Africa will endeavour to maintain and improve its long-standing good relations with the Republic of China.[42]

In several newsletters, CASA pointed out that its objective was to safeguard the community's interests and it was necessary to be open to contact with all parties who could have some bearing on its future. It was emphasized that CASA's contact with anyone, be it the government, the African National Congress, the ROC/Taiwan or the PRC did not necessarily imply support for their policies.[43]

From 1992 speculation in the media and government circles centred on whether or not South Africa and PRC would establish diplomatic ties. China had long supported the anti-apartheid cause, assisting liberation movements, and the dismantling of apartheid opened the way for formal relations with South Africa. A stumbling block however was South Africa's long-standing official recognition of ROC/Taiwan.[44] It appeared inevitable that South Africa would be caught between the political power of the PRC and the undeniable economic muscle of the ROC/Taiwan.

The Foreign Ministers of both PRC and South Africa exchanged unofficial visits and in October 1992, the president of the African National Congress (ANC), Nelson Mandela, visited mainland China, holding talks with both the Premier and the Communist Party general secretary. High level visits between the two countries continued and a particular emphasis was placed on forging trade and investment links. Contacts among businessmen were encouraged by trade fairs and exhibitions. The Great Wall Group under the control of the PRC's Ministry of Foreign Economic Relations and Trade established headquarters in Bedfordview, Transvaal, in March 1993. In the previous year, the PRC's official news agency, *Xinhua*, opened offices in Johannesburg.

Nelson Mandela visited ROC/Taiwan in July 1993 to raise funds for the ANC's election campaign and secured a promise for substantial contributions towards a vocational training centre. After the visit controversy flared over a news report from China that an ANC-led government would sever ties with ROC/Taiwan if it came to power. The ANC issued a statement 'to correct' the report, saying: 'While the ANC stands ready to build a new relationship with the government of Taiwan, whatever our past differences, it will not abandon its long-standing friends.'[45]

After South Africa's historic all-race elections, ROC/Taiwan's President Lee Teng-Hui and Foreign Minister Frederick Chien visited South Africa to attend Mandela's inauguration as the country's new State President on 10 May 1994. Later in the year a South African Foreign Affairs spokesman said any decision on the issue of the 'two Chinas' had to be 'taken on the basis of national interest and international precedent'.[46] The debate continues to rage, with ROC/Taiwan advocating that South Africa initiate a policy of dual recognition while PRC has refused to establish full diplomatic relations unless South Africa downgrades its existing ties with ROC/Taiwan.

Political analysts have argued that South Africa should 'capitalize on President Mandela's prestige — and the country's newfound influence as a regional power — to recognize "both Chinas".' Diplomats on the other hand have pointed out that only 28 minor countries recognize ROC/Taiwan, and that South Africa should fall in line with the United Nations and move the South African embassy from Taipei to Beijing.[47]

Summarizing the significance of the 'China issue' in post-apartheid South Africa and stating that it should be addressed against a wider international backdrop, foreign relations analyst Deon Geldenhuys said:

> This is not merely a triangular matter involving Pretoria, Taipei and Beijing. Most countries have previously dealt with the same dilemma. But the issue is not dead, for Taipei and its supporters are campaigning for full diplomatic recognition of the ROC, including membership of the United Nations. The way South Africa handles the question may indeed influence the international fortunes of the two Chinese states.[48]

The competition for influence in South Africa between ROC and PRC continued to precipitate tensions among Chinese organizations. Neutrality in dealing with both sides was propounded as an option, but being seen as a supporter of one or other side affected all sectors of the community, whether they were political, cultural, social or sporting groups.

SOUTH AFRICA'S CHINESE IN THE 1990s

Both South Africa and the Chinese community were confronted by new challenges in the 1990s. Reform had to provide for the needs of a population numbering 38.5 million, comprising 76% Blacks, 3% Asians, 9% Coloureds and 13% Whites in 1991.[49] For a minority such as the Chinese, the decade heralded significant changes in its numbers, composition and profile. The population had increased substantially — from 11 020 in 1980[50] to an estimated 20 000 or more in 1995. The steady influx of new immigrants had transformed the community from a closely-knit, relatively homogeneous group into an extended, multilingual mix of Chinese from ROC/Taiwan, Hong Kong, mainland China and elsewhere.

ADVERSE PUBLICITY

With the increased numbers came a dramatic shift in image from the former stereotype of Chinese as a quiet, law-abiding, low-profile community. In the early 1990s the media focused on malpractices and controversial activities by Chinese such as gill-net fishing, seal-culling, rhino horn and elephant tusk poaching, credit card frauds, gang warfare and labour abuse. One incident which attracted much publicity was the treatment of South African workers aboard Taiwanese trawlers. More than 30 suffered frostbite-related injuries, losing all or some of their fingers. Compensation was paid to the injured workers by the ROC/Taiwan government.[51]

The publicity increased tensions between the local Chinese and the new immigrants as newspapers reported on the wrongdoings of 'Chinese'. A marked 'us' and 'them' attitude developed since other South Africans could not differentiate between the two 'groups'. In a letter to a major newspaper, a Chinese South African expressed outrage at the 'behaviour of those Taiwanese who have exploited our resources' and ruined the image of the community. Replying, other Chinese questioned whether any good was achieved 'by singling out the Taiwanese for censure' and said this had only created further discord in the community.[52]

The ROC/Taiwan Industrialists Association also entered the fray, stating in its newsletter that the old and new immigrants did not understand each other. Although there had been embarrassing incidents, this was limited to a minority and had nothing to do with the community. It said all Chinese should be proud of the investments in South Africa by the new immigrants totalling US $2 billion and the creation of 50 000 jobs which had contributed greatly to the economy. The industrialists' newsletter appealed for greater understanding and more contact between the two groups.

THE CITIZEN Thursday 29 August 1991

Two deny receiving R1,6-m rhino horn in police trap

By Carol Hills

TWO Republic of China men yesterday denied in the Johannesburg Magistrate's Court receiving 204,75 kg of rhino horn with a street value of about R1,63 million.

6 SUNDAY TIMES, February 23 1992

Gangs fight

Murder, extortion and kidnap linked to 'Chinese mafia'

By DIANA STREAK

CHINESE gang warfare over the rights to a multi-million-rand shark-fin industry has boiled over into murders, a kidnapping and shootouts on the streets of South African cities.

IT'S TONGS VERSUS TRIADS

Taiwanese seen as marine marauders

By Jacqueline Myburgh

Taiwan is in danger of being labelled "public enemy number one", according to some conservationists.

Numerous calls to The Star have revealed that the public perceives the South African Government as turning a blind eye to Taiwan's marine malpractices in order to safeguard relations between the two countries.

The public has been outraged by the announcement that Jiuh Wueh Industries, a Taiwanese-owned factory in Port Nolloth, has been granted a permit to harvest 30 500 seal cubs and bulls next month.

The following incidents appear to have ruined Taiwan's reputation, on the environmental score:

- A rhino horn smuggling operation operating between South Africa and Taiwan was uncovered last year. Rhino horn is the East's equivalent of aspirin, according to Dr John Ledger, director of the Endangered Wildlife ...

Rhino horn, ivory worth ... seized

SA Chinese abhor fishing practices

Police seize ivory worth R2 million

PHILIP ZOIO

Chinese hit the headlines again in the 1990s. A spate of newspaper articles focused public attention on activities such as gillnetting, ivory poaching and gang warfare.

The Transvaal Chinese Association answered in its newsletter:

> That the new immigrants have invested over US$2 billion and employed 50 000 people in SA should be seen as a double-edged sword. This may have been good for the South African economy as a whole, but it is also important to note that it happened during the time when anti-apartheid groups were most successful in their calls for sanctions against South Africa. Both the 'new' and the 'old' immigrants should bear in mind that the interpretation could exist that the Republic of China on Taiwan (and therefore all Chinese) supported apartheid.

It concluded that each group should coexist without friction. Co-operation and unification should be encouraged, but neither group should feel threatened by the other.[53] CASA held a special conference in March 1992 to seek avenues for co-operation between old and new immigrants, and committed itself to encouraging closer contacts among all Chinese.

ILLEGAL IMMIGRATION

By the 1990s the Chinese became more diversified economically. No longer only shopkeepers and professionals, they spanned the full spectrum of occupational pursuits, being involved in the manufacturing industries, property development, restaurants, the trades, small businesses and street-hawking. It was, however, this latter occupation which again sparked public attention. Chinese vendors selling jeans, watches and knick-knacks on the streets of Johannesburg became conspicuous in the latter part of 1992

Lesotho Riots

More than 300 Chinese were forced to flee from Maseru, the capital of neighbouring Lesotho, when race riots flared in May 1991. After the death of a Black woman caught shoplifting, mobs went on the rampage, looting shops, stoning vehicles and setting fire to the property of Chinese and Indians.

According to press reports, local people 'had become increasingly resentful of Taiwanese immigrants who were running the majority of small businesses and industries in Lesotho.' Several people died in the rioting, and one Chinese survivor recounted a frightening tale of how he and his wife were forced to strip and were then stoned as they escaped from a mob.[54]

The Chinese, who had immigrated from Taiwan and mainland China since the late 1980s, sought refuge in the South African town of Ladybrand in the Orange Free State, a few kilometres from the border. Local White residents came to their aid, as did Chinese countrywide with food and clothing to meet their immediate needs. Substantial contributions towards relief aid for the refugees were made by ROC/Taiwan and the People's Republic of China, with donations also coming from the Chinese Association of South Africa and individuals.

when Black hawkers appealed for them to be removed.

Objecting to the presence of 'foreign traders', they claimed that hundreds of Chinese and Koreans had 'flooded' the pavements of Johannesburg.[55] Many of the immigrants, from mainland China and Taiwan, were found to have entered the country legally as tourists, but remained without the requisite residence or work permits. Some had entered South Africa as refugees after the unrest in Lesotho in May 1991.

Newspapers revealed that illegal immigrants from mainland China had been lured to South Africa by conmen who promised to find them work and homes. After paying up to R25 000 to agents, these immigrants found themselves abandoned in South Africa and turned to selling goods on the streets to survive.[56] Some illegal immigrants were reported to have bribed officials to issue permanent residence certificates or used agencies to obtain false documents. It was noted that the number of Chinese immigrants to South Africa had more than quadrupled in two years — from 460 in 1989 to 1 959 in 1991.[57] How many arrived as visitors and remained as illegal immigrants can only be estimated, but press reports speculated the figure could be as high as 8000.[58]

CASA held meetings with the Department of Home Affairs, the African Council for Hawkers and Informal Business (ACHIB) and the illegal immigrants. CASA said it was understandable that those who had left China sought a better life in the same way as the forefathers of the local community, but 'the current political climate in South Africa is not conducive to absorbing people without skills.' South Africa's high unemployment rate and poor economy increased the potential for racial conflict when Chinese hawkers competed with Black hawkers who themselves had fought for years for the right to sell on the streets.[59]

To promote understanding between the Black hawkers and Chinese, CASA arranged for the hawkers, through ACHIB, to meet manufacturers belonging to the Association of Chinese Industrialists in South Africa. The hawkers were offered the opportunity to buy goods direct from factories at competitive prices. The industrialists further agreed to channel the profits from their dealings with the hawkers into education and training schemes.[60] These initiatives, however, foundered because of a lack of organizational structures among the hawkers.

CASA said although the community had sympathy for the plight of fellow Chinese, there were serious consequences should the illegal influx continue. The Eastern Province Chinese Association and the Port Elizabeth Chinese provided accommodation and food for 14 hawkers for more than six months after they had been arrested for being in the country illegally, and were awaiting the outcome of civil court cases.[61]

To stem the influx of illegal immigrants, the South African Department of Home Affairs made requirements for visitors' visas and work permits for citizens of PRC more stringent and the PRC introduced additional screening measures for applicants for work permits.

FORGING A NEW COMMUNITY

Despite its growing numbers, the Chinese community retained a fair level of social and cultural cohesiveness. Community organizations provided a full social calendar, from dances and sports tournaments to Chinese New Year and 'Double Ten' celebrations. The assimilation of new immigrants prompted greater awareness of the need to speak Chinese, with many young people enrolling for either Mandarin or Cantonese classes.

Through its embassy and consulates-general, the government of the ROC/Taiwan supported a host of cultural and related activities in the community. A substantial loan was made for the establishment of the Chinese Cultural Centre, in August 1982, in the vacated premises of the Kuo Ting Chinese School, in Johannesburg. The centre offered classes in Chinese cooking, tai-chi, kung-fu and Chinese languages. Financial aid was also provided for organizing sports tournaments, Double Ten functions and various cultural gatherings. An Amity Conference of Overseas Chinese in Africa was organized every two years in various centres, coinciding with the African Regional Conference of the Grand Alliance for the Reunification of China under the Three Principles of the People.

The ROC/Taiwan government donated US$300 000 to CASA to assist the TCA in its project to build a community centre for Chinese in the Johannesburg area. Former Ambassador H.K. Yang made a personal donation of R20 000 to this cause in 1989. For young people in the community, a travel highlight was the youth tour to Taiwan and Hong Kong, organised by CASA and TCA in December each year. The tour, sponsored by the ROC/Taiwan's Overseas Chinese Affairs Commission, offered young people under 25 years of age the opportunity to meet Chinese from other parts of the southern hemisphere, to learn about Chinese culture and to tour Taiwan.

Whenever called upon to support good causes, the community rallied around and donated generously. Substantial sums were raised for causes such as:

- Riot relief in Port Elizabeth in mid-1990, when more than 20 Chinese families had their shops and homes looted and burned (More than R36 000 was raised.);
- Supply of food, clothing and shelter for more than 300 Chinese forced to flee the riots in Lesotho in May 1991;
- Flood relief in China in mid-1991 when several provinces were declared disaster areas, leaving at least two million homeless. Fund organizers, Jackson Leong and Ma Yip, with a China Flood Relief Fund committee raised more than R250 000 (nearly US $90 000);
- Tiananmen Square relief fund to aid those involved in the student unrest in June 1989. Difficulties were however encountered in transmitting the funds to China and money was either refunded or donated to the Hong Ning Chinese Aged Home;
- Floods in Natal, Orange Free State and Northern Cape when many South Africans lost their homes and possessions in 1987 and 1988. (R35 000 was given to the national Flood Disaster Fund);
- Hepatitis B blood testing to establish the incidence of the virus in the Chinese community, undertaken by Dr Ernest Song and researchers of the Liver Cancer Research Unit of the University of the Witwatersrand, in early 1983;
- Restoration of the historic tombstone of Chow Kwai For in the Braamfontein cemetery, Johannesburg, in 1983;
- Paying for a security guard to patrol the Chinese section of the Newclare cemetery after several visitors to the cemetery had been attacked and robbed in 1992;
- The purchase of a wheelchair for a young Chinese man, paralyzed in a racial shooting incident in which his brother was killed and a friend injured, in August 1992;
- Funding research costs for the South African Chinese History Project to collect information on the history of the community.

These were only some of the many projects in which Chinese throughout South Africa were collectively involved. Although many organizations formed in the 1990s served the interests of Taiwanese exclusively, they nonetheless enriched cultural awareness, added a different approach to functions, and extended the reach of the Chinese as a community.

CHINESE AND THE FRANCHISE

On 2 February 1990 State President F.W. de Klerk set South Africa on course for a more democratic society. In his landmark address to Parliament he announced the repeal of apartheid legislation, the unbanning of liberation movements and the release of political prisoners, including African National Congress leader, Nelson Mandela. From 1991 race as a criterion was eliminated from the statute books with the repeal of the Population Registration Act, the Group Areas Act and the Land Acts.

The unresolved issue of rights for the Chinese had remained a source of concern and perhaps embarrassment to the Government — to the extent that the issue was specifically raised in meetings with the Chinese Association of South Africa shortly after President De Klerk's historic 1990 speech. Foreign Minister R.F. (Pik) Botha told CASA representatives that he had long been fighting against the injustices caused by the anomalous status of the Chinese in South Africa and there had, 10 years previously, been an agreement between ROC/Taiwan Premier Sun Yun-Suan and President P.W. Botha that the situation would be addressed. He said the South African government was prepared to adhere to its commitment to grant full rights to the Chinese but wished to ascertain the community's views before proceeding.[62]

Community meetings were held around the country by CASA's regional members to obtain a consensus of opinion and CASA thereafter notified the government that since South Africa was entering a new era, it was unnecessary to single out the Chinese for special consideration. The Chinese felt more fundamental issues needed to take precedence and when the new South Africa came into being, constitutional rights for the Chinese would fall in line with those granted to all other South Africans. CASA also expressed the community's 'earnest desire to contribute towards the shaping of the new South Africa' whether directly or indirectly in the forthcoming negotiations process.[63]

CASA representatives also held meetings with the Deputy Minister of Constitutional Development and Planning, Roelf Meyer, and the Minister of Home Affairs, G. Louw, to discuss its stance on constitutional rights. On the question of the possible role the community could play in negotiations, it was pointed out that only political parties with some following would participate. Although it was suggested that the Chinese consider forming a political party, CASA felt it was nonsensical for the community to group itself racially in order to take part in the political processes. CASA also pointed out that the community had for generations been part of the disadvantaged in South Africa and was in a unique position since it understood both the frustrations of Blacks and the fears of Whites.[64]

The negotiating forum, the Convention for a Democratic South Africa (CODESA) eventually paved the way, from December 1991, for the country's new transitional democratic government. Becase CASA had an 'ethnic' constituency rather than a political one, it was not permitted to participate but continued to convey the community's views in meetings with parties across the political spectrum, including the Pan Africanist Congress, the African National Congress, the National Party, the Democratic Party and the Inkatha Freedom Party.[65]

South Africa's historic all-race elections were held on 27 and 28 April 1994 marking the first time the Chinese were entitled to vote as South African citizens. It was an emotional occasion, symbolizing the attainment, finally, of full rights for this small minority as well as the country's overwhelming Black majority. Despite rumours of right wing attacks as well as violence and bombings in urban areas in the days leading up to the elections, millions of South Africans stood for hours in long queues at polling stations countrywide to cast their votes. Tales abounded of the spirit of hope and exhilaration which had pervaded the nation. Despite numerous hitches in the overall organization, South Africa emerged peacefully from its first democratic elections and a new era had begun.

In Retrospect

The story of the Chinese in South Africa has been one of adaptation — an account of a numerically insignificant minority trying to find its place in a society stratified along colour lines. Beginning more than 300 years ago with the exile of Chinese convicts to the Cape, it has unfolded as a record of a people who were both 'needed' yet 'rejected'.

Chinese labour was in demand by various government departments and farmers in the 19th century Cape. From 1814 several groups of Chinese artisans and labourers worked in the western Cape, eastern Cape and Natal — but the largest Chinese importation scheme was the recruitment of some 63 000 labourers from 1904 to revive South Africa's gold mining industry after the second Anglo-Boer War. Needed for their labour alone, the Chinese were specifically excluded from skilled occupations and promptly sent back from whence they had come when their contracts expired.

'Free' Chinese settlers, not contracted labourers, started arriving from the 1870s, attracted by the country's new found mineral wealth and driven by conditions of poverty and economic decline in China. Equipped with little more than the will to make a living, they established themselves in small shops and laundries, later sending home for their wives and children. Restrictive immigration laws soon made it clear they were not wanted ... the Cape's Chinese Exclusion Act of 1904 and later the Union's Immigrants Regulation Act of 1913 prohibited all adult male immigration and by 1953 a total bar on the entry of Chinese was enforced.

Minuscule in terms of South Africa's total population (0.04% in 1990), the Chinese always constituted a distinctly identifiable minority which did not *belong* or fit readily into the country's major racial compartments, namely Black, Coloured, Indian and White. It was this lack of size which defined its role in South African society and worked both to its advantage and detriment as a community. The Chinese skirted the edges of the lives of other South Africans. Because they posed no numerical 'threat', they were usually ignored or even forgotten. They lived and traded among all races and when apartheid began to enforce the rigid separation of groups, they were, perhaps more than others, permitted the flexibility to continue straddling the colour line. Being 'in-between' gave them the rare opportunity to understand the frustrations and fears on both sides, yet also left them in the vulnerable position of not belonging to either. Their need to 'belong' found expression in the surge of nationalistic fervour during the Sino-Japanese War from 1937 to 1945 as Chinese countrywide made substantial sacrifices to aid China's war effort. When the Communist Party gained control of mainland China and the Chinese found themselves cut off from their motherland, they were made to realize the necessity of securing their future in South Africa.

The Chinese experience in South Africa was one of life by exemption. Prior to World War II they were permitted limited social 'privileges' in terms of access to White public transport and cinemas, but generally were subjected to most restrictions imposed on people of colour. In the apartheid era concessions continued under a permit system. The government's decision to grant 'honorary White' status to the Japanese in 1961 marked a watershed in the stringent application of apartheid laws to the Chinese. It was the first time that the authorities themselves compromised the rigid divisions between Whites and non-Whites, and because the general populace could not differentiate between Japanese and Chinese, the precedent paved the way for easing restrictions on the Chinese.

Because the Chinese sought basic rights, synonymous in South Africa with White rights, their path to social acceptance lay in increasing westernization. Through education they achieved greater social mobility, adopting western habits, language and social customs. To 'belong', they became almost chameleon-like as a community, adapting to changing circumstances to survive. Those who found adaptation to apartheid unacceptable led the community's 'brain drain' from the 1960s to countries where merit, not colour, determined their prospects.

By emphasizing racial difference, apartheid made the Chinese more aware of what it meant to be Chinese. Isolated on the tip of Africa, the community, without new immigration and an influx of Chinese cultural ideas, became somewhat insular and self-reliant, always aware that their status was tenuous, based largely on privileges, rather than rights. Stereotyped as a group, individuals felt answerable for the actions of other Chinese and conscious that whatever they did would have an impact on the community. The need for a sense of communal responsibility not only deprived Chinese of the freedom to live their lives as individuals, but it also made most of them conform to the behaviour expected of the 'quiet, industrious, law-abiding community'.

By definition, apartheid aimed to separate the races and therefore discouraged racial intermingling. The Chinese generally kept to themselves socially, but co-existed peacefully wherever possible with the other race groups. As shopkeepers with businesses in Black, Coloured and White areas, they tried to establish sound relations with their customers by offering an honest service, credit when needed and making donations to causes within the different communities where they traded.

In many ways apartheid gave the Chinese a stronger sense of identity, encouraged the formation of many Chinese organizations and perhaps enabled the community to retain its Chineseness longer than other Chinese communities which settled in the western world. The influx of new immigrants from Taiwan, Hong Kong and mainland China changed the nature of the Chinese community, increased its numbers and contributed towards its cultural diversity.

With the dawning of the new South Africa, race was removed from the statute books as a determinant of basic rights but it will continue to be a major factor in redressing past imbalances and instituting affirmative action policies. The change from White minority rule to Black majority rule has left the Chinese in the same no-man's land they have always occupied between the different racial groups. Although they have been given the franchise, the outstanding question remains whether or not the Chinese, so long perceived as 'foreigners' in the land of their birth, will finally be accepted as equal citizens.

Lists of Acknowledgments

Many institutions allowed us access to their facilities and we acknowledge our indebtedness to the libraries and librarians of :

University of the Witwatersrand, Johannesburg
Johannesburg Public Library
State Archives in Pretoria, Cape Town and Pietermaritzburg.
Kimberley Public Library
McGregor Museum, Kimberley
South African Library, Cape Town
The State Library, Pretoria
Don Africana Library, Durban Municipal Library
Local History Museum, Durban
Cory Library for Historical Research, Rhodes University
Port Elizabeth City Library
University of Durban-Westville
Barlow Rand Archives
Chamber of Mines of South Africa
South African Institute of Race Relations
Public Record Office, Surrey, England
Chinese Chamber of Commerce, Port Louis, Mauritius

Friends and community members have been generous in their support and we wish to record our sincere appreciation for encouragement, hospitality and assistance to:

Affat family
Raymond & Yvonne Ah Sing
Aou Chung Nan
Molly Au
Alan Chan Yan
Ronald & Stella Chong
Victor Chong
Shiang & Eileen Chum
Percy Date Chong
Seu Lau Fok
Albert Fontbin
Rae Graham
Henion Han
Lucia & Henry Hau Yoon
Choy & Lillian Ho
Les Hoy
Consul-General Wei Jen Hu
Dr Linda Human

Mr & Mrs L.S. Hwang
Gary & Delphine Junkin
Mr & Mrs H. Kew
Carston Kim Sing
Terry & Mary Lai King
Leonard Lam
Jerrold Law
Errol Lee Son
Jackson Leong
James Leong
Calvin Low Ah Kee
Gordon & Phyllis Loyson
Diana & Clifford Luk
Ma families of Durban
Man and Fokming families
Ralph & Jean Pakshong
Pow Chong families
Eileen Song
Norman Tam
Consul-General George Tuan
Lawrence Wilson
Norman Yan
Steven Yap
Eric Ying

Conference support

- World Chinese Conference in Mauritius 1991
- Luodi-Shenggen Conference in San Francisco 1992

Our work was greatly assisted by those who kindly provided books, photographs, documentary material, services facilitating the research and snippets of information which directed us along new paths. We are most grateful to:

Anchor Life Assurance
Ms Vivienne Affat
Mr James C. Armstrong
Ms Diana Arnott
Mrs Rosie Ah Chow
Mrs Violet Ah Chow
Mr & Mrs Roger Ah Kun
Mr Hymie Alper
Dr & Mrs W.F. Barron
Professor Belinda Bozzoli
Mrs Esme Bull
Mr Wayne Changfoot
Mrs Molly Chong
Mr Peter Coates
Ms Anna Cunningham
Ms Shelagh De Wet
Mr Ted Clayson
Mr Cecil Date Chong
Mr Ronald Date Chong
Mr Alkis Doucakis
Mr Donald Dunne
Eastern Province Chinese Association
Engineering Data Systems
Ms Helen Fairbairn
Mrs Yvonne Fokming
Ms Cecilia Ford
Ms Pamela Ford
Ms Deirdre Fripp
Consul-General John Hirsch
Mr Allan Ho
Mr Donald Ho
Mr Peter Holden
Mr William Hone
Mrs Sybil Hunt
Mr & Mrs Errol Jack Kee
Ms Esdre Keller
Mr & Mrs Winston King
Mr Sidney Kim Sing
Mr Edward Kin
Mr Alan Kolling
Mr Edward Kow
Mr Alan Kwon Hoo
Mrs Lily Lai
Lai Hin Family
Mr Mario Lee
Mr Cecil Leong
Mr Pak Seong Leong
Mrs Nancy Lo Pong
Mr Jeff Lok
Mr Kaye Luk
Mr Cheong Lun
Mrs Lung
Ms Jenny McGhee
Mr Michael Mong
Ms Moira Moore
Mr John Morrison
Professor Bruce Murray
Professor Reuben Musiker
Ms Dee Nash
Ms Margaret Northey
Dr & Mrs Oscar Norwich
Ms Marie Peacock

Mr & Mrs Eddie Pearce (Cosmos Films)
Ms Michele Pickover
Ms Gillian Pow Chong
Mr Werner Schlebach (Procolor)
Simmer & Jack Mine
Mr Basil Song
Mrs Esme Stephens
Mr Philip Stickler
Ms Beth Strachan
Mr Jonathan B. Thompson
Mr Bruce Titlestad
Mr Allan Toi
Uitenhage Chinese Association
Ms Aja Verhagen
Mr Nam Dat Way
Mr Percy Whyte
Mr Ernest Wing King
Mr & Mrs Graham Wingnean
Ms Dorothy Wheeler
Ms Wendy Whittaker
Ms Dorothy Wong
Ms Judy Yung
Ms Janet Zambri

PERSONS INTERVIEWED

Many people gave willingly of their time to tell us of their reminiscences and to allow us access to personal documents and photographs. While we spoke to many more community members than the list below reflects, we would like to record our sincere thanks to the following people in different parts of South Africa, as well as former South Africans who gave us information during visits back to the country.

Johannesburg and environs

Mr Ah Tong (Boksburg)
Mrs Inmie Brown
Mr Ho Sue Chong
Mr Tsang Ho Chun
Mr Willie Date Ling
Mr Donald Dunne
Mr Yung Fah
Mr Eric Ford
Mr Wellington Ford
Mr Cecil Fortoen
Mrs Eileen Foy
Mr Lam Foy
Mr Lee (Consular Gazette)
Mr Sung Himpoo
Consul-General Wei Jen Hu
Mr Ah Hue
Mr & Mrs Kee Fah Johnson
Mr Lew Johnson
Mr Fok Yu Kam
Mr C.C. Kan
Mr Edward Kin
Mr Jack Lau King
Mr Ignatius King
Mr Oscar Kwan
Mr Kelly Lai
Mrs Wan Yuk Lee
Mr Wilfred Lee
Mrs Lau Hoi Lee
Mr Kim Yen Leetion
Sr Lily Lee Sun
Mr & Mrs Leong Pak Seong
Mr and Mrs Richard Lohlun
Mrs Margie Lok
Mr and Mrs Stanley Luk
Mrs Ping Che Man
Mr Stanley May
Mr Keith Chen Ming
Mr Alec Oshry
Mr Ah Song
Dr Colin Song
Mrs Kwan Lai Thouw
Mr Jong Tin
Mr A.H. Tong
Fr Michael Tuohy
Mr Dang Sui Wah
Mrs Soy Yan
Mr Leslie Yenson
Mr Henry Yenson

Pretoria

Mr Shiang Chum
Mr Kenneth Fung
Mr Su Won Ho
Mr Chen Hong
Mr Douglas Kee
Mr Wing Ki
Mr Lewis Fu Law
Ambassador H.K. Yang

Vereeniging

Mr Quan Ba
Mr Sun Hing
Mr Li Kom

Durban

Mr Les Chapson
Mr Peter Chen
Mr Albert Fontbin
Mr Ma Wing Fut
Mr & Mrs Jack Hoption
Mr H.K. Kew
Mr Ralph Pakshong
Mr Gumm Timm
Mr Ma Wing Yip

Port Elizabeth

Mr James Affat
Mr Ah Ling
Mr Wally Ah Yui
Mrs Chantson
Mr T.F. Date Chong
Mr Percy Date Chong
Mrs N.F. Date Chong
Mrs Date Line
Mr W.J. Gin
Mr Godfrey Gin
Mr & Mrs Norman Huang
Mr Edward Jack Kee
Mr Hyman Li Green
Mr & Mrs D. Lin
Mr David Low Ah Kee
Mr James Low Ah Kee
Mr Gordon Loyson
Fr Ignatius Ou
Mr Archie Pow Chong
Mr S.S. Pow Chong
Mr W.S. Pow Chong
Mr Harry Simpson
Mrs Amy Singmin
Mr Enfield Song Loong
Miss M.K. Whiteley
Mr and Mrs Y. Whiteley
Mr Pan Ngian Wong
Mr Herman Wong On
Mrs Yee Loong

Uitenhage

Mr Raymond Ah Sing
Mrs Ah Sing
Mr George Lau
Mr Gordon Lee Sun
Mr Joey Long King
Mr Y.S. Manlee

East London

Mr Huey Chan
Mr Ley Changfoot
Mr Ken Eason
Mr John Louis Fontbin
Dr Stanley Himpoo
Mr Y.S. Lee
Mr Errol Lee Son
Mr Hop Sin Lee Sun
Mrs Radloff
Mr & Mrs L. Sent
Mr Harry Wong Kun

Eastern Cape

Mr & Mrs Wing On Ah Yui
Mrs W.S. Ah Yui
Mr William Y.S. Chan Henry
Mr Jack Chan Henry
Mr & Mrs E.H. Kingston
Mrs Chong Lai Lam
Mrs Nancy Lo Pong

Ciskei

Mr John Aou
Mr Andrew Aou
Mr Tony Huang
Mr Lawrence Ting
Mr Peter Tsai
Mr Robert Tsung

Kimberley

Mr & Mrs W.S. Chan Yan
Mr Meng Chan Yan
Mr Isaac Changfoot
Mr Choy Ho
Mr Henry Kim Sing
Mr Horace King
Mrs Kwon Hoo
Mr Jimson Ou Lee

Cape Town

Mr Victor Chong
Mr & Mrs Sam Chong
Mr Les Hoy
Mrs S.F. Hunt
Mr Leslie Kwongsee

Mr Bertram Lee
Mr Lionel Yankee Liang
Mr K.Y. Chong Ling
Mr George Ming
Mr & Mrs Edmund Quat
Mr L.A. Ying

Overseas

Mrs Nancy Ah Chuen
Mrs Florence Chang
Dr George Changfoot
Mrs Jacqueline Cheong
Dr Ted Wong Hoption
Dr Kwiton Jong
Mr Sidney Kim Sing (correspondent)
Mr Terry Lai King
Mr Jack Kolling
Ambassador Lo Ming Yuan
Mr W.K. Lew
Mr David K. Low
Mr Lee Sing Gen
Mr Ernest Wing King
Dr Norman Yenson
Mr A. York
Mrs Peggy Lai Yue

DONORS

Work on the South African Chinese History Project was made possible by generous donations from many organizations, businesses and individuals. We wish to express our gratitude to all who supported us financially, and also acknowledge the part played by Mrs Rae Graham and former Consul-General Wei Jen Hu who were both instrumental in securing major donations to enable us to launch the research.

Major Donors

Johannesburg City Council
Overseas Chinese Affairs Commission of the Republic of China
Barlow Rand Foundation
Transvaal Chinese Association
Kimberley Chinese Association
Anglo American and De Beers Chairman's Fund
Barclays National Bank Ltd.
Mr C.F. Hendson
Mr Quan Ba
Mr Aou Chung-Nan
Catholic Chinese Welfare Association
Pretoria Chinese Association
Sui Hing Hong
Foley and Law Photographic

All Donors

Bright Stars Sports Club
Western Province Chinese Association
Transvaal Chinese United Club
Mr Terry Lee
Mrs Doreen Chokie
Ambassador H.K. Yang
Mr & Mrs L.A. Ying
Mr Henry Huang
Mrs Peggy Lai Yue
Ambassador Lo Ming Yuan
Mr Ma Wing Tai
Mr Li Kom
Mr Ma Wing Yip
Mr Neville Son Hing
Mr and Mrs H. Lee Pan
The Man family
Mr & Mrs S. Himpoo
Association of Chinese Industrialists in South Africa
Mr & Mrs S. Lai How
Consul-General H.C. Chan
Mr W.S. Pow Chong
Mr S.S. Pow Chong
Mr Archie Pow Chong
Mr Ernest Low
Mr & Mrs Leslie Wing Law
Mr H.D. Lau
Mr Ah Tong
Mr Leong Hui
Mr Norman Li
Mr Julius Quan
Mr Norman Chan Tong
Eastern Province Chinese Association
Pick 'n Pay Stores
Metro Group Limited (E. Cape)
Mrs Y.S.M. Chang
Mr Jack Hoption
Mr Kenneth Fung
Mr Shiang Chum
Mr F.S. Tong
Mr Marlon Law
Mr Arthur Ma

Mr Wing Fat Ma
Mr H.K. Kew
Mr Ma Seung
Mr Li Ting Kong
Mr Robert Li
Mr Norman Ho
Mr Alfred Ah Ling
Mr Wilkie Leong
Mr Ho Winkee Leong
Mr Lau Chiu King
Mr Gerald Fok
Mr Fok Hong
Miss J. Law
Mr A.S. Nuen
Mr Norman Ho
Mr Jackie Sun Hing
Mr W.O. Ah Yui
Mr and Mrs A. Ah Yui
Mr F. Yee Loong
Mr & Mrs C. Ah Chow
Mr H. Simpson
Mr Y.S. Lee
Mr. H. Wong
Mr E. Lee Son
Mr W. Ah Yui
Mr E.H. Kingston
Mr and Mrs T. Kingston
Mr and Mrs G. Loyson
Mr E. Song Loong
Mr N. Tam
Mr K. Peking
Mr L.G. Chin
Mr J. Long King
Mr R. Ah Sing
Mr M. Chantson
St Francis Xavier Church
Mr V. Chan Yan
Mr A. Chan Yan
Mr C. Ho
Mr Chong Lai Lam
Mr & Mrs R. Low Kum
Mr L.C. Low Kum
Mr Desmond Low Kum
P.E. Chinese Catholic Association
Mr J. Affat
Mr P. Date Chong
Mr M. Lee
Mr S. Kin Yatt
Mr D. Lin
Mr T. Ah Yui
Mr E. Jack Kee
Mr P. Kin
Mr R.G. Shung
Ms G. Pow Chong
Mr D.K. Low
Mr R. Chong
Mr R. Pakshong
Mr Y. Chum
Mr P. Tam
Mr F. Law
Mr J. Ford
Mr E. Kamson
P. Leong
Mr A. York
Mrs Molly Pon
Mr E. Jackson
Mr A. Loyson
Mr M. Timkoe
Mr D. Ah Why
Mr A. Ah Kun
Mr E. Date Line
Mr R. Ahkee
Mrs R. Abrami
D. Chantson
Mr J. Knee Chong
Mr L. Knee Chong
Mr H. Li Green
Mr C. Low Yuen
Mr J. Chan Henry

We also acknowledge permission granted by Macmillan Press Ltd. to quote from Peter Richardson's *Chinese Mine Labour in the Transvaal*.

While we have made every effort to ensure that all our acknowledgments are complete, we must apologize to anyone whose name may inadvertently have been omitted from any of the above lists.

Notes

ABBREVIATIONS

BRA	Barlow Rand Archives
CAD	Cape Archives Depot, Cape Town
CASA	Chinese Association of South Africa
Cd	Command paper
EP	Eastern Province
EPCA	Eastern Province Chinese Association
NAD	Natal Archives Depot, Pietermaritzburg
OFS	Orange Free State
PE	Port Elizabeth
PRO	Public Record Office, Surrey
SAD	South African Archives Depot, Pretoria
TAD	Transvaal Archives Depot, Pretoria
TCA	Transvaal Chinese Association
UCLA	University of California, Los Angeles

CHAPTER 1 CONVICTS AND COOLIES: 1660-1880

1. J.J.L. Duyvendak, *China's discovery of Africa*, London: Arthur Probsthain, 1949, p. 7; F.C. He, The relationship between China and African history, *UCLA African Studies Center newsletter*, Fall 1987, p. 7.
2. Duyvendak, *China's discovery of Africa*, p. 7-10.
3. Duyvendak, *China's discovery of Africa*, p. 13-15.
4. P. Snow, *The Star Raft*, New York: Cornell U.P., 1989, p. 3-4.
5. Duyvendak, *China's discovery of Africa*, p. 23-27.
6. K.S. Chang, Africa and the Indian Ocean in Chinese maps of the fourteenth and fifteenth centuries, in *Imago mundi*, vol. 24, 1970, p. 21-25; O.I. Norwich, *Maps of Africa*, Johannesburg: Donker, 1983, p. 15.
7. Duyvendak, *China's discovery of Africa*, p. 32-35.
8. G. Caton-Thompson, *The Zimbabwe culture*, London: Oxford U.P., 1931, p. 67; C.E. Fripp, A note on mediaeval Chinese-African trade, in *NADA*, 1939, p. 94; F.R. Paver in The Asiatics in south-east Africa, *South African journal of science*, vol. 22, 1925, p. 516-522, points out that Sung dynasty pottery found in Pemba, as well as Chinese coins, dated between 845 and 1163, may well have been brought to the area in Chinese ships during the Ming dynasty.
9. R.A. Dart, A Chinese character as a wall motive in Rhodesia, *South African journal of science*, vol. 36, December, 1939, p. 474-476.

10. Snow, *The Star Raft*, p. 8.
11. R.A. Dart, The historical succession of cultural impacts upon southern Africa, *Nature*, vol. 115, p. 425-429.
12. R.A. Dart, *The oriental horizons of Africa*, Johannesburg: Hayne & Gibson, 1954, p. 13.
13. O.F. Mentzel, *A geographical-topographical description of the Cape of Good Hope*, part 3; revised and edited by H.J. Mandelbrote, Cape Town: Van Riebeeck Society, 1944, p. 95.
14. C.P. Thunberg, *Travels at the Cape of Good Hope*, 1772-1775, Cape Town: Van Riebeeck Society, second series no. 17, 1986, p. 246.
15. F.R. Paver, Far eastern contacts with southern Africa, *South African journal of science*, vol. 39, 1943, p.89-93.
16. E.H.L. Schwarz, The Chinese in Africa, *The South African nation*, February 12, 1927, p. 7-8; W.L. Speight, South Africa's Chinese visitors, *Africa revealed by word and picture*, vol. 5, no. 1, Jan. 1938, p. 42.
17. Schwarz, *The South African nation*, p. 8.
18. Speight, *Africa revealed by word and picture*, p. 42.
19. T.R.H. Davenport, *South Africa*, 2nd ed., Johannesburg: Macmillan, 1978, p. 18.
20. VOC – Verenigde Oostindische Compagnie, an abbreviation for 'de Generale Vereenighde Nederlantse G'octroieerde Oost Indische Compagnie'. A.J. Boeseken, *Slaves and free Blacks at the Cape 1658-1700*, Cape Town: Tafelberg, 1977, p. 5.
21. L. Guelke, The white settlers, 1652-1780, in *The shaping of South African society*, 1652-1820, edited by R. Elphick & H. Giliomee, Cape Town: Longman Penguin, 1979, p. 41-45.
22. R. Elphick & R. Shell, Intergroup relations: Khoikhoi, settlers, slaves and free blacks, 1652-1795, in *The shaping of South African society, 1652-1820*, edited by R. Elphick & H. Giliomee, Cape Town: Longman Penguin, 1979, p. 145.
23. H.C.V. Leibbrandt, *Precis of the Archives of the Cape of Good Hope, letters and documents received*, 1649-1662, part I, 1898, p. 84.
24. Dispatches of 4 December 1656 and 31 January 1657, quoted by I.D. MacCrone in *Race Attitudes in South Africa*, London: Oxford U.P., 1937, p. 27.
25. *The Oxford history of South Africa*; vol. 1, ed. by M. Wilson & L. Thompson, Oxford: Clarendon, 1969, p. 300.
26. J.C. Armstrong, The Chinese at the Cape in the Dutch East India Company period 1652-1795, Unpublished paper, 1986, p. 4.; H. Ly-Tio-Fane Pineo, *Chinese Diaspora in Western Indian Ocean*, Mauritius: Editions de l'Ocean Indien & Chinese Catholic Mission, 1985, p. 210.
27. Armstrong, The Chinese at the Cape ..., p. 4-5.
28. Armstrong, The Chinese at the Cape..., p. 13.
29. A.J. Boeseken, *Slaves and Free Blacks at the Cape 1658-1700*, Cape Town: Tafelberg, 1977, p. 30.
30. Armstrong, The Chinese at the Cape ..., p. 5-6.
31. *Internos*, vol. 1, no 2, September 1976, p. 7.
32. Elphick & Shell, in *The shaping of South African society*, p. 116.
33. H.J. van Aswegen, *Geskiedenis van Suid Afrika tot 1854*, Pretoria: Academica, 1989, p. 140-141.
34. Armstrong, The Chinese at the Cape..., p. 11.
35. Elphick & Shell, in *The shaping of South African society*, p. 146.
36. Armstrong, *The Chinese at the Cape* ..., p. 13.
37. Mentzel, *A geographical-topographical description of the Cape of Good Hope*, part II, vol. 6, 1925, p. 91.
38. Armstrong, The Chinese at the Cape ..., p. 7.
39. Armstrong, The Chinese at the Cape ..., p. 9.
40. Mentzel, *A geographical-topographical description of the Cape of Good Hope*, part II, vol. 6, p. 150.
41. Mentzel, *A geographical-topographical description of the Cape of Good Hope*, part II, vol. 6, 1925, p. 92. 'Granelen' – A diminutive species of crab with a soft, edible shell (footnote in original).
42. Mentzel, *A geographical-topographical description of the Cape of Good Hope*, p. 92.
43. A. Sparrman, *A voyage to the Cape of Good Hope towards the Antarctic Polar Circle round the world and to the country of the Hottentots and the Caffres from the year 1772-1776*; edited by V.S. Forbes, Cape Town: Van Riebeeck Society, 1975, p. 167.
44. Thunberg, *Travels at the Cape of Good Hope* 1772-1775, p. 22.
45. Armstrong, The Chinese at the Cape ..., p. 10.
46. S.A. *Law Journal*, vol. 23, 1906, p. 245-246.

47. Leibbrandt, *Precis of the Archives of the Cape of Good Hope, Requesten (Memorials) 1715-1806*, vol 1. p. 242.
48. Leibbrandt, *Precis of the Archives of the Cape of Good Hope, Requesten* p. 246.
49. Leibbrandt, *Precis of the Archives of the Cape of Good Hope, Requesten*, vol. 3, p. 886-887.
50. CAD/CJ, vol. 802, ref. 6. Court of Justice, Crown vs. Simon Arnold, [7 May 1807]. [Thanks to Dee Nash for this ref.]
51. Mentzel, *A geographical-topographical description of the Cape of Good Hope*, part II, vol. 6, 1925, p. 150.
52. Elphick & Shell, in *The shaping of South African society*, p. 140-141.
53. Leibbrandt, *Precis of the Archives of the Cape of Good Hope, Requesten*, p. 672 and 687.
54. Armstrong, The Chinese at the Cape..., p. 6.
55. Mentzel, *A geographical-topographical description of the Cape of Good Hope*, part I, 1921, p. 128.
56. Sparrman, *A voyage to the Cape of Good Hope ...*, p. 49.
57. Thunberg, *Travels at the Cape of Good Hope 1772-1775*, p. 49.
58. Armstrong, The Chinese at the Cape ..., p. 13; The reference to the two Chinese women is contained in James Armstrong's current research, outlined in his letter to the South African Chinese History Project, 13 November 1995. He states: 'Of the two Chinese women, one voluntarily accompanied her exiled husband to the Cape. Their story did not end happily, as they were robbed, murdered and their house fired by fellow-Chinese at the Cape. There were no children recorded. The other spent 10 years in the Slave Lodge, but died a free and comparatively wealthy woman. Also no children.'
59. H.R. Hahlo & E. Kahn, *The Union of South Africa*, London: Stevens, 1960, p. xxii.
60. Davenport, South Africa, p. 19; *The Oxford history of South Africa*, vol. 1, p. 272-279 and p. 233-246.
61. J. Barrow, *An account of travels into the interior of Southern Africa*, second vol., London: Cadell and Davies, 1904, p. 430-431.
62. G. Thompson, *Travels and adventures in Southern Africa*, ed. by V.S. Forbes, Cape Town: Van Riebeeck Society, 1968, parts 2 & 3, p. 168.
63. CAD/CO, vol. 3380, ref. 611. Letter to the Earl of Caledon, Governor of the Cape of Good Hope, 31 December 1810.
64. B.B. Brock & B.G. Brock, *Historical Simon's Town*, Cape Town: Balkema, 1976, p. 87.
65. Brock & Brock, *Historical Simon's Town*, p. 87.
66. R. Lewcock, Chinese craftsmen, in *Standard encyclopaedia of Southern Africa*, vol. 2, Cape Town: Nasou, 1971, p. 197.
67. CAD/CO, vol. 3941, ref. 36. Memorial to Governor dated 26 March, 1829.
68. Title Deed No. 175 of 1830. Erf 963 Cape Town. Transfer effected on 26 November, 1830.
69. T. Cross, *St Helena: including Ascension Island and Tristan da Cunha*, Newton Abbot: David & Charles, 1980, p. 32.
70. O. Blakeston, *Isle of St Helena*, London: Sidgwick and Jackson, 1957, p. 23.
71. P. Gosse, *St Helena 1502-1938*, London: Cassell, 1938, p. 246.
72. A. Beatson, *Tracts relative to the island of St Helena*, London: Bulmer, 1816. p. 186-187.
73. *St Helena almanack and annual register for the year of Our Lord 1884*, St Helena: Watson, [18..], p. 41.
74. J.C.Melliss, *St Helena*, 1875, [part reprint and with photographs] by Robin Castell, Chesham: Wensley Brown, 1979, p. 13.
75. CAD/MOOC, vol. 6/9/8, ref. 1475. Atim of China, death notice, 5 May 1836.
76. CAD/MOOC, vol. 6/9/41, ref. 8693, death notice Chinaman Attick (or Artick), 3 November 1846.
77. *Cape of Good Hope Gazette*, 1 May, 1840.
78. In the early 1980s the Chinese Association of Cape Town (called the Western Province Chinese Association in the 1990s) discovered they were still regarded as the titleholders to the property. After a fire on Signal Hill, they received a bill for damage from the Cape Town Fire Department ... and a copy of the 1830 map demarcating the cemetery.
79. R.R. Langham-Carter, Cape Town's first graveyards, *Cabo*, vol. 2 no. 1, June 1973, p. 18.
80. CAD/CO, vol. 3941, ref. 36. Petition to Governor dated 26 March 1829.
81. Title deed no. 175 of 1830, Erf 963, Cape Town.
82. CAD/GH, vol. 1/201, ref. 324. Petition from William Assue to Governor of the Cape, 17 April 1838.
83. CAD/GH, vol. 1/201, ref. 324. Petition from William Assue to Governor of the Cape, 5 May, 1838.
84. *Eastern Province Herald*, 20 January 1849; reprinted in *Internos*, vol. 1, no 2, September 1976, p. 7.

85. CAD/CO, vol. 4068, ref. 214, memorials received. Despatch from Henry, Duke of Newcastle to Lieutenant Governor Darling, 11 June, 1853.
86. *Cape Argus*, 1 June 1872.
87. *Cape Argus*, 17 September 1872.
88. Cape of Good Hope. Ministerial Department of Crown Lands and Public Works. Report on immigration and labour supply for the year 1875, p. 1. in Appendix I to the Votes and Proceedings of Parliament. Vol. IA. App I, 1876.
89. *Argus*, 24 February, 1876; from *Pall Mall Gazette* of 19 January, 1876.
90. CAB/CO, vol. 4227, ref. 122 , C.B. Smith to Colonial Secretary, 9 October 1882.
91. *Eastern Province Herald*, 11 November, 1881.
92. *Cape Argus Weekly Edition*, 25 November 1881, p. 6.
93. *The Friend of the Free State*, 8 December, 1881.
94. *Diamond Fields Advertiser*, 16 December 1881.
95. *Cape Argus Weekly Edition*, 20 December 1881, p. 11.
96. *Graaff Reinet Advertiser*, 15 November 1881.
97. *Natal Mercury*, 28 October, 1881.
98. *Cape Argus Weekly Edition*, 8 November 1881, p. 9.
99. *Eastern Province Herald*, 16 December 1881, p. 8.
100. NAD/CSO, vol. 890, ref. 1883/186. Colonial Secretary, Cape Town, forwards copy of a letter from Colonial Secretary, Hong Kong, 30 December 1882.
101. *Eastern Province Herald*, 2 October 1882.
102. *Graaff Reinet Advertiser*, 30 September 1881.
103. *Eastern Province Herald*, 13 October 1882.
104. *Graaff Reinet Herald*, 18 October 1882, p. 3.
105. *Eastern Province Herald*, 1 November 1882.
106. *Graaff Reinet Herald*, 4 November 1882. p. 3.
107. *Eastern Province Herald*, 1 November 1882, p. 4.
108. *Graaff Reinet Herald*, 20 December 1882.
109. *The Oxford history of South Africa*, p. 378-381 and 387.
110. E.H. Brookes & C. de B. Webb, *A history of Natal*, Pietermaritzburg: University of Natal Press, 1965, p. 82.
111. Brookes & Webb, *A history of Natal*, p. 82-86.
112. Natal Government Gazette, notice no. 223, 7 July, 1874.
113. NAD/CSO vol. 578, ref. 1877/216, letter from Immigration Agent to Protector of Immigrants Natal, 15 May 1875.
114. Interview with Mr Yung Fah, Johannesburg, 1986.
115. NAD/CSO, vol. 525, ref. 1875/2469, Protector of Immigrants, Natal to Colonial Secretary, 21 Aug 1875; *Natal Mercury*, 17 August 1875, p. 3.
116. *Natal Mercury*, 17 August 1875, p. 3.
117. *Natal Mercury*, 19 August 1875.
118. *Natal Mercury*, 8 February 1876.
119. NAD/MSCE, vol. 4, ref. 219/1876, intestate estate Simcaw alias 'Akou', 1876.
120. NAD/CSO, vol. 525, ref. 1875/2500.
121. *Natal Mercury*, 7 September 1875.
122. NAD/CSO, vol. 649, ref 1878/2413, 18 June, 1878.
123. *Natal Mercury*, 7 September 1875.
124. D.P. Carnegie, *Chinese emigration to Natal discussed and its defence answered*, Durban: Cullingworth, 1875, p. 2.
125. *Natal Mercury*, 9 September 1875.
126. *Natal Mercury*, 18 September 1875 and 21 September 1875.
127. *Natal Mercury*, 14 October 1875.
128. *Natal Mercury*, 19 October 1875.
129. *Natal Mercury*, 27 November, 1875.
130. *Natal Mercury*, 18 January 1876.
131. Natal Harbour Board, Chairman's minute and departmental reports for 1886 and 1887.

132. CAD/GH, ref. 23/39, Minute No. 1/35 of 9 March 1891 from Cape of Good Hope High Commissioner's Office. Telegram to Lord Knutsford and letter from Lord Knutsford to the Governor of the Cape, 5 May 1891.

CHAPTER 2 FROM CHINA TO SOUTH AFRICA

1. T. Chi, *A short history of Chinese civilisation*, London: Gollancz, 1942, p. 301.
2. J. Needham, *Science and civilisation in China*, London: Cambridge U.P., 1954, p. 93.
3. K.S. Latourette, *The Chinese: their history and culture*, 4th edition, New York: Macmillan, 1964, p. 247.
4. J. Chesneaux, M. Bastid and M. Bergere, *China from the Opium Wars to the 1911 Revolution*, Hassocks: Harvester, 1977, p. 47.
   Authors state figures from the Ministry of Revenue in Peking are not wholly accurate, but specialists say the government statistics are lower than the real ones. They do, however, indicate a general tendency.
   Population of China
   1770 - 213 613 163
   1800 - 295 273 311
   1820 - 353 377 694
   1830 - 394 784 681
   1840 - 412 814 828
5. Chesneaux, Bastid & Bergere, *China from the Opium Wars*, ... p. 48.
6. J. Chesneaux, *Peasant revolts in China, 1840-1949*, London: Thames and Hudson, 1973, p. 23.
7. Latourette, *The Chinese: their history and culture*, p. 287.
8. C. Schirokauer, *A brief history of Chinese and Japanese civilizations*, New York: Harcourt Brace Jovanovich, 1978, p. 380.
9. Chesneaux, Bastid & Bergere, *China from the Opium Wars* ..., p. 50.
10. Schirokauer, *A brief history of Chinese and Japanese civilizations*, p. 383.
11. H.F. MacNair, *Modern Chinese history*, Shanghai: Commercial, 1923, p. 2-9, quoted in Chesneaux, Bastid & Bergere, *China from the Opium Wars* ..., p. 59.
12. Chesneaux, Bastid & Bergere, *China from the Opium Wars* ...,p. 53-55.
13. Schirokauer, *A brief history of Chinese and Japanese civilizations*, p. 387-388.
14. Latourette, *The Chinese: their history and culture*, p. 274.
15. Ta Tsing Lu Li, *Laws and precedents of the Ch'ing Dynasty*, vol. XX, p. 11, quoted in H. Ly-Tio-Fane Pineo, *Chinese diaspora in western Indian Ocean*, Mauritius: Editions de l'Ocean Indien and Chinese Catholic Mission, 1985, p. 32.
16. T.T.W. Tan, *Your Chinese roots*, Singapore: Times Books, 1986. p. 42.
17. P. Li, *The Chinese in Canada*, Toronto: Oxford U.P., 1988, p. 136, quoting R. L. Irick, *Ch'ing policy toward the coolie trade, 1847-1878*, China: Chinese Materials Center, 1982, p. 4, and *Chambers 20th Century dictionary*.
18. Latourette, *The Chinese: their history and culture*, p. 231.
19. T. Chi, *A short history of Chinese civilisation*, p. 206.
20. Latourette, *The Chinese: their history and culture*, p. 233.
21. M.F. Farley, The Chinese coolie trade, 1845-1875, *Journal of Asian and African studies*, p. 259.
22. P.C. Campbell, *Chinese coolie emigration to countries within the British Empire*, London: King, 1923, p. 95.
23. P. Snow, *The Star Raft*, New York: Cornell U.P., p. 44.
24. Farley, *Journal of Asian and African studies*, p. 259-262.
25. Farley, *Journal of Asian and African studies*, p. 267.
26. S.W. Wang, The attitude of the Ch'ing court toward Chinese emigration, *Chinese culture*, vol. 9, no. 4, Dec. 1968, p. 68-69.
27. Cape of Good Hope. Parliament. Correspondence and papers on the subject of immigration from India and China. G39-1875, p. 12.
28. Wang, *Chinese culture*, p. 70; Cape of Good Hope. Parliament. Appendix I to the Votes and Proceedings of Parliament. Vol. Ic, 1875, p. 2.
29. Wang, *Chinese culture*, p. 70.
30. Wang, *Chinese culture*, p. 63, 75-76.

31. Chesneaux, Bastid & Bergere, *China from the Opium Wars ...*, p. 72.
32. Chesneaux, *Peasant revolts in China 1840-1949*, p. 24.
33. Chesneaux, *Peasant revolts in China 1840-1949*, p. 24-29.
34. Schirokauer, *A brief history of Chinese and Japanese civilizations*, p. 392; J. Robottom, *Twentieth Century China*, London: Wayland, 1971, p. 8.
35. Latourette, *The Chinese: their history and culture*, p. 292.
36. Tan, *Your Chinese roots*, p. 44.
37. Wang, *Chinese culture*, p. 64.
38. G.L. King, *Domestic religious beliefs and practices amongst the Chinese in Johannesburg*, M.A. thesis, University of the Witwatersrand, Johannesburg, 1974, p. 37-38.
39. Ly-Tio-Fane Pineo, *Chinese diaspora in western Indian Ocean*, p. 284.
40. King, *Domestic religious beliefs ...*, p. 37.
41. Ly-Tio-Fane Pineo, *Chinese diaspora in western Indian Ocean*, p. 284.
42. Blake, *Ethnic groups and social ...*, p. 8.
43. Tan, *Your Chinese roots*, p. 176.
44. Blake, *Ethnic groups and social ...*, p. 50.
45. Blake, *Ethnic groups and social ...*, p. 8, 50-52; G. Campbell, *Origins and migrations of the Hakkas*, [S.l.: s.n.], 1912, p. 11; S. Couling, The encyclopaedia Sinica, Shanghai: Kelly and Walsh, 1917, reprinted Taipei: Ch'eng Wen, 1973; E. Huntington, *The character of races*, New York: Arno, 1977, p. 393; C.P. Fitzgerald, *China: a short cultural history*, New York: Praeger, 1958, p. 621; Ly-Tio-Fane Pineo, *Chinese diaspora in western Indian Ocean*, p. 53; *Mei-hsien ti chu=Meixian prefecture*, p. 213.
46. *Mei-hsien ti chu=Meixian prefecture*, Pei Ching: Chung Kuo Kuo Chi Kung Po Kung Su, 1987, p. 78.
47. C.F. Blake, *Ethnic groups and social change in a Chinese market town*, Hawaii: University Press of Hawaii, 1981, p. 10.
48. J. Chen, *The Chinese of America*, San Francisco: Harper and Row, 1981, p. 9; S.S. Minnick, *Samfow: The San Joaquin Chinese Legacy*, Fresno, California: Panorama West, 1988, p. 5; Blake, *Ethnic groups and social*, p. 10.
49. Blake, *Ethnic groups and social ...*, p. 50.
50. Latourette, *The Chinese: their history and culture*, p. 438.
51. L. Pan, *Sons of the Yellow Emperor*, London: Secker and Warburg, 1990, p. 107; Tan, *Your Chinese roots*, p. 27;
52. Pan, *Sons of the Yellow Emperor*, p. 106.
53. Tan, *Your Chinese roots* p. 47-48.
54. D. Divine, *These splendid ships*, London: Muller, 1960, p. 102-106.
55. Ly-Tio-Fane Pineo, *Chinese diaspora in western Indian Ocean*, p. 24-25.
56. Ly-Tio-Fane Pineo, *Chinese diaspora in western Indian Ocean*, p. 88-92.
57. Ly-Tio-Fane Pineo, *Chinese diaspora in western Indian Ocean*, p. 93-96.
58. Ly-Tio-Fane Pineo, *Chinese diaspora in western Indian Ocean*, p. 257: Table XVII: Movement of the free Chinese population between Mauritius and the principal ports of South Africa 1880-1930.
59. D.J. Soares-Rebelo, The Chinese extraction Group in Mocambique, Unpublished paper, [July 1966].
60. Interview with Mr Jack Chan Henry, July 1987. Also mentioned by a number of community members.

CHAPTER 3 UNDER BRITISH RULE

1. *The Oxford history of South Africa*, vol. 2, ed. by M. Wilson & L. Thompson, Oxford: Clarendon, 1975, p. 1-12.
2. E. Rosenthal, *Schooners and skyscrapers*, Cape Town: Timmins, 1963, p. 76-82 and 105-119.
3. *The Oxford history of South Africa*, vol. 1, ed. by M. Wilson & L. Thompson, Oxford: Clarendon, 1969, p.380-381.
4. *Indian Opinion*, 22 February 1908, p. 96.
5. *Natal Mercury*, 18 September 1875, p. 3.
6. *Natal Mercury*, 18 September 1875 and 21 September 1875.
7. *Natal Mercury*, 28 October, 1881.
8. *The Friend*, 8 December 1881.

9. NAD/CSO, vol. 990, ref.1884/4714. Letter from Baker and Laughton to Colonial Secretary, 27 November 1884.
10. NAD/CSO, vol. 1078, ref. 1886/1881. Letter from Baker and Laughton to Acting Colonial Secretary, 29 April 1886 enclosing petition.
11. NAD/CSO, vol. 1078, ref. 1886/1881. Draft bill.
12. B. Pachai, *The international aspects of the South African Indian question, 1860-1971*, Cape Town: Struik, 1971, p. 8.
13. Cape of Good Hope. Parliament. Results of a census of the Colony of the Cape of Good Hope, as on the night of Sunday, the 5th April, 1891, Cape Town: Richards, 1892.
14. NAD/CSO, ref. 2001 / 1897. Letter from W. R. Poynton to the Colonial Secretary, dated 24 March 1897.
15. *The collected works of Mahatma Gandhi*, vol. III (1898 - 1903), Delhi: Ministry of Information and Broadcasting, 1960, p. 34-36.
16. Natal. Report of the Immigration Restriction Officer for the year 1897, Pietermaritzburg: Davis, 1897, p. 8.
17. Natal. Reports of the Immigration Restriction Department for the years 1900 to 1904. Pietermaritzburg: 'Times', 1901-5.

Restricted immigrants (Chinese) Males (M)

Year	*Males (M)/ Females (F)*	*Children*	*Total*
1900	111 (M) 2 (F)	4	117
1901	218 (M) 0 (F)	0	218
1903	257 (M) 0 (F)	0	257
1904	159 (M) 0 (F)	0	159

Unrestricted Chinese

Year	*Males (M)/ Females (F)*	*Children*	*Total*
1900	13 (M) 0 (F)	–	13
1901	20 (M) 0 (F)	–	20
1903	19 (M) 2 (F)	–	21

18. NAD/IRD, vol. 55, ref. IRD 974/1906 and NAD/IRD, vol. 44, ref. IRD 1138/1905.
19. NAD/CSO, vols. 151 and 152, ref. 1897/4317 and 1897/4530.
20. NAD/IRD, vol. 20, ref. IRD 780/1903.
21. NAD/CSO, vol. 1771, ref. 1904/8473. Letter from W.E. Fitch, advocate, to Colonial Secretary, 20 September 1904 enclosing petition.
22. SAD/BNS, vol. 1/1/309, ref. 13/74A. Letter from the Principal Immigration Officer of Natal to the Secretary of the Interior, 23 March 1923.
23. J.J. Redgrave, *Port Elizabeth in bygone days*, Wynberg: Rustica, 1947, p. 470.
24. Cape of Good Hope. Parliament. Results of a census of the Colony...
25. Interview with Mr Henry Kim Sing, Kimberley, September 1987.
26. B. Roberts, *Kimberley*, Cape Town: Philip, 1976, p. 220.
27. *Graaff Reinet Advertiser*, 15 October 1891, reprinting an article from a Kimberley newspaper.
28. TAD/SS, vol. 0, refs. R6829/90. R775/90, R7048/90. Landdrost Christiana, re uitlewering Chinees Lochin.
29. *Diamond Fields Advertiser*, 14 November 1881 and 16 December 1881.
30. Letter to the *Investors' Guardian*, Kimberley, reprinted in *Graaff Reinet Advertiser*, 20 December 1881, p. 3.

31. *Diamond Fields Advertiser*, 18 June 1890.
32. *Diamond Fields Advertiser*, 6 June, 14 June, 28 June, 18 July 1890.
33. *Diamond Fields Advertiser*, 25 September, 1891, p. 4.
34. *Diamond Fields Advertiser*, 3 October, 1891, p. 3.
35. *Diamond Fields Advertiser*, 27 October, 1891, p. 3.
36. *Diamond Fields Advertiser*, 12 November, 1891, p. 4.
37. *Diamond Fields Advertiser*, 24 May 1890.
38. Interviews with Mr Henry Kim Sing and Mr Ho Choy, Kimberley, September 1987.
39. Cape of Good Hope. Parliament. Results of a census of the colony of the Cape of Good Hope, as on the night of Sunday, the 17th April, 1904. Cape Town: Cape Times, 1905.
40. *South Africa's yesterdays*; ed. by P. Joyce, Cape Town: Reader's Digest, 1981, p. 52-53; J.J. Redgrave, *Port Elizabeth in bygone days*, p. 37.
41. *Looking back*, vol. VI, March 1966, p. 8 and Vol. XII, December 1972, p. 103.
42. CAD/3/UIT, vol. 9, ref. 306. Census of Chinamen living in Uitenhage, 15 October 1901.
43. Interviews with Mrs W.O. Ah Yui and Mr Lai Lam, Somerset East, July 1987.
44. *Eastern Province Herald*, 18 November 1881, p. 8.
45. Ly-Tio-Fane Pineo, *Chinese diaspora in western Indian Ocean*, Mauritius: Editions de l'Ocean Indien-Chinese Catholic Mission, 1985, p. 257; Cape of Good Hope. Parliament. Results of a census ... 5th April, 1891.
46. Ly-Tio-Fane Pineo, *Chinese diaspora in western Indian Ocean*, p. 257. Tabulating the movement of the free Chinese between Mauritius and the principal ports of South Africa, Ly-Tio-Fane Pineo records these figures for Chinese arriving in Port Elizabeth's Algoa Bay:

1888	23
1889	32
1890	45
1891	16
1892	7
1893	120
1894	53
1895	77
1896	571
1897	154
1898	524
1899	–
1900	23
1901	44
1902	71
1903	2
1904	2

47. Ly-Tio-Fane Pineo, *Chinese diaspora in western Indian Ocean*, p. 219, 257.
48. *Graaff Reinet Advertiser*, 14 May 1890.
49. *Graaff Reinet Advertiser*, 20 May 1897.
50. *Graaff Reinet Advertiser*, 20 May 1897 and 13 April 1898.
51. *Graaff Reinet Advertiser*, 23 and 28 September 1898.
52. Interviews with Messrs W.J., A. and S.S. Pow Chong and Mr Y. Whiteley, Port Elizabeth, July 1987.
53. C.G. Green, An old man remembers, in *Looking back*, vol. VIII no. 3, September 1968, p. 74.
54. L.G. Green, *Harbours of memory*, Cape Town: Timmins, 1969, p. 88.
55. *Star Weekly Edition*, 21 January, 1899, p.26.
56. Interview with Mr J. Chan Henry, Uitenhage, July 1987.
57. *Port Elizabeth year book and directory for 1901*, [S.l.: s.n.], 1901, p. 229.
58. *Port Elizabeth year book and directory for 1905*, [S.l.: s.n.], p. 188 and 331.
59. Letter by hon. secretary of King Edward's Hospital Fund for London to Nam Hoi and Sun Tak Club, 6 January 1903.

60. *A report on the Asiatic problem in Port Elizabeth*, presented to the Port Elizabeth Municipality by the Chief Sanitary Inspector. Port Elizabeth: Walton, 1911, p. 5.
61. *Graaff Reinet Advertiser*, 25 March 1903, p. 2.
62. Port Elizabeth Voters Register, Cape Town: Cape Times, 1905, p. 440.
63. Cape of Good Hope. Parliament. Results of a census of the colony ... on the night of Sunday, the 17th April, 1904.
64. CAB/CO, vol. 8570, ref. 22. Application for letters of naturalization.
65. *Studies in the history of Cape Town*, vol. 4, edited by C. Saunders, H. Phillips and E. van Heyningen, Cape Town: Univ. of Cape Town: 1981, p. 97.
66. *Studies in the history of Cape Town*, vol. 4, p. 97.
67. Cape of Good Hope. Parliament. Results of a census of the colony ... on the night of Sunday, the 17th April, 1904.
68. *Graaff Reinet Advertiser*, 18 September 1903.
69. *Star Weekly Edition*, 7 May, 1904, p. 30.
70. Interview with Mr Sam Chong, Cape Town, March 1987.
71. This reference appeared time and again in Chinese documents donated to the researchers, and led to many fruitless searches for 36 different pieces of legislation specifically affecting Chinese. Only much later was it realized this colloquial tag had been coined by the Chinese specifically for the Chinese Exclusion Act.
72. *Standard encyclopaedia of South Africa*, vol. 9, Cape Town: Nasou, 1973, p. 378.
73. CAD/CO, vol. A31, ref. C150/12. Correspondence between Colonial Secretary's Office and the Secretary for Public Works, Sept/Oct, 1904.
74. Interview with Mr L.A. Ying, Cape Town, 17 March 1987 – claims Cape Town Chinese Association was formed around 1902; NAD/IRD, vol. 42, ref. IRD 880/1905. Letter stating Mr W. Singson was president of Port Elizabeth Chinese Association; CAD/GH, vol. 23/84. Letter referring to actions of East London Chinese Association.
75. CAD/GH, vol. 23/84, ref. 23. General despatches. Complaint of Chinese residents in East London, 23 December 1904.
76. TAD/GOV, vol. 874, ref. PS 37/23/05. Chinese – allegations of Thomas Ah See.
77. CAD/T, vol. 897, ref. 247. Trading licences to Chinamen, 1905.
78. CAD/AG, vol. 1659, ref. 10318. Report from Commissioner of Urban police to Secretary of Law Department, 29 December 1905.
    Note: A Mr A.W. Baker, born in Pietermaritzburg in 1856, recorded his life's work in 'Grace Triumphant', a book published by Pickering & Inglis, Glasgow and London, in 1939. Although he mentions encounters with Chinese mineworkers who had converted to Christianity in the Transvaal (p. 112-114), he does not appear to be the 'Reverend Baker' who assisted the Cape Chinese during this period.
79. Cape of Good Hope. Parliament. Appendix II to the Votes and Proceedings of Parliament. Volume II, Report of the Select Committee on Asiatic Grievances, September 1908, Cape Town: Cape Times, p. 38- 42 and vi-viii.
80. Cape of Good Hope. Parliament. Appendix II to the votes ..., p. 42.
81. Cape of Good Hope. Parliament. Appendix II to the votes ..., p. vi.
82. CAD/PMO, vol. 238, ref. 342/08. Correspondence between Prime Minister of Cape of Good Hope and Imperial Chinese Consulate-General, July 1908.
83. CAD/PMO, vol. 238, ref. 342/08. Letter from Imperial Chinese Consulate-General, 13 June 1909.
84. CAD/PMO, vol. 238, ref. 342/08. Cover sheet on 'Chinese Exclusion' circulated from Prime Minister's Office on 17 June 1909.
85. CAD/PMO, vol. 238, ref. 342/08. Letter from Prime Minister of Cape of Good Hope, 22 June 1909.

CHAPTER 4 UNDER BOER RULE

1. H.R. Hahlo & E. Kahn, *The Union of South Africa*, London: Stevens, 1960, p. 6.
2. *The Oxford history of South Africa*; vol. 2, ed. by M. Wilson & L. Thompson, Oxford: Clarendon, 1969, p. 405-409.
3. T. R. H. Davenport, *South Africa*, 2nd ed., Johannesburg: Macmillan, 1978, p. 39- 40; B. A. le Cordeur,

Boer/British conflict: perspectives on the Southern African past, Cape Town: University of Cape Town, Centre for African Studies, 1979, p. 154.

4. *The Oxford history of South Africa*, vol. 1, p. 431.
5. *The Oxford history of South Africa*, vol. 1, p. 425-6.
6. *Illustrated guide to Southern Africa*, 3rd ed. Cape Town: Reader's Digest, 1982, p. 204.
7. *Johannesburg: one hundred years 1886-1986*, Johannesburg: Chris van Rensburg, 1986, p. 4.
8. *The Oxford history of South Africa*, vol. 1. p 429-430.
9. Davenport, *South Africa*, p. 64.
10. OFS Law Book, Chapter XXXIII, Sect. 2, 1890; Tung Miao, *Legal status of Chinese in the Union of South Africa*, Johannesburg: Chiao Sheng Pao, 1947, p.11-12.
11. Admission of Persons to Union Regulation Act, no. 22 of 1913, sect. XVII.
12. *Illustrated guide to Southern Africa*, p. 257.
13. TAD/SS, vol. 0, ref. R1929/76, 25 July 1876.
14. *Cape Argus*, 23 September 1886.
15. *Cape Argus*, 25 January 1887.
16. S.S. Minnick, *Samfow: the San Joaquin Chinese legacy*, Fresno: Panorama West, 1988, p. 11-23.
17. *Johannesburg: one hundred years*, p. 11.
18. TAD/SS, vol. 0, ref. R15335/90, 4 November, 1890. Petition signed by 121 Chinese living in Johannesburg.
19. Hahlo & Kahn, *The Union of South Africa*, p. 806.
20. Report of the Asiatic Inquiry Commission, U.G. 4, 1921, p. 4; M. Vane, *The South African Indians*, Johannesburg: Society of the Friends of Africa, [1948], p. 13.
21. Report of the Asiatic Inquiry Commission, p. 4.
22. B. Pachai, *The international aspects of the South African Indian question, 1860-1971*, Cape Town: Struik, 1971, p. 15.
23. J.R. Shorten, *The Johannesburg saga*, Johannesburg: Shorten, 1970, p. 97.
24. *Star Weekly Edition*, 14 August 1897, p. 25.
25. Vane, *The South African Indians*, p. 14.
26. Report of the Asiatic Inquiry Commission, p. 6.
27. TAD/SS, vol. 0, ref. R11697/88, 24 December 1888.
28. TAD/SS, vol. 0, ref. R10227(A)/89, 27 September 1889.
29. TAD/SS, vol. 0, ref. R4095/87. Petition to the State President and Executive Council of the South African Republic, December 1889.
30. TAD/SS, vol. 0, ref. R15335/90, 4 November 1890.
31. TAD/SS, vol. 0, ref. R1894/93. Letter from Nederlandse Afrikaanse Spoorweg Maatskappy in Lourenco Marques to Mine Commissioner, Barberton, 2 January 1893.
32. *Star Weekly Edition*, 7 May 1898, p. 15.
33. Report of the Asiatic Inquiry Commission, p. 9.
34. TAD/SP, vol. 41, ref. SPR42/94.
35. *The Star*, 9 September 1893, p. 5.
36. TAD/SS, vol. 0, ref. R14392/93.
37. *Standard and Diggers News*, 15 February 1894, p. 2.
38. TAD/SS, vol. 0, ref. R6654/96.
39. NAD/CSO, vol. 1468, ref. 1896/3151.
40. *Star Weekly Edition*, 11 June 1898, p. 19.
41. TAD/SS, vol. 0, ref R1959/93.
42. TAD/SS, vol. 0, ref. R7695/94.
43. TAD/SS, vol. 0, ref. R2739/93, 28 February 1893.
44. TAD/SP, vol. 60, ref. SPR855/95, 29 January 1895.
45. TAD/SS, vol. 0, ref. R4794/93, 28 February 1893.
46. TAD/SS, vol. 0, ref. R692/93.
47. TAD/SS, vol. 0, ref. R6670/98, 27 May 1898.
48. *Star Weekly Edition*, 4 September 1897, p. 18.
49. TAD/SS, vol. 0, ref. R2473/97, 17 February 1897.
50. TAD/SS, vol. 0, ref. R4772/98, 19 April 1898.

51. TAD/SS, vol. 0, ref. R2471/97, 17 January 1897.
52. TAD/SS, vol. 0, ref. R6670/98, November 1898, and ref. R16671/98, 15 December 1898.
53. TAD/SS, vol. 0, ref. R3898/98, 28 February 1898.
54. TAD/SS, vol. 0, ref. R15335/90, 4 November 1890.
55. TAD/SS, vol. 0, ref. R11952/91, 28 September 1891.
56. *Star Weekly Edition*, 9 October 1897 and 18 December 1898.
57. Volksraad resolution, 13 February 1899; TAD/ SS, vol. 0, ref. R2567/99, R2717/99 and R3360/99.
58. *Standard encyclopaedia of Southern Africa*, vol. 4, Cape Town: Nasou, 1971, p.473; A.H. Smith, *Johannesburg street names*, Cape Town: Juta, 1971, p. 158.
59. *Longland's Johannesburg and districts directory*, 1893, p. 61-91.
60. *Star Weekly Edition*, 18 December 1897, p. 20.
61. TAD/GOV, vol. 156, ref. Gen 760/04.
62. *Star Weekly Edition*, 23 October 1897, p. 29.
63. *Star Weekly Edition*, 19 March 1898, p. 18.
64. *Star Weekly Edition*, 14 August 1897, p. 25.
65. *Star Weekly Edition*, 17 October 1903, p. 22.
66. *Star Weekly Edition*, 2 October 1897, p. 9.
67. *Star Weekly Edition*, 16 April 1898, p. 8, and 30 April 1898, p. 21.
68. TAD/SS, vol. 0, ref. R15335/90, 4 November 1890.
69. TAD/SS, vol. 0, ref. R13636/92, 14 July 1892.
70. TAD/RAD, vol. 129, ref. 3215.
71. TAD/SS, vol. 0, ref. R627/97, 8 January 1897.
72. TAD/SS, vol. 0, ref. R13935/98. Petition dated 25 October 1898.
73. TAD/CS, vol. 303, ref. 5117/03.
74. TAD/CS, vol. 303, ref. 5117/03.
75. *Collected works of Mahatma Gandhi*, vol. V (1905-1906), Delhi: Ministry of Information and Broadcasting, 1961, p. 65.
76. Chun-Tu Hsueh, Sun Yat-sen, Yang Ch'u-yun, and the early revolutionary movement in China, *Journal of Asian Studies*, vol. 19, pt. 3, 1960, p. 313.
77. TAD/SS, vol. 0, ref. R13493/99.
78. F. Addington Symonds, *The Johannesburg story*, London: Frederick Muller, 1953, p. 147.
79. TAD/SS, vol. 0, ref. R848/00.
80. TAD/CS, vol. 15, ref. 1754/01.
81. TAD/CS, vol. 18, ref. 2155/01 and vol. 20, ref. 2448/01.
82. Peace Preservation Ordinance, no. 38 of 1902, as amended by Ordinance no. 5 of 1903.
83. TAD/CIA, vol. 27, ref M4. Letter dated 20 July 1905 to the Colonial Secretary's Office.
84. Pachai, *The South African Indian question*, p. 25.
85. TAD/CS, vol. 280, ref. 3676/03; TAD/CS, vol. 304, ref. 5186/03. Correspondence between the Governor's Office, Johannesburg and the Chief Secretary for Permits and Registrar of Asiatics, 28 December 1903 and 9 January 1904.
86. BRA/HE, file 140, no. 210, 20 May 1903.
87. TAD/CS, vol. 257, ref. 2356/03; TAD/LD, vol. 1328, ref. AG 4218/06, 25 March 1903.
88. TAD/RAD, vol. 129, ref. 3215.
89. TAD/RAD, vol. 84, ref. 2004.
90. Report of the Asiatic Inquiry Commission, p.10; Tung Miao, *Legal status of Chinese in the Union of South Africa*, p. 16 and 31.
91. TAD/MGP, vol. 130, ref. 14460A/01.
92. TAD/CS, vol. 199, ref. 16692/02 and vol. 364, ref. 8392/03.
93. TAD/WLD, vol. 0, ref. 38/1909. Judgment in Witwatersrand High Court in matter between Leung Quinn vs other members of Chinese Association, 1 April 1909.
94. *The Star*, 31 May 1905, p. 7.
95. 1904 census records 907 Chinese men and 5 women in the Transvaal. A report on the occupations of Chinese by March 1905 however reflects the presence of 1 059 Chinese men over the age of 16; TAD/ CIA, vol. 1, A279, ref. 22/M1.
96. *The Friend*, 12 January 1904.

97. *Eastern Province Herald*, 15 January 1904.
98. BRA/HE, file 140, no. 210. *Hong Kong Daily Press*, 30 May 1903.
99. BRA/HE, file 140, no. 210. Letter from Chinese Commercial Guild in Africa published in *Swatow Daily News*, 20 May 1903.
100. BRA/HE, file 140, no. 210. Letter to editor of *Chung Kwok Po*, 29 May 1903.

CHAPTER 5 ON THE GOLD MINES

1. P. Richardson, *Chinese mine labour in the Transvaal*, London: Macmillan, 1982, p. 180.
2. *Like it was: The Star 100 years in Johannesburg*, Johannesburg: Argus, 1987, p. 38; E. Rosenthal, *Encyclopaedia of South Africa*, 6th ed. London: Warne, 1973, p. 110.
3. Richardson, *Chinese mine labour in the Transvaal*, p. 8.
4. A.H. Jeeves, *Migrant labour in South Africa's mining economy*, Johannesburg: Witwatersrand U.P., 1985, p. 7.
5. Richardson, *Chinese mine labour in the Transvaal*, p. 13; J.A. Reeves, *Chinese labour in South Africa 1901-1910*, M.A. thesis, University of the Witwatersrand, Johannesburg, 1954, p. 12 states that the pre-war wage rate of 45 shillings per month had been reduced to 20 shillings during the war, and the rate after the war was between 30 shillings and 35 shillings.
6. D.J.N. Denoon, The Transvaal labour crisis, 1901-6, *Journal of African history*, vol. 8 no. 3, 1967, p. 482; P.C. Campbell, *Chinese coolie emigration to countries within the British Empire*, London: King, 1923, p. 164; Reeves, *Chinese labour in South Africa 1901-1910*, p. 22.
7. Denoon, *Journal of African history*, p. 485; H.J. and R.E. Simons, *Class and colour in South Africa 1850-1950*, Harmondsworth: Penguin, 1969, p. 52.
8. Richardson, *Chinese mine labour in the Transvaal*, p. 18.
9. A.A. Mawby, *The political behaviour of the British population of the Transvaal, 1902-1907*, Ph.D. thesis, University of the Witwatersrand, Johannesburg, 1969, p. 91; R. Davies, Mining capital, the state and unskilled white workers in South Africa, 1901-1913, *Journal of Southern African studies*, vol. 3 no. 1, Oct. 1976, p. 49-51.
10. Report of Mr. H. Ross Skinner furnished to Witwatersrand Labour Association: the result of his visit to the East to enquire into the prospects of obtaining Asiatic labourers for the mines of the Witwatersrand, Roodepoort, 1903, p. 3.
11. Report of Mr H. Ross Skinner furnished to the Witwatersrand Labour Association ..., p. 8.
12. Transvaal. Foreign Labour Department, Johannesburg. Annual report 1904-5, p. 12.
13. Reeves, *Chinese labour in South Africa 1901-1910*, p. 93, 103-109; Campbell, *Chinese coolie emigration to countries within the British Empire*, p. 174-175.
14. D. Ticktin, White labour's attitude, 1902-1904, towards the importation of indentured Chinese labourers by the Transvaal Chamber of Mines, in *University of Cape Town. Centre for African Studies. African seminar*. Vol. 1, 1978, p. 70-75; Reeves, *Chinese labour in South Africa 1901-1910*, p. 95-6, says not all these accusations were proved.
15. Cd. 1895. Further correspondence relating to the affairs of the Transvaal and Orange River Colony, London: HMSO, 1904, p. 13.
16. Cd. 1895. Further correspondence relating to the affairs of the Transvaal and Orange River Colony, p. 13; Campbell, *Chinese coolie emigration to countries within the British Empire*, p. 172.
17. Ticktin, in *University of Cape Town. Centre for African Studies. African seminar*, p. 64; Davies, *Journal of Southern African studies*, p. 44.
18. CAD/GH, vol. 35/62, ref. 5. Petition to the Governor of the Cape Colony from protesters in George, Paarl, Queenstown, Hanover, King Williams Town and Somerset West, 1903; Deputation from the White League to Lord Milner. His Excellency's reply, [S.l.: s.n., 1903], p. 19; Cd. 1899. Further correspondence regarding the Transvaal labour question, London HMSO, 1904, p. 13.
19. Reeves, *Chinese labour in South Africa 1901-1910*, p. 87-88; Campbell, *Chinese coolie emigration to countries within the British Empire*, p. 174.
20. Deputation from the White League to Lord Milner. His Excellency's reply, 3rd June 1903, p. 3.
21. *Collected works of Mahatma Gandhi*, vol. III (1898-1903), Delhi: Ministry of Information and Broadcasting, 1960, p. 452.

22. Mawby, *The political behaviour of the British population of the Transvaal*, p. 117.
23. C.C. Eldridge, *Victorian imperialism*, London: Hodder & Stoughton, 1978, p. 216.
24. B.W. Tuchman, *The proud tower*, New York: Macmillan, 1966, p. 356.
25. Richardson, *Chinese mine labour in the Transvaal*, p. 5.
26. Official programme of the great demonstration in Hyde Park, [S.l.: s.n.], 1904, p. [3]; Richardson, *Chinese mine labour in the Transvaal*, p. 5-6.
27. Richardson, *Chinese mine labour in the Transvaal*, p. 33.
28. Cd. 2788. No. 5, quoted in Campbell, *Chinese coolie emigration to countries within the British Empire*, p. 202-3.
29. Richardson, *Chinese mine labour in the Transvaal*, p. 22; D.J.N. Denoon, 'Capitalist influence' and the Transvaal during the Crown Colony period, 1900-1906, *Historical journal*, vol. 11 no. 2, 1968, p. 314-5; Cd. 1895, Further correspondence ... p. 13; Reeves, *Chinese labour in South Africa 1901-1910*, p. 67.
30. Denoon, *Journal of African history*, p. 494; Richardson, *Chinese mine labour in the Transvaal*, p. 30; M. Legassick, *The analysis of 'racism' in South Africa: the case of the mining economy*, IDEP/UN International Seminar on Socio-Economic Trends and Policies in southern Africa. Dar-es-Salaam, December 1-8, 1975, p. 44-46.
31. Ticktin, in *University of Cape Town. Centre for African Studies. African seminar*, p.79-80.
32. Richardson, *Chinese mine labour in the Transvaal*, p. 32.
33. PRO/CO 291/75/7860. Minutes of meeting between Chinese and British Governments re Engagement of Chinese Labourers, 24 Feb 1904, enc. in FO to CO, 4 Mar 1904, quoted in Richardson, *Chinese mine labour in the Transvaal*, p. 33-34.
34. Cd. 1945. Correspondence respecting the introduction of Chinese labour into the Transvaal, no. 6, p. 3-4; Reeves, *Chinese labour in South Africa 1901-1910*, p. 142-3.
35. Cd. 2026. Further correspondence relating to the Transvaal Labour Importation Ordinance, no. 2, p. 3.
36. Richardson, *Chinese mine labour in the Transvaal*, p. 36; Campbell, *Chinese coolie emigration to countries within the British Empire*, p. 178.
37. Convention between the United Kingdom and China respecting the employment of Chinese labour in British Colonies and Protectorates, signed at London, May 13, 1904. (Treaty series no. 7). London: HMSO, 1904, p. 4.
38. *Men of the times*, [Johannesburg]: Transvaal Pub. Co., 1905, p. 231-232.
39. TAD/FLD, vol. 130, ref. 19.2. Consular matters.
40. TAD/FLD vol. 130, ref. 19/3. Consular matters. Letter from F. Perry to Chamber of Mines 10 Dec. 1904.
41. Richardson, *Chinese mine labour in the Transvaal*, p. 37.
42. Extract from Circular No. 404 issued by the Chamber of Mines Labour Importation Agency Ltd. and Letter from F. Perry to Acting Imperial Chinese Consul General, 11 April 1908. (Chamber of Mines Archives, Ch. Consular fees.)
43. TAD/FLD, vol. 130, ref. 19/3. Consular matters.
44. Richardson, *Chinese mine labour in the Transvaal*, p. 47-63.
45. Richardson, *Chinese mine labour in the Transvaal*, p. 40-42.
46. See Chapter 4 for detailed discussion.
47. Richardson, *Chinese mine labour in the Transvaal*, p. 73-95.
48. J. Chesneaux, M. Bastid & M. Bergere, *China from the Opium Wars to the 1911 revolution*. Hassocks: Harvester, 1970, p. 328; Richardson, *Chinese mine labour in the Transvaal*, p. 109, 116 and 121.
49. Richardson, *Chinese mine labour in the Transvaal*, p. 104, 126.
50. Richardson, *Chinese mine labour in the Transvaal*, p. 66-67, 73-74.
51. Richardson, *Chinese mine labour in the Transvaal*, p. 148.
52. Reeves, *Chinese labour in South Africa 1901-1910*, p. 174.
53. Richardson, *Chinese mine labour in the Transvaal*, p. 159.
54. Richardson, *Chinese mine labour in the Transvaal*, p. 151-8, 164 & 192; Cd. 2401. Further correspondence relating to the labour in the Transvaal mines, London: HMSO, 1905, p. 82-3.
55. Reeves, *Chinese labour in South Africa 1901-1910*, p. 185.
56. F. Wilson, *Migrant labour*, Johannesburg: SACC & SPROCAS, 1972, p. 10.
57. Cd. 2401. Further correspondence relating to the labour in the Transvaal mines, p. 84.
58. Reeves, *Chinese labour in South Africa 1901-1910*, p. 187.
59. Report of the Special Committee appointed to inquire into the present conditions in regard to the

control of Chinese indentured labourers in the Witwatersrand district. Johannesburg: Argus, 1906, p. 5.

60. C. van Onselen, *Chibaro*, Johannesburg: Ravan, 1988, p. 151.
61. Transvaal. Foreign Labour Department, Johannesburg. Annual report 1904-5, Pretoria: Govt. Printer, 1906, p. 23.
62. Transvaal. Foreign Labour Department, Johannesburg. Annual report 1904-5, p. 12.
63. Cd. 2401. Further correspondence relating to the labour in the Transvaal mines, p. 82; Transvaal. Foreign Labour Department, Johannesburg. Annual report 1905-6, p. 9.
64. Report of the Special Committee appointed to inquire into the present conditions in regard to the control of Chinese indentured labourers in the Witwatersrand district, p. 8.
65. Richardson, *Chinese mine labour in the Transvaal*, p. 169-171; Denoon, *Journal of African history*, p. 491; Reeves, *Chinese labour in South Africa 1901-1910*, p. 191-2.
66. Reeves, *Chinese labour in South Africa 1901-1910*, p. 188.
67. Figures quoted in Richardson, *Chinese mine labour in the Transvaal*, p. 256, and obtained from FLD's Register of deaths, FLD, 1904-10 and BRA/HE 254, f. 137, no. 1210.
68. Transvaal. Foreign Labour Department, Johannesburg. Annual report 1904-5, p.18-21 and Annual report 1905-6, p. 25-27, Appendix 6.
69. Cd. 2819. Further correspondence ..., p. 48.
70. Report of the Special Committee appointed to inquire into the present conditions in regard to the control of Chinese indentured labourers in the Witwatersrand district. Johannesburg: Argus, 1906.
71. Transvaal. Foreign Labour Department, Johannesburg. Annual report, 1904-5, p. 15.
72. Cd. 2401. Further correspondence relating to the labour in the Transvaal mines, no. 28, p. 52-40.
73. Campbell, *Chinese coolie emigration to countries within the British Empire*, p. 194.
74. Transvaal, Foreign Labour Department, Johannesburg. Annual report 1905-6, p. 3, 7 & 24.
75. Reeves, *Chinese labour in South Africa 1901-1910*, p. 196-200.
76. *Transvaal Leader Weekly Edition*, 13 Jan. 1906, p. 1; 27 Jan. 1906, p. 14.
77. Summary of circulars issued by the Chamber of Mines Labour Importation Agency Ltd., from May 1904 to December 1906, for the guidance of mines employing Chinese labour, [1906], p. 22.
78. *Transvaal Weekly Illustrated*, 6 June 1908, p. 5.
79. Richardson, *Chinese mine labour in the Transvaal*, p. 127; Reeves, *Chinese labour in South Africa 1901-1910*, p. 195; Cd 2819. Further correspondence ..., p. 55.
80. Summary of circulars ..., p. 33.
81. Reeves, *Chinese labour in South Africa 1901-1910*, p. 196, 256.
82. *Transvaal Leader Weekly Edition*, 27 January & 3 February 1906.
83. Reeves, *Chinese labour in South Africa 1901-1910*, p. 195-6. *Transvaal Leader Weekly Edition*, 1 December 1906.
84. Transvaal. Foreign Labour Department, Johannesburg. Annual report 1905-6, p. 11.
85. *Transvaal Critic*, 15 June, 1906, p. 665.
86. TAD/LD, vol. 1433, ref. AG1544/07.
87. Transvaal. Foreign Labour Department, Johannesburg. Annual report 1904-5, p. 12-13.
88. TAD/FLD, vol. 145, ref 27/1-3. Religious Matters.
89. *Transvaal Leader Weekly Edition*, 1 December 1905, p. 24.
90. Denoon, *Journal of African history*, p. 491; Reeves, *Chinese labour in South Africa 1901-1910*, p. 191-2.
91. Cd. 2026. Further correspondence relating to the Transvaal Labour Importation Ordinance, p.37-8.
92. Richardson, *Chinese mine labour in the Transvaal*, p. 171-2.
93. Denoon, *Journal of African history*, p. 491-2.
94. Cd. 2819. Further correspondence ..., p. 27; Richardson, *Chinese mine labour in the Transvaal*, p. 171-2.
95. Cd. 2819. Further correspondence ..., p. 47-55. Report on the treatment of the Chinese labourers by Eugenio Bianchini.
96. E.G. Payne, *An experiment in alien labor*, Chicago: Univ. of Chicago Press, 1912, p. 63.
97. Transvaal. Foreign Labour Department, Johannesburg. Annual report 1905-6, p. 4-6.
98. TAD/FLD, vol. 225, ref. 62/51.
99. Cd. 2819. Further correspondence ..., p. 2-4.
100. TAD/FLD, vol. 224, ref. 62. Letter from Lieutenant-Governor to the Acting President of the Chamber of Mines, May 1905.
101. Transvaal. Foreign Labour Department, Johannesburg. Annual report 1905-6, p. 4.

102. T. Pakenham, *The Boer War,* Johannesburg: Jonathan Ball, 1982, p. 575.
103. Transvaal. Foreign Labour Department, Johannesburg. Annual report 1904-5, p. 13.
104. Denoon, *Journal of African history,* p. 491-2; Campbell, *Chinese coolie emigration to countries within the British Empire,* p. 194.
105. Transvaal. Foreign Labour Department, Johannesburg. Annual report 1905-6, p. 11.
106. Cd. 3025, p. 81, quoted by Campbell, *Chinese coolie emigration to countries within the British Empire,* p. 198.
107. *Transvaal Leader Weekly Edition,* 4 May, 1907, p. 4.
108. TAD/FLD, vol. 1410, ref. AG674/07. Letter from A.W. Baker to Attorney-General, 31 January 1907.
109. Richardson, *Chinese mine labour in the Transvaal,* p. 175.
110. Reeves, *Chinese labour in South Africa 1901-1910,* quoting H. Chilvers, *Out of the crucible,* p. 197.
111. Reeves, *Chinese labour in South Africa 1901-1910,* p. 213.
112. Transvaal. Foreign Labour Department, Johannesburg. Annual report 1904-05, p. 15.
113. Cd. 3025, p. 82, quoted in Campbell, *Chinese coolie emigration to countries within the British Empire,* p. 210.
114. Transvaal. Foreign Labour Department, Johannesburg. Annual report 1905-6, p. 11.
115. Richardson, *Chinese mine labour in the Transvaal,* p. 174-175.
116. *Daily Mail,* 25 Sept. 1905.
117. Cd. 2786. Further correspondence ..., no. 16, p. 9-10.
118. TAD/LD, vol. 1435, ref. AG 4304/06. Affidavit by A. P. Mooney published in *The Prince* on 22 September 1906.
119. A. K. Russell, *Liberal landslide: the general election of 1906,* Newton Abbot: David & Charles, 1973, p. 197.
120. Cd. 2788, no. 5, quoted in Campbell, *Chinese coolie emigration to countries within the British Empire,* p. 202-3.
121. Campbell, *Chinese coolie emigration to countries within the British Empire,* p. 206.
122. Richardson, *Chinese mine labour in the Transvaal,* p. 183.
123. N.G. Garson, 'Het Volk': the Botha-Smuts party in the Transvaal, 1904-11, *Historical journal,* vol. 9 no. 2, 1966, p. 113-115.
124. J. Mervis, *The fourth estate,* Johannesburg: Jonathan Ball, 1989, p. 25.
125. Campbell, *Chinese coolie emigration to countries within the British Empire,* p. 214-215; Richardson, *Chinese mine labour in the Transvaal,* p. 183-184.
126. TAD/GOV, vol. 988, ref. PS 37/5/06.
127. Richardson, *Chinese mine labour in the Transvaal,* p. 182.
128. *Transvaal Leader Weekly Edition,* 4 May 1907.
129. *Star Weekly Edition,* 2 June 1906; *Transvaal Leader Weekly Edition,* 21 July 1906, 3 and 10 August 1907.
130. Simons, *Class and colour in South Africa 1850-1950,* p. 53; Reeves, *Chinese labour in South Africa 1901-1910,* p. 266; Richardson, *Chinese mine labour in the Transvaal,* p. 176.
131. TAD/FLD, vol. 240, ref. 76, 1909.
132. *Transvaal Leader Weekly Edition,* 10 August 1907.
133. TAD/CS, vol 682, ref. H402, 1906-7; *Krugersdorp 100 jaar/years,* Krugersdorp: Town Council of Krugersdorp, 1987, p. 138-139.
134. TAD/GOV, vol. 1238, ref. PS 37/2/10. Attorney-General's Office, Report, 21 February 1910. 'Remission of sentences of Chinese labourers at present undergoing sentences of imprisonment in Transvaal Prisons.'
135. TAD/GOV, vol. 1238, ref. PS 37/2/10.
136. *South Africa today,* written in Chinese by Hon Chong Wing King under the pseudonym Deng Yee Tsung (One Clever Boy), published in Hong Kong, 1971.
137. Interview with Mr Eric Ford, Krugersdorp, March 1988.
138. Richardson, *Chinese mine labour in the Transvaal,* p. 180.
139. Mervis, *The fourth estate,* p. 24, quoting from Chilvers, *Out of the crucible.*
140. Census records for 1904 enumerate 1380 Chinese in the Cape of Good Hope and 910 in the Transvaal. The Chinese in Natal were not recorded separately.
141. Richardson, *Chinese mine labour in the Transvaal,* p. 35.
142. Mervis, *The fourth estate,* p. 29.
143. Convention between the United Kingdom and China ..., p. 4.

CHAPTER 6 PASSIVE RESISTANCE AND THE CHINESE

1. Its proponent in South Africa, Mohandas K. (Mahatma) Gandhi, defined this philosophy as a spiritual force, or 'soul force' which could 'only be cultivated or wielded by those who will entirely eschew violence.' B. Pachai, *The international aspects of the South African Indian question, 1860-1971*, Cape Town: Struik, 1971, p. 37.
2. TAD/CS, vol. 657, ref. 8132; TAD/CS, vol. 630, ref. 5859. Colonial Secretary's answer to question from Mr Solomon in Legislative Council, 24 July 1905. Annexure to M. Chamney's 'Report on the position of Asiatics in the Transvaal (irrespective of Chinese indentured labour) in relation especially to their admission and registration, 17 April 1906.
3. TAD/CS, vol. 630, ref. 5859. Registrar and Protector of Asiatics, M. Chamney's 'Report on the position of Asiatics in the Transvaal (irrespective of Chinese indentured labour) in relation especially to their admission and registration', 17 April 1906, p. 16.
4. Cd. 3308. Correspondence relating to legislation affecting Asiatics in the Transvaal. No. 16: Governor to the Secretary of State, 13 Oct. 1906, p. 16-21.
5. Cd. 3308. Correspondence relating to legislation ... Enclosure 1 in no. 16. Resolution 4, p. 21.
6. TAD/GOV, vol. 202, ref. Gen 1005/06.
7. TAD/PM, vol. 5, ref. 14/1/07 and 14/6/07. Correspondence between Foreign Office, Prime Minister's Office and Colonial Office including letter from Wang Tahsieh and petition from Chinese in Transvaal dated 27 September 1906, 6 March 1907; TAD/GOV, vol. 202, ref. GEN 1005/06.
8. This letter also appears in *The collected works of Mahatma Gandhi*, vol. VI (1906-1907), Delhi: Ministry of Information and Broadcasting, 1961, p. 59-60.
9. TAD/CS, vol. 630, ref. 5859.
10. R.A. Huttenback, *Gandhi in South Africa: British imperialism and the Indian question 1860-1914*, Ithaca: Cornell U.P., 1971, p. 177-178.
11. *Indian Opinion*, 30 March 1907, p. 2.
12. *Indian Opinion*, 6 April 1907.
13. *Indian Opinion*, 20 April 1907, p. 150.
14. Quoted in *Indian Opinion*, 20 April 1907.
15. *Indian Opinion*, 11 May 1907, p. 177.
16. Cd. 3887. Secretary of State to Governor, 9 May 1907.
17. *The selected works of Mahatma Gandhi*, vol. 3, ed. by Shriman Narayan, Ahmedabad: Navajivan, 1968, p. 172.
18. *Indian Opinion*, 1 June 1907, p. 206.
19. TAD/FLD, vol. 183, ref. 38/54.
20. TAD/FLD, vol. 183, ref. 38/54.
21. TAD/PM, vol. 5, ref. 14/6/1907, 11 June 1907.
22. TAD/PM, vol. 5, ref. 14/6/1907.
23. Letter to *Johannesburg Star*, reprinted in *Indian Opinion*, 29 June 1907.
24. *Indian Opinion*, 13 July 1907, p. 265.
25. *Indian Opinion*, 17 August 1907, p. 331.
26. *Indian Opinion*, 12 October 1907.
27. *Indian Opinion*, 23 April 1909.
28. *Indian Opinion*, 20 August, 1910.
29. *Indian Opinion*, 26 October 1907.
30. *Indian Opinion*, 31 August 1907.
31. *Indian Opinion*, 31 August 1907.
32. J. Chen, *The Chinese of America*, San Francisco: Harper & Row, 1981, p. 172-173.
33. Chen, *The Chinese of America*, p. 168. Chen states the US Chinese population numbered 107 488 in 1890 and 88 863 in 1900.
34. *Indian Opinion*, 5 and 12 October 1907.
35. *Indian Opinion*, 5 October 1907.
36. *Transvaal Weekly Illustrated*, 2 November 1907.
37. *Indian Opinion*, 9 November 1907.
38. *Indian Opinion*, 9 November 1907.

39. *The collected works of Mahatma Gandhi*, vol. VII (June-Dec 1907), p. 297.
40. *Indian Opinion*, 7 December 1907, p. 317.
41. *The selected works of Mahatma Gandhi*, vol. 3, p. 200.
42. *Indian Opinion*, 5 October 1907.
43. *Indian Opinion*, 12 October 1907.
44. *Indian Opinion*, 26 October 1907.
45. TAD/FLD, vol. 183, ref. 38/54; *Indian Opinion*, 9 November 1907.
46. *Indian Opinion*, 16 November, 1907.
47. *Transvaal Weekly Illustrated*, 16 November 1907, p. 11.
48. *Indian Opinion*, 7 December 1907, p. 317.
49. *The collected works of Mahatma Gandhi*, vol. VII (June-Dec 1907), p. 395.
50. *Indian Opinion*, 23 November 1907, p. 484.
51. *Indian Opinion*, 23 November 1907, p. 493.
52. *Transvaal Leader*, 6 January 1908, p. 8.
53. *The collected works of Mahatma Gandhi*, vol. VII (June-Dec 1907), p.470.
54. *Indian Opinion*, 4 January 1908, p. 2.
55. *Indian Opinion*, 4 January 1908.
56. *Indian Opinion*, 4 January 1908, p. 4.
57. *Transvaal Leader*, 14 January 1908, p. 7.
58. Huttenback, *Gandhi in South Africa*, p. 200.
59. Transvaal. Legislative Assembly. Correspondence between Colonial Secretary's Office and leaders of the Asiatic and Chinese communities, 28-30 January 1908. [T.A. 4-'08], Pretoria: Government Printer, August 1908.
60. *Transvaal Leader*, 1 February 1908, p.9.
61. *Transvaal Leader*, 12 February 1908, p. 7.
62. *Transvaal Leader*, 14 February 1908, p. 8.
63. *The collected works of Mahatma Gandhi*, vol. VIII (Jan-Aug 1908), p. 107.
64. Cd. 4327. Further correspondence relating to legislation affecting Asiatics in the Transvaal. No. 2: despatch of 17 February 1908 from Governor to Secretary of State, 9 March 1908.
65. *Transvaal Leader*, 15 February 1908, p. 10.
66. *Indian Opinion*, 29 February 1908.
67. Huttenback, *Gandhi in South Africa*, p. 191-2.
68. *Indian Opinion*, 4 July 1908, p. 295.
69. TAD/GOV, vol. 1135, ref. PS 15/1/08 and PS 15/4/08. Letter from J. C. Smuts to the Earl of Selborne, dated 26 June 1908.
70. *Indian Opinion*, 1 August 1908, p. 346.
71. *Indian Opinion*, 22 August 1908, p. 379.
72. TAD/WLD, vol. 0, ref. 38/1909; TAD/WLD, vol. 5/129, ref. 51/1909. Illiquid case Leung Quinn vs Ho Ling and others.
73. *Indian Opinion*, 13 February 1909, p. 76.
74. TAD/WLD, vol. 0, ref. 38/1909.
75. *Indian Opinion*, 14 March 1908, p. 126.
76. *Yorkshire Daily Post*, reprinted in *Indian Opinion*, 30 May 1908, p. 231.
77. *Indian Opinion*, 9 May 1908, p. 205.
78. *Rand Daily Mail*, 19 April 1909, p. 7.
79. *Rand Daily Mail*, 19 April 1909, p. 7.
80. *The Star*, 19 April 1909, p. 9; *Transvaal Weekly Illustrated*, 24 April 1909, p. 31.
81. *Rand Daily Mail*, 19 April 1909, p. 7.
82. *Transvaal Weekly Illustrated*, 24 April 1909, p. 31.
83. *The Star*, 19 April 1909, p. 9.
84. *Rand Daily Mail*, 20 April 1909, p. 7.
85. *Indian Opinion*, 1 May 1909, p. 194 & 201.
86. *Indian Opinion*, 16 October 1909, p. 451.
87. *Indian Opinion*, 16 October 1909, p. 451.
88. *Indian Opinion*, 16 October 1909, p. 445.

89. *Indian Opinion*, 27 November 1909, p.510-511.
90. *Indian Opinion*, 27 November 1909, p. 510-511.
91. TAD/WLD, vol. 0, ref. 38/1909.
92. TAD/LA, vol. 14, ref. 230/08.
93. *Indian Opinion*, 13 March 1909, 20 March 1909.
94. TAD/GOV, vol. 1193, ref. PS 15/1/25/09.
95. TAD/PM, vol. 5, ref. 14/2/1909.
96. Cd. 4584. Further correspondence relating to legislation affecting Asiatics in the Transvaal. Enclosure in no. 19.
97. TAD/PM, vol. 5, ref. 14/2/1909; TAD/LA, vol. 14, ref. 230/08; TAD/FLD, vol. 183, ref. 38/54. Lai Ky informed the Registrar of Asiatics of the activities of those whom he called agitators urging other Chinese to continue the struggle. He named C F J Frank as chairman of the resisters, and other followers as Dixon or Luk Mun, Fok Ting, Fok Tim, all of 90 Kerk Street, Fok Cho of 92 Bree Street, as well as Li Kam, Fok Yee and M. Easton, all of 6 Alexander Street. All had been registered but had burnt their certificates a few months previously.
98. *Indian Opinion*, 17 April 1909, p. 177.
99. *Indian Opinion*, 1 May 1909, p. 192.
100. *Indian Opinion*, 31 July 1909, p. 337.
101. *Indian Opinion*, 28 September 1909, p. 383.
102. *Indian Opinion*, 7 March 1908, p. 112.
103. *Indian Opinion*, 4 September 1909, p. 385.
104. *Indian Opinion*, 11 September 1909, p. 399.
105. TAD/LD, vol. 1756, ref. AG 1774/09. Correspondence between Acting Imperial Chinese Consul- General for RSA and Secretary to the Law Department, 31 August 1909 and 13 September 1909.
106. TAD/LD, vol. 1756, ref. AG1774/09; *Indian Opinion*, 4 September 1909, p. 385.
107. Cd. 5363. Letter from Gandhi to Colonial office, 2 September 1909 and 18 September 1909, p. 34-8.
108. *Indian Opinion*, 25 September 1909, p. 417 and 9 October 1909, p. 444.
109. *Indian Opinion*, 4 December 1909.
110. *Indian Opinion*, 13 November 1909, p. 488 and 26 February 1910, p.72.
111. *Indian Opinion*, 15 January 1910, p. 25.
112. *Indian Opinion*, 29 January, 1910, p. 38.
113. *Indian Opinion*, 5 March 1909, p. 81.
114. *Indian Opinion*, 23 July 1910.
115. *Indian Opinion*, 9 October 1909; *Transvaal Weekly Illustrated*, 11 September 1909.
116. *Indian Opinion*, 4 December 1909, p. 515.
117. *Indian Opinion*, 25 September 1909, p.414 and 4 December 1909, p. 515.
118. *The selected works of Mahatma Gandhi*, vol. 3, p. 305.
119. Huttenback, *Gandhi in South Africa*, p. 205.
120. *Indian Opinion*, 7 May 1910, p.150-1.
121. Huttenback, *Gandhi in South Africa*, p. 204.
122. *Indian Opinion*, 23 July 1910.
123. *Indian Opinion*, 20 August 1910.
124. NAD/IRD, vol. 85, ref. IRD 1265/1910.
125. NAD/IRD, vol. 85, ref. IRD 1263/1910.
126. *Indian Opinion*, 29 October 1910, p.356.
127. *Indian Opinion*, 12 November 1910.
128. *Indian Opinion*, 31 December 1910, p.436.
129. NAD/IRD, vol. 86, ref. IRD 1541/1910.
130. *Indian Opinion*, 21 January 1911.
131. NAD/IRD, vol. 90, ref. IRD 689/1911; NAD/IRD, vol. 87, ref. IRD 5/1911; *Indian Opinion*, 25 February 1911.
132. Ly-Tio-Fane Pineo, *Chinese Diaspora in western Indian Ocean*, p. 254-255.
133. Letter from M.K. Gandhi to C. Lane, 29 April 1911; *Indian Opinion*, 27 May, 1908.
134. Letter to C. Lane, 20 May 1911; *Indian Opinion*, 27 May 1911, p. 209 and 10 June 1911, p. 233.
135. *Indian Opinion*, 29 April 1911.

136. *Indian Opinion*, 27 May 1911.
137. SAD/GG, vol. 1208, ref 51/926.
138. Ly-Tio-Fane Pineo, *Chinese diaspora in western Indian Ocean*, p. 239.
139. *The selected works of Mahatma Gandhi*, p. 200.
140. H.J. and R.E. Simons, *Class and colour in South Africa 1850-1950*, Harmondsworth: Penguin, 1969, p. 72.

CHAPTER 7 DISCRIMINATION IN THE UNION OF SOUTH AFRICA

1. The *Oxford history of South Africa*, vol. 2, ed. by M. Wilson & L. Thompson, Oxford: Clarendon, 1975, p. 343-347.
2. H.R. Hahlo & E. Kahn, *The Union of South Africa*, London: Stevens, 1960, p. 121.
3. T.R.H. Davenport, *South Africa*, 2nd ed., Johannesburg: Macmillan, 1978, p.165-169.
4. Hahlo & Kahn, *The Union of South Africa*, p. 122.
5. *The Oxford history of South Africa*, vol. 2, p. 356.
6. *The Oxford history of South Africa*, vol. 2, p. 361-362, p. 332-333.
7. *The Oxford history of South Africa*, vol. 2, p. 364.
8. Hahlo & Kahn, *The Union of South Africa*, p. 793-811.
9. TAD/GOV, vol. 991, ref. PS 37/37/06. Lew Yuk Lin requested Governor Selborne to allow Chinese the right to have liquor for their personal use. Request refused.
10. SAD/GG, vol. 991, ref. 37/27 and 37/28. Letter to Minister of Interior, 20 November 1910.
11. SAD/GG, vol. 991, ref. 37/27 and 37/28. Letter to Lord Gladstone, 5 December 1910.
12. SAD/GG, vol. 762, ref. 20/97, 20/99 & 20/104.
13. SAD/GG, vol. 773, ref. 20/926 & 20/903.
14. SAD/GG, vol. 722, ref. 15/1018. Letters 29 April 1920 and 14 May 1920.
15. Correspondence of Uitenhage Chinese Association, 1923-1926; Minutes of the Transvaal Chinese United Club, 1916-1926.
16. Minutes of the Transvaal Chinese United Club, 1916-1926.
17. SAD/GG, vol. 717, ref. 15/706. Letter dated 28 April 1914.
18. SAD/GG, vol. 717, ref. 15/706 and 15/724.
19. From official census statistics published by the three colonies and by the Office of Census and Statistics in Pretoria.
20. SAD/CIA, vol. 4, ref. M31. Letter from Principal Immigration Officer to the Secretary for the Interior, 1 October 1918.
21. SAD/CIA, vol. 4, ref. M31. Letter from Chinese Association Port Elizabeth to Minister for the Interior, 27 September 1916, relating to question of recognizing Chinese marriages.
22. SAD/CIA, vol. 4, ref. M31. Letters from American Vice-Consul in charge of Chinese Interests to Secretary for the Interior, 20-24 September 1918.
23. SAD/CIA, vol. 4, ref. 18/M/31. Letter from Principal Immigration Officer to American Vice-Consul in charge of Chinese Interests, 17 December 1918.
24. SAD/CIA, vol. 4, ref. 13/M/358. Letter from Principal Immigration Officer, Cape Province, to Commissioner for Immigration and Asiatic Affairs, 13 September 1928.
25. TAD/GOV, vol. 951 & 952, ref. PS 15/12/06. Correspondence between Protector of Asiatics and SA ConsTADulary, February 1906.
26. SAD/BNS, vol. 1/1/310, ref. 13/74, parts 1-7. Letter to Consul Feng Wang from the Commissioner for Immigration and Asiatic Affairs, 3 April 1933, with reports from South African Police, 22 March 1933 and Immigration Officer, 2 March 1933.
27. SAD/BNS, vol. 1/1/310, ref. 55/74, parts 1-7. Sworn statements, June 1924-July 1925.
28. SAD/BNS, vol. 1/1/310, ref. 13/74, parts 1-7. Correspondence between Feng Wang, Consul-General and Commissioner for Immigration and Asiatic Affairs, February-April 1933.
29. SAD/BNS, vol. 1/1/58, ref. 55/74, parts 1-7. Petition from Leong Song, presented to House of Assembly, 5 July 1920; Cape of Good Hope. Parliament. Appendix II to the Votes and Proceedings of Parliament, Vol II, 1908. Report of the Select Committee on Asiatic Grievances [A16-'08], petition from Hing Woo.

30. Cape of Good Hope. Parliament. Appendix I to the Votes and Proceedings of Parliament, Vol. 1, 1907. Report on immigration and labour for the year ending 31 December 1906, p. 8.
31. SAD/GG, vol. 990, ref 37/4. Petitions forwarded by Acting Imperial Chinese Consul-General, 9 June 1910.
32. SAD/GG, vol. 991, ref. 37/27, 37/28 & 37/61. Letter Acting Secretary for the Interior, 21 November 1910.
33. SAD/CIA, vol. 7, ref. M86.
34. SAD/CIA, vol. 35, ref. M358.
35. SAD/CIA, vol. 4, ref. M31 and 31/M/31. Correspondence between Secretary for the Interior and the Commissioner for Immigration and Asiatic Affairs, March-May 1929.
36. SAD/CIA, vol. 4, ref. M347. Annual report of Principal Immigration Officer for 1932.
37. Official Year Book of the Union and of Basutoland, Bechuanaland Protectorate, and Swaziland, no, 14, 1931-1932, p.829; *Cape Times*, 9 January 1924.
38. SAD/GG, vol. 728, ref. 15/1188A and 15/1188B. Memorandum from Governor-General Athlone to the Colonial Office, London, 22 February 1924.
39. Union Gazette Extraordinary, 5 January 1924.
40. *Cape Times*, 16 February 1924.
41. Letter in Chinese from PE Chinese Association to Consul-General, 14 January 1924, in Uitenhage Chinese Association papers.
42. *Sunday Times*, 10 February 1924.
43. Letter to Consul-General Liu Ngai from Secretary to the Prime Minister, D.F. Malan, 18 March 1926, in Uitenhage Chinese Association papers.
44. South Africa. Parliament. Report of the Asiatic Inquiry Commission, Cape Town: Cape Times, 1921, [U.G. 4-'21]; South Africa. Parliament. Report of the Select Committee on Asiatics in Transvaal, Cape Town: Cape Times, 1930, [S.C. 7-'30]; Land Tenure by Asiatics and South African Coloured People in the Transvaal, *Race Relations Journal*, vol. 2, no. 5, November 1935, p. 43;
45. SAD/JUS, vol. 1290, ref. 1/149/32. Petition from Executive Council of the Chinese Association of the Transvaal, 26 August 1932; SAD/GG, vol. 728, ref. 15/1462, petition from the Chinese Community of the Transvaal, cover sheet of file, 16 August 1932.
46. *The Star*, 8 February 1933.
47. *The Star* and *Rand Daily Mail*, 8 February 1933.
48. South Africa. Parliament. Report of the Transvaal Asiatic Land Tenure Act Commission, Pretoria: Govt Printer, 1934, [U.G. 7-1934], parts I-II, p. 246-249.
49. South Africa. Parliament. Report of the Transvaal Asiatic Land Tenure Act Commission, p. 57, 127-128.
50. *Cape Times*, 22 December 1936.
51. Tung Miao, *Legal status of Chinese in the Union of South Africa*, Johannesburg: Chiao Sheng Pao, 1947, p. 20.
52. The Asiatics (Transvaal Land and Trading) Act (Act No. 28 of 1939); the Asiatics (Transvaal Land and Trading) Amendment Act (Act No. 28 of 1941); the Trading and Occupation of Land (Transvaal and Natal) Restriction Act (Act No. 35 of 1943); the Asiatic Land Tenure and Indian Representation Act (Act No. 28 of 1946).
53. SAD/ARG, Vol. 10, ref. ACT1/1/2/3/1. Petition from Chinese community of the Transvaal; SAD/ARG, Vol. 8, ref. ACT1/1/1/3/12. Memorandum from Natal Chinese Association.
54. Liquor Licensing Ordinance, No. 32 of 1902; SAD/JUS, vol. 353, ref. 3/743/22. Petition of the Transvaal Chinese Association to the Acting Consul, 9 February 1918.
55. TAD/GOV, vol. 991, ref. PS 37/37/1906;, TAD/LD, vol. 1487, ref. AG 3156/07.
56. South Africa. Parliament. Select Committee on working of Transvaal Liquor Laws [S.C. 2-'18]. Minutes of evidence, April 1918, p. 491-492.
57. SAD/JUS, vol. 353, ref. 3/743/22 and 1/417/28.
58. SAD/JUS, vol. 353, ref. 3/743/22 and 1/417/28. Letter from TCA to American Vice-Consul for Chinese Interests, 25 November 1918.
59. SAD/JUS, vol. 353, ref. 3/743/22 and ref. 1/417/28. Correspondence between Consul- General Liu Ngai and Minister for Justice, March-April 1922.
60. SAD/JUS, vol. 353, ref. 3/743/22 and 1/417/28. Correspondence between Dr J.B. Bok, Secretary for

Justice and Major A.E. Trigger, CID, 28 April 1925 and 5 May 1925.

61. SAD/JUS, vol. 353, ref. 3/743/22 and ref. 1/417/28; SAD/GG, vol. 851, ref. 24/398, 7/4339, 7/4324 and 15/1433. Letter from Minister of Lands to Minister of Justice, 3 May 1933.
62. Act No. 30 of 1928; SAD/JUS, vol. 353, ref. 3/743/22 and 1/417/28; SAD/GG, vol. 851, ref. 24/398, 7/4339, 7/4324 and 15/1433. Correspondence between Consul-General Liu Ngai, Secretary for External Affairs and Secretary for Justice, October-November 1928.
63. SAD/JUS, vol. 353, ref 3/743/22 and 1/417/28. Letter from Consul-General Liu Ngai to the Minister of Justice, 4 December 1928, accompanied by petition signed by 30 Natal Chinese. Letter from Eugene Renaud & Mooney to the Minister of Justice, 21 February 1934, accompanied by petition signed by 26 Chinese resident in Durban and Pietermaritzburg. Petition from Natal Chinese Association to Minister of Justice, 23 January 1942.
64. SAD/JUS, vol. 353, ref. 3/743/22 and 1/417/28;SAD/GG, vol. 851, ref. 24/398, 7/4339, 7/4324 and 15/1433. Letter from Commissioner of Police to Secretary for Justice, 14 January 1929.
65. SAD/JUS, vol. 618, ref. 2173/36, 7934/29 and 1/417/28, Memorandum from Commissioner of Police appended to correspondence between the Departments of External Affairs, Interior and Justice, July-August 1936.
66. SAD/JUS, vol. 618, ref. 2173/36. Letter from Minister of External Affairs to British Ambassador in Peking, 25 September 1936.
67. SAD/JUS, vol. 618, ref. 2173/36.
68. SAD/JUS, vol. 353 and 618, ref. 1/417/28.
69. *Rand Daily Mail*, 8 April 1940.
70. SAD/JUS, vol. 353 and 618, ref. 1/417/28. Letter from Consul-General to Minister of Justice, 8 April 1940.
71. SAD/JUS, vol. 353 and 618, ref. 1/417/28, Letter from Secretary for Justice to Secretary for External Affairs, 19 April 1940.
72. SAD/JUS, vol. 618, ref. 1/4178. Petition from Natal Chinese Association to Minister of Justice, 23 January 1942.
73. South Africa. Government Gazette, 24 September 1943. Proclamation No. 177 of 1943.
74. Durban Alienation of Land Ordinance, No. 14 of 1922; The Borough and Townships Land Ordinance, No. 5 of 1923; The Townships Ordinance, No. 11 of 1926.
75. Tung Miao, *Legal Status of Chinese in the Union of South Africa*, p. 28-29.
76. TAD/MM, vol. 198, ref. MM690/08.
77. Ordinance 14 of 1904; *The Oxford History of South Africa*, vol. 2, p. 30.
78. Tung Miao, *Legal status of Chinese in the Union of South Africa*, p. 37.
79. Cape statistics from: Appendix I to the Votes and Proceedings of Parliament, 1907. Report on Immigration and Labour for the year ending 31 December 1906, p. 9; Transvaal statistics from: TAD/CIA, vol. 1 A279, ref 22/M1. Statistics for 1905 on occupations of Chinese.
80. Half Holiday Act of 1905 and General Dealers' Licensing Act 1906, required traders to close shops on Wednesday afternoons and at 8 pm every evening.
81. TAD/CS, vol. 417, ref. 387/04.
82. *Indian Opinion*, 22 February 1908, p. 96.
83. A report on the Asiatic problem in Port Elizabeth presented by the Chief Sanitary Inspector, Port Elizabeth: Walton, 1911. Annexure: Port Elizabeth Retail Traders Association letter, 23 November 1910.
84. A report on the Asiatic problem ..., p. 2-4.
85. A report on the Asiatic problem ..., p. 3.
86. SAD/GG, vol. 714, ref. 15/466.
87. SAD/GG, vol. 715, ref. 15/557.
88. SAD/GG, vol. 715, ref. 15/557.
89. SAD/GG, vol. 715, ref. 15/557; *Pretoria News*, September 1913.
90. SAD/CIA, vol. 22 ref. M1, part 1; *Rand Daily Mail*, 16 August 1918.
91. SAD/GG. vol. 727, ref. 15/1433; *Rand Daily Mail*, 15 January 1929.
92. SAD/GG, vol. 727, ref. 15/1433.
93. SAD/GG, vol. 727, ref. 15.1443. Minutes of evidence taken before the Select Committee on Asiatics in Transvaal, 26 March 1930, p. 206-231.

94. C. van Onselen, *Studies in the social and economic history of the Witwatersrand 1886-1914*, vol. 2: New Nineveh, Johannesburg: Ravan, 1982, p. 96-97.
95. *Transvaal Weekly Illustrated*, 20 February 1909, p. 6.
96. *The Star*, 22 November 1907.
97. *The Star*, 13 March 1908.
98. Van Onselen, *Studies in the social* ..., p. 97.
99. NAD/IRD, vol. 59, ref. IRD 69/1907; NAD/IRD vol. 50, ref. IRD 398, 1906; NAD/MSCE, ref. 23926/1936.
100. A report on the Asiatic problem ..., p. 4.
101. *Port Elizabeth year book and directory for 1910*, p. 97.
102. CAD/3/PEZ, vol. 4/1/1/1495, ref. 25/102. Memorandum on provision of public wash houses and laundries, Port Elizabeth, 12 October 1925.
103. CAD/3/ELN, vol. 996, ref. 1287. Reports to the Chief Sanitary Inspector, East London, 19 July 1912.
104. Interview with Mr Les Hoy, Cape Town, March 1987.
105. CAD/3/CT, vol. 4/1/4/257 ref. E411/4.
106. CAD/3/CT, vol. 4/1/4/238, ref. E125/4.
107. B.M. Titlestad, *Penetrating the invisible society: an examination of the emergence and decline of Chinese participation in the 'Kaffir' eating house trade*, unpublished seminar paper, Department of Geography and Environmental Studies, University of the Witwatersrand, Johannesburg, 1984, p. 13.
108. C.M. Rogerson, 'Shisha Nyama': The rise and fall of the Native eating house trade in Johannesburg, in *The Making of Class*, History Workshop, University of the Witwatersrand, February 1987, p. 8-9.
109. *Indian Opinion*, 26 June 1909, p. 84.
110. Rogerson, *The making of class*, p. 11-13.
111. TAD/SS, vol. 0, ref. R14109/98.
112. TAD/LD, vol. 1472, ref. AG2667/07.
113. TAD/LD, vol. 229, ref. AG24/03.
114. SAD/JUS, vol. 830, ref. 1/580/24.
115. SAD/JUS, vol. 830, ref. 1/580/24, *Rand Daily Mail*, July 1914.
116. SAD/JUS, vol. 830, ref. 1/580/24.
117. CAD/AG, vol. 1846, ref. 17352.
118. CAD/T, vol. 1220, ref. 215.
119. TAD/FLD, vol. 103, ref. 38/55.
120. Letter from Consulate-General to Mr L.A. Ying, Cape Town, 13 June 1950.
121. G.H. Pirie, Racial segregation on Johannesburg trams: procedures and protest, 1904-1927, *African Studies*, vol. 48, no. 1, 1989, p. 42 and 53.
122. TAD/JHM, vol. 8, ref. 316(A).
123. Arms and Ammunition Act (No. 10 of 1907). The later Arms and Ammunition Act (No. 28 of 1937) stipulated licences could only be issued to persons other than Europeans with the special approval of the Minister of Justice.
124. Law 3 of 1897, regulating the Marriage of Coloured Persons within the South African Republic. Coloured persons were any person belonging to or being a descendant of any native race in South Africa and persons being descendants of one of the native races of Asia.
125. TAD/DCU, vol. 66, ref. 173/06. Customs report on anticipated attempt by a Chinese to smuggle opium from Lourenco Marques into the Transvaal, 17 January 1906.
126. TAD/CS, vol. 678, ref 9389. Refusal of application by Sing For for permit to purchase opium for his personal use, 10 November 1906 and letter from A.W. Baker to Attorney-General, 31 January 1907.
127. CAD/PMO, vol. 239, ref. 415/08.
128. Interview with Mr Harry Simpson, Port Elizabeth, July 1987.
129. Interview with Mr Edmund Quat, Cape Town, September 1988.
130. *Transvaal Weekly Illustrated*, 4 July 1908, p. 6.
131. Opium Trade Regulation Amendment Act, 1909.
132. L. Pan, *Sons of the Yellow Emperor*, London: Secker & Warburg, 1990, p. 121.
133. CAD/AG, vol. 1740, ref. 8314.

CHAPTER 8 COMMUNITY ORGANIZATIONS FLOURISH

1. From official census statistics published by the three colonies and by the Office of Census and Statistics in Pretoria. Distribution figures by province for 1946 are not available.
2. SAD/BNS, vol. 1/1/58, ref. 55/74, parts 1-7. Petition from Leong Song, presented to the House of Assembly, 5 July 1920.
3. Natal. Census of the Colony of Natal, April, 1904. Pietermaritzburg: Davis, 1905; South Africa. Office of Census and Statistics. Sixth census of the population of the Union of South Africa, enumerated 5th May 1936. Pretoria: Government Printer, 1938-1942. Vol. 5: Birthplaces, period of residence and nationality, p. 116. Table 26 on the number of Asiatics in the principal towns and their suburbs shows 75 Chinese in Durban and suburbs and 7 in Pietermaritzburg and suburbs.
4. NAD/IRD, vol. 78, ref. IRD 1292/1909.
5. Interview with Mr Bertram Lee, Cape Town, March 1988.
6. SAD/JUS, vol. 353, ref. 1/417/28. Petition to Minister of Justice, from the Chinese Community resident in the province of Natal, despatched by Consul-General Liu Ngai, 4 December 1928.
7. Interviews with Dr Ted Wong Hoption, Johannesburg, November 1987 and Mr Ralph Pakshong, Durban, March 1988.
8. Interview with Dr Ted Wong Hoption, Johannesburg, November 1987. Well-known community member, Mr C.P. Yenson, was a regular patron of the Edward Hotel in Durban throughout the 1920s and 1930s.
9. Interview with Mr Henry Kim Sing, Kimberley, September 1987.
10. Interview with Mr W.S. Chan Yan, Kimberley, September 1987.
11. South Africa. Office of Census and Statistics. Sixth census of the population of the Union of South Africa, enumerated 5 May 1936.
12. B. Roberts, *Kimberley: turbulent city*, Cape Town: Philip, 1976, p. 384.
13. Interviews with Mr W.S. Chan Yan and Mr Meng Chan Yan, Kimberley, September 1987.
14. Interviews with Mr Ley Changfoot, East London, July 1987; Mr Sung Himpoo, Johannesburg; Dr Stanley Himpoo, East London; and group interview with Mrs Yan, Mrs Kwan Thouw and Mrs M. Lok, Johannesburg, August 1987.
15. Interview with Mr L.A. Ying, March 1987.
16. CAD/AG, vol. 1848, ref. 17584. Police record no. 3310, case no. 4193, 8 Sept. 1908, Rex vs Ching Chong.
17. Constitution and Rules of the Chinese Republic United Association of No. 170 Loop Street, Cape Town, in the Union of South Africa, 1 April 1921.
18. South Africa. Office of Census and Statistics. Sixth census of the population of the Union of South Africa, enumerated 5 May 1936.
19. Deed of Transfer executed on 17 October 1944 on Lot No. 39 of the farm 'Welgelegen', in Mowbray; Interview with Mr George Ming, Cape Town, March 1987.
20. *Cape Times*, October 1945.
21. Interviews with Mr Harry Wong, East London, July 1987 and Mr Peter Chen, Durban, May 1988.
22. Letter from East London Chinese Association to Uitenhage Chinese Association, 30 January 1924.
23. Interviews with Mr John Louis Fontbin, East London, July 1987 and Mr Lee Sing Gen, Johannesburg, April 1990.
24. South Africa. Office of Census and Statistics. Sixth census of the population of the Union of South Africa, enumerated 5 May 1936.
25. *New China*, October 1946 – November 1947.
26. R. Trehaven, A note on the 'Spanish flu' of 1918 in Port Elizabeth. *Looking back*, vol. 27, no. 2, September 1988, p. 32-33.
27. South Africa. Office of Census and Statistics. Sixth census of the population of the Union of South Africa, enumerated 5 May 1936.
28. NAD/IRD, vol. 42, ref. IRD 880/1905.
29. TAD/GOV, vol. 874, ref. PS 37/23/05. A man named Thomas Ah See claimed he was being paid £1000 by 'Chinese communities' in the Eastern Cape to take a petition relating to the Chinese Exclusion Act to the Chinese Minister in London. Cape Chinese, however, seemed to have communicated directly with the Minister and had their grievances redressed before Mr Ah See reached London.
30. Draft report of the Chinese Association, Port Elizabeth, written in Chinese by Mr Y. Whiteley, June

1935 and translated by Mr Stanley May.

31. Reorganized rules and regulations, Chinese Association, Port Elizabeth, South Africa, 1 November 1919.
32. Reorganized rules and regulations, Chinese Association, Port Elizabeth.
33. Draft report of the Chinese Association, Port Elizabeth, June 1935 (in Chinese).
34. Draft report of the Chinese Association, Port Elizabeth.
35. Letter to Port Elizabeth City Engineer's Department, 25 May 1938, states a new building had been erected at 64 Evatt Street and requests permission to purchase street to the rear of the building. That the erection of the premises took place in 1937 is substantiated by interviews with Mr Harry Simpson and Mr Y. Whiteley, Port Elizabeth, July 1987.
36. A. Heard, 'My Chinese pupil'.
37. SAD/CIA, vol. 37, ref. M819. Letter from H. Polakow, 24 January 1942.
38. SAD/CIA, vol. 37, ref. M819. Letter from Commissioner for Immigration and Asiatic Affairs to Secretary for the Interior, 25 February 1942.
39. Amended Constitution of Moi Yean Commercial Association of Port Elizabeth, South Africa, 1918 (in Chinese).
40. Rules and Regulations, Cantonist United Benefit Society, Port Elizabeth, South Africa, established 1 January 1918.
41. Interviews with Mr Harry Simpson and Mr Y. Whiteley, Port Elizabeth, July 1987.
42. Interview with Mr Gordon Lee Sun, Uitenhage, July 1987 — stated that his father told him the Chinese Association had been formed prior to the Chinese Republic in 1911. Mr Joey Long King, interviewed in Uitenhage in July 1987, stated he had heard the association was older than the Chinese Association in Port Elizabeth.
43. All these documents were donated to the SA Chinese History Project.
44. Interviews with Mr Joey Long King and Mr Raymond Ah Sing, Uitenhage, July 1987.
45. Interview with Mr Edward Jack Kee, Port Elizabeth, July 1987.
46. Letter from Mr Sidney Kim Sing, Vancouver, Canada, 1990.
47. Interview with Mr Edward Jack Kee.
48. Interviews with Mrs Nee Fook Date Chong, Port Elizabeth, August 1987 and Mr Leslie Kwongsee, Cape Town, April 1988. Mr Singer is said to have married a White woman in Port Elizabeth and had one daughter. He was eventually forced to leave when authorities discovered his illegal presence in the city.
49. Interview with Mr Edmund Quat, Cape Town, September 1988.
50. Interview with Mrs Chantson, Port Elizabeth, July 1987.
51. Interview with Mr Y. Whiteley.
52. South Africa. Office of Census and Statistics. Sixth census of the population of the Union of South Africa, enumerated 5 May 1936.
53. SAD/BNS, vol. 1/1/346, ref. 82/74. Chinese societies and associations.
54. SAD/JUS, vol. 353, ref. 3/743/22. Petition of the Transvaal Chinese Association to the Acting Consul of the Chinese Republic, Johannesburg, 9 February 1918.
55. SAD/GG, vol. 717 and 222, ref. 15/706, 15/742, 15/1018, 19/M/31.
56. Petition to Dr D.F. Malan, Minister of the Interior, accompanied by letter dated 26 December 1924 from Mr C P Yenson.
57. South Africa. Parliament. Report of the Select Committee on Asiatics in Transvaal [S.C. 7-30], Cape Town: Cape Times, 1930, p. 206-231.
58. The same signatories' names appear on a petition to the Governor-General of South Africa, the Earl of Clarendon, SAD/GG, vol. 728, ref. 15/1462, 16 August 1932. In this petition, however, the six stated that they were delegates for the Transvaal Chinese Union.
59. Interview with Mr Alec Oshry, Johannesburg, January 1988.
60. The Asiatic Act: the conditions and status of the Chinese community in the Union of South Africa, compiled by Mr. Ah York (Lai Shu Kai), joint secretary and senior executive member of the Transvaal Chinese Association and chairman of the Transvaal Chinese School Board of Trustees, 30 June 1947, p. 5.
61. The Asiatic Act ..., p. 10; Interview with Mr Wellington Ford, November 1987.
62. TAD/GOV, vol. 991, ref. PS 37/37/06. Letter from Acting Chinese Consul-General Liu Ngai to Lieutenant-Governor for the Transvaal, 13 October 1906.

63. Cantonese Club membership certificate, issued to Ah Chung on 24 December 1919.
64. TAD/JHM, vol. 8, ref. 316.
65. Interviews with Mr Yung Fah, Johannesburg, 1985 and Mr Leslie Yenson, Johannesburg, October 1987.
66. Cantonese Club membership certificate (in Chinese); Certificate of Conversion to Freehold Title, registered no. 9514 on stand 221, Ferreiras, 8 October 1943.
67. Interview with Mr Yung Fah.
68. Minutes of Transvaal Chinese United Club. Letter to *Chung Hing* newspaper, 13 September 1909, p. 31.
69. Minutes of Transvaal Chinese United Club. Notice dated 26 April 1909, p. 15.
70. TAD/MHG, vol. 0, ref. 1470/58. Transvaal Chinese United Club, ex parte application of Tong King, 1958, p. 5.
71. Interview with Mr Wellington Ford.
72. Memorandum of Association of Chee Kung Tong Trust Limited, Stand 247, Ferreiras, at Johannesburg Deeds Office.
73. Minutes of Transvaal Chinese United Club, 10 September 1919.
74. SAD/BNS, vol. 1/1/309, ref. 13/74AA.
75. Minutes of Transvaal Chinese United Club, 10 September 1919.
76. Interview with Mr Ho Sue Chong, Johannesburg, October 1987.
77. Interviews with Mr Edward Kin, Johannesburg, November 1987 and Mr Ho Sue Chong.
78. Chinese Constitution of Transvaal Chinese Traders Association.
79. Interview with Mr Lew Johnson, Johannesburg, March 1983. Mr Johnson said a business association called the 'Seong Fooi' was concerned with licensing issues in the 1920s.
80. Interview with Mr Edward Kin.
81. Interview with Mr Jong Tin, Johannesburg, May 1983.
82. Interview with Mrs Wan Yuk Lee, Johannesburg, November 1990.
83. S.C. Hau, Birth of the Young Chinese Cultural League, in *50th Anniversary Pretoria Chinese School 1984*, p.47.
84. Interview with Mr Lew Johnson.
85. Interview with Mr Leslie Yenson.
86. Interviews with Mr Leslie Yenson and Mrs Wan Yuk Lee.
87. P. Knox & T. Gutsche, *Do you know Johannesburg?*, Vereeniging: Unie Volkspers, 1947, p. 66-67.
88. *Handbook on race relations in South Africa,* edited by E. Hellmann, New York: Octagon, 1975.
89. Correspondence between E.P. Chinese Association and Consulate-General, from March 1963-June 1964; Minutes of E.P. Chinese Association committee meeting, 6 January 1965.
90. Interview with Mrs Wan Yuk Lee.
91. J.S. Chum, The Pretoria Chinese Association and the School, in *50th Anniversary Pretoria Chinese School 1984*, p. 153.
92. Interview with Lewis Fu Law, Pretoria, July 1988.
93. The establishment of the Pretoria Chinese School, in *50th Anniversary Pretoria Chinese School 1984*, p. 61.
94. Interview with Mr Su Won Ho, Pretoria, April 1988.
95. Chen So Chiang, *Overseas Chinese revolutionary movements*, Taichung: Jianxing Printing Works, 1985, p. 136. Dr Chen also states that branches of the 'Hing Jung Hwei', translated as the 'Re-establish China Society', were established in Johannesburg and Pietermaritzburg in 1897.
96. *The new Encyclopaedia Britannica*, vol. 8, 15th ed. 1987.
97. Press clipping, source unknown but most likely an Eastern Cape newspaper, circa June 1921.
98. Interviews with Mr Henry Kim Sing and Mr W.S. Chan Yan.
99. Press clipping, source unknown but most likely an Eastern Cape newspaper, circa June 1921.
100. C.M. Wilbur, *Sun Yat-Sen, frustrated patriot,* New York: Columbia U.P., 1976, p. 50-52 and 307, note 51.

CHAPTER 9 WAR IN CHINA: THE COMMUNITY RESPONDS

1. NAD/CSO, vol. 1801, ref. 1905/9374. Refusal by Transvaal Government to allow Japanese merchant to enter Transvaal; TAD/LTG, vol. 97, ref. 97/14. Position of Japanese in the Transvaal.
2. TAD/GG, vol. 707, ref. 15/92 & 15/188. Application of Mr. K. Furuya. Office of the Governor-General

of South Africa, minute 39, 13 January 1911.

3. S. Jones & A. Muller, *The South African economy 1910-90*, New York: St Martin's, 1992, p. 116-120.
4. SAD/GG, vol. 988 & 1312, ref. 36/334. Asiatic immigration. Dr Malan's speech in the House of Assembly, reported in *The Star*, 5 March 1931 and editorial comment in same issue.
5. South Africa. Office of Census and Statistics. Third census of the population of the Union of South Africa enumerated 3 May 1921, part VIII, Non-European Races. [U.G. 20-24]. This census lists the number of Japanese males as 83 and females as 15, totalling 98. A special report by the Assistant Director of Census, No. 14: 'The Asiatic Population of the Union: An Historical Survey', p. 9, however states that the number of Japanese in the 1921 census was inflated because of the presence of a Japanese boat in Durban harbour with a crew of 44.
6. SAD/GG, vol. 851, ref. 24/398. Letter from Minister of External Affairs, J.B.M. Hertzog, to the Secretary of State for Dominion Affairs, 12 February 1929.
7. SAD/JUS, vol. 353, ref. 3/743/22 & 1/417/28 ; SAD/GG, vol. 851, ref. 24/398, 7/4339, 7/4324 & 15/1433. Letter from the Secretary for External Affairs to the Secretary for Justice, 21 November 1928 and petition from the Chinese community of Natal to the Minister of Justice, under a covering letter from Consul-General Liu Ngai, 4 December 1928.
8. SAD/GG, vol. 851, ref. 24/398. Letter from the Secretary for External Affairs to the Chinese Consul-General, 5 February 1929.
9. South Africa. Sixth census of the population of the Union of South Africa, enumerated 5th May, 1936. Volume V, Birthplaces, period of residence and nationality of the European, Asiatic and Coloured population [U.G. 24, 1942], p. 121. Tabulated according to nationality, this census records 1882 males and 1062 females, a total of 2944 Chinese.
10. South Africa. Parliament. Notes exchanged between the Union Government and the Japanese Consul in the Union concerning Japanese immigration into South Africa, February 1931, [A1-31].
11. SAD/GG, vol. 988 & 1312, ref. 36/334. Press clippings from *Rand Daily Mail*, 27-28 February 1931; *The Star*, 4 March 1931.
12. SAD/GG, vol. 988 & 1312, ref. 36/334. *Rand Daily Mail* 28 March 1931.
13. *Rand Daily Mail*, 3 March 1931.
14. *The Star*, 5 March 1931.
15. *Rand Daily Mail*, 15 July 1931.
16. South Africa. Office of Census and Statistics. Sixth census of the population of the Union of South Africa, enumerated 5 May 1936.
17. SAD/GG, vol. 727, ref. 15/1433. *The Star*, 16 January 1929.
18. *The Star*, 25 February 1929; *Cape Times*, 28 February 1929.
19. *Rand Daily Mail*, 23 April 1929.
20. Interviews with Mr Lew Johnson, March 1983, and Mr Tsang Ho Chun, May 1983.
21. *The Star*, 1 May 1929.
22. *Rand Daily Mail*, 18 July 1929.
23. *Rand Daily Mail*, 7 November 1929.
24. *The Star*, 30 August 1930.
25. *The Star*, 30 August and 8 September 1930; *Rand Daily Mail*, 30 August and 8 September 1930.
26. *Rand Daily Mail*, 8 September 1930.
27. *The Star*, 8 September 1930.
28. *Rand Daily Mail*, 8 September 1930.
29. W. King, Thirty years of the Johannesburg Chinese School, *Johannesburg Chinese Kuo Ting High School annual*, 1956.
30. K.S. Latourette, *The Chinese: their history and culture*, 4th edition, New York: Macmillan, 1964, p. 351.
31. K. Furuya, *Chiang Kai Shek, his life and times*, New York: St John's University, 1981; abridged English edition by Chun-ming Chang, p. 555-557.
32. B. Crozier, *The man who lost China*, New York: Scribner, 1976, p. 207.
33. *Chronicle of 20th Century history*, ed. by J.S. Bowman, London: Bison, 1989, p. 116.
34. Interview with Dr Ted Wong Hoption, 4 November 1987.
35. A.S. Moore Anderson, The Chinese allies we insult, *The Forum*, 24 October 1942, p. 7; *The China Week News*, East London, 13-18 December 1943, published by China War Relief Fund, p. 4.

36. Interview with Miss M. Whiteley and Mr Gordon Loyson, Port Elizabeth, July 1987.
37. Interview with Mr Ho Su Won, Pretoria, April 1988.
38. Interview with Mr Gordon Loyson.
39. Pamphlet dated 20 November 1938 and receipts in possession of Mr P.S. Leong, Johannesburg.
40. SAD/JUS, vol. 353 and 618, ref. 1/417/28, Letter from Consul-General to Minister of Justice, 13 February 1942.
41. Interview with Mrs Wan Yuk Lee, Johannesburg, November 1990.
42. Report of South African Transvaal Chinese Women's Association, 30th year of the Republic of China, (1941), published in Chinese.
43. Interview with Mrs Ivy Leong, Johannesburg, 13 November 1991.
44. *Chinese Consular Gazette*, 6 July 1943.
45. *Cape Times*, 25 December 1937.
46. Records of Mr Y. Whiteley, Chinese secretary of Eastern Province Chinese Association, undated. Translated from Chinese by Mr Stanley May.
47. Certificate in possession of Mr Sun Hing, interviewed in Vereeniging, May 1987.
48. *China at war*, pamphlet published by Chinese War Relief Fund, 1 April 1943; Messages from General J.C. Smuts, Prime Minister, and Dr Colin Steyn, Minister of Justice, p. 1 & 8. (Strange Africana Library).
49. Sundry correspondence, including letter from the National Union of South African Students' Councillor, H.T. Bonfa, of Howard College, Durban, to J. Rollnick, 6 June 1938; Undated letter by C.R. Robb, on behalf of the Chinese Relief Fund Committee of the Students Representative Council, University of the Witwatersrand (AD 843/RJ/Pn 8.2.); Letter from Mr J.D. Rheinallt Jones dated 28 June 1938, (AD 843/RJ/Kb5) (University of the Witwatersrand Library).
50. *China at war*, p. 4.
51. Copies lodged at the Strange Africana Library, Johannesburg.
52. *Cape Times*, 14 April 1943.
53. Interview with Mr L.A. Ying, Cape Town and correspondence from 'Help for Free China Fund', 2 October 1943.
54. *Cape Times*, 3 February 1944.
55. Personal documents of Mr L.A. Ying, including Liberty Cavalcade letterhead featuring China section committee.
56. Letter from Mr Sidney Kim Sing, 8 March 1989.
57. Report on Queenstown contribution, published in *South Africa and China*, by the China War Relief Fund, 1944, p. 3.
58. *South Africa and China*, p. 3.
59. Report on Durban contribution, published in *South Africa and China*, p. 3.
60. SAD/CIA, vol. M819, ref. M721/47. Memoir re Chinese seamen, 6 July 1943.
61. SAD/JUS, vol. 353 and 618, ref. 1/417/28. Letter from Consul-General to Minister of Justice, 13 February 1942.
62. NAD/MSCE, vol. 0, ref. 35366/1942.
63. Interviews with Mr Ralph Pakshong and Mr Albert Fontbin, Durban, May 1988.
64. Interview with Mr L.A. Ying, Cape Town, March 1987.
65. Letter from Consul-General Dekien Toung to shipping companies, 6 May 1943. (Personal papers of Mr L.A. Ying).
66. Letter from Consul-General C.Y. Shih, 11 December 1944.
67. National Chinese Welfare Council, special publication, New York, July 1990.
68. Letter from Mr David Low, 13 June 1991.
69. National Chinese Welfare Council, special publication, p. 21-24.
70. Moore Anderson, *The Forum*, p. 7-8.
71. A.J. Friedgut, How we treat the gallant Chinese, *The Forum*, 7 August 1943, p. 5-6 and 27.
72. Undated pamphlet headlined 'Emphatically Yes, we do says Mr Anthony Eden'. (Strange Africana Library).

CHAPTER 10 EDUCATION: FROM SHOPS TO UNIVERSITIES

1. Transvaal Education Act, no. 25 of 1907, Natal Education Act, no. 6 of 1910 and Cape Consolidated Education Ordinance, no. 10 of 1930.
2. Tung Miao, *Legal status of Chinese in the Union of South Africa*, Johannesburg: Chiao Sheng Pao, 1947, p. 39-41.
3. B.K. Murray, *Wits – the early years*, Johannesburg: Witwatersrand U.P., 1982, pp. 297-300.
4. D.Y.H. Wu, The construction of Chinese and non-Chinese identities, *Daedalus*, vol. 120 no. 2, Spring 1991, p. 163.
5. J.W. Loewen, *The Mississippi Chinese: between black and white*, 2nd edition, Prospect Heights: Waveland, 1971, p. 66. Chinese parents started Chinese schools in an attempt to avoid discrimination against their children, who were excluded from White schools.
6. Interview with Mr Lew Johnson, Johannesburg, March 1983. Mr Johnson attended the night school started by the Chinese Consulate in the 1930s. Consular staff taught Mandarin as well as English/ Chinese translation. Other teachers were employed to offer lessons in English and bookkeeping to older students.
7. Wu, *Daedalus*, p. 163.
8. Interview with Mr S.S. Pow Chong, Port Elizabeth, July 1987.
9. Teacher at the Johannesburg Kuo Ting High School, Mr F Y Kam, said in the 1940s and 1950s the ratio of Chinese to English teaching was 70% – 30% for the lower classes, changing gradually to 30% – 70% as children reached higher classes. Former chairman of the Chinese High School board in Port Elizabeth, Mr S. Kim Sing said that prior to 1950 (when the Group Areas Act was introduced) the Eastern Province Chinese Association's education policy was to teach English for 3 hours and Chinese for 3 hours per day. 'This worked well for maintaining Chinese culture and identity but was not practical for life in South Africa ... This education policy was abandoned because pupils' English standards were low. They experienced problems in high school ... So after 1950, EPCA policy was to provide a western-style higher education, with unavoidable consequential cultural disintegration.'
10. History of St Francis Xavier Church, taken from the Community of the Resurrection Sisters' Records, Grahamstown and the Church records. Extract from Occasional Letter, November 1918 and Annual report of work in 1918, p. 1.
11. History of St. Francis Xavier Church, p. 2.
12. Interview with Mr Archie Pow Chong, Port Elizabeth, July 1987.
13. *Blue Banner*, Chinese High School, Port Elizabeth, 1977, p. 6-8; History of St Francis Xavier Church, p. 2.
14. Draft report presented by the Chinese Association, Port Elizabeth, South Africa, June 1935, p. 7. The C.R. Sisters state the teacher's arrival date as September 1923 while the Draft report of the Chinese Association states that 'in 1922 a teacher was engaged ...'. As Mr Yip had to arrive from China, he probably was appointed in 1922 and only arrived by ship in 1923.
15. Draft Report presented by the Chinese Association, Port Elizabeth, June 1935, p. 5-7.
16. L. Human, *The Chinese People of South Africa: freewheeling on the fringes*, Pretoria: Unisa, 1984, p.48; *Blue Banner*, 1977, p. 6-8. In History of St Francis Xavier Church, p. 5, it is stated that in 1935 the sisters were no longer permitted entry to the day school and had started a Sunday school.
17. Interview with Mr Wong Pan Ngian, Port Elizabeth, July 1987.
18. Deed of Transfer in favour of the Trustees of the E.P. Chinese Primary School, 16 May 1942.
19. Interview with Mr Harry Simpson, Port Elizabeth, July 1987.
20. Interviews with Mrs Foong Chong, Mr Harry Simpson and Mr Wally Ah Yui, Port Elizabeth, July 1987.
21. *The Crozier*, December 1966, p. 6.
22. Interviews with Mr Sun Hing of Vereeniging, who attended the Market & Becker Street school in 1916, and Mr Ah Tong of Boksburg who attended school in Ferreirastown in the mid-1920s.
23. W. King, Thirty years of the Johannesburg Chinese School, *Johannesburg Chinese Kuo Ting High School annual*, 1956; Interviews with Mr Ah Tong of Boksburg, Mr Chen Hong of Pretoria and Mr S May of Johannesburg.
24. A. Macmillan, *The Golden City Johannesburg*, London: Collingridge, [1933], p. 303.
25. Interview with Mr Fok Yu Kam, Johannesburg.
26. Interview with Mr Leong Pak Seong, Johannesburg.

27. King, *Johannesburg Chinese Kuo Ting High School annual*, 1956, translated by Mr Stanley May.
28. SAD/BNS, vol. 1/1/375, ref. 192/74. Letter from Consul-General Fartsan T. Sung to the Minister for the Interior, 26 July 1939.
29. SAD/BNS, vol. 1/1/35, ref. 192/74.
30. Interviews with Mr Fok Yu Kam, Mr Lam Foy, and others.
31. SAD/BNS, vol. 1/1/375, ref. 192/74. Petition to the Hon. the Minister of the Interior re: Fok Ling Kien, presently headmaster of the Chinese School, Alexander Street, Ferreiras, August 1939.
32. SAD/BNS, vol. 1/1/375, ref. 192/74, Letter from Commissioner for Immigration and Asiatic Affairs to Secretary for the Interior, 10 August 1939.
33. King, *Johannesburg Chinese Kuo Ting High School annual*, 1956.
34. *Kuo Ting Chinese School*, 1942, published in Chinese, translated by Mr Stanley May. (Donated by Mr Donald Dunne).
35. King, *Johannesburg Chinese Kuo Ting High School annual*, 1956.
36. SAD/CIA, vol. 29, ref. M8, vol 2. Letter from Secretary, Transvaal Education Department to the Commissioner for Immigration and Asiatic Affairs, 6 October 1943.
37. SAD/TPB, vol. 2333, ref. TALG197/5734. Letter from Mr W. King of Johannesburg Chinese Kuo Ting School, to the Administrator of the Transvaal.
38. SAD/TPB, vol. 2333, ref. TALG 197/5734.
39. King, *Johannesburg Chinese Kuo Ting High School annual*, 1956.
40. *Johannesburg Chinese Kuo Ting High School*, 21st anniversary publication, 1971, p. 111.
41. Interview with Mr Lew Johnson.
42. S.C. Hau, The establishment of the Pretoria Chinese School, *50th anniversary Pretoria Chinese School*, 1984, p. 61-62.
43. S.C. Hau, The establishment of the Pretoria Chinese School, *50th Anniversary Pretoria Chinese School*, 1984, p. 48.
44. Interviews with Mr L. Yankee-Liang, Cape Town, April 1988, and Mr C. Lun, Johannesburg, 1989.
45. SAD/CIA, vol. 29, M8, vol. 2. Letter from Secretary of Transvaal Education Department to the Commissioner for Immigration and Asiatic Affairs, 6 October 1943.
46. W.M. Kee, The school building fund, *50th Anniversary Pretoria Chinese School*, 1984, p. 82.
47. Interview with Mr W.S. Chan Yan, Kimberley, September 1987.
48. Interviews with Mr Joey Long King and Mr Raymond Ah Sing, Uitenhage, July 1987.
49. Interviews with Mr Harry Wong, and Mr Ken Eason, East London, July 1987.
50. Group interview, East London, July 1987.
51. Interview with Mr Harry Wong.
52. Interview with Mr L.A. Ying, Cape Town, March 1987.
53. Marist Brothers and the South African Chinese, *Vinculum*, newsletter of the Catholic Chinese Association, Johannesburg, vol. 10A, December 1977, p. 14-15.
54. Interview with Mrs Peggy Lai Yue (nee Liang), Johannesburg, May 1987.
55. Interview with Dr Norman Yenson, Johannesburg, November 1989.
56. Interview with Fr Michael Tuohy, Johannesburg, October 1987.
57. Interview with Mr Bertram Lee, Cape Town, March 1988.
58. G. Beckett, *The school that is our own: Auckland Park Preparatory School*, Pretoria: Sigma Press, 1991, p. 143-146.
59. Interview with Mr Schalk van H. Spies, Johannesburg, November 1991. As a pupil at the Volkshoerskool in Heidelberg, Mr Spies said there were two Chinese children, a girl and a boy, in his class in 1942 or 1943.
60. Interview with Mr L. Yankee Liang, Cape Town, April 1988. Through contacts with the local Queenstown newspaper editor and a Cape Member of the Provincial Council, representations were made for Chinese girls to be given special permits to attend a White government primary school.
61. Murray, *Wits – the early years*, p. 297-300.
62. Murray, *Wits – the early years*, p. 297; Transvaal Technical Institute minute book, 23 March 1906; University of the Witwatersrand, Johannesburg. Memorandum for Committee on admission of non-Europeans, Misc.C/82/53. No record can be found of a Chinese student in the registers of the Transvaal Technical Institute or the School of Mines and Technology between 1904 and 1910.
63. Local girl is Chinese hero, in *China at war*, published by China War Relief Fund, 1 April 1943, p. 5.

64. Statement for the consideration by the Prime Minister of the Union of South Africa, the Honourable Dr D. F. Malan, 27 March 1954, by Ting Shao and L.N. Liang.
65. Interview with Dr Ted Wong Hoption, Johannesburg, November 1987.
66. B.K. Murray, Wits University, student politics, and the coming of apartheid, *Perspectives in education*, vol. 12, no. 1, Summer, 1990, p. 57, quoting SRC Minutes, 14 May & 1 June 1948.
67. Murray, *Perspectives in education*, p. 62.
68. Murray, *Perspectives in education*, p. 64, quoting Sutton to SRC President, 8 March 1954, File B19/3.
69. Interview with Dr Norman Yenson.
70. *A survey of race relations in South Africa*, 1953-54, Johannesburg: South African Institute of Race Relations, 1954, p. 107.
71. *The open universities in South Africa*, Johannesburg: Witwatersrand U.P. 1957; *The open universities in South Africa and academic freedom 1957-1974*, Cape Town: Juta, 1974; *A survey of race relations in South Africa, 1957-1958*, Johannesburg: South African Institute of Race Relations, [1958], p. 194-202.
72. M. Kim Sing, The problem of the Chinese student, *E. P. Chinese Review*, vol. 1. no. 4, Nov- Dec. 1964, p. 12-13.
73. Interviews with Mr Albert Fontbin and Mr Ralph Pakshong, Durban, May 1988.
74. Presenting 'C.S.S.' (Chinese Students Society), [Johannesburg: the Society, 1948], p. 3.
75. Wang Gungwu, Among non-Chinese, *Daedalus*, vol. 120, no. 2, Spring 1991, p. 144-146.

CHAPTER 11 GRAND APARTHEID

1. *Standard encyclopaedia of Southern Africa*, vol. 1, Cape Town: Nasou, 1970, p. 472.
2. M. Legassick, *The analysis of 'racism' in South Africa: the case of the mining economy*, IDEP/UN International Seminar on Socio-Economic Trends & Policies in Southern Africa, Dar-es-Salaam, December 1-8, 1975, p. 1, 28 and 48.
3. G. Gerhart, *Black power in South Africa, the evolution of an ideology*, Berkeley: University of California Press, 1978, p. 85.
4. The Study Project on Christianity in Apartheid Society, *Anatomy of apartheid*, Johannesburg: Spro-cas, 1970, p. 9.
5. South Africa. Bureau of Census and Statistics. Population census, 7th May 1946, Pretoria: Govt Printer, 1949-1954, 5 v.
6. The Immigrants Regulation Act, no. 22 of 1913 declared all Asiatics to be 'prohibited immigrants' and permitted entry only to wives and children of legal residents; Chapter XXXIII of the Orange Free State Law Book, Section 2 of 1890, stated 'No Arab, 'Chinaman', Coolie or other Asiatic Coloured person ... may settle in this State for the purpose of carrying on a commercial business or farming or otherwise remain there for longer than two months ....'.
7. South Africa. Government Gazette, 6 March 1959. Proclamation no. 46 of 1959. Definition of Coloured groups in terms of Section Five of the Population Registration Act, 1950.
8. *Laws affecting race relations in South Africa, 1948-1976*, Johannesburg: South African Institute of Race Relations, 1978, p. 16.
9. *The Star*, 8 March 1962, 'Chinese is officially declared White'.
10. *Rand Daily Mail*, 23 March 1962, 'Racial Absurdity'.
11. *Rand Daily Mail*, 18 May 1962, 'Built-in Hypocrisy'.
12. L.N. Smedley, *A sociological analysis of some aspects of the life of South Africa's Chinese community*, D.Litt thesis, University of South Africa, Pretoria, 1980, p. 23.
13. *The law of South Africa*, vol. 21, Durban: Butterworths, 1984, p. 403 and 421.
14. H.R. Hahlo & E. Kahn, *The Union of South Africa*, London: Stevens, 1960, p. 797.
15. Interview with Mr M.P. Lombaard, Chief Director: Civic Affairs, Department of Home Affairs, 10 November 1994.
16. *The Star*, 8 March 1962, Chinese is officially declared White – Mr Song proves he is 'generally accepted'.
17. *Rand Daily Mail*, 16 March 1962, Song White – but wife 'is still Coloured'.
18. *Cape Times*, 3 May 1962, 'Classify Song family white, pleads M.P.'
19. *Rand Daily Mail*, 16 May 1962, 'Mistake in Song Case says Fagan.'
20. South Africa. Parliament. House of Assembly. Debates, 18 October 1966, col. 3909-3911.

21. *Chinese Consular Gazette*, 26 April 1947.
22. *Chinese Consular Gazette*, 23 April 1947.
23. Personal notes of Mr S.C. Wing King, Port Elizabeth, 19 June-10 August 1950.
24. Amendments to the constitution of the Chinese Association of South Africa, adopted on 4 April 1954 at a General Representative Conference.
25. Preamble to Constitution of Chinese Association, adopted at General Representative Conference on 4 April 1954.
26. Constitution of the Central Chinese Association of South Africa, adopted at the General Conference held in Johannesburg, 13-14 August 1960, p. 2.
27. Constitution of the Central Chinese Association of South Africa, p. 1-2.
28. Memorandum for the consideration of the Hon. Minister for the Interior of the Union of South Africa. Submitted by the Chinese Association of South Africa, 10 February 1951, p. 6-7.
29. Circular letter of resignation as chairman of Central Chinese Association, by Dr N. Yenson, 11 July 1967; Report on the general conference of the Central Chinese Association held on 9 July 1967 by the Chinese Students Society delegates.
30. Letters from Consul-General Wei to Mr S.C. Wing King, chairman of EPCA, 30 January 1963 & 22 February 1963.
31. Interviews with Mr Albert Fontbin, Durban, May 1988 and Mr Ernest Wing King, Johannesburg, April 1989.
32. These were: Central Chinese Association, Cantonese Club, Moi Yean Association, Pretoria Chinese Association, E.P. Chinese Association, Moi Yean Commercial Association, E.P. Chinese Sports Association, Cape Town Chinese Association, East London Chinese Association and Durban Chinese Association.
33. Letters and circular from EPCA to 35 Chinese organizations, 25 April 1964.
34. K. Kirkwood, *The Group Areas Act*, Johannesburg: South Africa Institute of Race Relations, [195-], p. 5.
35. M. Horrell, *The Group Areas Act – its effect on human beings*, Johannesburg: South African Institute of Race Relations, 1956, p. 25.
36. Kirkwood, *The Group Areas Act*, p. 6.
37. *Daily Dispatch*, 17 February 1953.
38. M.Y.D. Dinath, *Asiatic population settlement in the Transvaal (1881-1960) with special reference to the Johannesburg municipality*, B.A. (Hons) thesis, University of the Witwatersrand, Department of Geography, 1963, p. 100.
39. Precious and Base Metals Act, no. 35 of 1908.
40. Letter from the Central Chinese Association of South Africa to the Group Areas Board, 25 May 1956, p. 3.
41. Community Development Act, no. 3 of 1966; M. Festenstein & C. Pickard-Cambridge, *Land and race: South Africa's group areas and land acts*, Johannesburg: South African Institute of Race Relations, 1987, p. 25; *The law of South Africa*, vol. 10, p. 418-421.
42. Chinese Association of South Africa memorandum to regional associations, (in Chinese), 16 March 1953.
43. Letter from Central Chinese Association of South Africa to Group Areas Board, 25 May 1956, p. 2-3.
44. Statement for the consideration by the Prime Minister of the Union of South Africa, the Hon. Dr D F Malan, by Ting Shao and L.N. Liang, 27 March 1954.
45. Group Areas Bill – 1st reading on 24 April 1950; 2nd reading on 29 May 1950; 3rd reading on 13 June 1950 and passed on 7 July 1950.
46. Interviews, Mr Leong Pak Seong, June 1987, Mr Stanley May, February 1994 and Mr Jack Lau, 3 August 1992. The first issue of *Good Hope Magazine* was published on 20 February 1953 and the second on 20 May 1953.
47. Horrell, *The Group Areas Act – its effect on human beings*; Letter from Central Chinese Association of South Africa to Group Areas Board, 25 May 1956.
48. According to the *Rand Daily Mail*, 1 November 1956, the Krugersdorp Municipality agreed to support the establishment of a residential Chinese area in the Transvaal and to permit Chinese to retain their current premises in Krugersdorp until an area was proclaimed.
49. *Rand Daily Mail*, 3 June 1959, 'Ruin faces many as Africans move from township'; *Rand Daily Mail*, 2 September 1960, 'Nigel Indians hold protest meeting'.

50. *Rand Daily Mail*, 29 June 1955; *New Age*, 7 July 1955.
51. *Survey of Race Relations in South Africa*, 1961, Johannesburg: South African Institute of Race Relations, 1962, p. 164.
52. *Rand Daily Mail*, 16 February 1960.
53. *Rand Daily Mail*, 31 August 1965.
54. *Rand Daily Mail*, 26 January 1966; *Pretoria News*, 1 April 1966.
55. *Rand Daily Mail*, 2 February 1967.
56. Letters from Central Chinese Association of South Africa to Group Areas Board, 25 and 26 May 1956.
57. Interview with Mr Stanley May, Johannesburg, November 1984.
58. T. Lodge, Political mobilisation during the 1950s: an East London case study, in: *The politics of race, class and nationalism in twentieth-century South Africa*, edited by S. Marks & S. Trapido, London: Longman, 1987, p. 313.
59. *The Star*, 22 May 1953.
60. Letter from [Central Chinese Association of South Africa] to Group Areas Board, 16 January 1957, p. 3.
61. *Rand Daily Mail*, 21 November 1956, 'Chinese shopkeepers told to quit homes, shops in Sophiatown'; *Rand Daily Mail*, 1 April 1957, 'Chinese will not know where to sleep tonight'; *Cape Times*, 19 April 1957, 'Family waits for eviction'; *Rand Daily Mail*, 19 April 1957, 'Chinese, under eviction order, wait in fear'; *Rand Daily Mail*, 24 April 1957, 'Chinese family may have six weeks respite from eviction'; *The Star*, 23 April 1957, 'Chinese home demolition deadline today'; *Rand Daily Mail*, 25 April 1957, 'Chinese fate: questions in Parliament'; *Cape Times*, 27 April 1957, 'Removal of Chinese families'.
62. *The Star*, 20 July 1958.
63. Address by the Chairman of the Transvaal Chinese Association Mr Wellington Ford, to the Group Areas Board in connection with the hearing of an inquiry to be held at the City Hall, Johannesburg, 15 September 1958. p. 5.
64. A. Paton, *The people wept, being a brief account of the origin, contents, and application of that unjust law of the Union of South Africa known as The Group Areas Act of 1950 (since consolidated as Act No. 77 of 1957)*, Kloof: A. Paton, [1958?], p. 3 and 32.
65. Interview with Group Areas Board, 6 December 1960.
66. *Rand Daily Mail*, 4 April 1967.
67. *Sunday Times*, 11 February 1968; *The Star*, 13 September 1968.
68. Letter from Minister of Community Development to Consul-General, 19 February 1971.
69. Letter from the Chairman, Transvaal Chinese Association, to the Minister of Community Development, 3 September 1971.
70. Letter from Private Secretary, Ministry of Community Development and of Public Works, to the Chairman, Transvaal Chinese Association, 8 October 1971.
71. *Eastern Province Herald*, 23 February 1972; *The Star*, 28 February 1972.
72. Interviews with Mr L.A. Ying and Mr L. Kwongsee; Letter from L.A. Ying to the Minister of the Interior, 12 June 1962.
73. Horrell, *The Group Areas Act – its effect on human beings*, p. 72, 77-79; The size of the Chinese population is erroneously reflected as 1300, but according to community appeals of the time, the number was in fact 300; *Cape Times*, 29 July 1955: Black River Vigilance Association collected 86 signatures of residents opposed to Chinese area.
74. *Rand Daily Mail*, 21 November 1960.
75. Representations submitted by the Chinese Association of Cape Town on behalf of all Chinese residents of Cape Town in respect of proposed Group Areas for Chinese, [1960?].
76. Interviews with Mr L.A. Ying and Mr L. Kwongsee; Letter from L.A. Ying to the Minister of the Interior, 12 June 1962.
77. *Daily Dispatch* editorial, 17 February 1953.
78. SAD/BEP, vol. 373, ref. G7/324. Letter from East London Chinese Association to Land Tenure Advisory Board, [February/March 1953]; *Daily Dispatch*, 17 February 1953.
79. South Africa. Government gazette, 31 July 1959. Proclamation no. 157 of 1959.
80. South African Institute of Race Relations. Report by Research Officer on the Group Areas Proclamation for Kimberley, 10 September 1959, RR. 181/59 Spe., p. 11.
81. Letter to Minister of Community Development from Consul-General Lo Ming Yuan, 21 March 1968.
82. *Natal Mercury*, 2 July 1970.

83. South Africa. Government gazette. Proclamation no. 78 of 1973.
84. Letter and memorandum from Uitenhage Chinese Association to the Eastern Cape Committee of the Group Areas Board, 30 October 1956.
85. *Natal Mercury*, 2 July 1970.
86. Horrell, *The Group Areas Act – its effect on human beings*, p. 96.
87. *Eastern Province Herald*, 6 December 1952.
88. City of Port Elizabeth. Provisional Town Planning Scheme No. 1. Objection. Memorandum from Eastern Province Chinese Association to Town Clerk of Port Elizabeth, 23 January 1953.
89. *Eastern Province Herald*, 10 October 1956; *Evening Post*, 24 October 1956.
90. *Evening Post*, 20 November 1956.
91. *Evening Post*, 28 November 1956.
92. South Africa. Government gazette, 30 May 1961. Proclamation no. 144 of 1961.
93. Interview with Mr Ernest Wing King, Johannesburg, April 1989.
94. Interview with Mr Harry Simpson, Port Elizabeth, July 1987.
95. Letter from Regional Representative, Department of Community Development to EPCA, 7 December 1967; Letter from EPCA to Chinese Consulate-General, 11 June 1970; Letter from Chinese Consul-General to EPCA, 20 January 1971.
96. Delegate's report to meeting of Central Chinese Association on 9 July 1967.
97. Smedley, *A sociological analysis of some aspects of the life of South Africa's Chinese community*, p. 24.
98. Letters from Divisional Council of Port Elizabeth to EPCA, 7 and 26 April 1964; Letter from EPCA to Divisional Council, 20 May 1970.
99. Interviews with Mr W.J. Pow Chong, Mr S.S. Pow Chong and Mr A. Pow Chong, Port Elizabeth, July 1987.
100. Memorandum from the EPCA to the Minister of Community Development, Mr W.H. du Plessis, for meeting held on 30 September 1974.
101. Notice in *Eastern Province Herald*, 14 January 1976; Letter from the Department of Community Development to Consul-General, 18 April 1976.
102. Letter from EPCA to Regional Representative, Department of Planning and Environment, 30 January 1976.
103. *Sunday Tribune*, 16 October 1966, 'The families who live in a shadow'.
104. South Africa. Parliament. House of Assembly. Debates, 18 October 1966, col. 4579.
105. South Africa. Parliament. House of Assembly. Debates, 11 October 1966, col. 3909-3910.
106. *Rand Daily Mail*, 25 August 1971, 'Chinese live in "twilight zone". '
107. *Sunday Times*, 22 August 1971, 'Displaced persons' fear hangs over Rand Chinese'.
108. *Rand Dail Mail*, 3 November 1966, 'Chinese can't live in air – magistrate.'
109. *Rand Daily Mail*, 18 February 1970.
110. *Laws affecting race relations in South Africa, 1948-1976*, p. 75, quoting Hansard 4 of 1977, cols. 402-4.
111. Smedley, *A sociological analysis of some aspects of the life of South Africa's Chinese community*, p. 24.
112. Report of the Technical Committee of Enquiry into the Group Areas Act, 1966, the Reservation of Separate Amenities Act 1953 and related legislation, Pretoria: Government Printer, 1983, p. 63.
113. South Africa. Parliament. House of Assembly. Debates, vol. 21, 27 June 1984, cols. 9962 and 9966.
114. Race relations survey 1991/2, Johannesburg: South African Institute of Race Relations, 1992, p. 339.
115. Statement for the consideration by the Prime Minister ..., 27 March 1954.
116. Letter from Secretary for External Affairs to Consul-General Ting Shao, 26 February 1955.
117. Letter from [Central Chinese Association] to Minister of the Interior, 17 June 1957.
118. South Africa. Parliament. House of Assembly. Debates, 21 July 1970, cols. 93-94.
119. Letter from Transvaal Chinese Association to Minister of the Interior, September 1975.
120. Statement for the consideration of the Prime Minister ..., 27 March 1954.
121. Letter from Secretary for External Affairs to Consul-General Ting Shao, 26 February 1955.
122. Statement for the consideration of the Prime Minister ..., 27 March 1954.
123. SAD/BNS, vol. 1/1/751, ref. 27/74. Illegal immigration. General Matters. Letter from Commissioner for Immigration and Asiatic Affairs to Secretary for the Interior, 24 September 1954; Letter from Secretary for External Affairs to Consul-General Ting Shao, 26 February 1955.
124. *The Star*, 23 May 1967, 'Chinese used infiltration tactics – Pelser'.
125. SAD/BNS, vol. 1/1/751, ref. 27/74. Illegal immigration. General matters. Letter from Commissioner for

Immigration and Asiatic Affairs to Secretary for the Interior, 24 September 1954; SAD/BNS, vol. 1/1/757, ref. 47/74.

126. SAD/BNS, vol. 1/1/751, ref. 27/74.
127. Petition to King George VI of Great Britain, Johannesburg, 17 February 1947. (Mr A. York).
128. Criminal Procedure Amendment Act, no. 96 of 1965; *Race relations as regulated by law in South Africa, 1948-1979*, p. 236; EPCA Chinese notice to community, 28 January 1967.
129. *Rand Daily Mail*, 28 January 1967, 'Three 180-day detainees have killed themselves'; Motala, *Behind closed doors*, p. 21-22.
130. *Rand Daily Mail*, 20 January 1967, 'Detainee used socks to hang himself'; *The Star*, 19 January 1967, 'Detainees' evidence not sought'; Motala, *Behind closed doors*, p. 21-22.
131. S. Motala, *Behind closed doors*, Johannesburg: South African Institute of Race Relations, 1987, p. 21-22.
132. EPCA circular, 12 January 1967 containing summary of letter from Consul-General Lo Ming Yuan.
133. Chinese circulars from Central Chinese Association of South Africa, 21 February 1967 and Consulate-General, 20 February 1967.
134. Letter from Central Chinese Association to EPCA, enclosing Chinese circular issued by Central, 21 February 1967.
135. Letter from Dr N. Yenson, Acting Chairman, Central Chinese Association, to Mr S. Kim Sing of EPCA, 21 February 1967.
136. Letter from EPCA chairman, Mr S. Kim Sing, to Dr N. Yenson, 28 February 1967.
137. The Chinese man convicted was Mr Benny Low (Lau). The Department of Immigration official was Mr Petrus Venter. *Dagbreek en Sondagnuus*, 28 Mei 1967, 'Lot van Rooi Sjinese in SA Onseker. Korrupte amptenaar het honderde land laat inkom'; *A survey of race relations in South Africa*, 1967, p. 56.
138. *Dagbreek en Sondagnuus*, 28 May 1967.
139. *The Star*, 29 May 1967, '400 Chinese seeking permission to stay.'
140. *Die Vaderland*, 29 May 1967, 'Sjinese vra SA om hier te bly'.
141. Interview with Mr Shiang Chum, Pretoria, April 1988.
142. Interview with Lo Ming Yuan, Johannesburg, October 1989.
143. Interview with Mr Ignatius King, Johannesburg, August 1994.
144. J.S. Chum, Lo Ming Yuan Scholarship, *50th anniversary Pretoria Chinese School*, 1984, p. 195.
145. Matters concerning Admission to and Residence in the Republic Amendment Act, no. 53 of 1986.
146 G.H. Pirie, *Racial segregation on public transport in South Africa, 1877-1989*, Ph.D thesis, University of the Witwatersrand, Johannesburg, 1990, p. 12-13.
147. *Race relations as regulated by law in South Africa, 1948-1979*, p. 49.
148. Statement for the consideration of the Prime Minister ... 27 March 1954; Reply by Secretary for External Affairs, 26 February, 1955.
149. Letter to Chairman, Kimberley Chinese Association, from Director of Hospital Services, Provincial Administration of the Cape, 14 September 1960.
150. Interviews with Terry and Mary Lai King, Johannesburg, January 1989.
151. Letter from Prime Minister's Office to Fr M. Tuohy, 1 February 1963 and Fr Tuohy's correspondence files.
152. Copy of draft memorandum, drafted by attorneys and apparently submitted to the Ministers of Community Development and the Interior, 4 January 1962, p. 15. No signatures but seems to have been commissioned by Central Chinese Association.
153. *Race relations as regulated by law in South Africa, 1948-1979*, p. 54-59, 168-169; South Africa. Government Gazette. Proclamation no. R26 of 12 February 1965.
154. Letter from Mr M. Chan Yan, Kimberley Chinese Association to Dr W.L.D.M. Venter, Member of Parliament, 4 August 1965.
155. *The Star*, 18 June 1965 – 'A Chinese gesture ...'
156. Letter from TCA to Minister of Interior, 7 April 1965; Report from EPCA delegate at conference of Central Chinese Association, 9 July 1967; Correspondence of Fr M. Tuohy from Department of the Interior on disability grant for Mr Sun Ford, 11 September 1969.
157. South Africa. Parliament. House of Assembly. Questions and replies, vol. 40, 25 April 1972, col. 905.
158. South Africa. Parliament. House of Assembly. Questions and replies, vol. 40, 4 February 1972, col. 72; 18 February 1972, col. 284; 22 February 1972, col. 302.
159. South Africa. Parliament. House of Assembly. Questions and replies, vol. 40, 4 February 1972, col. 71-72.

160. *The Star,* 2 February 1962, 'Pretoria refuses Chinese players'; *Cape Argus,* 22 June 1962, 'Chinese bar: UCT out of basketball'; *The Star,* 18 July 1962, 'Chinese not allowed to take up post'; *Rand Daily Mail,* 28 July 1962, 'He lay in pain as colour muddle untangled'; *Evening Post,* 4 September 1965, 'Two Chinese Owners were not there'.
161. *Rand Daily Mail,* 3 February 1962, '... 6000 Chinese are Coloured'.
162. *Die Vaderland,* 19 October 1959, ''n Skroef los by Jan Smuts?'
163. Pirie, *Racial segregation on public transport in South Africa, 1877-1989,* p. 24-26.
164. *Daily News,* 26 November 1970, 'Chinese: Blaar's decision defied'; *Natal Mercury,* 26 November 1970, 'Chinese Students segregated.'
165. Letter from EPCA to Consul-General Lo Ming Yuan, 11 June 1970.
166. *The Star,* 2 October 1967, 'Doctor's bid to work in group area is rejected.'
167. *Cape Argus,* 9 December 1975, 'Twilight world of SA Chinese'.
168. *Daily Dispatch,* 25 April 1970, 'Now Chinese must see show with non-whites'.
169. *Rand Daily Mail,* 13 April 1970, 'Parents told Ava to quit contest' and 'Chinese Puzzle'; *Rhodeo,* 26 March 1970, 'Rag Queen fracas taints Rag'; *Cape Argus,* 9 December 1975, 'Twilight world of SA Chinese'.
170. *Daily Dispatch,* 6 and 7 April 1970; *Sunday Times,* 12 April 1970.
171. *Eastern Province Herald,* 9 April 1970, 'Beachfront fun spots closed to Chinese'; *Eastern Province Herald,* 10 April 1970, 'Billiard saloons forced to bar City Chinese'.
172. *Daily Dispatch,* 25 May 1970, 'Chinese barred – so tour is called off'.
173. *Daily Dispatch,* 23 and 24 June 1970, 'Protest over ban on Chinese' and 'Wits weight-lifters withdraw after Free State bars Chinese'.
174. *Cape Times,* 13 July 1970, 'Chinese boys ordered out'; *The Star,* 22 July 1970, 'Why Chinese were asked to leave'; *Daily News,* 22 July 1970, 'Tests not suited to Chinese'; *Rand Daily Mail,* 23 July 1970, 'When a Chinese is not Chinese'.
175. *Rand Daily Mail,* 27 June 1970, 'Silent – and the Chinese prefer it', by Lin Menge.
176. *Natal Mercury,* 29 June 1970, 'Let Chinese Alone' plea.
177. *Daily News,* 30 June 1970, 'The Chinese – a re-appraisal'.
178. *The Star,* 8 July 1970, 'Protests do us harm, say Chinese'; *Daily News,* 3 July 1970, 'Chinese – S.A.'s tragic forgotten community'.
179. *The Star,* 7 July 1970; *Sunday Times,* July 1970.
180. *Eastern Province Herald,* 20 August 1970, 'Chinese ruling applies to all in S.A.'; *Rand Daily Mail,* 23 July 1970, 'U.P. gets blame for Chinese affair'.
181. *The Star,* 29 July 1970, ' "Sad comment" on S.A. Society'.
182. *Rand Daily Mail,* 20 August 1970, 'Chinese Checkers'; *Natal Mercury,* 21 August 1970, 'S.A.'s Chinese Puzzle'.
183. *Eastern Province Herald,* 27, 28 and 29 May 1971, 'Rhodes boycott call over Chinese ban', 'Strong reaction over Chinese', 'Chinese students: U.P.E. guided by govt.'
184. *Race Relations as regulated by law in South Africa, 1948-1979,* p. 50.
185. *Sunday Times,* 20 April 1975, 'For the Chinese in SA ... life in no man's land'; *Natal Mercury,* 27 October 1975, 'U.P. to debate Chinese vote'.
186. *Eastern Province Herald,* 6 February 1978, 'Aronson motion on SA Chinese', and 7 February 1978, 'Appeal over Chinese'.
187. *Inter Nos,* published by the Port Elizabeth Chinese Catholic Association, vol. 3, no. 1, March 1978, p. 16-17.
188. South Africa. Parliament. House of Assembly. Debates, 13 April 1978, col. 4625.
189. *Laws affecting Race Relations in South Africa, 1948-1976,* p. 20.
190. Interview with Fr M. Tuohy; *Vinculum*: newsletter of the Catholic Chinese Welfare Association, [July, 1994], p. 5.
191. Interview with Fr Ignatius Ou, Port Elizabeth, July 1987.
192. *The law of South Africa,* vol. 10, 1980, p. 352.
193. Interview with Mr M.P. Lombaard, Chief Director: Civic Affairs, Department of Home Affairs, November 1994.
194. *The law of South Africa,* vol. 16, 1992, p. 27.
195. *Sunday Chronicle,* 5 February 1964, 'Insight into South Africa's Chinese – Life in the shadows' and 12 September 1965, 'No place in the sun for the Chinese ... Silent community are like rabbits in a storm'.

CHAPTER 12 SEEKING SOME CONCESSIONS

1. Tentative agenda for the Advisory Conference on the Betterment of Living Conditions of Chinese People in the Union, Johannesburg, 19-20 September 1959, p. 3.
2. Notes on interview with Minister of the Interior on 6 December 1960, attended by Wellington Ford and Norman Song, representing the Central Chinese Association and Lew Johnson and Lai Hing representing the Transvaal Chinese Association.
3. Notes on interview with Chairman and member of the Group Areas Board, 6 December 1960.
4. T.R.H. Davenport, *South Africa,* 2nd ed., Johannesburg: Macmillan, 1978, p. 288.
5. Letter from [C. P. Yenson] to Minister of Foreign Affairs, 1 May 1960.
6. *A survey of race relations in South Africa,* 1962, Johannesburg: South African Institute of Race Relations, 1963, p. 229-231.
7. *Rand Daily Mail,* 13 November 1962, 'We stand loyal to S.A., say Chinese.'
8. S. Jones & A. Muller, *The South African economy, 1910-90,* New York: St Martin's, 1992, p. 216-221.
9. South Africa. Parliament. House of Assembly. Debates, 14 April 1961, col. 4532.
10. *Sunday Express,* 5 November 1961, 'S.A. makes Japs "White" to boost trade'; *The Star,* 22 November 1961, 'White status for Japanese, but not Chinese.'
11. South Africa. Parliament. House of Assembly. Debates, 1 May 1962, col. 4767; *Sunday Times,* 26 September 1965, 'Dr V. tells why Japanese are 'White' ... and why 8000 Chinese are not'.
12. South Africa. Parliament. House of Assembly. Debates, 30 April 1962, col. 4630.
13. *The Star,* 29 November 1961, 'The law still says Japanese are not White' and 8 February 1962, 'Honorary Whites'.
14. *Rand Daily Mail,* 22 January 1962, 'Japanese gymnasts spark row'.
15. *Sunday Times,* 4 February 1962, 'Strength through Pig-iron'.
16. *The Star,* 31 January 1962, 'National issue raised by ban on Japanese'; *Cape Times,* 31 January 1962, 'Pretoria will ban visiting Jap swimmers'; *Cape Times* 1 February 1962, 'Japanese swimmer ban row spreads'; *The Star,* 2 February 1962, 'Swimming ban lifted'.
17. *Rand Daily Mail,* 13 February 1962, 'Council is silent over bus blunder'; *The Star,* 13 February 1962, 'Japan accepts apology by Pretoria'.
18. *The Star,* 27 September 1965, 'Confucion'; *The Star,* 2 May 1962, 'Japanese are in a Chinese puzzle'; *Rand Daily Mail,* 19 July 1962, 'When a Japanese is almost white...'
19. *Pretoria News,* 21 November 1961, 'One gets race privilege but both are same, says expert.'
20. *Rand Daily Mail,* 10 January 1962, 'Unprincipled'.
21. South Africa. Parliament. House of Assembly. Debates, 1 May 1962, col. 4767.
22. South Africa. Parliament. House of Assembly. Debates, 1 May 1962, cols. 4769-4770.
23. *The Argus,* 2 May 1962, 'Japanese question as tangled as Chinese puzzle'.
24. *The Star,* 24 February 1970, ' "White" – if it's trade'; *Rand Daily Mail,* 28 November 1970, 'Japanese feel race pinpricks, says top man'.
25. *Rand Daily Mail,* 5 May 1970, 'Japanese are "White" – in business only'; *Daily News,* 10 May 1970, 'Sailors are White'.
26. *Rand Daily Mail,* 10 December 1974, 'How bright the rising sun?'
27. *Finansies & tegniek,* vol. 49, no. 29, 22 Jul 1988, p. 9, 'Japan voer meer na SA uit'.
28. *Finansies & tegniek,* vol. 40, no. 20, 20 Mei 1988, p. 12, 'Skaduwee oor Japanse handel'.
29. Draft memorandum re The Chinese of South Africa to be presented to the Ministers of Community Development and the Interior, unsigned, January 1962. From correspondence it appears that this memorandum was also seen by Prime Minister, Dr H. Verwoerd.
30. Draft memorandum re The Chinese of South Africa, January 1962.
31. *Sunday Times,* 26 September 1965, 'Dr V. tells why Japanese are "White"... and why 8000 Chinese are not'.
32. M. Chan Yan, Letter to the editor, *E.P. Chinese Review,* vol. 2, no. 3, November/December 1965.
33. M. Kim Sing, What of the future? *Spectrum,* newsletter of the Cape Town Chinese Students Society, October 1965, p. 2.
34. L. Human, *The Chinese people of South Africa: freewheeling on the fringes,* Pretoria: University of South Africa, 1984, p. 78.

35. L.N. Smedley, *A sociological analysis of some aspects of the life of South Africa's Chinese community*, D.Litt thesis, University of South Africa, Pretoria, 1980, p. 315-345.
36. Circular letter in Chinese from Consul-General Lo Ming Yuan to regional associations, [1968].
37. Circular letter in Chinese from Consul-General Lo Ming Yuan to regional associations, [1968]; Agenda for the 3rd General Conference of the South African Trade Mission Committee, 28 July 1967.
38. *Rand Daily Mail,* 30 January 1973, 'Rand Show "prejudice" so Taiwan pulls out'; *Rand Daily Mail,* 2 February 1973, 'Chinese aren't a problem, says Bosman'.
39. An interview with the Chinese consul in Cape Town, Mr Lee, *Spectrum,* [1973], p. 7-12.
40. Kim Sing, *Spectrum,* October 1965, p. 2.
41. Interview with Mr Ley Changfoot, East London, July 1987.
42. Interview with Dr George Changfoot, Johannesburg, December 1985.
43. Interview with Mr Douglas Kee, Johannesburg, November 1995.
44. L. Pan, *Sons of the Yellow Emperor,* London: Secker & Warburg, 1990, p. 122; *Drum,* September 1952, p. 6-7, 'Fah Fee: Secrets of the "house of the numbers".'
45. Letter from Central Chinese Association of South Africa to Minister of Interior, [1956?], p. 7-8.
46. Interview with Mr Alec Oshry, Johannesburg, January 1988.
47. Statement for the consideration by the Prime Minister of the Union of South Africa, the Hon. Dr D F Malan, by Ting Shao and L.N. Liang, 27 March 1954, p. 6; Minutes of EPCA meeting, 9 January 1968.
48. Dr C. Chan Yan reported that the pay ratio was 10:7:6 for White: Chinese, Indian, Coloured: and Bantu respectively. In the Cape the hospitals were more liberal. Chinese students have worked in white hospitals except when nurses complained. In: EPCA committee minutes, 22 February 1971, item 12.
49. *The Star,* 17 July 1962; *Cape Times,* 20 July 1962.
50. *A survey of race relations in South Africa,* 1964, p. 238-239.
51. South African Institute of Race Relations, News release RR. 161/65, 5 January 1966.
52. *Rand Daily Mail,* 7 April 1967, 'A "brain drain" of S. African Chinese'; *Evening Post,* 8 April 1967, 'Why Chinese are pulling up roots in S.A.'; Speech by Dr Norman Yenson, Acting Chairman of the Central Chinese Association at the farewell dinner given by the association in honour of the visiting trade mission from Formosa, 6 April 1967.
53. *Evening Post,* [January], 1977, 'Why some Chinese have left South Africa'.
54. *Rand Daily Mail,* 7 February 1976, 'Portrait of SA's Chinese'.
55. *Race Relations survey,* 1988/89, Johannesburg: South African Institute of Race Relations, 1989, p. 409.
56. Statistics from the University of the Witwatersrand Medical School, courtesy of Mr M.Y. Dinath.
57. *Handbook on Race Relations in South Africa,* New York: Octagon Books, 1975, originally published 1949.
58. *Rand Daily Mail,* 2 February 1962, 'And now — Chinese softball players banned'; *The Star,* 15 September, 1965, 'Basketball has race laws poser'; *Die Transvaler,* 7 October 1965, 'Chinese in W.P.-span: Minister antwoord'.
59. Letter from EPCA to Chinese Consulate-General, 11 June 1970; *The Star,* 19 August 1970, 'Apartheid eased for Chinese'.
60. *The Week End Review Annual,* Johannesburg, February 1955, p. 30.
61. SA Chinese Softball Tournament programme, Port Elizabeth, 26-27 December 1954, p. 1.
62. *The Crozier,* November 1971, p. 4. 'PE Church which serves Chinese may soon move'.
63. A. Song, *The effects of Protestant Christianity on the Chinese cult of ancestors as practised in the Johannesburg area,* Ph.D. thesis, University of Durbvan Westville, 1989, p. 155-162.
64. Interview with Mr S.S. Pow Chong, Port Elizabeth, July 1987.
65. Interview with Dr George Changfoot, Johannesburg, December 1985.
66. *E.P. Chinese Review,* vol. 1, no. 1, April 1964, p. 1.
67. *The Voice of South African Chinese,* vol. 2. no. 1. January 1968.
68. Pan, *Sons of the Yellow Emperor.* p. 376-377; Professor Wang Gungwu outlined the four major patterns of Chinese migration, as that of the trader (*huashang*), the coolie (*huagong*), the sojourner (*huaqiao*) and the re-migrant (*huayi*) in: Wang Gungwu, *China and the Chinese overseas,* Singapore: Times Academic, 1991, p. 4-10.
69. SA Chinese community: leaderless, rudderless. *The Voice,* vol. 2, no. 2, February 1968, p. 4-5; Speech by Dr Norman Yenson, acting chairman of the Central Chinese Association at the farewell dinner given by the Association in honour of the visiting trade mission from Formosa, 6 April 1967.
70. Kim Sing, *Spectrum,* October 1965, p. 3.

71. E. Wing King, How Chinese are we? *E.P. Chinese Review,* vol. 1, no. 4, Nov-Dec 1964, p. 5.
72. T. Gin, Decline of Chinese civilisation in S.A., *Spectrum*, August 1963, p. 6.
73. Editorial, *Spectrum*, October 1967.
74. Editorial, *Vinculum*, October 1972.
75. Chinese New Year : Year of the Rabbit brochure, 28 January 1987, published by Chung Wah Sports Club.
76. R.F. Ford, The dilemma of being born a South African Chinese, *Vinculum*, December 1972, p. 27.
77. Editorial, *Vinculum*, vol. 7A, Easter issue, April 1974.
78. Human, *The Chinese people of South Africa: freewheeling on the fringes*, p. 87-88 and 100-108.
79. Wang, *China and the Chinese Overseas*, p. 20.

CHAPTER 13 THE END OF AN ERA

1. D. Geldenhuys, The head of government and South Africa's foreign relations, in: *Malan to De Klerk: leadership in the apartheid state*, London: Hurst, 1994, p. 273-274.
2. Geldenhuys, *Malan to De Klerk: leadership in the apartheid state*, p. 276-281.
3. *A survey of race relations in South Africa*, 1980, Johannesburg: South African Institute of Race Relations, 1981, p. 4-7.
4. *Rand Daily Mail*, 7 October 1980, 'What we really think of the President's Council'.
5. *The Citizen*, 19 March 1980, 'Better status'.
6. Submissions tabled at the meeting of Chinese organizations held in Johannesburg on 13-14 September 1980.
7. *Pretoria News*, 27 September 1980, 'City Jaycee is first Chinese for Council'.
8. *Pretoria News*, 29 September 1980, 'Chinese 'shocked' by acceptance'.
9. J.S. Chum, chairman of the Chinese Association of South Africa, press statement, 2 October 1980; *Rand Daily Mail*, 3 October 1980, 'Chop for Chinese member'.
10. *Pretoria News*, 27 September 1980, 'City Jaycee is first Chinese for Council'; *Evening Post*, 8 October 1980, 'Businessman replies to Chinese critics'; *Pretoria News*, 6 October 1980, 'Winchiu puts his case'.
11. *Sunday Times*, 14 June 1981, 'At last the dragon stirs'.
12. Constitution of the Chinese Association of South Africa as adopted on 22 March 1981 in Johannesburg.
13. *Sunday Times*, 14 June 1981, 'At last the dragon stirs'.
14. *A survey of race relations in South Africa*, 1982, p. 1-6.
15. South Africa. Parliament. House of Assembly. Debates, vol. 3, 7 May 1985, col. 5041.
16. South Africa. Parliament. House of Assembly. Debates, vol. 114, 4 May 1984, col. 5781-5782.
17. *Eastern Province Herald*, 7 May 1984, 'Getting the Chinese out of limbo'.
18. Letter from Chairman, CASA, to Ministers of Constitutional Development and Planning and Internal Affairs, 25 May 1984.
19. Group Areas Amendment Act, no. 101 of 1984; *Rand Daily Mail*, 23 June 1984, 'Chinese in line for new deal'; *Eastern Province Herald*, 23 June 1984, 'Chinese in line for white vote'; *Weekend Post*, 23 June 1984, 'Chinese confused on position in white political dispensation'.
20. *The Star*, 18 August 1986, 'Chinese checkers'.
21. *Race relations survey* 1987/88, Johannesburg: South African Institute of Race Relations, 1988, p. xxxi-xxxvii.
22. *The Star*, 5 July 1988, 'Call for Chinese voting rights'.
23. *The Star*, 7 July 1988, 'Call for Chinese vote is welcomed'.
24. Letter from Chairman, CASA, to State President, P.W. Botha, 3 August 1988.
25. SAD/GG, vol. 773, ref. 20/926, 27 November 1919.
26. In 1930 Chong Lawson was appointed Chinese consular agent in Port Elizabeth, SAD/GG, vol. 788, ref. 20/1853, 4 July 1930; In 1932 Dr L.N. Liang was appointed honorary consul for China in Lourenco Marques (Portuguese East Africa) and in 1933 acting vice-consul during Ting Shao's absence on leave, SAD/GG, vol. 789, ref. 20/1905, 23 March 1932 and ref. 20/1960, 6 July 1933.
27. Geldenhuys, *Malan to De Klerk: leadership in the apartheid state*, p.281; D. Geldenhuys, *Some foreign policy implications of South Africa's 'Total National Strategy', with particular reference to the '12-point plan'*, Johannesburg: South African Institute of International Affairs, 1981, p. 34.
28. Geldenhuys, *Some foreign policy implications ...*, p. 34.

29. *Sunday Times*, 19 October 1980, 'After Taiwan ... Chinese may become full citizens'.
30. South Africa. Parliament. House of Assembly. Questions and replies, vol. 97, col. 49-50, 87, 104-105.
31. OFS Law Book, Chapter XXXIII, Section 2, 1890.
32. *Sunday Express*, 28 August 1983, 'Rejected Bibi turns to school 340 km away.'
33. Matters concerning Admission to and Residence in the Republic Amendment Act, no. 53 of 1986, paragraph 13 repealed Chapter XXXIII of the OFS Law Book, Section 2, 1890.
34. *Laws affecting race relations in South Africa, 1948-1976*, Johannesburg: South African Institute of Race Relations, 1978, p. 218.
35. J. Wilhelm, Something new from the East, *The Executive*, September 1988, p. 21-25.
36. C.C. Kan, The Republic of China: the future hope for all Chinese. Paper presented at the Fifth Biennial Conference of the Chinese Association of South Africa, 15 April 1989; C.C. Kan, *Chinese industrial investment in Southern Africa*, Johannesburg: Association of Chinese Industrialists in Southern Africa, 26 July 1992.
37. C. Liao, The Chinese investor in southern Africa in retrospect and futurity. Speech given at the Biennial Conference of the Chinese Association of South Africa, 6-7 April 1991.
38. *Financial Mail*, 30 April 1993, 'No miracles, just commonsense'.
39. Kan, *Chinese industrial investment in Southern Africa;* Interview, 18 November 1994.
40. *The Citizen*, 25 May 1990, 'Chinese opposed to "exclusive" areas'; *The Star*, 25 May 1990, 'Chinese reject group areas'.
41. *TCA Newsletter*, no. 79, 5 March 1993.
42. *TCA Newsletter*, no. 74, 9 April 1992.
43. *TCA Newsletter*, no. 74, 9 April 1992 and no. 76, 19 August 1992.
44. *Business Day*, 24 January 1992, 'China to cement ties once apartheid ends' and 'SA unlikely to switch allegiances over China'.
45. *Free China Journal*, vol. X, no. 52, 6 August 1993, 'Mandela pledges friendly relations with ROC'; *The Citizen*, 19 August 1993, 'Mandela's alleged promise on China "corrected" '; *Business Day*, 19 August 1993, 'Snags emerge over ANC-Taiwan links'.
46. *The Star*, 19 August 1994, 'Decision soon on two Chinas'.
47. *Sunday Times*, 11 June 1995, 'South Africa's Chinese puzzle'; *Business Day*, 15 August 1995, 'Time has come to confront the problem of the two Chinas' (S. Camerer); *Free China Journal*, 14 July 1995.
48. D. Geldenhuys, *South Africa and the China question: a case for dual recognition*, Johannesburg: University of the Witwatersrand, International Relations Department, East Asia Project, working paper series 6, 1995, p. 4.
49. *Race relations survey*, 1991/92, p. 1.
50. Letter from Central Statistical Services to University of the Witwatersrand Library, 22 April 1983.
51. *The Star*, 2 July 1990, 'Taiwanese seen as marine marauders'; *The Citizen*, 6 July 1990, 'SA Chinese abhor fishing practices'; *Cape Times*, 13 September 1990, 'Compensation for hurt SA seamen'.
52. *TCA Newsletter*, no. 72, 12 December 1991; *Sunday Times*, 6 October 1991, 'Chinese values mocked'.
53. *TCA Newsletter*, no. 72, 12 December 1991.
54. *Sunday Times*, 26 May 1991, 'Locals accuse settlers of stealing their jobs', 'Naked couple stoned in Lesotho race frenzy'.
55. *Saturday Star*, 5 September 1992, 'Threat to foreign traders'.
56. *Sunday Times*, 20 September 1992, 'Conmen rob Chinese in come-to-SA racket'.
57. *Saturday Star*, 26 September 1992, 'Illegal immigrants bribe way into SA'.
58. *Sunday Times*, 27 December 1992, 'Chinese will be deported'; *The Citizen*, 28 December 1992, 'Illegal Chinese immigrants to be deported'.
59. *TCA Newsletter*, no. 78, 9 December 1992.
60. *TCA Newsletter*, no. 79, 5 March 1993.
61. *TCA Newsletter*, no. 79, 5 March 1993 and no. 81, 12 August 1993.
62. Notes of meeting between Minister of Foreign Affairs and CASA delegation in Cape Town, 5 March 1990.
63. Letter from CASA Chairman to Minister of Foreign Affairs, 19 March 1990.
64. Notes on CASA discussions held with Deputy Minister of Constitutional Development and Planning in Cape Town, 5 June 1990 and with Minister of Home Affairs and National Education in Cape Town, 15 June 1990.
65. Interview with Mr Rodney Man, October 1994.

Selected Bibliography

BOOKS, ARTICLES AND THESES

Addington Symonds, F. *The Johannesburg story*. London: Frederick Muller, 1953.

Armstrong, James C. *The Chinese at the Cape in the Dutch East India Company period 1652-1795*. Unpublished paper, 1986.

Baker, A.W. *Grace Triumphant*. Glasgow: Pickering & Inglis, 1939.

Barrow, J. *An Account of travels into the interior of Southern Africa*. London: Cadell & Davies, 1904.

Beatson, Alexander. *Tracts relative to the island of St Helena; written during a residence of five years*. London: Bulmer, 1816.

Beckett, G. *The school that is our own: Auckland Park Preparatory School*. Pretoria: Sigma Press, 1991.

Blake, C. Fred. *Ethnic groups and social change in a Chinese market town*. Hawaii: University Press of Hawaii, 1981. (Asian studies at Hawaii; 27)

Blakeston, Oswell. *Isle of St Helena*. London: Sidgwick & Jackson, 1957.

Boeseken, Anna J. *Slaves and free Blacks at the Cape 1658-1700*. Cape Town: Tafelberg, 1977.

Brookes, Edgar H. & Webb, Colin de B. *A history of Natal*. Pietermaritzburg: University of Natal Press, 1965.

Campbell, G. *Origins and migrations of the Hakkas*. [S.l.: s.n.], 1912.

Campbell, Persia C. *Chinese coolie emigration to countries within the British Empire*. London: King, 1923.

Carnegie, D.P. *Chinese emigration to Natal discussed and its defence answered*. Durban: Cullingworth, 1875.

Caton-Thompson, G. *The Zimbabwe culture: ruins and reactions*. London: Oxford Univ. Press, 1931.

Chang, Kuei-Sheng. Africa and the Indian Ocean in Chinese maps of the fourteenth and fifteenth centuries. *Imago mundi*, vol. 24, 1970, p. 21-30.

Chen, Jack. *The Chinese of America: from the beginnings to the present*. San Francisco: Harper & Row, 1982.

Chen So Chiang. *Overseas Chinese revolutionary movements*. Taichung: Jianxing Printing Works, 1985.

Chesneaux, Jean, Bastid, Marianne & Bergere, Marie-Claire. *China from the Opium Wars to the 1911 Revolution*. English translation. Hassocks: Harvester Press, 1977.

Chesneaux, Jean. *Peasant revolts in China, 1840-1949*. Translated by C.A. Curwen. London: Thames & Hudson, 1973.

Chi, Tsui. *A short history of Chinese civilization*. London: Gollancz, 1942.

Chinese New Year: Year of the Rabbit brochure. Johannesburg: Chung Wah Sports Club, Jan 1987.

Chronicle of 20th Century history. Ed. by J.S. Bowman. London: Bison, 1989.

The collected works of Mahatma Gandhi. vol. I-XI. Delhi: Ministry of Information and Broadcasting, 1960-.

Cross, Tony. *St Helena: including Ascension Island and Tristan da Cunha*. Newtown Abbot: David & Charles, 1980.

Crozier, B. *The man who lost China*. New York: Scribner, 1976.

Couling, S. *The encyclopaedia Sinica*. Shanghai: Kelly & Walsh, 1917, reprinted Taipei: Ch'eng Wen, 1973.

Dart, Raymond A. A Chinese character as a wall motive in Rhodesia. *South African journal of science*, vol. 36, Dec. 1939, p. 474-6.

Dart, Raymond A. The historical succession of cultural impacts upon southern Africa. *Nature*, vol. 115, p. 425-9.

Dart, Raymond A. *The oriental horizons of Africa*. Johannesburg: Hayne & Gibson, 1954.

Davenport, T.R.H. *South Africa*. 2nd ed. Johannesburg: Macmillan, 1978.

Davies, Robert. Mining capital, the state and unskilled white workers in South Africa, 1901-1913. *Journal of Southern African studies*, vol. 3 no. 1, Oct. 1976, p. 41-69.

Denoon, D.J.N. 'Capitalist influence' and the Transvaal during the Crown Colony period, 1900-1906. *Historical journal*, vol. 11 no. 2, 1968, p. 301-31.

Denoon, D.J.N. The Transvaal labour crisis, 1901-6. *Journal of African history*, vol. 8 no. 3, 1967, p. 481-94.

Dinath, M.Y.D. *Asiatic population settlement in the Transvaal (1881-1960) with special reference to the Johannesburg municipality*. B.A. (Hons) thesis, University of the Witwatersrand, Department of Geography, 1963.

Divine, A.D. *These splendid ships*. London: Muller, 1960.

Duyvendak, J.J.L. *China's discovery of Africa*. London: Arthur Probsthain, 1949.

Eldridge, C.C. *Victorian imperialism*. London: Hodder & Stoughton, 1978.

Elphick, Richard & Shell, Robert. Intergroup relations: Khoikhoi, settlers, slaves and free blacks, 1652-1795. In *The shaping of South African society, 1652-1820*, ed. by R. Elphick & H. Giliomee, Cape Town: Longman, 1979, p. 116-169.

"Emphatically Yes, we do, says Mr. Anthony Eden". [S.l.:s.n., 194-]

Farley, M. Foster. The Chinese coolie trade 1845-1875. *Journal of Asian and African studies*, vol. 3, 1968, p. 257-70.

Festenstein, M. & Pickard-Cambridge, C. *Land and race: South Africa's group areas and land acts*. Johannesburg: South African Institute of Race Relations, 1987.

Fitzgerald, C.P. *China: a short cultural history*. New York: Praeger, 1958.

Ford, R.F. The dilemma of being born a South African Chinese. *Vinculum*, Dec. 1972, p. 27.

Friedgut, A.J. How we treat the gallant Chinese. *The Forum*, 7 Aug 1943.

Fripp, C.E. A note on mediaeval Chinese-African trade. *NADA*, 1939, p. 88-96.

Furuya, Keija. *Chiang Kai Shek: his life and times*. New York: St John's University, 1981; abridged English edition by Chun-ming Chang.

Garson, Noel G. 'Het Volk': the Botha-Smuts party in the Transvaal, 1904-11. *Historical journal*, vol. 9 no. 2, 1966, p. 101-20.

Geldenhuys, Deon. The head of government and South Africa's foreign relations. In *Malan to De Klerk: leadership in the apartheid state*, ed. by Robert Shrire. London: Hurst, 1994, p. 245-90.

Geldenhuys, Deon. *Some foreign policy implications of South Africa's "Total National Strategy", with particular reference to the "12-point plan"*. Johannesburg: South African Institute of International Affairs, 1981.

Geldenhuys, Deon. *South Africa and the China question: a case for dual recognition*. Johannesburg: University of the Witwatersrand, International Relations Department, East Asia Project, 1995. (Working paper series; 6).

Gerhart, Gail M. *Black power in South Africa: the evolution of an ideology*. Berkeley: University of California Press, 1978.

Gin, Trevor. Decline of Chinese civilisation in S.A. *Spectrum*, Aug 1963, p.6-7.

Gosse, Philip. *St Helena 1502-1938*. London: Cassell, 1938.

Green, C.G. An old man remembers. *Looking back*, vol. VIII no. 3, Sept 1968.

Green, Lawrence G. *Harbours of memory*. Cape Town: Howard Timmins, 1969.

Guelke, Leonard. The white settlers, 1652-1780. In *The shaping of South African society, 1652-1820*, ed. by R. Elphick and H. Giliomee. Cape Town: Longman, 1979, p. 41-74.

Hahlo, H.R and Kahn, Ellison. *The Union of South Africa: the development of its laws and constitution*. London: Stevens, 1960.

Handbook on race relations in South Africa. Ed. by E. Hellmann. New York: Octagon, 1975.

He, Fangchuan. The relationship between China and African history. *UCLA African Studies Center newsletter*, Fall 1987.

Historical Simon's Town: vignettes, reminiscences & illustrations ... ed. by B.B. and B.G. Brock, Cape Town: Balkema, 1976.

Horrell, Muriel. *The Group Areas Act - its effect on human beings*. Johannesburg: South African Institute of Race Relations, 1956.

Hsueh, Chun-Tu. Sun Yat-sen, Yang Ch'u-yun, and the early revolutionary movement in China. *Journal of Asian studies*, vol. 19, pt. 3, 1960, p. 307-318.

Human, Linda. *The Chinese people of South Africa: freewheeling on the fringes*. Pretoria: University of South Africa, 1984.

Huntington, E. *The character of races*, New York: Arno, 1977.

Huttenback, Robert A. *Gandhi in South Africa: British imperialism and the Indian question 1860-1914*. Ithaca: Cornell Univ. Press, 1971.

Illustrated guide to Southern Africa. 3rd ed. Cape Town: Reader's Digest, 1982.

Jeeves, Alan H. *Migrant labour in South Africa's mining economy*. Johannesburg: Witwatersrand Univ. Press, 1985.

Johannesburg: one hundred years 1886-1986. Johannesburg: Chris van Rensburg, 1986.

Johannesburg Chinese Kuo Ting High School annual, 1956.

Johannesburg Chinese Kuo Ting High School. 21st anniversary publication, 1971.

Jones, S. & Muller, A. *The South African economy, 1910-90*. New York: St Martin's, 1992.

Kim Sing, Maureen. The problem of the Chinese student. *E.P. Chinese Review*, vol. 1, no. 4, Nov-Dec. 1964, p. 10-15.

Kim Sing, Maureen. What of the future? *Spectrum*, Oct 1965, p. 2-4.

King, Gloria Luksun. *Domestic religious beliefs and practices amongst the Chinese in Johannesburg*. M.A. thesis, University of the Witwatersrand, Johannesburg, 1974.

Kirkwood, K. *The Group Areas Act*. Johannesburg: South Africa Institute of Race Relations, [195-].

Knox P. & Gutsche, T. *Do you know Johannesburg?* Vereeniging: Unie Volkspers, 1947.

Krugersdorp 100 jaar/years. Krugersdorp: Town Council of Krugersdorp, 1987.

Kuo Ting Chinese School, 1942.

Land Tenure by Asiatics and South African Coloured People in the Transvaal, *Race Relations journal*, vol. 2, no. 5, November 1935.

Langham-Carter, R.R. Cape Town's first graveyards. *Cabo*, vol. 2 no. 2, June 1973, p. 16-22.

Latourette, Kenneth Scott. *The Chinese: their history and culture*. 4th ed. New York: Macmillan, 1964.

Law of South Africa. Ed. by W.A. Joubert. vol. 1- Durban: Butterworths, 1984-

Laws affecting race relations in South Africa, 1948-1976. Compiled by Muriel Horrell. Johannesburg: South African Institute of Race Relations, 1978.

Le Cordeur, B.A. Boer/British conflict. In *Perspectives on the Southern African past*. Cape Town: University of Cape Town, Centre for African Studies, 1979, p. 153-162. (Occasional papers; 2).

Legassick, M. *The analysis of "racism" in South Africa: the case of the mining economy*. IDEP/UN International Seminar on Socio-Economic Trends and Policies in southern Africa. Dar-es-Salaam, December 1-8, 1975.

Leibbrandt, H.C.V. *Precis of the Archives of the Cape of Good Hope. Letters and documents received, 1649-1662*. part 1, 1898.

Leibbrandt, H.C.V. *Precis of the Archives of the Cape of Good Hope. Requesten (memorials) 1715-1806*. vol. 1-5, 1903-. Reprinted Cape Town: South African Library, 1988-9.

Lewcock, Ronald. Chinese craftsmen. In *Standard encyclopaedia of Southern Africa*, vol. 2. Cape Town: Nasou, 1971, p. 197.

Li, Peter S. *The Chinese in Canada*. Toronto: Oxford Univ. Press, 1988.

Like it was : The Star 100 years in Johannesburg. Johannesburg: Argus, 1987.

Lodge, Tom. Political mobilisation during the 1950s: an East London case study. In *The politics of race, class and nationalism in twentieth-century South Africa*, ed. by S. Marks & S. Trapido. London: Longman, 1987.

Loewen, James W. *The Mississippi Chinese: between black and white*. 2nd edition. Prospect Heights: Waveland, 1971.

Longland's Johannesburg and districts directory, 1893.

Ly-Tio-Fane Pineo, Huguette. *Chinese diaspora in western Indian Ocean*, Mauritius: Editions de l'Ocean Indien

& Chinese Catholic Mission, 1985.
MacCrone, I.D. *Race attitudes in South Africa*. London: Oxford Univ. Press, 1937.
Macmillan, A. *The Golden City Johannesburg*. London: Collingridge, [1933].
Mawby, A.A. *The political behaviour of the British population of the Transvaal, 1902-1907*. Ph.D thesis, University of the Witwatersrand, Johannesburg, 1969.
Mei-hsien ti chu=Meixian prefecture. Pei Ching: Chung Kuo Kuo Chi Kung Po Kung SSu, 1987.
Melliss, John Charles. *St. Helena*, 1875. [part reprint and with photographs] by Robin Castell. Chesham: Wensley Brown, 1979.
Men of the times. [Johannesburg]: Transvaal Pub. Co., 1905.
Mentzel, Otto Friedrich. *A geographical-topographical description of the Cape of Good Hope*. Parts 1-3; revised and edited by H.J. Mandelbrote. Cape Town: Van Riebeeck Society, 1921-1944. (Van Riebeeck Society for the publication of South African historical documents)
Mervis, Joel. *The fourth estate*. Johannesburg: Jonathan Ball, 1989.
Minnick, Sylvia Sun. *Samfow: the San Joaquin Chinese legacy*. Fresno, California: Panorama West, 1988.
Moore Anderson, A.S. The Chinese Allies we insult. *The Forum*, 24 Oct 1942.
Motala, S. *Behind closed doors*. Johannesburg: South African Institute of Race Relations, 1987.
Murray, Bruce K. *Wits - the early years*. Johannesburg: Witwatersrand Univ. Press, 1982.
Murray, Bruce K. Wits University, student politics, and the coming of apartheid. *Perspectives in education*, vol. 12 no. 1, 1990, p. 55-68.
Needham, Joseph. *Science and civilisation in China*. Cambridge: Cambridge Univ. Press, 1954.
New Encyclopaedia Britannica. vol. 8, 15th ed. 1987.
Norwich, Oscar J. *Maps of Africa*: an illustrated and annotated carto-bibliography. Johannesburg: Ad. Donker, 1983.
Official programme of the great demonstration in Hyde Park. [S.l.: s.n.], 1904.
Open universities in South Africa. Johannesburg: Witwatersrand Univ. Press, 1957.
Open universities in South Africa and academic freedom 1957-1974, Cape Town: Juta, 1974.
Oxford history of South Africa. Vol. 1-2, edited by Monica Wilson & Leonard Thompson. Oxford: Clarendon Press, 1969-1975.
Pachai, Bridglal. The history of the "Indian Opinion" 1903-1914. In *Archives year book for South African history*, vol. 24. Cape Town: Government Printer, 1963.
Pachai, Bridglal. *The international aspects of the South African Indian question, 1860-1971*. Cape Town: Struik, 1971.
Pakenham, Thomas. *The Boer War*. Johannesburg: Jonathan Ball, 1982.
Pan, Lynn. *Sons of the Yellow Emperor*. London: Secker & Warburg, 1990.
Paton, Alan. *The people wept, being a brief account of the origin, contents, and application of that unjust law of the Union of South Africa known as The Group Areas Act of 1950 (since consolidated as Act No 77 of 1957)*. Kloof: A. Paton, [1958?]
Paver, F.R. The Asiatics in south-east Africa. *South African journal of science*, vol. 22, 1925, p. 516-522.
Paver, F.R. Far eastern contacts with southern Africa. *South African journal of science*, vol. 39, 1943, p. 88-94.
Payne, E.G. *An experiment in alien labor*. Chicago: University of Chicago Press, 1912.
Pirie, G.H. Racial segregation on Johannesburg trams: procedures and protest, 1904-1927. *African Studies*, vol. 48, no. 1, 1989.
Pirie, G.H. *Racial segregation on public transport in South Africa, 1877-1989*. Ph.D. thesis, University of the Witwatersrand, Johannesburg, 1990.
Politics of race, class and nationalism in twentieth-century South Africa. Ed. by S. Marks & S. Trapido, London: Longman, 1987.
Port Elizabeth year book and directory, [S.l.: s,n.], 1901-.
Race relations as regulated by law in South Africa, 1948-1979. Compiled by Muriel Horrell. Johannesburg: South African Institute of Race Relations, 1982.
Race relations survey. See: Survey of race relations in South Africa.
Redgrave, J.J. *Port Elizabeth in bygone days*. Wynberg: Rustica, 1947.
Reeves, J.A. *Chinese labour in South Africa 1901-1910*. M.A. thesis, University of the Witwatersrand, Johannesburg, 1954.
Richardson, Peter. *Chinese mine labour in the Transvaal*. London: Macmillan, 1982.
Roberts, B. *Kimberley: turbulent city*. Cape Town: David Philip, 1976.

Robottom, John. *Twentieth Century China*. London: Wayland, 1971.

Rogerson, C.M. 'Shisha Nyama': the rise and fall of the Native eating house trade in Johannesburg. In *The Making of Class*, History Workshop, University of the Witwatersrand, February 1987, p. 1-36.

Rosenthal, Eric. *Encyclopaedia of South Africa*. 6th ed. London: Warne, 1973.

Rosenthal, Eric. *Schooners and skyscrapers*. Cape Town: Howard Timmins, 1963.

Ross Skinner, H. Report ... furnished to Witwatersrand Labour Association: the result of his visit to the East to enquire into the prospects of obtaining Asiatic labourers for the mines of the Witwatersrand, Roodepoort, 1903.

Russell, A.K. *Liberal landslide: the general election of 1906*. Newton Abbot: David & Charles, 1973.

Schirokauer, Conrad. *A brief history of Chinese and Japanese civilizations*. New York: Harcourt Brace Jovanovich, 1978.

Schwarz, E.H.L. The Chinese in Africa. *The South African nation*, Feb 12, 1927, p. 7-8.

The Selected works of Mahatma Gandhi. Vol 3, ed. By Shriman Narayan, Ahmedabad: Navajivan, 1968.

The Shaping of South African society, 1652-1820. ed. by Richard Elphick and Hermann Giliomee. Cape Town: Longman, 1979.

Shorten John R. *The Johannesburg saga*. Johannesburg: Shorten, 1970.

Simons, H.J. and R.E. *Class and colour in South Africa 1850-1950*, Harmondsworth: Penguin, 1969.

Smedley, Linda N. *A sociological analysis of some aspects of the life of South Africa's Chinese community*. D.Litt thesis, University of South Africa, Pretoria, 1980.

Smith, Anna H. *Johannesburg street names*. Cape Town: Juta, 1971.

Snow, Philip. *The Star Raft: China's encounter with Africa*. New York: Cornell Univ. Press, 1989.

Soares-Rebelo, D.J. *The Chinese extraction group in Mocambique*. Unpublished paper, [July 1966].

Song, Arthur. *The effects of Protestant Christianity on the Chinese cult of ancestors as practised in the Johannesburg area*. Ph.D. thesis, University of Durban Westville, 1989.

South Africa today. Written in Chinese by Hon Chong Wing King under the pseudonym Deng Yee Tsung. Hong Kong, [s.n.], 1971.

South Africa's yesterdays. Ed. by P. Joyce. Cape Town: Reader's Digest, 1981.

Sparrman, Anders. *A voyage to the Cape of Good Hope towards the Antarctic Polar Circle round the world and to the country of the Hottentots and the Caffres from the year 1772-1776*. ed. by V.S. Forbes, transl. from the Swedish revised by J. & I. Rudner. Cape Town: Van Riebeeck Society, 1975. (Vol 1, second series no. 6)

Speight, W.L. South Africa's Chinese visitors. *Africa revealed by word and picture*, vol. 5, no. 1, Jan. 1938, p. 42.

St Helena Almanack and annual register for the year of Our Lord 1884. St Helena: Watson, [18-].

Standard Encyclopaedia of Southern Africa. Vol. 1-. Cape Town: Nasou, 1970-.

Studies in the history of Cape Town. Vol. 4, ed. by C. Saunders, H. Phillips and E. van Heyningen. Cape Town: University of Cape Town: 1981.

Study Project on Christianity in Apartheid Society. *Anatomy of apartheid*. Johannesburg: SPROCAS, 1970.

Summary of circulars issued by the Chamber of Mines Labour Importation Agency Ltd., from May 1904 to December 1906, for the guidance of mines employing Chinese labour, [Johannesburg: Chamber of Mines, 1906].

Survey of race relations in South Africa, 1953-, Johannesburg: South African Institute of Race Relations, 1954-. (Also published as *Race relations survey*).

Tan, Thomas Tsu-wee. *Your Chinese roots: The overseas Chinese story*. Singapore: Times Books, 1986.

Thompson, George. *Travels and adventures in Southern Africa*. Ed. by V.S. Forbes. Parts 2 & 3. Cape Town: Van Riebeeck Society, 1968. (Van Riebeeck Society; 49).

Thunberg, Carl Peter. *Travels at the Cape of Good Hope, 1772-1775*. Ed. by V.S. Forbes. Translation from the Swedish revised by J. & I. Rudner. Cape Town: Van Riebeeck Society, 1986. (Van Riebeeck Society, 2nd series; 17).

Ticktin, David. White labour's attitude, 1902-1904, towards the importation of indentured Chinese labourers by the Transvaal Chamber of Mines. In *University of Cape Town. Centre for African Studies. African seminar*. vol. 1, 1978, p. 64-93.

Titlestad, Bruce Martin. *Penetrating the invisible society: an examination of the emergence and decline of Chinese participation in the 'Kaffir' eating house trade*. Unpublished seminar paper, Department of Geography and Environmental Studies, University of the Witwatersrand, Johannesburg, 1984.

Trehaven, Rose. A note on the 'Spanish flu' of 1918 in Port Elizabeth. *Looking back*, vol. 27 no. 2, Sept 1988, p. 31-41.

Tuchman, Barbara W. *The proud tower: a portrait of the world before the war 1890-1914*. New York: Macmillan,

1966.
Tung Miao. *Legal status of Chinese in the Union of South Africa*. Johannesburg: Chiao Sheng Pao, 1947.
Van Aswegen, H.J. *Geskiedenis van Suid Afrika tot 1854*. Pretoria: Academica, 1989.
Van Onselen, Charles. *Chibaro*. Johannesburg: Ravan Press, 1988.
Van Onselen, Charles. *Studies in the social and economic history of the Witwatersrand, 1886-1914*. vol. 2: New Nineveh. Johannesburg: Ravan Press, 1982.
Vane, Michael. *The South African Indians*. Johannesburg: Society of the Friends of Africa, [1948]. (South African affairs pamphlets. 3rd series; 17)
Wang, Gungwu. Among non-Chinese. *Daedalus*, vol. 120, no. 2, Spring 1991, p. 135-158.
Wang, Gungwu. *China and the Chinese overseas*. Singapore: Times Academic, 1991.
Wang, Sing-wu. The attitude of the Ch'ing court toward Chinese emigration. *Chinese culture*, vol. 9, no. 4, Dec. 1968, p. 62-76.
Wilbur, C. Martin. *Sun Yat-Sen: frustrated patriot*. New York: Columbia Univ. Press, 1976.
Wilhelm, Janet. Something new from the East. *The Executive*. Sept 1988, p. 21-5.
Wilson, F. *Migrant labour*. Johannesburg: SACC & SPROCAS, 1972.
Wing King, Ernest. How Chinese are we? *E.P. Chinese Review*, vol. 1, no. 4, Nov-Dec 1964, p.3-5.
Wu, David Yen-ho. The construction of Chinese and non-Chinese identities. *Daedalus*, vol. 120, no. 2, Spring 1991, p. 159-180.
50th Anniversary Pretoria Chinese School 1984. Pretoria: 50th anniversary Committee for the Pretoria Chinese school.

OFFICIAL SOURCES – PUBLISHED

Great Britain

Command papers Cd. 1895, 1899, 1945, 2026, 2401, 2786, 2788, 2819. Correspondence relating to labour in the Transvaal mines.
Command papers Cd. 3308, 3887, 4327, 4584, 5363. Correspondence relating to legislation affecting Asiatics in the Transvaal.

South Africa

Cape of Good Hope. Parliament. Appendix I to the Votes and Proceedings of Parliament, Vol. 1A, App 1, 1876. Ministerial Department of Crown Lands and Public Works. Report on immigration and labour supply for the year 1875.
Cape of Good Hope. Parliament. Appendix I to the Votes and Proceedings of Parliament, Vol. 1, 1907. Report on immigration and labour for the year ending 31 December 1906.
Cape of Good Hope. Parliament. Appendix II to the Votes and Proceedings of Parliament. Volume II, Report of the Select Committee on Asiatic Grievances, September 1908, Cape Town: Cape Times, 1980.
Cape of Good Hope. Parliament. Correspondence and papers on the subject of immigration from India and China. [G39-1975].
Cape of Good Hope. Parliament. Results of a census of the Colony of the Cape of Good Hope, as on the night of Sunday, 5th April, 1891. Cape Town: Richards, 1892.
Cape of Good Hope. Parliament. Results of a census of the Colony of the Cape of Good Hope, as on the night of Sunday, 17th April, 1904. Cape Town: Cape Times, 1905.
Convention between the United Kingdom and China respecting the employment of Chinese labour in British Colonies and Protectorates, signed at London, May 13, 1904. London: HMSO, 1904. (Treaty series; 7)
Deputation from the White League to Lord Milner. His Excellency's reply, 3rd June 1903.
Natal. Census of the Colony of Natal, April 1904. Pietermaritzburg: Davis, 1905.
Natal. Report of the Immigration Restriction Officer for the year 1897. Pietermaritzburg: Davis, 1897.
Natal. Reports of the Immigration Restriction Department for the years 1900 to 1904. Pietermaritzburg: "Times",

1901-5.

Natal Harbour Board. Chairman's minute and departmental reports for 1886 and 1887.

Official Year Book of the Union and of Basutoland, Bechuanaland Protectorate, and Swaziland, no. 14, 1931-1932.

Port Elizabeth Municipality. A report on the Asiatic problem in Port Elizabeth, presented to the Port Elizabeth Municipality by the Chief Sanitary Inspector. Port Elizabeth: Walton, 1911.

Port Elizabeth Voters Register. Cape Town: Cape Times, 1905.

Report of the Technical Committee of Enquiry into the Group Areas Act, 1966, the Reservation of Separate Amenities Act 1953 and related legislation. Pretoria: Government Printer, 1983.

South Africa. Office of Census and Statistics. Third census of the population of the Union of South Africa enumerated 3 May 1921, part VIII, Non-European Races. [U.G. 20-24].

South Africa. Office of Census and Statistics. Sixth census of the population of the Union of South Africa, enumerated 5th May, 1936. Pretoria: Government Printer, 1938-42. Volume V, Birthplaces, period of residence and nationality of the European, Asiatic and Coloured population [U.G. 24, 1942].

South Africa. Bureau of Census and Statistics. Population census, 7th May 1946, Pretoria: Government Printer, 1949-1954, 5 v.

South Africa. Parliament. House of Assembly. Questions and replies.

South Africa. Parliament. House of Assembly. Debates.

South Africa. Parliament. Report of the Asiatic Inquiry Commission, Cape Town: Cape Times, 1921, [U.G. 4-'21];

South Africa. Parliament. Report of the Select Committee on Asiatics in Transvaal, Cape Town: Cape Times, 1930, [S.C. 7-'30].

South Africa. Parliament. Report of the Transvaal Asiatic Land Tenure Act Commission, parts I-II. Pretoria: Government Printer, 1934, [U.G. 7-1934].

South Africa. Parliament. Select Committee on working of Transvaal liquor laws [S.C. 2-'18].

South Africa. Parliament. Notes exchanged between the Union Government and the Japanese Consul in the Union concerning Japanese immigration into South Africa, February 1931, [A1-31].

Transvaal. Foreign Labour Department, Johannesburg. Annual report 1904- Pretoria: Government Printer, 1906-.

Transvaal. Legislative Assembly. Correspondence between Colonial Secretary's Office and leaders of the Asiatic and Chinese communities, 28-30 January 1908. Pretoria: Government Printer, Aug 1908. [T.A. 4-'08]

Transvaal. Report of the Special Committee appointed to inquire into the present conditions in regard to the control of Chinese indentured labourers in the Witwatersrand district. Johannesburg: Argus, 1906.

NEWSPAPERS, PERIODICALS AND PAMPHLETS

Blue Banner
Business Day
Cape Argus
Cape of Good Hope Gazette
Cape Times
Chiao Sheng Pao (Chinese Consular Gazette)
China at War
China Week News
The Citizen
The Crozier
Dagbreek en Sondagnuus
Daily Dispatch
Daily Mail
Daily News
Diamond Fields Advertiser
Eastern Province Herald
E.P. Chinese Review
Evening Post
Financial Mail
Finansies & Tegniek
Free China Journal
The Friend
Graaff Reinet Advertiser
Graaff Reinet Herald
Indian Opinion
Internos
Natal Mercury
New China
Pretoria News
Rand Daily Mail
South Africa and China
Spectrum
Standard and Diggers News
The Star

Sunday Chronicle
Sunday Express
Sunday Times
Sunday Tribune
TCA newsletter
Transvaal Critic
Transvaal Leader
Transvaal Leader Weekly Edition
Transvaal Weekly Illustrated
Die Transvaler
Die Vaderland
Vinculum
Voice of South African Chinese
Weekend Post

OFFICIAL SOURCES – UNPUBLISHED

CAD. Cape Archives Depot, Cape Town.
Files AG, CO, GH, MOOC, PMO, T, 3/CT, 3/ELN, 3/PEZ.
NAD. Natal Archives Depot, Pietermaritzburg.
Files CSO, IRD, MSCE.
SAD. South African Archives Depot, Pretoria.
Files ARG, BEP, BNS, CIA, JUS, TPB.
TAD. Transvaal Archives Depot, Pretoria.
Files CIA, CS, DCU, FLD, GOV, JHM, LA, LD, MGP, MHG, MM, PM, RAD, SP, SS, WLD.

OTHER SOURCES – UNPUBLISHED

Associations in the Chinese community:
Eastern Province Chinese Association
Uitenhage Chinese Association
BRA. Barlow-Rand Archives.
H. Eckstein & Co. Papers.
Chamber of Mines of South Africa Archives.
Rhodes University. Cory Library for Historical Research.
Noel Ross Papers.
South African Institute of Race Relations.
University of the Witwatersrand.
Rheinallt Jones Papers.
University Archives.

Index